HANDBOOK OF
EYEWITNESS PSYCHOLOGY

HANDBOOK OF EYEWITNESS PSYCHOLOGY

Volume 2

MEMORY FOR PEOPLE

EDITED BY

Rod C. L. Lindsay
Queen's University, Ontario

David F. Ross
University of Tennessee, Chattanooga

J. Don Read
Simon Fraser University, British Columbia

Michael P. Toglia
State University of New York, Cortland

Psychology Press
Taylor & Francis Group

New York London

Editorial Director: Steve Rutter
Editorial Assistant: Anthony Messina
Cover Design: Tomai Maridou
Full-Service Compositor: MidAtlantic Books & Journals, Inc.

This book was typeset in 11/13 pt Goudy Old Style, Italic, Bold, and Bold Italic. Headings were typeset in Americana, Bold, Italic and Bold Italic.

First Published by Lawrence Erlbaum Associates, Inc., Publishers
10 Industrial Avenue
Mahwah, New Jersey 07430

Reprinted 2010 by Psychology Press

CIP information for this volume can be obtained by contacting the Library of Congress.

ISBN   978-0-8058-5152-6—0-8058-5152-8 (case)
ISBN   978-1-4106-1491-9—0-8058-1491-3 (e book)

Contents

Preface

The initial intention of the editors of this volume was to update the Ross, Read, and Toglia (1994) volume on adult eyewitness research. The intervening decade had dramatically increased the eyewitness literature. Early on, we decided that the literature had become so large that a comprehensive volume attempting to bring together the eyewitness area in a single volume would be useful for both the research community and legal practitioners. Because the literature had become so extensive, we subsequently divided the work into two more manageable volumes. One volume is concerned with what once was called the psychology of report (e.g., Whipple, 1909, 1912) and perhaps more recently memory for events. Memory for events is critical to the determination of what actually occurred and whether a crime has been committed. Such concerns have generated the large and diverse literature discussed in our other volume: *Handbook of Eyewitness Psychology: Memory for Events* (Toglia, Read, Ross, & Lindsay, 2007).

The current volume contains 21 chapters by researchers from Australia, Canada, England, Germany, Scotland, South Africa, and The United States of America plus a concluding chapter by a legal expert discussing the implications of the current state of the eyewitness literature from an applied and legal perspective. This volume addresses issues of memory for people. Such memories are critical to the apprehension and prosecution of criminal suspects and also to avoid the conviction of innocent people. Of particular importance, errors of commission, or false identification, have long been claimed to be a serious source of miscarriages of justice (e.g., Borchard, 1932) and recently have been proven conclusively to be a major source of wrongful convictions (Connors, Lundregan, Miller, & McEwen, 1996; Gross, Kristen, Matheson, Montgomery, & Patel, 2004). This volume addresses the extensive literature on a variety of forensically relevant topics related to memory for people.

Concern for the application of the research results was a priority throughout the volume. Many of the chapters are directly relevant to police procedures for obtaining evidence from witnesses, others address issues of interpretation of such evidence, and still others are concerned with the impact of eyewitness evidence in court.

First, suspects must be found, often using descriptions, mug shots, and composites. Research on these topics is critical. The guilty can not be punished if they are not found. Equally important, the innocent are at risk to the extent that descriptions, mug shots, and composite faces lead to their being categorized as suspects. Once a suspect has been determined, eyewitnesses may be asked to "identify" them. The selection (identification) of suspects is addressed in terms of the procedures used to accomplish this task (voice and facial recognition from show ups and lineups). The techniques currently used to construct and assess the fairness of lineups are discussed as well as potential alternatives to current procedures. Uncontrollable factors that affect selection accuracy also are discussed such as witness race, age (both child and elderly witnesses), and arousal level, as well as delay between the crime and identification attempt. The need for theories addressing eyewitness identification accuracy is discussed and an attempt to fill this gap is made.

The accuracy of eyewitness evidence is of importance only to the extent that such evidence has impact in court; thus, the degree to which eyewitness testimony is credible and believed is critical. Chapters address factors that may permit the discrimination of accurate from inaccurate witnesses ("postdicting") based on information obtained from witnesses (e.g., confidence) or their performance (e.g., speed of identification). The impact of "legal safeguards" (e.g., expert testimony) on the belief of eyewitnesses also is addressed.

Long ago the failure to consider adequately the position of police, lawyers, and judges provided serious impediments to progress in understanding eyewitness issues and applying scientific results in the field (e.g., Munsterberg, 1908; Wigmore, 1909). The concluding chapter provides a perspective on the literature from the legal perspective in hopes of avoiding a repetition of such past errors.

REFERENCES

Borchard, E. M. (1932). *Convicting the innocent: Sixty-five actual errors of criminal justice*. Yale University Press: New Haven, Connecticut.

Connors, E., Lundregan, T., Miller, N., & McEwen, T. (1996). *Convicted by juries, exonerated by science: Case studies in the use of DNA evidence to establish innocence after trial*. Washington, D.C.: National Institute of Justice.

Gross, S. R., Kristen, J., Matheson, D. J., Montgomery, N., & Patel, S. (2004). Exonerations in the United States: 1989 through 2003. www.law.umich.edu/NewsAndInfo/exonerations-in-us.pdf

Munsterberg, H. (1909). *On the Witness Stand*. McClure: New York.

Toglia, M., Read, J. D., Ross, D. F., & Lindsay, R. C. L. (2007). *Handbook of Eyewitness Psychology: Memory for Events*. Lawrence Erlbaum and Associates, Mahwah, New Jersey: Lawrence Erlbaum & Assoc.

Whipple, G. M. (1909). The observer as reporter: A survey of the 'psychology of testimony'. *Psychological Bulletin, 6*, 153–170.

Whipple, G. M. (1912). Psychology of testimony and report. *Psychological Bulletin, 9*, 264–269.

Wigmore, J. H. (1909). Professor Muensterberg and the psychology of testimony: Being a report of the case of Cokestone v. Muensterberg. *Illinois Law Review, 3*, 399.

About the Editors

Dr. J. Don Read is Professor of Psychology and Director of the *Law and Forensic Psychology Program* at Simon Fraser University. Dr. Read received a B.A. degree from the University of British Columbia followed by M.Sc. and Ph.D. degrees from Kansas State University. His research investigates eyewitness memory, face recognition, reconstructive memory, recollections of childhood abuse, and long-term autobiographical memory and has been funded by the National Sciences and Engineering Research Council of Canada, NATO, and the Alberta Law Foundation. Dr. Read has published some 70 papers and chapters and co-edited four other books including *Recollections of Trauma* (1997), *Eyewitness Memory* (1997), and *Adult Eyewitness Memory* (1994). Dr. Read was recently the Chair of the Society for Applied Research in Memory and Cognition (1998-2002) and the North American Editor of *Applied Cognitive Psychology*. He is currently Editorial Board member of *Applied Cognitive Psychology*, *Law and Human Behavior*, *Legal and Criminological Psychology*, and The Oxford Press *Psychology and Law Book Series*.

Rod Lindsay is Professor of Psychology, Queen's University, Canada and Honorary Professor of Psychology, University of Aberdeen, Scotland. He holds a Ph.D. in social psychology from the University of Alberta (1982) and conducts empirical studies on issues in the legal system such as eyewitness reliability, police procedures for obtaining eyewitness evidence, methods of obtaining superior evidence from eyewitnesses, and the effects of eyewitness evidence on jurors. He has published more than 50 articles in social science journals and also has published in law jounals. He has consulted and testified on eyewitness issues in North America, Europe, and Africa (Rwandan War Crimes Tribunal). He has consulted widely on issues of policy concerning eyewitness identification procedures including being a co-author of the National Institute of Justice publication: *Eyewitness Evidence: A Guide for Law Enforcement* (1999). He has been extensively involved in training of judges, police, and prosecutors in Canada.

Dr. Michael Toglia holds the rank of Professor in the Department of Psychology at State University of New York-Cortland. Since 2003 he has served as the Executive Director of the international organization the Society for Applied Research in Memory and Cognition (SARMAC). He has over 50 scientific publications which in addition to this Handbook include 7 books, most of which are edited volumes devoted to issues on eyewitness memory and testimony. Other editorial experience includes: editor service for 13 journals, a term as Action Editor for the journal *Memory*, a current appointment on the editorial board for SARMAC's official journal *Applied Cognitive Psychology*, and reviewer of NSF grant proposals. Similarly, he recently completed a two-year position as a consultant on a

NIH grant concerning false memory in special populations. He has testified and/or consulted in numerous cases involving the suggestibility of memory, been interviewed by several national newspapers, and appeared on Public Television in the documentary *What Jennifer Knew* narrated by Susan Saint-James. He is a Fulbright Senior Specialist as well as a Fellow in Division 3 (Experimental), and Division 41 (Psychology and the Law) of the American Psychological Association.

David F. Ross, Ph.D. is a UC Foundation Professor of Psychology at the University of Tennessee at Chattanooga. Dr. Ross received his Ph.D. in Developmental and Social Psychology from Cornell University. Over the last 15 years he has conducted research on factors that influence the accuracy of eyewitness testimony in children and adults, and the psychology of jury behavior. He has published five scientific volumes on psycholegal issues including *Children's Eyewitness Memory* (Ceci, Ross, & Toglia, Eds.); *Perspectives on Children's Testimony* (Ceci, Toglia, & Ross, Eds.); *Adult Eyewitness Testimony: Current Trends and Developments* (Ross, Read, and Toglia, Eds); *Handbook of Psychology Volume 1: Memory for Events* (Toglia, Read, Ross, and Lindsay, Eds., 2006); *Handbook of Psychology Volume 2: Memory for People* (Lindsay, Ross, Read, and Toglia, Eds., 2006). Dr. Ross has published numerous articles in top-tier scientific journals; he was invited on two occasions to present his work at NATO conferences on eyewitness memory in children and adults and jury behavior; and he received funding from the National Institute of Justice and from the National Science Foundation for his psycholegal research that subsequently resulted in an award from the American Psychology and Law Society. Dr. Ross is also a member of the editorial board for Law and Human Behavior; and he served as a guest editor for a volume on hearsay testimony and the child witness that appeared in *Psychology, Public Policy, and Law*, a journal published by the University of Arizona College of Law and the University of Miami School of Law. Most recently Dr. Ross published an invited article on child witnesses that appeared in *Law and Contemporary Problems*, a journal that is published by the Duke University School of Law. Additionally, Dr. Ross has provided numerous educational seminars to legal and mental health professionals on how to interview the child witness, the accuracy of adult eyewitness testimony, the psychology of jury behavior and jury selection, and techniques for jury persuasion. Dr. Ross has also served as a consultant to lawyers on trial strategy, conducting mock trials, designing opening and closing statements, evaluating eyewitness testimony in children and adults, witness preparation, and jury selection. Dr. Ross also has a specialization in serving as a mitigation expert in death penalty cases. Finally, Dr. Ross has testified as an expert witness on the accuracy of eyewitness testimony in state and federal courts throughout the United States.

HANDBOOK OF
EYEWITNESS PSYCHOLOGY

I

FINDING SUSPECTS

1

Person Descriptions as Eyewitness Evidence

Christian A. Meissner
University of Texas at El Paso

Siegfried L. Sporer
University of Giessen, Germany

Jonathan W. Schooler
University of British Columbia, Canada

Two teenage girls were enjoying their family vacation in a hotel hot tub one evening. Shortly after their parents had left them, the girls were approached by a stranger, who proceeded to join them in the hot tub. Following several minutes of conversation, the stranger attempted to molest the older girl by touching her "private parts." The older girl struck the stranger in the face and told him to stop, and instructed the younger girl to find their parents. After the older girl shouted "rape" several times, the stranger finally exited the hot tub, gathered his belongings, and ran from the area. The girls would later describe the stranger as a male in his twenties, with no shirt, wearing tan/brown shorts and a shell necklace. He had dark hair, and a dark/suntanned complexion. Upon receiving the description, detectives released a BOLO ("be on the lookout"), and a suspect matching the description was detained 45 minutes later as he walked on the beach about a half-mile from the hotel. The girls were brought to the suspect and together identified him as the stranger they had encountered. The suspect was arrested for the crime, but prosecutors would later drop the charges when the suspect provided a detailed (and corroborated) alibi for his whereabouts at the time of the incident. Simply put, detectives had detained the wrong person.

Person descriptions represent an important element for detectives in the investigation of any crime. Unfortunately, the descriptions provided by witnesses or victims tend to be rather nondistinct and, like the description provided by the teenage girls above, can frequently apply to many people in the vicinity of the crime. Although descriptions are most often useful for locating a suspect in the immediate aftermath of an incident, they are also used throughout a criminal investigation to identify potential suspects from mug books, to construct sketches or composites of a suspect, and as a basis for selecting fillers when investigators are constructing a lineup identification parade and subsequently assess the "fairness" of that lineup. In addition, witness descriptions are regularly introduced at trial as a means for demonstrating the congruence between the suspect and a witness's memory. In *Neil v. Biggers* (1972), the U.S. Supreme Court indicated that witness descriptions could be used as one basis for determining the accuracy of a witness. However, as discussed in this chapter, the relationship between a witness's description and his or her ability to perceptually identify the actual perpetrator is not clear-cut.

Given the importance of person descriptions as eyewitness evidence, psychologists and criminologists have conducted a wealth of research aimed at establishing what is known about the content and veracity of person descriptions, as well as factors that may positively or negatively influence a witness's ability to provide an accurate description. The current chapter provides a review of this research, including a discussion of psychological factors that may influence person descriptions at encoding (e.g., alcohol, stress, illumination, distance, etc.), the effects of delay and repeated descriptions over time, the role of person variables (e.g., age, gender, race, etc.) and individual differences, and the influence of misinformation from investigators and/or co-witnesses. In addition, we address the variety of recall techniques that have been explored to improve the quality and quantity of person descriptors, and the relationship between such description procedures and witnesses' subsequent attempts at perceptual identification of a suspect (i.e., the verbal overshadowing effect, Schooler & Engstler-Schooler, 1990; or the use of person descriptions as retrieval cues, Cutler, Penrod, & Martens, 1987; Sporer, in press).

CONTENTS OF PERSON DESCRIPTIONS IN REAL CASES

Quantity and Quality of Descriptors

A number of archival studies have examined the content of person descriptions in real cases. Likely the most well-known study was conducted by Kuehn (1974). This study involved the analysis of person descriptions contained in 100 police protocols of cases of bodily injury, rape, and robbery in Seattle, Washington. Statements were taken from the witnesses immediately after the incident, and all perpetrators in the sample were strangers. Unfortunately, it is not clear from Kuehn's report whether the descriptions were rendered as free descriptions or were the result of some standardized questioning scheme employed by the local police. The number of details contained in the descriptions was fairly meager overall (with a maximum of nine descriptors)—on average there were 7.2 descriptors, whereas most witnesses reported 8 or 9 features. Only four victims were unable to provide any details at all. In descending order of frequency, gender, age, height, build, race, weight, complexion, and hair color were mentioned. With the exception of eye color (23%), all features were named by more than 70% of all victims. Kuehn concluded from these data that witnesses were able to convey a general impression about the perpetrator but could not provide more specific features, like hair or eye color.

In contrast to Kuehn (1974), Yuille and Cutshall (1986) examined a single shooting incident, involving a total of 21 witnesses, of which 13 collaborated in a follow-up research interview. Surprisingly, the witnesses' reports were remarkably elaborate and highly accurate, even after the 5-month delay between the incident and the research interviews. Based on these results, the authors questioned typical laboratory findings that have capitalized on witness errors since the heyday of eyewitness testimony research by Stern (1902) and Munsterburg (1908). However, one potential explanation for the findings of Yuille and Cutshall may be that the type of case, which apparently was quite spectacular, was likely to have involved multiple interviews of the witnesses, many conversations between witnesses and family/friends, as well as ample opportunity to read about the events in the local press. We speculate that these multiple information exposures may have served as opportunities for witnesses to rehearse these events and thus improve recall (for more on the role of verbal and visual rehearsal in eyewitness recall, see Read, Hammersley, Cross-Calvert, & McFadzen, 1989; Sporer, 1988, 1989).

Overall, Yuille and Cutshall (1986) found that the police interview had rendered a total of 392 action, 180 person description, and 78 object description details, many of which turned out to be correct (82%, 76%, and 89%, respectively). These figures were even higher for the research interview, which asked additional questions that were of primary interest to a memory researcher but not to a police investigator. Yet, despite the large number of correct details elicited by both the police and the researchers in the interviews there were also some errors in the person descriptions, most of which referred to estimates of height, weight, and age (23% errors out of a total of 46 such statistics in the police interview). Such estimates were deemed errors if they were outside of an acceptable range determined by the authors (i.e., plus or minus 2 inches or years, or 5 pounds). Second in errors were faulty descriptions of style and color of hair, as well as style and color of clothing (18%). Problems with descriptions of clothing, particularly memory for colors, were noted long ago by Munsterberg (1908). Cutshall and Yuille (1989) were subsequently able to elicit a greater number of details (although not a greater proportion of accurate details) than the police from witnesses of shootings and of bank robberies up to 2 years after the incident.

Sporer (1992a) analyzed criminal records containing 100 witnesses (46 male, 54 female) who provided a total of 139 person descriptions of perpetrators of capital crimes (mostly cases of robbery and rape). About half of the descriptions were from witnesses who were themselves victims or bystanders involved in the criminal action; the other half were from persons who had observed the criminal outside the context of the crime itself. Overall, person descriptions tended to be rather poor; the number of descriptive details mentioned ranged from 1 to 48 details (M = 9.71; SD = 7.03). Almost one-fourth of all descriptive details referred to general information such as height, age, and race, where height estimates frequently referenced some (unknown) population norm (e.g., "average height", "normal body figure," etc.). Another 31% of descriptors referred to clothes, and 30% described the face of the perpetrator. Some witnesses also mentioned jewelry or the dialect spoken. Close to 5% of the descriptors referenced personality characteristics (which are useless when investigators are trying to find a person to arrest, but may promote subsequent recognition of the person because of the deeper level of processing possibly involved at encoding; see Sporer, 1991). It is also noteworthy that quantity and pattern of descriptions found in this archival study closely resembled those of a staged event study in which a confederate had interrupted a lecture to take away a slide projector (Sporer, 1992b).

Of the facial descriptors analyzed by Sporer (1992a), the majority referred to the upper half of the face, particularly the hair of the perpetrator. This finding confirms earlier studies on contents of facial descriptions (Ellis, Shepherd, & Davies, 1980; Laughery, Duval, & Wogalter, 1986; Shepherd, Ellis, & Davies, 1977) and on the importance of upper portions of the face in the recognition process (e.g., Fisher & Cox, 1975). In fact, the cheek and chin (but also the forehead) were rarely mentioned in these descriptions. Although reference to hair (about 16% of all descriptors) appeared to be the most dominant single descriptor, it is also the most problematic and is likely to be of little help in the pursuit of a criminal because hair style can be most readily altered in comparison with other more permanent features (e.g., inner features of a face). Similarly, the large number of references to the clothing of the perpetrator is generally of limited value when police are attempting to locate a perpetrator.

Lindsay, Martin, and Webber (1994) examined the descriptions of 105 criminals published in the Kingston, Ontario newspaper (*The Whig Standard*) and compared their completeness with that of 100 descriptions (across five targets) obtained from a series of laboratory studies. Participant-witnesses viewing staged crimes were most likely to report clothing (99%), hair color (90%), and height (86%), whereas less than 50% reported such obvious descriptors as gender, age, or race/ethnicity. The most frequently reported feature of the face was the eyes (43%), and all other features were reported less than 25% of the time. Witnesses to real crimes were significantly more likely to report gender (96%), hair color (38%), clothing (60%), and race/ethnicity (25%), and facial features were provided in less than 10% of the sample. Although the results of Lindsay et al. indicated that laboratory witnesses provided more complete descriptions than real witnesses (7.35 vs. 3.94 features, respectively), they more generally concluded: "The data strongly support our concern that eyewitness descriptions are frequently vague" (p. 531).

Van Koppen and Lochun (1997) reported a large-scale archival analysis of person descriptions in 431 robbery cases. A total of 1313 witnesses provided 2299 descriptions of the offenders. Descriptors were subdivided into 24 permanent descriptors (e.g., gender, skin color) and 19 temporary characteristics (e.g., particulars of clothing, type of mask). Similar to Sporer's (1992a) findings, the completeness of the descriptions was rather poor. Of the possible maximum of 43 descriptors, the median number provided by each witness was 8 (interquartile range = 6). Permanent features were mentioned more frequently (median = 5, interquartile range = 5) than temporary characteristics (median = 2, interquartile range = 3). Considering that gender, appearance (including race), and skin color were among the most frequently mentioned permanent characteristics (characteristics that are likely the most obvious to any observer), the paucity of these descriptions becomes even more dramatic. Less than 5% of the descriptors referred to inner features of a face (eye color, nose, face color or complexion, mouth, eye shape, teeth, earrings, chin, ear size, ears protruding), which are considered most important for identifying another person (Ellis, 1992). Of the temporary characteristics, the majority of descriptors referred to hats (51%) and hat color (31%), as well as jackets (28%), coats (25%), and trousers (26%), and their respective colors (28%, 22%, and 18%).

Van Koppen and Lochun's (1997) analysis was not restricted to the quantity of information recalled as in Sporer's (1992a) study, but also sought to analyze the accuracy of descriptions by validating the descriptions by witnesses against the descriptions contained in the police database used in the Netherlands. Although more elements of the descrptors were correct than incorrect, the majority of crucial facial descriptors were wrong (e.g., accuracy of facial descriptors included: eye color = 36%; nose = 35%; mouth = 39%; chin = 38%). Most strikingly, almost all descriptors of facial hair (beard and mustache) failed to match the police database. Given that perpetrators may have changed these aspects of their appearance over time, however, the latter finding is difficult to interpret. Interestingly, there was a negative correlation between accuracy and completeness, indicating that when witnesses did provide more extensive descriptions their accuracy suffered.

Estimates of Height and Weight

Almost all person descriptions contain references to the perceived height, weight, and age of the perpetrator (Kuehn, 1974; Sporer, 1992a; van Koppen & Lochun, 1997; Yuille & Cutshall, 1986); however, authors differ in their interpretation of existing data regarding the extent to which such estimates are accurate. Some authors have defined accuracy as estimates falling within a certain range of "true" values (e.g., true value plus or minus 2 inches or 5 pounds; see Yarmey & Yarmey, 1997; Yuille & Cutshall, 1986), concluding that estimates appear to be rather accurate. Then again, treating values with a difference of 4 inches (almost 10 cm) in height as "accurate" would allow an estimate of 170 cm to be equivalent to one of 180 cm, values that are substantially below or above the population average (see Flin & Shepherd, 1986; Sporer, 1996).

When the accuracy of estimates for height and weight are defined as the correlation between the actual values and their estimates, these correlations are well below their maximum possible value. For example, Janssen and Horowski (1980) reported that the average correlations between the actual and estimated heights in a series of studies with students aged 10 to 18 fluctuated between $.26 < rs < .90$. As might be expected, the correlations were smaller for younger children than for older teenagers. This age effect could be either a function of the restricted experience of the smaller children with numbers (see also Davies, 1996) or a result of the smaller children's own height, which seems to assist adults in gauging their estimates of another person.

Next to the target's true height and weight, probably the most important determinant of this type of estimate is the witness's own height and weight, perhaps modified by his or her knowledge (or better, supposition) of what the average population norm might be for a typical middle-aged male or female. Flin and Shepherd (1986) have presented a comprehensive and representative study on this topic. The authors had 588 participants estimate the height and weight of male targets (using a total of 14 targets of differing heights and weights). Each target was accompanied by a second person, the context person, who asked the participant for directions. Thereafter, the context person returned to the participant and asked for an estimate of the target's height and weight, as well as the participant's own height and weight. Overall, Flin and Shepherd found evidence for an own-anchor effect in which participants used their own height or weight as a reference to judge that of the target person. In contrast, neither the context person's height nor his or her weight appeared to influence participants' estimates, as might have been expected if participants were to compare the two individuals side by side. Generally, participants underestimated the target person's height and weight. There was also a tendency for participants to underestimate the height of taller targets and to overestimate the height of shorter targets—a finding that could be interpreted as regression to the mean. Flin and Shepherd explained this finding with reference to subjects' knowledge of population norms, which might induce observers to shy away from extreme judgments. Hence, very tall or very heavy targets were more likely to be underestimated.

FACTORS THAT INFLUENCE DESCRIPTION ACCURACY/COMPLETENESS

Consistent with any memory task, the accuracy or completeness of person description is likely to be influenced by a host of factors, including those present at encoding (e.g., opportunity to view, anxiety or stress, etc.) or throughout the retention interval (e.g., length of the interval, post-event misinformation, etc.). The current section will review the available laboratory, field, and archival research on such factors, as well as witness or target variables (e.g., age, race/ethnicity, gender, etc.) or other individual difference variables that might influence description performance. Finally, various methods for obtaining person descriptions are discussed here for their influence on accuracy and completeness.

Encoding-Based Factors

Opportunity to View. It has been assumed that many if not most crimes happen at night; however, few studies have directly assessed the influence of illumination levels on person descriptions. From the perception literature we know that color vision is dramatically reduced at low levels of illumination, which implies that descriptions of clothing or hair color given under these conditions must be treated with caution. In addition, less information can be extracted under low levels of illumination (G. R. Loftus, 1985; Reinhardt-Rutland, 1986), which should lead to poorer descriptions. One study conducted by Yarmey (1986) has confirmed these extrapolations to person descriptions. More specifically, Yarmey examined eyewitness recall and identification of an event under conditions representing daylight, beginning of twilight, end of twilight, and night vision. His results indicated a significant influence of illumination level on witness recall, including details of the perpetrator, the victim, and the environment. As might have been expected, recall was superior during the daylight and beginning of twilight conditions.

Although it has been assumed that the opportunity to view a target person (i.e., distance between or duration of the event) should significantly influence the accuracy or completeness of person descriptions, only a handful of field studies have attempted to investigate such factors. For example, Yarmey, Jacob, and Porter (2002) conducted a study in which participants interacted with a target person for 5 seconds or 30 seconds and were subsequently asked to describe the encounter. As expected, their results indicated that person descriptions (particularly for clothing) were superior when participants had a longer time to observe the target person. Another aspect that appears to be important regards whether the witness encodes information about a perpetrator with the intent of later recalling it from memory. Along these lines, Yarmey (2004) found that instructions to intentionally encode information from the event for a subsequent memory test led to superior recall of person descriptions (again particularly for articles of clothing).

Although both laboratory and field research on such factors has been minimal, there are some archival analyses of criminal records that have explored the importance of viewing conditions. Despite claims for the superior ecological validity of archival studies (Yuille & Cutshall, 1986), the problem with archival analyses is that the accuracy of the descriptions generally cannot be determined—rather, a proxy for accuracy must be created with respect to the precision of the description, or its relative consistency with that of the individual found guilty for the crime. In Sporer's (1992a) study, the mean number of descriptors, length, and precision of person descriptions were coded and related to low, medium, and high levels of a host of potentially relevant factors, including illumination, duration of event, and time to observe. The categories "low," "medium," and "high" are not to be taken literally, as they may take on different meanings with respect to the particular variable coded (e.g., "high illumination" was operationalized as bright daylight or good artificial lighting). Level of illumination had the expected effect (such that greater illumination led to more complete person descriptions), whereas duration of the incident and time estimated for the target to be in view did not seem to influence description completeness. Similarly, van Koppen and Lochun (1997) found that better illumination and shorter distances between the witness and perpetrator were associated with greater frequency of person descriptors. Whereas both of these studies supported the predicted linear relationship between opportunity to view and recall, Kuehn's (1974) archival analysis found worse performance for twilight conditions than for observations either at bright daylight or at night.

Stress or Anxiety. Eyewitness events are generally considered anxiety-provoking situations in which the victim or witness is likely to experience a great deal of stress during the encoding process. Consistent with this notion, a number of studies of eyewitnesses have suggested that high levels of stress or anxiety impair memory by restricting attentional and executive processes at encoding and thereby prevent the consolidation of information into a coherent event sequence (see Deffenbacher, 1983, 1994). On the other hand, other studies suggest that stress may increase participants' memory for central details (Christianson, 1992) and that the negative effects of stress (at least in some cases) may reverse with the passage of time (Burke, Heuer, & Reisberg, 1992; Christianson, 1984; for a general review see Deffenbacher, Bornstein, Penrod, & McGorty, 2004;

Schooler & Eich, 2000.) With regard to person descriptions, several laboratory studies have demonstrated impairment in accuracy and completeness as a result of stress or anxiety. For example, Clifford and Hollin (1981) varied the violence of a to-be-remembered event and found that participants in the violent conditions were less likely to recall details of the perpetrator (see also Loftus & Burns, 1982). In their recent meta-analysis on the topic, Deffenbacher et al. (2004) found that heightened anxiety led to significant decrements in recall accuracy (Cohen's $d = -.31$) across studies.

The presence of a weapon, which may be accompanied by stress or fear, has also been shown to divert a witness's attention away from the face of the offender. A number of studies have investigated the possibility that the presence of a weapon is associated with impaired recall of details of the perpetrator or event. Consistent with the aforementioned research, studies of the "weapon focus" effect have generally demonstrated a significant influence of the presence of a weapon on person description accuracy (see meta-analysis by Steblay, 1992). Recent research by Pickel (1998, 1999) has indicated that the unusual or unexpected nature of a weapon may be responsible for the observed effect on description accuracy, when contrasted with the "threat" posed by the object.

Archival studies of eyewitness testimony have also attempted to assess the influence of anxiety, stress, or the presence of a weapon on the accuracy or completeness of person descriptions. Given that stress in criminal situations could not be observed (or manipulated) directly, the amounts of anxiety and arousal were coded retrospectively by classification of an event on the basis of the reports emerging from police records (e.g., presence of a deadly weapon, bodily injury, etc.) or of self-reports of anxiety provided by the witnesses in the course of testimony. In Sporer's (1992a) study, three groups of witnesses were compared: victims, bystanders participating in the event without being victims, and other witnesses who were questioned by the police about the perpetrator during the investigation but were not themselves directly involved in the case (e.g., the owner of a gunshop where the perpetrator bought his weapon). Overall, the most striking finding of this analysis was that none of the various ways in which stress had been coded seemed to indicate the expected deterioration in witness recall for high levels of stress and its associated variables. In fact, there even appeared to be a (linear) increase in descriptive details as a function of some of these stress-related variables (e.g., greater reported anxiety was associated with a greater number of details). An analysis of stress conducted by Yuille and Cutshall (1986) showed similar results, whereas an analysis conducted by van Koppen and Lochun (1997) demonstrated results consistent with the laboratory and field research reported earlier (i.e., high levels of stress associated with impaired recall performance). A more recent archival study by Wagstaff et al. (2003) demonstrated null effects on the accuracy or completeness of person descriptions. The general inconsistency observed between laboratory or field research and archival research may potentially be accounted for by length of the retention interval. Laboratory studies have typically used short retention intervals that are known to sometimes give an advantage to nonstressful memories, whereas archival studies typically involve longer retention intervals, which sometimes afford advantages to more stressful memories (Kleinsmith & Kaplan, 1963, 1964). It also possible that stressful experiences may be more likely to incur rehearsal, which could increase the amount of details recalled. Importantly, in none of these archival studies was it possible to ascertain the accuracy of the descriptions, so all conclusions from the archival data must be drawn with caution.

Alcohol or Drugs. The consumption of alcohol or drugs is frequently associated with criminal activity (Yuille, 1986). Laboratory research has consistently demonstrated that alcohol consumption inhibits the encoding process when administered beforehand and thereby impairs subsequent recall of information (for a review see Sayette, 1999). However, research has been somewhat limited in examining the influence of alcohol or drug usage on the accuracy or completeness of eyewitness descriptions. One of the few empirical studies examining the effect of alcohol consumption on witness recall was conducted by Yuille and Tollestrup (1990). In general, the authors found that consumption of alcohol significantly impaired participants' ability to recall details (in both frequency and accuracy of recall) of the event and/or target person, regardless of whether the participant recalled immediately (and under the continued influence of alcohol) or 1 week later. Read, Yuille, and Tollestrup (1992; Experiment 1) subsequently found similar effects. In his archival analysis, Sporer (1992a) also found that when witnesses had consumed alcohol they were less able to report details about the perpetrator's appearance.

More recently, Yuille and his colleagues (Yuille, Tollestrup, Marxsen, Porter, & Herve, 1998) investigated the effects of marijuana use on eyewitness memory. Prior research had generally shown detrimental effects of marijuana on memory recall (cf. Murray, 1986). The results of Yuille et al. demonstrated that marijuana use significantly impaired the completeness of witnesses' recall regarding the event or target person. This effect, however, was moderated by the timing of recall such that the impairment of recall associated with marijuana use was present only when participants were questioned immediately after the event. When participants in the marijuana and control conditions were questioned after a 1-week delay, no differences in completeness of recall were observed. In contrast to completeness of recall, no significant effects of marijuana use were found when accuracy of recall was considered. It is apparent that further research is needed to evaluate the influence of alcohol and drugs on eyewitness recall.

Retention Factors

To the layperson it may sound like a truism that accurate retrieval of information should deteriorate following increased levels of delay; however, the form of the postulated forgetting function varies with the type of material (e.g., visual vs. verbal) as well as the form of the memory test (e.g., recall vs. recognition; see Shepherd, Ellis, & Davies, 1982; Shepherd, 1983; Sporer, 1989; Wixted & Ebbesen, 1997). The current section discusses the available research (laboratory, field, and archival) regarding the influence of retention factors on person descriptions, including the length of the delay, the strength of the memory trace, and the intrusion of post-event information.

In general, laboratory research has shown significant detrimental effects of delay in the accuracy and completeness of person descriptions. For example, Ellis, Shepherd, and Davies (1980) had participants describe one face immediately after viewing it, and another either 1 hour, the next day, or 1 week following exposure. Participants remembered significantly fewer details after 1 week compared with the two shorter retention intervals, and memory loss was rather equally distributed across specific facial features. The accuracy of person descriptions also declined significantly with the longer delay interval. In a similar laboratory experiment, Meissner (2002) found significant losses in both the completeness and the accuracy of facial descriptors when participants provided a description either immediately or following a 1-week delay.

In their archival analysis, van Koppen and Lochun (1997) observed a pattern consistent with the aforementioned laboratory studies, such that witnesses provided fewer person descriptors following longer retention intervals. In contrast to this study, Yuille and Cutshall (1986) and Cutshall and Yuille (1989) emphasized strikingly high levels of recall from witnesses of real crimes as late as 2 years after the incidents. As mentioned previously, these high levels of performance were likely mediated by repeated questioning (and rehearsal) prior to recall at the time of the study (see Sporer, 1989).

It should be noted that the course of time alone is unlikely to have a detrimental effect on recall; rather, both the strength of the initial memory trace and interference from a variety of activities during the delay interval are likely the major influence of a witness's ultimate recall of person descriptors. Generally referred to as "post-event information," witnesses may obtain information during the retention interval (either deliberately or unintentionally) through a number of sources or tasks that they engage in. For example, overhearing a description provided by another person or being shown an erroneous facial composite or sketch can lead the witness to incorporate erroneous details into his or her own description of the perpetrator, and the likelihood of such post-event information influencing subsequent recall has been shown to increase following a long retention interval (Loftus & Greene, 1980; Loftus & Ketcham, 1983; Shaw, Garven, & Wood, 1997; Sporer, 1996b). The related effects of misleading questioning by investigators (referred to as "misinformation") and collaborative recall with another witness (or "co-witness" effects) are discussed below.

Witness and Target-Person Variables

As in the eyewitness identification literature, a number of witness and target variables (e.g., gender, age, ethnicity, etc.) appear to influence the accuracy and completeness of person descriptions. This section reviews the available literature on such variables.

Gender.   Although many studies on eyewitness memory have included both male and female participants, few have analyzed gender differences. Several studies conducted by Yarmey (1986, 1993, 2004) have generally indicated few differences in the recall of men and women. When differences were noted, they typically involved responses to specific attributes that women may have been more likely to attend to at encoding (e.g., jewelry, hair color or length, and weight; see Yarmey, 2004), or they involved more complex interactions between variables (such as levels of illumination; see Yarmey, 1986). In several studies, Yarmey noted that men appeared more confident in their responses than women (Yarmey, 1986, 1993).

MacLeod and Shepherd (1986) have drawn attention to gender differences in an archival study of criminal assault cases. Similar to research by Yarmey (1986, 2004), gender differences were found to covary in a complex manner with such variables as the type of questions analyzed (e.g., action details vs. descriptive details; statements referring to self, victim, accused, or periphery) and the type of incident (involving injury of the victim or not). In his archival analysis, Sporer (1992a) reported that male witnesses provided on average longer descriptions than females (M = 7.50 vs. 7.10 number of lines in the protocol, respectively). In contrast, the number of descriptors and rated precision of statements showed an opposite but nonsignificant trend favoring females. Thus, it appears that although females may have said less quantitatively, they did not necessarily convey less information.

Child Witnesses.   Although some studies have found that the relative accuracy in reports of children may not differ from that of adults (Goodman & Reed, 1986; Leippe, Romanczyk, & Manion, 1991; Marin, Holmes, Guth, & Kovac, 1979), adults' statements are likely to be much longer and more detailed than those of children (Davies, Tarrant, & Flin, 1989; Dent & Stephenson, 1979; Leippe et al., 1979; Marin et al., 1979). In contrast, a recent study conducted by Pozzulo and Warren (2003, Experiment 1) observed both greater accuracy and completeness of person descriptions provided by adults versus youths (ages 10 to 14). Further analyses indicated that adults were more likely to report features of the face, aspects of the body (i.e., height, weight, and build), and race of the perpetrator, whereas youths were more likely to report various accessories (e.g., belt or glasses). With regard to accuracy, youths were significantly less accurate than adults in describing interior facial features (e.g., eyes, nose, or mouth), aspects of the body, and the age of the perpetrator. In a follow-up study using a live event, Pozzulo and Warren (Experiment 2) observed the more classic pattern involving a greater frequency of person descriptors by adults when compared with youths, but no differences in the overall accuracy of features reported. The analysis of specific features was largely consistent with the first study, except that aspects of the target's clothing were more likely to be reported by adults in the sample. Recent research by Lindholm (2005) has also suggested that witnesses, particularly children and young adults, may actually perform better when recalling descriptions of target persons matching their own age group. Such own-age effects (similar to the cross-race effects discussed below) may result from a variety of experiential or motivational factors (cf. Sporer, 2001a), and further research on this topic seems warranted.

Saywitz (1995) has suggested that it may be important to adapt one's language when interviewing children such that questions are more comprehensible to young children. In particular, interviewers should use short sentences with a simple grammatical structure, common phrases, and proper names. They should avoid the passive voice, double negatives, and indirect questions. Before estimates are obtained, interviewers should also make sure that children understand concepts like size, distance, weight, age, and time, as well as particular body parts and various color names. For example, Dent (1982) reported large inaccuracies in estimates with children between 8 and 13 years of age. Furthermore, age estimates may suffer from children's lack of knowledge of facial cues to aging (Ellis, 1992). Providing children (and adults) with possible ranges or specific anchors (Dent, 1982; Sporer, 1996b) or a color plate or color wheel may lead to better results for some aspects of person descriptions than free descriptions. In contrast, specific questions (e.g., *What was the color of her hair?*) may lead not only to more information but also to more inaccurate information than general questions (e.g., *What was her appearance?*; Dent & Stephenson, 1979).

One challenge in understanding the influence of misinformation on children relative to adults is that children may be both more likely to forget details of the original experience (including the appearance of the perpetrator) and more likely to forget any misinformation they receive about the individual after the fact (Schooler, 1998; Schooler & Loftus, 1993). Thus, it is possible that testing children following a delay (when they have had the opportunity to forget the misinformation) may provide the best opportunity for achieving veridical recall. In their classic review of the topic, Ceci and Bruck (1993) also posited that certain cognitive (e.g., memory trace strength or source-monitoring ability) and social (e.g., conformity to an authority figure) activities can mediate a child's susceptibility to suggestion in recall. Although the authors caution against the perils of suggestive questioning, they warn against completely discounting children's recall. In their own words, "children are able to encode and retrieve large amounts of information, especially when it is personally experienced and highly meaningful" (p. 434).

Elderly Witnesses.   Aging in late adulthood has been shown to affect both the perceptual and memory abilities of witnesses (for a review, see Yarmey, 1996). Elderly witnesses (i.e., above 65 years), for example, are increasingly more likely to demonstrate deficits in their visual acuity at night, and in their ability to perceive depth and to adapt to darkness. Both color vision (particularly blue and blue-green) and memory for colors are also likely to decline with age. At later age levels, individuals are also more likely to demonstrate difficulty with source monitoring (Cohen & Faulkner, 1989; Henkel, Johnson, & de Leonardis, 1998), which may be crucial in many eyewitness situations (e.g., to counter the influence of suggestive questioning).

In a field experiment in which both showup and lineup identifications were administered to participants ranging in age between 18 and 65 (Yarmey, Yarmey, & Yarmey, 1994), 651 individuals were randomly approached in public places and asked for directions by one of two young adult, female confederates. The duration of exposure to the target was approximately 15 seconds. Two minutes later the witness was approached by a female investigator and was asked to describe the target and to identify her face and voice. With regard to description accuracy, young adults (18–29 years of age) were significantly superior (M = 72%) to middle-aged witnesses (30–44 years of age) (M = 61%), who in turn were superior to older adults (45–65 years of age) (M = 54%). These results comport with prior research conducted by Yarmey and his colleagues (e.g., Yarmey & Kent, 1980), which indicated that "young adults on average were twice as complete and 20% more accurate in free narration in their descriptions of a criminal incident than were the elderly" (Yarmey, 1996, p. 268). Recent research by Searcy, Bartlett, Memon, and Swanson (2001) has demonstrated similar effects on person description completeness and accuracy for young versus elderly adults. However, to the extent that most of these studies have used only young adults as targets to be observed and described, these studies may reflect as much an in-group bias in the form of an own-age effect (Sporer, 2001a) as deficits in the memory of elderly witnesses.

Cross-ethnic Differences.   Although more than 60 studies have investigated recognition memory for own- versus other-race faces (for reviews see Chance & Goldstein, 1996; Meissner & Brigham, 2001b; Sporer, 2001a), very few studies have attempted to determine whether participants differ in the way they describe faces of their own and another race (Sporer, 2001b). Those that have investigated descriptions of own- versus other-race faces have suggested that individuals attend to features deemed relevant to own-race faces and further attempt to apply this encoding scheme inappropriately when examining other-race faces (Ellis, Deregowski, & Shepherd, 1975; Shepherd & Deregowski, 1981). For example, Ellis and colleagues (1975) demonstrated several differences in the type of features that black and white participants recalled (regardless of the race of face). Although Ellis and colleagues did not assess descriptions for accuracy or discriminability, they did note that white participants often reported rather "redundant" descriptions of black faces (e.g., "he has black skin, black, kinky hair and brown eyes") that would likely be indiscriminant upon later assessment (p. 123).

Fallshore and Schooler (1995) compared Caucasian undergraduates' ability to identify and describe African American and Caucasian faces. As is typically found, they observed the cross-race effect for lineup identification decisions, such that participants were better able to recognize Caucasian relative to African American faces. However, when description accuracy was assessed with the use of a communication accuracy paradigm in which subject-judges attempted to identify the faces based on witnesses' verbal descriptions, no cross-race effect was observed (although a numerical advantage was shown for the identification of other-race faces). Fallshore and Schooler speculated that differences in the pattern of results associated with cross-racial face recognition versus face description may be due to differential reliance on configural versus featural processing for own versus other race faces, respectively (see Rhodes, Brake, Taylor, & Tan, 1989). Accordingly, if the source of the own-race face recognition advantage were an enhanced ability to rely on configural information (Sporer, 2001a), then it follows that verbal description ability, which typically relies on featural knowledge (see Farah, Wilson, Drain, & Tanaka, 1998; Wells & Turtle, 1987), should not reveal such differences. Thus, although the relative dearth of studies on the topic clearly suggests the need for additional research, the absence of evidence for an own-race advantage for person description may reflect fundamental differences in the processes associated with face recognition versus description.

Methods for Obtaining Person Descriptions

Several methods of eliciting a person description have been developed over the years, from standard free recall approaches to feature checklists and techniques based upon

principles of cognitive psychology (e.g., the cognitive interview). In this section, we discuss research on the generation of person descriptions and their positive and negative
effects. Along the way, we also address the role of leading questions and attempts at permitting witnesses to collaborate in generating a description, and we consider the effect
of repeated questioning on the accuracy and completeness of person descriptions.

Free Recall vs. Leading Questions.   Likely the most common technique used by
investigators to obtain a person description involves a request for the witness to simply
recall what he or she remembers about the perpetrator of the crime. Although such free
recall descriptions are often quite accurate, unfortunately they rarely satisfy investigators,
because of their likelihood of being incomplete with regard to critical details (Lipton,
1977). Thus, investigators will frequently follow up with more specific, close-ended questions to complete the description (e.g., *Do you remember the color of the man's hair?*). In
addition, investigators may have previously received information regarding the perpetrator and so will attempt to confirm this information by inquiring about more specific details (e.g., *Did the man have red hair with long sideburns?*) or may include this information
in the context of inquiring about another detail (e.g., *This man with the red hair and long
sideburns, did he have any facial hair?*). Unfortunately, such leading questions can have rather
harmful consequences for the witness's attempts at subsequent recall, as studies indicate
that witnesses are quite likely to incorporate potentially inaccurate information ("misinformation") into their person descriptions (Loftus, 1975, 1979; Loftus & Zanni, 1975).
For example, Loftus and Greene (1980) observed that participants who viewed a face
and then heard a description of the face that was attributed to another witness later incorporated the verbal expressions of that witness into their description, even when the
description was in error.

Feature Checklists.   As noted above, one primary drawback to the use of free recall
tasks regards the incompleteness of person descriptions. Witnesses will often vary in their
output criterion for recalling details of an event (Koriat & Goldsmith, 1996), and a common difficulty with person descriptions involves the limited vocabulary that individuals
have for describing the human face. In an attempt to alleviate this problem, researchers
have sought to develop feature checklists that might aid witnesses in providing more
complete (and useful) descriptions of the perpetrator they viewed. For example, Shepherd (1986; see also Shepherd & Ellis, 1996; Sporer, in press) and his colleagues have
developed the Aberdeen Face Rating Schedule, which consists of some 50 items on
which witnesses are asked to rate individual features of a face on five-point scales (for a
published version of these scales, see Sporer, in press). Using these forms, observers are
prompted to use certain features that otherwise they might omit or forget. However, accuracy of these descriptions might be poor, as people may frequently mark the middle
("normal") value of the scale when they either don't remember or guess the information
(Sporer, in press). Nonetheless, forms of this type are useful both for communicating information to other agencies and for conducting computerized searches to identify individuals in mug shot databases who might be presented to the witness (cf. Pryke, Lindsay,
& Pozzulo, 2000). A prototype of such a system was developed by psychologists at the

University of Aberdeen (see Shepherd, 1986; Shepherd & Ellis, 1996), and another similar system, SIGMA-IRIS, was used by the Austrian police (Zima & Zeiner, 1982).

One potential problem with the use of feature checklists regards their presentation of a rather exhaustive list of person descriptors, many of which the witness may never have attended to at encoding. The information elicited is either not very informative (as when witnesses mark default, "normal" values) or even incorrect, and the accuracy of the information is not related to the accuracy of a later identification (Sporer, in press). When the witness signifies the recollection of several features that are incongruent with the actual perpetrator, this may cause interference quite similar to the misinformation effects discussed above. In several studies, Wogalter (1991, 1996) has shown that such feature checklists (in contrast to a free recall or imaging task) can produce more incorrect features and subsequently interfere with witnesses' ability to identify the perpetrator. As a result, feature checklists may not provide the best means for collecting eyewitness information.

Collaborative Recall. Should witnesses be permitted to discuss their memory for the event with one another in generating a common, agreed-upon description for the perpetrator? There are, of course, potential benefits from collaborative recall, but there would also be potential costs of cross-contamination if witnesses were to share erroneous information with one another. Psychologists have studied this problem in the context of person descriptions, attempting to understand any benefits of permitting collaborative recall on the accuracy and completeness of descriptions, and the extent to which witnesses may adopt erroneous information provided by another witness into their descriptions. For example, Warnick and Sanders (1980) investigated the influence of group discussion of a previously viewed event on individual witness's subsequent recall. Their results indicated superior accuracy and completeness of recall for participants who had discussed the event in a group when compared with participants who recalled the information independently. Yarmey and Morris (1998) conducted a similar study, but had some participants also provide a consensus description of the perpetrator and event (some immediately, others following a 1-week delay). The results of Yarmey and Morris also indicated that group discussions led to more correct details being recalled when compared with individual attempts at recall, but no similar increase in erroneous details.

Given that witnesses' person descriptions are generally quite accurate, it seems reasonable that collaborative recall would have some positive effects on the amount of information recalled. But are witnesses particularly susceptible to adopting erroneous details that might be provided by another witness? To explore such a "conformity effect," Gabbert, Memon, and Allan (2003) created a situation in which witnesses viewed events differing in several key features. Witnesses were then later asked to discuss the event with another witness before providing a description independently. Consistent with previous studies of the misinformation paradigm (cf. Shaw et al., 1997), a rather substantial percentage of participants (71%) incorporated erroneous details provided to them by the co-witness. Thus, to the extent that a co-witness might provide erroneous information, collaborative recall may contaminate the person descriptions of others who participate in the discussion.

Repeated Questioning. Witnesses may be asked to provide a description of the perpetrator and event on multiple occasions, including immediately following the event, throughout the investigative process, in depositions and pretrial hearings, and finally (but most importantly) on the witness stand before a jury. To what extent might repeated questioning influence the veridicality of the information provided by the witness? The general cognitive literature has shown both positive and negative effects of repeated recall (Brown, 1923). For example, individuals may benefit from repeated attempts by recalling information or items that had not previously been reported (Payne, 1987; Roediger & Challis, 1989). To avoid confusion, we adopt the distinction between *hypermnesia*, that is, an increase in net recall (number of new details minus number of items lost), and *reminiscence*, that is, the gross recall of details provided at least once across a number of trials (Payne, 1987; Turtle & Yuille, 1994). In their study of eyewitnesses, Scrivner and Safer (1988) demonstrated hypermnesia during the repeated recall of event and perpetrator details from a previously viewed crime. Turtle and Yuille (1994) partially replicated these findings with longer retention intervals between successive recall episodes, demonstrating reminiscence but not hypermnesia. Bornstein, Liebel, and Scarberry (1998) further demonstrated that repeated testing can improve recall for details of a negatively arousing event.

In addition to the possibility of more complete descriptions, repeated testing has also been shown to preserve an individual's memory by strengthening associations that are retrieved (see Bjork, 1988). One important moderator, however, regards the retention interval prior to the first attempt at retrieval—to the extent that the retention interval is brief, more information may be preserved by the act of retrieval (Bahrick, 2000; Ebbesen & Rienick, 1998; Shaw, Bjork, & Handal, 1995). Ebbesen and Rienick (1998) varied the interval between exposure to a target and the first recall attempt (1 day, 7 days, or 28 days), and all participants provided a second recall attempt after 4 weeks. Their results indicated that, across all conditions, participants recalled about one less descriptor at the 4-week test ($M = 8.50$) than at all other tests ($M = 9.50$). Although the authors stress the fact that there was virtually no decline in the recall of personal attributes once a recall attempt was made, the percentage of errors for facial features, clothing color, and clothing style was still substantial. Even recall for the ethnicity of the person who participants had interacted with showed error rates between 13% and 23%. Nonetheless, these results do appear to demonstrate the predicted protection of person description memory afforded by repeated questioning. In a similar fashion, Dunning and Stern (1992) reported two experiments in which participants showed a (nonsignificant) tendency to recall more person information correctly, with no change in incorrect or confabulated details, over repeated reports. The interval between reports, however, was only 5 minutes, which is functionally quite different from the situation in which witnesses are repeatedly asked about events at different occasions separated by days or even months (Sporer, 1992a; van Koppen & Lochun, 1997).

In contrast to the benefits of increased completeness and maintenance of the memory, Roediger and his colleagues have demonstrated that repeated testing can also have rather paradoxical effects in which erroneous information may be reported and incorporated into subsequent recall episodes (see Roediger, McDermott, & Goff, 1997; Roediger, Wheeler, & Rajaram, 1993). For example, a study by Roediger, Jacoby, and McDermott (1996) demonstrated that when participants were encouraged to recall erroneous information from a previously viewed crime, they were more likely to report that information in later attempts at recall (cf. Schooler, Foster, & Loftus, 1988). Meissner (2002) subsequently replicated the pervasive effects of self-generated misinformation in the context of person descriptions, particularly when participants were forced to report descriptors that they were unsure of.

Cognitive Interview. Over the years, researchers have been interested in devising techniques that might improve the accuracy and completeness of information obtained from witnesses. Likely the most well-known technique is the cognitive interview, which was initially developed by Geiselman and Fisher in the early 1980s (for a review, see Fisher & Geiselman, 1992). Overall, the cognitive interview consists of four main components: (1) context reinstatement, which includes mentally reinstating the environmental and personal context of the original event; (2) instruction to "report all" information, including partial information, even if it seems unimportant; (3) recounting the event in a variety of temporal orders; and (4) reporting the events from a variety of perspectives. With the use of the cognitive interview, a host of studies have shown that descriptions of persons, objects, and events can be reliably improved when compared with other standard (free recall) interview techniques.

In the first of these studies, Geiselman et al. (1984) obtained 11.00 correct details in response to open-ended questions about characteristics of a person from witnesses instructed with the cognitive interview, compared with 7.38 details by witnesses in a standard interview condition. Importantly, the cognitive interview did not lead to an increase in incorrect details. Whereas this basic pattern of results has been confirmed in studies with real witnesses (Fisher, Geiselman, & Amador, 1989), other studies have noted an increase in the recall of incorrect details gathered with the cognitive interview. For example, a study by Finger and Pezdek (1999) found that the cognitive interview increased the recall of both correct and incorrect facial descriptors when compared with a standard interview procedure. Confirming this pattern, a recent meta-analysis of 42 studies by Koehnken, Milne, Memon, and Bull (1999) revealed a large increase in the number of correct details elicited by the cognitive interview and a smaller, yet significant, increase in the number of incorrect details elicited. Furthermore, the meta-analysis indicated that accuracy rates elicited with the cognitive interview were about the same as accuracy rates achieved with traditional interview methods (84% vs. 82%, respectively). It should be noted that the majority of studies examining the cognitive interview have not focused on obtaining person descriptions per se, so further research in this direction seems worthwhile.

THE RELATIONSHIP BETWEEN PERSON DESCRIPTIONS AND EYEWITNESS IDENTIFICATION

So far our discussion has focused on the nature and quality of person descriptions. An important related issue involves the relationship between the description and identification of faces. This in turn leads to two distinct (albeit related) questions. First, what is the relationship between the quality with which a witness describes a face and the accuracy with which he or she subsequently identifies it? Second, what is the influence of describing a face on its subsequent identification? As will be seen, the answers to both of these questions are not as intuitive as one might expect.

The Description-Identification Relationship

It seems quite reasonable that witnesses who are better at describing a perpetrator should also be better at identifying him. The intuitive nature of this relationship is inherent in the arguments in many eyewitness cases where inconsistencies between a witness's initial description of a perpetrator and the appearance of the suspect are highlighted to undermine the credibility of the identification. Both the U.S. Supreme Court (*Neil v. Biggers*, 1972) and the German Supreme Court have used the quality of person descriptions as indicators to evaluate the accuracy of person identifications in criminal trials (see Sporer & Cutler, 2003). Despite the appeal of the belief that a strong relationship should exist between face description quality and identification accuracy, research reveals that this relationship is at best very weak and often nonexistent. Although Sporer (1992b) reported a significant positive relation (assessed by a point-biserial correlation) between the number of descriptors and identification accuracy in a staged event study ($r = .28$), other studies have not confirmed this finding when focusing on the accuracy of descriptions. For example, Grass and Sporer (1991) staged another event in a classroom and then 1 week later had participants describe the target's appearance and respond to prompted questions about the target's appearance. Participants were then presented live simultaneous, live sequential, or photographic sequential lineups. These authors found no relationship between two judges' assessments of either the completeness ($r = -.06$) or accuracy ($r = -.04$) of the descriptions and identification performance. Similar failures to find a relationship between face description quality and recognition performance have been observed in a number of other studies (Pigott & Brigham, 1985; Sporer, in press). Furthermore, Wells and Leippe (1981) actually found a nonsignificant, yet sizable, negative relationship ($r = -.41$) between the accuracy of witnesses verbal recall of other aspects of the scene of a simulated crime and their identification of the target individual.

Although an absence of a relationship between person description quality and identification performance is by far the most common result, there are a few circumstances under which a relationship has been observed. Using the communication accuracy paradigm, Fallshore and Schooler (1995) examined the relationship between a description's quality and the ability of another individual to use a given description to identify the individual described from among a set of distractors. In the context of describing and identifying own- versus other-race faces, the authors found no significant relationship between description accuracy and identification performance for own-race faces ($r = .12$), but a significant relationship in performance on other-race faces ($r = .36$). This finding further supports the view that other-race faces may be recognized in a more featural manner than own-race faces (Rhodes et al., 1989; Sporer, 2001a). Accordingly, inasmuch as the recognition of other-race faces depends on the quality of witnesses' memory of individual features, the veracity of the witnesses' memory for those features (as revealed by the quality of their descriptions) becomes predictive of their recognition performance. This finding also potentially offers a key for understanding why face description quality bears so little relationship to identification performance with own-race faces—namely, the two tasks may draw on fundamentally different types of knowledge, with the former depending on participants' memory for distinctive features and the latter depending on their nonverbal knowledge of the face in its entirety (see Farah et al., 1998; Wells & Turtle, 1987).

A second exception to the typical absence of a relationship between description quality and face recognition quality comes from studies that have compared the relative ease with which different faces can be described versus recognized. Wells (1985) showed participants multiple faces and then examined their ability to both describe and recognize each face. He found that distinctive faces tended to be easier to describe and to recognize than less distinct faces, thereby leading to a modest relationship between recognition accuracy and description quality ($r = .27$) across faces. Although this modest correlation does suggest that certain distinctive faces can be recognized on the basis of individual features, it certainly does not undermine the more common conclusion that typically little relationship between verbal description quality and recognition accuracy can be expected.

A final exception to the absence of a relationship between description quality and recognition performance has been observed in studies in which participants were forced to generate rather elaborate descriptions of faces and were later asked to identify these individuals in a lineup identification task (cf. Meissner, Brigham, & Kelley, 2001). In these studies, it appears that the elicitation of elaborate verbal descriptions may lead participants to generate inaccurate details, which then impairs their recognition performance. Indeed, several studies using such a paradigm (Finger & Pezdek, 1999; Meissner, 2002; Meissner et al., 2001) have found that incorrect details reported in participants' descriptions are predictive of subsequent identification errors.

In short, it seems that despite the clear intuition that witnesses who are better at describing a target should also be better at recognizing it, this relationship has proved to be quite elusive and generally weak. Though the absence of such a relationship may undermine this frequently relied-upon method for assessing the credibility of witnesses, it also provides an important link in our understanding of the nature of person descriptions—namely, that person descriptions may draw upon knowledge or cognitive processes that are very different from those invoked in the identification of a face. More specifically, person descriptions appear to encourage a focus upon verbalizable features of the face that are not always useful for perceptually individuating a given face from among similar distractors. In contrast, recognition of faces has been shown to involve a configural process in which features combine to create a nonverbalizable perceptual set that is stored and later accessed for pattern recognition (Farah et al., 1998). The exceptions to the incompatibility of these processes appear to involve faces that are recognizable based upon a distinctive local feature, or conditions in which retrieval of a face description distorts the veracity of the memory trace and interferes with subsequent identification.

The Influence of Person Descriptions on Identification: Verbal Overshadowing

The fundamental difference between describing a face and recognizing it also contributes to some counterintuitive findings regarding the influence of verbally describing a face on subsequent recognition of that face. Intuitively we might expect that describing a face would be helpful for subsequent memory performance, because it constitutes a form of verbal rehearsal, and verbal rehearsal is well known to enhance memory performance (e.g., Darley & Glass, 1975; Glenberg & Adams, 1978; see Sporer, 1989). There is some evidence that visually rehearsing a face, even after being prompted by a verbal description cue, may indeed improve recognition (Sporer, 1988). However, a growing body of research suggests that contrary to this intuition, efforts to describe a previously seen face can actually *impair* subsequent memory performance, at least under some circumstances.

In the original documentation of this counterintuitive effect of verbal description on face recognition (termed *verbal overshadowing*), Schooler and Engstler-Schooler (1990) showed participants a videotape of a bank robbery. Some participants were instructed to describe the robber in as much detail as possible while others engaged in an unrelated filler activity. Finally, all participants were shown a lineup containing the robber and seven foils. The results revealed that participants who had described the robber were markedly less accurate in recognizing him compared with no-description controls. Follow-up experiments by Schooler and Engstler-Schooler were largely consistent with the verbal overshadowing hypothesis that the negative effects of verbalization were due to a mismatch between the visual information or processes associated with the original experience and the verbal information or processes associated with the act of verbal description. For example, the negative effects of verbal description generalized to another type of nonverbal stimuli (i.e., colors), but not to more readily verbalized stimuli (i.e., the contents of what the robber said). Similarly, whereas verbal rehearsal repeatedly disrupted performance, visualizing the robber's face had no effect on subsequent identification.

Since its original demonstration, the verbal overshadowing phenomenon has been replicated numerous times (Dodson, Johnson, & Schooler, 1997; Fallshore & Schooler, 1995; Ryan & Schooler, 1998; Schooler, Ryan, & Reder, 1996; Sporer, 1989). At the same time, however, it has also failed to replicate on a number of occasions (Lovett, Small, & Engstrom, 1992; Yu & Geiselman, 1993). A meta-analysis of the verbal overshadowing effect was recently conducted by Meissner and Brigham (2001a). Across a sample of 15 studies (29 effect size comparisons; $N = 2018$), Meissner and Brigham observed a small, yet significant, verbal overshadowing effect ($Zr = -.12$) demonstrating that participants who described a target face were 1.27 times more likely to later *misidentify* the face from a lineup recognition task when compared with participants who did not generate a description prior to identification.

Although the verbal overshadowing effect is a reliable phenomenon, it nevertheless appears to be somewhat fragile. Moreover, while research following the original demonstration of verbal overshadowing is largely (if not entirely) consistent with the claim that it is associated with discrepancies between the modality of the original visual encoding, the precise mechanism responsible for the effect remains an issue of some contention. We briefly review the research surrounding this topic and then consider the merits of several current explanations. As will be seen, there is compelling evidence in support of each of the primary accounts, yet no single explanation can accommodate all of the extant findings suggesting that multiple mechanisms may be involved.

Recoding Interference. In their original account of the verbal overshadowing effect, Schooler and Engstler-Schooler (1990) proposed that it results from recoding interference in which "the verbalization of a visual memory can foster the formation of a nonveridical verbally biased representation corresponding to the original stimulus" (p. 62). Such an account generally explains why the overshadowing effect is exclusively observed with nonverbal stimuli such as faces that are difficult to put into words, but not with stimuli that are more easily described.

More recently, Meissner and his colleagues (Meissner, 2002; Meissner et al., 2001) have provided additional support for the recoding interference account by demonstrating that the influence of verbalization is mediated by the amount of incorrect descriptors that participants are encouraged to generate. Specifically they found that verbal disruption was maximized when participants were "forced" to provide elaborate descriptions of the face. Under such forced recall conditions, Meissner and colleagues (2001) found that participants were more likely to include erroneous elements in their descriptions and subsequently demonstrated verbal overshadowing in their poor performance on a lineup identification task (27% accuracy) when compared with participants in a no-description control condition (52% accuracy). In contrast, another group of participants were warned to provide very accurate descriptions and not to guess at any particular features. Those in this warning condition actually demonstrated verbal enhancement (63% accuracy) when compared with participants in the control or forced conditions. Meissner and colleagues have replicated this "instructional bias" effect in several studies (Meissner, 2002; Meissner et al., 2001; see also Finger & Pezdek, 1999; MacLin, Tapscott, & Malpass, 2002) and have found that the effect persists despite delays of 30 minutes or 1 week, despite instructions to source monitor, and across repeated attempts at recall prior to identification. Taken together, these results suggest that extensive verbalization can lead to the production of a self-generated misinformation effect whereby participants are misled by the erroneous details present in their own descriptions. Further support of this account has also come from a moderator analysis conducted by Meissner and Brigham (2001a) demonstrating that variations in the reliability of verbal overshadowing studies could be reconciled by differences in the procedure used by various researchers. In particular, studies that utilized elaborative description procedures led to more reliable verbal overshadowing effects than those that utilized a standard free-recall procedure.

Transfer Inappropriate Processing Shift. Although the recoding interference account nicely accommodates many verbal overshadowing findings, there are some results that it does not easily handle (for a review see Schooler, Fiore, & Brandimonte, 1997; Schooler, 2002). First, whereas a relationship between verbalization quality and recognition performance has been observed in some studies (e.g., Finger & Pezdek, 1999,

Meissner, 2002; Meissner et al., 2001), other studies have failed to find such a relationship (e.g., Schooler & Engstler-Schooler, 1990). If verbal overshadowing is due to inaccuracies present in the verbal description, then, as Meissner and others have noted, such inaccuracies should be predictive of performance. The failure to find such a relationship across all studies, regardless of the type of recall instructions or task provided, is therefore potentially problematic for this account (Schooler, 2002).

A second problem for the recoding interference account involves studies demonstrating that verbalization can interfere with the recognition of other nonverbalized faces. For example, Dodson and colleagues (1997) presented participants with two faces (a male and a female face) and then had them describe just one of them. On a subsequent recognition test, they observed that verbalization interfered with the recognition of the nonverbalized face as much as it did with the verbalized face. Additional studies have demonstrated that even describing a parent's face from memory can interfere with recognition of a recently encoded (and unrelated) face. More recently, Brown and Lloyd-Jones (2002, 2003) have introduced a novel overshadowing paradigm in which participants are asked to encode a series of faces. Half of the participants are then asked to provide a description of the final face they viewed, and the second group of participants is asked to complete an unrelated filler task. Thereafter, all participants are provided with a recognition test in which a series of faces are shown to them (both novel faces and those from the study set). Brown and Lloyd-Jones have consistently found that describing the final face produces a verbal overshadowing effect in the recognition of all faces from the study set.

If verbal overshadowing is the product of relying on an inaccurate verbal code, then it is hard to understand why verbalization would have comparable effects when the face in question was itself never actually verbalized. Given these concerns, Schooler and his colleagues have suggested an alternative to the recoding interference account, originally termed "transfer inappropriate retrieval" (Schooler et al., 1997) but subsequently renamed "transfer inappropriate processing shift" (TIPS) (Schooler, 2002), based upon evidence that *retrieval* per se may not be a critical component of the process. According to Schooler and colleagues, verbal descriptions may induce a general processing shift that dampens the subsequent application of nonverbal configural processes. In effect, verbal description causes participants to become "stuck" in a verbal mode of processing faces, which is then applied (inappropriately transferred) to the recognition test, resulting in disruption.

The TIPS account nicely accommodates the basic finding that verbalization impairs recognition of nonverbal stimuli (such as faces), but not stimuli that are easily verbalizable (as only the former would be disrupted by an excessive focus on verbal processing). It also accounts for the findings that verbalizing one face can interfere with recognition of a different face (because of the general nature of the processing shift). Finally, TIPS is consistent with the influence of other manipulations (e.g., focusing on individual elements of composite figures) that disrupt face recognition performance (Macrae & Lewis, 2002) and provides a useful way of conceptualizing a variety of situations in which the engagement in one task can impair performance on subsequent tasks. At the same time, however, it does not offer a simple account of why a relationship is sometimes observed between the quality of verbal descriptions and recognition performance.

Criterion Shifts.   Until recently, the debate regarding the mechanisms underlying the negative effects of verbal description on face recognition were limited to the recoding interference and transfer inappropriate processing accounts. However, a third account has been suggested in which verbalization is said to more simply induce a criterion shift such that individuals who provide a description are subsequently less likely to make a positive identification (irrespective of accuracy). In a target-present lineup (used by the majority of researchers investigating the verbal overshadowing effect), such a shift would lead to a greater frequency of misses and thus to reduced accuracy. In testing this hypothesis, Clare and Lewandowsky (2004) found that verbal description of a previously presented face impaired performance on suspect present lineups when participants were provided a "not present" option, but not when they were forced to select from among the faces presented. Moreover, on a target-absent lineup, verbalization actually improved performance (being more cautious necessarily leads to less false identifications)—a finding that the authors note is not predicted by either the recoding interference or TIPS accounts.

While representing an important additional account of verbal overshadowing effects, Clare and Lewandowsky (2004) acknowledge that this approach cannot explain all the extant findings. Specifically, a number of studies have found verbal overshadowing effects with paradigms that either did not include a "not present" option (e.g., Fallshore & Schooler, 1995) or assessed performance on target-absent lineups (e.g., Meissner, 2002). In addition, the recognition paradigm introduced by Brown and Lloyd-Jones (2002, 2003) permitted the calculation of signal detection measures of discrimination and response criterion, but found an overshadowing effect on the former measure. Taken together, these findings prove difficult for a criterion shift account and encourage further research on the precise mechanism of the verbal overshadowing effect.

Summary of Verbal Overshadowing Findings.   In the end it seems that all three current accounts of the negative effects of verbal description on face recognition have merit. Under some conditions, such as when individuals provide elaborate descriptions of a face and a relationship between description quality and recognition accuracy exists, it seems quite likely that verbalization produces a self-generated misinformation effect in which participants rely upon their erroneous description at the expense of their more veridical visual memory. Under other conditions, particularly when no relationship between description performance and recognition accuracy is observed and/or when verbalization is observed to impair the recognition of faces other than those described, it seems likely that verbalization induces a transfer inappropriate processing shift, whereby featural processing operations are inappropriately applied to a recognition test that would be better served by nonverbal, configural processes. Under still other situations, particularly when not present options are included, and the negative effects of verbalization are limited to increased misses, a criterion shift may be in operation. Clearly future research is needed to sort out more precisely when each of these respective mechanisms may be at play. Nevertheless, such research seems greatly warranted, given that verbal description is an inherent element in many eyewitness situations, and that understanding the precise mechanisms by which such descriptions can impair memory is certain to be critical to minimizing the negative effects that such descriptions might otherwise have. In the meantime, investigators should be cautioned against encouraging elaborate descriptions of a perpetrator, so as to minimize the effects of self-generated misinformation on later identification.

CONCLUSIONS AND FUTURE DIRECTIONS

A pervasive theme of research on eyewitness performance is that memory is not particularly reliable. Unfortunately, this theme appears to be particularly pronounced in the context of person descriptions. Person descriptions tend to be vague and nondiscriminative and are susceptible to many of the sources of error that plague other forms of eyewitness memory (e.g., the effects of arousal, poor encoding conditions, misinformation, declines with age, etc.). At the same time, there appear to be some aspects of person descriptions that are uniquely problematic. For example, whereas in general it is useful for witnesses to generate as much information about a witnessed event as possible (e.g., Fisher et al., 1989), in the context of person description, encouraging people to spend extensive time generating their descriptions can actually impair face recognition (Finger & Pezdek, 1999) and result in the generation of a greater proportion of inaccurate details (Meissner et al., 2001).

Although much has been learned about person description, there is still more that needs to be discerned. Theoretically, an important area for future research is to further flesh out the shared and unique processes that contribute to individuals' ability to recognize as opposed to describe faces. A variety of converging lines of evidence suggest that person descriptions may draw on processes that are distinct from those involved in face recognition. Whereas face recognition benefits from focusing on the global qualities of a face (Farah et al., 1998), face description benefits more from consideration of individual features (Wells & Turtle, 1987). Similarly, whereas face recognition consistently reveals an own-race advantage (a process known to rely on configural processing), face description has generally failed to show such a difference (Meissner & Brigham, 2001b; Sporer, 2001a, 2001b). These findings, in conjunction with a rather low or inconsistent relationship between the quality of face descriptions and recognition performance, as well as the verbal overshadowing phenomenon, suggest that face recognition and face description may rely on fundamentally different processes.

From this perspective it appears that future research might benefit from more precisely delineating the distinct processes contributing to person description versus recognition and explicating the behavioral and neurocognitive underpinnings of those processes. For example, recent research has found that face recognition performance is impaired if, between encoding and test, participants are shown large letters composed of small letters and are asked to attend to the smaller letters—a procedure believed to promote featural processing (Macrae & Lewis, 2002). However, what would be the effect of such a manipulation on person description? Given the hypothesis that person description relies more on featural processing, it seems quite plausible that although a focus on local processing impairs face recognition, it may actually improve face description! It has also been observed that focusing on large letters in this task can enhance face recognition; however, according to the current perspective, a configural process might actually impair person description. It also seems quite plausible that person description and face recognition may differentially draw upon separate areas of the brain, with face recognition relying more on the nonverbal operations associated with the right hemisphere (Leehey, Carey, Diamond, & Cahn, 1978) and face description relying more on the verbal operations associated with the left hemisphere (Hellige, 1993). Further investigation of the unique and sometimes conflicting processes associated with person recognition and description may be crucial to enhancing our theoretical understanding of these two critical elements of eyewitness memory.

In addition to suggesting important theoretical directions for future research, the present analysis also points to some critical applied issues that must be resolved if we are to maximize the efficacy of person descriptions in eyewitness contexts. As noted, it appears that the value of person descriptions critically depends upon how much information individuals are required to generate, with extensive descriptions leading to both more inaccurate and more disruptive descriptions. However, determining the precise amount of information that will lead to maximum description quality has yet to be determined. Exactly how much information should witnesses be asked to provide? If details are not spontaneously offered, should they be probed for? And if so, which details are acceptable to inquire about, and which details may lead to elaborative interference? If a witness does offer an extensive description that is potentially more riddled with inaccuracies, are there some details (e.g., hair color) that might be more likely to be accurate than others (e.g., shape of face)? Are the details that are generated first more likely to be accurate than those generated later, and, if so, can the utility of person descriptions be enhanced by differentially emphasizing details that are more likely to be accurate from those that are more suspect? Although clearly there is much more that we need to research, we are in a far better position to know when and how to use this critical source of eyewitness information by recognizing the unique issues that affect person description processes.

ACKNOWLEDGMENTS

The writing of this manuscript was supported by a grant from the National Science Foundation to the first author (CAM) and a grant from the *Deutsche Forschungsgemeinschaft* (German Science Foundation) to the second author (SLS).

REFERENCES

Bahrick, H. (2000). Long-term maintenance of knowledge. In E. Tulving & F. I. M. Craik, *The Oxford handbook of memory* (pp. 347–362). New York: Oxford University Press.

Bjork, R. A. (1988). Retrieval practice and the maintenance of knowledge. In M. M. Gruneberg, P. E. Morris, & R. N. Sykes (Eds.), *Practical aspects of memory* (Vol. 2, pp. 396–401). London: Wiley.

Bornstein, B. H., Liebel, L. M., & Scarberry, N. C. (1998). Repeated testing in eyewitness memory: A means to improve recall of a negative emotional event. *Applied Cognitive Psychology, 12*, 119–131.

Brown, W. (1923). To what extent is memory measured by a single recall trial. *Journal of Experimental Psychology, 6*, 377–382.

Brown, C., & Lloyd-Jones, T. J. (2002). Verbal overshadowing in a multiple face presentation paradigm: Effects of description instruction. *Applied Cognitive Psychology, 16*, 873–885.

Brown, C., & Lloyd-Jones, T. J. (2003). Verbal overshadowing of multiple face and car recognition: Effects of within- versus across-category verbal descriptions. *Applied Cognitive Psychology, 17*, 183–201.

Burke, A., Heuer, F., & Reisberg, D. (1992). Remembering emotional events. *Memory & Cognition, 20*, 277–290.

Ceci, S. J., & Bruck, M. (1993). Suggestibility of the child witness: A historical review and synthesis. *Psychological Bulletin, 113*, 403–439.

Chance, J. E., & Goldstein, A. G. (1996). The other-race effect and eyewitness identification. In S. L. Sporer, R. S. Malpass, & G. Koehnken (Eds.), *Psychological issues in eyewitness identification* (pp. 153–176). Mahwah, NJ: Lawrence Erlbaum Associates.

Christianson, S. (1984). The relationship between induced emotional arousal and amnesia. *Scandinavian Journal of Psychology, 25*, 147–160.

Christianson, S. (1992). Emotional stress and eyewitness memory: A critical review. *Psychological Bulletin, 112*, 284–309.

Clare, J., & Lewandowsky, S. (2004). Verbalizing facial memory: Criterion effects in verbal overshadowing. *Journal of Experimental Psychology: Learning, Memory, & Cognition, 30*, 739–755.

Clifford, B. R., & Hollin, C. R. (1981). Effects of the type of incident and the number of perpetrators on eyewitness memory. *Journal of Applied Psychology, 66*, 364–370.

Cohen, G., & Faulkner, D. (1989). Age differences in source forgetting: Effects on reality monitoring and on eyewitness testimony. *Psychology & Aging, 4*, 10–17.

Cutler, B. L., Penrod, S. D., & Martens, T. K. (1987). Improving the reliability of eyewitness identifications: Putting context into context. *Journal of Applied Psychology, 72*, 629–637.

Cutshall, J., & Yuille, J. C. (1989). Field studies of eyewitness memory of actual crimes. In D. C. Raskin (Ed.), *Psychological methods in criminal investigation and evidence* (pp. 97–124). New York: Springer.

Darley, C. F., & Glass, A. L. (1975). Effects of rehearsal and serial list position on recall. *Journal of Experimental Psychology, 93*, 83–89.

Davies, G. M. (1996). Children's identification evidence. In S. L. Sporer, R. S. Malpass, & G. Koehnken (Eds.), *Psychological issues in eyewitness identification* (pp. 233–258). Mahwah, NJ: Lawrence Erlbaum Associates.

Davies, G., Tarrant, A., & Flin, R. (1989). Close encounters of the witness kind: Children's memory for a simulated health inspection. *British Journal of Psychology, 80*, 415–429.

Deffenbacher, K. A. (1983). The influence of arousal on reliability of testimony. In S. M. A. Lloyd-Bostock & B. R. Clifford (Eds.), *Evaluating witness evidence* (pp. 235–251). Chichester, England: Wiley.

Deffenbacher, K. A. (1994). Effects of arousal on everyday memory. *Human Performance, 7*, 141–161.

Deffenbacher, K. A., Bornstein, B. H., Penrod, S. D., & McGorty, E. K. (2004). A meta-analytic review of the effects of high stress on eyewitness memory. *Law & Human Behavior, 28*, 687–706.

Dent, H. (1982). The effects of interviewing strategies on the results of interviews with child witnesses. In A. Trankell (Ed.), *Reconstructing the past* (pp. 279–298). Stockholm: Norstedt.

Dent, H., & Stephenson, G. (1979). An experimental study of the effectiveness of different techniques of questioning child witnesses. *British Journal of Social & Clinical Psychology, 18*, 41–51.

Dodson, C. S., Johnson, M. K., & Schooler, J. W. (1997). The verbal overshadowing effect: Why
descriptions impair face recognition. *Memory & Cognition, 25*, 129–139.

Dunning, D., & Stern, L. B. (1992). Examining the generality of eyewitness hypermnesia: A close
look at time delay and question type. *Applied Cognitive Psychology, 6*, 643–657.

Ebbesen, E. B., & Rienick, C. B. (1998). Retention interval and eyewitness memory for events
and personal identifying attributes. *Journal of Applied Psychology, 5*, 745–762.

Ellis, H. D. (1992). The development of face processing skills. *Proceedings of the Royal Society,
Series B, 335*, 105–111.

Ellis, H. D., Deregowski, J. B., & Shepherd, J. W. (1975). Descriptions of white and black faces
by white and black subjects. *International Journal of Psychology, 10*, 119–123.

Ellis, H. D., Shepherd, J. W., & Davies, G. M. (1980). The deterioration of verbal descriptions of
faces over different delay intervals. *Journal of Police Science & Administration, 8*, 101–106.

Fallshore, M., & Schooler, J. W. (1995). The verbal vulnerability of perceptual expertise. *Journal
of Experimental Psychology: Learning, Memory, & Cognition, 21*, 1608–1623.

Farah, M. J., Wilson, K. D., Drain, M., & Tanaka, J. W. (1998). What is "special" about face perception? *Psychological Review, 105*, 482–498.

Finger, K., & Pezdek, K. (1999). The effect of verbal description on face identification accuracy:
"Release from verbal overshadowing." *Journal of Applied Psychology, 84*, 340–348.

Fisher, G. H., & Cox, R. L. (1975). Recognizing human faces. *Applied Ergonomics, 6*, 104–109.

Fisher, R. P., & Geiselman, R. E. (1992). *Memory-enhancing techniques for investigative interviewing.* Springfield, IL: Charles C. Thomas.

Fisher, R. P., Geiselman, R. E., & Amador, M. (1989). Field test of the cognitive interview:
Enhancing the recollection of actual victims and witnesses of a crime. *Journal of Applied Psychology, 74*, 722–727.

Flin, R. H., & Shepherd, J. W. (1986). Tall stories: Eyewitnesses' ability to estimate height and
weight characteristics. *Human Learning, 5*, 29–38.

Gabbert, F., Memon, A., & Allan, K. (2003). Memory conformity: Can eyewitnesses influence
each other's memories for an event? *Applied Cognitive Psychology, 17*, 533–543.

Geiselman, R. E., Fisher, R. P., Firstenberg, I., Hutton, L. A., Sullivan, S. J., Avetissian, I. V.,
et al. (1984). Enhancement of eyewitness memory: An empirical evaluation of a cognitive
interview. *Journal of Police Science and Administration, 12*, 74–80.

Glenberg, A., & Adams, F. (1978). Type I rehearsal and recognition. *Journal of Verbal Learning
and Verbal Behavior, 17*, 455–163.

Goodman, G. S., & Reed, R. S. (1986). Age differences in eyewitness testimony. *Law & Human
Behavior, 10*, 317–332.

Grass, E., & Sporer, S. L. (1991, March). *Richtig oder falsch? Zur Vorhersage von Identifi-
zierungsleistungen durch weitere Aussagen von Zeugen* [Correct or false? Post-dicting eyewitness identification accuracy from verbal statements]. Paper presented at the 33rd Tagung
experimentell arbeitender Psychologen in Giesen, Germany.

Hellige, J. B. (1993). Unity of thought and action: Varieties of interaction between the left and
right cerebral hemispheres. *Current Directions in Psychological Science, 2*, 21–25.

Henkel, L. A., Johnson, M. K., & De Leonardis, D. M. (1998). Aging and source monitoring:
Cognitive processes and neuropsychological correlates. *Journal of Experimental Psychology:
General, 127*, 251–268.

Janssen, J. P., & Horowski, A. C. (1980). Schueler schaetzen Koerpergroessen: Akzentuierungs-
tendenz als kognitiver Stil der Personenwahrnehmung [Children estimate height: Accentu-
ation tendencies as a cognitive style in person perception]. *Zeitschrift für Entwicklungspsy-
chologie und Paedagogische Psychologie, 10*, 167–176.

Kleinsmith, L. J., & Kaplan, S. (1963). Paired-associate learning as a function of arousal and
interpolated interval. *Journal of Experimental Psychology, 65*, 190–193.

Kleinsmith, L. J., & Kaplan, S. (1964). Interaction of arousal and recall interval in nonsense syllable paired-associate learning. *Journal of Experimental Psychology, 67,* 124–126.

Koehnken, G., Milne, R., Memon, A., & Bull, R. (1999). The cognitive interview: A meta-analysis. *Psychology, Crime & Law, 5,* 3–27.

Koriat, A., & Goldsmith, M. (1996). Monitoring and control processes in the strategic regulation of memory accuracy. *Psychological Review, 103,* 490–517.

Kuehn, L. L. (1974). Looking down a gun barrel: Person perception and violent crime. *Perceptual & Motor Skills, 39,* 1159–1164.

Laughery, K. R., Duval, C., & Wogalter, M. S. (1986). Dynamics of facial recall. In H. D. Ellis, M. A. Jeeves, F. Newcombe, & A. Young (Eds.), *Aspects of face processing* (pp. 373–387). Dordrecht: Martinus Nijhoff.

Leehey, S., Carey, S., Diamond, R., & Cahn, A. (1978). Upright and inverted faces: The right hemisphere knows the difference. *Cortex, 14,* 411–419.

Leippe, M. R., Romanczyk, A., & Manion, A. P. (1991). Eyewitness memory for a touching experience: Accuracy differences between child and adult witnesses. *Journal of Applied Psychology, 76,* 367–379.

Lindholm, T. (2005). Own-age biases in verbal person memory. *Memory, 13,* 21–30.

Lindsay, R. C. L., Martin, R., & Webber, L. (1994). Default values in eyewitness descriptions: A problem for the match-to-description lineup foil selection strategy. *Law & Human Behavior, 18,* 527–541.

Lipton, J. P. (1977). On the psychology of eyewitness testimony. *Journal of Applied Psychology, 62,* 90–95.

Loftus, E. F. (1975). Leading questions and the eyewitness report. *Cognitive Psychology, 7,* 560–572.

Loftus, E. F. (1979). *Eyewitness testimony.* Cambridge, MA: Harvard University Press.

Loftus, E., & Burns, T. E. (1982). Mental shock can produce retrograde amnesia. *Memory & Cognition, 10,* 318–323.

Loftus, E. F., & Greene, E. (1980). Warning: Even memory for faces may be contagious. *Law & Human Behavior, 4,* 323–334.

Loftus, E. F., & Ketcham, K. E. (1983). The malleability of eyewitness accounts. In S. M. A. Lloyd-Bostock and B. R. Clifford (Eds.) *Evaluating witness evidence* (pp. 159–171). New York: John Wiley & Sons.

Loftus, E. F., & Zanni, G. (1975). Eyewitness testimony: The influence of the wording of a question. *Bulletin of the Psychonomic Society, 5,* 86–88.

Loftus, G. R. (1985). Picture perception: Effects luminance on available information and information extraction rate. *Journal of Experimental Psychology: General, 114,* 342–356.

Lovett, S. B., Small, M. Y., & Engstrom, S. A. (1992, November). *The verbal overshadowing effect: Now you see it, now you don't.* Paper presented at the annual meeting of the Psychonomic Society, St. Louis, MO.

MacLeod, M. D., & Shepherd, J. W. (1986). Sex differences in eyewitness reports of criminal assaults. *Medicine, Science & the Law, 26,* 311–318.

MacLin, O. H., Tapscott, R. L., & Malpass, R. S. (2002). The development of a computer system to collect descriptions of culprits. *Applied Cognitive Psychology, 16,* 937–945.

Macrae, C. N., & Lewis, H. L. (2002). Do I know you?: Processing orientation and face recognition. *Psychological Science, 13,* 194–196.

Marin, B. V., Holmes, D. L., Guth, M., & Kovac, P. (1979). The potential of children as eyewitnesses. *Law & Human Behavior, 3,* 295–305.

Meissner, C. A. (2002). Applied aspects of the instructional bias effect in verbal overshadowing. *Applied Cognitive Psychology, 16,* 911–928.

Meissner, C. A., & Brigham, J. C. (2001a). A meta-analysis of the verbal overshadowing effect in face identification. *Applied Cognitive Psychology, 15,* 603–616.

Meissner, C. A., & Brigham, J. C. (2001b). Thirty years of investigating the own-race bias in memory for faces: A meta-analytic review. *Psychology, Public Policy, & Law, 7*, 3–35.

Meissner, C. A., Brigham, J. C., & Kelley, C. M. (2001). The influence of retrieval processes in verbal overshadowing. *Memory & Cognition, 29*, 176–186.

Munsterberg, H. (1908). *On the witness stand. Essays on psychology and crime.* New York: Doubleday, Page.

Murray, J. B. (1986). Marijuana's effects on human cognitive functions, psychomotor functions, and personality. *Journal of General Psychology, 113*, 23–55.

Neil v. Biggers, 409 U.S. 188 (1972).

Payne, D. G. (1987). Hypermnesia and reminiscence in recall: A historical and empirical review. *Psychological Bulletin, 101*, 5–27.

Pickel, K. L. (1998). Unusualness and threat as possible causes of "weapon focus." *Memory, 6*, 277–295.

Pickel, K. L. (1999). The influence of context on the "weapon focus" effect. *Law & Human Behavior, 23*, 299–311.

Pigott, M., & Brigham, J. C. (1985). Relationship between accuracy of prior description and facial recognition. *Journal of Applied Psychology, 70*, 547–555.

Pozzulo, J. D., & Warren, K. L. (2003). Descriptions and identification of strangers by youth and adult eyewitnesses. *Journal of Applied Psychology, 88*, 315–323.

Pryke, S., Lindsay, R. C. L., & Pozzulo, J. D. (2000). Sorting mug shots: Methodological issues. *Applied Cognitive Psychology, 14*, 81–96.

Read, J. D., Hammersley, R., Cross-Calvert, S., & McFadzen, E. (1989). Rehearsal of faces and details in action events. *Applied Cognitive Psychology, 3*, 295–311.

Read, J. D., Yuille, J. C., & Tollestrup, P. (1992). Recollections of a robbery: Effects of arousal and alcohol upon recall and person identification. *Law & Human Behavior, 16*, 425–446.

Reinhardt-Rutland, A. H. (1986). Note on nonveridical visual perception and pedestrian accidents at night. *Perceptual & Motor Skills, 63*, 371–374.

Rhodes, G., Brake, S., Taylor, K., & Tan, S. (1989). Expertise and configural coding in face recognition. *British Journal of Psychology, 80*, 313–331.

Roediger, H. L., & Challis, B. H. (1989). Hypermnesia: Improvements in recall with repeated testing. In C. Izawa (Ed.), *Current issues in cognitive processes: The Tulane Flowerree Symposium on Cognition* (pp. 175–199). Hillsdale, NJ: Lawrence Erlbaum Associates.

Roediger, H. L., Jacoby, J. D., & McDermott, K. B. (1996). Misinformation effects in recall: Creating false memories through repeated retrieval. *Journal of Memory and Language, 35*, 300–318.

Roediger, H. L., McDermott, K. B., & Goff, L. M. (1997). Recovery of true and false memories: Paradoxical effects of repeated testing. In M. A. Conway (Ed.), *Recovered memories and false memories* (pp. 118–149). Oxford: Oxford University Press.

Roediger, H. L., Wheeler, M. A., & Rajaram, S. (1993). Remembering, knowing, and reconstructing the past. In D. L. Medin (Ed.), *The psychology of learning and motivation: Advances in research and theory* (pp. 97–134). San Diego: Academic Press.

Ryan, R. S., & Schooler, J. W. (1998). Whom do words hurt?: Individual differences in susceptibility to verbal overshadowing. *Applied Cognitive Psychology, 12*, 105–126.

Sayette, M. A. (1999). Cognitive theory and research. In K. Leonard & H. Blume (Eds.), *Psychological theories of drinking and alcoholism* (2nd ed., pp. 247–291). New York: Guilford press.

Saywitz, K. J. (1995). Improving children's testimony: The question, the answer, and the environment. In M. S. Zaragoza, J. R. Graham, G. C. N. Hall, R. Hirschman, & Y. S. Ben-Porath (Eds.), *Memory and testimony in the child witness* (pp. 113–140). London: Sage.

Schooler, J. W. (1998). The distinctions of false and fuzzy memories. *Journal of Experimental Child Psychology, 71*, 130–143.

Schooler, J. W. (2002). Verbalization produces a transfer inappropriate processing shift. *Applied Cognitive Psychology, 16,* 989–997.

Schooler, J. W., & Eich, E. (2000). Memory for emotional events. In E. Tulving & F. I. M. Craik, *The Oxford handbook of memory* (pp. 379–392). New York: Oxford University Press.

Schooler, J. W., & Engstler-Schooler, T. Y. (1990). Verbal overshadowing of visual memories: Some things are better left unsaid. *Cognitive Psychology, 22,* 36–71.

Schooler, J. W., Fiore, S. M., & Brandimonte, M. A. (1997). At a loss *from* words: Verbal overshadowing of perceptual memories. In D. Medin's (Ed.), *Handbook of learning and motivation* (Vol. 37). Orlando, FL: Academic Press.

Schooler, J. W., Foster, R. A., & Loftus, E. F. (1988). Some deleterious consequences of the act of recollection. *Memory and Cognition, 16,* 243–251.

Schooler, J. W., & Loftus E. F. (1993). Multiple mechanisms mediate individual differences in eyewitness accuracy and suggestibility. In H. W. Reese and J. M. Puckett (Eds.), *Mechanisms of practical cognition* (pp. 177–203). Hillsdale, NJ: Lawrence Erlbaum Associates.

Schooler, J. W., Ryan, R. S., & Reder, L. M. (1996). The costs and benefits of verbalization. In D. Herrmann, M. Johnson, C. McEvoy, C. Hertzog, & P. Hertels (Eds.), *Basic and applied memory: New findings* (pp. 51–65). Mahwah, NJ: Lawrence Erlbaum Associates.

Scrivner, E., & Safer, M. A. (1988). Eyewitnesses show hypermnesia for details about a violent event. *Journal of Applied Psychology, 73*(3), 371–377.

Searcy, J. H., Bartlett, J. C., Memon, A., & Swanson, K. (2001). Aging and lineup performance at long retention intervals: Effects of metamemory and context reinstatement. *Journal of Applied Psychology, 86,* 207–214.

Shaw, J. S., Bjork, R. A., & Handal, A. (1995). Retrieval-induced forgetting in an eyewitness-memory paradigm. *Psychonomic Bulletin and Review, 2*(2), 249–253.

Shaw, J. S., Garven, S., & Wood, J. M. (1997). Co-witness information can have immediate effects on eyewitness memory reports. *Law & Human Behavior, 21,* 503–523.

Shepherd, J. W. (1983). Identification after long delays. In S. M. A. Lloyd-Bostock & B. R. Clifford (Eds.), *Evaluating witness evidence* (pp. 173–187). Chichester: Wiley.

Shepherd, J. W. (1986). An interactive computer system for retrieving faces. In H. D. Ellis, M. A. Jeeves, F. Newcombe, & A. Young (Eds.), *Aspects of face processing* (pp. 398–409). Dordrecht/Boston/Lancaster: Martinus Nijhoff.

Shepherd, J. W., & Deregowski, J. B. (1981). Races and faces: A comparison of the responses of Africans and Europeans to faces of the same and different races. *British Journal of Social Psychology, 20,* 125–133.

Shepherd, J. W., & Ellis, H. D. (1996). Face recall—Methods and problems. In S. L. Sporer, R. S. Malpass, & G. Koehnken (Eds.), *Psychological issues in eyewitness identification* (pp. 87–115). Mahwah, NJ: Lawrence Erlbaum Associates.

Shepherd, J. W., Ellis, H. D., & Davies, G. M. (1977). *Perceiving and remembering faces.* Technical report to the Home Office under Contract no. POL/73/1675/24/1.

Shepherd, J. W., Ellis, H. D., & Davies, G. M. (1982). *Identification evidence: A psychological examination.* Aberdeen: Aberdeen University Press.

Sporer, S. L. (in press). Person descriptions as retrieval cues: Do they really help? *Psychology, Crime, and Law.*

Sporer, S. L. (1988). Long-term improvement of facial recognition through visual rehearsal. In M. M. Gruneberg, P. E. Morris, & R. N. Sykes (Eds.), *Practical aspects of memory* (pp. 182–188). London: Wiley.

Sporer, S. L. (1989). Verbal and visual processes in person identification. In H. Wegener, F. Lösel, & J. Haisch (Eds.), *Criminal behavior and the criminal justice system* (pp. 303–324). New York/Berlin: Springer.

Sporer, S.L. (1991). Encoding strategies and the recognition of human faces. *Journal of Experimental Psychology: Human Learning, Memory and Cognition, 17,* 323–333.

Sporer, S. L. (1992a, March). *An archival analysis of person descriptions*. Paper presented at the Biennial Meeting of the American Psychology-Law Society in San Diego, California.

Sporer, S. L. (1992b). Post-dicting eyewitness accuracy: Confidence, decision-times and person descriptions of choosers and non-choosers. *European Journal of Social Psychology, 22,* 157–180.

Sporer, S. L. (1996a). Describing others: Psychological issues. In S. L. Sporer, R. S. Malpass, & G. Koehnken (Eds.), *Psychological issues in eyewitness identification* (pp. 53–86). Mahwah, NJ: Lawrence Erlbaum Associates.

Sporer, S. L. (1996b). Experimentally induced person mix-ups through media exposure and ways to avoid them. In G. M. Davies, S. Lloyd-Bostock, M. McMurran, & C. Wilson (Eds.), *Psychology and law: Advances in research* (pp. 64–73). Berlin: De Gruyter.

Sporer, S. L. (2001a). Recognizing faces of other ethnic groups: An integration of theories. *Psychology, Public Policy, & Law, 7,* 36–97.

Sporer, S. L. (2001b). The cross-race bias: Beyond recognition of faces in the laboratory. *Psychology, Public Policy, and Law, 7,* 170–200.

Sporer, S. L., & Cutler, B. L. (2003). Identification evidence in Germany: Common sense assumptions, empirical evidence, guidelines, and judicial practices. In P. J. van Koppen & S. D. Penrod (Eds.), *Adversarial vs. inquisitorial justice: Psychological perspectives on criminal justice systems* (pp. 191–208). New York: Plenum.

Steblay, N. M. (1992). A meta-analytic review of the weapon focus effect. *Law & Human Behavior, 16,* 413–424.

Stern, L. W. (1902). Zur Psychologie der Aussage [Psychology of report]. *Zeitschrift für die gesamte Strafrechtswissenschaft, 22,* 315–370.

Turtle, J. W., & Yuille, J. C. (1994). Lost but not forgotten details: Repeated eyewitness recall leads to reminiscence but not hypermnesia. *Journal of Applied Psychology, 79,* 260–271.

van Koppen, P., & Lochun, S. (1997). Portraying perpetrators: the validity of offender descriptions by witnesses. *Law and Human Behavior, 21,* 661–685.

Wagstaff, G. F., MacVeigh, J., Boston, R., Scott, L., Brunas-Wagstaff, J., & Cole, J. (2003). Can laboratory findings on eyewitness testimony be generalized to the real world? An archival analysis of the influence of violence, weapon presence, and age on eyewitness accuracy. *Journal of Psychology: Interdisciplinary & Applied, 137,* 17–28.

Warnick, D. H., & Sanders, G. S. (1980). The effects of group discussion on eyewitness accuracy. *Journal of Applied Social Psychology, 10,* 249–259.

Wells, G. L. (1985). Verbal descriptions of faces from memory: Are they diagnostic of identification accuracy. *Journal of Applied Psychology, 70,* 619–626.

Wells, G. L., & Leippe, M. R. (1981). How do triers of fact infer the accuracy of eyewitness identifications? Using memory for peripheral detail can be misleading. *Journal of Applied Psychology, 66,* 682–687.

Wells, G. L., & Turtle, J. W. (1987). What is the best way to encode faces? In M. M. Gruneberg, P. E. Morris, & R. N. Sykes (Eds.), *Practical aspects of memory: Current research & issues* (pp. 163–168). New York: Wiley & Sons.

Wixted, J. T., & Ebbesen, E. B. (1997). Genuine power curves in forgetting: A quantitative analysis of individual subject forgetting functions. *Memory & Cognition, 25,* 731–739.

Wogalter, M. S. (1991). Effects of post-exposure description and imaging on subsequent face recognition performance. *Proceedings of the Human Factors Society, 35,* 575–579.

Wogalter, M. S. (1996). Describing faces from memory: Accuracy and effects on subsequent recognition performance. *Proceedings of the Human Factors and Ergonomics Society, 40,* 536–540.

Yarmey, A. D. (1986). Verbal, visual, and voice identification of a rape suspect under different levels of illumination. *Journal of Applied Psychology, 71,* 363–370.

Yarmey, A. D. (1993). Adult age and gender differences in eyewitness recall in field settings. *Journal of Applied Social Psychology, 23,* 1921–1932.

Yarmey, A. D. (1996). Age and eyewitness memory. In S. L. Sporer, R. S. Malpass, & G. Koehnken (Eds.), *Psychological issues in eyewitness identification* (pp. 259–278). Mahwah, NJ: Lawrence Erlbaum Associates.

Yarmey, A. D. (2004). Eyewitness recall and photo identification: A field experiment. *Psychology, Crime & Law, 10*, 53–68.

Yarmey, A. D., Jacob, J., & Porter, A. (2002). Person recall in field settings. *Journal of Applied Social Psychology, 32*, 2354–2367.

Yarmey, A. D., & Kent, J. (1980). Eyewitness identification by elderly and young adults. *Law & Human Behavior, 4*, 359–371.

Yarmey, A. D., & Morris, S. (1998). The effects of discussion on eyewitness memory. *Journal of Applied Social Psychology, 28*, 1637–1648.

Yarmey, A. D., & Yarmey, M. (1997). Eyewitness recall and duration estimates in field settings. *Journal of Applied Social Psychology, 27*, 330–344.

Yarmey, A. D., Yarmey, A. L., & Yarmey, M. J. (1994). Face and voice identifications in showups and lineups. *Applied Cognitive Psychology, 8*, 453–464.

Yu, C. J., & Geiselman, R. E. (1993). Effects of constructing identi-kit composites on photo-spread identification performance. *Criminal Justice & Behavior, 20*, 280–292.

Yuille, J. C. (1986). Meaningful research in the police context. In J. C. Yuille (Ed.), *Police selection and training: The role of psychology* (pp. 225–246). Dordrecht, the Netherlands: Martinus Nijhoff.

Yuille, J. C., & Cutshall, J. L. (1986). A case study of eyewitness memory of a crime. *Journal of Applied Psychology, 71*, 291–301.

Yuille, J. C., & Tollestrup, P. A. (1990). Some effects of alcohol on eyewitness memory. *Journal of Applied Psychology, 75*, 268–273.

Yuille, J. C., Tollestrup, P. A., Marxsen, D., Porter, S., & Herve, H. F. M. (1998). An exploration on the effects of marijuana on eyewitness memory. *International Journal of Law & Psychiatry, 21*, 117–128.

Zima, H., & Zeiner, W. (1982). Das Versuchsprojekt "Sigma." Neue Wege zur Erfassung und Auswertung von Signalementdaten [Project "Sigma": New way of gathering and evaluating person descriptions]. *Kriminalistik, 36*, 593–596.

2

Mug Books: More Than Just Large Photospreads

Hunter A. McAllister
Southeastern Louisiana University

On the surface, mug books and photospreads seem to be somewhat similar procedures; both involve eyewitnesses looking at mug shots in an attempt to identify a perpetrator. It is perhaps because of the surface similarity to photospreads that research on mug books has been very limited. Why would we need to conduct research on mug books when there is an extensive literature on lineups and photospreads; aren't mug books just large photospreads? In spite of the surface similarities, there are, in fact, significant differences in procedures. Lineups and photospreads (from this point on the term *lineup* is used as the general term to apply to both lineup and photospread procedures) are used when the police have a suspect. The inclusion of lineup members other than the suspect is for the purpose of protecting an innocent suspect; most lineups contain only six members. In contrast, mug book searches are conducted when the police do not have a suspect; the purpose of having the eyewitness look at the mug book pictures is to find a possible suspect. The hope is that the perpetrator of the crime has been booked for another crime in the past, and the eyewitness will recognize the perpetrator's mug shot in the process of looking through the mug book—a process that could involve looking through literally thousands of pictures.

There are, in fact, some issues that have relevance to both lineups and mug books, such as what poses should be used, whether color makes a difference, and whether pictures should be presented one at a time or in groups. Although these are questions that have relevance for both lineups and mug books, we shall see that the answers are not always the same for the two procedures. Other mug book issues have little relevance to lineups, such as techniques for sorting mug shots, size of mug books, etc. We begin with topics that show some commonality and progress to topics unique to mug books.

MUG BOOK CONTENT

In constructing a mug book, one of the most basic questions is the content of the book. Presumably, the better the quality of the information, the better the eyewitness's performance will be. Laughery, Alexander, and Lane (1971) provided the earliest information about the nature of the mug shots. They argued that a portrait pose might be the most effective pose because it contains features of both a front and a profile view. To test this prediction, research participants were shown four candid slides of a male target. Participants were then randomly assigned to view mug books in which all 150 pictures (149 decoys and 1 target) were presented in front view, profile view, left portrait, or right portrait. Laughery et al. (1971) created a rather unusual accuracy measure that combined a participant's yes or no decisions about a picture with their confidence in this judgment. The target measure ranged from a score of 6, indicating complete confidence that this was the target, to 1, indicating complete confidence that this was not the target. For decoys a 6 indicated complete confidence that this was not the target and a 1 complete confidence that it was. When target picture scores were analyzed, there were no significant differences in accuracy rates for the various poses. Scores ranged from 2.8 to 3.6 on the 6-point scale. The scores for the 149 decoys were totaled and analyzed; again, there was no effect for pose. The average score that each decoy received ranged from 5.55 to 5.72. Similar to their predictions concerning pose, Laughery et al. argued that color photographs should provide more information than black-and-white (B & W) photographs. They conducted an experiment that included a manipulation of whether color pictures or B & W mug shots were used. The procedure was similar to that of the earlier experiment, except that the target person was seen live rather than in slides. There were no significant effects of the type of photograph on correct identifications of the target; the mean scores for color and B & W were an identical 4.9 for both conditions. Analysis of the decoy scores show no significant effect for type of photograph; the average decoy score in the color condition was 5.89, and the average score in the B & W condition was 5.78. In summary, neither pose nor color had an impact on mug book performance; thus, there was no support for presumably more informative pictures being more useful.

Although Laughery et al. (1971) did not find that mug shots that presumably contained more information were more effective, their attempts to make mug shots more realistic may have been too weak. Research on lineups has shown that more realistic modes of presentation (videotape and live) result in improved performance (Shapiro & Penrod, 1986; Cutler, Berman, Penrod, & Fisher, 1994). Melara, DeWitt-Richards, and O'Brien (1989) found that target identification rates were higher when voices were included in photospread procedures. Schiff, Banka, and de Bordes Galdi (1986) created a dynamic display in which the foils and targets were filmed in motion while sitting in a slowly rotating chair, yielding a 180° scan of the face from right to left profile. Their dynamic display produced recognition rates superior to those of the more traditional static photospread procedures. Could dynamic information be used to improve mug book performance?

When considering the use of dynamic information with mug books, a practical problem immediately arises. Adding a 30-second clip of a person walking and talking would lengthen a 6-person photospread by 3 minutes; in contrast, the viewing time for a 1,000-person mug book would increase by over 8 hours. One solution to this problem would be to present this dynamic information for only some of the mug shots. In the process of searching a mug book, there will be many pictures that a witness knows immediately are not of the perpetrator; providing dynamic cues for these pictures would be pointless. Allowing a witness to chose whether or not dynamic information is presented for a particular case could solve the practical problem of using such information with mug books.

McAllister, Bearden, Kohlmaier, and Warner (1997) conducted an experiment to test the effectiveness of a computerized mug book, allowing witnesses to choose dynamic information. Witnesses to a 5-minute videotape of simulated computer crime attempted to identify the perpetrator from one of three types of mug books: (a) dynamic no-choice—where every static mug shot was followed by the presentation of a 30-second video that contained 10 seconds each of a full body view of the person walking, a head shot where the person is talking, and a head shot where the view is rotated through 360°; (b) dynamic choice—where static mug shots were followed by the dynamic information only when chosen by the participant; and (c) static—where just the static mug shot was presented. The picture of the perpetrator was always present and appeared in position 70. There were significantly fewer false positive identifications of the 69 foils preceding the perpetrator in the Dynamic Choice condition (M = 2.87) than in the Static condition (M = 4.87). There were no significant differences in the ability to identify the perpetrator; identification rates for the Dynamic Choice, Dynamic No-Choice, and Static conditions were 77.4%, 68.6%, and 76.7%, respectively. Participants in the dynamic choice condition chose to have the dynamic information presented an average of 8.54 times for the 69 foils preceding the perpetrator, with 80.4% requesting it for the perpetrator. Dynamic information seemed to be chosen judiciously, with the result of improving mug book performance.

Choosing dynamic information in the study by McAllister et al (1997) increased the amount of time taken to conduct the mug book search by an average of less than 5 minutes; however, this might still be too burdensome when dealing with larger mug books. McAllister, Blair, Cerone, and Laurent (2000) speculated that it might be possible to cut down on the amount of search time by giving witnesses even greater control. Witnesses could be allowed to choose not only whether dynamic information would be presented, but also how much dynamic information would be presented. The impact of allowing witnesses to choose the type of cues presented was explored in two experiments. In Experiment 1, participants viewed the same video used in McAllister et al. (1997) and attempted to identify the perpetrator from one of three types of mug books: (a) dynamic-combined—the same as the dynamic choice condition in McAllister et al. (1997), (b) dynamic-separable—participants could sequentially chose which of the three types of cues to present with the ability to stop at any point, and (c) a static control. The picture of the perpetrator was always present and appeared in position 70. As in the earlier research, there were no significant differences for correct identifications; identification rates for the Dynamic-Combined, Dynamic-Separable, and Static conditions were 76.8%, 66.1%, and 69.7%, respectively. There were significantly fewer false positives in the dynamic-separable condition (M = 2.76) than for the static control (M = 4.50); however, the dynamic separable was not significantly different from the dynamic-combined (M = 3.27). Allowing greater choice reduced the amount of time for presenting dynamic information with no apparent loss in performance.

Both McAllister et al. (1997) and McAllister et al. (2000) employed relatively small mug books. Would witnesses still choose dynamic information when mug books become larger? McAllister, Stewart, and Loveland (2003) included a position of the perpetrator factor. Witnesses to a videotaped, simulated crime attempted identifications from mug books where the perpetrator and 69 preceding foils appeared in positions 1–70, 71–140, or 141–210. When the foils appeared in positions 1 to 69, dynamic information was chosen an average of 7.54 times; this is very similar to the 8.54 times in McAllister et al. (1997) and the 7.45 times in McAllister et al. (1999). There was a significant decline in dynamic information use when the foils appeared in positions 71 to 140 (2.23 times) and in positions 141 to 210 (1.30 times). The use of dynamic information for the perpetrator also dropped as the number of preceding pictures increased; only 33% of witnesses used dynamic information when the perpetrator was in position 210. The drastic decrease in the use of dynamic information that occurred as the number of mug shots viewed increased calls into question the usefulness of dynamic mug books for larger sets of mug shots. If dynamic mug books are to be useful, they would have to be used in conjunction with a technique to prune the mug book down to a size where the dynamic information would be utilized.

ONE-AT-A-TIME OR GROUPED DISPLAY

Another basic question about mug book construction is how to display the various pictures. A careful reading of the procedures in mug book research reveals that sometimes the pictures are presented one at a time and other times in groups. Research conduced with lineups would suggest there might be differences in the effectiveness of these two approaches. Lindsay and Wells (1985) introduced the sequential lineup procedure as a technique for reducing the problem, in which witnesses use the relative judgment strategy of comparing the lineup members with each other and then selecting the one who most resembles the perpetrator. Lindsay and Wells (1985) found that sequential lineups reduced the number of false positives at no cost to correct identifications; their findings have been replicated many times (see Steblay, Dysart, Fulero, & Lindsay, 2001).

When considering simultaneous and sequential procedures in mug books, certain differences with lineups immediately become apparent. Because mug books contain a large number of pictures, it will generally be not possible to have a truly simultaneous procedure in which all of the pictures are presented at the same time. Rather, a small subset of the pictures is simultaneously presented on a page followed by subsequent pages, each with its own small group of pictures. Stewart and McAllister (2001) referred to such a procedure as a "grouped" procedure rather than a simultaneous procedure. Clearly, a grouped procedure is not a purely simultaneous procedure, because each small group of simultaneous pictures is presented sequentially. Stewart and McAllister (2001) had eyewitnesses to a simulated crime attempt to identify the perpetrator from a computerized mug book. Half of the witnesses attempted identifications from mug books in which the 216 pictures were presented sequentially, one picture per page (screen); for the other half of the witnesses, the mug shots were presented in groups of 12 mug shots per page. Contrary to the findings with lineups, the sequential procedure of Stewart and McAllister (2001) produced a significantly *greater* number of false positive identifications than the grouped procedure. Consistent with the past findings on lineups, there were no differences between simultaneous and sequential mug book procedures on correct identifications of the perpetrator.

Why was the simultaneous procedure more effective in mug books than in lineups? It is possible that the different natures of a lineup task and a mug book task cause witnesses to use different cognitive processes in making their decisions. Witnesses in simultaneous lineups use a relative strategy of determining the person who most resembles the perpetrator because they believe that the perpetrator is present in the one and only lineup that they will be viewing (Wells, 1984). In contrast, witnesses viewing grouped mug book pictures may have little interest in relative comparisons on a particular screen because they know that additional screens of mug shots are to follow; furthermore, because there is no suspect, no particular screen is any more likely than the next to contain the perpetrator. Without the need for relative judgments, the grouped procedure may actually encourage a more natural style of face recognition. Presenting witnesses with a group of pictures allows them to scan the pictures in much the same way that they would scan a crowd looking for a friend—quickly passing over the faces of strangers rather than analyzing them in fine detail, as might be done when pictures are presented sequentially. Although, it is intuitively appealing, it should be noted that at this point there is only very limited support for this explanation. McAllister, Michel, Tarcza, Fitzmorris and Nguyen (2006) found that witnesses using grouped mug book procedures made their judgments more rapidly than those using sequential mug books; this was just the opposite of the pattern that they found with lineups.

This is one occasion where the recommendation based on research findings may be directed more to eyewitness researchers than to law enforcement. Many of us conducting research on mug books also conduct research on lineups; it was only natural that we would use the same techniques found to be effective in our lineup research when conducting mug book research. In contrast to the lab, many of the computerized mug book programs currently used by police present the witness with groups of pictures rather than one-at-a-time. Mug book researchers should consider using grouped presentation for its ecological validity as well as its effectiveness.

EFFECT OF VIEWING MUG BOOKS ON LINEUP PERFORMANCE

Given the field's greater interest in lineups than in mug books, it is not surprising that one of the most researched topics is the impact that viewing mug books has on subsequent lineup performance. Although most of the researchers in this area would agree that viewing a mug book can adversely affect lineup performance, they differ in terms of their explanations for why this might occur. Not surprisingly, different theoretical perspectives led to differences in the types of designs and research procedures employed.

Interference Effects—No Overlap Between Mug Book and Lineup

One possible explanation of the negative impact of mug books on lineups is that it is the simple exposure to the many pictures in a mug book that interferes with the original memory of the perpetrator. A minimum requirement for a test of interference is that there is no overlap between the pictures in the mug book and pictures in the lineup. Without this minimum requirement, declines in performance could be due to such things as source confusion (i.e., you remember that you have seen someone in the lineup before but cannot remember whether it was at the crime scene or in the mug book). Davies, Shepherd, and Ellis (1979) were the first to provide such a test of interference. Participants in this research viewed a brief videotape of three men playing cards and then were assigned to one of four conditions. In three of the conditions, the participants viewed 100 mug shots of innocent foils: (a) in a standard search condition the participant was told to search the pictures for a card player; (b) a second group was also told to search for a card player, but after the search was informed that no card player's picture had occurred in those pictures; (c) a group viewed the 100 mug shots, but merely rated each picture on pleasantness. In addition to the three groups viewing mug shots, there was a group that did not view any mug shots but spent an equal amount of time listening to a comedy tape. Participants from all condition groups then performed a recognition task that consisted of 36 mug shots, 3 of which were of the card players from the video, and none of which were from the 100 interpolated mug shots. Compared with the other three conditions, the standard search condition produced the fewest correct identifications as well as the fewest false positives. The simplest explanation of these results is that the effect of viewing mug shots is to make an individual less likely to choose anyone from a subsequent lineup. Although Davies et al. (1979) were hesitant to completely rule out the possibility that simple interference can occur, they leaned toward criterion-change explanations of the effects of mug book viewing on lineups.

A second test of the interference effects of mug books was provided by Cutler, Penrod, and Martens (1987). In this research, after witnessing a videotaped robbery, half of the witnesses were asked to search a mug book containing 44 mug shots. The mug book did not contain the perpetrator or any of the members of a subsequent lineup. After the mug book task, witnesses viewed a lineup. Reminiscent of one of the Davies et al. (1979) control conditions, witnesses in the mug book condition were told before viewing the lineup that the perpetrator had not been in the mug book pictures. The lineup consisted of eight pictures; for half of the witnesses the perpetrator was present in the lineup, and for half he was not present. There were no effects of mug book viewing on lineup performance. These findings are actually quite consistent with those of Davies et al. (1979). Davies et al. (1979) argued that including information that the perpetrator's picture had not been in the mug book should remove any criterion shift. Procedures such as that of Cutler et al. (1987) that included such information would not produce a criterion shift, and hence there would be no impact on lineup performance.

A final experiment that could be said to be testing the interference effects of mug book viewing on lineup performance was Experiment 1 of Dysart, Lindsay, Hammond, and Dupuis (2001). This more recent test had a number of improvements over Davies et al. (1979) and Cutler et al. (1987): (a) a more realistic 600-picture mug book was used, as opposed to the relatively small mug book sizes of 44 and 100 used in the earlier research; (b) a more standard lineup size of 6 was used, as opposed to 8 and 36 in the earlier research; and (c) there was no statement to the witness that the mug book did not contain the perpetrator. Like the work of Cutler et al. (1987), the research also included a perpetrator present or absent factor that provided for a much cleaner look at the shift of criterion hypothesis than could be provided by Davies et al. (1979), which used only perpetrator present lineups. The findings of Dysart et al. (2001) were the same as those of Cutler et al. (1987)—there were no significant differences between those witnesses who viewed mug shots and those who did not. It is important to note that Dysart et al. (2001) did not inform witnesses that the perpetrator had not been in the mug book; thus, the possible explanation of the failure to find effects in Cutler et al. (1987) was not a viable explanation in this case.

Conclusion

What can be said about the impact of viewing a set of mug shots that do not contain anyone that appears in the lineup? From the three experiments that have addressed the issue, there seems to be little danger. All three experiments show that there is no increased danger to the innocent suspect, and only one of the three found a reduced ability to identify the guilty suspect. None of the experiments found any support for the interference hypothesis. At worst, it seems that viewing a mug book that does not contain someone in the lineup causes the witness to adopt a more stringent criterion for making an identification in the lineup

Familiarity and Commitment Effects— Overlap Between Mug Book and Lineup

The above research dealt with the situation where there is no overlap between the mug book and the lineup; however, in many cases there is an overlap. In the ideal case, the witness identified the perpetrator in the mug book, the perpetrator was apprehended, and the witness then identified the perpetrator in a lineup. But what of the case where a person was viewed in the mug book and was not the perpetrator and yet appeared in the lineup? Is this person at greater risk for being identified in the lineup because their picture appeared in the mug book? Brown, Deffenbacher, and Sturgill (1977) were the first to address this issue. They were concerned about a witness who might recognize a face but not recall the circumstances under which that face had first been encountered. Was this face encountered at the scene of the crime, or was it perhaps in mug book pictures viewed subsequent to the crime? This confusion has been referred to at various times as unconscious transference, the source-monitoring error, and the familiarity effect. Although three experiments were conducted, only Experiments 2 and 3 were really relevant to the effect of mug books on lineup performance. Given that the experiments were conceptually similar, with similar results, only Experiment 3 is discussed here. In Experiment 3, witnesses viewed two targets as they entered class; one had handed them their exam questions, and the other had handed them an answer sheet. They later viewed a 12-person mug book that contained 10 fillers, a target who would subsequently appear in the line-up, and a nontarget who would subsequently appear in the lineup. Following the mug book, participants were shown a four-person lineup that contained (a) the target who had appeared in the mug book, (b) the target who did not appear in the mug book, (c) a nontarget who was seen in the mug book, and (d) a nontarget seen only in the lineup. As expected, there did appear to be a familiarity effect. The target seen in the mug book was more likely to be identified than the target seen only in the lineup. The more dra-matic effect was that the target not seen in the mug book was not significantly more likely to be identified than the nontarget seen in the mug book. The finding that some-one seen only in a mug book was just as likely to be identified as the perpetrator as the actual perpetrator is a very disturbing finding. Such a finding naturally generated a num-ber of follow-up experiments designed to explore situations where mug books and line-ups overlap.

Although not denying the possibility of a familiarity effect, Gorenstein and Ellsworth (1980) were concerned with a different type of problem that could occur when mug books and lineups overlap. They were concerned with situations in which a witness makes an incorrect false-positive identification in a mug book and is then subsequently asked to make an identification in a lineup. Is the commitment to this mug book choice so strong that this same person would even be selected in a lineup that also contained the actual perpetrator? To test for such a commitment effect, Gorenstein and Ellsworth (1980) had a female confederate enter a psychology class and ask the professor if she could look for her wallet. At the end of the class the experimenter asked half of the stu-dents to remain behind to look at an array of 12 pictures. The array did not contain the target person; however, the instructions were such that witnesses were required to choose someone from the 12. All witnesses (those who had viewed the array and those who had not) were asked to select the target person from a lineup. For those who were in the mug book condition the six-person lineup consisted of the person incorrectly chosen from the mug book, the actual target, two faces from the mug book that were not selected, and two faces not seen before. Each witness in the no-mug-book control group was given a lineup with the same six pictures as one of the mug book witnesses. Witnesses who viewed a mug book were more likely to chose a picture in the lineup that they had in-correctly chosen in the mug book (44%) than the actual target (22%). There was no ev-idence of a simple familiarity effect above and beyond this commitment effect; pictures that had been seen in the mug book but were not chosen were no more likely to be cho-sen in the lineup than pictures that were encountered for the first time in the lineup.

One of the limitations of the research by Gorenstein and Ellsworth (1980) was that in order to examine the effects of commitment to an incorrect identification in a mug book, they strongly pressured witnesses to choose someone from the mug book (even though the perpetrator was not present). Although this technique did ensure that every-one would make an incorrect choice that permitted the test of commitment, Brigham and Cairns (1988) argued that the technique suffered from low mundane reality/external va-lidity. Brigham and Cairns (1988) attempted to improve on the procedure by using unbiased instructions (i.e., the perpetrator may or may not be present) for witnesses in the mug book conditions. Witnesses to a videotaped, staged attack were assigned to one of four conditions: (a) a mug book condition in which they made a public choice that the experimenter could see, (b) a mug book condition in which they made a private choice, (c) a control condition in which witnesses rated the attractiveness of the mug shots used in the mug book conditions, and (d) a no-photo control group. The three mug book conditions viewed 18 photos that did not include the perpetrator's picture. All witnesses then viewed a six-person, perpetrator-present lineup. In addition to the perpetrator, there were three pictures used in the mug book and two filler faces never seen by any of the witnesses before. For those witnesses in the mug book conditions who chose one of the mug book pictures, this picture was substituted for one of the mug book pictures in the lineup. Lineup performance was similar to that observed by Gorenstein and Ellsworth (1980). Those witnesses who made a choice in the mug book were likely to choose this person again in the lineup, even though the actual perpetrator was present; as in the study by Gorenstein and Ellsworth, there were actually more selections of the incorrect mug book choice than of the perpetrator. Those witnesses who did not make a choice in the mug book were generally less likely to choose anyone in the lineup, although when they did choose they usually correctly identified the perpetrator.

In some ways the procedure of Brigham and Cairns (1988) was an improvement over Gorenstein and Ellsworth's (1980) procedure of forcing witnesses to make a choice from a perpetrator absent mug book. Brigham and Cairns (1988) allowed witnesses to either choose or not choose a picture from the mug book. If they chose a picture from the mug book, it would be included along with the target's picture. The fact that their tests of commitment are based primarily on only some of their participants (the 54% of the witnesses who chose someone from the mug book) could be seen as a limitation of the research. Another limitation of both Gorenstein and Ellsworth (1980) and Brigham and Cairns (1988) was the extremely small size of the mug books. In an attempt to improve on the earlier tests of a commitment effect, Dysart et al. (2001) used a procedure that solved both the problem of getting all of the witnesses to make an unforced choice and using a more realistically sized mug book. The mug book procedure was one developed by Lindsay, Nosworthy, Martin, and Martynuck (1994), who proposed that mug books should be viewed simply as an investigative tool to aid in locating suspects. Rather than asking a witness to answer just yes or no, researchers could also allow the witness to answer maybe. They argued that the task should be viewed as one in which the goal is to develop a group of suspects to investigate further, rather than an identification technique. When used in conjunction with relatively large mug books, virtually all witnesses make at least some incorrect choices, making this technique an ideal procedure for testing commitment effects.

In the Dysart et al. (2001) test of commitment effects, witnesses to a purse snatching viewed a mug book that contained 600 pictures (the perpetrator was not present), or the witnesses were in a no-mug-book control. Using the Lindsay et al. technique of allowing maybe responses, all witnesses in the mug book conditions chose pictures that at least might have been of the perpetrator. All lineups were perpetrator absent and contained one picture from the mug book and five new foils not seen in the mug book. Sets of three witnesses viewed the same lineups. The lineup contained one of the pictures selected by one of the three witnesses during the mug book phase. This allowed a test of commitment. A second witness who also viewed the mug book, but had not selected this picture, viewed the same lineup. This second witness allowed for a test of familiarity, as he or she had seen the picture, but not selected it. A third witness yoked to the other two witnesses saw the same lineup, but did not view a mug book. This third witness was the control with which the other two were compared. There was a significant effect of commitment. Witnesses who had chosen an innocent person in the mug book were significantly more likely to choose this person in a lineup than either the witness who had seen but not chosen the person in the mug book or the witness who had not viewed a mug book. There was no evidence of familiarity, in that the witness who had seen but not chosen the innocent suspect was not significantly different from the control in selecting this person in the lineup; in fact, there were actually more false positives of the innocent suspect in the control condition.

Memon, Hope, Bartlett, and Bull (2002) provide the most recent test of commitment and familiarity effects. In this research participants viewed a video clip of a car theft; some of the witnesses then viewed a mug book. The mug book consisted of 12 pictures that fit the perpetrator's general description in terms of age, hair color, hair length, no facial hair, and no glasses. One of these pictures was designated as the Critical Foil (CF) and was placed in the sixth position of the sequentially presented mug book pictures. This critical foil was the only individual from the mug book who appeared in a subsequent lineup. The perpetrator-absent lineup consisted of six pictures, one of which was the CF. The lineup performances of three groups were compared: mug book choosers, mug book nonchoosers, and controls who were not exposed to a mug book. Mug book choosers had a significantly higher proportion of CF choices (.40) than either nonchoosers (.16) or controls (.13). If these choosers had selected the CF in the mug book, this would have been consistent with the commitment hypothesis; however, only 13 of 73 of the mug book choosers actually chose the CF. When these 13 were dropped from the analysis, the results remained essentially the same, with 35% of those who had chosen someone other than the CF in the mug book now choosing the CF in the lineup. Although Memon et al. (2002) did not deny the effect that commitment can have (of the 13 that had chosen the CF in the mug book, 61% again selected the CF in the lineup), their data did provide support for the familiarity effect. However, the support for familiarity had a qualification not mentioned in past research—familiarity had an impact only for those who chose someone from the mug book. Choosing anyone from a mug book made it more likely that a witness would choose a person from the lineup who was also in the mug book. Nonchoosers did not show an effect for familiarity.

The study of Lindsay et al. (1994) was the only follow-up to Brown et al. (1977) that dealt with the situation in which the overlap between mug book and lineup involved the perpetrator (i.e., it is a picture of the perpetrator who appeared in both the mug book and the lineup. In their Experiment 1, witnesses to a staged theft of the experimenter's purse attempted to locate the perpetrator in mug books that always contained the perpetrator. The perpetrator's picture occurred after 100, 300, 500, or 700 other photos had been shown. As discussed earlier, witnesses were encouraged to use a lenient criteria and were allowed a maybe response. After witnesses had completed the mug book, they were allowed to review all of their choices in order to eliminate any that on reflection they realized were not of the perpetrator. Following this review, witnesses in the 100 and 500 mug book conditions attempted to identify the perpetrator in a perpetrator-present or perpetrator-absent six-person lineup. Results were compared with the lineup performance witnesses not viewing a mug book. There were more correct identifications of the perpetrator and fewer false-positive identifications of the innocent suspect in the mug book conditions than in the no-mug-book control condition. Lindsay et al. attributed these findings to the fact that the perpetrator had been present in the mug book, and any witness who had selected the perpetrator would have seen his picture again in the final review of selected pictures occurring before the mug book; thus, the approximately 60% of witnesses choosing the perpetrator from the mug book had seen his picture three times before they began the lineup. It is possible that commitment or familiarity could explain the slightly better performance of those viewing mug books compared with the control.

Conclusion

The conclusions about the impact of mug books and lineups overlapping are not quite as straightforward as most summary statements of this area would suggest. Although often summarized in a one-sentence warning about the negative effect of viewing mug books, the findings are much more complex than this. Although seemingly addressing the same topic, the way in which mug books and lineups overlapped varied considerably across experiments.

Let us first consider overlaps involving the perpetrator. In an ideal case, the perpetrator is present in the mug book and appears in the lineup. Will the mug book experience influence witnesses' performance in the lineup? Only two of the articles reviewed speak to this issue. In both Brown et al. (1977) and Lindsay et al. (1994), the witnesses who had seen the perpetrator in the mug book were more likely to select him in the lineup than witnesses who saw him only in the lineup. This could have been due to increased familiarity or to commitment to having chosen him in the mug book (as many witnesses did). Although it was not tested by the other researchers, it is fair to say that they would agree with the conclusion that viewing the perpetrator in a mug book would not hurt the ability to identify the perpetrator in a lineup. Some of the research in which the perpetrator did not appear in the mug book but did appear in the lineup also provides information about the impact of mug book viewing on identifying the perpetrator in lineups. Both Gorenstein and Ellsworth (1980) and Brigham and Cairns (1988) used mug books that did not contain the perpetrator; however, the lineups in this research contained the perpetrator as well as an innocent individual seen only in the mug book. Gorenstein and Ellsworth (1980) found that there was a smaller percentage of correct identifications in the mug book condition than in the no-mug-book control, although this difference was not significant. Brigham and Cairns (1988) found that those who had viewed mug books were significantly lower in correct identifications than those in the no-mug-book control condition. The effect in both experiments appears to be due to witnesses being committed to a choice made in the mug book. When an innocent person chosen in the mug book is also present in a lineup containing the actual perpetrator, a number of witnesses will remain committed to their original choice, thereby reducing the correct identifications of the perpetrator. This is a negative influence of mug books, but it is an influence that is easily controllable. If the suspect (perpetrator) being evaluated in the lineup did not appear in the mug book, then the lineup should not contain the picture of anyone seen in the mug book. This would convert the situation into one in which there is no overlap between the mug book and the lineup, a situation where two of the three studies showed no effect of mug book viewing on identification of the perpetrator. In conclusion, viewing mug books does not seem to be a major problem, as far as correct identification of a perpetrator is concerned. The situations where it could produce a problem are controllable.

In spite of the above optimistic comments about accurate identifications of perpetrators, it should be recognized that the major concern of those conducting research in this area was with the situation where an innocent person appearing in both the mug book and the lineup is selected as a perpetrator. It has been suggested that there are two possible reasons why this might occur: (a) commitment to an innocent face selected from the mug book and/or (b) familiarization with the face due to the mug book experience. There was strong support for commitment; all of the research found that selecting an innocent person from a mug book increased the likelihood that a witness would identify that person again in a subsequent lineup. Unfortunately the literature does not provide much help in determining how the commitment effect might be removed. Based on work from social psychology dealing with conformity, Brigham and Cairns (1988) attempted to show that the less public the choice, the smaller the commitment effect would be; however, they found no effect for their public/private manipulation. If the commitment effect is not due to some concern about how others would view a lack of consistency, this would suggest that less controllable factors (e.g., actual memory) might be involved. However, before giving up on explanations of commitment that involve a need to seem consistent to others, additional research is needed. Brigham and Cairns (1989) acknowledged that their manipulation may not have been strong enough and, furthermore, that if a larger number of participants had been used, patterns consistent with their hypotheses might have been significant. If it could be found that a public/private manipulation changed the commitment effect, it would give hope that the effect could be reduced through procedural changes (e.g., instructions given before the lineup). However, for the present the best advice for police would be that witnesses who identify someone in a mug book search should not be asked to make an identification of this same person in a lineup. When police do ask a witness to attempt a lineup identification, it should be recognized that the only new information that could be gained would be if the witness did not identify this person; simply another identification of this person really tells little about whether their mug book choice was correct or not.

The other major concern when mug books and lineups overlap is that a person who was merely seen (but not chosen) in a mug book is in danger of being selected in a subsequent lineup because of a familiarity effect. There is much less agreement on this effect than on the commitment effect. Brown et al. (1977) favored a familiarity effect interpretation of their results; however, they did not report data that would allow us to separate how much of the effects were due to familiarity and how much to commitment. Memon et al. (2002) also claimed support for a familiarity effect, but only for those witnesses who had made a choice in the mug book task. Choosers in the mug book task were more likely to choose someone who had been seen in the mug book (regardless of whether it was the person they chose in the mug book or not). In contrast to the two articles claiming some support for familiarity, Dysart et al. (2001) found in Experiment 2 a significant effect of commitment, but no evidence at all of a familiarity effect. The cause for the differing results is likely to be found in procedural differences. The two articles supporting familiarity effects involved extremely small mug books (15 mug shots or less). The study by Dysart et al. (2001) was the only research to use large mug books (up to 600 mug shots) and was the one study that did not find familiarity effects. Although both Dysart et al. (2001) and Memon et al. (2002) suggest that mug book size may be the critical factor, whether this is, in fact, the case can only be determined by additional research. In the meantime, it would appear that both Dysart et al. (2001) and Memon et al. (2002) would agree that if a witness has not made a choice in the mug book, there is little danger in that witness viewing a lineup containing someone who was in the mug book. The disagreement comes when the witness has selected someone from the mug book who is not to be in the lineup; only Memon et al. (2002) advises against having this witness view the lineup.

EFFECTS OF MUG BOOK SIZE ON MUG BOOK PERFORMANCE

In the last section, mug book size was speculated to be a possible cause for the discrepant findings concerning the effect of mug books on *lineup* performance, and the call was for future research. But what about the impact of mug book size on *mug book* performance? Laughery et al. (1971) provided the first data relevant to this issue. In Experiment 1 participants who had viewed four slides of one human face attempted to identify this face in a mug book consisting of 150 sequentially presented slides. The critical variable was whether the target face appeared in position 40 or position 140. Technically speaking, this is not a manipulation of mug book size; however, it is clearly relevant to the mug book size issue. Two other variables were manipulated in this research—viewing time of the target (10 s or 32 s) and knowledge that a mug book task would follow exposure to the target (knowledge or no knowledge). For each picture a yes or no judgment was made, as was a degree of confidence measure. These two measures were combined into a 6-point scale for the target as well as for each foil. When the target measure was analyzed, there was a significant main effect for position; better performance was found when the target was in position 40 than when it was in position 140. When the foil measure was analyzed, there was a significant main effect for prior knowledge and a significant three-way interaction. Lower false-positive scores were found when participants knew that they were going to view a mug book; this was particularly true when the target had been seen for 32 s and was in position 40.

As to why witnesses were better able to identify the target in the early position, Laughery et al. (1971) speculated that this effect could be due to the interference of the additional decoy pictures seen or to the greater amount of time elapsed when the target appeared in the later position. In an attempt to determine which of these two explanations could best account for the position effect, Laughery, Fessler, Lenorovitz, and Yoblick (1974) conducted four experiments. In Experiment 1, the key manipulation was the delay between the initial exposure to the target and the subsequent mug book search; there were six levels of delay, ranging from 4 minutes to 1 week. When the correct identification measure and the false-positive measure were analyzed, there was no significant effect for delay. Not finding any support for a decay explanation, Laughery et al. (1974) went on to explore the interference explanation. They reasoned that if interference was the problem, then the more similar the foils to the target, the greater the interference would be. The strongest test of their hypothesis occurred in Experiment 2c, where there was both a manipulation of similarity of foils to the target and of the position of the target in the mug book. Participants were run in two separate trials. To the extent that the position effect was due to interference, there should have been a greater effect of position on correct identifications when the mug books were made up of similar pictures than when the pictures were dissimilar; this interaction pattern was, in fact, significant, but only for the Trial 2 replication of the design. When false positives were analyzed, a significant effect of similarity was found such that there were more false positives when the pictures were similar, but this effect occurred only in Trial 1. Although the results were not completely consistent with predictions, it did appear that the danger of viewing larger mug books might come from the increased number of pictures that would be encountered that were similar to the perpetrator.

In contrast to the Laughery research, Lindsay et al. (1994) actually manipulated mug book size. In Experiment 1, witnesses to a staged theft attempted to identify the perpetrator from mug books that contained 127, 327, 527, or 727 mug shots. The perpetrator's picture was always 27 pictures from the end of the mug book. Consistent with the earlier findings, the smaller, 100-picture mug book produced significantly more correct identifications than the larger 500- and 700-picture mug books. Mug book size also seemed to have an impact on false positives. Although not statistically tested, false-positive choices steadily decreased as the number of pictures seen increased. Lindsay et al. (1994) suggested that one interpretation of this data is that it is due to a criterion shift; as more and more nontargets were seen, witnesses became less and less likely to make an identification response to any picture. Lindsay et al. 1994 sought to determine whether the negative effects of larger mug books might be attributable to the increase in the number of pictures similar to the perpetrator rather than just simply the greater number of pictures. In Experiment 3 of Lindsay et al. (1994), witnesses to a staged theft attempted an identification from a mug book containing the perpetrator and (a) 199 pictures selected from a pool of 727 based on similarity to the perpetrator, (b) 199 pictures randomly selected from the pool of 727 pictures, and (c) the entire pool of 727 pictures.

The correct identifications of the perpetrator in the mug book with 200 similar were roughly equal to the correct identifications in the 727-picture mug book. This suggests that it was the number of similar pictures (which would have been the same in the two mug books) and not the total number of pictures that was critical. Further support for this argument is the finding that these two mug books produced marginally significantly fewer correct identifications than the mug book with 200 random selection pictures (which contained fewer similar pictures than the other two conditions). Thus, Lindsay et al. (1994) have a somewhat qualified view of the negative impact of larger mug books—the greater the number of mug book pictures *similar to the perpetrator*, the less likely it is that the perpetrator will be identified.

The most recent experiment relevant to the issue of mug book size was conducted by McAllister, Stewart, and Loveland (2003), who included a position of the perpetrator factor. Witnesses to a videotaped, simulated crime attempted identifications from mug books where the perpetrator and 69 preceding foils appeared in positions 1–70, 71–140, or 141–210. The mug books also varied as to whether they were static or dynamic. Consistent with past research, correct identifications of the perpetrator were lower the later the perpetrator's picture appeared. In contrast to the other experiments, the same set of foils preceded the perpetrator's picture in all conditions. This allowed for a less confounded look at false positives made late in a mug book as compared with those made early. The later the set of 69 foils occurred in the mug book, the fewer the false positives selected from the set. Similar to the findings in Experiment 1 of Lindsay et al. (1994), as the number of pictures viewed increased, the likelihood of making an identification (correct or incorrect) decreased. Experiment 2 of McAllister et al. (2003) explored the impact of similarity. Identifications were attempted in mug books that contained either 69 pictures pruned by a computer facial recognition algorithm for their similarity to the perpetrator or a random selection of 69 pictures. Contrary to the finding of Lindsay et al. (1994), similarity of mug book pictures did not affect mug book performance. One possible reason for the different results is that McAllister et al. (2003) used computer facial recognition similarity ratings to select pictures, whereas Lindsay et al. (1994) used human similarity rating. Some support for this as an explanation came from Experiment 3 of McAllister et al.'s (2003), where it was found that when mug book pictures were rated for similarity to the perpetrator both by the computer algorithm and by humans, the correlation between the two ratings was virtually zero. In summary, McAllister et al. (2003) found support for the idea that larger mug books would reduce correct identification rates, but that larger mug books would not place an innocent individual at greater risk. They failed to find support for similarity as defined by a computer recognition algorithm as being a critical factor.

It does appear that the larger the mug book, the less likely it is that a witness will be able to make a correct identification of the perpetrator; the extent to which similarity is involved still requires further research. One often-advocated solution to the mug book size problem has been to prune mug books down to just those individuals who could possibly be the perpetrator. The next section deals with the literature on how successful pruning mug books might be.

PRUNING OR SORTING MUG BOOKS

Before the advent of computers, only the grossest type of pruning was practical (e.g., gender, age, race, type of crime, etc.). Computers have dramatically changed the level of pruning possible. Computers can be used to compare a witness's description of the perpetrator with each mug shot in the mug book in order to narrow the search. Laughery, Rhodes, and Batten (1981) made a distinction between two different approaches to this comparison process—a matching approach as opposed to a sequencing approach. The matching approach eliminates mug shots that do not fit the witness's input; this is a true pruning procedure. A sequencing approach orders pictures in terms of their similarity to the witness's input; thus, when discussing computerized mug books with the use of a sequencing approach, the term *sorting* will be used, rather than *pruning*. Most of the techniques to be described in this section use the sequencing approach.

Early work on the use of computers to sort faces was based on categorizing faces as a function of various facial features. The features of each face in a mug book would be input to the computer, based on ratings provided by human judges who rated the features or on physical measurement of the features made by the computer (e.g., width of lips, distance between eyes). The witnesses would then enter information about the features of the perpetrator, and a comparison would be made with each picture in the mug book.

Harmon (1973) was one of the first to use a sorting procedure based on human judgments of features. Harmon had 10 trained observers rank 256 faces on 35 features (only 21 were actually used in the mug book procedure). The value of each feature for each picture was the average of the 1 to 5 scale value assigned by the 10 observers. In a test of the computerized mug book, a witness was given the front, three-quarter, and profile pictures of one member of the database, and then the witness entered his or her description of this person feature by feature into the computer. The witness entered features in decreasing order of how extreme they considered them to be. After each feature was entered, the computer would sort the pictures so that pictures with the most similar feature scores would be highest in the rankings. After the witness had entered those features that they considered most extreme (usually four or less), they could use an automatic feature selection that involved the computer asking them about particular features based on the features that most efficiently separated the members of the population. The procedure was stopped after 10 steps. Results were impressive; the correct face appeared in the tenth place or better in 99% of the trials. By the tenth sorting, the target had risen to the first position for 70% of the trials.

There are certain limitations to the method of Harmon (1973) that should be mentioned. First, it appears that the target picture was present the entire time that it was being described by a witness. A second limitation involves the small number of pictures in the database. Success with sorting 256 pictures does not guarantee success with a more realistically sized pool. Finally, a system based around having every picture in a mug shot pool judged by 10 different individuals would obviously be extremely costly to implement in a real-world setting.

Lee and Whalen (1995) attempted to improve on the work begun by Harmon (1973). Rather than having each picture in the database rated by 10 raters as Harmon had done, Lee and Whalen (1995) used only one rater. However, this rater made ratings on 90 features rather than the 35 features used in the Harmon system; each feature was coded on a 5-point scale. The database consisted of 640 pictures of known offenders, in contrast to the 256 pictures of nonoffenders used by Harmon (1973). Three experiments were conducted to test the system. All three of the experiments involved participants viewing a picture randomly selected from the database for 10 seconds. After a 1-minute delay, they were asked to recall the target on each of the 90 features. The mean retrieval ranks for the three experiments were 17.4, 4.1, and 9.7. These figures are an obvious improvement over the 320 photographs that an average witness would have to go through before reaching the target if the target had been randomly placed in the mug book.

The effectiveness of the Lee and Whalen (1995) system has been replicated in a number of other experiments. Lee and Whalen (1996) conducted a series of five experiments to explore the impact of the number of raters used to scale pictures in a database. The basic procedure was similar to the earlier approach, with a minor change. As in the earlier research, the retrieval rates were impressive. The main new finding was that adding a second rater did improve system performance; however, the addition of a third, fourth, or fifth rater did not improve the retrieval rates. Most recently, Lee, Whalen, Jollymore, Read, and Swaffer (1998) replicated the findings of Lee and Whalen (1995, 1996) with the use of live targets rather than photo targets and testing over varying delays. The system worked well with live targets, required only two raters per picture, and was not affected by delays of up to 4 weeks. Not only was the system effective; it was more practical than the similar system proposed by Harmon (1973). The Lee and Whalen system needed only one or two raters, in contrast to the 10 used by Harmon (1973).

Adachi (1994) proposed yet another computer-based retrieval system using human ratings of the features of each face in the database. In common with Lee and Whalen, only one rater was used; however, in contrast to the 90–107 features used by Lee and Whalen, Adachi used 605 features. Witnesses using this system simply described the target; they were not prompted by the system asking about specific features. In the test of this system, the database consisted of 100 pictures that had been rated on the 605 features. Pictures selected at random were presented to 12 participants for 30 seconds. Fifteen seconds later the participants freely described the features of the face. Each of the described features was assigned by an operator to one feature in the set; witnesses were not asked about specific features. The pool of 100 pictures was then sorted on the match with features derived from the witness's description. The performance score that was emphasized was hit rate, which was defined as bringing the target picture to the first position; this occurred 35% of the time. Although bringing the target to the first position was emphasized, information was also provided for other positions. For example, the target was brought to one of the top five positions 60% of the time and to one of the top 10 positions 80% of the time. This performance on a database of 100 is clearly not as impressive as the performances with Lee and Whalen's system on databases ranging from 640 to 1,000 pictures.

To this point in the discussion, all of the sorting techniques have categorized faces based on human judgments about their features; however, other work attempted to use physical measurement of features. Bledsoe's (1966) facial recognition algorithm utilized such physical measurement of features as the distance between eyes and the width of lips. In Bledsoe's (1966) system, a human operator would extract the coordinates of various facial features, and from these coordinates the computer could compute distance between eyes, width of mouth, etc. One operator could process 40 pictures per hour, an obvious reduction in man-hours over any of the procedures based on human judgments. Once the database of pictures was coded according to the physical measurements, then it would be possible to input a target picture and have the computer locate those pictures that were most similar to the target. One difficulty in developing a mug book from such a procedure is that humans do not encode faces as a set of measurements; witnesses would be at a loss to give the number of centimeters between the perpetrator's eyes. This problem was addressed by Shepherd and colleagues (1986; Ellis, Shepherd, Flin, Shepherd, & Davies, 1989).

Shepherd developed a computerized mug book that used both subjective ratings similar to those of Harmon (1973) and physical measurements similar to those of Bledsoe (1966). The database consisted of 1,000 pictures and was coded on 47 parameters for each face. Ten graduate students rated 38 attributes on five point scales (e.g., breadth of face, length of hair) and 9 attributes on dichotomous scales (e.g., presence or absence of facial hair); mean values were used for each parameter. A second stage involved taking physical measurements and scaling them to values on a 5-point scale using linear regression; this made it possible to know what a human scale score of 3 on breath of face translated into in actual physical measurement. Where no physical measurement was possible, the original human rating was used. Because of this translation between physical measurements and scale scores, witnesses could provide information about facial features in a more natural way. They could much more easily respond on a scale going from 1 (close set) to 5 (wide spaced) than trying to give physical measurements.

Shepherd (1986) reported the results of three experiments to test this FRAME system. All three experiments used the same basic procedure with a few minor modifications. The third experiment that was reported by both Shepherd (1986) and Ellis et al. (1989) was the most interesting of the three because it permitted a comparison with a standard album. Much of the research in this area focuses just on the usefulness of the system in bringing the target picture to the front of the mug book. However, a second issue concerns the recognition performance by the witness. By including a standard album condition, it is possible to see the effect of the computerized search on witness identification performance as well. In this experiment, participants were exposed to a picture for 10 seconds. For half of the participants, the face was one that had been rated as distinctive, and for the other half, the face was one rated as typical. After describing the target, half of the participants then attempted to locate the target in an album search. The participant was given four albums, each containing 250 faces; the target's picture was placed in one of four positions. The other half of the participants were in the computer search condition. The computer search began with the experimenter asking the participants to describe the target. The experimenter then had the participants rate each of the features mentioned in their free descriptions that corresponded to one of the 47 rating scales. Only features mentioned in the free descriptions were entered. These ratings were used to sort the database. The most similar pictures were presented in order. A successful retrieval was defined as the target appearing in this set of six pictures and the participant identifying him. If the participants were not successful in this first search, they could choose to modify the search parameters either by changing the values or by using values from faces that seemed similar to the target. This process could be repeated up to four times. Performance was broken down into hits (the target was retrieved and identified), false positives (an incorrect identification was made before the target was retrieved), misses (the target was retrieved but not identified), or nonretrieval (the target was not retrieved in the four searches). The results showed that hit rates for distinctive faces were not significantly different for the album (78%) and computer search (75%) conditions. Only 9% of the computer searches failed to retrieve the target picture. For the more difficult task of a target with a typical face, the hit rate for the computer search (69%) was significantly higher than for the album search (44%), in spite of the fact that 22% of the computer searches failed to retrieve the target's picture.

One of the criticisms that could be made of sorting faces by features is that this is not the way that faces are normally processed. Natural face recognition is a holistic process rather than an analytic process; rather than analyzing a face feature by feature, we focus more on the configural pattern of faces. Levi, Jungman, Ginton, Aperman, and Noble (1995) developed a technique where pictures could be judged with the use of more holistic judgments of facial similarity. Levi et al. (1995) conducted three experiments, all of which used the same basic system. First, a witness would be required to describe the target, based on a small set of categories (e.g., age, eye color, blemish), and give a confidence rating. Presumably these features had previously been rated by judges, although this process is not described. The computer would then sort the 1,200 pictures in the database according to their similarity to the description of the target. Up to this point the procedure is similar to that of Ellis et al. (1989); however, from this point on it differs significantly. Following the initial sorting based on features, the 24 pictures with the highest rankings were presented to the witness who chose up to five photos that were similar to the target. These pictures were then used to sort the pictures in the database based on their similarity to the selected pictures. Similarity was based on coding done by a single rater. The rater had compared each of the 1,200 pictures in the database with 80 reference photos; each picture was scored as being similar or dissimilar to each of the 80 reference photos. Ratings were done such that each photo would have approximately 35 pictures described as dissimilar and 45 as similar. To the extent that a picture in the data base had been judged as dissimilar to the same reference photos as a picture that was chosen by the witness, it would be moved up in mug booking ranking.

In Experiment 1, participants attempted to locate a well-known public figure. After the sorting based on the description was completed, the picture was placed in the 808th position, and the first set of 24 pictures was presented. Participants selected the most similar pictures, and the pictures were resorted. This continued until the participant reached the target, or 24 screens had been seen (576 photos). The 76% that reached the target picture before the cutoff point viewed a median of 8 screens; 79% correctly identified the target when it was reached. Participants in Experiment 2 briefly viewed a male target live, and then searched the database with the use of the procedure used in Experiment 1. The 78% who reached the target viewed a median of 15 screens; 23% identified the target when it was reached. In Experiment 3, after viewing the photograph of a familiar or unfamiliar target, participants went through the same computerized mug book procedure as in the first two experiments. The 84% of searches that reached the target before the 24-screen cutoff did so in a median of four screens.

Levi et al. (1995) demonstrated that computerized sorting procedures using similarity judgments could be effective. However, Levi et al. (1995) were not suggesting that similarity judgments should replace feature judgments, but rather that they could be used in conjunction with features. In contrast, others have viewed feature approaches and similarity approaches as competitors (Pryke, Lindsay, & Pozzulo, 2000). Pryke et al. (2000) tested the relative effectiveness of the two approaches. A database of 600 pictures was rated on features and on similarity by five raters. The 54 features included the 47 used by Ellis et al. (1989). The similarity judgments involved rating the similarity of each picture to each of 16 comparison faces on a 10-point scale. Participants first viewed a picture of either a distinctive or an average face for 1 minute. They then rated this target face on the various features, followed by rating the similarity of the face to each of the 16 comparison faces (order was reversed for half of the participants). This process was then repeated for a second target face; if the first face had been average, this second face would then be distinctive. Sorting by description produced a higher percentile for the target than sorting by similarity; this difference was significantly more pronounced for distinctive faces than for average faces.

One limitation of the study by Pryke et al. (2000) is that it does not use the iterative features that were used by certain of the descriptive and similarity approaches. Both the descriptive approach used by Ellis et al. (1989) and the similarity approach used by Levi et al. (1995) allowed (required) witnesses to make a series of sortings. If no identification was made after the first six pictures had been viewed, Ellis et al. (1989) allowed witnesses to amend the search parameters for the next sorting; this would be repeated for up to four sets of pictures. After the first 24 pictures were viewed in the study by Levi et al. (1995), witnesses were asked to select up to five faces that were similar to the target, and, based on these choices, the pool would be sorted; this would be repeated for up to 24 sets of pictures. The findings of Pryke et al. (2000) may not generalize to systems using iterative procedures.

The most recent advances in sorting procedures involve the use of computer facial recognition algorithms that break the face down into low-level image features (not the same as human descriptions of features such as eyes, nose, or ears). In these systems, a picture of the target's face is entered into the computer, which then uses a computer facial recognition algorithm to convert it to an image code. Based on the similarity of the image codes of the target picture and the pictures in the mug shot pool, the top matches are returned. The problem for using such a system with eyewitnesses is how to get an initial image from them in order to conduct the sorting.

Pentland, Picard, and Sclaroff (1996) described a solution to the initial image problem for the mug book program Photobook. In their approach, a witness would simply begin to look through an initial set of pictures in the mug book; when the witness determined that one of the pictures was somewhat similar to the perpetrator, the program would sort the mug book based on this picture. The witness would then look through the sorted pictures until another face similar to the perpetrator was found, and the mug book would be resorted. This process would continue until an identification was made, or the search was terminated. In contrast to this iterative approach involving multiple sortings of mug book pictures, a second approach involves just one sorting based on one picture—a composite picture constructed by the witness. Computerized composite systems have been developed to the point that they can produce images that are close to photographic level and are recognizable by the facial recognition algorithms. In fact, some of the composite programs use the same facial recognition algorithms used in the computerized mug books. Other computerized composite systems are built around the more traditional feature-oriented approach.

Although both iterative and composite approaches have been used on the first image problem, there is a dearth of evidence of their relative effectiveness. Baker (1999) provides the only direct comparison of the two approaches in mug books using computer facial recognition algorithms. After viewing the picture of a target person, participants in this research were asked to construct a composite of the target with the use of a computerized composite system. In a within-subjects design, these same participants were asked to search the database with the use of an iterative strategy. Participants were told that they would be given 20 pictures at a time. They picked the one picture from this group that was most similar to the target, after which the computer ordered the 4,500 pictures according to which the computer considered most similar and presented them in order of similarity. From that point on, the participant could conduct this sorting process as little or as much as desired. The iterative strategy produced a target percentile rank of 65%; this would be an unacceptable figure in a large mug book. The composite approach produced a percentile rank of 80%, which though superior to the iterative strategy, is still not particularly impressive.

There is other research that also demonstrates problems with using an iterative approach with programs using computer facial recognition algorithms. Rivas (1999) had participants view a 3-minute videotape of an interaction between a shopkeeper and a customer. Following the video, participants were asked to locate the customer in a computerized mug book. The interface of the mug book program was somewhat similar to the one used by Baker (1999); however, it was based on a related but different algorithm. The mug shot pool consisted of 505 randomly ordered pictures, with the exception that the target photo was located in position 490. Only 43% of participants reached the target picture before the cutoff of 505 pictures was reached. Of the 43% who actually reached the target's picture, the mean percentile rank was 48%. These results suggest that the computerized program might actually be harmful to a search. Everyone using a sequential procedure, methodically going through the mug book, would have reached the picture at the 490th position, as opposed to 57% of the participants in the experimental condition, who had not reached the picture by position 505.

Given the poor results with an interactive strategy, the composite approach may offer the most promise. However, basing a sorting procedure around a composite is not without its problems. Research on composites constructed with some of the more widely used electronic programs has shown that witnesses are not able to produce good likenesses of faces, particularly when the composites are constructed from memory (Davies, Van der Willik, & Morrison, 2000; Koehn & Fisher, 1997; Kovera, Penrod, Papas, & Thill, 1997). But what does saying that these composites are not good likenesses actually mean? What determines what a good likeness is?

A technique that is often used to evaluate the quality of a composite is to show it to someone who was not involved in the construction of the composite and see if this person can recognize the target person based on this composite. However, in order to evaluate the quality of a composite for use as the initial picture in a mug book search, the composite must be submitted to the computerized mug book to see if it can recognize the target. It is possible that the best composite construction system as determined by human recognition is not the best as determined by computer recognition. Clearly this is a topic that deserves future research.

It is a fairly safe prediction that the mug books of the future will be computer-based systems that allow witnesses to sort the pictures. What will be the basis for this sorting process? The bulk of the research to date has focused on systems that involve the mug shot pool being rated by human judges either on features or on similarity. This research is of importance because it showed that computerized mug books can be effective; however, although some have seen some very limited use in the field, it is unlikely that these systems will ever be widely adopted. For one thing, there would be overwhelming practical problems. Consider New York City, where there are 800 arrest warrants issued each day. If each picture took 5 minutes to code and required coding from two judges, it would take a team of 20 people just to keep up with the daily coding, not to mention coding of the hundreds of thousands of mug shots taken before the system was in place. Police would see this as simply too costly. A system that could automatically code the faces through computer recognition algorithms and thus require minimal human intervention seems much more practical. Many of the same companies already dealing with the criminal justice system on high-technology security issues also produce mug book programs using computer facial recognition; these companies are in an excellent position to market their products. In spite of the fact that these will be the systems used by many police departments in the very near future, there has been extremely limited published research in this direction. Although there has been a significant amount of research on how the computer facial recognition algorithms themselves work, there has been very little on how an eyewitness might interact with these algorithms in a computerized mug book. Research on the effectiveness of computerized mug books using facial recognition algorithms is perhaps the highest priority for future mug book research.

CONCLUSION

The case has been made that mug books are not just large photospreads that require little additional research. Even on issues where mug books and photospreads seemingly overlap, mug book research is still necessary. As was shown by Stewart and McAllister (2001), clearly established findings with lineups, such as the impact of sequential procedures, do not necessarily carry over to mug books. In addition, there are a number of topics unique to mug books that still have generated little research interest. Perhaps the most critical of the uniquely mug book topics is sorting mug files with computer facial recognition programs. Computerized mug book programs have been developed and have already been adopted by police departments. Psychology must become much more involved in researching the most effective way for witnesses to interact with these programs.

REFERENCES

Adachi, K. (1994). Computer-based retrieval of witnessed faces using inter-feature similarity. *Japanese Psychological Research, 36*, 233–238.

Baker, E. J. (1999). The mug-shot search problem: A study of the eigenface metric, search strategies, and interfaces in a system for searching facial image data. Doctoral dissertation, Harvard University, 1999. *Dissertation Abstracts International, 60*(3), 1156B.

Bledsoe, W. W. (1966). *Man-machine facial recognition*. Report No. PRI-22. Palo Alto, CA: Panoramic Research.

Brigham, J. C., & Cairns, D. L. (1988). The effect of mug shot inspections on eyewitness identification accuracy. *Journal of Applied Social Psychology, 18*, 1394–1410.

Brown, E., Deffenbacher, K., & Sturgill, W. (1977). Memory for faces and the circumstances of encounter. *Journal of Applied Psychology, 62*, 311–318.

Cutler, B. L., Berman, G. L., Penrod, S., & Fisher, R. P. (1994). Conceptual, practical, and empirical issues associated with eyewitness identification test media. In D. F. Ross, J. D. Read & M. P. Toglia (Eds.), *Adult eyewitness testimony: current trends and development* (pp. 163–181). New York. Cambridge University Press.

Cutler, B. L., Penrod, S. D., & Martens, T. K. (1987). Improving the reliability of eyewitness identifications: Putting context into context. *Journal of Applied Psychology, 72*, 629–637.

Davies, G., Shepherd, J., & Ellis, H. (1979). Effects of interpolated mug shot exposure on accuracy of eyewitness identification. *Journal of Applied Psychology, 64*, 232–237.

Davies, G., van der Willik, P., & Morrison, L. J. (2000). Facial composite production: A comparison of mechanical and computer-driven systems. *Journal of Applied Psychology, 85*, 119–124.

Dysart, J. E., Lindsay, R. C. L., Hammond, R., & Dupuis, P. (2001). Mug shot exposure prior to lineup identification: Interference, transference, and commitment effects. *Journal of Applied Psychology, 86*, 1280–1284.

Ellis, H. D., Shepherd, J. W., Flin, R. H., Shepherd, J., & Davies, G. M. (1989). Identification from a computer-driven retrieval system compared with a traditional mug-shot album search: A new tool for police investigations. *Ergonomics, 32*, 167–177.

Gorenstein, G. W., & Ellsworth, P. C. (1980). Effect of choosing an incorrect photograph on a later identification by an eyewitness. *Journal of Applied Psychology, 65*, 616–622.

Harmon, L. D. (1973). The recognition of faces. *Scientific American, 229*, 70–82.

Koehn, C., & Fisher, R. P. (1997). Constructing facial composites with the Mac-a-Mug Pro system. *Psychology, Crime and Law, 3*, 209–218.

Kovera, M. B., Penrod, S. D., Pappas, C., & Thill, D. L. (1997). Identification of computer-generated facial composites. *Journal of Applied Psychology, 82*, 235–246.

Laughery, K. R., Alexander, J. F., & Lane, A. B. (1971). Recognition of human faces: Effects of target exposure time, target position, pose position and type of photograph. *Journal of Applied Psychology, 55*, 477–483.

Laughery, K. R., Fessler, P. K., Lenorovitz, D. R., & Yoblick, D. A. (1974). Time delay and similarity effects in facial recognition. *Journal of Applied Psychology, 59*, 490–496.

Laughery, K. R., Rhodes, B., & Batten, G. (1981). Computer-guided recognition and retrieval of facial images. In G. Davies, H. Ellis, & J. Shepherd (Eds.), *Perceiving and remembering faces* (pp. 251–271). London: Academic Press.

Lee, E., & Whalen, T. (1995). Computerized feature retrieval of images: Suspect identification. *Ergonomics, 38,* 1941–1957.

Lee, E., & Whalen, T. (1996). Feature approaches to suspect identification: Effects of multiple raters on system performance. *Ergonomics, 39,* 17–34.

Lee, E., Whalen, T., Jollymore, G., Read, C., & Swaffer, M. (1998). The effects of delay on the performance of computerized feature systems for identifying suspects. *Behaviour & Information Technology, 17,* 294–300.

Levi, A. M., Jungman, H., Ginton, A., Aperman, A., & Noble, G. (1995). Using similarity judgments to conduct a mugshot album search. *Law and Human Behavior, 19,* 649–661.

Lindsay, R. C. L., Nosworthy, G. J., Martin, R., & Martynuck, C. (1994). Using mug shots to find suspects. *Journal of Applied Psychology, 79,* 121–130.

Lindsay, R. C. L., & Wells, G. L. (1985). Improving eyewitness identifications from lineups: Simultaneous versus sequential lineup presentation. *Journal of Applied Psychology, 70,* 556–564.

McAllister, H. A., Bearden, J. N., Kohlmaier, J. R., & Warner, M. D. (1997). Computerized mug books: Does adding multimedia Help? *Journal of Applied Psychology, 82,* 688–698.

McAllister, H. A., Blair, M. J., Cerone, L. G., & Laurent, M. J. (2000). Multimedia mug books: How multi should the media be? *Applied Cognitive Psychology, 14,* 277–291.

McAllister, H. A., Michel, L. L. M., Tarcza, E. V., Fitzmorris, M., & Nguyen, K. H. T. (2006). Mug shot presentation procedures in lineups and mug books. Manuscript submitted for publication.

McAllister, H. A., Stewart, H. A., & Loveland, J. (2003). Effects of mug book size and computerized pruning on the usefulness of dynamic mug book procedures. *Psychology, Crime, & Law, 9,* 265–278.

Melara, R. D., Dewitt-Rickards, T. S., & O'Brien, T. P. (1989). Enhancing lineup identification accuracy: Two codes are better than one. *Journal of Applied Psychology, 74,* 706–713.

Memon, A., Hope, L., Bartlett, J., & Bull, R. (2002). Eyewitness recognition errors: The effects of mugshot viewing and choosing in young and old adults. *Memory & Cognition, 30,* 1219–1227.

Pentland, A., Picard, R., & Sclaroff, S. (1996). Photobook: Tools for content-based manipulation of image databases. *International Journal of Computer Vision, 18,* 233–254.

Pryke, S., Lindsay, R. C. L., & Pozzulo, J. D. (2000). Sorting mug shots: Methodological issues. *Applied Cognitive Psychology, 14,* 81–96.

Rivas, R. K. (1999). *Comparing traditional mug shot albums with those using computer facial recognition algorithms.* Unpublished master's thesis, Southeastern Louisiana University.

Schiff, W., Banka, L., & de Bordes Galdi, G. (1986). Recognizing people seen in events via dynamic "mug shots." *American Journal of Psychology, 99,* 219–231.

Shapiro, P. N., & Penrod, S. D. (1986). Meta-analysis of facial identifications studies. *Psychological Bulletin, 100,* 139–156.

Shepherd, J. W. (1986). An interactive computer system for retrieving faces. In H. D. Ellis, M. A. Jeeves, F. Newcombe, & A. W. Younge (Eds.), *Aspects of face processing* (pp. 278–285). Dordrecht: Martinus Nijhoff.

Steblay, N., Dysart, J., Fulero, S., & Lindsay, R. C. L. (2001). Eyewitness accuracy rates in sequential and simultaneous lineup presentations: A meta-analytic comparison. *Law and Human Behavior, 25,* 459–473.

Stewart, H. A., & McAllister, H. A. (2001). Simultaneous versus sequential mug book procedures: Some surprising results. *Journal of Applied Psychology, 86,* 1300–1305.

Wells, G. L. (1984). The psychology of lineup identifications. *Journal of Applied Social Psychology, 14,* 89–103.

3

Facial Composites: Forensic Utility and Psychological Research

Graham M. Davies
University of Leicester, United Kingdom

Tim Valentine
Goldsmiths' College, United Kingdom

Police composites are impressions of a suspect's facial appearance derived from a witness description. Such disembodied faces stare out from the pages of our newspapers and television screens, coupled with a plea to members of the public to get in touch with the police if they believe they know someone or may have seen an individual bearing a resemblance to the composite. In the United Kingdom, just 10% of composite faces are released to the media. The remainder are used for internal police enquiries: around half are shown to informants familiar with the appearance of local criminals, and another third are used for house-to-house enquiries in the hope that they will cue a tentative identification (Kitson, Darnbrough, & Shields, 1978). Inevitably, many composites end up neglected in police files or thumbtacked to bulletin boards, awaiting the arrest of a suspect by other means. How effective are composite systems in practice? And can they be improved through psychological research?

In this chapter we review four generations of composite systems, together with the psychological research they have provoked. The earliest technique still in use is the artist's impression of a face, rendered from a witness description. The second generation is represented by mechanical systems, such as the Identikit and Photofit, which build up a face from component features (eyes, noses, mouths, etc.) selected by the witness. A third generation based on software systems, like Mac-a-Mug and E-fit, uses the same principle of witness-guided feature selection, but uses a computer to synthesize and manipulate an image of a face on a video screen. A fourth generation based on the use of genetic algorithms is at the development stage; such systems seek to capitalize on a witness's powers to discriminate between whole faces, rather than identify individual features. We conclude by considering whether the fit between the qualities of human memory and the demands of the composite process means that all systems place an unrealistic burden on the witness: perhaps the quest for the "perfect" composite system may be illusory.

ARTISTS' IMPRESSIONS

The use of an artist to sketch a likeness of a suspect from a witness's description has a long history in forensic science. As early as 1911, the technique was used in the hunt for Dr. Crippen, who had fled London, shortly before the remains of his wife were discovered buried in his cellar. The Metropolitan Police circulated an artist's impression of Crippen's current appearance, and he was subsequently identified as a passenger traveling under an assumed name on a transatlantic liner. In more recent times, the hunts for the Unabomber and the perpetrators of the Oklahoma and Bali bombings have also involved widespread publicity for artists' impressions (Taylor, 2001).

Construction Methods

Despite the publicity surrounding their work, there is little consensus among police artists about the appropriate method for constructing a likeness and no international standards for such sketches. The International Association for Identification has a Forensic Art Certification Board, and the American FBI runs an annual training course, but the influence of such bodies appears limited (Domingo, 1984).

Most artists work directly with the witness, but FBI operatives are taught to work at a distance, from a description provided by a field officer (Clifford & Davies, 1989). A number of experienced artists have written of their own methods (e.g., Cormack, 1979; Homa, 1983; Taylor, 2001), but their views differ on such matters as whether photographic reference material should be used or whether the artist should rely upon freehand drawings; whether caricature should be used to emphasize distinctive features; and the time to be allocated to capturing characteristic expressions (Davies, 1986b).

Taylor (2001) has described in detail her own approach to obtaining a likeness. In the *Pre-Interview Stage*, the artist and the investigator review the circumstances of the crime and the opportunities the witness had to view the suspect. Drawings should not be attempted if the witness had very limited or fragmentary views. In the *Rapport Building Stage*, the artist gets to know the witness as a person and explains the goal of composite art. The artist is aiming for an impression, not a finished portrait. In the *Initial Drawing Stage*, the artist elicits a detailed verbal description, which forms the basis of an outline drawing, with priority given to features emphasized by the witness. At the *Fine-Tuning Drawing Stage*, the drawing is progressively refined; reference material in the form of mugshots exemplifying particular features or groups of features may be shown to help the witness. The final *Finishing Touches* involve a review of individual features and perhaps attention to expression. The witness may be encouraged to give a score out of 10 for degree of likeness. According to Taylor, police artists take from 1 to 3 hours to evolve a satisfactory drawing.

Research on the Effectiveness of Artist's Sketches

Apart from demonstrations of the effectiveness of caricature (Benson & Perrett, 1991; Rhodes, 1996), little empirical research appears to have been conducted on the assumptions and recommendations of individual artists (but see Davies, 1986b; Davies & Little, 1990). Anecdotal accounts testify to the success of individual artists in capturing likeness (Garcia & Pyke, 1977; Boylan, 2000), but there appear to have been no systematic attempts to gauge their overall effectiveness under police operational conditions. It would be difficult to arrive at an overall estimate, given the widespread differences in the way that individual artists work. To be effective, a sketch artist must not only be good at portraiture, but also possess the interviewing skills needed to elicit relevant information from the witness (Taylor, 2001). Some artists regularly employ the Cognitive Interview to elicit the necessary facial description (Frowd et al., 2005). Not surprisingly, a combination of interviewing and artistic talents is rare, and such individuals tend to be brought in by the police on an ad hoc basis for high-profile cases. The United States has over 500 sheriff's departments, but only 18 full-time artists (Poole, 2004). According to one U.S. sheriff, "It is a dying art" (Penserga, 2003), and, for most cases, police increasingly rely upon mechanical or computer-based composite production systems.

MECHANICAL SYSTEMS

The Identikit

The need for a uniform system that could reproduce facial resemblance without the intervention of a skilled police artist was recognized by Hugh MacDonald, a California police officer, who introduced a device called the Identikit in 1959. The original Identikit consisted of some 568 drawings of different facial features: chins, eyebrows, eyes, hairstyles, lips, and noses reproduced on transparent acetate sheets. MacDonald advocated that witnesses be asked to provide a verbal description of each feature in turn. The operator would then select the acetate foil that best fit the description, and the foils would be superimposed to yield a composite face. The witness could then refine this first composite by exchanging and adjusting features until a satisfactory likeness emerged. Foils were number coded, enabling the rapid transmission of likeness information from one force to another in the days before facsimile transmission. No systematic investigation seems to have been undertaken of the level of accuracy achievable by the system or of its operational effectiveness, although there are striking stories of isolated successes, in both the United States (Sondern, 1964) and the United Kingdom (Jackson, 1967).

Photofit

One perceived weakness of the original Identikit was the absence of realism in the monochrome drawings. Subsequent research has shown that the naming of even famous faces from simple line drawings is very poor. It is necessary to add the depth cues and shading normally present in photographs before such drawings are readily identified (Davies, Ellis, & Shepherd, 1978b; Bruce, Hanna, Dench, Healey, & Burton, 1992).

In 1970, the British inventor Jacques Penry persuaded the police in the United Kingdom to adopt and develop a composite system based on actual photographs of facial features: the Photofit system. In its final form, Photofit, like Identikit, contained examples of some 560 facial features: hairstyles, pairs of eyes and eyebrows, noses, mouths, and chins, of which hair formed the single largest group (213 different styles). Each example was printed on thin card and could be superimposed, jigsaw fashion, within a special frame to produce a composite face. Complementary to the features was a directory or "Visual Index" reproducing each of the features in miniature for consultation by the witness. Like the original Identikit, Photofit also contained a range of accessories, such as hats and spectacles, to enhance the final likeness.

Photofit was supplied with no specific instructions as to use, apart from a book illustrating Penry's approach to physiognomy (Penry, 1971). However, most operators were taught to begin by eliciting a verbal description from the witness, whose attention would then be directed by the operator to particular features in the Visual Index that appeared to correspond to the description. The selected features would then be assembled in the frame and the initial likeness shown to the witness for comment and subsequent amendment. Plain acetate sheets and wax pencils were also provided for amending the image through the addition of scars, tattoos, etc. Like the Identikit, there were no formal trials of the system, though its introduction was overseen by a working party of police identification personnel (King, 1971).

System Development

After its introduction, Photofit spread to some 20 countries, and Identikit was also extensively marketed, latterly in a revised form that featured photographic levels of realism in its features (Identikit II; see Owens, 1970). Additional kits were produced for rendering likenesses of women as well as men and to model different-race faces, such as Asian and African-Caribbean. Police forces in other countries developed their own systems, such as those in France (Portrait Robot), Germany, and Italy, but all were based on the same principle of the recognition of individual features and their fusion into a composite face (see Allison, 1973; Davies, 1981, for reviews).

Early Evaluations of Photofit

An initial attempt to gauge the likely accuracy of the Photofit kit was reported by Ellis, Davies, and Shepherd (1975). In one study, witnesses worked with a trained operator to reproduce a likeness after briefly viewing a photograph of one of a number of white male targets. The resulting composite was then viewed by panels of judges who attempted to choose the correct face from an array of 36 different faces. The accuracy of the judges for this task was generally poor: although there were isolated examples of likenesses that were readily recognised, overall accuracy was generally poor, with just 12.5% of judges' first selections being correct, which increased to 25% if their second and third choices were taken into account.

Davies, Ellis, and Shepherd (1978a) asked participants to make Photofit composites of two faces, one immediately following observation and a second after a delay of 1 week. Degree of likeness of the composites was assessed by rating scales and an identification task. Overall level of accuracy was again poor, and there was no measurable change in quality of likeness between composites made immediately and those made after a delay, despite a follow-up study confirming that recognition memory for the faces had deteriorated significantly in the interval. The authors concluded that this was further evidence for the insensitivity of the system.

Ellis, Davies, and Shepherd (1978a) compared Photofit composites made in the presence of a photo of the target face with those made from memory. Again, no differences in rated quality of likeness emerged as a result of viewing condition, a finding again suggestive of low sensitivity in the system. In an attempt to probe memory for the face independent of the composite, the witnesses themselves made sketches of the faces. These drawings showed significant differences in rated quality between those made from memory and those made in the presence of the target, again suggesting gross insensitivity in the composite system.

Two exceptions to this insensitivity rule concern the impact of race and age. Facial recognition within racial groups is generally better than across groups (e.g., Chance & Goldstein, 1996; Chiroro & Valentine, 1995). Ellis, Davies, and McMurran (1979) reported that composites of a white face made from memory by black South African participants were matched by judges to the correct faces significantly less accurately than those made by white Scots. However, there was no corresponding advantage for black witnesses on the black faces: both groups produced composites that were poorly matched against the correct faces by the judges. The authors attributed this finding to the smaller range of features included in the black Photofit kit. However, all of the judges were white, and the possibility that a black panel might have produced a different pattern of results cannot be excluded.

Children show marked developmental improvements in their ability to recognize faces with age (see Davies, 1996, for a review). Flin, Markham, and Davies (1989) asked children to briefly observe a photograph of a male face before compiling a Photofit from memory. Both the initial verbal descriptions and the subsequent composites produced by children aged 8–9 years were matched to the correct photographs significantly less accurately by adult judges than those made by 11–12-year-olds. The accuracy of the verbal descriptions produced by children of different ages was not significantly linked to the quality of the composites they produced, suggesting that verbal description and composite production may draw upon rather different skills.

Mention of the preliminary verbal descriptions raises one of the most surprising results for Photofit reported by the research team. One of the assumptions of all composite systems is that the visual image of the face is a more powerful aid to identification than the verbal description from which it is derived: an impression of a face should be worth a thousand words. Christie and Ellis (1981) compared the relative effectiveness of the initial verbal description elicited from experimental participants with the finished Photofit composite as a guide to likeness. Verbal descriptions were a consistently better guide to likeness than the Photofit composites. Moreover, a combination of description plus composite was no better than description alone.

Taken together, the results of these experimental studies suggest that Photofit is a very imprecise tool for conveying facial likeness. Is this result typical of all mechanical composite systems, or is it confined solely to Photofit?

Evaluation of the Identikit

The only other system to be extensively researched was the original Identikit, studied by Laughery and his colleagues. Laughery and Fowler (1980) had volunteers converse with a target for 7–8 minutes before working with a trained Identikit technician or a police artist to produce a likeness of the target's face. Subsequently, technician and artist constructed a likeness with the target present. The composites were then assessed for degree of likeness by rating scales and a computerized search task of a database that included the target faces. Irrespective of the race or gender of the witness, the ratings showed a very similar pattern. Artist's sketches were judged as superior to Identikit composites. Moreover, whereas sketches made from memory received lower ratings than those made in the presence of the target, no such difference was found for the Identikit, precisely paralleling the findings obtained with Photofit. Both artists and the Identikit performed poorly in the computerized search task. Identikits were at chance except for a subgroup of composites that received particularly high ratings of likeness, but even here, high-rated sketches were superior (Laughery & Smith, 1978).

Other results also show parallels to those reported for Photofit. For instance, for delay, McNeil et al. (1987) could detect no change in quality for Identikits made after 3 weeks, compared with those constructed immediately after observation (though a later study by Green and Geiselman, 1989, did detect a decline in quality with a delay after a week with Identikit II). Like Photofit, the Identikit did show sensitivity to age. Schwartz-Kenney, Norton, Chalkley, Jewett, and Davis (1996) had children aged 5–6 or 8–9 years of age interact with a stranger for 15 minutes before attempting to build a likeness of his face. Identikit portraits made by the older children were rated as better likenesses compared with those of the younger children, with no effect for gender of child.

Possible Limitations on Experimental Studies

From these experimental studies, it appears that mechanical composite systems are of questionable forensic value. However, before such systems are condemned wholesale, some of the limitations of the experimental work should be underlined.

For instance, many of the Photofit studies used very brief exposure intervals and photographs rather than an actual person as the target. It could be argued that composites are rarely compiled after such a brief exposure to the suspect. However, extending the exposure interval led to no demonstrable increase in the quality of likeness of the composite (Ellis et al., 1978). Equally, although the use of an actual person as a target provides the witness with greater depth and shape cues than a photograph, Ellis, Davies, and Shepherd (1976) could detect no difference in composite quality when live and photographic targets were directly compared. Furthermore, all of Laughery and Fowler's studies of the Identikit used long exposure intervals combined with actual persons as targets and results were just as disappointing as they were for Photofit. Another criticism is that in most of the studies reported, accuracy was assessed by such methods as ranking composites in terms of degree of likeness, sorting, or matching composites against photographs of the target faces. These methods certainly lack the forensic realism of the identification from an array, the task employed by Ellis et al. (1975), but they produce accuracy scores that are reliable and significantly intercorrelated, suggesting that they are tapping a common underlying process (Davies et al., 1978a). Finally, most of the studies cited make no attempt at forensic realism: the witnesses do not believe a crime is taking place, and there is little personal investment in constructing an accurate likeness of the "offender." There is certainly room for more ambitious experimental attempts at simulated crimes, though evidence from the field studies reviewed below does not suggest that accuracy of witnesses is likely to be enhanced by real crime settings.

A more subtle point concerns the choice of dependant variables. Operationally, police do not necessarily seek a pinpoint likeness, but rather try to isolate a subset of persons from whom the suspect is drawn and, equally importantly, to eliminate people who bear no resemblance to the suspect. Thus, if a witness compiles a round, pudgy-faced Photofit, investigators may switch enquiries away from lean-faced suspects to focus on the fuller faced (Davies, Ellis, & Shepherd, 1985). How effective are such composite systems at conveying such type-likeness information? Christie, Davies, Shepherd, and Ellis (1981) explored this issue by asking subjects to attempt to match Photofit composites gathered from memory under experimental conditions to an array of photographs of men's faces, one of which was always the target. The faces had previously been assessed for degree of likeness to each other, by asking other judges to sort the faces into groups on the basis of likeness and then using hierarchical clustering analysis to isolate groups of physiognomically similar faces. When the matching scores were assessed by the traditional criterion of perfect likeness, only 23% of choices proved correct. However, when the criterion was relaxed to include a correct type likeness, then some 48% were satisfactory. Clearly, there is information present in the average composite that can be forensically useful, but the 52% of composites that failed to meet even the type likeness criterion must continue to be a source of concern, as such composites could lead police to disregard the actual perpetrator.

One final consideration concerns the skills of the operator. A composite system is only as good as the technician using it. As has been noted, Photofit contained no explicit instructions on how it was to be deployed operationally, and training courses for operatives, with input from psychologists, were a comparatively late development (Davies, Shepherd, Shepherd, Flin, & Ellis, 1986). Evidence for the value of expertise in compiling composites emerges from later studies that compared the quality of composites made in the presence of a photograph of the target and those made from memory. Early studies of both the Identikit and Photofit suggested no difference in assessments of quality underlining the apparent insensitivity of the systems. However, later studies of Photofit using a very experienced operator, who had compiled many hundreds of composites, produced reliable differences in quality between composites made from memory and those from view (Christie et al., 1981). The same expert operator took part in a further study when her skills were assessed against those of a novice operator who was familiar with the mechanics of the kit but had little practical experience of its use (Davies, Milne, & Shepherd, 1983). Both were required to compile two target faces described to them by individual witness subjects. The composites produced by the expert were rated as better likenesses and were sorted more accurately than those made by the novice. Analysis of the process of composite production suggested that the expert took longer over the verbal description phase and tended to elicit richer and more elaborate descriptions compared with the novice. This strategy had also been noted by Laughery, Duval, and Wogalter (1986) among successful police artists.

Will real witnesses to crime do any better than research volunteers in the laboratory? The most systematic survey on the operational effectiveness of Photofit was conducted by the British Home Office (Kitson et al., 1978) and suggests that the laboratory findings are broadly representative of field outcomes. Over a 6-month period, Kitson et al. followed up some 729 composites made in the course of police enquiries by 15 different police forces. After 2 months, 140 cases had been cleared up, and the investigating officer was contacted to establish what role Photofit had played in this. According to the officers, in some 5% of cases Photofit was entirely responsible for solving the case: the image produced by the witness was immediately identified and the suspect arrested. In 50% of cases, it was "very useful" (17%) or "useful" (33%) in solving the crime: typically a good type likeness that narrowed the focus of the enquiry. However, in 45% of cases, the composites proved either "not very useful" (20%) or "no use at all" (25%). These would be examples of composites that diverted enquiries and wasted police time. A later survey of Photofits produced by the Metropolitan Police produced rather similar proportions, albeit from a much smaller sample of resolved cases (Bennett, 1986). Research suggests that these disappointing findings are not unique to Photofit. Levi (1997) reported that of 243 cases in which Identikit II was used by the Israeli police, 54 led to convictions, but only 5 were deemed to have been significantly aided by the presence of the composite. Experimental evidence suggested that the "successful" composites were not better guides to likeness than those that did not lead to convictions.

Evaluation of the Mechanical Systems

From these findings, it is hard to argue that the laboratory research paints an overly pessimistic picture of the forensic utility of mechanical composite systems. Publicized successes need to be balanced against complete failures to render an effective likeness. The particular combinations of witness characteristics, suspect appearance, and viewing conditions that are likely to lead to a good-quality composite remain elusive. In a study where witnesses made pairs of Photofit composites, the rated quality of one likeness was essentially unrelated to the other (Davies et al., 1978a). It remains to be asked why mechanical systems are so relatively poor at rendering likenesses.

One problem is the range and representativeness of the features in the kits. Although the number of features appeared large and the possible different combinations impressive, the features represented reflected intuition rather than the result of any systematic research. It was evident that although the kit could make some faces well, others were impossible to make with the supplied set of parts (Ellis et al., 1976). Research employing multidimensional scaling of the likeness judgments made on large populations of faces suggested that age, face shape, and quality and distribution of hair are important dimensions of judgment of likeness (Ellis, 1986; Shepherd, Davies, & Ellis, 1981). As Bruce and Young (1998) have observed, age and face shape are global dimensions involving multiple features that are very difficult for mechanical systems to model. One common complaint of Photofit operators was the lack of youthful features in the kit, which gave most composites a middle-aged look (Davies et al., 1985).

One answer to this was the introduction of the Aberdeen Supplement to the Photofit male kit, which included an additional 80 features selected from the female kit and judged as sufficiently androgynous to pass as "young" masculine features. Despite the disproportionate number of hair sections included, shifting fashions in hair styles have always presented a particular difficulty for composite systems. The Aberdeen Supplement included a number of female hairstyles to try to cope with the vogue for longer hair among younger men in the 1980s. However, these were stopgap measures, which did not address the wider issues of achieving global change in faces created by all mechanical composite systems.

Another difficulty inherent in mechanical systems was the way in which the use of fixed components inevitably constrained the aspects of the face that could be changed. Thus, the distance between the eyes or the eyebrow-to-hairline distance can have a major impact on degree of likeness (Haig, 1986). However, mechanical systems like Photofit and Identikit cannot readily accommodate changes of this kind. In Photofit, eyes and eyebrows came as a single piece, and it was up to the operator to try to amend the composite with a wax pencil if a witness liked the eyes but took exception to the brows or vice versa. Global changes, such as making a face longer or wider, involved either laborious exchanges of individual features or very extensive overdrawing on top of the basic composite, which were not always successful in achieving the appropriate outcome (Gibling & Bennett, 1994).

Finally, there was the rationale of the systems, which assumed that witnesses could readily parse a remembered face into component features and relate such features to the foils in the Identikit or the examples included in the visual index of Photofit. Research on the process of face recognition suggests that faces are normally encoded not as a string of features, but rather as an overall gestalt in which feature information is subsumed within a general impression of the face as a whole (Tanaka & Farah, 2003; Rakover,

2002). Encoding a face in terms of an overall impression (configural processing) is an ideal strategy for facial recognition but may hinder the recall of individual features where a feature-based approach is required (Wells & Hryciw, 1984). A demonstration of the difficulties of extracting feature information accurately from memory of an overall face was provided by Davies and Christie (1982). Participants had an extended opportunity to observe a male target before rating the similarity of 30 mouths drawn from the Photofit kit. Judgments were made from memory, and participants viewed the mouths as isolated features or embedded in a composite face resembling the target. Ratings in these two conditions were essentially uncorrelated. However, if judges then made ratings on the features in the presence of the target face, these ratings were highly correlated with those made when the mouths were placed in a composite face, but not with the features in isolation. This result implies that judgments of features from memory are more veridical when made within a schematic face than when made in isolation.

It appears that the very process embodied in mechanical systems of synthesizing a completed face from judgments on individual features may be psychologically flawed. The face is more than the sum of its parts, and to achieve a maximum likeness, witnesses need to be able to manipulate a total face rather than make discriminations based on isolated feature information. The ability to make such global changes and to store large and more representative repertoires of features required the abandonment of mechanical methods for the versatility and power of the modern computer.

SOFTWARE SYSTEMS

Gillenson and Chandrasekaren (1975) demonstrated the potential of computer graphics to provide a composite tool of great versatility. The Computer-Aided Design Centre (CADC) in Cambridge built a working prototype system, with the use of a powerful mainframe computer, at the request of the British Home Office in 1978. The system used the features from the Photofit system in digitized form that could be called up onto a screen. Programs to warp or stretch features or groups of features provided additional flexibility, and an averaging algorithm eliminated the skin tone boundaries between components to produce a more lifelike face (Kitson et al., 1978). However, results from early trials that compared degree of likeness achieved relative to a conventional Photofit kit were disappointing: composites produced from memory with the CADC prototype were no more accurately recognized than those made by the traditional mechanical method (Christie et al., 1981), and further progress had to await the arrival of the desktop computer and cheaper, more versatile graphics packages.

A number of manufacturers entered the market with rival composite systems (see Clifford & Davies, 1989; Shepherd & Ellis, 1996, for reviews). Two representative systems, which have been subject to extensive research, are Mac-A-Mug Pro, designed for the Apple Macintosh computer, and the E-fit system, which utilizes the Windows technology of the PC. Both are based on the traditional approach of synthesizing the desired face from a library of features.

Mac-a-Mug Pro

Mac-a-Mug Pro (Shaherazam, 1986) uses a modest database of line-drawn facial features (184 hairlines, 117 eyebrows, 13 ears, 65 noses, 80 mouths, and 45 chins). However, much greater variety is claimed through the use of specialized editing processes. Features, for instance, can be enlarged or shrunk, age lines and skin complexion darkened, eyes moved farther apart, and hairlines and facial hair trimmed or extended. The manufacturers offer no guidance as to how the system should be employed, but most technicians begin by eliciting a brief verbal description, which is then used as a guide to relevant features that may be viewed on screen or in a visual reference catalogue. Once features have been selected, and modified if necessary, a composite face is synthesized on screen for the witness's evaluation; further fine-grain changes can be accomplished with the use of specialized graphics packages (Koehn & Fisher, 1997).

Cutler, Stocklein, and Penrod (1988) compared the value of photographs of targets and Mac-a-Mug composites as aids to identifying faces in a photographic array. An experienced operator who was able to continually refer to photographs of the targets compiled the composites. Participants searched for the targets in the presence of the likenesses or from memory. Judgments were well above chance in all conditions, and those made in the presence of the likenesses were superior to those made from memory, but the composites were as effective as the photographs in the memory condition. This study demonstrates that under ideal circumstances, the Mac-a-Mug system is capable of generating a highly recognizable composite. Wogalter and Marwitz (1991) used volunteer witnesses to compile six composites of different target faces, first from memory and later from a photograph. Composites made from a photograph were rated as better likenesses than those made from memory, suggesting a basic sensitivity in the system, though this result was not repeated when judges attempted to match targets to sample faces. In a study of greater forensic realism, Koehn and Fisher (1997) allowed participants to meet a stranger before being asked to compile the stranger's face with Mac-a-Mug Pro. The resulting composites were then rated for degree of likeness: 69% of the composites shared the lowest two ratings on a 10-point scale. When judges attempted to use the composites to match to the target face in a six-photo array, just 4% were correctly matched. When other judges performed the same task, using composites of the target generated by the trained operator from life, the matching score rose to 77%, emphasizing that the problem with reconstruction did not lie in the inability of the system to make the requisite face, but in witness's memory. Contrary to earlier findings reported by Davies and Milne (1985) for Photofit, instructions designed to encourage visualization and context reinstatement were no more effective than standard instructions.

Similar disappointing results emerged from a series of experiments reported by Kovera, Penrod, Pappas, and Thill (1997). An important feature of their studies was the use of familiar faces as targets, rather than total strangers. Students compiled composites of former teachers and classmates. These were then shown to fellow students, who were familiar with the targets, who attempted to discriminate them from unfamiliar composites. Judgments were made in terms of familiarity, confidence, and, where possible, naming. Despite being informed of the origins of the composites, just 3 out of 167 names offered by judges were correct! Moreover, constructor's ratings of familiarity of the target and quality of the composite were unrelated to identification accuracy on any measure. The authors concluded that "In the light of the results from this study, it appears that the Mac-a-Mug system's facility for producing recognisable composites under laboratory conditions is severely limited" (Kovera et al., 1997, p. 241).

E-Fit

Are the negative results unique to Mac-a-Mug Pro, or are they common to all face construction software? Both Koehn and Fisher (1997) and Kovera et al. (1997) speculate that a composite system that made more concessions to a configural rather than a feature-based approach to face construction might fare better when witnesses must construct faces from memory. One system that explicitly seeks to accommodate a configural approach is the E-fit system (Aspley Limited, 1993), used extensively in the United Kingdom and elsewhere. E-fit owes much to the CADC system and, unlike Mac-a-Mug, uses features of photographic quality. It is also marketed with explicit guidance on its use and regular training courses are offered (Clark, 2000). The method recommended involves an extensive initial interview to establish whether the witness saw enough of the suspect's face to make an attempt at a composite worthwhile, which may involve the use of the Cognitive Interview to facilitate witness recall (Finger & Pezdek, 1999). Then witnesses provide a verbal description of the suspect's facial features, cued by on-screen multiple-choice questions. These answers in turn drive an algorithm that selects the most appropriate features from the E-fit database, and these features are displayed as a total face. The witness can then amend this by scrolling through alternative features within the context of the face until an acceptable likeness emerges. Finally, fine-grain changes, such as trimming or lengthening hair or the addition of scars or tattoos, can be accomplished with the use of a standard graphics package.

Davies, van der Willick, and Morrison (2000) compared the effectiveness of E-fit with the old Photofit system in constructing familiar and unfamiliar faces. The composites were then shown to a panel of judges familiar with the appearance of the targets, who rated them for familiarity, provided names where possible, and, finally, attempted to match the composites to photographs of the targets. Performance across all three tasks produced a similar pattern. Consistent with earlier findings from Mac-a-Mug, familiar faces constructed in E-fit in the presence of the target were disproportionately better than any other condition. Judges averaged 83% accuracy for matching such composites to correct targets. However, in the memory conditions, whether composites were of familiar or unfamiliar faces, no discernible difference in performance between E-fit and Photofit was detectable. As in the Kovera et al. (1997) study, naming was problematic. None of the composites made in either system by witnesses initially unfamiliar with the appearance of the target were ever named correctly, though judges gave many incorrect identifications.

Findings interpreted as more favorable to E-fit were reported by Brace, Pike, and Kemp (2000). An experienced E-fit operator constructed pairs of composites for a series of 48 famous personalities, the first from memory and second with the aid of a reference photograph. A second condition involved a witness describing the same faces to the operator, first from memory and then with the photograph present. Judges were able to correctly identify 35% of the pairs of composites made by the operator and 25% of the pairs made from witness descriptions. However, the design precluded judgments being provided exclusively on composites made from memory, and rates of incorrect identifications were also not reported. When given feedback as to the identity of the person described, judges rated composites made by the witness from memory as poorer likenesses than those made with the aid of a photograph. Less favorable findings were reported by Davies and Oldman (1999). Witnesses assisted an operator in constructing one of four famous faces, first from memory and then with a reference picture continuously present. As in the Brace et al. study, E-fits made from memory received lower rankings than those made from views. However, when judges were asked to name the persons, just 10% of the composites made from view and less than 6% of those made from memory were identified. Moreover, this was coupled with a 25.2% false naming rate.

One way of boosting identification rates might be to publish all witnesses' attempts at a likeness, either as a set or in the form of a single image, morphed from the constituent likenesses. However, placing a good likeness with three poor ones reduces the identification rate compared with one good likeness alone (Brace, Pike, Kemp, Turner, & Bennett, 2001). Morphed composites appear to have advantages over a single good likeness for the recognition of familiar faces, but this is lost for unfamiliar faces made from memory, arguably the most forensically relevant condition (Bruce, Ness, Hancock, Newman, & Rarity, 2002).

Could a changed method of composite construction more successfully foster retrieval of configural information? Certainly, there was no evidence in the Davies et al. (2000) study to suggest that the approach encouraged by E-fit was different from the traditional Photofit; they were indistinguishable in terms of the order of construction and the time taken to select features.

Evaluation of Software Systems

Software-based facial reconstruction systems allow much greater control over the manipulation of the configural properties of a face than was possible with mechanical systems. Credible and readily identifiable composites can be built by these systems, provided a reference photograph of the target is available to the operator or witness at the time of construction. Problems over the range and representativeness of features seem to have been solved, at least for white Caucasian male faces. However, the problems of constructing a good likeness from memory appear to remain for most witnesses. In the Davies et al. (2000) study, facial composites produced from memory by a sophisticated software system were of no greater utility than composites produced by an old mechanical system.

Why do such software systems produce such disappointing results under laboratory tests? One weakness could be the continuing reliance on a *logical* rather than a *psychological* analysis of face encoding (Davies et al., 1985). A more successful approach might start from a thorough analysis of how faces are perceived and remembered and then use

these insights to construct a system. This is the premise of the fourth generation of composites, which attempt to evolve a remembered facial image within a face space.

THE FOURTH GENERATION: EVOLVING FACES

The task of building a facial composite requires that the witness synthesize a given
face by retrieving individual facial features. However, as has been noted, the available
evidence suggests that face perception does not normally involve analyzing the face
into its constituent parts. The conflict between the nature of facial encoding and task
demands may be the underlying cause of the poor utility of mechanical and software
systems.

Face-Space

A face similarity space, commonly referred to as "face-space," provides a useful framework for understanding face recognition. The central idea is that faces are encoded in
a multidimensional similarity space (Valentine, 1991a, b, 1995, 2001). This framework
permits face-processing phenomena to be understood in terms of the similarity within a
population of faces, without necessarily defining the dimensions on which faces are encoded. Face-space has provided a useful single framework for understanding disparate
face-processing phenomena, including the effects of distinctiveness and race (Byatt &
Rhodes, 1998; Chiroro & Valentine, 1995; Valentine & Endo, 1992), inversion (Valentine, 1991), caricature (Lee, Byatt, & Rhodes, 2000), and the development of face
recognition (de Haan, Humphreys, & Johnson, 2002). Two recent theoretical developments have now been applied to develop a fourth generation of facial composite systems. First, principal component analysis has been used to implement a face-space, and,
second, genetic algorithms have been used to search the space to converge on a desired
facial likeness.

Use of Principal Component Analysis
to Implement Face-Space

Principal component analysis (PCA) can be used to extract a set of dimensions (known as
eigenfaces) from a sample of faces on which they can be encoded (Sirovich & Kirby, 1987;
Turk & Pentland, 1991). The eigenfaces can be used to encode and reconstruct the appearance of the original sample and new faces from the same population. In effect, the
principal components provide the dimensions of the face-space. More precisely, this similarity space is an image-space, as the principal components are derived from one specific
image of each face. Each eigenface is holistic because it codes variance across the entire
image; faces are not encoded in terms of their parts. Some principal components can be
interpreted, for example, appearing to code gender (O'Toole, Abdi, Deffenbacher, &
Valentin, 1995), but many components are not interpretable. The eigenface representa-

tion shows an important property postulated by the face-space framework: faces closer together in the PCA space are perceived as more similar to each other (Tredoux, 2002).

A face can be reconstructed by combination of the eigenfaces (or principal components) in the correct proportions. Any face, from the same population as the sample used to derive the PCA, can be coded as a set of weights of a given set of eigenfaces. Thus artificial faces can be constructed by any novel combination of weights.

There are some caveats that should be added. First, faces can be viewed as having two aspects to their appearance: texture and shape. Texture is given by the greyscale or color information in the image of a face. Shape is defined by the position of landmark features (e.g., the corners of the eyes and mouth). The construction of synthetic faces from PCA works well only if the faces in the sample are "shape-free"; that is, the landmarks are located at the same position in each face image. Therefore, all of the fourth-generation composite systems morph faces to the average shape of the faces in the sample, with the use of a technique introduced by Craw and Cameron (1991). PCA is carried out separately on the texture and shape information. Shape and texture can be combined with the use of a further PCA into an active appearance model that gives a single set of optimally compact parameters (Cootes, Edwards, & Taylor; 1998; Cootes & Taylor, 2001).

A second caveat is that PCA does not reconstruct the texture of hair accurately. The solution adopted in both Evo-fit and Eigen-fit involves selecting a hair style from a database in the same manner as earlier face reconstruction systems, prior to commencement of the evolutionary search, and restricting the PCA to the face excluding the hair. Fortunately, the style, length, texture, and color of hair are attributes that witnesses find relatively easy to describe verbally.

Evolving Faces to Navigate the Face-Space

PCA can be combined with a genetic algorithm (GA) to converge on the desired facial image. The genetic algorithm is so named because it uses two principles of evolution: random variation (or mutation) and selection. The construction of a facial composite begins by the generation of a random set of (artificial) facial images within the PCA space. The witness then selects the image or images that are most similar to the appearance of the culprit. In the initial set there will be a wide range of facial appearances, and none are likely to closely resemble the culprit. The selection made by the witness is then used to "breed" a new set of images introducing mutations around the "parent" face or faces. The process is repeated iteratively, with successive "generations" becoming more similar to the culprit and to each other. The process continues until the witness cannot choose because all of the faces resemble the culprit equally well, or it becomes clear that the GA has failed to converge on the desired appearance.

Systems under Development

Three research teams are developing facial reconstruction systems based on these principles. Hancock, Frowd, and colleagues (Stirling University, Scotland) are developing a system called Evo-fit (Hancock, 2000). Solomon and colleagues (University of Kent, England) are developing a system known as Eigen-fit (Gibson, Pallares Bejarano, & Solomon, 2003). Tredoux, Rosenthal, and colleagues (University of Cape Town, South Africa) are developing a system known as ID (previously E-face; Tredoux, Rosenthal, Nunez, & da Costa, 1999). Both Tredoux and Solomon recombine shape and texture into an active appearance model, allowing the witness to choose between facial images that differ in shape and texture. Hancock uses separate PCA spaces of shape and texture. Witnesses are asked to choose a best likeness from both a set of images that vary in shape and another set of images that differ in texture. It is possible to select the texture of one face with the shape of another.

The challenge is to develop a system that produces lifelike images, converges quickly on the desired appearance, and is easy for the witness to use. Quick convergence and ease of use can be conflicting requirements. The witness may provide rich information, for example, by providing a numerical rating of every image in a "generation" for similarity to the target. However, the demands placed on the witness are relatively high. Alternatively, the witness may be asked simply to pick the face from a set that is most similar to the target appearance. This task is easier for the witness but provides less information to guide the evolution of the next generation and may require many generations to produce a recognizable reconstruction. Evolution can arise from crossover (e.g., between the appearance of two "parents") and mutation (random variation of single appearance from one generation to the next). Algorithms that allow crossover and mutation will tend to produce more variation within each generation.

Gibson, Pallares Bejarano, and Solomon (2003) identify three evolutionary algorithms:

Scale Rating (SR).   All of the images in each generation are rated on a numeric scale for similarity to the target. Two faces are selected to breed the next generation, enabling both crossover and mutation. Hancock (2000) used a similar approach.

Select Multiple Mutate (SMM).   The witness chooses the best likeness. This image is then reproduced with random mutation in all but one of the faces of the next generation. Tredoux et al. (1999) describe a similar approach that they term *Population Based Incremental Learning* (PBIL).

Follow the Leader.   One new face is displayed with the current best likeness. The witness simply chooses the best likeness of the two faces. The new face displayed at each iteration is produced by breeding of the current best likeness with a new face. The recent evolutionary history is used to determine the future trajectory of the evolution. If the process has followed a well-defined direction, a preference for this direction can be used in subsequent generations.

The allure of using genetic algorithms lies in the gradual holistic changes to faces that exploit the witness's natural ability to recognize the culprit's face, rather than require the witness to undertake the very difficult task of verbally describing facial features. However, sometimes a witness will comment that the likeness would be improved by a change to a specific feature (e.g., a smaller chin, thicker eyebrows). The evolutionary nature of a genetic algorithm makes it impossible to make a specific change to a local feature easily. Therefore all of the systems described include a facility to make specified changes to the features or position of features of the current best likeness. The modified face can then be used to breed a new generation.

Evaluation of GA Systems

All of the fourth-generation systems are still under development, so there have been few evaluations of their performance to date. Gibson et al. (2003) report trials based on simulated witness behavior in which the Select Multiple Mutate algorithm required 150 iterations, and the Follow-The-Leader algorithm required 350 iterations to produce a "quasi-perfect" composite. A human operator produced a good composite of an unfamiliar target face, which was in view throughout the process, after viewing 162 faces, over 27 iterations, and took approximately 20 minutes (see Figure 3–1). A recognizable composite of Tony Blair was produced from memory after 23 iterations and viewing of 138 faces (see Figure 3–2). Both of these composites were constructed with the SMM genetic algorithm. Formal human experimental evaluation of the Eigen-fit system is currently in progress.

Frowd, Hancock, and Carson (2004) found that naïve judges could name 10% of Evo-fit composites of celebrities produced from memory, compared with 17% of composites produced by an E-fit operator. The poorer performance of Evo-fit could have been attributable to the age range of the celebrities being inappropriate to the database used to generate the PCA space for Evo-fit. The age range of celebrities was appropriately restricted in a second experiment, in which the target faces were visible during the production of the composite. The naming rate of Evo-fit composites was 25% under these conditions, which is similar to comparable data for E-fit.

Frowd et al. (2005) evaluated the utility of Evo-fit, E-fit, Profit, FACES, and a police sketch artist under more forensically realistic conditions. The "witness" viewed a target face of a celebrity. The celebrities were not very famous and were chosen to be unfamiliar to each witness. After a 2-day delay, each witness underwent a cognitive interview and worked with an appropriately trained operator to construct a composite. The utility of the composites was evaluated by three groups of participants, each of whom

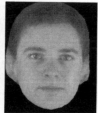

FIGURE 3–1.   SMM human trial with target face visible: (a) Starting face, (b) and (c) are intermediate points in the evolutionary process, (d) final generated composite after 27 iterations (162 faces viewed), (e) the actual target face.

FIGURE 3–2.   SMM human trial for famous face from memory: (a) Starting face, (b) and (c) are intermediate points in the evolutionary process, (d) final generated composite after 23 iterations (138 faces viewed), (e) addition of hair to facial composite.

was given one of three tasks: naming, sorting, and identification. The sorting task required participants to match composites to the appropriate face from an array of all of the targets. The identification task required participants to match the composite to the target face from a lineup including distracters chosen to be similar in appearance. The naming rate was very low, even when conditionalized by the number of participants who were familiar with the target celebrities. The naming rate of sketches (8.1%) was significantly higher than for PROfit (1.3%) and E-fit (0%) but did not achieve a statistically significant difference compared with Evo-fit (3.6%) and FACES (3.2%). The sorting task produced a much higher level of performance but a similar result. Performance was significantly better for the sketches (54%) than for Evo-fit (39%) and the other systems (25–42%). There was no significant difference in the performances of any of the composite systems. E-fit performed best in the identification task (60% compared with 47% for sketches and 31% for Evo-fit). Performance with E-fit was significantly better than that of all other systems except sketches. However, performance on the identification task was not correlated with performance on naming. In contrast, sorting performance showed a significant correlation with naming rate. Naming is usually considered to be the most forensically relevant test; therefore the lack of an association between "identification" performance and naming suggests that the identification task should be interpreted with caution.

The use of genetic algorithms is an exciting development, which exploits the contemporary theory of face processing. The GA technique can perform at levels similar to those of the current composite systems, but it remains to be demonstrated whether they will prove more effective than current composite methods. Like all systems, the GA methods incorporate certain psychological assumptions about memory for faces that deserve to be more rigorously evaluated. First, research suggests that for Caucasian faces, hair is the single most salient cue for witnesses (Ellis, 1986). Although hair style is selected at an early stage in some systems, it is divorced from the choice of Eigenfaces. Second, many systems require witnesses to grade the similarity of faces, but earlier research suggests that perhaps only half the composites produced by witnesses are of an appropriate physiognomic type (Christie et al., 1981) and that witnesses are also poor at making absolute judgments of similarity with any degree of accuracy from memory (Clark, 2000). There is also the danger that viewing approximate likenesses may interfere with memory for the original face. Moreover, a skilled police artist can still outperform all current systems that have been evaluated so far.

CONCLUSIONS

Skilled police artists remain the benchmark against which all systems must be compared, and no mechanical or software system has yet to equal or outperform them. However, although artists are quick to trumpet their successes, they have also had their failures, and the overall level of accuracy is hard to compute for a skill so idiosyncratic and poorly understood. After three decades of intensive research, it is still unclear for any technique what predicts or postdicts a successful interview. Witnesses are inconsistent in the quality of composites they reproduce from one face to another and over time (Davies et al., 1978a). Neither the witnesses themselves nor the operators are effective in estimating when a likeness is likely to prove to be of good or poor quality (Kovera et al., 1997). A good likeness appears to depend upon an elusive combination of a face whose features may be readily reproduced, an observant and articulate witness, and a skilled operator who knows how to ask the right questions (Davies et al., 1983).

This is not to deny the progress that has been achieved through research and development. Some of the more obvious sources of error evident in earlier systems have been identified and removed. These include a lack of relevant features and sufficient flexibility of size and positioning to model the full range of faces. For the male Caucasian face, most software systems now allow the skilled operator to fashion a recognizable likeness from life or a photograph (Brace et al., 2000; Cutler et al., 1988). Likewise, fourth-generation systems permit witnesses to work on total faces rather than use the traditional approach emphasizing individual features (Gibson et al., 2003).

One area of continuing controversy concerns the possible inhibiting effect of verbal description on facial recall. Dodson, Johnson, and Schooler (1997) demonstrated experimentally that recognition for faces can be impaired if the observer is required to verbally describe them prior to recognition: the "verbal overshadowing effect." It has been recently demonstrated that providing detailed verbal descriptions impairs the witness's ability to subsequently select appropriate features (Wells, Charman, & Olson, 2005). Clark (2000), too, reported that for E-fit, the recommended practice of re-interviewing the witness about the suspect's appearance midway through construction had a detrimental effect upon final composite quality, a finding consistent with overshadowing. However, verbal overshadowing is not an inevitable consequence of describing a face, even under laboratory conditions (Meissner & Brigham, 2001), and delay serves to reduce any potential impairment (Finger & Pezdek, 1999). The conditions under which verbal encoding interferes with facial memory remain poorly understood. The retrieval-based interference explanation assumes that verbalization impairs the original memory trace of the face (Meissner, Brigham, & Kelley, 2001). However, in some circumstances it appears that verbal recall and visual recognition processes function independently (Davies, 1986a), and an explanation of the verbal overshadowing effect in terms of a criterion shift seems at least as plausible (Clare & Lewandowsky, 2004).

One consideration that perhaps has been insufficiently challenged is the belief that memory for a briefly observed and unfamiliar face is sufficiently detailed to construct a successful composite. This belief appears to be based on the frequently iterated statement that face recognition is far superior to face recall, and our ability to recognize faces, often after many years, testifies to a robust and unique encoding system for all faces. More recent research on face recognition suggests, however, that familiar and unfamiliar faces are encoded in different ways which results in striking differences in subsequent ease of recognition (Bruce & Young, 1998). Even degraded images of familiar individuals caught on CCTV are readily recognized (Burton, Wilson, Cowan, & Bruce, 1999), but unfamiliar faces seen on CCTV are matched to an appropriate photograph very inaccurately indeed, even when participants have continuous access to an image of the face as they carry out the task (Bruce, Henderson, Newman, & Burton, 2001; Davies & Thasen, 2000; Kemp, Towell, & Pike, 1997).

Research from other areas of face processing suggests that memory for the appearance of novel faces may be fragmentary and inadequate. Ellis (1984) noted that verbal descriptions, both in the presence of the face and from memory, were selective and incomplete. Even in recognition memory for novel faces, faces that share certain dominant attributes such as hair style and face shape are readily confused (Davies, Shepherd, & Ellis, 1979). Learning a face takes time and repeated exposure under different viewing conditions (Bruce, 2003).

Schema theory has demonstrated that where memory is imperfect, then plausible reconstruction is likely to take place, which may or may not be accurate (Brewer, 1996). In a task like constructing a face, which requires exhaustive recall of all features, there are opportunities for attitudes and assumptions to fill gaps and color the constructive process. Some years ago, Shepherd, Ellis, McMurran, and Davies (1978) demonstrated the impact of negative and positive stereotypes on Photofit reconstructions. Witnesses constructed composites that were judged as more intelligent and handsome when they were told the man was a lifeboat captain than when he was described as a murderer (see also Oliver, Jackson, Moses, & Dangerfield, 2004, for an example of the influence of racial stereotyping on face recall). More recently, Davies and Oldman (1999) replicated the finding of Shepherd et al. with the use of familiar faces and showed that attitudes also influenced quality of likeness. Faces made by persons who disliked the target were of a better quality than those made by persons who liked them. As the authors observed, contempt appears to breed familiarity.

It seems likely that the largest distortions due to affect and stereotyping will occur on unfamiliar faces viewed for fleeting periods, often the conditions prevailing when witnesses to crime view actual suspects. In these circumstances, it may be that for many witnesses, composite production imposes an unrealistic burden upon them, with inevitable consequences for composite quality, irrespective of the system employed. Perhaps, in the light of recent findings, composite production should be reserved for witnesses who have had extensive experience of the person concerned. Perhaps feature selection should be confined to items mentioned by witnesses in their verbal descriptions. Intelligent systems could be developed that could accurately "suggest" missing features from existing choices of other parts of the face, rather than rely on guesses fueled by feelings and stereotypes.

Probably the first encounter between psychologists and the Identikit was described by Connolly and McKeller (1963): "Having seen this device, and having been subjects in a demonstration, we consider this to be a marked improvement [over verbal descriptions] but also a 'psychological Pandora's box'" (p. 22), adding that "the problem of identification would repay psychological enquiry" (p. 23). Four generations of composite systems have now been reviewed together with the psychological enquiry they have provoked. Although measurable progress has been made and all systems may claim successes, perhaps the quest for the perfect system may be illusory and we must learn to live within the limitations of witness memory.

REFERENCES

Allison, H. C. (1973). *Personal identification*. Boston: Holbrook Press.

Aspley Limited. (1993). *E-fit*. Hatfield, UK: Author.

Bennett, P. (1986). Face recall: A police perspective. *Human Learning, 5*, 197–202.

Benson, P. J., & Perrett, D. L. (1991). Perception and recognition of photographic quality caricatures: Implications for the recognition of natural images. *European Journal of Cognitive Psychology, 3*, 103–135.

Boylan, J. (2000) *Portraits of guilt: The woman who profiles the faces of America's deadliest criminals*. New York: Pocket Books

Brace, N. A., Pike, G. E., & Kemp, R. I. (2000). Investigating E-fit using famous faces. In A. Czerederecka, T. Jaskiewicz-Obydzinska, & J. Wojcikiewicz (Eds.), *Forensic psychology and law: Traditional questions and new ideas* (pp. 272–276). Krakow, Poland: Institute of Forensic Research Publishers.

Brace, N. A., Pike, G. E., Kemp, R. I., Turner, J., & Bennett, P. (2001) *Does the presentation of multiple facial composites improve suspect identification?* Unpublished paper, Department of Psychology, the Open University.

Brewer, M. B. (1996). When stereotypes lead to stereotyping: The use of stereotypes in person perception. In C. N. Macrae, C. Stangor, & M. Hewstone (Eds.), *Stereotypes and stereotyping* (pp. 254–275). New York: Guilford.

Bruce, V. (2003). *Getting to know you—How we learn new faces*. Final report to the Economic and Social Research Council. Swindon: ESRC

Bruce, V., Hanna, E., Dench, N., Healey, P., & Burton, M. (1992). The importance of "mass" in the line drawings of faces. *Applied Cognitive Psychology, 6*, 619–628.

Bruce, V., Henderson, Z., Newman, C., & Burton, A. M. (2001). Matching identities of familiar and unfamiliar faces caught on CCTV images. *Journal of Experimental Psychology: Applied, 7*, 207–218.

Bruce, V., Ness, H., Hancock, P. J. B., Newman, C., & Rarity, J. (2002). Combining face composites yields improvements in face likeness. *Journal of Applied Psychology, 87*, 894–902.

Bruce, V., & Young, A. (1998). *In the eye of the beholder: The science of face perception*. Oxford: Oxford University Press

Burton, A. M., Wilson, S., Cowan, M., & Bruce, V. (1999). Face recognition in poor-quality video. *Psychological Science, 10*, 243–248.

Byatt, G., & Rhodes, G. (1998). Recognition of own-race and other-race caricatures: Implications for models of face recognition. *Vision Research, 38*, 2455–2468.

Chance, J., & Goldstein, A. (1996). The other-race effect and eyewitness identification. In S. L. Sporer, R. Malpass, & G. Koehnken (Eds.), *Psychological issues in eyewitness identification* (pp. 153–176). Mahwah, NJ: Lawrence Erlbaum Associates.

Chiroro, P., & Valentine, T. (1995). An investigation of the contact hypothesis of the own-race bias in face recognition. *Quarterly Journal of Experimental Psychology, 48A,* 879–894.

Christie, D., Davies, G., Shepherd, J., & Ellis, H. (1981). Evaluating a new computer-based system for face recall. *Law and Human Behavior, 5,* 209–218.

Christie, D., & Ellis H. (1981). Photofit constructions versus verbal descriptions of faces. *Journal of Applied Psychology, 66,* 358–363.

Clare, J., & Lewandowsky, S. (2004). Verbalising facial memory: Criterion effects in verbal overshadowing. *Journal of Experimental Psychology: Learning, Memory and Cognition, 30,* 739–755.

Clark, C. (2000). *Interviewing for facial identification.* Report to the Home Office Police and Reducing Crime Unit. London: Home Office.

Clifford, B. R., & Davies, G. M. (1989). Procedures for obtaining identification evidence. In D. Raskin (Ed.), *Psychological methods in investigation and evidence* (pp. 47–96). New York: Springer-Verlag.

Connolly, K., & McKeller, P. (1963). Forensic psychology. *Bulletin of the British Psychological Society, 16,* 16–24.

Cootes, T. F., Edwards, G. J., & Taylor, C. J. (1998). Active appearance models. In H. Burkhardt & B. Neumann (Eds.), *Proceceeding of the European Conference on Computer Vision* (Vol. 2, pp. 484–498). Berlin: Springer-Verlag.

Cootes, T. F., & Taylor, C. J. (2001). Statistical models of appearance for medical image analysis and computer vision. *Proceedings of SPIE Medical Imaging, 3,* 138–147.

Cormack J. (1979). *The police artists' reference.* Pewaukee, WI: Waukesha County Technical Institute.

Craw, I., & Cameron, P. (1991). Parametising images for recognition and reconstruction. In P. Mowforth (Ed.), *Proceedings of the British Machine Vision Conference 1991* (pp. 367–370). New York: Turing Institute Press and Springer-Verlag.

Cutler, B., Stocklein, C. J., & Penrod, S. (1988). Empirical examination of a computerised facial composite production system. *Forensic Reports, 1,* 207–218.

Davies, G. (1981). Face recall systems. In G. Davies, H. Ellis, & J. Shepherd (Eds.), *Perceiving and remembering faces* (pp. 227–250). London: Academic Press.

Davies, G. M. (1986a). The recall and reconstruction of faces: Implications for theory and practice. In H. D. Ellis, M. A. Jeeves, & A. Young (Eds.), *Aspects of face processing* (pp. 388–398). Dordrecht, the Netherlands: Nijhoff.

Davies, G. M. (1986b). Capturing likeness in eyewitness composites: The police artist and his rivals. *Medicine. Science and the Law, 26,* 283–290.

Davies, G. M. (1996). Children's identification evidence. In S. L. Sporer, R. S. Malpass, & G. Koehnken (Eds.), *Psychological issues in eyewitness identification* (pp. 233–258). Mahwah, NJ: Lawrence Erlbaum Associates.

Davies, G., & Christie, D. (1982). Face recall: An examination of some factors limiting composite production accuracy. *Journal of Applied Psychology, 67,* 103–109.

Davies, G., Ellis, H., & Shepherd, J. (1978a). Face identification. The influence of delay upon accuracy of Photofit construction. *Journal of Police Science and Administration, 6,* 35–42.

Davies, G., Ellis, H., & Shepherd, J. (1978b). Face recognition accuracy as a function of mode of representation. *Journal of Applied Psychology, 63,* 180–187.

Davies, G. M., Ellis, H. D., & Shepherd, J. W. (1985, May 16). Wanted—Faces that fit the bill. *New Scientist,* no. 1456, 26–29.

Davies, G., & Little, M. (1990). Drawing on memory: Exploring the expertise of the police artist. *Medicine, Science and the Law, 30,* 345–353.

Davies, G., & Milne, A. (1985). Eyewitness composite production. A function of mental or physical reinstatement of context. *Criminal Justice and Behavior, 12,* 209–222.

Davies, G., Milne, A., & Shepherd, J. (1983). Searching for operator skills in face composite reproduction. *Journal of Police Science and Administration, 11,* 405–409.

Davies, G., & Oldman, H. (1999). The impact of character attribution on composite production: A real world effect? *Current Psychology, 18*, 128–139.

Davies, G. M., Shepherd, J. W., & Ellis, H. D. (1979). Similarity effects in face recognition. *American Journal of Psychology, 92*, 507–523.

Davies, G., Shepherd, J. W., Shepherd, J., Flin, R., & Ellis, H. (1986). Training skills in police Photofit operators. *Policing, 2*, 35–46.

Davies, G., & Thasen, S. (2000). Closed-circuit television: How effective an identification aid? *British Journal of Psychology, 91*, 411–426

Davies, G. M., van der Willik, P., & Morrison, L. (2000). Facial composite production: A comparison of mechanical and computer-driven systems. *Journal of Applied Psychology, 85*, 119–124.

De Haan, M., Humphreys, K., & Johnson, M. (2002). Developing a brain specialized for face perception: A converging methods approach. *Developmental Psychobiology, 40*, 200–212.

Dodson, C. S., Johnson, M. K., & Schooler, J. W. (1997). The verbal overshadowing effect: Source confusion or strategy shift? *Memory & Cognition, 25*, 129–139.

Domingo, F. (1984, June). Composite art: The need for standardization. *Identification News*, pp. 7–15.

Ellis, H. D. (1984). Practical aspects of face memory. In G. Wells & E. Loftus (Eds.), *Eyewitness testimony* (pp. 12–37). Cambridge: Cambridge University Press.

Ellis, H. (1986). Face recall: A psychological perspective. *Human Learning, 5*, 189–196.

Ellis, H., Davies, G., & McMurran, M. (1979). Recall of white and black faces by white and black witnesses using the Photofit system. *Human Factors, 21*, 55–59.

Ellis, H., Davies, G., & Shepherd, J. (1976). *An investigation of the Photofit system for recalling faces.* Final report, grant no. HR 3123/1. Swindon: Social Science Research Council.

Ellis, H., Davies, G., & Shepherd, J. (1978). A critical examination of the Photofit system for recalling faces. *Ergonomics, 21*, 297–307.

Ellis, H., Davies, G., & Shepherd J. (1978b). Remembering pictures of real and unreal faces: Some practical and theoretical considerations. *British Journal of Psychology, 69*, 467–1174.

Ellis, H., Shepherd, J., & Davies, G. (1975). An investigation of the use of the Photofit technique for recalling faces. *British Journal of Psychology, 66*, 29–37.

Finger, K., & Pezdek, K. (1999). The effect of the cognitive interview on face identification accuracy: Release from verbal overshadowing. *Journal of Applied Psychology, 84*, 340–348.

Flin, R., Markham, R., & Davies, G. M.(1988). Making faces: Developmental trends in the construction and recognition of face composites. *Journal of Applied Developmental Psychology, 10*, 123–137.

Frowd, C., Hancock, P. J. B., & Carson, D. (2004). EvoFIT: A holistic evolutionary facial imaging technique for creating composites. *Association for Computing Machinery Transactions on Applied Psychology, 1*, 1–21.

Frowd, C., Carson, D., Ness, H., McQuiston-Surrett, D., Richardson, J. Baldwin, H., et al. (2005). Contemporary composite techniques: The impact of a forensically-relevant target delay. *Legal and Criminological Psychology, 10*, 63–81.

Garcia, E., & Pyke, C. (1977). *Portraits of crime*. New York: Condor.

Gibling, F., & Bennett, P. (1994). Artistic enhancement in the production of Photofit likenesses: An examination of its effectiveness in leading to suspect identification. *Psychology, Crime and the Law, 1*, 93–100.

Gibson, S., Pallares Bejarano, A., & Solomon, C. (2003). Synthesis of photographic quality facial composites using evolutionary algorithms. In R. Harvey & J. A. Bangham (Eds.), *Proceedings of the British Machine Vision Conference 2003* (pp. 221–230). London: British Machine Vision Association.

Gillenson, M., & Chandrasekaren, B. (1975). A heuristic strategy for developing human facial images on a CRT. *Pattern Recognition, 7*, 187–196.

Green, D. L., & Geiselman, R. E. (1989). Building composite facial images: Effect of feature saliency and delay of construction. *Journal of Applied Psychology, 74,* 714–721.

Haig, N. D. (1986). Investigating face recognition with an image processing computer. In H. D. Ellis, M. A. Jeeves, & A. Young (Eds.), *Aspects of face processing* (pp. 410–425). Dordrecht, the Netherlands: Nijhoff.

Hancock, P. J. B. (2000). Evolving faces from principal components. *Behaviour Research methods, Instruments and Computers, 32,* 327–333.

Homa, G. (1983). *The law enforcement composite sketch artist.* West Berlin, NJ: Author.

Jackson, R. L. (1967). *Occupied with crime.* London: Harrap.

Kemp, R., Towell, N., & Pike, G. (1997). When seeing should not be believing: Photographs, credit cards and fraud. *Applied Cognitive Psychology, 11,* 211–222.

King, D. (1971). The use of Photofit 1970–1971: A progress report. *Police Research Bulletin, 18,* 40–44.

Kitson, A., Darnbrough, M., & Shields, E. (1978). Let's face it. *Police Research Bulletin,* no. 30, pp. 7–13.

Koehn, C., & Fisher, R. P. (1997). Constructing facial composites with the Mac-a-Mug Pro system. *Psychology, Crime and Law, 3,* 209–218.

Kovera, M. B., Penrod, S., Pappas, C., & Thill, D. (1997). Identification of computer-generated facial composites. *Journal of Applied Psychology, 82,* 235–246.

Laughery, K., Duval, C., & Wogalter, M. (1986). Dynamics of face recall. In H. Ellis, M. Jeeves, F. Newcombe, & A. Young (Eds.), *Aspects of face processing* (pp. 373–387). Dordrecht: Nijhoff.

Laughery, K., & Fowler, R. (1980). Sketch artist and Identikit procedures for recalling faces. *Journal of Applied Psychology, 65,* 307–316.

Laughery, K., & Smith, V. L. (1978). Suspect identification following exposure to sketches and Identikit composites. *Proceedings of the Human Factors Society, 22nd Annual Meeting, Detroit* (pp. 631–635).

Lee, K. J., Byatt, G., & Rhodes, G. (2000). Caricature effects, distinctiveness and identification: Testing the face-space framework. *Psychological Science, 11,* 379–385.

Levi, A. M. (1997). *Police composites: Do they contribute to convictions?* Unpublished manuscript. Jerusalem: Division of Identification and Police Science, Israeli Police Headquarters.

McNeil, J. E., Wray, J. L., Hibler, N. S., Foster, W. D., Rhyne, C. E., & Thibault, R. (1987). Hypnosis and the identi-kit: A study to determine the effect of using hypnosis in conjunction with the making of identi-kit composites. *Journal of Police Science and Administration, 15,* 63–67.

Meissner, C. A., & J. C. Brigham. (2001). A meta-analysis of the verbal overshadowing effect in face identification. *Applied Cognitive Psychology, 15,* 603–616.

Meissner, C. A., Brigham, J. C., & Kelley, C. M. (2001). The influence of retrieval processes in verbal overshadowing. *Memory and Cognition, 29,* 176–186.

Oliver, M. B., Jackson, R. L., Moses, N. N., & Dangerfield, C. L. (2004). The face of crime: Viewers' memory of race-related facial features of individuals pictured in the news. *Journal of Communication, 54,* 88–104.

O'Toole, A. J., Abdi, H., Deffenbacher, K. A., & Valentin, D. (1995). A perceptual learning theory of the information in faces. In T. Valentine (Ed.), *Cognitive and computational aspects of face recognition: Explorations in face space* (pp. 159–182). London: Routledge.

Owens, C. (1970, November). Identikit enters its second decade—Ever growing at home and abroad. *Finger Print and Identification Magazine,* pp. 3–8, 11–17.

Penry, J. (1971). *Looking at faces and remembering them: A guide to facial identification.* London: Elek Books.

Penserga, B. (2003, October 20). Police sketch artists yield to computer composites. *The Daily Times* (Delaware),

Poole, O. (2004, January 21). I know what it's like to want justice. *The Daily Telegraph* (London), p. 14

Rakover, S. (2002). Featural vs. configurational information in faces: A conceptual and empirical analysis. *British Journal of Psychology, 93,* 1–30.

Rhodes, G. (1996). *Superportraits: Caricatures and recognition.* Psychology Press. Hove.

Schwartz-Kenney, B. M., Norton, C., Chalkley, B., Jewett, J., & Davis, K. (1996, February). *Building a composite of a stranger: Young children's use of the Identi-Kit.* Paper presented at the Biennial Conference of the American Psychology-Law Society, Hilton Head, NC.

Sergent, J. (1984). An investigation into component and configurational processes underlying face perception. *British Journal of Psychology, 75,* 221–242.

Shaherazam (1986). *The Mac-a-Mug pro manual.* Milwaukee, WI: Shaherazam.

Shepherd, J., Davies, G., & Ellis, H. (1981). Studies of cue saliency. In G. Davies, H. Ellis, & J. Shepherd (Eds.), *Perceiving and remembering faces* (pp. 105–132). London: Academic Press.

Shepherd, J. W., & Ellis, H. D. (1996). Face recall—methods and problems. In S. L. Sporer, R. S. Malpass, & G. Koehnken (Eds.), *Psychological issues in eyewitness identification* (pp. 87–116). Mahwah, NJ: Lawrence Erlbaum Associates.

Shepherd, J. W., Ellis, H. D., McMurran, M., & Davies, G. M. (1978). Effect of character attribution on Photofit construction of a face. *European Journal of Social Psychology, 8,* 263–268.

Sirovich, L., & Kirby, M. (1987). Low dimensional procedure for the characterization of human faces. *Journal of the Optical Society of America A, 4,* 519–524.

Sondern, F. (1964, April). The box that catches criminals. *Readers' Digest,* pp. 37–44.

Tanaka, J. W., & Farah, M. J. (2003). The holistic representation of faces. In M. A. Peterson & G. Rhodes. *Perception of faces, objects and scenes* (pp. 53–74). Oxford: Oxford University Press.

Taylor, K. T. (2001). *Forensic art and illustration.* Boca Raton, FL: CRC Press.

Tredoux, C. (2002). A direct measure of facial similarity and its relation to human similarity perceptions. *Journal of Experimental Psychology: Applied, 8,* 180–193.

Tredoux, C., Rosenthal, Y., Nunez, D., & da Costa, L. (1999). *Face reconstruction using a configural, eigenface-based composite system.* Paper presented to the third meeting of the Society for Applied Research Memory and Cognition, Boulder, Colorado, July 1999. Retrieved May 12, 2003 from http://web.uct.ac.za/depts/psychology/plato/

Turk, M., & Pentland, A. (1991). Eigenfaces for recognition. *Journal of Cognitive Neuroscience, 3,* 71–86.

Valentine, T. (1991a). A unified account of the effects of distinctiveness, inversion and race in face recognition. *Quarterly Journal of Experimental Psychology, 43A,* 161–204.

Valentine, T. (1991b). Representation and process in face recognition. In R. Watt (Ed.), *Pattern recognition by man and machine* (pp. 107–124). (Vol. 14 in 'Vision and Visual Dysfunction' series edited by J. Cronly-Dillon) London: Macmillan Press.

Valentine, T. (1995). *Cognitive and computational aspects of face recognition: Explorations in face space.* London: Routledge.

Valentine, T. (2001). Face-space models of face recognition. In: M. J. Wenger & J. T. Townsend (eds.) *Computational, geometric, and process perspectives on facial cognition: Contexts and challenges* (pp. 83–113). Mahwah: LEA.

Valentine, T., & Endo, M. (1992). Towards an exemplar model of face processing: The effects of race and distinctiveness. *Quarterly Journal of Experimental Psychology, 44A,* 671–703.

Wells, G., Charman, S. D., & Olson, E. A. (2005). Building face composites can harm lineup identification performance. *Journal of Experimental Psychology: Applied, 11,* 147–157.

Wells, G., & Hryciw, B. (1984). Memory for faces: Encoding and retrieval operations. *Memory and Cognition, 12,* 338–344.

Wogalter, M., & Marwitz, D. (1991). Face composite construction: In-view and from-memory quality and improvement with practice. *Ergonomics, 34,* 459–468.

II

IDENTIFYING SUSPECTS: SYSTEM VARIABLES

4

Remembering Faces

Vicki Bruce
University of Edinburgh

Mike Burton
University of Glasgow

Peter Hancock
University of Stirling

This handbook is about eyewitness psychology. The eyewitness to a crime is notoriously poor at being able to recognize or reconstruct—using composites—the faces of people seen at the crime. Yet our everyday lives are characterized by successful recognition and identification of people we know. Recent research has helped us to understand the paradox that we are both remarkably good (when people are familiar) and dramatically poor (when people are unfamiliar) at recognizing faces. In this chapter we review the evidence for the distinction between unfamiliar and familiar face recognition, and consider both the theoretical and practical implications of this distinction. At a theoretical level, we suggest a simple model of the process of familiarization, which could account for the apparently qualitative differences in processing that arise from familiarity. At a practical level, we consider the implications of our research for the identification of suspects, particularly when CCTV images are available to assist with identification.

The chapter begins by considering some of the differences that have been observed between familiar and unfamiliar face recognition and asks whether these differences arise because of the additional availability of nonvisual coding for familiar faces, or whether there is (additionally) evidence for a difference in the visual representation of familiar compared with unfamiliar faces. We then review the nature of the differences in visual representation of familiar compared with unfamiliar faces, before turning finally to consider how such apparently qualitative differences in processing may arise through simple exposure to more images of faces. The chapter concludes with a brief discussion of the practical implications of our work.

DIFFERENCES BETWEEN FAMILIAR
AND UNFAMILIAR FACE RECOGNITION

Neuropsychological evidence of a double dissociation between familiar and unfamiliar face recognition and matching has been reported (see Bruce & Young, 1986). Some prosopagnosic patients, who have profound difficulties in recognizing friends and acquaintances in their daily lives, can have normal ability in tasks of face matching. In contrast, not all people who are poor at matching unfamiliar faces are prosopagnosic. In a careful study of a large group of patients injured by gunshot wounds in the World War II, Young, Newcombe, de Haan, Small, and Hay (1993) produced further evidence of this double dissociation. Patient P.G., with a right hemispheric lesion, was highly deficient at two separate tasks of familiar face recognition, but performed quite normally at both the Benton task of unfamiliar face matching (Benton, Hamsher, Varney, & Spreen, 1983) and a sequential matching task using unfamiliar faces. Conversely, patient S.J. performed normally at familiar face recognition but was significantly impaired both at the Benton task and at the sequential face matching task.

The framework for human face recognition proposed by Bruce and Young (1986) almost two decades ago first articulated a possible reason for some differences between familiar and unfamiliar face processing. Bruce and Young argued that the visual representations mediating face recognition comprised two different kinds of code—"pictorial" codes—emphasizing details of a particular "picture" or view of a face, and "structural" codes—a more abstract representation of a face that allowed generalization beyond details of particular views or pictures. However, this distinction alone cannot readily account for the double dissociation described above, because the Benton task requires matching across subtle differences in viewpoint. However, in addition to distinctions at the level of visual coding processes, familiar faces gain access to other information about personal identity—what Bruce and Young termed "identity-specific" structural codes— what someone does for a living, and what his or her name is. It is possible that a patient with preserved abilities to match unfamiliar faces but who is unable to recognize familiar ones has intact pictorial and structural coding systems, but has lost the ability to recognize the familiarity of known faces or to retrieve information about other aspects of personal identity. Conversely, a person who can retrieve identities but not match unfamiliar faces may be able to activate familiarity and personal identity information from an impoverished visual representation system, much as we can all achieve when recognizing familiar faces from poor-quality images.

Ability to Deal with Degraded Information

Burton, Wilson, Cowan, and Bruce (1999) examined recognition of people shown in low-quality CCTV video footage. Participants were shown video clips of 10 people, and later were shown high quality photographs of 20 people—half of them encountered in the video and half novel. Participants were required to decide which were photographs of people seen earlier. Students familiar with the people shown in the photographs were near perfect at this task, whereas those who were unfamiliar with the individuals per-formed almost at chance. This result can be explained if the poor-quality videos pre-served enough visual information to allow familiar participants to recognize the identities of those viewed. Their later memory performance could then be mediated by recollec-tion either of the visual forms or of the nonvisual associations (knowledge of the personal identities, perhaps including names). For the unfamiliar participants the only way they could perform the later recognition task would be to match across from the poor-quality visual information to the higher-quality photographs—clearly a near-impossible task. A further experiment confirmed that the familiar participants were recognizing the faces from the videos, because when faces were concealed, their identification performance was very much reduced. So here we have another example of dissociation between fa-miliar and unfamiliar face recognition performance, but again it might be differences in the *non*visual codes that explain the effects. Are there any differences between the *visual* representations available for familiar and unfamiliar faces?

Ability to Deal with Changes in Viewpoint

Bruce (1982) demonstrated that recognition memory for pictures of unfamiliar faces was impaired significantly by a change in the picture between study and test. After studying 24 unfamiliar male faces for 8 seconds each, in an old-new recognition test, participants were 90% correct when the same pictures were repeated. A change in expression or view-point reduced recognition to 76%, and a change in both expression and viewpoint re-duced it to 61% correct, with a false-positive rate of 12% shown for new items in the test phase. This dramatic effect of changing view was seen, even though there was a good deal of visible clothing and distinctive hairstyles that remained constant between study and test phases. In contrast, when the faces were shown to participants who were familiar with them, hit rates were 95% whether pictures were identical or changed at test (false-positive rates of 8%). Other studies have shown that unfamiliar face matching and/or recognition is impaired by a change in lighting direction (Hill & Bruce, 1996), perspective (Liu & Chaudhuri, 2003), and spatial frequency content (Liu, Collin, Rainville, & Chaud-huri, 2000; Biederman & Kalocsai, 1997). These findings suggest that our representa-tions of unfamiliar faces are based on relatively "raw" image properties. It seems that our lifetime experience with the class of faces does not allow us to view a face in one image and readily generalize to a different picture of the face in which the image properties dif-fer. In Bruce and Young's (1986) terms, it seems that unfamiliar face recognition is dom-inated by pictorial codes.

This dependency on "pictorial" coding of unfamiliar faces was demonstrated rather dramatically in studies conducted in our group on matching faces from security video images. Bruce et al. (1999) set up matching tasks in which participants were invited to state whether or not a male face shown in a high-quality video frame, with unlimited in-spection time, appeared in an array of similar looking male faces shown immediately be-side the face for comparison. There was no memory load at all in this task, and yet per-formance was only 70% accurate when viewpoint and expression matched in the target and array faces. As viewpoint or expression was changed, performance declined further. This poor performance reflected the fact that even when high-quality images of the same face are taken on the same day, different cameras and slightly different poses produce variations in image, such that different images of the same face can look very different, and two different people's faces can look very similar. In contrast, when the faces to be matched are identical pictures, or the face images vary but the faces are familiar, such matching tasks are trivially easy (see Bruce et al., 2001, for direct comparisons of familiar and unfamiliar face matching from video images).

Again, it may be that it is the availability of different nonvisual codes that allows good generalization across viewpoint for familiar faces. To see if there is some specifically visual component to this ability, it would be better to examine a task where any overt memory or comparison element is minimized, and so the strategic use of nonvisual coding is less appropriate. Repetition priming is a form of implicit memory where previous exposure to an item makes it easier to recognize that item later, even though there is no explicit linkage between the earlier and later events. Familiar faces are recognized more quickly in a test phase if they have earlier been seen in the same or a different picture, but there is no priming of familiarity decisions from earlier encounters with the person's name, showing that face priming must be associated in some way with the system representing the visual form of the face rather than with a person's identity (Bruce & Valentine, 1985; Ellis et al., 1987). Priming is greatest from same compared with different pictures, showing that a component of priming arises from "pictorial" coding, but robust priming is found even across quite substantial delays from different pictures seen in quite different contexts (Bruce et al., 1998). Jenkins, Burton, and Ellis (2002) showed that repetition priming is found even when participants cannot remember having seen the images in the first phase, making it extremely unlikely that priming is itself based upon the same kinds of coding processes that underlie overt memory.

Roberts and Bruce (1989) compared the repetition effect for familiar and unfamiliar faces in a task where participants were asked to decide whether or not each face they saw was one of four target people. Target faces could be repeated immediately or, after an intervening item, in the same picture or a picture different from that just encountered. For familiar faces, a repetition advantage for repeated compared with nonrepeated items was found for changed as well as constant pictures, and across intervening items as well as for immediately repeated ones. For unfamiliar items, in contrast, repeating identical pictures gave an advantage, but there was no repetition advantage for changed items. In this experiment there was no explicit requirement for remembering faces, or even for comparing them from one trial to another. Yet the experiment found evidence for pictorial priming of unfamiliar faces and priming across different pictured viewpoints for familiar ones. Such findings bolster the view that representations of familiar faces are somehow based upon "structural" codes that combine information from different images and viewpoints in a way that facilitates recognition across a variety of transformations.

In the next section we explore in more detail the differences there may be between these pictorial and structural coding systems.

VISUAL REPRESENTATIONS OF FAMILIAR AND UNFAMILIAR FACES

Representation of Different Parts of the Face

There is some evidence that there is a qualitative difference in visual representations between unfamiliar and familiar faces. Ellis et al. (1979) showed that recognition memory for unfamiliar faces was dominated by external face features, whereas recognition of familiar faces depended much more on internal features. Young et al. (1985) confirmed the relative importance of internal features for familiar faces with the use of matching tasks. The importance of the external features for unfamiliar face matching was demonstrated again by Bruce et al. (1999) in the video array-matching task. Performance at matching to the array was only slightly impaired if only the external face features of the target face were shown, but performance was extremely poor if only internal features were shown.

This change can be seen as faces become familiarized in novel ways. O'Donnell and Bruce (2001) investigated the initial stages of familiarization by asking participants to memorize names for a small set of men who were studied in video clips until all names were correctly remembered. There was then a test phase where pairs of faces were shown and participants had to decide whether the faces were identical or slightly different. Differences could be found in subtle changes to eyes or mouth (internal features), hair or chin (external features). We compared the accuracy with which these differences could be detected for the familiarized faces with a set of similar men who were novel (unfamiliar) in the test phase. Different subgroups of participants learned different sets of faces as familiar, so no observed differences between familiarized and unfamiliar items could be attributed to differences in the items per se. Two experiments showed that for unfamiliar faces, only changes to the hair were well detected. For the familiarized items, changes to hair and eyes were accurately detected. The effect of familiarization on the detection of changes to the eyes was particularly dramatic. Changes that were virtually undetectable when faces were unfamiliar were recognized with very high accuracy for the familiarized items.

In three further experiments we tracked this shift toward an internal feature advantage as subjects were familiarized with a larger set of initially unfamiliar faces. Participants were asked to learn a set of 24 faces from video images and complete a face-matching task on three consecutive days. In the matching task participants were shown pairs of faces—taken from different, high-quality image formats (one video still, one photograph) and asked to decide if the pairs showed the same person or two different people. One member of each pair could be shown just in external features, internal features, or as the whole face—the other face was always shown intact. We examined performance in terms of accuracy and speed, as some of the faces became familiar during the course of the experiment. In Experiment 1 (reported in Bonner, Burton, & Bruce, 2003), half of the faces were learned from moving images, whereas the others were learned from static images to determine whether movement was necessary to produce the internal advantage found for matching of familiar faces. We found that by the end of the three days, performance on the internal features had improved and was equivalent to performance on the external features. In contrast, matching of the external features remained at a relatively constant level across the experiment. Faces were learned equally well from moving and static images, suggesting that movement is not necessary to promote learning of the internal features. Two further unpublished experiments used similar methodology (Bruce & Burton, 2002). In Experiments 2 and 3 all faces were learned from static images, but their presentation varied. In Experiment 2 we compared massed presentation of successive views of the same face with spaced presentation. In Experiment 3 we compared presenting different instances of the same face with constant or varied semantic information about (fictitious) personal identity. The aim in all three experiments was to see whether face learning was facilitated by conditions that might lead to the "binding" of different views of the same individual together (i.e., moving sequences, massed sequences, and consistent context might all promote binding). In the event all three experiments revealed the same pattern—learning was dominated by internal features, but there was no effect of variations in the learning environment.

The learning tasks employed by O'Donnell and Bruce (2001) and Bonner et al. (2003), however, are artificial. In a recently completed project in Stirling and Glasgow (Bruce & Burton, 2002), we attempted to use a more realistic simulation of the learning of new faces. Participants were recruited to view a soap opera series with actors and characters with which they were initially unfamiliar (the soap operas came from Irish television, and the participants were recruited in Scotland). We found representations shifted toward internal feature dominance after very little exposure and, within the limits of experiments conducted to date, this shift appeared to be little influenced by whether the faces were viewed in coherent episodes or in scrambled scenes. Our tentative conclusions, then, are that the learning of robust visual representations of faces is relatively uninfluenced by the precise circumstances of the learning—what matters is the variation in visual instances encountered.

EFFECTS OF MOVEMENT

Recent research has suggested that representations of familiar faces may contain, or be accompanied by, information about their characteristic movement patterns. Knight and Johnston (1997) demonstrated that famous faces made difficult to recognize by photographic negation became easier to recognize if they are shown in a moving rather than a static image. Lander, Christie, and Bruce (1999) attempted to determine whether the effect was due to the multiple views seen in moving clips or to the movement per se. They showed that recognition of faces shown in thresholded (black-on-white) images was better if the faces were moving rather than static, and that this advantage was greatest if the sequence was shown in a way that preserved its original dynamic characteristics. The same set of frames shown moving more slowly, or in a different order of presentation, was less effective as a trigger for recognition. Lander and Bruce (2004) reported benefits for repetition priming if faces were seen moving in the study phase. Moving clips primed later familiarity judgments made about famous faces better than still images—even surpassing the priming shown by direct repetition of the same still images between study and test. All of these studies combine to suggest that the characteristic movements of familiar faces may somehow be represented in memory and can be revealed in experiments where recognition is suboptimal for other reasons.

This demonstration of the use of dynamic information for face recognition may have practical consequences too—Lander, Bruce, and Hill (2001) demonstrated how motion could act to reveal identities of faces apparently masked by blurring or pixellation, typically used to preserve anonymity in television documentaries. A face that appears unrecognizable by someone unfamiliar with the person depicted (e.g., a TV editor) could quite easily be recognized by friends or family when he or she is shown moving in the TV program.

In contrast, there are rather few convincing effects of movement demonstrated on the recognition of previously unfamiliar faces. Positive benefits of moving sequences were reported by Pike et al. (1997), who showed that recognition memory for unfamiliar faces was better when these had been studied moving, rather than when they were seen in multiple or single still images, and Hill, Schyns, and Akamatsu (1997) also found recognition memory to be better if faces were studied in an animated sequence rather than in randomly ordered frames. But a number of other studies have failed to find any benefit for moving over multiple static images (Christie & Bruce, 1998; Lander & Bruce, 2003; Bonner, Burton, & Bruce, 2003). Some possible reconciliation of these conflicting findings may be that movement *can* help build 3D representations, but this may aid recognition in only rather limited circumstances. For example, Hill et al.'s (1997) benefit for moving sequences was shown when faces were presented as 3D surface faces, devoid of visible texture, and recognition of such items is likely to be particularly dependent on the kind of 3D structural representation revealed by motion. Although it would seem plausible that seeing unfamiliar faces move would be beneficial to building robust representations, there is little support for this as a general conclusion. On balance, then, we think that what is important for *building* a representation is exposure to *multiple variations* in pose and expression. The additional benefits of dynamic presentation found with highly familiar faces may rely on a longer-term familiarity that allows the characteristic motions made by people expressing and speaking to be learned.

HOW DO DIFFERENCES BETWEEN UNFAMILIAR AND FAMILIAR FACES EMERGE?

How do the varied images that we encounter when meeting an initially unfamiliar face become coded or consolidated as "structural codes" that characterize processing of familiar faces? In this section we review the prototype effect in visual pattern recognition and suggest that the formation of prototypes from varied exemplars is a promising way to think about the consolidation of structural codes.

The "prototype" effect in visual memory describes the tendency of people to find familiar the "average" of a set of images even when it hasn't been studied. It was first demonstrated by Posner and Keele (1968), who used random dot patterns. When a set of instances of dot patterns was created through systematic distortion of an underlying prototype pattern, participants later found the unstudied prototype to be at least as familiar as the instances they had actually been exposed to. There have been several demonstrations of such effects in face memory. Using Identikit faces, Solso and McCarthy (1981) created a prototype from a particular set of face features and then produced variants by changing one or more of the components from the prototype. Participants exposed to a set of these exemplars later recognized the unstudied prototype with greater confidence than the studied exemplars. Bruce et al. (1991) found a similar effect when exemplars were created by varyiation of the spacing of the internal features of faces.

Cabeza, Bruce, Kato, and Oda (1999) extended the investigation of prototype effects in face recognition in several important directions. They used images of real faces whose feature positions or head angles were varied. Prototype effects were shown much more strongly when variations were made to feature position within a face than when the prototype was an unstudied head angle. Such observations may indicate that different instances of faces are combined to form a prototype within but perhaps not between different viewpoints.

How might such prototype effects be conceived? To understand this, we need to review basic visual representations and think about how additional exposure operates.

The statistical technique Principal Components Analysis (PCA) has been used to suggest ways in which faces might be represented, both by human perceivers and for artificial computer-based face recognition systems (Kirby & Sirovich, 1990; Turk & Pentland, 1991). The technique works by taking a set of faces (i.e., face images) and deriving from these a core set of components that can be recombined in a weighted sum to reconstruct any face image, illustrated in Figure 4–1. Formally, these components are the eigenvectors from the PCA on the original images and are known as *eigenfaces* in this literature. The computational advantage of the approach is that it provides efficient storage: one needs relatively few eigenfaces to provide a good representation of a face (typically about 50 in the literature we review here), giving a substantial saving by comparison with the thousands of values one needs to represent a face pixel by pixel.

PCA has been used with considerable success to provide models of face recognition. A set of eigenfaces is used to code a database of "known" faces. A novel face is then introduced to the system and coded in these same eigenfaces. Recognition takes the form

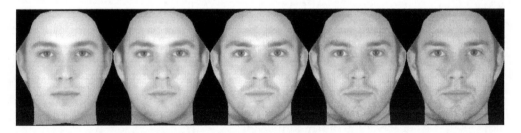

FIGURE 4–1.   Left image, an average face; right image, an original face. Center images, reconstructions using 10, 20, and 50 principal components.

of a simple match: does the database contain a face with a coding sufficiently similar to signal recognition? A number of researchers have shown that this approach can provide rather good levels of recognition (e.g., Valentin, Abdi, & O'Toole, 1994). In fact, using the array task described above (Bruce et al., 1999), we have shown that PCA can actually outperform human subjects in matching unfamiliar faces (Burton et al., 2001). Furthermore, we have suggested that PCA offers a good way to capture the visual codes described above, and that when combined with a higher-level representation of personal information, it may provide an understanding of face recognition linking vision and meaning (Burton, Bruce, & Hancock, 1999).

Although PCA is normally used to study face *recognition*, it appears to have some attractive qualities for the study of other aspects of face processing. For example, it can provide a good analysis of facial emotion, in particular showing how faces signal their identity and expression independently (Calder et al., 2001; Cottrell, Branson, & Calder, 2003), a proposal first made on the basis of psychological dissociations rather than physical analysis of face images (Bruce & Young, 1986). We have also shown that the similarity between faces, as perceived by human viewers, corresponds to physical proximity in the eigenface encoding, suggesting that this representation is a useful model of human face representation (Hancock, Burton, & Bruce, 1996).

One very interesting use of PCA, which has a bearing on the issue of face learning, is the proposal that it might provide an account of the "other race effect" (O'Toole, Deffenbacher, Valentin, & Abdi, 1994; Furl, Phillips, & O'Toole, 2002). It is well established that our memory for same-race faces is better than that for different-race faces. O'Toole and her colleagues have suggested that this could be because the variations in other-race faces may not be captured well by the dimensions with which we code same-race faces. This is an inherent property of PCA. So, if we were to derive eigenfaces from a set of people who all had the same hair color, then hair color would not emerge as a significant dimension, that is, it would not be coded in the eigenfaces, which (by definition) are derived to capture as much variance as possible in the set. If we now use these same eigenfaces to try to recognize people whose hair color does vary, then this dimension will not be well coded in the eigenfaces, and so it will be hard to use this characteristic to recognize someone. In other words, our representation of faces is derived from those we have seen. If we grow up learning how the faces around us vary and derive representations of this (akin to eigenfaces), then these will not allow us to perform well when we are suddenly exposed to a set of faces that vary in different ways.

O'Toole's proposal gives us an insight into how PCA may be used to think about face learning. The "training set" of faces is those we see early in life, and these form the basis of our face representations, in just the same way that our language comprehension is tuned early in life to the languages we hear while growing up. However, this is not the only important aspect of face learning. In fact, we learn new faces all the time, throughout life, and the very significant differences between familiar and unfamiliar face processing, described above, are striking precisely because all familiar faces start as unfamiliar.

In some recent work we have begun to ask whether PCA can capture this aspect of adult face learning. The approach we have taken is to compare systems built using different numbers of images of the same person. Most PCA systems are derived from a single image of many individuals. Here we have asked how systems perform when the eigenfaces are derived from a set that contains many instances of each person. By varying the numbers of images of each person, we try to model the level of familiarity a viewer might have with each face. So, for example, a particular version of the system might be very familiar with Tony Blair (i.e., have seen many images of him) but less familiar with Britney Spears (have seen fewer images of her).

We have approached this project in two different ways, broadly corresponding to exemplar and to prototype-based systems. In exemplar models, we build eigenfaces from each face image that the model is deemed to know. So, for example, the eigenfaces might be derived from nine Tony Blair images, four Britney Spears images, and so on. In the prototype models, we derive eigenfaces from a single image of each person, but this image is the *average* of all those the model knows (i.e., the average of nine Tony Blairs, the average of four Britney Spears, etc.). We can derive image averages because, prior to all our PCA studies, we morph images to the same shape, such that the face outline and features always fall in the same part of the image. This shape normalization is a technique introduced by Craw (1995; Craw & Cameron, 1991).

Figure 4–2 shows the image average of nine Tony Blairs. The results of these analyses (Burton et al., 2005) show a very interesting pattern. First, prototype systems perform much better than exemplar systems. Even though the images used are those of celebrities, and so we have no control over lighting, contrast, and so forth, a prototype system can achieve very high recognition rates. Second, prototype systems get systematically better as more images contribute to the average. This appears to echo learning: the more exposure one has to a particular face, the more robust is one's recognition of that person.

We should be clear that we are not claiming a general superiority of prototype over exemplar-based recognition systems. Our claim is only that this particular characterization of learning appears to have several attractive properties, and these need to be explored further. Of particular interest is the fact that this average/prototype representation appears to be quite robust; as it develops, it can be recruited to match a wider variety of images of the represented person. We suggest that this might be a way to understand the development of pictorial and structural codes, as described above. If one is forced to use pictorial codes to recognize or match a face, then one has to cope with any number of image variations that are specific to that picture and do not have any relevance to the person's identity. For example, if the light is coming from a particular direction, it may give the nose a certain appearance. Despite our general familiarity with faces, it is diffi-

FIGURE 4–2.   An average of nine pictures of Tony Blair.

cult to judge how the nose will look with light from a different direction. If one is unfamiliar with this person, then it will be difficult to do the match. However, if one is basing one's judgment on the average/prototype of many images of that person, then such variations in lighting direction will cancel one another out. In fact, over many instances, the average will eventually eliminate all such variations, which are incidental to the person's identity. As it does so, the prototype will come to look less and less like a *photo* of the person (see the image above) but will eventually carry only identity-specific, and not image-specific, information. This may, therefore, be the way that structural codes develop. For a familiar face, a new image is compared with this structural model, and a match between images is established not by comparing them with each other, but by comparing each with the internal model. Since averaging makes sense within but not, on the whole, between different viewpoints, it is possible that the prototypes we store are separately structured around different viewpoints (cf. Cabeza et al., 1999).

This proposal also has the feature that unfamiliar face recognition and familiar face recognition actually operate by the same process. In both cases, one is matching an incoming image to a stored representation. However, the difference is that the stored representation for a face one has seen only once carries a lot of image-specific information. One is therefore (in principle) unable to disambiguate those aspects of the image due to variations in the individual person (structural codes) and those due to the particular instance (pictorial codes). This rather simplistic notion of learning is in contrast to the theory, described above, that people undergo a processing change as a face becomes familiar. The idea that internal features become more important than external features during learning might therefore reflect the stability of these facial characteristics over many instances; for example, hairstyles will change regularly, but eyes noses and mouths less so. The transition toward internal features may therefore reflect the development of the prototype rather than the development of a processing strategy on behalf of the viewer.

SUMMARY AND CONCLUSIONS

In this chapter we have contrasted our facility at recognizing familiar faces with the fragility of unfamiliar face processing—a fragility that gives rise to many of the difficulties in remembering faces reported elsewhere in this volume. We have argued that our expertise with familiar faces arises in a simple way, through the accumulation and averaging of innumerable different images of a person's face.

This theoretical position—that expertise with individual faces arises from quantity rather than quality of processing, is given additional support by an intriguing finding reported by Troje and Kersten (1999). They showed that observers were relatively poor at recognizing a profile view of their own face, compared with a full-face view, whereas for other known faces there was no difference in processing of full-face and profiles. If general expertise and familiarity with faces were responsible for our capacity to deal with differing viewpoints, then it would seem reasonable to suggest that this would allow good processing of an unfamiliar view of one's own face. If, on the other hand, it is mere exposure to variations in viewpoint and expression that creates expertise with a face, then one will rarely encounter one's own face in anything other than the full-face view seen in a mirror.

What are the practical implications of the work reviewed here? For unfamiliar faces, memories and indeed perceptual impressions are image-specific, and the capacity to generalize from one image to another is quite limited. Impressions can be affected by viewpoint and lighting, and we must be very careful not to assume that an apparent resemblance between two images of faces implies that they are identical. Our studies of matching from CCTV images to photographs have revealed how readily images of two different but similar-looking people can be mistakenly taken to belong to the same person, and judges and juries should be alerted to the dangers of inferring identity from mere resemblance. This is not a problem that arises just with low-quality images—similar-looking people in extremely high-quality images can be mistaken for each other, as happened in our published studies. In contrast, however, even low-quality images of familiar faces can be extremely effective prompts to recognition. The best use of CCTV images of faces will be to provoke recognition of the protagonists by people already familiar with them.

REFERENCES

Benton, A. L., Hamsher, K. de S., Varney, N., & Spreen, O. (1983). *Contributions to neuropsychological assessment: A clinical manual*. Oxford: Oxford University Press.

Biederman, I., & Kalocsai, P. (1997). Neurocomputational bases of object and face recognition. *Philosophical Transactions of the Royal Society, B352*, 1203–1219.

Bonner, L., Burton, A. M., & Bruce, V. (2003). Getting to know you: How we learn new faces. *Visual Cognition, 10*, 527–536.

Bruce, V. (1982). Changing faces: Visual and non-visual coding processes in face recognition. *British Journal of Psychology, 73*, 105–116.

Bruce, V., & Burton. A. M. (2002). *Getting to know you—How we learn new faces*. Final report on ESRC grant: http://www.regard.ac.uk/research_findings/R000238357/report.pdf

Bruce, V., Carson, D., Burton, A. M., & Kelly, S. (1998). Prime time advertisements: Repetition priming from faces seen on subject recruitment posters. *Memory & Cognition, 26*, 502–515.

Bruce, V., Henderson, Z., Greenwood, K., Hancock, P., Burton, A. M., & Miller, P. (1999). Verification of face identities from images captured on video. *Journal of Experimental Psychology: Applied, 5*, 339–360.

Bruce, V., Henderson, Z., Newman, C., & Burton, A. M. (2001). Matching identities of familiar and unfamiliar faces caught on CCTV images. *Journal of Experimental Psychology: Applied, 7*, 207–218.

Bruce, V., & Valentine, T. (1985). Identity priming in the recognition of familiar faces. *British Journal of Psychology, 76*, 373–383.

Bruce, V., & Young, A. (1986). Understanding face recognition. *British Journal of Psychology, 77*, 305–327.

Burton, A. M., Bruce, V., & Hancock, P. J. B. (1999). From pixels to people: A model of familiar face recognition. *Cognitive Science, 23*, 1–31.

Burton, A. M., Jenkins, R., Hancock, P. J. B., & White, D. (2005). Robust representations for face recognition: The power of averages. *Cognitive Psychology, 51*, 256–284..

Burton, A. M., Miller, P., Bruce, V., Hancock, P. J. B., & Henderson, Z. (2001). Human and automatic face recognition: a comparison across image formats. *Vision Research, 41*, 3185–3195.

Burton, A. M., Wilson, S., Cowan, M., & Bruce, V. (1999). Face recognition in poor quality video: Evidence from security surveillance. *Psychological Science, 10,* 243–248.

Cabeza, R., Bruce, V., Kato, T., & Oda, M. (1999). The prototype effect in face recognition: Extension and limits. *Memory & Cognition, 27,* 139–151.

Calder, A. J., Burton, A. M., Miller, P., Young, A. W., & Akamatsu, S. (2001). A principal component analysis of facial expressions. *Vision Research, 41,* 1179–1208.

Christie, F., & Bruce, V. (1998). The role of movement in the recognition of unfamiliar faces. *Memory & Cognition, 26*(4), 780–790.

Cottrell, G. W., Branson, K., & Calder, A. J. (2002). Do expression and identity need separate representations? In *Proceedings of the 24th Annual Cognitive Science Conference, Fairfax, Virginia.* Mahwah, NJ: Lawrence Erlbaum Associates.

Craw, I. (1995). A manifold model of face and object recognition. In T. Valentine (Ed.), *Cognitive and computational aspects of face recognition.* London: Routledge.

Craw, I., & Cameron, P. (1991). Parameterising images for recognition and reconstruction. In P. Mowforth (Ed.), *Proceedings of the British Machine Vision Conference, 1991.* Berlin: Springer-Verlag.

Ellis, H. D., Shepherd, J. W., & Davies, G. M. (1979). Identification of familiar and unfamiliar faces from internal and external features—Some implications for theories of face recognition. *Perception, 8,* 431–439.

Furl, N., Phillips, P. J., & O'Toole, A. J. (2002). Face recognition algorithms and the other-race effect: computational mechanisms for a developmental contact hypothesis. *Cognitive Science, 26,* 797–815.

Hancock, P. J. B., Burton, A. M., & Bruce, V. (1996). Face processing: Human perception and principal components analysis. *Memory & Cognition, 24,* 26–40.

Hill, H., & Bruce, V. (1996). Effects of lighting on the perception of facial surfaces. *Journal of Experimental Psychology: Human Perception and Performance, 22,* 986–1004.

Hill, H., Schyns, P. G., & Akamatsu, S. (1997). Information and viewpoint dependence in face recognition. *Cognition, 62,* 201–222.

Jenkins, R., Burton, A. M., & Ellis, A. W. (2002). Long-term effects of covert face recognition. *Cognition, 86,* B43–B52.

Kirby, M., & Sirovich, L. (1990). Applications of the Karhunen-Loeve procedure for the characterization of human faces. *IEEE: Transactions on Pattern Analysis and Machine Intelligence, 12,* 103–108.

Knight, B., & Johnston, A. (1997). The role of movement in face recognition. *Visual Cognition, 4,* 265–273.

Lander, K., & Bruce, V. (2003). The role of motion in learning new faces. *Visual Cognition, 10,* 897–912.

Lander, K., & Bruce, V. (2004). Repetition priming from moving faces. *Memory & Cognition, 32,* 640–647.

Lander, K., Bruce, V., & Hill, H. (2001). Evaluating the effectiveness of pixilation and blurring on masking the identity of familiar faces. *Applied Cognitive Psychology, 15,* 101–116.

Lander, K., Christie, F., & Bruce, V. (1999). The role of movement in the recognition of famous faces. *Memory & Cognition, 27,* 974–985.

Liu, C. H., & Chaudhuri, A. (2003). Face recognition with perspective transformation. *Vision Research, 43,* 2393–2402.

Liu, C. H., Collin, C. A., Rainville, S. J. M., & Chaudhuri, A. (2000). The effects of spatial frequency overlap on face recognition. *Journal of Experimental Psychology: Human Perception and Performance, 26,* 956–979.

O'Donnell, C., & Bruce, V. (2001). Familiarisation with faces selectively enhances sensitivity to changes made to the eyes. *Perception, 30*(6), 755–764

O'Toole, A. J., Deffenbacher, K. A., Valentin, D., & Abdi, H. (1994). Structural aspects of face recognition and the other race effect. *Memory & Cognition, 22,* 208–224.

Pike, G. E., Kemp, R. I., Towell, N. A., & Phillips, K. C. (1997). Recognizing moving faces: The relative contribution of motion and perspective view information, *Visual Cognition, 4,* 409–437.

Posner, M. I., & Keele, S. W. (1968). On the genesis of abstract ideas. *Journal of Experimental Psychology, 77,* 353–363.

Roberts, T., & Bruce, V. (1989). Repetition priming of face recognition in a serial choice reaction-time task. *British Journal of Psychology, 80,* 201–211.

Solso, R. L., & McCarthy, J. E. (1981). Prototype formation of faces—A case of pseudo-memory. *British Journal of Psychology, 72,* 499–503.

Troje, N. F., & Kersten, D. (1999). Viewpoint-dependent recognition of familiar faces. *Perception, 28,* 483–487.

Turk, M., & Pentland, A. (1991). Eigenfaces for recognition. *Journal of Cognitive Neuroscience, 3,* 71–86.

Valentin, D., Abdi, H., & O'Toole, A. (1994). Categorization and identification of human face images by neural networks: A review of the linear autoassociative and principal component approaches. *Journal of Biological Systems, 2,* 413–423.

Young, A. W., Hay, D. C., & McWeeny, K. H. (1985). Matching familiar and unfamiliar faces on internal and external features. *Perception, 14,* 737–746.

Young, A. W., Newcombe, F., de Haan, E. H. F., Small, M., & Hay, D. C. (1993). Face perception after brain injury: selective impairments affecting identity and expression. *Brain, 116,* 941–959.

5

The Psychology
of Speaker Identification and
Earwitness Memory

A. Daniel Yarmey

University of Guelph, Canada

This chapter describes and explores variables that contribute to the accuracy of speaker identification and earwitness memory. An examination is made of (1) the history of voice identification in the courts; (2) differences between earwitness memory and eyewitness memory; (3) why speakers are difficult to identify; (4) a review of different witness/suspect factors and situational factors; (5) investigative procedures that play a role in earwitness memory; and finally, (6) some recommended procedures and guidelines for the administration of voice lineups.

SPEAKER IDENTIFICATION
AND EARWITNESS MEMORY

Victims or witnesses who are visually handicapped or a perpetrator whose face is disguised, or who commits a crime that occurs in the dark, or over the telephone, are examples of individuals and situations that could lead to *earwitness testimony* being given at court. Earwitness identification evidence refers to the process of a witness hearing the voice(s) of a perpetrator(s) and encoding that information in memory, retrieving the stored information when called to describe the speaker's voice and/or identify the speaker in a voice lineup, and finally, testifying or communicating these responses to a police officer, trial judge, and/or jury. Speaker recognition is differentiated from speaker identification; the former refers to general familiarity with one or more voices within a voice sample for whatever reason, whereas speaker identification is the process of discriminating a particular person's voice from a single speech sample or from a number of different voice samples.

Analysis of speaker identification generally has followed two different procedures. The first approach, referred to as *aural-perceptual analysis*, involves testing the effectiveness of human listeners in identifying a speaker through auditory procedures, such as a voice lineup. The second approach, called the *acoustic procedure*, involves machine/computer analyses (see Hollien, 1990, 2002; Nolan, 1996; Ormerod, 2002; Rose, 2002). Forensic acoustic phonetics pertains to computerized/machine analyses of selected voice samples for the frequency and intensity of speech sound waves and resonance. Acoustic examinations yield numerical calculations and/or graphic illustrations of voice pitch and the examination of vowels and consonants and voice quality. Given this procedure, phoneticians can test whether a taped speech sample uttered by an unknown speaker involved in a crime matches a taped reference sample uttered by a known speaker, the suspect.

It should be noted at the outset that all reviewers of the scientific literature on earwitness memory have concluded that extreme caution must be taken by the legal system when voice identification evidence is used. Neither the aural-perceptual approach nor the acoustic approach can uniquely characterize a person's voice. Speakers cannot be identified with certainty from either auditory or acoustic procedures (see Baldwin & French, 1990; Bonastre et al., 2003; Bull & Clifford, 1999; Deffenbacher et al., 1989; Wilding, Cook, & Davis, 2000; Yarmey, 1995a, 1995b). Although acoustic examinations are important for legal proceedings, this type of analysis is beyond the scope of this chapter and is not covered in this review.

Aural-perceptual speaker identifications are difficult and error prone. However, as would be expected, some witnesses are significantly superior to others in their accuracy of speaker identification for both familiar and unfamiliar speakers (e.g., Yarmey, 1995a; Yarmey, Yarmey, Yarmey, & Parliament, 2001). According to Read and Craik (1995), the probability of correct identification of an unfamiliar speaker from a voice lineup who was heard only once and for a brief amount of time is about 30%. Misidentification of unfamiliar speakers from target-absent lineups also can be very high. For example, in three field experiments conducted by this writer, only 2% (Yarmey, Yarmey, & Yarmey, 1994), 16% (Yarmey, 2003a), and 28% (Yarmey, 2001a) of the witnesses correctly rejected the six-voice target-absent lineups, respectively. Nonetheless, speaker identification is not impossible and may be reliable for a substantial number of earwitnesses, given certain witness/suspect characteristics, situational characteristics, and police investigative procedures.

The Courts and Earwitness Identification

Although research on eyewitness testimony dates back to the late nineteenth century, the first scientific experiments on speaker identification were conducted by McGehee (1937, 1944). Apart from a recent review of the literature by Solan and Tiersma (2003), there has been limited historical analysis of the courts' use of earwitness evidence. Furthermore, reviews of the historical background of witness psychology generally have overlooked the theoretical and empirical research on earwitness testimony (e.g., Levine & Tapp, 1973; Loh, 1981; Sporer, 1982). Because recommendations and conclusions regarding the problematic nature of earwitness reports are made by the courts, often without guidance from science, a brief overview of the history of speaker identification is presented in the next section.

The first record of a court evaluating the probative value of earwitness testimony dates from the 1660 trial in England of William Hulet. Hulet was accused of regicide in the execution of King Charles I. The critical evidence against Hulet came from Richard Gittens, who was familiar with Hulet's voice through their membership in the same military regiment. Although the face of the executioner was hidden, Gittens stated that he knew that Hulet was the executioner "by his speech" when he heard him beg the king's forgiveness. Hulet was found guilty of high treason by the jury. Subsequently, the original hangman of King Charles I confessed to the execution, and "the court, being sensible of the injury done to Hulet, procured his reprieve" (Solan & Tiersma, 2003, p. 394).

The first documented evidence of a case involving earwitness testimony in North America occurred in 1861 when a New York trial judge permitted the testimony of a witness who claimed that he could identify the defendant's dog by hearing its bark as one of the two dogs that had killed his sheep (*Wilbur v. Hubbard*, 1861). The dog reportedly had a distinctive, coarse, harsh bark. The court ruled that "if a person can be identified through his/her voice alone, the same could be done with a barking dog" (cited in Tosi, 1979, p. 1). Early in the twentieth century in a case involving the rape of a white woman by an unfamiliar black man whose face was obscured, a Florida judge concluded that the voice identification based on hearing two sentences "I have got you now" and "I don't want your money" was likely to be accurate (Hollien, 2002, p. 19). The judge reasoned:

> The manner, time, and place of his assault on her threw her instantly into the highest state of terror and alarm, when all of her senses and faculties were at the extreme of alert receptiveness, when there was nothing within her reach by which to identify her assailant but his voice. Who can deny that under these circumstances that voice so indelibly and vividly photographed itself upon the sensitive plate of her memory as that she could forever promptly and unerringly recognize it on hearing its tones again. (*Mack v. Florida*, 1907, p. 709)

Clearly, the assumption was made that there is a positive correlation between the emotional arousal and stress of a victim and the accuracy of speaker identification. Unfortunately, as reported later in the chapter, there has been little empirical study of this relationship.

Perhaps the most celebrated American case involving speaker identification occurred in New York in 1933 following the kidnap and murder of the infant son of Colonel Charles Lindbergh, the celebrated hero and first man to fly solo across the Atlantic ocean. Soon after the kidnapping Lindbergh talked and negotiated over the telephone with a man claiming to be the kidnapper. Lindbergh again heard the man's voice at night at a cemetery where $50,000 in gold certificates was to be delivered by his associate, Dr. John Condon. While waiting by his car nearly 100 yards away from where the ransom was to be delivered, Lindbergh heard the words "Hey, doctor! Over here, over here," pronounced by a speaker with a foreign accent. Twenty-nine months later German-born Bruno Richard Hauptmann was accused and convicted of this crime, partly on the basis of Lindbergh's speaker identification (*New Jersey v. Hauptmann*, 1935). Interestingly, prior to trial, Lindburgh told a grand jury that "it would be very difficult to sit here and say that I could pick a man by that voice." Later that day the district attorney asked Lindburgh, "Would you like to see the man who kidnapped your son?" (Solan & Tiersma,

2003, p. 373). The following day Hauptmann was brought to the D.A.'s office and asked to say the following phrase, "Hey, doctor. Here, doctor, over here" in front of Lindburgh and a group of detectives. At this point Lindburgh told the D.A. that he recognized the voice of Hauptmann as that of the kidnapper. At trial, Lindburgh testified that he heard the voice of the kidnapper at the cemetery and that it was the same voice that he heard in the office of the district attorney. The inherent suggestibility of this one-person (showup) voice identification, and other factors such as cross-ethnic identification, length of the retention interval, and the size of the voice sample all question the fairness, reliability, and validity of this identification. The conviction and execution of Bruno Hauptmann remain controversial to this day.

This trial is also important in another way; it served as the stimulus for the first aural-perceptual experiments on speaker identification (McGehee, 1937, 1944). In these experiments McGehee presented student research participants with passages of phrases read by an unfamiliar person standing behind a screen. Subsequently, participants were tested for their recognition memory of the target and four other speakers. Factors such as the effects of delay (ranging between 1 day and 5 months); gender differences; ethnicity differences; and voice disguise on recognition memory were investigated. Unfortunately, because the experimental research designs involved a confound between treatment conditions and speakers, McGehee's results are difficult to interpret (Thompson, 1985). Nevertheless, Frances McGehee's historical experimental contributions did set the stage for contemporary, empirically based, scientific research.

Solan and Tiersma's (2003) review of court cases in the United States that focus on trials involving voice identification evidence shows that this topic has been readily addressed in criminal courts (see, for example, *Commonwealth v. Miles*, 1995; *United States v. Duran*, 1993; *Yeatman v. Inland Property Management, Inc.*, 1994). Conversely, in Canada and England, with a couple of exceptions (see Komulainen, 1988; Ormerod, 2001, 2002), the courts have given little attention to the issues related to voice identification.

From the Court to the Laboratory:
Earwitness Memory

The following two cases show how trial judges have made judgments regarding different factors that influence speaker identification. It is possible, of course, that the judges' conclusions are correct and have been guided by knowledge of relevant scientific literature on earwitness testimony. It is my guess, however, that most judges' conclusions about earwitness evidence are based on their trial experience, their knowledge of eyewitness identification, and commonsense beliefs. However, as this chapter shows, the processes that underlie earwitness identification differ in some respects from that of eyewitness identification.

In *Commonwealth v. Miles* (1995) the State Supreme Court of Massachusetts drew the following conclusions:

> After consulting with the office of the district attorney, the police used a voice identification procedure that adequately protected the defendant's rights. There was no one-on-one confrontation

between the victim and the defendant. The victim could not see the participants during the procedure, nor could they see her. The defendant selected the order in which he would read. The participants read the same innocuous passage from a fifth-grade reader. Defense counsel attended the procedure and, although consulted, never objected to it. In addition, we have viewed a videotape of the voice identification procedure, and conclude that the procedure was not impermissibly suggestive. The defendant's voice did not stand out because of his age, nor did any other aspect of the procedure direct undue attention to the defendant's voice. Hence, we conclude that the judge properly denied the defendant's motion to suppress the voice identification. (cited in Solan & Tiersma, 2003, p. 380)

Similarly, in *United States v. Duran* (1993), the Ninth Circuit affirmed a conviction for bank robbery in which the primary evidence consisted of voice identification at trial by a bank teller. The Court concluded:

Again, both tellers had ample opportunity to listen to Duran's voice during the robbery. Duran ordered the tellers to raise their hands and demanded money. He ordered [a] teller to escort him into the vault and to open it up. Inside the vault, Duran continued to holler at [the teller], demanding the keys to the vault, telling her to hurry, and asking where all the money was. He ordered [the teller] back to the teller area and demanded the keys to the remaining cash drawers, As Duran left, he threatened everyone in the bank: "don't move or we'll kill you." Both tellers were likely very attentive during the robbery given Duran's weapon and threats, as evidenced by their accurate descriptions of Duran and his distinctive voice and the fact that neither teller equivocated in her identification of Duran's voice. Moreover, the in-court identifications occurred just three months after the bank robbery. (cited in Solan & Tiersma, 2003, p. 383)

Both of these legal analyses contain several assumptions about factors that influence earwitness descriptions and identification, such as the opportunity to observe; the perpetrator's quality, loudness, and tone of voice during the commission of the crime; the effects of stress and weapon focus on voice identification; the length of the retention interval; the number of suspects in a voice lineup; the selection of foils (fillers); the use of a live lineup; and the nature of the voice script to be uttered by the suspect and the foils in the lineup. These assumptions and the different factors that influence speaker descriptions and identification are reviewed in the following sections.

Differences Between Earwitness Memory and Eyewitness Memory

Contrary to one American judge who stated that there is no scientific evidence that voice identification was as dangerous as visual identification (Ormerod, 2001), earwitness and eyewitness researchers would hardly agree. Although it has been assumed that estimator variables and system variables that influence eyewitness memory function in the same manner with earwitness memory (Clifford, 1980), this assumption is not true for all factors.

The processes that underlie earwitness identification and eyewitness identification are not identical (Hollien 1996). Accuracy of identification is superior with faces compared to that obtained with voices (Hollien, Bennett, & Gelfer, 1983; McAllister, Dale,

& Keay, 1993; Yarmey et al., 1994). For example, in the Yarmey et al. (1994) investigation, the mean correct identification scores for the same targets presented in photo showups and photo lineups were 57% and 46%, respectively. In contrast, the mean correct identification scores for these targets in voice showups and voice lineups were 28% and 9%, respectively.

Contrary to logic, witnesses who can both see and hear a perpetrator do not give greater attention to or have better memory for auditory information as lighting gets poorer (Yarmey, 1986). Furthermore, when witnesses both see and hear a perpetrator, speech is attended to first of all for meanings, emotions, and attitudes rather than for identification purposes. Also, when witnesses both see and hear a perpetrator, the presence of auditory information interferes only slightly with visual identification of the target. In contrast, visual information clearly interferes with speaker identification (McAllister, Dale, Bregman, McCabe, & Cotton, 1993). This experiment showed that speaker identification was significantly superior in an auditory condition ($M = 61\%$) compared with an auditory-visual condition ($M = 33\%$) when a voice lineup was used. However, when a visual lineup was used, facial identifications in a visual condition ($M = 75\%$) were similar and not significantly different from identifications in an auditory-visual condition ($M = 64\%$). These results indicate that visual information can interfere with the processing of auditory information. A face overshadowing effect also has been demonstrated such that the voice of an unfamiliar speaker is better remembered if the target's face was not observed at the time of encoding (Cook & Wilding, 1997a, 2001).

More trust should be given by the justice system in eyewitness confidence than in earwitness confidence of the accuracy of identification (Olsson, Juslin, & Winman, 1998). Earwitnesses also are significantly more vulnerable to post-event information than are eyewitnesses (McAllister, Bregman, & Lipscomb, 1988). In two separate experiments participants witnessed a videotaped automobile accident either visually or auditorily, and then were exposed to post-event questioning. Although accuracy of speed estimations was greatest in the visual condition, the auditory condition proved most vulnerable to post-event information in both experiments.

The courts' dealings with aural-perceptual identifications tend to be guided by those principles that govern visual identification (Komulainen, 1988). However, there is a danger in considering these practices to be equivalent (Broeders & Rietveld, 1995). Whereas suspects can easily modify their voices as they speak for a voice lineup, suspects in a visual stand-up lineup or photo array are less able to alter their appearance apart from changes in head hair, facial hair, and normal aging. Some jurisdictions such as the courts of New South Wales in Australia have stricter rules for voice identification than for visual identification (Heydon, 1994). Voice identification evidence is allowed only when the speaker (suspect) is highly familiar to the witness, or the voice of the accused is particularly distinctive (*Regina v. Smith*, 1984; *Regina v. Brownlowe*, 1987). In contrast, courts in the United States and Canada generally allow witnesses who believe that they recognize a voice simply to take the stand and say so. Unfortunately, the courts in these two countries are often mistaken in their assumptions regarding the reliability of witnesses' accuracy of voice identification (Solan & Tiersma, 2003).

Processing Information for Voice Identification

What differences exist between speakers' voices that allow for identification? In spite of potential problems of speaker distortion arising from system effects (e.g., poor telephone transmission, background noise, etc.) and person effects (e.g., fear, anxiety, health problems, alcohol, intentional disguise, etc.), voice identification is possible, given certain factors. Identification is facilitated by relatively long speech samples showing an overall consistency in pitch, habits, and other distinctive characteristics in the total configuration of sound factors (Ladefoged & Ladefoged, 1980). Even with relatively short speech samples, the greater the variety in speech sounds, the better the subsequent identification (Roebuck & Wilding, 1993). Speaker identification is facilitated when listeners use a pool of voice parameters from which they select subsets for auditory recognition, such as pitch level, pitch patterns and variability, vocal intensity patterns, dialect, articulation, general voice and speech quality, and prosody (the timing and/or melody of speech) (Hollien, 2002). If one parameter lacks usefulness, recognition and identification can still occur if one or more parameters are sufficiently distinctive. It is unlikely that a sole characteristic determines identification of an individual from all other speakers; besides, the critical parameters are not the same for all speakers (Lavner, Gath, & Rosenhouse, 2000; van Lancker, Kreiman, & Emmorey, 1985a; van Lancker, Kreiman, & Wickens, 1985b). Listeners use a variety of different types of problem-solving strategies to recognize and identify both familiar and unfamiliar speakers. There is no single way and no unique characteristic that ensures accurate aural-perceptual voice identification (Hanley, Smith, & Hadfield, 1998; Hanley & Turner, 2000; Yarmey, 1995b).

Because of everyday experiences in listening and learning to distinguish between the voices of family, friends, and acquaintances, people often believe that speaker identification is routine and highly accurate (*Regina v. Morin*, 1995; Yarmey et al., 2001).Under ideal conditions many familiar and unfamiliar speakers can be recognized and distinguished relatively accurately by their voice because of *between-speaker* or *inter-speaker variation* (Rose, 2002). That is, because of physiological differences in the structure of speech mechanisms and use of the voice tract, as well as the influence of geographical, educational, and socioeconomic factors, different speakers have different-sounding voices. However, it is also the case that *within-speaker* or *intra-speaker variations* exist. A particular speaker rarely pronounces a given word or phrase in an identical way on different occasions, even if the second utterance is produced in succession (Hollien, 1990). Some speakers sound differently from time to time because of within-speaker changes in intentions, mood states, emotion and stress, thought distractions, situational demands, and changes in health and physical status.

Witnesses asked to identify a speaker from a voice lineup will always have to deal with between-speaker differences and within-speaker differences. Even if the perpetrator is in a lineup, he or she may sound differently in spite of the fact that the words spoken during the crime are repeated in the lineup. Given these considerations, the criminal justice system must operate on the belief that a witness's voice identification will be based on larger between-speaker variations (foils vs. suspect) than within-speaker variations (suspect's voice on different occasions).

CHARACTERISTICS OF THE WITNESSES
AND SUSPECTS IN SPEAKER IDENTIFICATION

Individual Differences

Apart from a few studies on the effects of age and gender, there is an absence of empirical research on the influence of individual differences, especially personality and intelligence, and their effects on voice identification. Studies on individual differences need to be done because of the possible light they may shed on such important issues as susceptibility to accepting suggestions and earwitness accuracy (see Schooler & Loftus, 1993; Tomes & Katz, 1997), as well as individual differences in source monitoring (e.g., did I hear that speaker, or did I just imagine hearing him speak? Johnson, Hashtroudi, & Lindsay, 1993). Suggestion has been shown to be capable of evoking false auditory memories. Vernon and Nelson (2000) presented participants with a short film followed by a series of questions that included a question about what the principal person had said in a particular situation, when in fact he had not spoken in that context. Twenty-three of 30 participants recalled hearing him speak and specifically recalled a suggested statement.

> ***Developmental Differences in Voice Recognition.*** Child development studies indicate that voice recognition is present soon after birth (e.g., DeCasper & Fifer, 1980; DeCasper & Prescott, 1984). Newborn infants prefer their mothers' voices over unfamiliar female voices and can discriminate familiar whispered voices from unfamiliar whispered voices (Spence & Freeman, 1996). Identification of familiar voices in nursery school children, although inferior to that of adults, is significantly better than chance (Bartholomeus, 1973; Murray & Cort, 1971). Children between the ages of 6 and 9 are equivalent to the performance of adult listeners in gender classification of adult speakers (Bennett & Montero-Diaz, 1982). Voice identification significantly improves between the ages of 6 and 10 for recently learned unfamiliar voices, and the ability of some 10-year-olds is equivalent to that of adults (Mann, Diamond, & Carey, 1979). Children as young as 3 years recognize familiar cartoon characters' voices significantly better than chance, although they perform significantly more poorly than 4- and 5-year-olds. Furthermore, all children are more accurate at identifying more familiar than they are at identifying less familiar voices (Spence, Rollins, & Jerger, 2002). These results indicate that characteristics of a speaker's voice and identity are stored in long-term memory at a very young age. It should be noted, however, that some children with disabilities, such as autism, are impaired in recognizing and identifying familiar voices and are impaired in voice-face matching tasks (Boucher, Lewis, & Collis, 1998).
>
> Unfortunately, little attention has been given to the examination of children's ability to identify speakers in forensic-type situations. In a field experiment involving children between 3 and 8 years of age after a visit to the dentist, Peters (1987) found poor performance and no significant differences in lineup identifications for target voices. Children and adults have been shown to be equally poor at voice lineup identification (Clifford, 1997; Clifford & Toplis, 1996). Young children aged 5–6 years are highly suggestible in voice identification. Although instructed that the target voice may or may

not be present, young children make a high number of false alarms in target absent line-ups. False positives in voice identification decrease with increasing age of witnesses (Clifford & Toplis, 1996). Comparisons of young adults with middle-aged adults indicate that listeners between the ages of 21 and 40 are superior in speaker identification to those over age 40 (Bull & Clifford, 1984).

Older Adults. Elders, in comparison to young adults, have a deficit in remembering the source of specific vocal information. Older adults have been found to confuse words they actually said from words they imagined saying, and words one person said from words another person said (Hashtroudi, Johnson, & Chrosniak, 1989). When older adults listen to two speakers and have to decide later who said what, and are engaged in multitask processing, they are less likely to differentiate the source of their information (Johnson, De Leonardis, Hashtroudi, & Ferguson, 1995). Because hearing loss is common with advanced age, especially for high-frequency sounds, it would be expected that voice identification would show a steady decline with increasing age (Yarmey, 2000). Research on the elder earwitness is needed, with special attention given to the differences between young-old, medium-old, and old-old participants.

Gender Differences. Several investigations have failed to find gender differences in speaker identification for either familiar or unfamiliar voices (e.g., Thompson 1985; van Lancker et al., 1985a, 1985b; Yarmey, 1986; Yarmey & Matthys, 1992; Yarmey et al., 2001). However, Roebuck and Wilding (1993) found women to be superior to men, but only in identification of female speakers. Similarly, Wilding and Cook (2000) found no significant differences for men in the recognition of male and female voices, but women were significantly better at recognizing female than at recognizing male voices.

Blind Listeners

Visually handicapped witnesses have given earwitness testimony in court (*State v. Ferris*, 1982). It could be assumed that individuals who lack eyesight compensate by having enhanced hearing performance, including superior performance in speaker identification. Studies have shown that the blind are superior to the sighted in sound localization, the ability to identify very short intervals between two consecutive noise bursts, and speech discrimination (Muchnik, Efrati, Nemeth, Malin, & Hildesscheimer, 1991). Similarly, the blind have been shown to be superior to the sighted in identifying speech at low sound levels, particularly in the presence of competing environmental noise (Niemeyer & Starlinger, 1981). However, these superior auditory functions have not been shown to differentially facilitate sound recognition or speaker identification.

Cobb, Lawrence, and Nelson (1979) found no significant differences in sound recognition between congenitally blind participants (77% accurate) and sighted individuals (78%) on a test for 194 naturalistic sounds after a 7-day retention period. Winograd, Kerr, and Spence (1984) presented blind and sighted adults with 20 unfamiliar voices and 7 seconds later gave a recognition memory test for the 20 original voices mixed with 20 new speakers. No significant differences were found.

In contrast, in a more forensically relevant experiment, Bull, Rathborn, and Clifford (1983) presented blind and sighted participants with a single phrase, "I'll meet you outside the National Westminister Bank at six o'clock tonight," followed 5 seconds later with a voice lineup of several speakers, all repeating the same originally presented phrase. Participants were told the target's voice was in the lineup. Participants were given six trials, with a different target and different foils used in each trial. Blind participants were superior to sighted individuals, but there were no significant differences within the blind participants as a function of degree of blindness. (e.g., totally blind, blind with perception of light, blind with residual sight, and blind with goodish sight). More recently, Elaad, Segev, and Tobin (1998) conducted a staged experiment testing the accuracy of voice identification by three groups of participants: voice identification experts, totally blind individuals, and a group of sighted listeners involved in a mock theft. In contrast to the Bull et al. (1984) experiment, participants were told that the target may or may not be present in the lineup. Experts were significantly better at identification than the other two groups, which did not differ significantly from each other. However, the blind indicated significantly less confidence than the sighted in the accuracy of their decisions. Elaad et al. concluded that although the blind may be superior to the sighted on some auditory tasks, this does not include an enhanced sensitivity to speaker identification.

In summary, blind individuals may be superior to sighted individuals in sound localization and speech discrimination but do not appear to be superior in voice identification lineups in which proper lineup instructions are given (e.g., "The target may or may not be present in the lineup").

Confidence-Accuracy Correlations

Jurors' perceptions of eyewitness evidence (and presumably earwitness evidence) are influenced by witnesses' confidence in their judgments of identification; however, witness confidence levels are highly malleable (Devenport, Studebaker, & Penrod, 1999; Wells, Ferguson, & Lindsay, 1981). Confidence-accuracy correlations in most studies on voice identification for unfamiliar speakers are nonsignificant or are relatively low (e.g., Procter, 2002, $r = .26$; Saslove &Yarmey, 1980, $r = .26$).

Confidence-accuracy correlations of voice identification are moderated by conditions present during observation, such as voice-sample durations, tone and quality of the speaker's voice, and the familiarity of the speaker's voice. For instance, Yarmey and Matthys (1992) found a significant negative confidence-accuracy relationship with short voice-sample durations (18 seconds). In contrast, no reliable relationships (with one exception) were found for slightly longer durations (36 seconds). For relatively long voice-sample durations of 120 seconds and 6 minutes, significant positive correlations were found. Note that although these confidence-accuracy relationships were statistically significant, they were not high ($r < .50$ in each case). Orchard and Yarmey (1995) found that voice distinctiveness yielded significant negative confidence-accuracy correlations. That is, the more confident participants were in the accuracy of their identifications with speakers who had distinctive voices, the less correct they were on both target-present and target-absent lineups. In contrast, the confidence-accuracy relationships for non-distinctive voices were not significant on either type of lineup. Participants who heard the perpetrator whisper in contrast to speaking in a normal tone of voice during the commission of the crime also showed significantly different confidence-accuracy correlations. Significant confidence-accuracy correlations were found in the target-absent lineup for targets who spoke in a normal tone of voice during the commission of a crime and were tested with a normal tone voice lineup. In contrast, no significant confidence-accuracy correlations were found for targets who whispered during the crime and were tested with a whisper on the voice lineups. Yarmey (1986) has also shown that the amount of illumination available during the commission of a crime (daylight, start of twilight, end of twilight, and darkness) has no significant effect on either accuracy of voice identification or reported confidence in judgments.

More recently, Olsson et al. (1998) showed that identification for unfamiliar voices is typically made with overconfidence; accuracy is often low; and there is little relationship between confidence and accuracy. Similarly, Yarmey (2003a) found that earwitnesses were significantly more confident in the accuracy of their lineup identifications when (1) they knew at the time of encoding that they would be tested for speaker identification as opposed to not being prepared for an identification test; (2) they spoke to the target over the telephone and subsequently were given a voice lineup over the telephone, in contrast to witnesses who interacted with the target in field situations; and (3) they were given a one-person showup rather than a six-person lineup. With one exception, the confidence-accuracy correlations across the different conditions were not significant.

Research is needed to determine whether there is a relationship between confidence and accuracy of identification as a function of those witnesses who choose a voice from a lineup versus those witnesses who do not pick a voice from the lineup (see Sporer, Penrod, Read, & Cutler, 1995). It is probable that confidence-accuracy relationships are low (positive or negative) in most studies or not significant because of "floor effects." That is, accuracy of identification (hits) for unfamiliar speakers is typically low, and false-alarm rates in target-absent lineups usually exceed the hit rate across most research studies. Participants, however, are just as confident in their selections on the target-absent lineup as they are in their decisions on the target-present lineup.

It may be concluded that witnesses' confidence in their identification decisions for unfamiliar speakers are not reliable predictors of accuracy of identification. However, Yarmey et al. (2001) found significant confidence-accuracy correlations for witnesses who were highly familiar (family members, best friends) with a speaker's normal tone of voice, in contrast to speakers who were only moderately familiar (co-worker, teammate) or unfamiliar (stranger). Confidence-accuracy correlations as a function of voice familiarity were not significant when the speaker whispered his or her utterances.

Witness Descriptions

According to the Supreme Court of the United States, the more accurate the original descriptions of a suspect, the greater the likelihood of identification accuracy (*Neil v. Biggers*, 1972). Studies by Yarmey (2001a, 2003a) show that participants in face-to-face field situations and in telephone-transmitted speech situations describe only four or five voice characteristics of the target in spite of being repeatedly prompted to remember additional characteristics (see also Künzel, 1994). Most witnesses tend to describe specific characteristics, that is, pitch, enunciation, and tone of voice, in their free recall. Other characteristics, such as rate of speech, rate variation, tremor, expressive style, pauses, and nasality, are seldom mentioned by witnesses.

Contrary to the beliefs of the U.S. Supreme Court (*Neil v. Biggers*, 1972), accuracy of voice identification has not been found to be related to witnesses' completeness of descriptions of voice characteristics, or accuracy in recall of what was said by the perpetrator during the crime, or recall of specific words stated during the crime (Yarmey, 2001a). Furthermore, accuracy of identification, although significantly better than chance, does not differ as a function of the lineup containing only phrases taken from the crime versus a lineup consisting of nonidentical phrases. These results support Hammersley and Read's (1996) recommendation that lineups should not reproduce what the perpetrator allegedly said. Accuracy of identification is significantly superior, however, if the witness participates in a conversation with the target person, in contrast to simply overhearing the target's voice (Nolan & Grabe, 1996). Hammersley and Read (1985) found recognition to be three times better for a conversational partner than for an overheard voice.

Witness descriptions (ratings) of characteristics of distinctive voices are superior, however, to descriptions of nondistinctive voices (Yarmey, 1991a). Whereas ratings of distinctive voices were found to be reliable over a 1-week retention period, ratings of characteristics of nondistinctive voices were inconsistent over a 24-hour retention interval. Randomly selected distinctive and nondistinctive voices chosen from the general community vary considerably from each other in voice quality (see also Aiken, Jamieson, & Parsa, 1999; Kreiman, Gerratt, Precoda, & Berke, 1992). However, Yarmey (1994) found that ratings made by undergraduate and graduate students of the voices of five police officers who served as foils in a real-life lineup in California were similar to each other on a number of characteristics and differed significantly from ratings made of the suspect's voice.

Speech-language clinicians, in contrast to naive listeners, attend to different aspects of voice quality when judging the similarity of voices for both normal and pathological voices (Kreiman, Gerratt, & Precoda, 1990). This suggests that when police choose foils for voice lineups they should be aware that not all witnesses' descriptions of voice characteristics upon which the lineup may be constructed will be as reliable as others. Furthermore, police must be sensitive to the variability among voice characteristics across individuals who may have either distinctive or nondistinctive voices and to the variability among police officers who must listen to the suspect's voice and select matching foils. Police may wish to involve the expertise of speech-language clinicians or phonetic experts in their selection of foils in the construction of voice lineups. Clearly, witness descriptions of voices must be treated with utmost caution.

Verbal Overshadowing Effect

It is possible that witnesses' descriptions of a perpetrator's voice can impair subsequent speaker identification accuracy (the verbal overshadowing effect). Perfect, Hunt, and

Harris (2002) found significantly poorer identification (24% correct) compared with a control condition (50% correct) when lineups were administered soon after witnesses gave verbal descriptions of a target's voice. However, studies by Carlucci and Meissner (2003) and Clifford (2003) failed to find a verbal overshadowing effect. The differences in the results among these three experiments are probably accounted for by differences in the research designs employed, such as the types of instructions given to participants, the length of the retention interval between participants' verbal descriptions of the target and the presentation of the voice lineup, and the types of research participants used. The verbal overshadowing effect needs further investigation.

Naive Witnesses versus Phonetic Experts

Most crimes associated with earwitness evidence involve ordinary citizens who do not have professional training in phonetics. It is possible, however, that experts on occasion could be earwitnesses to a crime. Trained experts in phonetics have been found to be superior to naive listeners in aural-perceptual speaker identification (Elaad et al., 1998; Schiller & Köster, 1998). In addition, people who have musical talents or professional training in singing have been shown to be superior to their nonmusical counterparts in speaker recognition (Köster, Hess, Schiller, & Künzel, 1998). Differences in expertness might make these individuals more credible witnesses than laypeople, given both types of witnesses and the same observational conditions in a criminal event.

Research has also shown that there are differences within expert forensic phoneticians themselves in their ability to identify voices. Not all experts are as accurate in speaker identification as other experts (Köster et al., 1998). As a consequence, triers of fact could be faced with the problem of determining the weight of testimony from opposing phoneticians. In contrast, there is no evidence to show that police officers are experts in voice identification or that their training makes them superior to naive listeners. However, the courts often make the assumption that police who briefly hear a voice are credible witnesses (Solan & Tiersma, 2003).

Ethnicity and Other-Race and Accented Voices

How likely is it that witnesses can accurately recognize the ethnicity/race of someone just by hearing their voice? Is the own-race bias that is found in facial identification (i.e., people are better at recognition of faces of people of their own race than those of other races; see Meissner & Brigham, 2001) also found in voice recognition?

Research by Lass, Mertz, and Kimmel (1978) confirmed several earlier studies that white listeners are capable of accurately judging race (white, black) and sex identification from recorded speech samples. More recent research shows that speakers' ethnicity is judged by American listeners through nonstandard dialect or racial speech cues. Furthermore, very small amounts of speech (the single word *hello* suffices) are needed to discriminate between dialects of African American Vernacular English, Chicano English, and Standard American English (Purnell, Idsardi, & Baugh, 1999). These empirical findings are inconsistent with the deductions of defense attorney Johnnie Cochran, the lead lawyer for the 1995 murder trial of O. J. Simpson (*People of the State of California v.*

Orenthal James Simpson, 1995). Cochran objected to a question put by prosecutor Christopher Darden to a witness: "The second voice that you heard sounded like the voice of a black man; is that correct?" Cochran's objection that basing racial identification on speech was racist and should not be allowed in court was overruled by the trial judge (Baugh, 2000). The Supreme Court of Kentucky also has affirmed the legality of judged racial identity from speech by a lay witness (*Clifford v. Kentucky*, 1999).

Nevertheless, judging racial identity from heard speech is not always straightforward. Research conducted in Wales shows that most (80%) third-generation black immigrants from the West Indies are misidentified as white speakers of the same socioeconomic background (Giles & Bourhis, 1982). The differences between this study and studies conducted in the United States suggest that accents differ as a function of factors other than simply race/ethnicity. Circumstances such as socioeconomic factors, education, historical and political groupings over time, and geographical regions of various sizes all may play a role in affecting accents. In addition, the validity of judged racial identity from heard speech depends upon the use of fair and proper testing procedures.

Studies on own-race/ethnicity versus other-race/ethnicity speaker identification are now starting to show some consistency in findings. One of the first investigations to examine this issue was conducted by Goldstein, Knight, Bailis, and Conover (1981). Listeners (African American and white) were asked to identify speakers with and without foreign accents soon after hearing them speak. No significant differences were found. In contrast, Thompson (1987) found that monolingual English-speaking listeners were superior in identification of bilingual targets' voices after a 1-week retention interval on spoken English, followed by English spoken with a heavy Spanish accent, and poorest speaking in Spanish. These results were replicated by Goggin, Thompson, Strube, and Simental (1991), who found that voice identification improved by nearly 200% when the listener was familiar with the language, in contrast to when statements were spoken in a foreign language (see also Doty, 1998; Hollien, Majewski, & Doherty, 1982; Köster & Schiller, 1997; Köster, Schiller, & Künzel, 1995; Schiller & Köster, 1996).

It may be concluded that just as there is an own-race bias effect in face identification, there is a consistent own-race/ethnicity speaker identification effect.

Emotional Arousal/Stress of the Perpetrator and the Victim

The effects of emotionality/stress on earwitness memory have received little attention from researchers. Perpetrators often experience stress, anger, and anxiety, which will be reflected in various speech characteristics, such as speaking rate, duration, and number of speech bursts (Hollien, Saletto, & Miller, 1993). Construction of voice lineups seldom captures the tone of voice used by perpetrators during the commission of crimes. If a suspect is heard yelling in a loud, angry tone of voice during a crime, accuracy of lineup identification is significantly poorer if witnesses are given voices of suspects speaking in normal conversational tones of speech than if they were tested with loud, angry voices (Saslove & Yarmey, 1980). Solan and Tiersma (2003) report a New Jersey case in which a rapist was very calm and soft-spoken while committing the assault. Later when the victim was confronted with a voice through an open door at the police station, she failed to make a positive identification when the man was speaking in an angry and abusive tone. However, when he calmed down and spoke in a normal tone of voice, the victim claimed to recognize his voice immediately (New Jersey Superior Court, 1976). The emotional state and emotional tone of voice of the speaker are not given much consideration as such by the courts (Solan & Tiersma, 2003).

Victims/witnesses of crime also may experience heightened or even traumatizing levels of emotional arousal or stress, which may be expected to influence attention, memory, and verbal reports (Christianson, 1992). However, the emotional arousal or stress of a victim may or may not interfere with speaker identification. At the present time, there is no research on this topic. The effects of different types of stress on speaker identification need to be explored (see Yuille & Daylen, 1998).

Weapon Focus Effect

One variable that may or may not be related to emotional arousal, but is related to witness interest or saliency of attention, is the weapon focus effect, that is, the hypothesis that the presence of a weapon held by a perpetrator during the commission of a crime interferes with an eyewitness's ability to later identify the perpetrator. Although this effect has been found with facial identification (Steblay, 1992), only one published study has investigated whether it negatively affects speaker identification (Pickel, French, & Betts, 2003). Participants viewed a videotaped crime showing a man holding a weapon or a neutral object while speaking to a female employee of a bar and grill. Results showed that the presence of the weapon failed to affect the accuracy of voice identification or memory for the target's voice characteristics. However, people participating in the presence of the weapon were less able to recall the semantic content for difficult-to-comprehend communications in contrast to less difficult speech materials. The failure to find a weapon focus effect on voice identification supports the unpublished findings of Yarmey and Pauley (see Yarmey, 1995b).

Witness Preparation

Witnesses to crimes sometimes are aware of the incident and prepare themselves to remember the perpetrator to the best of their ability. In contrast, other witnesses may not know that a crime is occurring and do not give special attention to the perpetrator. Witness preparation has been found to significantly facilitate accuracy of speaker identification (Armstrong & McKelvie, 1996; Saslove & Yarmey, 1980; but also see Perfect et al., 2002, who found no differences between prepared and nonprepared witnesses). Saslove and Yarmey (1980) also showed that some voices are so distinctive that they are readily identified without preparation. More recently, Yarmey (2003a) found that prepared witnesses in contrast to nonprepared witnesses asked to freely describe a target's voice paid particular attention to the pitch, quality of enunciation, and tone of voice. These results were consistent for witnesses in two different contexts, that is, telephone-transmitted speech and face-to-face field conditions. Witnesses gave few descriptions of voice characteristics (M = 4.77, SD = 4.38), and accuracy of identification was low both in line-ups (M = 27%) and showups (M = 28%). However, prepared witnesses were significantly more accurate than nonprepared witnesses in their identifications.

Although several studies suggest that restoring the context of the original event does not influence earwitness identification (Cook & Wilding, 1997a; Kerstholt, Jansen, Van Amelsvoort, & Broeders, 2004; Memon & Yarmey, 1999), further research should investigate whether context reinstatement procedures would differentially facilitate the recall and identification performance of prepared witnesses in contrast to unprepared witnesses.

Speaker Familiarity

When people talk with friends, relatives, and fellow workers (Bricker & Pruzansky, 1966; Schmidt-Nielsen & Stern, 1985), or when listeners hear familiar public persons such as politicians and movie/television celebrities (Meudell, Northen, Snowden, & Neary, 1980), identification is facilitated by the use of private forms of greetings, pet expressions, nicknames, stereotypical phrases, and other contextual information. Familiar voices consist of relatively unique dimensional patterns; however, perceptions of these patterns may change as a function of changes in context and expectations (van Lancker et al., 1985a, b).

Several studies show near-perfect scores for recognition of familiar speakers (e.g., Abberton & Fourcin, 1978; Hollien et al., 1983; LaRiviere, 1972). In contrast, other researchers have found that familiarity of speakers is not a guarantee of voice identification (e.g., Bartholomeus, 1973; Clarke & Becker, 1969; Goldstein & Chance, 1985; Read & Craik, 1995). Misidentification of familiar persons can occur for many reasons, one of which is unconscious transference, a process that has been demonstrated in eyewitness identification (e.g., Ross, Ceci, Dunning, & Toglia, 1994). Unconscious transference and voice identification, such as the inability of a shopkeeper to distinguish between the voice of a familiar but innocent customer and a masked perpetrator heard at the scene of a crime, has yet to be empirically investigated.

Misidentification of a familiar speaker also can occur through witness expectations. Recognition of familiar persons often depends on the closed set of people likely to be encountered in particular settings. People tend to hear who they expect to hear. Thus, if observers (police) expect to hear a particular person answer a telephone, misidentification of a familiar speaker may occur if someone else actually answers the call (Ladefoged & Ladefoged, 1980).

To test the hypothesis that expectations affect the recognition of familiar voices, one study examined the ability of experienced phoneticians to identify the voices of highly familiar laboratory colleagues (Ladefoged, 1978). Given two unfamiliar African American speakers among a larger set of white speakers, 5 out of 10 experts misidentified the speakers as one of the two familiar African Americans who worked in their laboratory.

In another study, and using himself as the sole subject, P. Ladefoged recognized 9 out of 29 familiar voices (31% accuracy) on hearing the word *hello*, recognized 66% from a single sentence, and recognized 83% from 30 seconds of continuous speech. Ladefoged did not recognize his own mother's voice both when she said *hello* and when she spoke a single sentence, but recognized her from a 30-second passage (Ladefoged & Ladefoged, 1980). These results were supported by Goldstein and Chance (1985) in a study involving 20 listeners who attempted to discriminate the voices of 9 very familiar friends from 11 unfamiliar speakers. Speakers were tape-recorded uttering the same seven short messages. Only 12 of the listeners recognized all 9 familiar voices. In contrast, only one listener correctly rejected 9 of the 11 unfamiliar voices as strangers. Six of the 11 unfamiliar foils could not be distinguished from members of the familiar group.

Recognition of familiar voices from a close-knit network of speakers (university students who have lived together in residence with each other for 2 years) shows wide differences across speakers (Foulkes & Barron, 2000). Some familiar speakers are readily identified, whereas others are consistently misidentified. One listener was found to misidentify his own voice, and strangers were misidentified as network members. Speakers with the most distinctive regional accents and other idiosyncratic feature were easiest to identify, as were speakers with high and low pitch values. In contrast, speakers with average pitch values were the most difficult to identify.

Rose and Duncan (1995) found an 85% accuracy rate in the identification of highly familiar voices and a 30% false-alarm rate for strangers' voices after listening to taped 45-second voice samples. Similarly, Yarmey et al. (2001) found significant differences in speaker identification for familiar voices as a function of different levels of familiarity (i.e., high familiar: an immediate family member or best friend; moderate familiar: a co-worker, teammate, or general friend; and low familiar: a casual acquaintance, such as a next-door neighbor). In one of two experiments 85% of high familiar speakers were correctly identified, with 5% false identifications and 10% misses. For moderate familiar speakers 79% were identified, with 13% false identifications and 8% misses. For low familiar speakers 49% were identified, with 23% false identifications and 28% misses. And finally, 55% of strangers were correctly rejected, but 45% were falsely identified as a familiar person. Both high familiar and moderate familiar voices were more readily identified than low familiar and unfamiliar voices. A separate group of participants (potential jurors) asked to predict the percentage correct performance for each of these groups stated that 99%, 96%, 89%, and 84% of listeners would be correct for each of the respective conditions. These results, along with those of Rose and Duncan (1995), suggest that a 15% error rate in identification may be expected with very familiar speakers.

The second experiment of Yarmey et al. (2001) confirmed the results of the first experiment but, in addition, showed that when speakers whispered, only 77% of high familiar speakers were correctly identified (91% were predicted to be accurate), 35% moderate familiar were identified (81% predicted), 22% low familiar were identified (86% predicted), and 20% unfamiliar voices were correctly rejected (74% predicted). Forty percent of the unfamiliar speakers were falsely identified as a familiar person. It is apparent that whispered voices do not lead to high identification rates and that potential jurors vastly overestimate the accuracy of identification with both normal tone and whispered voices. Laypeople are also highly unrealistic in their commonsense predictions of the accuracy of speaker identifications of unfamiliar voices from both showups and lineups; that is, voice identifications are significantly overestimated (Yarmey, 1995b).

It may be concluded that with normal tones of speech, speaker identification is relatively accurate only with the most familiar voices (5% false identification rate and 10% "don't knows"). False identification rates increase as voice familiarity decreases. Most troubling for the courts is the finding of exceedingly high false identifications (45%) for the voices of strangers, even though participants were permitted to state they did not know. Also troubling is the fact that the laypeople in these two experiments, all of whom were potential jurors, have an unrealistic sense of the difficulties in the identification of moderate familiar and less familiar speakers with normal tones of speech, let alone with whispers.

Voice Disguise

In order to avoid detection, Brazilian kidnappers reportedly place a pencil between their front teeth and under the tongue to disguise their ransom demands (de Figueiredo & de Souza Britto, 1996). A whispered voice is an effective disguise because it conceals the most salient vocal characteristics, such as pitch, inflection, and intonation (Reich & Duke, 1979). Whispered voices are significantly more difficult to identify than normal-tone voices, regardless of the duration of the voice sample (30 seconds or 8 minutes) (Orchard & Yarmey, 1995). Even presenting whispered speech over three spaced exposures as opposed to a single massed presentation does not improve recognition performance, in contrast to normal-tone voices (Procter & Yarmey, 2003). Allowing research participants to freely disguise their voices, except for "foreign dialects" or whispers, also impairs recognition performance (Hollien et al., 1982). Most people are able to consistently change their pitch in order to create a preferred disguise. Speakers with a higher-than-average pitch tend to increase their pitch levels, whereas those with a lower-than-average pitch prefer to disguise their voices by lowering their pitch (Künzel, 2000; see also Manning, Fucci, & Dean, 2000)). Intoxication also is known to shift most voices to a higher level of pitch (Hollien & Martin, 1996). Speaking tempo, pauses, and hesitations in speech all change as a function of higher levels of alcohol intoxication (Künzel, Braun, & Eysholdt, 1992). Imitation is another form of disguise. A Swedish study showed that most witnesses asked to identify the voice of a highly familiar politician who was present in a lineup accompanied by the voice of an impersonator correctly selected the politician. However, in a target-absent lineup, which included the voice of the impersonator but not the voice of the politician, most participants misidentified the impersonator's voice as the voice of the politician (Schichting & Sullivan, 1997). Clearly, disguise affects many of the acoustic features that allow for speaker identification. Perpetrators who wish to avoid identification through disguise unfortunately will often be successful.

Speakers' Appearance and Voice Cues

It is common for behavioral scientists and police agencies to study crime scenes, to interview witnesses, and to obtain all types of other evidence in order to construct a criminal profile of the type of person(s) who committed a particular crime. Given that kidnappers or terrorists may telephone their ransom demands or bomb threats, how effective would estimations of these callers' ages, heights, weights, occupational categories, and personality characteristics be, based only on hearing their voices?

Listeners are able to judge speaker age, height, and weight from speech samples significantly better than would be expected from chance. Krauss, Freyberg, and Morsella (2002), using randomly selected participants strolling in Central Park, New York City, as speakers and undergraduate students as judges found that estimations made from voice recordings of age, height, and weight significantly correlated with speakers' actual age, height, and weight (r's = .61, .54, and .55, respectively). The average absolute differences in age, height, and weight estimations were 7.11 years, 2.94 inches, and 25.59 lbs., respectively. These results suggest that there are (undetermined) voice cues that correlate with physical characteristics. Similarly, van Dommelen and Moxness (1995) found significant correlations between estimated height and weight and actual height and weight based on voice recordings. However, these correlations were found only for male speakers. Neither male nor female judges accurately estimated female speaker height or weight, and all of the judgments were underestimations. Unlike the results found by Krauss et al. (2002), the differences between men's and women's average estimates and actual speaker height and weight were marginal, which may reflect greater heterogeneity among strollers in a city park than in the heights and weights found among undergraduate students (see also Künzel, 1989; Yarmey, 1992).

Not all studies on age estimations, however, have been as accurate as that of Krauss et al. (2002). Cerrato, Falcone, and Paoloni, (2000) assessed listeners' ability to give reliable age estimations of unknown speakers by listening to their voices over the telephone. Listeners were asked to identify the speaker's age by choosing one of seven age groups: 18–24, 25–31, 32–38, 39–45, 46–52, 53–59, and 60–66. Listeners rarely were correct with young speakers and generally overestimated their age. Older speakers' ages were underestimated, particularly the 60–66-year age group, who were judged as 46–52-year-old speakers. The most accurate age estimation was for speakers in the 46–52-year age group. The overall percentage of correct answers was only 27%. Cerrato et al. (2000) recommend that age estimations be bound within general descriptions such as "young adult," "middle," and "older adult" age categories.

Stereotypes and Voice Characteristics

Judgments of speakers' physical characteristics can be confounded with stereotypes. Listeners given tape recordings of different speakers show high consensus of agreement on the speakers' personality traits, physical appearance, and profession, and these categorizations influence estimations of speakers' characteristics (Aronovitch, 1976; Yamada, Hakoda, Yuda, & Kusuhara, 2000; Yarmey, 1993). In addition, Yarmey (1993) showed that listeners were superior in voice recognition for stereotyped good guys (medical doctors, engineers, and clergyman) in contrast to bad guys (sexual assault felons, armed robbers, and mass murderers). Thus, stereotypes not only are elicited from judged voices;

they also can influence recognition memory for perceived criminal and noncriminal speakers.

Listeners stereotype voices on the basis of powerful or powerless styles (Erickson, Lind, Johnson, & O'Barr, 1978), pitch and loudness (Scherer, 1974), and attractiveness (Berry, 1990; Zuckerman & Driver, 1989). Each of these factors can contribute to witnesses' credibility and persuasiveness. Brimacombe, Quinton, Nance, and Garrioch (1997) demonstrated in an eyewitness memory experiment that when young adults judge the testimony of an older eyewitness, the speech of older eyewitnesses is perceived as noticeably weaker than that of younger eyewitnesses. In contrast to young adults, older eyewitnesses more often prefaced their statements with negative qualifiers (e.g., "I think," "I'm not sure, but"). High credibility in both young adults and older adults was associated with utterances containing very few negative qualifiers.

If jurors stereotype defendants and witnesses on the basis of voice characteristics, the concepts of fairness and due process could be violated (Lown, 1977; *Reynolds v. United States*, 1878). For example, Baldwin and French (1990) describe a British case in which a German with a very marked Bavarian accent was accused of fraud. The trial judge was concerned that the English jury would be prejudiced by listening to taped speech samples of the perpetrator. According to Baldwin and French (1990), in addition to being a German national, the defendant's "disposition and demeanor during the investigations and as heard on the admitted sample . . . seemed to embody every negative and unpleasant characteristics that could be associated with Germans in English eyes" (p. 15). The trial judge concluded that the jury could not listen to the taped speech samples in an objective way, and ruled the samples inadmissible. As a consequence, all charges against the accused were dropped.

SITUATIONAL FACTORS AFFECTING EARWITNESS MEMORY

Voice-Sample Durations

Voices can be recognized under optimal conditions with better than chance expectations with speech samples of 2 seconds or less (Bricker & Pruzansky, 1966). The longer the opportunity to listen to a speaker, the greater the accuracy of identification (Cook & Wilding, 1997b; Hammersley & Read, 1985; Orchard & Yarmey, 1995; Read & Craik, 1995; Yarmey, 1991b; Yarmey & Matthys, 1992). Note, in addition to differences in hit scores, the later two studies by Yarmey also showed that longer voice samples (18 seconds to 8 minutes) led to increased false-alarm rates. In contrast, Orchard and Yarmey (1995) did not find that false alarms increased with longer exposure durations. Similarly, Kerstholt et al. (2004) found that listeners made significantly fewer false identifications in a target-absent condition following a 1-week delay when the original voice sample was long (70 seconds) rather than short (30 seconds). Because of the inconsistent false-alarm rates across these four experiments, conclusions about mistaken identification as a function of voice-sample duration are not warranted at the present time.

Distributed Exposures of Speech Samples

Length of speech samples matters; however, this may be less important for purposes of identification than whether a speaker is heard over distributed exposures such as three separate exposures of 1 minute each, than one massed exposure of 3 minutes in total duration. Goldstein and Chance (1983) introduced listeners to a single massed presentation or three distributed exposures of a speaker's voice over three consecutive days. Distributed exposures significantly increased voice identification relative to the massed presentation. Yarmey and Matthys (1992) replicated these findings but found that only two distributed voice samples rather than three distributed samples were significantly better than a massed trial. Consistent with these findings, Procter and Yarmey (2003) also found that two but not three distributed exposures significantly improved identification performance relative to one massed trial. It is possible that after two distributed exposures attention to voice characteristics and effort is maximized, whereas a third exposure is redundant with a subsequent decrease in attention and effort (Dempster, 1996). As mentioned before, the identification of a disguised voice (whispers) was not improved by distributed exposures.

Duration Estimations

Although longer opportunities to listen to perpetrators may increase the credibility of voice identifications (*Neil v. Biggers*, 1972), knowledge of event durations usually is based on witnesses' estimations, and estimated duration of speech events has been shown to be error prone. Speech lasting between 15 seconds and 8 minutes is significantly overestimated, with women giving substantially greater overestimations than men (e.g., Yarmey et al., 1994; Orchard & Yarmey, 1995). For relatively long conversations of 20 minutes and 40 minutes involving face-to-face encounters between a witness and a researcher, two-thirds of the participants underestimated and the remainder overestimated the actual durations of the two timed events (Yarmey, 1990).

Retention Intervals

Several studies show that memory for an unfamiliar voice tends to decline over time (e.g., Clifford, Rathborn, & Bull, 1981; Papcun, Kreiman, & Davis, 1989). Voice identification has been found to decline over 1-week, 2-week, and 3-week delays in testing from 50% and 43% accuracy to 9% accuracy, respectively (Clifford, 1983). Similarly, Bull and Clifford (1984) found a significant reduction in voice identification after a 3-week delay but no significant difference between 1- and 2-week delays. In another study, Clifford (1980) found significant changes in performance from 41% to 19% accuracy over a range of retention intervals of 10 minutes, 24 hours, 7 days, and 14 days. Little loss in voice recognition is apparent over a 24-hour period (Legge, Grossman, & Pieper, 1984; Saslove & Yarmey, 1980; Yarmey, 1991b). Yarmey and Matthys (1992) found that correct identifications did not differ for voices tested over a 1-week period, but false alarms significantly increased over this period, especially for a perpetrator's voice initially heard with short (18 seconds and 38 seconds) exposure durations. In contrast, Hammersley and Read (1985) found that when a witness is involved in natural conversation with a target, recognition is not affected over retention intervals of between 2 and 14 days. Broeders and Rietveld (1995), in contrast to most studies, found little loss in identification performance over 3 weeks, with 84% accuracy after 1 week and 80% accuracy at 3 weeks.

Beyond stating that speaker identification will decline over time, the effects of delay on voice identification over a relatively short period (3 weeks or less) are difficult to predict because the effects depend upon a number of factors. That is, performance also depends on attention, differences in voice distinctiveness, ease of acquisition, the length of the original voice sample, changes in voice quality between the original observation and test, and so forth.

Multiple Perpetrators

Crimes involving multiple perpetrators should inhibit witnesses' memorial abilities because of cognitive interference. Legge et al. (1984), in a traditional laboratory experiment on memory for unfamiliar voices, found that recognition performance showed significant improvement as the number of voices to be learned decreased from 20 to 5. Similarly, Carterette and Barneby (1975) found a decline in recognition memory for voices as the number of voices increased with 2, 3, 4, or 8 target voices. No research has been conducted on the effects of multiple perpetrators on speaker identification in forensic-type situations.

Telephone-Transmitted Speech

Speaker identifications involving the use of the telephone may have particular problems to overcome, such as different distortions in transmission from different telephone lines. Degradations of the speech signal, particularly in the loss of high-frequency energy, are common because telephone lines typically transmit a band of frequencies between 300 and 3,400 Hertz, whereas human voices may contain components up to about 12,000 Hertz (Künzel, 1994; Pollack, Pickett, & Sumby, 1954). As a consequence, important dimensions needed for identification may be filtered out. Also, noisy backgrounds such as music or other voices heard at the same time can interfere with attention (Hollien 1990; Rose, 2002). Quite different speakers may sound very similar to each other when distortions occur in telephone-transmitted speech (Rothman, 1977).

The first forensically oriented study to investigate speaker recognition over the telephone was conducted by Rathborn, Bull, and Clifford (1981). Participants from the general public listened to one of four taped conditions: (1) target voices recorded on a tape and then tested with a tape-recorded message; (2) target voices recorded on a tape and then tested over the telephone; (3) target voices taped over the telephone and then tested from a tape recorder; and (4) target voices taped over the telephone and then tested over the telephone. Participants were tested with six-person target-present lineups immediately after hearing the target voices utter a 13-word sentence. Listeners were significantly better at recognizing the target voice from condition 1 than the other three conditions, which did not differ from each other. These results demonstrate that identification of a target voice heard originally from a tape recorder and tested with a tape recorder is significantly better than identification of voices involved with telephone transmissions because the context keeps voice quality consistent. Telephone lines introduce distortions or, perhaps, restrict energy frequencies that minimize recognition performance. However, these results also indicate that if a voice is heard over the telephone and tested over the telephone, accuracy of performance is equivalent to that in which participants originally heard the voice over the telephone and then were tested directly with a tape-recorded lineup. This suggests that police would not have to replicate the telephone-telephone conditions in order to find reliable results.

More recently, Yarmey (2003a) compared telephone transmitted speech with face-to-face speech in field situations. Because most of the findings of this study have already been described (see sections on Confidence, Witness Descriptions, and Witness Preparation), only a brief statement is needed here. Although speaker identification was significantly better than chance, no significant differences were found on target-present and target-absent showups or six-person lineups for telephone-transmitted speech and testing conducted *in situ*. Unlike the results of Rathborn et al. (1981), tape-recorded identification tests transmitted over the telephone did not distort speech relative to tape-recorded lineups given face to face. Künzel (1997) found that the only difference between face-to-face speech and telephone-transmitted speech is the greater frequency in telephone speech of filled pauses among the total number of pauses. Speakers use filled pauses to signal their intent to continue to speak, which in face-to-face communication is communicated by facial expressions or gestures. Yarmey's (2003a) findings have been supported by Perfect et al. (2002). Hearing a voice recorded through a telephone, in contrast to hearing it directly from a tape recorder, showed no significant differences in accuracy of identification, although less confidence was associated with the telephone voice. These results suggest that telephone recordings of voice lineups could be used for speaker identification without loss in accuracy of identification.

Finally, Yarmey (2003a) showed that witnesses were more than twice as likely to falsely identify the most similar-sounding foil in a target-absent showup condition than they were in a six-person target-absent lineup in both telephone-transmitted speech and face-to-face situations. Innocent suspects appear to be at risk in speaker identification when showups are conducted, regardless of the mode of speech.

INVESTIGATIVE PROCEDURES

Unlike witness/suspect factors and situational factors, system variables such as investigative interviews and the construction and administration of voice lineups are under the control of police. In 1967 the Supreme Court of the United States recognized that the lineup is a critical stage vis-à-vis the constitutionality of police practices and procedures in obtaining identifications (*United States v. Wade*, *Gilbert v. California*, and *Stovall v. Denno*). A word of caution, however, is appropriate here. An identification of a suspect from a voice lineup only suggests that the individual could be the perpetrator, as opposed to proving he/she definitely is the perpetrator (Hammersley & Read, 1996). The selection of a suspect may merely indicate that the chosen voice bears a strong resemblance to the voice of the perpetrator. Because voice identification is recognized to be a difficult task, a positive selection made with high confidence should always be supported by independent corroborative evidence. Similarly, failure to select a voice from a lineup does not prove that the perpetrator is not present. It may simply indicate that the witness made a false-negative response or miss, rather than a correct rejection of the lineup. The following section covers system variables that have been shown to influence speaker identification and will finish with a set of guidelines and recommendations for earwitness lineups.

Investigative Interviews and Earwitness Memory

Several investigative interview techniques of witness/victims and suspects are available, such as statement analysis, hypnosis, the cognitive interview, and the structured interview (Turtle & Watkins, 1999; Yarmey, 2001b). The cognitive interview, in particular, has received considerable attention from researchers and the police (Fisher & Geiselman, 1992). In contrast to the standard police interview, the cognitive interview elicits significantly more accurate and complete information with no demonstrable increase in errors or plausible guesses (Memon & Bull, 1991). Similarly, the structured interview, which emphasizes the social psychological components of communication, such as rapport building and interviewer social skills, offers another effective interview technique for eyewitness recall (Memon, Wark, Holley, Bull, & Koehnken, 1997). However, with the exception of a study by Memon and Yarmey (1999), no attention has been given to the interaction between different interview procedures and earwitness memory. A comparison between the cognitive interview and the structured interview failed to show that earwitness descriptions and earwitness identifications are differentially facilitated by these two interview strategies. Because witnesses' voice descriptions are so poor, research is needed to show whether one or more investigative interviewing techniques may best be used to facilitate witness/victims' voice recall.

Lineup Construction

A number of problems remain unresolved regarding the construction of voice lineups. In order to be fair to the suspect, his/her voice should not stand out in the lineup as being different from the foils based on the earwitness's earlier descriptions of his/her voice, or any other factors that would draw special attention to him/her. Even with relatively good recording conditions, a suspect's voice will appear salient if his/her voice sample is based on recordings of spontaneous speech and all of the foils are recorded reading these same words or phrases (Laubstein, 1997). Spontaneous speech is obtained by surreptitious recording of the suspect's voice and is typically edited and re-recorded by police for the voice lineup. [The laws of some countries prohibit the taking of surreptitious recordings, but this is not the case in the United States and Canada.] According to Laubstein, the splicing out of the suspect's voice can unintentionally produce perceived changes in pitch and loudness, such that the listener may erroneously conclude that a single voice is actually two voices. Similarly, read speech differs from spontaneous speech in terms of pitch, speech rate, speaking tempo, pauses, and hesitations (Künzel, 1997). As a consequence, differences in speech styles between the suspect and fillers may inadvertently be built into the lineup and could contribute to subsequent distortions of identification. In spite of potential distortion from within-speaker and between-speaker differences, it is recommended that the suspect and foils all read the same passage of materials, which should be long enough (approximately 60 seconds) to provide for a reasonable presentation of all phonetic and idiosyncratic speech characteristics. In addition, a second voice lineup containing spontaneous speech of the same length and fidelity of the suspect and foils could be recorded and provided to witnesses. The problem with these suggestions, however, is that multitask procedures would probably be considered inefficient and burdensome, resulting in a lack of support by the police. Recommended procedures for police practices should minimize complexity and be practical and specific enough not to lead to the conviction of an innocent person (Ormerod, 2001).

In contrast to lineups containing four or eight speakers, Bull and Clifford (1999) found that lineups of six speakers lead to the most accurate performance. As mentioned earlier, lineups need not be constructed with identical phrases remembered from the crime. Lineups containing identical phrases or words used by the offender have not been found to yield higher accuracy of identification (hits) or lower false identifications of innocent suspects than lineups containing nonidentical phrases (Yarmey, 2001a).

Lineup Identifications: Remember or Just Know

In order to explore the retrieval process involved in voice identification of an unfamiliar speaker, Procter and Yarmey (2003) asked participants who had selected a voice from a lineup to indicate whether they *remembered* the voice of the perpetrator, or if they simply *just knew* that the voice was the same (Tulving, 1985). Results showed that a "remembered" voice was more likely to be correct than a "just know" voice. However, this main effect was qualified by several interaction effects. "Remembered" voices were more accurately identified than "just know" voices when witnesses were given a single massed trial as opposed to two or three distributed exposures to the target's voice during the acquisition stage; when witnesses were given short (18 seconds) in contrast to long (6 minutes) voice-sample durations; and when the perpetrator whispered as opposed to speaking in a normal tone of voice. "Remembered" voices of unfamiliar speakers are probably recognized more correctly because processing involves feature analysis to a greater extent than pattern recognition. Pattern recognition is more likely to be the preferred processing strategy for identification of familiar speakers (see van Lancker et al., 1985a, b). However, "remember" versus "just know" retrieval strategies for the identification of familiar voices remains to be investigated. Further research is needed to explore the retrieval processes involved in voice identification for different variables such as race/ethnicity, showups versus multiple-person lineups, and so forth.

Single-Person (Showups) versus Many-Person Lineups

Single-person identifications usually occur shortly after the occurrence of a crime when the police find a person who matches the general description of the suspect. The victim/ witness may then be presented with a one-person in-field confrontation. Earwitness showups are relatively rare but do occur on occasion (see *Stovall v. Denno*, 1967). Only two studies have compared the accuracy of speaker identification of one-person and six-person lineups, and both were conducted in naturalistic field situations (Yarmey et al., 1994; Yarmey, 2003a). In both experiments accuracy of identification in showups (28% and 28%, respectively) and in six-person lineups (9% and 27%, respectively) was poor. Furthermore, both experiments showed that significantly more false identifications of the "innocent" suspect were found in the showup than in the lineup condition. As stated earlier, an innocent "sound-alike" suspect is at significantly more risk of being misidentified in a single-person confrontation than in a many-person voice lineup.

Earwitness Identification: Guidelines and Recommendations

In the last few years steps have been taken by the Department of Justice in the United States (Technical Working Group for Eyewitness Evidence, 1999), in Canada (Manitoba, 2001), and in England (Kebbel & Wagstaff, 1999) to provide guidelines to the police in their eyewitness lineup procedures (see also Yarmey, 2003b). These guidelines should prove to be invaluable for both eyewitness and earwitness identification evidence. For example, the different guidelines recommend that the police officer who conducts a lineup should have no knowledge of the case; the officer should advise the witness that it is just as important to clear the innocent as it is to identify the suspect; all proceedings should be videotaped; all witness statements must be recorded verbatim and signed by the witness in order to minimize the possibility of contamination of a witness by other police officers or other witnesses; each witness should be escorted from the police station when the lineup is completed; and police officers should not speak with witnesses following their lineup decisions regarding their identification or their inability to identify anyone.

In addition, several experts, such as Broeders and Rietveld (1995); Bull and Clifford, (1999); Hammersley and Read (1996); Hollien (1996, 2002); Hollien, Huntley, Künzel, and Hollien, (1995); and Ormerod (2001), have suggested criteria for voice lineups, and the following recommendations have benefited from their advice:

1. *Witnesses.* Witnesses must be questioned about their level of hearing; preferably they should be tested by an audiologist.
2. *Delay in testing.* Witnesses should be interviewed as early as possible after the criminal event in order to construct a voice/speech profile of the perpetrator. Voice lineups should be conducted as soon as possible following the arrest of a criminal suspect.

3. *Tape recordings.* A voice lineup should be presented on high-quality audio equipment rather than by live presentation. The suspect and all foils must be taped-recorded with the same equipment, with the use of a separate tape for each participant. Each tape recording should be a minimum of 30–60 seconds in duration (200 words or longer).

4. *Disguise.* Speakers should be tape-recorded while using the same tone of speech as used by the perpetrator during the commission of the crime.

5. *Reproduction of the words used by the perpetrator.* In order to prevent deliberate distortion of specific words or phrases by a (guilty) suspect at the time of recording, the lineup should not contain words or phrases spoken by the perpetrator during the crime.

6. *Voice samples.* If possible, spontaneous speech uttered by the suspect speaking in a natural voice for 10 to 15 minutes should be recorded. The suspect's speech should not come from a police interview. A selected neutral portion of a continuous unedited utterance of 30–60 seconds' duration should be used as the voice lineup test materials. All foils should be asked to give spontaneous speech of the same duration and on the same neutral theme as that given by the suspect. If the selection of the suspect's test materials involves splicing from a longer tape, the selection of test materials for the foils also should involve splicing from a longer tape. Foils should not be allowed to hear the suspect's voice prior to tape recording. If recordings of spontaneous speech are not possible, the suspect and the foils should be recorded reading the same elementary school-level materials.

7. *Selection of foils.* Foils should be selected who match the witness's free descriptions of the perpetrator's voice. If there is more than one witness, separate lineups should be constructed for each witness, based on each witness's unique speaker descriptions. Because the suspect's voice must not be salient in the voice lineup, the voices of foils and the suspect should be matched generally in perceived voice similarity (pitch, tone, articulation, etc.) and for variables such as age, sex, race/ethnicity, education, socioeconomic level, and geographic background. In the case of cross-racial or cross-ethnic identification, it is recommended that those persons selecting voices of foils be of the same race/ethnicity as the suspect, or that forensic phoneticians be consulted whenever possible.

8. *Lineup size.* It is recommended that the lineup consist of the suspect's voice and five foils.

9. *Conduction of the lineup.* Each voice tape should be randomly selected from a pool of tapes hidden from view, and the witness should not be told the total number of voice tapes to be presented. The witness should be told that different speakers are presented on each tape, and the perpetrator may or may not be present. Also, the witness should be instructed that a particular tape will be presented once and only once, but may be repeatedly played on request before his/her decision is given. All of the tapes in the voice lineup should be presented, even if an identification is made on one or more earlier tapes.

10. *Certainty.* The witness's degree of certainty (preferably as a statement of percentage certainty) following an identification must be recorded and signed by the witness.

11. *Confrontations.* Voice lineups should be used, rather that one-person (showup) confrontations.

12. *Familiarity.* Because speaker familiarity ranges from low to high, voice lineups should be conducted for both familiar suspects and unfamiliar suspects.

13. *Telephone.* A speaker heard originally over the telephone may be tested with a taped voice lineup rather than over the telephone.

14. *Test for "fairness" of the lineup.* Prior to the conduction of the lineup, the fairness of a lineup should be determined by a test of whether a group of naive listeners would select the suspect, or any particular foil, significantly more frequently than by chance.

15. *Eyewitness and earwitness lineups.* If both eyewitness identifications and earwitness identifications are to be made, visual identifications should be attempted first. Whereas visual identifications can be made either from a live lineup or from a photo lineup, speaker identifications should be made from tape recordings. To ensure "fairness" in both types of lineups, independent attention must be given to the selection of suitable foils for the visual lineup, followed by a selection of suitable foils for the voice lineup.

16. *Judges' instructions.* Trial judges must emphasize the frailities of earwitness identification to the jury and the fact that, if errors do happen, mistaken speaker identification is more likely to occur than mistaken visual identification.

IN CONCLUSION

This chapter has shown that accuracy of identification of unfamiliar speakers heard only once and for a relatively short period is less than 50%. Misidentification of unfamiliar speakers is common and often exceeds the accuracy of identification in experimental research. Although familiar speakers are more likely to be correctly identified than strangers, misidentification of high and moderate familiar speakers can occur. Because earwitness memory is highly error-prone, prosecutors and trial judges should be very cautious in trying and hearing cases based solely on speaker identification evidence. Nevertheless, speaker identification is possible, and, if it is used as evidence, proper and fair pretrial procedures must be followed in the construction and administration of voice lineups. Mistaken speaker identification and mistaken facial identification are two of the greatest causes of actual or possible wrongful convictions.

ACKNOWLEDGMENTS

This research was supported by grant no. 410-2001-0010 from the Social Sciences and Humanities Research Council of Canada.

REFERENCES

Abberton, E., & Fourcin, A. (1978). Intonation and speaker identification. *Language and Speech, 21*, 305–318.

Aiken, S. J., Jamieson, D. G., & Parsa, V. (1999). Behavioural speaker identification: A forensic application. *Canadian Acoustics, 27*, 3–9.

Armstrong, H. A., & McKelvie, S. J. (1996). Effect of face context on recognition memory for voices. *Journal of General Psychology, 123*, 259–270.

Aronovitch, C. (1976). The voice of personality: Stereotyped judgments and their relation to voice quality and sex of speaker. *Journal of Social Psychology, 99*, 207–220.

Baldwin, J., & French, P. (1990). *Forensic phonetics*. London: Pinter.

Bartholomeus, B. (1973). Voice identification by nursery school children. *Canadian Journal of Psychology, 27*, 464–472.

Baugh, J. (2000). Racial identification by speech. *American Speech, 75*, 362–364.

Bennett, S., & Montero-Diaz, L. (1982). Children's perception of speaker sex. *Journal of Phonetics, 10*, 113–121.

Berry, D. S. (1990). Vocal attractiveness and vocal babyishness: Effects on stranger, self, and friend impressions. *Journal of Nonverbal Behavior, 14*, 141–153.

Bonastre, J.-F., Bimbot, F., Boë, L.-J., Campbell, J. P., Reynolds, D. A., & Magrin-Chagnolleau, I. (2003). Person authentication by voice: A need for caution. Available at http://www.acp-parole.org/doc/AFCP_Sp1C_HotTopicsEurospeech03_final.pdf

Boucher, J., Lewis, V., & Collis, G. (1998). Familiar face and voice matching and recognition in children with autism. *Journal of Child Psychology and Psychiatry, 39*, 171–181.

Bricker, P. D., & Pruzansky, S. (1966). Effects of stimulus content and duration on talker identification. *Journal of the Acoustical Society of America, 40*, 1441–1449.

Brimacombe, C. A. E., Quinton, N., Nance, N., & Garrioch, L. (1997). Is age irrelevant? Perceptions of young and old adult eyewitnesses. *Law and Human Behavior, 21*, 619–634.

Broeders, T., & Rietveld, T. (1995). Speaker identification by earwitnesses. In A. Braun & J.-P. Köster (Eds.), *Studies in forensic phonetics* (pp. 1–11). Trier: Wissenschaftlicher Verlag.

Bull, R., & Clifford, B. R. (1984). Earwitness voice recognition accuracy. In G. L. Wells & E. F. Loftus (Eds.), *Eyewitness testimony: Psychological perspectives* (pp. 92–123). New York: Cambridge University Press.

Bull, R., & Clifford, B. (1999). Earwitness testimony. In A. Heaton-Armstrong, E. Shepherd, & D. Wolchover (Eds.), *Analysing witness testimony* (pp. 194–206). London: Blackstone Press.

Bull, R., Rathborn, H., & Clifford, B. R. (1983). The voice recognition accuracy of blind listeners. *Perception, 12*, 223–226.

Carlucci, M., & Meissner, C. A. (2003, July). *The influence of intstructional bias on earwitness memory*. Paper presented at the meeting of the Society for Applied Research in Memory and Cognition. Aberdeen, Scotland.

Carterette, E. C., & Barneby, A. (1975). Recognition memory for voices. In E. Cohen & G. Nottebohn (Eds.), *Structure and processes in speech perception* (pp. 246–265). New York: Springer.

Cerrato, L., Falcone, M., & Paoloni, A. (2000). Subjective age estimation of telephone voices. *Speech Communication, 31*, 107–112.

Christianson, S. -Å. (1992). Emotional stress and eyewitness memory: A critical review. *Psychological Bulletin, 112*, 284–309.

Clarke, F. R., & Becker, R. W. (1969). Comparisons of techniques for discriminating among talkers. *Journal of Speech and Hearing Research, 12*, 747–761.

Clifford v. Kentucky, 7 SW3d 371 Ky 1999.

Clifford, B. R. (1980). Voice identification by human listeners: On earwitness reliability. *Law and Human Behavior, 4*, 373–394.

Clifford, B. R. (1983). Memory for voices: the feasibility and quality of earwitness evidence. In S. M. A. Lloyd-Bostock & B. R. Clifford (Eds.), *Evaluating witness evidence* (pp. 189–218). Chichester: Wiley.

Clifford, B. R. (1997). *A comparison of adults' and children's face and voice identification.* Paper presented at the 5th European Congress of Psychology, July 6–11. Dublin, Ireland [cited in Bull & Clifford (1999)].

Clifford, B. R. (2003, July). *Do children or adults exhibit a verbal overshadowing effect?* Paper presented at the International Conference on Psychology and Law, Edinburgh, Scotland.

Clifford, B. R., Rathborn, H., & Bull, R. (1981). The effects of delay on voice recognition accuracy. *Law and Human Behavior, 5,* 201–208.

Clifford, B. R., & Toplis, R. (1996). A comparison of adults' and children's witnessing abilities. In N. Clark & G. Stephenson (Eds.). *Investigative and forensic decision-making: Issuers in criminological and legal psychology* (pp. 76–83). Leicester, British Psychological Society.

Cobb, N. J., Lawrence, D. N., & Nelson, N. D. (1979). Report on blind subjects' tactile and auditory recognition for environmental stimuli. *Perceptual and Motor Skills, 48,* 363–366.

Commonwealth v. Miles, 648 N.E.2d 719, 728–29 (Mass. 1995).

Cook, S., & Wilding, J. (1997a). Earwitness testimony 2: Voice, faces and context. *Applied Cognitive Psychology, 11,* 527–541.

Cook, S., & Wilding, J. (1997b). Earwitness testimony: Never mind the variety, hear the length. *Applied Cognitive Psychology, 11,* 95–111.

Cook, S., & Wilding, J. (2001). Earwitness testimony: Effects of exposure and attention on the face overshadowing effect. *British Journal of Psychology, 92,* 617–629.

DeCasper, A. J., & Fifer, W. P. (1980). Of human bonding: Newborns prefer their mother's voice. *Science, 208,* 1174–1176.

DeCasper, A. J., & Prescott, P. A. (1984). Human newborns' perception of male voices: Preference, discrimination and reinforcing value. *Developmental Psychology, 5,* 481–491.

Deffenbacher, K., Cross, J., Handkins, R., Chance, J., Goldstein, A., Hammersley, R., & Read, J. D. (1989). Relevance of voice identification research to criteria for evaluating reliability of an identification. *Journal of Psychology, 123,* 109–119.

de Figueiredo, R. C., & de Souza Britto, H. (1996). A report on the acoustic effects of one type of disguise. *Forensic Linguistics, 3,* 168.

Dempster, F. N. (1996). Distributing and managing the conditions of encoding and practice. In E. L. Bjork & R. A. Bjork (Eds.), *Memory* (pp. 317–344). New York: Academic Press.

Devenport, J. L., Studebaker, C. A., & Penrod, S. D. (1999). Perspectives on jury decision-making. In F. T. Durso (Ed.), *Handbook of applied cognition* (pp. 819–845). Chichester, UK: Wiley.

Doty, N. D. (1998). The influence of nationality on the accuracy of face and voice recognition. *American Journal of Psychology, 111,* 191–214.

Elaad, E., Segev, S., & Tobin, Y. (1998). Long-term working memory in voice identification. *Psychology, Crime & Law, 4,* 73–88.

Erickson, B., Lind, A., Johnson, C., & O'Barr, W. (1978). Speech style and impression formation in a court setting: The effect of "powerful" and "powerless" speech. *Journal of Experimental Social Psychology, 14,* 266–279.

Fisher, R. P., & Geiselman, R. E. (1992). *Memory-enhancing techniques for investigative interviewing.* Springfield, IL: Charles C. Thomas.

Foulkes, P., & Barron, A. (2000). Telephone speaker recognition amongst members of a close social network. *Forensic Linguistics, 7,* 181–198.

Gilbert v. California, 388 U. S. 263 (1967).

Giles, S. G., & Bourhis, R. Y. (1982). A reply to a note on voice and racial categorization in Britain. *Social Behavior and Personality, 10,* 249–251.

Goggin, J. P., Thompson, C. P., Strube, G., & Simental, L. R. (1991). The role of language familiarity in voice identification. *Memory and Cognition, 19*, 448–458.

Goldstein, A. G., & Chance, J. E. (1983, October). *The effect of temporal distribution of the study trials on voice recognition: The spacing effect.* Paper presented at the Biennial Convention of the American Psychology-Law Society, Chicago, IL.

Goldstein, A. G., & Chance, J. E. (1985, May). *Voice recognition: The effects of faces, temporal distribution of "practice" and social distance.* Paper presented at the annual meeting of the Midwestern Psychology Association, Chicago, IL.

Goldstein, A. G., Knight, P., Bailis, K., & Conover, J. (1981). Recognition memory for accented and unaccented voices. *Bulletin of the Psychonomic Society, 17*, 217–220.

Hammersley, R., & Read, J. D. (1985). The effect of participation in a conversation on recognition and identification of the speakers' voices. *Law and Human Behavior, 9*, 71–81.

Hammersley, R., & Read, J. D. (1996). Voice identification by humans and computers. In S. L. Sporer, R. S. Malpass, & G. Koehnken (Eds.), *Psychological issues in eyewitness identification* (pp. 117–152). Mahwah, NJ: Lawrence Erlbaum Associates.

Hanley, J. R., Smith, S. T., & Hadfield, J. (1998). I recognize you but I can't place you: An investigation of familiar-only experiences during tests of voice and face recognition. *Quarterly Journal of Experimental Psychology, 51A*, 179–195.

Hanley, J. R., & Turner, J. M. (2000). Why are familiar-only experiences more frequent for voices than for faces? *Quarterly Journal of Experimental Psychology, 53A*, 1105–1116.

Hashtroudi, S., Johnson, M. K., & Chrosniak, L. D. (1989). Aging and source monitoring. *Psychology and Aging, 4*, 106–112.

Heydon, D. (1994). Lawyer's response to forensic linguistics. In J. Gibbons (Ed.), *Language and the law* (pp. 440–442). New York: Longman.

Hollien, H. (1990). *The acoustics of crime.* New York: Plenum.

Hollien, H. (1996). Considerations of guidelines for earwitness lineups. *Forensic Phonetics, 3*, 14–23.

Hollien, H. (2002). *Forensic voice identification.* New York: Academic Press.

Hollien, H., Bennett, G., & Gelfer, M. P. (1983). Criminal identification comparison: Aural versus visual identification resulting from a simulated crime. *Journal of Forensic Sciences, 28*, 208–221.

Hollien, H., Huntley, R., Künzel, H., & Hollien, P. A. (1995). Criteria for earwitness lineups. *Forensic Linguistics, 2*, 143–153.

Hollien, H., Majewski, W., & Doherty, E. T. (1982). Perceptual identification of voices under normal, stress and disguise speaking conditions. *Journal of Phonetics, 10*, 139–148.

Hollien, H., & Martin, C. A. (1996). Conducting research on the effects of intoxication on speech. *Forensic Linguistics, 3*, 107–128.

Hollien, H., Saletto, J. A., & Miller, S. K. (1993). Psychological stress in voice: A new approach. *Studia Phonetica Posnaniensia, 4*, 5–17.

Johnson, M. K., De Leonardis, D. M., Hashtroudi, S., & Ferguson, S. A. (1995). Aging and single versus multiple cues in source monitoring. *Psychology and Aging, 10*, 507–517.

Johnson, M. K., Hashtroudi, S., & Lindsay, D. S. (1993). Source monitoring. *Psychological Bulletin, 114*, 3–28.

Kebbel, M. R., & Wagstaff, G. F. (1999). *Face value? Evaluating the accuracy of eyewitness information.* Police Research Series, Paper 102. London: The Home Office.

Kerstholt, J. H., Jansen, N. J. M., Van Amelsvoort, A. G., & Broeders, A. P. A. (2004). Earwitnesses: Effects of speech duration, retention interval and acoustic environment. *Applied Cognitive Psychology, 18*, 327–336.

Komulainen, E. K. (1988). Subjective voice identification: The literal meaning of "talking yourself behind bars." *Alberta Law Review, 26*, 521–547.

Köster, O., Hess, M. M., Schiller, N. O., & Künzel, H. J. (1998). The correlation between auditory speech sensitivity and speaker recognition ability. *Forensic Linguistics, 5*, 22–32.

Köster, O., & Schiller, N. O. (1997). Different influences of the native language of a listener on speaker recognition. *Forensic Linguistics, 4,* 18–28.

Köster, O., Schiller, N. O., & Künzel, H. J. (1995). The influence of native-language background on speaker recognition. In K. Elenius & P. Branderud (Eds.), *Proceedings of the Thirteenth International Congress of Phonetic Sciences, Stockholm* (Vol. 4, pp. 306–309).

Krauss, R. M., Freyberg, R., & Morsella, E. (2002). Inferring speakers' physical attributes from their voices. *Journal of Experimental Social Psychology, 38,* 618–625.

Kreiman, J., Gerratt, B. R., & Precoda, K. (1990). Listener experience and perception of voice quality. *Journal of Speech and Hearing Research, 33,* 103–115.

Kreiman, J., Gerratt, B. R., Precoda, K., & Berke, G. S. (1992). Individual differences in voice quality perception. *Journal of Speech and Hearing Research, 35,* 512–520.

Künzel, H. J. (1989). How well does average fundamental frequency correlate with speaker height and weight? *Phonetica, 46,* 117–125.

Künzel, H. J. (1994). On the problem of speaker identification by victims and witnesses. *Forensic Linguistics, 1,* 45–57.

Künzel, H. J. (1997). Some general phonetic and forensic aspects of speaking tempo. *Forensic Linguistics, 4,* 48–83.

Künzel, H. J. (2000). Effects of voice disguise on speaking fundamental frequency. *Forensic Linguistics, 7,* 149–179.

Künzel, H. J., Braun, A., & Eysholdt, U. (1992). *Einfluss von alkohol auf sprache und stimme.* Heidelberg: Kriminalistik-Verlag [cited in Künzel (1997)].

Ladefoged, P. (1978). Expectation affects identification by listening. *UCLA—Working Papers in Phonetics, 41,* 41–42.

Ladefoged, P., & Ladefoged, J. (1980). The ability of listeners to identify voices. *UCLA—Working Papers in Phonetics, 49,* 43–51.

LaRiviere, C. (1972). Some acoustic and perceptual correlates of speaker identification. *Proceedings of the Seventh International Congress of Phonetic Sciences,* 558–564.

Lass, N. J., Mertz, P. J., & Kimmel. K. L. (1978). The effect of temporal speech alterations on speaker race and sex identifications. *Language and Speech, 21,* 279–290.

Laubstein, A. S. (1997). Problems of voice lineups. *Forensic Linguistics, 4,* 262–279.

Lavner, Y., Gath, I., & Rosenhouse, J. (2000). The effects of acoustic modifications on the identification of familiar voices speaking isolated vowels. *Speech Communication, 30,* 9–26.

Legge, G. E., Grossmann, C., & Pieper, C. M. (1984). Learning unfamiliar voices. *Journal of Experimental Psychology: Learning, Memory, and Cognition, 10,* 298–303.

Levine, F. J., & Tapp, J. L. (1973). The psychology of criminal identification: The gap from Wade to Kirby. *University of Pennsylvania Law Review, 121,* 1079–1131.

Loh, W. D. (1981). Perspectives on psychology and law. *Journal of Applied Social Psychology, 11,* 314–355.

Lown, C. (1977). Legal approaches to juror stereotyping by physical characteristics. *Law and Human Behavior, 1,* 87–100.

Mack v. Florida, 44 So. 706 (Fla. 1907).

Manitoba. (2001). *The inquiry regarding Thomas Sophonow: The investigation, prosecution and consideration of entitlement to compensation.* Winnipeg, MB: Department of Justice. Available at www.gov.mb.ca/justice/sophonow/recommendations/english.html

Mann, V., Diamond, R., & Carey, S. (1979). Development of voice recognition: Parallels with face recognition. *Journal of Experimental Child Psychology, 27,* 153–165.

Manning, R. K., Fucci, D., & Dean, R. (2000), College-age males' ability to produce the acoustic properties of an aging voice. *Perceptual and Motor Skills, 94,* 767–771.

McAllister, H. A., Bregman, N. J., & Lipscomb, T. J. (1988). Speed estimates by eyewitnesses and earwitnesses: How vulnerable to postevent information? *Journal of General Psychology, 115,* 25–35.

McAllister, H. A., Dale, R. H. I., Bregman, N. J., McCabe, A., & Cotton, C. R. (1993). When eyewitnesses are also earwitnesses: Effects on visual and voice identifications. *Basic and Applied Social Psychology, 14,* 161–170.

McAllister, H. A., Dale, R. H., & Keay, C. E. (1993). Effects of lineup modality on witness credibility. *Journal of Social Psychology, 133,* 365–376.

McGehee, F. (1937). The reliability of the identification of the human voice. *Journal of General Psychology, 17,* 249–271.

McGehee, F. (1944). An experimental study of voice recognition. *Journal of General Psychology, 31,* 53–65.

Meissner, C. A., & Brigham, J. C. (2001). Thirty years of investigating the own-race bias in memory for faces: A meta-analytic review. *Psychology, Public Policy, & Law, 7,* 3–35.

Memon, A., & Bull, R. (1991). The cognitive interview: Its origins, empirical support, evaluation and practical implications. *Journal of Community and Applied Social Psychology, 1,* 291–307.

Memon, A., Wark, L., Holley, A., Bull, R., & Koehnken, G. (1997). Eyewitness performance in cognitive and structured interviews. *Memory, 5,* 639–656.

Memon, A., & Yarmey, A. D. (1999). Earwitness recall and identification: Comparison of the cognitive interview and the structured interview. *Perceptual and Motor Skills, 88,* 797–807.

Meudell, P. R., Northen, B., Snowden, J. S., & Neary, D. (1980). Long term memory for famous voices in amnesic and normal subjects. *Neuropsychologia, 18,* 133–139.

Muchnik, C., Efrati, M., Nemeth, E., Malin, M., & Hildesheimer, M.(1991). Central auditory skills in blind and sighted subjects. *Scandinavian Audiology, 20,* 12–23.

Murray, T., & Cort, S. (1971). Aural identification of children's voices. *Journal of Auditory Research, 11,* 26–262.

Neil v. Biggers, 409 US 188 (1972).

New Jersey v. Hauptmann, 180 A. 809 (1935).

New Jersey Superior Court, Appeal Division, 351 A.2d 787, 789, 1976.

Niemeyer, W., & Starlinger, I. (1981). Do the blind hear better? Investigations on auditory processing in congenital or early acquired blindness. *Audiology, 20,* 12–23.

Nolan, F. J. (1996). Speaker recognition and forensic phonetics. In W. Hardcastle & J. Laver (Eds.), *The handbook of phonetic sciences* (pp. 744–766). Oxford: Blackwell.

Nolan, F. J., & Grabe, E. (1996). Preparing a voice lineup. *Forensic Linguistics, 7,* 74–94.

Olsson, N., Juslin, P., & Winman, A. (1998). Realism of confidence in earwitness versus eyewitness identification. *Journal of Experimental Psychology: Applied, 4,* 101–118.

Orchard, T. L., & Yarmey, A. D. (1995). The effects of whispers, voice-sample duration, and voice distinctiveness on criminal speaker identification. *Applied Cognitive Psychology, 9,* 249–260.

Ormerod, D. (2001). Sounds familiar? Voice identification evidence. *Criminal Law Review* (October), 95–622.

Ormerod, D. (2002). Sounding out expert voice identification. *Criminal Law Review* (October), 771–790.

Papcun, G., Kreiman, J., & Davis, A. (1989). Long-term memory for unfamiliar voices. *Journal of the Acoustical Society of America, 85,* 913–925.

Perfect, T. J., Hunt, L. J., & Harris, C. M. (2002). Verbal overshadowing in voice recognition. *Applied Cognitive Psychology, 16,* 973–980.

Peters, D. P. (1987). The impact of naturally occurring stress on children's memory. In S. J. Ceci, M. P. Toglia, & D. F. Ross (Eds.), *Children's eyewitness memory* (pp. 122–141). New York: Springer-Verlag.

Pickel, K. L., French, T. A., & Betts, J. M. (2003). A cross-modal weapon focus effect: The influence of a weapon's presence on memory for auditory information. *Memory, 11,* 277–292.

Pollack, J., Pickett, J. M., & Sumby, W. H. (1954). On the identification of speakers by voice. *Journal of the Acoustical Society of America, 26,* 403–406.

Procter, E. E. (2002). The effect of distributed learning on the identification of disguised voices. Unpublished M.A. thesis, University of Guelph, Guelph, ON, Canada.

Procter, E. E., & Yarmey, A. D. (2003). The effect of distributed learning on the identification of normal-tone and whispered voices. *Korean Journal of Thinking & Problem Solving, 13,* 17–29.

Purnell, T., Idsardi, W., & Baugh, J. (1999). Perceptual and phonetic experiments on American English dialect identification. *Journal of Language and Social Psychology, 18,* 10–24.

Rathborn, H., Bull, R., & Clifford, B. R. (1981). Voice recognition over the telephone. *Journal of Police Science and Administration, 9,* 280–284.

Read, J. D., & Craik, F. I. M. (1995). Earwitness identification: Some influences on voice recognition. *Journal of Experimental Psychology: Applied, 1,* 6–18.

Regina v. Brownlowe, 7 NSWLR 461 (1987).

Regina v. E. J. Smith, [1984] 1 NSWLR 462; (1986) 7 NSWLR 444.

Regina v. Morin, 37 C.R. (4th) 395 (Ontario Ct. App. 1995).

Reich, A., & Duke, J. (1979). Effects of selected vocal disguises upon speaker identification by listening. *Journal of the Acoustical Society of America, 66,* 1023–1028.

Reynolds v. United States, 98 U.S. 145 (1878).

Roebuck, R., & Wilding, J. (1993). Effects of vowel variety and sample length on identification of a speaker in a lineup. *Applied Cognitive Psychology, 7,* 475–481.

Rose, P. (2002). *Forensic speaker identification.* London: Taylor & Francis.

Rose, P., & Duncan, S. (1995). Naive auditory identification and discrimination of similar voices by familiar listeners. *Forensic Linguistics, 10,* 1–17.

Ross, D. F., Ceci, S. J., Dunning, D., & Toglia, M. P. (1994). Unconscious transference and lineup identification: Toward a memory blending approach. In D. F. Ross, J. D. Read, & M. P. Toglia (Eds.), *Adult eyewitness testimony: Current trends and developments* (pp. 80–100). Cambridge: Cambridge University Press.

Rothman (1977). A perceptual (aural) and spectographic identification of talkers with similar sounding voices. *Proceedings of the International Conference on Crime Countermeasures—Science and Engineering (July)* [cited in Rathborn, Bull, & Clifford (1981)].

Saslove, H., & Yarmey, A. D. (1980). Long-term auditory memory: Speaker identification. *Journal of Applied Psychology, 65,* 111–116.

Scherer, K. R. (1974). Voice quality analysis of American and German speakers. *Journal of Psycholinguistic Research, 3,* 281–297.

Schichting, F., & Sullivan, K. P. H. (1997). The imitated voice—A problem for voice lineups? *Forensic Linguistics, 4,* 148–165.

Schiller, N. O., & Köster, O. (1996). Evaluation of a foreign speaker in forensic phonetics: A report. *Forensic Linguistics, 3,* 176–185.

Schiller, N. O., & Köster, O, (1998). The ability of expert witnesses to identify voices: A comparison between trained and untrained listeners. *Forensic Linguistics, 5,* 1–9.

Schmidt-Nielsen, A., & Stern, K. R. (1985). Identification of known voices as a function of familiarity and narrow-band coding. *Journal of the Acoustical Society of America, 77,* 658–663.

Schooler, J. W., & Loftus, E. F. (1993). Multiple mechanisms mediate differences in eyewitness accuracy and suggestibility. In J. M. Puckett & H. W. Reese (Eds.), *Mechanisms of everyday cognition* (pp. 177–203). Hillsdale, NJ: Lawrence Erlbaum Associates.

Solan, L. W., & Tiersma, P. M. (2003). Hearing voices: Speaker identification in court. *Hastings Law Journal, 54,* 373–435.

Spence, M. J., & Freeman, M. S. (1996). Newborn infants prefer the maternal low-pass filtered voice, but not the maternal whispered voice. *Infant Behavior and Development, 19,* 199–212.

Spence, M. J., Rollins, P. R., & Jerger, S. (2002). Children's recognition of cartoon voices. *Journal of Speech, Language, and Hearing Research, 45,* 214–222.

Sporer, S. L. (1982). A brief history of the psychology of testimony. *Current Psychological Reviews, 2,* 323–340.

Sporer, S. L., Penrod, S., Read, D., & Cutler, B. (1995). Choosing, confidence, and accuracy: A meta-analysis of the confidence-accuracy relation in eyewitness identification studies. *Psychological Bulletin, 118*, 315–327.

State v. Ferris, 212 Neb. 835, 326, N.W.2d 185 (1982).

Steblay, N. M. (1992). A meta-analytic review of the weapon focus effect. *Law and Human Behavior, 16*, 413–424.

Stovall v. Denno, 388 U.S. 293, 302 (1967).

Technical Working Group for Eyewitness Evidence. (1999). *Eyewitness evidence: A guide for law enforcement*. Washington, DC: United States Department of Justice, Office of Justice Programs. Available at www.ojp.usdoj.gov

Thompson, C. P. (1985). Voice identification: Speaker identifiability and a correction of the record regarding sex effects. *Human Learning, 4*, 19–27.

Thompson, C. P. (1987). A language effect in voice identification. *Applied Cognitive Psychology, 1*, 121–131.

Tomes, J. L., & Katz, A. N. (1997). Habitual susceptibility to misinformation and individual differences in eyewitness memory. *Applied Cognitive Psychology, 11*, 233–251.

Tosi, O. (1979). *Voice identification: Theory and legal applications*. Baltimore: University Park Press.

Tulving, E. (1985). Memory and consciousness. *Canadian Psychology, 26*, 1–12.

Turtle, J., & Watkins, K. (1999). Investigative interviewing: Maximizing information and minimizing errors from witnesses, victims and suspects of crime. In G. M. Chayko & E. D. Gulliver (Eds.), *Forensic evidence in Canada* (2nd ed., pp. 53–82). Aurora, ON: Canada Law Book.

United States v. Duran, 4 F.3d 800 (9th Cir. 1993).

United States v. Wade, 388 U.S. 218 (1967).

van Dommelen, W. A., & Moxness, B. H. (1995). Acoustic parameters in speaker height and weight identifications: Sex-specific behaviour. *Language and Speech, 38*, 267–287.

van Lancker, D., Kreiman, J., & Emmorey, K. (1985a). Familiar voice recognition: Patterns and parameters. Part 1: Recognition of backward voices. *Journal of Phonetics, 13*, 19–38.

van Lancker, D., Kreiman, J., & Wickens, T. D. (1985b). Familiar voice recognition: Patterns and parameters. Part 2: Recognition of rate-altered voices. *Journal of Phonetics, 13*, 39–52.

Vernon, B., & Nelson, E, (2000). Exposure to suggestion and creation of false auditory memories. *Psychological Reports, 86*, 344–346.

Wells, G. L., Ferguson, T. J., & Lindsay, R. C. L. (1981).The tractability of eyewitness confidence and its implications for triers of fact. *Journal of Applied Psychology, 66*, 688–696.

Wilbur v. Hubbard, 35 Barb. 303 (N.Y. App. Div. 1861).

Wilding, J., & Cook, S. (2000). Sex differences and individual consistency in voice identification. *Perceptual and Motor Skills, 91*, 535–538.

Wilding, J., Cook, S., & Davis, J. (2000). Sound familiar? *The Psychologist, 13*, 558–562.

Winograd, E., Kerr, N. H., & Spence, M. J. (1984). Voice recognition: Effects of orienting task, and a test of blind versus sighted listeners. *American Journal of Psychology, 97*, 57–70.

Yamada, N., Hakoda, Y., Yuda, E., & Kusuhara, A. (2000). Verification of impression of voice in relation to occupational categories. *Psychological Reports, 86*, 1249–1263.

Yarmey, A. D. (1986). Verbal, visual and voice identification of a rape suspect under different levels of illumination. *Journal of Applied Psychology, 71*, 363–370.

Yarmey, A. D. (1990). Accuracy and confidence of duration estimates following questions containing marked and unmarked modifiers. *Journal of Applied Social Psychology, 20*, 1139–1149.

Yarmey, A. D. (1991a). Descriptions of distinctive and non-distinctive voices over time. *Journal of the Forensic Science Society, 31*, 421–428.

Yarmey, A. D. (1991b). Voice identification over the telephone. *Journal of Applied Social Psychology, 21*, 1868–1876.

Yarmey, A. D. (1992). The effects of dyadic discussion on earwitness recall. *Basic and Applied Social Psychology, 13*, 251–263.

Yarmey, A. D. (1993). Stereotypes and recognition memory for faces and voices of good guys and bad guys. *Applied Cognitive Psychology, 7,* 419–431.

Yarmey, A. D. (1994). Earwitness evidence: Memory for a perpetrator's voice. In D. F. Ross, J. D. Read, & M. P. Toglia (Eds.), *Adult eyewitness testimony: Current trends and developments.* New York: Cambridge University Press.

Yarmey, A. D. (1995a). Earwitness and evidence obtained by other senses. In R. Bull & D. Carson (Eds.), *Handbook of psychology in legal contexts* (pp. 262–273). New York: Wiley.

Yarmey, A. D. (1995b). Earwitness speaker identification. *Psychology, Public Policy, and Law, 1,* 792–816.

Yarmey, A. D. (2000). The older eyewitness. In M. B. Rothman, B. D. Dunlop, & P. Entzel (Eds.), *Elders, crime, and the criminal justice system: Myth, perceptions, and reality in the 21st century* (pp. 127–148). New York: Springer.

Yarmey, A. D. (2001a). Earwitness descriptions and speaker identification. *Forensic Linguistics, 8,* 113–122.

Yarmey, A. D. (2001b). Police investigations. In R. A. Schuller & J. R. P. Ogloff (Eds.), *Introduction to psychology and law: Canadian perspectives* (pp. 59–94). Toronto: University of Toronto Press.

Yarmey, A. D. (2003a). Earwitness identification over the telephone and in field settings. *Forensic Linguistics, 10,* 65–77.

Yarmey, A. D. (2003b). Eyewitness identification: Guidelines and recommendations for identification procedures in the United States and in Canada. *Canadian Psychology, 44,* 181–189.

Yarmey, A. D., & Matthys, E. (1992). Voice identification of an abductor. *Applied Cognitive Psychology, 6,* 367–377.

Yarmey, A. D., Yarmey, A. L., & Yarmey, M. J. (1994). Face and voice identifications in showups and lineups. *Applied Cognitive Psychology, 8,* 453–464.

Yarmey, A. D., Yarmey, A. L., Yarmey, M. J., & Parliament, L. (2001). Commonsense beliefs and the identification of familiar voices. *Applied Cognitive Psychology, 15,* 283–299.

Yeatman v. Inland Property Management, Inc., 845 F. Supp. 625, 628 (N.D. Ill. 1994).

Yuille, J. C., & Daylen, J. (1998). The impact of traumatic events on eyewitness memory. In C. P. Thompson, D. J. Herrmann, J. D. Read, D. Bruce, G. G. Payne, & M. P. Toglia (Eds.), *Eyewitness memory: Theoretical and applied perspectives* (pp. 155–178). Mahwah, NJ: Lawrence Erlbaum Associates.

Zuckerman, M., & Driver, R. E. (1989). What sounds beautiful is good: The vocal attractiveness stereotype. *Journal of Nonverbal Behavior, 13,* 67–82.

6

Show-up Identifications: Suggestive Technique or Reliable Method?

Jennifer E. Dysart
John Jay College of Criminal Justice, CUNY

R. C. L. Lindsay
Queen's University, Ontario

There are various methods of testing a witness's ability to identify a perpetrator, such as mug-shot searches, lineups, and the show-up identification procedure, where a witness is presented with only one person or photo. The show-up is a commonly used procedure in the United States. Flowe, Ebbesen, Burke, and Chivabunditt (2001) report that show-ups were used for 55% of identifications conducted in 488 sampled cases between 1991 and 1995 in a large U.S. metropolitan area. McQuiston and Malpass (2001) documented a show-up use rate of 30% for identification attempts conducted by police in El Paso County, Texas. Gonzalez, Ellsworth, and Pembroke (1993) enlisted the help of an Illinois detective to record all identifications (lineups and show-ups) in which he was involved over a designated period of time. Results from this field study indicated that 77% of identification tasks were show-ups. Thus, although the variance in use of show-ups may be large, they are used extensively.

Given the widespread use of show-ups, it is somewhat surprising that relatively little research has been conducted on this identification technique. A recent meta-analysis (Steblay, Dysart, Fulero, & Lindsay, 2003) comparing identification accuracy rates from show-ups and lineups was able to examine only 12 tests of the hypothesis from eight papers on the topic (seven published). Considering that there are over 200 lineup identification studies in the literature, it is clear that rigorous empirical investigation of the show-up technique is long overdue. Our review of the current knowledge concerning show-ups begins with a discussion of their theory and place in the identification literature followed by a review of the limited data available and finishes with a discussion of issues yet to be addressed.

IDENTIFICATION THEORY

Decision Accuracy

When a witness is presented with a perpetrator-present show-up (or target-present in the research context), two outcomes are possible: the witness could make a correct identification or an incorrect rejection (nonidentification). When a witness is presented with a perpetrator-absent show-up (or target-absent), again only two outcomes are possible: a correct rejection (nonidentification) or a false identification (witness identifies the innocent suspect as the perpetrator; Wells, 1984). An "identification" of the suspect increases the probability that the suspect is the criminal, whereas nonidentifications of the suspect reduce the probability that the suspect is the criminal (Charman & Wells, this volume; Wells, 1984, 1993; Wells & Lindsay, 1980; Wells & Turtle, 1986). From this perspective, it is considered critical to test the impact of any identification procedure or modification in identification procedures with both target-present and target-absent procedures.

Absolute and Relative Judgments

Wells (1984) suggested that when lineup members are presented at the same time, as in a simultaneous lineup, witnesses may compare the lineup members with each other and select the one who most closely resembles their memory of the perpetrator. This "relative judgment" strategy works well with target-present lineups, as the presence of the perpetrator provides the witness with a strong memory cue that enhances the likelihood of a positive identification. However, the relative judgment strategy is problematic when the target is absent, as a witness using the relative judgment strategy is still likely to choose the lineup member who most closely resembles the criminal, resulting in a false identification if the suspect is selected. In an attempt to reduce the use of relative judgments, Lindsay and Wells (1985) developed the sequential lineup, where witnesses are shown the members of the lineup one at a time. This procedure requires witnesses to make a yes or no decision at the time of presentation of each lineup member and does not allow them to view any lineup member again after an identification decision has been made. The sequential lineup has been successful in reducing false identifications because it encourages absolute memory judgments and renders the relative judgment strategy ineffective (because you can't go back, it does no good to decide that an already rejected lineup member looks most like the criminal).

A recent meta-analysis (Steblay, Dysart, Fulero, & Lindsay, 2001) revealed that sequential lineups were superior to simultaneous lineups because they dramatically reduce the frequency of false-positive choices from target-absent lineups, probably because they reduce reliance on relative judgments (Lindsay & Bellinger, 1999). An additional benefit of sequential lineups is that they decrease the impact of lineup biases, including instruction bias, where the witness is encouraged to select someone from the identification procedure; clothing bias, where the suspect is the only person presented in clothing similar to that recalled as being worn by the perpetrator; and foil bias, where the suspect is the only member of the lineup matching the description of the criminal provided by the witness (Lindsay et al., 1991). Instruction bias directly encourages the use of a relative judgment strategy (Malpass & Devine, 1981). Clothing and foil biases make the suspect stand out from the other lineup members (Lindsay, Wallbridge, & Drennan, 1987; Lindsay & Wells, 1980). Witnesses who use a relative judgment strategy readily select suspects who stand out. Thus, with lineups, when the identity of a police suspect is obvious, the lineup is considered unfair or biased (Doob & Kirshenbaum, 1973; Malpass, 1981; Wells, Leippe, & Ostrom, 1979). One of the strategies for reducing false identifications with lineups is to make certain that the suspect does not stand out from the other lineup members (Malpass & Lindsay, 1999).

Application of Relative versus Absolute Judgment to Show-ups

With show-ups it is clear who the suspect is, as only one person is presented to the witness. As a result, many researchers believe that the show-up identification procedure is flawed and more likely to lead to false identifications because of the suggestive nature of the procedure (Kassin, Tubb, Hosch, & Memon, 2001; Wagenaar & Veefkind, 1992; Yarmey, 1998).

Although many believe that the show-up procedure leads to higher rates of false identification, an alternative hypothesis with the show-up procedure is that, because only one person is presented, the witness must use an absolute judgment strategy. Therefore, as with sequential lineups, where absolute judgments are often used, show-ups could produce lower rates of false identification than are obtained with the simultaneous lineup technique. In addition, the potential introduction of psychological reactance, a perceived loss of freedom in one's environment (Brehm, 1966), might lead to a decrease in choosing behavior generally. For example, a witness might feel pressure from police to identify the suspect as the criminal when only one person is presented in the identification task. Resisting this pressure could lead to nonidentification of the suspect. The pressure to choose someone might also exist with lineup techniques; however, if the lineup is not biased, an innocent police suspect should not be obvious, and psychological reactance would play a smaller role in generating false identifications from lineups.

If the show-up procedure generates a lower choosing rate, correct identifications may occur less often from show-ups than lineups. On the other hand, lower overall choosing rates associated with show-ups may not result in lower rates of choosing innocent suspects than that found with lineups. With lineups, the innocent suspect is protected to some degree by the presence of other lineup members (referred to as *foils, fillers,* or *distracters*). When one assumes that a fair lineup procedure is used, such that there is only one suspect and all lineup members are similar in appearance to the suspect on all features mentioned by the witness in the description of the criminal (Charman & Wells, this volume; Wells, Rydell, & Seelau, 1993), and if the suspect is innocent, there is no reason, on average, for the suspect to be a more likely choice than any other lineup member for witnesses using either relative or absolute judgment strategies. As a result, the rate of false identification from a properly conducted identification procedure would be expected to be the rate of false-positive choices divided by the number of people shown to the witness. For a lineup, 6, 8, 10, or 12 people are presented to the witness (depending on the jurisdiction). As a result, the expected rate of false identification will be much lower than the rate of false-positive choices. For the show-up, only one person is shown to the witness, and thus all false-positive choices will be false identifications. Because of this difference between the lineup and show-up, it is possible for the show-up to generate a much lower false-positive rate than a lineup without improving the false identification rate. In fact, if we assume that about 50% of witnesses select someone from target-absent, simultaneous lineups, a false-positive choice rate of 6.25% from a show-up procedure would be better than expected from a six-person lineup (8.33%), equal to the expectation from an eight-person lineup (6.25%), and worse than expected from a 12-person lineup (4.12%). Following this principle, an advantage for the lineup is that the false identification rate can be reduced by an increase in lineup size, a variable completely under the control of the criminal justice system. There is no comparable adjustment to the show-up procedure that could guarantee a reduction in errors with the use of that procedure.

Of course, the probability that a given innocent suspect will be selected will vary randomly with the accidental degree of resemblance of the suspect and other line-up members to the true criminal. The rate of choosing people who vary in degree of similarity to the true criminal may also interact with the identification procedure. An innocent suspect who happens to closely resemble the true criminal may be protected by a line-up containing foils who also closely resemble the true criminal. Alternatively, the absence of any foil as similar to the criminal as the innocent suspect may make the innocent suspect stand out and increase the probability that the witness will select the suspect. The show-up identification may result in high rates of choice of a similar-looking innocent suspect because of the degree of match to memory, or a lower rate due to failure to be a precise match to memory or psychological reactance.

Next we examine the research on the effects of using show-ups on identification accuracy. Past research and future suggestions for research are presented under the umbrellas of system variables and estimator variables, respectively.

SHOW-UP ACCURACY: AN OVERVIEW

In an investigation of the overall effectiveness of show-ups versus line-ups, Steblay et al. (2003) found that show-ups yield lower overall choosing rates (27%) than line-ups (54%). The lower choice rate for show-ups was considered counterintuitive because of the inherent suggestiveness of the show-up procedure and the belief of eyewitness experts that show-ups would lead to higher rates of choosing and particularly false identifications than line-ups (Kassin et al., 2001). However, as just discussed, the fact that the choice rate for show-ups and line-ups imply different false identification rates means that we must consider the data separately for target-present and target-absent conditions to determine the risk of false identification. As a result, the expectations of experts could still be correct to the extent that the risk of false identification may be higher with show-ups than with line-ups, even though the overall rate of choosing is lower from show-ups.

The results did support the absolute judgment hypothesis and/or the psychological reactance theory described previously to the extent that the overall choosing rate was lower for show-ups than for line-ups. Further studies are needed in which these two hypotheses are directly tested to determine the effects of each on identification accuracy from show-ups. Psychological reactance theory will be somewhat more complicated to investigate because it is extremely difficult for researchers in a laboratory to replicate the inherent pressures of a real criminal investigation (e.g., a participant in an experiment knows that no one will go to jail based on his or her identification decision). Therefore, it is likely that field studies or collaborative efforts with police will be needed in order to parse out the effects of psychological reactance on identification accuracy from show-ups.

The results of the Steblay et al. (2003) meta-analysis also showed that the lower choosing rate associated with show-ups resulted in a different pattern of identification accuracy for show-ups and line-ups, depending on the presence versus absence of the target. In target-present conditions, show-ups (46%) produce a significantly lower rate of choosing than line-ups (71%). However, all show-up choices are correct, whereas a substantial number of line-up choices are not (foil selections). As a result, approximately the same correct identification rate occurs in line-ups (45%).

In target-absent conditions, show-ups (85%) produced a higher correct rejection rate than line-ups (57%), resulting in a tendency for witnesses not to identify the innocent suspect. However, all witnesses who identify a person from a target-absent show-up commit a false identification. Although 43% of witnesses selected someone from the line-ups, such choices include both suspect selections (false identifications) and foil selections (known errors). Because all of the lineups contained six members, the expected rate of false identification is 43%/6 or 7.17%, less than half the rate for show-ups (15%). This reasoning applies only if the innocent suspect is no more likely to resemble the true criminal than any other line-up member.

If the innocent suspect bears a stronger resemblance to the criminal than other line-up members, the results could be different. Two studies had designated the most similar line-up member as an innocent suspect. Those studies generated a 5% rate of choosing this person from a line-up, in comparison with 12% for the same suspects presented in show-ups. Thus, even when the innocent suspect bears a greater resemblance to the criminal than other line-up members, false identifications are more likely from show-ups than line-ups.

Overall, show-ups fair poorly when compared with line-ups. Correct identification rates are equal and false identification rates are about two to three times as high with show-ups compared with line-ups. However, this analysis considers only a general effect. Other variables of importance in the identification literature could interact with the identification procedure to influence the relative merits of line-ups and show-ups. For the most part, there are no data on these issues.

Finally, Steblay et al. (2003) argued at one point that because foil choices are known errors, it was reasonable to drop them from the analysis and compare the rates of false identification from show-ups and line-ups without this data. This procedure produces virtually identical rates of false identification from show-ups and line-ups. However, this analysis is highly questionable and clearly misleading. If 100 witnesses attempt identifications from target-absent show-ups and another 100 attempt identifications from target-absent line-ups, the best estimates from the meta-analysis are that 15 show-up witnesses and 7 line-up witnesses will falsely identify innocent suspects. The fact that some additional number of witnesses will make known errors by selecting foils from the line-ups is irrelevant. More innocent suspects will be at risk of wrongful conviction based on erroneous identification if show-ups are used.

SYSTEM AND ESTIMATOR VARIABLES

There are two classes of variables that affect eyewitness accuracy: (a) system variables, such as line-up instructions and structure, which are controlled by investigators, and (b) estimator variables, such as age and race, which are not controllable (Wells, 1978). Researchers have argued that system variable research is more beneficial because it can have a direct influence on police practice (Wells et al., 2000). This is true if system and estimator variables do not interact. Interactions between system and estimator variables would complicate the situation considerably. Some estimator variables have received attention: cross-race identification (e.g., Brigham, Meissner, & Bennett, this volume), cross-age identification accuracy (e.g., Bartlett & Memon, this volume; Pozzulo, this volume), and the confidence-accuracy relation (e.g., Leippe & Eisenstadt, this volume). Other than these topics, relatively little estimator variable research has been conducted in the eyewitness area, and even less has been conducted with show-ups. Because of this fact, we provide many suggestions for future research involving estimator variables and the show-up technique.

SYSTEM VARIABLES

Some of the system variables that have been investigated with show-ups include live versus photographic presentation, clothing bias, instruction bias, biased construction, whether a verbal description was given by the witness, and the amount of time delay between the event and the task.

Live versus Photographic Presentation

The majority of real-world show-ups are conducted live (e.g., Behrman & Davey, 2001; Flowe & Ebbesen, 2001). Empirical studies, however, have mostly used photographic presentation of the suspect in the show-up procedure. Only two empirical studies have used live presentation of the suspect with show-ups (Gonzalez et al., 1993; Yarmey et al., 1996). The Steblay et al. meta-analysis indicates that show-ups generate more correct rejections than lineups, regardless of whether the procedure is conducted live or with photographs. When the identification procedure is conducted with the use of photographs, there is no significant difference in correct identification rates between show-ups and line-ups. However, when the procedure is conducted live, line-ups generate more correct identifications than show-ups (Steblay et al., 2003). This latter result, however, should be interpreted with caution, as there was only one test of the hypothesis available for analysis and the manipulation was confounded with cross-race identification (Gonzalez et al., 1993).

Clothing Bias

Clothing bias occurs when a suspect is presented to the witness wearing clothing that matches the description of the criminal's clothing provided by the witness. Clothing bias is of particular concern with show-ups because they are often conducted within hours of the crime, and therefore there is an increased likelihood that the suspect will be apprehended based on the (clothing) description provided by the eyewitness. Consequently, suspects in show-ups may frequently be presented wearing clothing matching the description provided by the witness.

The effect of clothing bias on identification accuracy from target-present line-ups is generally nonsignificant (i.e., clothing bias does not lead to a significant increase in correct identifications of the target; e.g., Lindsay, Wallbridge, & Drennan, 1987). With target-absent line-ups, on the other hand, clothing bias does lead to a significant increase in false identifications of innocent suspects. The likely cause of these results is that the suspect stands out relative to the other members of the line-up because of the clothing match (to the witness's description). The data with regard to clothing bias and show-up identifications is clear (Dysart, Lindsay, & Dupuis, in press; Yarmey et al., 1996). When the target is presented in the same clothing or clothing similar to that worn during the event or described by the eyewitness, there is no significant increase in correct identifications. However, when a (highly or moderately) similar-looking innocent suspect is presented in similar clothing, there is a significant increase in false identifications. The clothing bias effect has not been supported with dissimilar-looking suspects, as it is likely that the mismatch between the suspects' face and the perpetrator's face outweighs the influence of similar-looking attire, and the witness is able to correctly reject the suspect.

The results of the show-up clothing bias studies conducted to date also indicate that the type of clothing worn by the suspect may have a differential influence on the biasing effect. For example, Dysart et al. (in press) presented suspects in distinct (Harley-Davidson t-shirt) and common (blue button-down dress shirt) clothing and only found the clothing bias effect for the distinct shirt. Common types of clothing (e.g., white t-shirt and blue jeans) may have a less damaging effect on false identifications because the probability of people other than the perpetrator being in the area and wearing clothing matching the description is much higher when the clothing described is commonly worn in the community. Replications of this effect would be useful. Regardless of the exact results, clothing bias is a potential source of identification bias for line-ups, show-ups, and even mug-shot searches (Lindsay, Nosworthy, Martin, & Martynuck, 1994).

Instruction Bias

Instruction bias occurs when the witness is led to believe that the true perpetrator is present in the identification procedure and that the witness's job is to "pick him out." The effect of instruction bias on identification accuracy from line-ups is well established in the identification literature (Steblay, 1997) and generally leads to an increase in false identifications and no increase in correct identifications of the target. With respect to the show-up procedure, there are no published studies on the effects of instruction bias on identification accuracy. As with line-ups, it is strongly recommended that police explicitly warn witnesses that the guilty party may not be presented to them.

Biased Construction

The biased construction of a line-up procedure involves using foils who do not resemble the description of the criminal, while the suspect does resemble the description of the criminal (Malpass & Lindsay, 1999). Because only the suspect is presented in a show-up, a show-up cannot be biased in this fashion. On the other hand, the reason that line-ups are perceived to be biased under such conditions is that the witness is able to determine which line-up member is the suspect without having to recognize the suspect as the person actually seen; that is, the suspect stands out. Because the identity of the suspect is always obvious in a show-up, the structure of show-ups is always biased by this criterion.

Verbal Overshadowing

In some identification situations, witnesses are not asked to provide a description of a perpetrator (e.g., when there are multiple witnesses to an event). However, witnesses often are asked to describe the person who committed the crime, resulting in a deficit in identification accuracy attributed to verbal overshadowing (Meissner & Brigham, 2001; Meissner, Sporer, & Schooler, this volume). Studies that have compared identification accuracy from line-ups and show-ups have not varied whether descriptions were obtained, and thus there are no tests of verbal overshadowing on identification accuracy using show-ups.

Delay

Delay in the identification situation refers to the amount of time between the event and the first identification attempt. After much searching and consultation with eyewitness experts and criminal defense lawyers, the only court decision pertaining to this delay appears to be *Neil vs. Biggers* (1972). The "Biggers criterion," which resulted from this decision, states that the time between the event and the identification plays a role in evaluating identification accuracy. However, there is no indication that the show-up identification procedure should or must be used within any particular time limit. Ironically, the identification in the Biggers case was from a show-up after a delay of 7 months. Although there is currently no specific rule, it should not be taken to mean that there is no effect of delay. The little available data on delay and identification accuracy from show-ups fails to indicate strong detrimental effects of delay (e.g., Dysart et al., in press). However, the research has only explored differences between a few minutes and a few days.

Dysart and Lindsay (this volume) review research supporting concern for identification accuracy from line-ups after long delays. The issue of whether or not delay has a more detrimental, equal, or less detrimental effect on show-ups than line-ups remains an empirical issue in need of investigation.

Future System Variable Research

Because there have been so few studies conducted on show-up identification accuracy, the section on future directions for research could be practically limitless. We provide suggestions for the areas of investigation that we believe are critical to understanding the strengths and weaknesses of the show-up identification technique.

Future research with regard to the effects of presenting the suspect live or via a photograph is imperative for evaluating the show-up procedure as it is actually conducted in the majority of real-world cases. Studies that examine the identification rates of the target and innocent suspect, presented live or with a photograph, are extremely important in determining the ability of witnesses to make a correct identification decision with the show-up procedure. Additional features of real-world criminal investigations, such as whether or not the show-up is conducted with the suspect sitting in the back seat of a police car or in handcuffs, also need to be explored, because of the inherent suggestiveness of these situations. It is more likely that a suspect presented live will be restrained in some way in order to reduce the risk of fight or flight. A suspect presented in a photograph obviously does not present such a risk, and therefore the additional suggestibility of restrained suspects presented live should be examined.

Clothing bias is potentially inherent in all show-up identifications conducted live, soon after the criminal event. Therefore, further study of the effects of various types of clothing on the false identification of innocent suspects is critical. It is likely that, regardless the type of clothing worn by the perpetrator, clothing bias will have some effect on identification accuracy. Furthermore, common clothing may have a stronger impact on a live than on a photo identification procedure and on procedures conducted shortly after the event rather than long after. These two factors may interact to produce a very strong clothing bias. Many people may wear t-shirts and jeans, but how many of them are within a block of the location of a robbery minutes after the event? This logic may make a suspect apprehended only minutes after the event and wearing clothing highly similar to that described by the witness difficult for the witness to reject.

One potential solution for eliminating clothing bias is for police or other investigators to disguise or hide the clothing worn by the suspect. This could easily be done by placing a blanket or police jacket around the suspect sitting in the police car and having the witness identify only the face. The combination of masking clothing cues and including an instruction to witnesses explaining why the clothing is being covered could be explored in future research.

Research on instruction bias has almost exclusively focused on the presence or absence of the "perpetrator may or may not be present" warning. Additional studies examining other, forensically relevant instructions are likely to be useful. For example, when a witness is presented with a suspect in the field, should additional instructions be used to warn the witness that the police have apprehended the suspect only because he was in the area and that no other evidence against the suspect is known at that time? Should the witness be told that their task is not only to identify a perpetrator, but to exculpate an innocent person? A recent examination of the use of "cautious" instructions with show-ups (Dysart & Lindsay, 2006) found that there was no significant decrease in false identifications with cautious instructions; however, there was a significant decrease in correct identifications of the target. Clearly this decrease in correct decisions is an undesirable result, and therefore further investigation of the effects of such manipulations is warranted.

The effects of verbal overshadowing have not been explicitly investigated with the show-up procedure. Therefore, any exploration of the effects of providing a description of the perpetrator on identification accuracy from show-ups would be useful. Also, the type of description provided, open-ended or multiple-choice format, would be worthy of investigation.

Very little is known about the effects of delay periods. The results from investigations of short delays (several hours to several days) are inconsistent. Is there a critical period of time after which show-ups become even more dangerous than they are shortly after the crime? Another topic that has yet to be investigated with show-ups is the effect of post-identification feedback on ratings of confidence and other estimates of the identification situation. Bradfield, Wells, and Olson (2002) found that confirming feedback from a line-up administrator had a significant effect on estimates of identification decision confidence, quality of view of the perpetrator, amount of attention paid to the event, clarity of memory for the perpetrator, etc. It is reasonable to expect that this type of feedback also would have an effect on witnesses who view a show-up, but the size of the effect is unknown and is subject to empirical investigation.

Another factor relating to eyewitness identification accuracy from show-ups that has yet to be thoroughly examined is the effect of multiple identification procedures on identification accuracy. In the one study that has investigated this phenomenon with show-ups, Behrman and Vayder (1994) asked half of their participants to make an identification from a show-up after viewing a videotaped event. All participants were then asked to make an identification from a line-up 5–7 days later. Participants who viewed the show-up were significantly more likely to select the innocent suspect from the line-up than were participants who did not view him in the show-up. The authors discouraged the use of such multiple procedures. This effect is similar to the "commitment" and "transference" effects reported after exposure to mug shots followed by a subsequent line-up (Dysart, Lindsay, Hammond, & Dupuis, 2001; Memon, Hope, Bartlett, & Bull, 2002). Future studies replicating this effect and testing the conditions in which it may or may not be more likely to occur are needed before any strong conclusions can be made on this issue.

ESTIMATOR VARIABLES

There are several estimator variables that have been investigated with line-ups that have yet to be (fully) explored with show-ups. These variables include cross-age identification, cross-race identification, weapon focus, the effects of multiple perpetrators on identification accuracy, and alcohol intoxication.

Age of Witness

Very little show-up research has been conducted with age of witness and age of perpetrator as independent variables. The results from two studies using children (preschool to kindergarten) as witnesses suggest that show-ups lead to a higher rate of correct identifications than do line-ups (Beal, Schmitt, & Dekle, 1995; Dekle, Beal, Elliott, & Hunneycutt, 1996). A third study found no difference in correct identification rate for children (Lindsay, Pozzulo, Craig, Lee, & Corber, 1997). The results from two studies using adults (18–65 years of age) showed a positive effect of using show-ups for target-present identification conditions. For children 8–15 years old and undergraduate students, there is no significant difference in correct identifications between show-ups and line-ups. The results for target-absent conditions are much less positive for show-ups. All of the studies with child witnesses (preschool to 15 years) indicate that much higher rates of false identification are likely with show-ups as compared with line-ups. Overall, show-ups are significantly more suggestive or leading with children (see Lindsay et al., 1997).

Cross-Race Identification

The cross-race effect occurs when the perpetrator or target and the witness are from different racial backgrounds. A recent meta-analysis of the cross-race identification literature found that there is a significant decrease in identification accuracy under these conditions (Meissner & Brigham, 2001). No published studies have examined the cross-race effect with the show-up identification procedure. Therefore, any examination of this phenomenon would be informative to the eyewitness literature. A recent comparison of simultaneous and sequential line-ups in the same-race and cross-race contexts found interactions with identification procedure, suggesting that the results with one procedure need not generalize to others (Lindsay, Brigham, Malpass, & Ross, 2003).

Weapon Focus

The weapon focus effect is a general effect in which any object that draws attention away from the target will lead to a decrease in identification accuracy (Steblay, 1992). This effect has generally been tested with weapons, such as knives and guns, but can also be found with unusual items that are inconsistent with the situation (Pickel, 1999, this volume). No published studies have examined the weapon focus effect with the show-up identification procedure.

Multiple Perpetrators

In situations where multiple perpetrators are involved in a crime, the witness may be required to try to identify more than one of the offenders. Although no published studies could be located on the effect of multiple perpetrators on identification accuracy from show-ups, research suggests that as the number of targets increases, the quality of target descriptions decreases (Clifford & Hollin, 1981; Sporer, 1996; van Koppen & Lochun, 1997). The effect of viewing multiple targets is likely to be a decrease in identification accuracy, as witness attention would be divided among the individuals, and details of the perpetrators would be more difficult to discern. Empirical tests of this hypothesis are needed to determine whether show-up identifications might lead to more accurate decisions because of the speed with which they can be conducted after an event or more false identifications because multiple suspects are being exposed to this suggestive procedure. As with the match of clothing and person, the fact that police produce multiple suspects, each to be presented shortly after the event, could increase inferences of guilt independently of true recognition.

Alcohol

To date, there is one published study on the effects of alcohol on identification accuracy from show-ups (Dysart, Lindsay, MacDonald, & Wicke, 2002). In addition, Dysart and Lindsay (2006) further investigated the show-up procedure's effectiveness at reducing identification errors with intoxicated participants, a group of witnesses who are rarely investigated in the eyewitness area. In fact, most studies conducted to date with intoxicated witnesses have exposed intoxicated witnesses to an event and then conducted an identification task at a later time when the witnesses were sober (Read, Yuille, & Tollestrup, 1992; Yuille & Tollestrup, 1990). Prior to the studies of Dysart et al. (2002) and Dysart and Lindsay (2006), no published research had explored the effects of intoxication on identification accuracy while the witness is still intoxicated. If a show-up procedure is used because a suspect has been apprehended relatively quickly after a crime, it is plausible that witnesses may be asked to attempt identification from show-ups while still intoxicated. The importance of conducting this type of research is supported by the fact that over 460,000 crimes of violence and theft occur every year in the United States in bars, restaurants, and nightclubs, where it is likely that at least some of the witnesses to these crimes are under the influence of alcohol (U.S. Department of Justice, 2003).

The effects of alcohol intoxication on eyewitness identification accuracy were predicted from alcohol myopia theory (Steele & Josephs, 1990). Alcohol myopia theory states that intoxicated individuals have restricted cognitive capacity and are only able to attend to the most salient aspects in their environment. Therefore, with regard to criminal investigations, there are many predictions that alcohol myopia theory can make in relation to the procedures that police might use. For example, if a police officer were to draw a witness's attention to a particular feature of the criminal, such as clothing, it is possible that an intoxicated witness would be more sensitive to that information and would perhaps be more likely to use it in his or her identification decision.

In the study by Dysart et al. (2002), witnesses at various levels of alcohol intoxication (0.00% to 0.20% blood-alcohol level) interacted with a target and were asked soon thereafter to try to identify that individual from a photo show-up. Participants viewed a target-present or target-absent show-up to determine the effects of alcohol intoxication on both correct identifications of the target and false identifications of an innocent, similar-looking person. The results of this study showed that alcohol intoxication had no effect on correct identifications of the target individual; however, as blood-alcohol level increased, witnesses were significantly more likely to make a false identification of the innocent suspect.

Dysart and Lindsay (2006) combined the effects of alcohol intoxication and two of the system variables already studied in the eyewitness area: clothing bias and instruction bias (Lindsay, Wallbridge, & Drennan, 1987; Steblay, 1997; Yarmey, Yarmey, & Yarmey, 1994, 1996). Clothing bias was manipulated in two ways: standard clothing bias, where the innocent suspect is presented in clothing worn by the culprit, and a match-to-description clothing bias, where the suspect was presented in clothing similar to that described by the witness after the event (regardless of whether or not the description was accurate). Both intoxicated and sober witnesses were affected by the match-to-description clothing bias manipulation, but, as predicted, the intoxicated witnesses were particularly affected.

Dysart and Lindsay (2006) also explored the effect of instruction bias on identification accuracy from show-ups. As stated earlier, research with instruction bias has focused on the effects of suggesting to witnesses that the criminal is present in the procedure and that their task is to "pick him out" or select him (i.e., leading instructions). The current research differed from this type of bias by focusing on the other end of the bias continuum: cautious instructions. For example, if a police officer wanted a witness to be careful when making a decision, what would be the effect of an additional warning of the possibility of identification error? Although this question had yet to be answered with sober witnesses, it was particularly interesting to investigate with intoxicated witnesses, as it would be reasonable for a police officer, when dealing with a witness under the influence of alcohol, to encourage a careful decision. The cautious instructions were influential for both sober and intoxicated witnesses, but, again, especially so for intoxicated witnesses. In fact, the most accurate group of witnesses in the experiment was the intoxicated witnesses exposed to a target-absent show-up after the cautious instructions (97% accurate).

Combined, the results of these experiments suggest that intoxicated witnesses presented with show-ups can be as accurate, or more accurate, than sober witnesses under certain circumstances. These results do not suggest that intoxicated witnesses are more accurate under all circumstances, and therefore more research with this group of witnesses is certainly needed.

CONCLUDING COMMENTS

Rates of correct identification vary widely from as high as 92% (Dysart et al., in press) to as low as 0% (Gonzalez et al., 1993) in studies using show-ups. The cause of the variation in correct identification rates is likely due to the level of similarity between the target and his photograph, the length of exposure, and possibly the type of exposure (live vs. videotape). Regardless of the overall level of correct identification, the research consistently indicates little or no difference between the show-up and line-up procedures in terms of correct identification, except for child and elderly witnesses in a few studies. Further exploration of this possible age effect is needed.

In a recent survey, 65% of eyewitness experts indicated that they believed that the show-up is a risky procedure (Kassin, Tubb, Hosch, & Memon, 2001). Their concern was for false rather than correct identifications. The data strongly support their concerns. The show-up is unduly suggestive, resulting in false identification rates consistently higher from show-ups than from line-ups. At the same time, the pattern in the literature is for witnesses to make a "not there" decision more often with a show-up than with a line-up identification procedure. Ironically, this produces a pattern in which show-ups produce both a higher rate of correct rejections and a higher rate of false identifications than line-ups. We need to communicate this effect to police and the courts so that they realize that the lower choice rate from show-ups does not translate into a lower false identification rate than obtained with line-ups.

There are two good reasons to continue studying the show-up procedure. First, there are so many unknowns at this point because so little research has been done that it is clearly premature to abandon the topic. For example, show-ups may be a technique of choice for elderly witnesses. Second, and most important, police will not abandon the show-up. If the procedure will be in use, we (and they) need to know much more about it.

ACKNOWLEDGMENT

Preparation of this chapter was supported by grants to R. Lindsay from the Social Sciences and Humanities Research Council of Canada.

REFERENCES

Beal, C. R., Schmitt, K. L., & Dekle, D. J. (1995). Eyewitness identification of children: Effects of absolute judgments, nonverbal response options, and event encoding. *Law and Human Behavior, 19,* 197–216.

Behrman, B., & Davey, S. (2001). Eyewitness identification in actual criminal cases: An archival analysis. *Law and Human Behavior, 25,* 475–491.

Behrman, B., & Vayder, L. T. (1994). The biasing influence of a police showup: Does the observation of a single suspect taint later identification? *Perceptual & Motor Skills, 79,* 1239–1248.

Bradfield, A. L., Wells, G. L., & Olson, E. A. (2002). The damaging effect of confirming feedback on the relation between eyewitness certainty and identification accuracy. *Journal of Applied Psychology, 87,* 112–120.

Brehm, J. W. (1966). *A theory of psychological reactance.* New York: Academic Press.

Clifford, B. R., & Hollin, C. R. (1981). Effects of the type of incident and the number of perpetrators on eyewitness memory. *Journal of Applied Psychology, 66,* 364–370.

Dekle, D. J., Beal, C. R., Elliott, R., & Hunneycutt, D. (1996). Children as witnesses: A comparison of line-up versus showup identification methods. *Applied Cognitive Psychology, 10,* 1–12.

Doob, A. N., & Kirshenbaum, H. M. (1973). Bias in police lineups—Partial remembering. *Journal of Police Science and Administration, 18,* 287–293.

Dysart, J. E., & Lindsay, R. C. L. (2006). Intoxicated witnesses: The effects of clothing and instruction bias on identification accuracy from show-ups. Under review.

Dysart, J. E., Lindsay, R. C. L., & Dupuis, P. R. (in press). Clothing matters: The effects of clothing bias on identification accuracy from show-ups. *Applied Cognitive Psychology.*

Dysart, J. E., Lindsay, R. C. L., Hammond, R., & Dupuis, P. (2001). Mug shot exposure prior to lineup identification: Interference, transference, and commitment effects. *Journal of Applied Psychology, 86,* 1280–1284.

Dysart, J. E., Lindsay, R. C. L., MacDonald, T. K., & Wicke, C. (2002). The intoxicated witness: Effects of alcohol on identification accuracy. *Journal of Applied Psychology, 87,* 170–175.

Flowe, H., Ebbesen, E., Burke, C., & Chivabunditt, P. (2001, June). *At the scene of the crime: An examination of the external validity of published studies on line-up identification accuracy.* Paper presented at the annual meeting of the American-Psychological Society, Toronto, Ontario, Canada.

Gonzalez, R., Ellsworth, P. C., & Pembroke, M. (1993). Response biases in line-ups and show-ups. *Journal of Personality and Social Psychology, 64,* 525–537.

Kassin, S. M., Tubb, V. A., Hosch, H. M., & Memon, A. (2001). On the "general acceptance" of eyewitness testimony research. *American Psychologist, 56,* 405–416.

Lindsay, R. C. L., & Bellinger, K. (1999). Alternatives to the sequential lineup: The importance of controlling the pictures. *Journal of Applied Psychology, 84,* 315–321.

Lindsay, R. C. L., Brigham, J. C., Malpass, R. S., & Ross, D. F. (2003, July). *Cross-race identification from simultaneous and sequential lineups.* Society for Applied Research in Memory And Cognition, Aberdeen, Scotland.

Lindsay, R. C. L., Lea, J. A., Nosworthy, G. J., Fulford, J. A., Hector, J., LeVan, V., et al. (1991). Biased line-ups: Sequential presentation reduces the problem. *Journal of Applied Psychology, 76,* 796–802.

Lindsay, R. C. L., Nosworthy, G. J., Martin, R., & Martynuck, C. (1994). Using mugshots to find suspects. *Journal of Applied Psychology, 79,* 121–130.

Lindsay, R. C. L., Pozzulo, J. D., Craig, W., Lee, K., & Corber, S. (1997). Simultaneous lineups, sequential lineups, and showups: Eyewitness identification decisions of adults and children. *Law and Human Behavior, 21,* 219–225.

Lindsay, R. C. L., Wallbridge, H., & Drennan, D. (1987). Do the clothes make the man? An exploration of the effect of lineup attire on eyewitness identification accuracy. *Canadian Journal of Behavioural Science, 19,* 463–478.

Lindsay, R. C. L., & Wells, G. L. (1980). What price justice? Exploring the relationship of lineup fairness to identification accuracy. *Law & Human Behavior, 4,* 303–313.

Lindsay, R. C. L., & Wells, G. L. (1985). Improving eyewitness identifications from line-ups: Simultaneous versus sequential line-up presentations. *Journal of Applied Psychology, 70,* 556–564.

Malpass, R. S. (1981). Effective size and defendant bias in eyewitness identification lineups. *Law and Human Behavior, 5,* 299–309.

Malpass, R. S., & Devine, P. G. (1981). Eyewitness identification. Lineup instructions & the absence of the offender. *Journal of Applied Psychology, 66,* 343–350.

Malpass, R. S., & Lindsay, R. C. L. (1999). Measuring lineup fairness. *Applied Cognitive Psychology, 13*(SI), S1–S7.

McQuiston, D., & Malpass, R. S. (2001, June). *Eyewitness identifications in criminal cases: An archival study.* Paper presented at the fourth biennial meeting of the Society for Applied Research in Memory and Cognition, Kingston, Ontario, Canada.

Meissner, C. A., & Brigham, J. C. (2001a). A meta-analysis of the verbal overshadowing effect in face identification. *Applied Cognitive Psychology, 15,* 603–616.

Meissner, C. A., & Brigham, J. C. (2001b). Thirty years of investigating the own-race bias in memory for faces: A meta-analytic review. *Psychology, Public Policy, & Law, 7,* 3–35.

Memon, A., Hope, L., Bartlett, J., & Bull, R. (2002). Eyewitness recognition errors: The effects of mugshot viewing and choosing in young and old adults *Memory & Cognition, 30,* 1219–1227.

Pickel, K. L. (1999). The influence of context on the "weapon focus" effect. *Law and Human Behavior, 23,* 299–311.

Pozzulo, J. D., & Lindsay, R. C. L. (1999). Elimination line-ups: An improved identification procedure for child eyewitnesses. *Journal of Applied Psychology, 84,* 167–176.

Read, J. D., Yuille, J. C., & Tollestrup, P. (1992). Recollections of a robbery: Effects of arousal and alcohol upon recall and person identification. *Law and Human Behavior, 16,* 425–446.

Sporer, S. L. (1996). Psychological aspects of person descriptions. In S. L. Sporer, R. S. Malpass, & G. Kohnken (Eds.), *Psychological issues in eyewitness identification* (pp. 53–86). Mahwah, NJ: Lawrence Erlbaum Associates.

Steblay, N. (1992). A meta-analytic review of the weapon focus effect. *Law and Human Behavior, 16,* 413–424.

Steblay, N. (1997). Social influence in eyewitness recall: A meta-analytic review of lineup instruction effects. *Law and Human Behavior, 21,* 283–297.

Steblay, N., Dysart, J. E., Fulero, S., & Lindsay, R. C. L. (2001). Eyewitness accuracy rates in sequential and simultaneous line-up presentations: A meta-analytic comparison. *Law and Human Behavior, 25,* 459–473.

Steblay, N., Dysart, J. E., Fulero, S., & Lindsay, R. C. L. (2003). Eyewitness accuracy rates in police showup and line-up presentations: A meta-analytic comparison. *Law and Human Behavior, 27,* 523–540.

Steele, C. M., & Josephs, R. A. (1990). Alcohol myopia: Its prized and dangerous effects. *American Psychologist, 45,* 921–933.

U.S. Department of Justice. (2003). *Criminal victimization in the United States, 2002 Statistical Tables.* NCJ Publication no. 200561. Washington, DC: Author.

van Koppen, P. J., & Lochun, S. K. (1997). Portraying perpetrators: The validity of offender descriptions by witnesses. *Law and Human Behavior, 21,* 661–685.

Wagenaar, W. A., & Veefkind, N. (1992). Comparison of one-person and many-person lineups: A warning against unsafe practices. In F. Losel, D. Bender, & T. Bliesner (Eds.), *Psychology and law: International perspectives* (pp. 275–285). Berlin: Walter De Gruyter.

Wells, G. L. (1978). Applied eyewitness-testimony research: System variables and estimator variables. *Journal of Personality and Social Psychology, 36,* 1546–1557.

Wells, G. L. (1984). How adequate is human intuition for judging eyewitness testimony? In G. L. Wells & E. F. Loftus (Eds.), *Eyewitness testimony: Psychological perspectives* (pp. 256–272). New York: Cambridge University Press.

Wells, G. L. (1993). What do we know about eyewitness identification? *American Psychologist, 48,* 553–571.

Wells, G. L., Leippe, M. R., & Ostrom, T. M. (1979). Guidelines for empirically assessing the fairness of a lineup. *Law and Human Behavior, 3,* 285–293.

Wells, G. L., & Lindsay, R. C. L. (1980). On estimating the diagnosticity of eyewitness nonidentifications. *Psychological Bulletin, 88,* 776–784.

Wells, G. L., Malpass, R. S., Lindsay, R. C. L., Fisher, R. P., Turtle, J. W., & Fulero, S. M. (2000). From the lab to the police station: A successful application of eyewitness research. *American Psychologist, 55,* 581–598.

Wells, G. L., Rydell, S. M., & Seelau, E. P. (1993). The selection of distractors for eyewitness line-ups. *Journal of Applied Psychology, 78,* 835–844.

Wells, G. L., & Turtle, J. (1986). Eyewitness identification: The importance of line-up models. *Psychological Bulletin, 99,* 320–329.

Wright, D. B., Boyd, C. E., & Tredoux, C. G. (2003). Inter-racial contact and the own-race bias for face recognition in South Africa and England. *Applied Cognitive Psychology, 17,* 365–373.

Yarmey, A. D. (1998). Person identification in showups and line-ups. In C. P. Thompson & D. J. Herrmann (Eds.), *Eyewitness memory: Theoretical and applied perspectives* (pp. 131–154). Mahwah, NJ: Lawrence Erlbaum Associates.

Yarmey, A. D., Yarmey, A. L., & Yarmey, M. J. (1994). Face and voice identifications in showups and line-ups. *Applied Cognitive Psychology, 8,* 453–464.

Yarmey, A. D., Yarmey, M. J., & Yarmey, A. L. (1996). Accuracy of eyewitness identification in show-ups and line-ups. *Law and Human Behavior, 20,* 459–477.

Yuille, J. C., & Tollestrup, P. (1990). Some effects of alcohol on eyewitness memory. *Journal of Applied Psychology, 75,* 268–273.

7

Lineup Construction and Lineup Fairness

Roy S. Malpass
University of Texas at El Paso

Colin G. Tredoux
University of Cape Town

Dawn McQuiston-Surrett
Arizona State University

Police lineups come from English criminal law and procedure. According to Devlin (1976), lineups were instituted through a Middlesex magistrate's order in the mid-nineteenth century. They were intended as a fair replacement for the practices of courtroom identification, and showups, which were widely used in nineteenth-century England but widely recognized as potentially unfair to the defendant. Their origin indicates that the notion of fairness is their *raison d'être*. They are intended to secure an identification that can potentially incriminate someone but is fair to those who are subjected to it, particularly those who are innocent of the crime.

Study of the case law in many countries, as well as recent DNA-based exonerations in the United States, indicate that lineups are not invariably fair—many innocent people are convicted after identification from a lineup by an eyewitness. The problem is significant because eyewitness evidence is cited as the most significant source of wrongful conviction (Scheck, Neufeld, & Dwyer, 2001). The DNA exoneration cases where the false conviction is established with near certainty show that eyewitness evidence has been largely responsible for false conviction in more than 70% of cases (www.innocenceproj .org). Wrongful identifications result from a number of failures of police procedure; however, many of these are minimized when the lineups presented to witnesses are fair. If witnesses are induced to make a lineup identification, a fair lineup will expose the innocent suspect to an identification risk of 1/the number of persons in the lineup. A lineup biased against the suspect (because s/he stands out in some manner) adds additional risk. A lineup in which only two members (the defendant and one other) fit the witness's description of the offender increases the identification risk to 1/2. It follows that we must be able to construct fair lineups and to diagnose the fairness of lineups.

The original guidelines of how to construct lineups, as they have come down to us in English law, contained these key ideas: (i) to put a "sufficient number of men" in a line, (ii) "who bear a reasonable resemblance to each other in physical appearance," (iii) "such that the identity of the suspect is not suggested to the witness." In practice, the "sufficient number" came to mean eight in England and six in the United States. The degree of resemblance proved impossible to specify precisely, but case law in England evolved to specify that the resemblance should extend to height, weight, clothing, and general appearance.

We can surmise from this that the original thinking behind the lineup was (i) that it should consist of a number of "plausible" fillers (i.e., nonsuspect lineup members who adequately resemble the suspect), and (ii) that the identity of the suspect should not be suggested by the manner of construction of a lineup, or the way in which it is conducted. From the beginning, then, these two principles persist:

- The suspect should not stand out from the other lineup members, and nor should any filler.
- Fillers should be equally good alternatives to the suspect.

LINEUP STRUCTURE

Decades of empirical research suggest that mistaken eyewitness identifications are more likely to occur when the suspect stands out in a lineup. Police lineups can even appear unfair to independent observers. For example, in a South African case where an eyewitness reported a robbery involving three Indian perpetrators, the police used a lineup containing three Indian suspects and three white fillers [*Pelwani v. S.*, 1963 (2) (PH) H237 (T)]. The court dismissed evidence of identification from the lineup, reasoning that the witness had pointed out the only three people on the lineup that he could have pointed out: that is, the lineup consisted in effect of only three members. A similar case in the United States, in which the suspect was described as a black man, used a six-person lineup containing one black suspect and five white fillers (Ellison & Buckhout, 1981). The egregious unfairness of these lineups is probably beyond dispute, but for many lineups the case is not as clear. Constructing lineups that are fair from the onset of the police investigation is important. Indeed, the National Institute of Justice Research Report titled *Eyewitness Evidence: A Guide for Law Enforcement*[1] (The Guide) (Technical Working Group, 1999) addresses this as the opening principle in the section on composing lineups: "Fair composition of a lineup enables the witness to provide a more accurate identification or nonidentification" (p. 29).

---

[1]The section of the Guide (Technical Working Group, 1999) on composing a photo lineup is quoted in Appendix 1.

Constructing Fair Lineups

Two separate but related constructs have been developed in psychological research on lineup fairness: lineup bias and lineup size (Malpass, 1981; Malpass & Devine, 1983; Wells, Leippe, & Ostrom, 1979).

Lineup Bias.   An unbiased lineup is one in which persons without the visual experience possessed by a witness choose the suspect with a frequency approximating chance expectation, where chance expectation is defined as 1/number of lineup members. Lineups can be biased toward the suspect (more identifications of the suspect than expected) or away from the suspect (fewer identifications than expected). From the perspective of protecting the potentially innocent suspect from false identification, the suspect should not stand out in the lineup as being physically different from the fillers so as to draw extra attention to him, or to suggest his status as "suspect." The Guide expresses this point in the following way: "The investigator shall compose the lineup in such a manner that the suspect does not unduly stand out" (p. 29). *Pelwani v. S.* (1963) provides an excellent example of a lineup that is unfair because it is biased toward the suspect—in that case, three of them! In a fair lineup, attempts should be made to include fillers in the lineup who have been matched on the suspect's general physical characteristics as stated in the verbal description of the suspect given by the witness, or, if an adequate description is not available, with reference to the appearance of the suspect or his/her lineup photo. When the suspect stands out in the lineup relative to the other lineup members, uncertain eyewitnesses may be cued to identify the suspect based simply on his distinctiveness rather than a true match between their memory of the culprit and that lineup member.

The concept of lineup bias is rather obvious. If the witness describes an offender with a scar on his right cheek and the suspect is the only person in the lineup with a scar on the right cheek, the lineup is clearly biased toward the suspect. The Guide provides this caution: "Create a consistent appearance between the suspect and fillers with respect to any unique or unusual feature (e.g., scars, tattoos) used to describe the perpetrator by artificially adding or concealing that feature" (p. 30). Any attribute of the photographs or their presentation that causes the suspect to stand out is potentially biasing.

Lineup size is the degree to which the fillers in the lineup are viable alternatives to the suspect based on the witness's description of the culprit or based on their physical similarity to the suspect. The Guide puts it this way: "Select fillers who generally fit the witness' description of the perpetrator. When there is a limited or inadequate description of the perpetrator provided by the witness, or when the description of the perpetrator differs significantly from the appearance of the suspect, fillers should resemble the suspect in significant features" (p. 29).

The effectiveness of the fillers in a lineup as alternatives to the suspect is of great importance. When a filler is not a plausible alternative to the suspect, the function of that individual in the lineup is reduced. The number of individuals in the lineup is an important matter. When the number of persons in a lineup is 6, a witness who cannot identify the offender but makes a lineup choice anyway will have a 1 in 6 chance of wrongfully choosing the innocent suspect when the offender is actually absent. The corresponding risk in a four person lineup is 25%. Few people would want to risk the loss of their free-dom on a 3:1 bet!

When a lineup includes members who do not fulfill their role as acceptable alter-nates to the suspect, the lineup is effectively smaller than its actual size. Fillers who are not viable alternatives serve no purpose, and the risk of mistaken identification is in-creased because the expectation that an innocent suspect will be chosen merely by chance increases dramatically. Two measures of lineup size based on this principle and an analysis of the contribution of individual fillers to lineup size have been discussed in the literature: Effective Size (Malpass, 1981; Malpass & Devine, 1983) and E' (Tredoux, 1998, 1999). Both measures adjust the size of the lineup downward to reflect the failure of one or more fillers to perform as viable alternatives to the suspect.

Lineups should not be composed of individuals who are too similar to one another. The extreme form of a high-similarity lineup is one where the lineup members are clones of each other. It is self-evident that such a lineup would render witnesses unable to make discriminatory identifications. Although it is argued that lineup members should resem-ble each other in terms of general physical appearance and characteristics based on a witness's description of the culprit, some degree of variation among them is desirable (Wells, 1993; Wells, Seelau, Rydell, & Luus, 1994). The Guide contains this instruction: "Consider that complete uniformity of features is not required. Avoid using fillers who so closely resemble the suspect that a person familiar with the suspect might find it difficult to distinguish the suspect from the fillers" (p. 30). Natural variation among lineup mem-bers is desirable because it allows a witness with a clear memory of the culprit to distin-guish between similar individuals, whereas a witness without a clear memory may be un-able to do so. Likewise, if the suspect is the offender, witnesses will be better able to make an identification, whereas when the suspect is not the offender witnesses will not be aided in identifying him. Variation in the physical appearance of lineup members is not bad unless it causes the suspect to stand out. The variation among lineup members should be meaningful to witnesses in the case where the suspect is actually the offender but not meaningful when the suspect is not the offender.

Selection of Fillers

A number of methods for selecting fillers in lineup construction have been proposed and studied.

Perceptual Similarity to Suspect. The traditional method of lineup construction is a procedure in which lineup fillers are selected based on their physical similarity to the suspect. There are at least two methods for achieving this. First, fillers can be judged per-ceptually (subjectively) by the investigator (police officer or researcher) as to their degree of similarity to the suspect. This is the approach adopted in most police practice, but it is also prevalent in laboratory and field studies of eyewitnesses. Second, filler-suspect similarity can be judged by persons independently of the lineup task, and some criterion can be set so as to utilize as fillers only those persons who exceed the criterion; for ex-ample, a specified proportion of judges may have to agree that the photo is appropriate for the lineup, or the photo must surpass a predetermined point on a scale representing similarity of the prospective filler to the suspect. This approach is taken in a number of studies, including those of Lindsay and Wells (1980) and Malpass and Devine, (1983). However, little is known, in fact, of the systematic relation between degree of suspect-filler similarity and the fairness of lineups, apart from the finding that lineups in which the fillers have low similarity to the suspect have high measures of bias and low measures of Effective Size (Malpass and Devine, 1983). A recent study by Tredoux (2002) reports a potential method for measuring the facial similarity of lineup members from a principal component analysis (PCA) of facial images. The physical measure of similarity derived from the PCA predicted both the result of lineup evaluation procedures based on "mock witnesses" (see below) and eyewitness performance from photospreads. However, whereas low-similarity lineups were shown to result in lineups with high bias and low Effective Size, low-similarity lineups led to greater accuracy, in terms of hits and correct rejections, than moderate- or high-similarity lineups when used with eyewitnesses.

These lineup construction methods are an important attempt to follow the guideline discussed above that the suspect not be physically distinctive from the fillers. Indeed, the similarity strategy is reportedly used most often by police (over 80% of the time) when they construct lineups and photospreads (Wogalter, Malpass, & McQuiston, 2004). However, a series of studies by Wogalter and colleagues suggest that this lineup construction method can actually result in bias or suggestiveness toward the suspect (Laughery, Jensen, & Wogalter, 1988; Marwitz & Wogalter, 1988; Wogalter & Jensen, 1986; Wogalter, Marwitz, & Leonard, 1992). Specifically, research indicates that choosing fillers with reference to physical similarity to the suspect can result in the suspect having unique properties, such as being the "prototype" or having the most familiar face of the group. Paradoxically, this suspect-matched lineup procedure can still result in the suspect standing out. Luus and Wells (1991) also argue that a suspect-matched lineup can result in the lineup members being too similar to one another.

Witness' Verbal Description of Culprit.   An alternative lineup construction method is the *description-matched* strategy, in which fillers are selected based on the witness's description of the culprit instead of the suspect's physical appearance. The rationale for the description-matched procedure is that it meets the criteria for constructing a fair lineup in which the suspect does not stand out relative to the fillers, and at the same time allows for all lineup members to vary on general physical characteristics so as to not make the lineup task impossible for an eyewitness who has a good memory of the culprit (see Wells, Rydell, Seelau, & Luus, 1994). Indeed, the research literature shows an advantage for description-matched lineups over suspect-matched lineups in promoting accurate identifications (e.g., Wells, Rydell, & Seelau, 1993). However, for this procedure to be effective a useful description of the offender is required from the witness(s). "White male, between 20 and 30 years old, 5'6" to 6'0" tall, brown hair and brown eyes wearing faded jeans, white athletic shoes and a black t-shirt" will not prove very helpful in constructing an acceptable lineup with the use of the description-matched procedure since it is quite vague. This underscores a common problem: although they may be accurate, verbal descriptions elicited from witnesses and recorded in police reports are often not very descriptive of the offender in ways that will help to differentiate him/her from others with similar general features.

An additional concern arises when there are multiple eyewitnesses to a crime, each of whom gives a separate description of the culprit to police. It is common for the general descriptions given by separate eyewitnesses to be similar, but for differences to appear in the more specific (and more useful) descriptors. If the descriptions are adequate for use of the match to description strategy, one way to deal with multiple eyewitnesses is to base the selection of fillers on a composite description of the culprit that incorporates the descriptors given by all of the witnesses. This, of course, depends largely on the degree of overlap between descriptions. If there are important differences between separate witness descriptions, it may be necessary to construct different lineups for each witness. Of course if the witness descriptions are inadequate, then a match-to-suspect approach would be more appropriate, and in that case variation in witness descriptions is not of great importance.

Modal Verbal Description of the Suspect.   If a verbal description of the culprit is impoverished or absent, there is an alternative means of choosing fillers based on descriptions. It is to obtain a number of descriptions of the *suspect* from persons similar to the witness(s) in age, sex, and ethnicity (and any other demographic variables thought appropriate to local conditions). The modal descriptors can be found and used to guide filler selection.

Our preference is to base filler choice on a verbal description of the culprit, if a useful one is available, and secondarily on physical similarity to the suspect (to augment the verbal description).

EVALUATING THE SUCCESS
OF LINEUP CONSTRUCTION

There are at least three contexts in which lineup fairness should be evaluated:

1. Law enforcement should evaluate and document the size and bias of their lineups prior to use.
2. Scholars using lineups in research should evaluate and document lineup size and bias as a matter of quantifying this aspect of the stimulus materials used in their work, as a guide to replication.
3. Defense attorneys should routinely evaluate the lineups that form the basis for an eyewitness identification in their cases. If the lineup can be shown to have been structurally or procedurally unfair, it may be possible to win a motion to suppress the identification evidence. Failing that, evidence of unfairness may be introduced in court.

It is not enough to follow the procedures outlined here to ensure that a fair lineup has been produced. Its degree of fairness should be demonstrated, and adjustments made if necessary. Psychologists have pioneered a methodology for doing this by developing techniques for constructing fair lineups and creating quantitative fairness measures. Research on lineup fairness started in earnest with a paper by Doob and Kirshenbaum (1973). They served as consultants in a Canadian case, *R v. Shatford*, which turned on a lineup identification made by a single eyewitness. The eyewitness made an identification at the lineup despite the fact that the only description of the perpetrator she was able to give was that he was "attractive." Doob and Kirshenbaum suspected that the witness was basing her identification on a "memory fragment" or perhaps even on her earlier insubstantial description to the police. The second possibility seemed to have some weight, because the suspect was particularly attractive. In order to test this possibility, Doob and Kirshenbaum had 20 naïve subjects rate members of the lineup for attractiveness. The suspect received an attractiveness rating substantially higher than that of any of the fillers, suggesting that the suspect could be selected by a witness who remembered only that he was attractive.

In a second stage of the study, Doob and Kirshenbaum showed a photograph of the lineup to 23 "mock witnesses" (persons who had not been present at the original crime), along with the original eyewitness description of the suspect. They reasoned that if the lineup was "fair," those who had not been present at the crime should not be able to identify the suspect, except by guessing. There were 12 people in the lineup, so the expected rate of guessing would be approximately 1/12. If significantly more mock witnesses than this selected the suspect, it would be evidence that the lineup was unfair, and that the structure of the lineup somehow suggested the identity of the suspect to the witnesses. Fourteen of the 22 witnesses selected the suspect, a result that would occur randomly with a probability less than 0.001. They concluded that the lineup was unfair, specifically that it was biased against the suspect.

This innovative research procedure pioneered more than 30 years ago by Doob and Kirshenbaum has become known as "mock witness evaluation" and is the basis for almost all further work on post-hoc assessment of lineup fairness. The purpose of mock witness evaluation is to assess the structural fairness of the lineup—whether the fillers are adequate alternatives to the suspect and whether the suspect stands out from the fillers. Its purpose is not to predict what witnesses would do. The central assumption is this: if persons who have had no exposure whatever to the suspect prior to viewing the lineup can select him from the lineup with a probability greater than chance, then the lineup is biased toward identification of the suspect.

If a lineup is structurally biased, when an actual witness identifies the suspect, one has to ask whether s/he makes the identification based on memory of the person from the witnessed event or whether s/he is merely using the same minimal information used by mock witnesses to make the same choice.

Evaluating an Existing Lineup: Principles

Evaluating an existing lineup is in principle very similar to lineup construction, using similar analytical concepts. The basic questions are:

- Does the suspect stand out from the other members of the lineup?
- Are the fillers adequate alternatives to the suspect?

The standard for answering these questions requires some clarification. Fairness evaluation is not based on replicating or simulating the perspective of actual witnesses. If we were to write an equation (or model) for predicting the response of a witness to an eyewitness identification lineup, it would include at least these factors/categories:

1. The amount/quality of the information (visual memory) the witness has about the offender,
2. These, and other factors, related to the likelihood of the witness making an identification (decision criterion), independent of the information they have of:
    a. The witness's understanding of the lineup identification task.
    b. The witness's willingness to cooperate with the perceived wishes of the administering officer.
    c. The degree to which the witness believes that the administering officer wants him/her to choose someone from the lineup.
3. The fairness of the lineup.

The first category of variables cannot be known by psychologists or by the criminal justice system independently of the identification process and are not under their control. The second category can be influenced to some degree by instructions/admonitions and other aspects of the lineup procedure. But these are matters of lineup administration rather than the structural fairness of the lineup itself. The structural fairness of the lineup, on the other hand, can be known in great detail and is completely under the control of the criminal justice system. The purpose of the mock witness procedure is to quantify structural lineup fairness, not to estimate the effects of the other two classes of influences on the eyewitness' lineup choice. In this way assessment of the role of lineup structure in the actual witness's response to the lineup is separated from the other factors that influence it.

The mock witness paradigm controls the first category of variables by holding them constant and eliminating them as contributors to the result of the mock witness process. It provides either no information about the suspect or very particular (but nonvisual) information. It instructs each mock witness to choose one of the members of the lineup. In this way the mock witness procedure is sensitive only to variations in the structure of a lineup (the relationships in physical and attributional appearance among the lineup members) or the structure of a lineup, given the descriptive information provided to the mock witnesses, and not other factors that might influence the likelihood of making a lineup choice at all.

When a witness makes an identification there may be ambiguity about how to interpret it. The identification could come about as a result of the witness choosing the suspect from the lineup solely on the basis of his or her memory that this specific person is the person he or she saw committing the witnessed crime. Or the identification could come from a more complex process: the witness may make a cluster of judgments that result in an identification. The witness may believe that s/he would not be called to examine a lineup if the police did not have a suspect, and furthermore that the police are seldom wrong, so it is highly likely that the actual culprit is in the lineup. Given these beliefs, it would be easy for the witness to approach the task by looking for the one member of the lineup who is most likely to be the culprit. In such a case a suspect who stands out from the fillers, even when factually innocent, is at risk of identification by a wholly rational, cooperative, and well-intentioned witness.

Witness identifications cannot be interpreted directly, in an absolute way. The basis for this is developed by Wells (1993) in the "lineups as experiments" analogy. In order to interpret an identification, a control comparison is required that allows the finders of fact to know the result of identifications made by people who had no visual information at all about the suspect in the lineup. Experiments include control groups because the effects of experimental treatments require interpretation against some base or standard condition. This idea also characterizes lineup identifications: the witness identification cannot be interpreted without information about the effects of background factors, prominent among them being the effect of the lineup's structure—its fairness in the sense of both size and bias.

When a lineup is biased toward the suspect, the witness may not need any memory at all of the criminal or the event in question in order to know which member of the lineup is the suspect. A good analogy for this is multiple-choice tests in educational settings: if a multiple-choice item is given to students in which the correct choice is known because all of the alternative choices are obviously false, the item is no test of knowledge of the subject.

Evaluating an Existing Lineup: Procedure

Information Given to Mock Witnesses

There is a range of information that can be provided to mock witnesses as a basis for their lineup choice. They could be given no information at all, and simply be asked to indicate which member of the lineup is the police suspect. If mock witnesses can reliably choose the suspect based on no particular information apart from a simple inspection of the lineup, then identification by an actual witness adds no information about the guilt of the suspect. Alternatively, mock witnesses could be given the verbal description the witness gave to law enforcement, as in the study by Doob and Kirshenbaum (1973). Another alternative is to provide mock witnesses with a modal or composite description of the suspect. Each of these is described below.

Culprit Description. Verbal descriptions collected by law enforcement appear not to be elicited with the purpose of obtaining individuating information. Many printed/ online forms used for police reports contain categories that are not conducive to this purpose. As a result, descriptions are often far less effective than they might be. In particular, they are less an aid to lineup construction than they could be.

If the lineup fillers were chosen on the basis of the culprit description, then one matter of interest is whether the suspect stands out with respect to the culprit description. In that case, the information given to mock witnesses is the description given by eyewitnesses as obtained from police records. This is the classic starting point for mock witness evaluation of lineups. If there are multiple but divergent descriptions given by a single witness, a composite description can be made. But if there are divergent descriptions given by multiple witnesses, then as many lineup evaluations must be made as there are divergent descriptions.

Suspect Description.   Suspects are "nominated" through many routes besides the verbal description of the culprit. The police will often pick a suspect based on knowledge of persons in the area, and through forms of information unrelated to facial appearance. For these and other reasons, the suspect may bear little similarity to the description(s) given by eyewitnesses. When this occurs, the question still is whether s/he stands out from the fillers. To evaluate this possibility, mock witnesses may be given a "modal" description of the suspect. To obtain a modal description, the investigator should obtain a photograph of the suspect taken close to the time of the offense. Then using that photograph, the investigator obtains a description of the suspect from a sample of judges who are of the same demographic categories as the witness, with respect to approximate age, sex, ethnicity, and social class (primarily because descriptive vocabulary may vary along these lines). Although the purpose is not to simulate the eyewitness, using descriptive language unfamiliar to the witness(es) may give a misleading conclusion as to whether or not the suspect stands out, as described.

There is at least one special instance in which a modal description can be useful. If the witness has seen or helped to construct a composite image of the culprit during the investigation process, his/her memory for the appearance of the culprit is likely to have been modified (Topp, McQuiston, & Malpass, 2003). In such a case it would be appropriate to use modal description information based on the composite image as the description given to mock witnesses.

No Description.   Mock witnesses may generally believe that their task is to choose based on the descriptive information provided them (McQuiston & Malpass, 2002). However, we know that there is more to lineup identifications than that. Research shows that if a lineup member's appearance fits a criminal appearance stereotype, his/her likelihood of being identified as the culprit is increased (McQuiston & Malpass, 2002). For this reason it is possible that the suspect may stand out from the fillers on a basis that is not related to culprit or suspect descriptions, but is based on other grounds that may not be clearly discernible. As argued above, the most basic evaluation of lineup fairness is one in which the lineup is displayed with no other information given. If mock witnesses choose the suspect with greater than chance frequency, the lineup is unfair in size, bias, or both.

Composite.   Composite images made during the course of an investigation are known to be highly variable in their similarity to the offender (see Davies & Valentine, this volume; Shepherd & Ellis, 1996). It may be of interest to show mock witnesses a copy of the composite image when the witness has constructed or has been shown a composite, and when the original witness description does not resemble the suspect. The rationale, of course, is to inquire into whether the witness's memory has been contaminated: Any identification of the suspect following viewing of a composite raises the question of whether the identification is based on the witness's memory for the face of the offender at the time of the offense or on their memory of the composite. Topp, McQuiston, and Malpass (2003) show that for witnesses who participated in constructing a composite and then subsequently viewed it at least once, there was a contamination of their memory for the target face in the direction of the composite.

Our recommended approach is to routinely do multiple mock witness evaluations based on no description at all, one of the description types, and on a composite if one was produced. This provides a rough quantitative dimension to the question of how much information is necessary for identification of the suspect: mock witnesses with no personal individuating information, mock witnesses with a verbal description of the offender, or an eyewitness with the unique individuating information that comes from having seen the person before, presumably committing the offense in question. Once more, the logic is that if one can identify the suspect based on the knowledge provided to mock witnesses in the first two of these, one does not need to have had the knowledge possessed by an eyewitness in the third, and the meaning of an eyewitness identification is ambiguous.

QUANTITATIVE MEASURES OF LINEUP FAIRNESS

To preserve the distinction between the size and bias aspects of lineups, we discuss these separately. Before proceeding with that discussion, however, the desired attributes of quantitative indicators of lineup fairness require a brief discussion.

Desiderata for Lineup Fairness Measures

What are the *desiderata* for measures of lineup size and bias? First, the measures must reflect the theoretical meaning of the concepts to be measured. Therefore, bias should reflect the degree to which the suspect in a lineup will be chosen at a rate above or below chance expectation (where chance expectation is based on the number of people in the lineup). Lineup size should reflect the adequacy of the individual fillers as alternatives to the suspect.

- The measures should be bounded by the range of the phenomenon. Size measures, for example, must never yield "sizes" that are greater than the number of persons in the lineup.
- The measures should be a calibrated monotonic function of changes in the underlying latent variable. This means that the numerical index representing size should increase or decrease proportionately with each increase or decrease in the adequacy of a filler, and the index representing bias should change proportionately with each change in preference for the suspect. As bias or size is manipulated by experimenters, the measures should respond in a calibrated monotonic manner.
- The measures should have a sampling distribution that allows for inferential statistical analysis.

- The measures should be accessible to law enforcement officers and the public, so that clear and understandable explanations of their meaning and interpretation can be given.

Does the Suspect Stand Out?
Measures of Lineup Bias

The mock witness procedure, as originally conceptualized by Doob and Kirshenbaum, uses a measure of lineup bias. Bias is the extent to which the proportion of mock witnesses choosing the suspect is greater or less than that expected by chance. When the proportion of mock witnesses choosing the suspect equals that expected by chance (i.e., $1/k$, where k is the number of lineup members), the lineup is unbiased. When it deviates from the expected value, it is biased. The measure has interpretable limits at both the upper and lower ends. As the proportion approaches unity, mock witnesses are choosing the suspect to the exclusion of the fillers, and when the proportion approaches zero, witnesses are failing to choose the suspect at all. However, one can expect the proportion to show random sampling variation, and an important question thus concerns how to interpret the observed proportion. For example, if 7 of 20 mock witnesses (35%) choose the suspect from a five-person lineup, we need to know whether this could reasonably be explained as chance variation from the expected value of 4 of 20 (20%). Doob and Kirshenbaum used a z-test to make this decision, but Tredoux (1998) recommends the direct calculation of binomial probabilities instead. The latter method does not make the assumption of an approximating distribution. Wells, Leippe, and Ostrom (1979) and Tredoux (1998) recommend reporting the proportion as a confidence interval rather than as a point estimate, and Tredoux (1998) refers readers to a formula that is more accurate than that regularly used for computing confidence intervals around proportions.

Usually, eyewitness researchers are interested in situations where the lineup is biased against the suspect (i.e., where the suspect is chosen by a higher proportion of mock witnesses than is expected by chance), but it is also possible that the lineup could be biased in favor of the suspect. Imagine a lineup where 1 of 30 mock witnesses (3%) chooses the suspect from a five-person lineup. This is significantly less than we would expect by chance (binomial $p < 0.01$). On the one hand, this might appear to be of no consequence to the police or to eyewitness researchers, as the suspect's liberty has not been jeopardized unfairly. However, this approach only recognizes the problem of false identifications and fails to recognize that a second kind of error can be committed when a lineup is used, namely the failure to identify a guilty perpetrator. Lineups in which suspects are chosen by mock witnesses at levels significantly below chance responding are poorly constructed and run the risk of committing the second kind of error. Such lineups may be rare, but it is useful to extend the reasoning behind the measure of lineup bias so that it can be used as a warning indicator for both types of fundamental error.

"Nominal," "Functional," and "Effective Size"

The nominal size of a lineup is simply the number of people appearing: suspect plus fillers. The nominal size sets a limit on the *a priori* risk to which an innocent person is exposed. For the most frequent nominal size used in the United States (6), the risk of a false identification from a perfectly fair lineup by a poor but willing eyewitness is 16.67%. A major step toward decreasing the risk of false identification to innocent suspects would be to increase the nominal size of the lineup. An increase to 12 reduces the risk to 8.3%. The degree of the false identification risk ought to be a matter for policy discussions. Assuming that the lineups are fair, increasing nominal size is a simple and effective method for reducing the probability of false alarms. The technology to support this is available where photospread or video lineups are considered acceptable alternatives to corporeal lineups.

A lot depends on whether lineups that contain 5 (or 11, or 19) fillers actually contain that many realistic alternatives to the suspect—whether they are fair in the "size" sense. A lineup containing a white suspect, two white fillers, an African American, a large dog, and a refrigerator has a maximum size of three (similar in effect to *Pelwani v. S*, 1963), and if the two other white fillers are very different from the suspect, the maximum is perhaps even lower. The problem here is to develop quantitative measures that reflect the number of lineup members who act as viable alternatives to the suspect, thus detecting whether the lineup size is effectively smaller than it appears.

Most legal jurisdictions prescribe the number of lineup members (e.g., 6 in most of the United States; 8, 10, or 12 in various parts of Canada; 9 or 10 in England), and fillers who are selected for the lineup are required to be reasonable matches to the suspect on general attributes such as height, weight, hair color, and facial appearance. The notion of a "plausible filler" is inscribed in legal understandings of what a fair lineup should be, and it is important therefore to attempt to measure the number of plausible members in a lineup. We can distinguish between the nominal size of a lineup (i.e., how many people are in it) and its "Effective Size" (i.e., the number of plausible lineup members) (Malpass, 1981).

Wells, Leippe, and Ostrom (1979) recognized this and proposed a proxy measure known as "Functional Size," which is the reciprocal of the proportion of mock witnesses choosing the suspect. Thus, if 10 of 20 people choose the suspect from a five-person lineup, the reciprocal is 20/10 = 2, and the lineup has a Functional Size of only 2. In the hypothetical lineups *d* and *e* of Table 7.1, Functional Size is 2 and 6 respectively, and this corresponds quite well to the apparent difference in the number of plausible fillers between the lineups (i.e., from visual inspection of the array frequencies).

The concept underlying Functional Size (i.e., to distinguish the number of nominal and plausible lineup members) is a good one, but there are a number of reasons to consider alternative measures. First, Functional Size is not a sufficient estimator: it takes account only of the number of mock witnesses choosing the suspect and does not consider the fillers, except in aggregate. It is possible to arrive at values of Functional Size that suggest a lineup with an acceptable number of plausible fillers, where this is clearly not the case. Such an example is shown in lineup *f* of Table 7.1.

Second, it is possible to arrive at values of Functional Size that cannot be interpreted in any reasonable sense as the number of plausible lineup members. In the case of lineup *g* in Table 7.1, for instance, the nominal size is 6, and the Functional Size is 100. This estimate is not meaningful in the sense of indicating the number of plausible lineup members.

TABLE 7.1.
Functional Size in a Number of Hypothetical Lineups

Lineup	Member						Not Present	Functional Size
	1	2	3	4*	5	6		
d	5	3	6	30	9	3	4	2
e	8	9	8	10	9	9	7	6
f	1	3	20	10	21	4	1	6
g	20	50	4	1	20	5	0	100

* = suspect.

Third, it is possible for the Functional Size of a lineup to be identical to its nominal size and for the distribution of identifications to exhibit a clearly different picture about the number of plausible fillers. Lineup f of Table 7.1 is one example. The Functional Size of the lineup is 6, suggesting six plausible lineup members, when there are only two. It is easy to imagine many other patterns of distribution of mock witness choices across the fillers that show a similar result.

At the heart of the matter is the fact that Wells et al.'s (1979) measure of Functional Size is not a size measure, but rather a bias measure. It is the reciprocal of the proportion of mock witnesses who choose the suspect, and although it may be possible to give it a quasi-size interpretation, its computational basis restricts it to a statement about how frequently the suspect is chosen.

Effective Size. Malpass (1981) suggested Effective Size as a measure of the number of plausible lineup members. Effective Size has a maximum of k, the number of lineup members, and a minimum of 1 (assuming that mock witnesses must choose one member of the lineup). Starting from the maximum value, a subtraction is made for each lineup member who is chosen at a rate that differs from chance expectation.

The assumption underlying the notion of Effective Size is appealing: one or more of the fillers in a lineup may present an inadequate test of a witness who has little more than general knowledge of the appearance of the offender, and we shouldn't take the ability of a witness to reject such fillers very seriously. The calculation of Effective Size acts on this assumption by reducing the nominal size of the lineup according to departures of proportionate identification of individual fillers from that expected by an equiprobability model (every lineup member drawing the same number of mock witness choices). For many distributions of identifications the measure gives an indication of the number of fillers that could reasonably be considered to be present, at least from visual inspection of array frequencies. Lineups h, i, and j in Table 7.2 are clear examples.

However, there are a number of weaknesses with the Effective Size measure (see Tredoux, 1998). Most importantly, there is no known sampling distribution for Effective Size, which weakens the kinds of conclusions researchers or practitioners can draw about particular lineups.

TABLE 7.2.
Effective Size in a Number of Hypothetical Lineups

Lineup Member	1	2	3	4*	5	6	E_a
h	0	25	5	25	3	2	2.83
i	10	10	9	10	11	10	5.90
j	1	0	12	12	0	11	3.17
k	7	7	7	24	8	7	4.60
l	12	6	9	13	14	6	5.10
m	6	19	3	20	8	10	4.45

E_a = Effective Size calculated with adjustment for null fillers.
* = suspect

Tredoux (1998) suggested an alternative computational formula for Effective Size that retains most of the desirable properties, with the important added benefit of a known sampling distribution. Specifically, the measure has a maximum of k, the number of lineup fillers, and a minimum of 1 (assuming that mock witnesses are required to choose a lineup member). If some lineup members attract more choices than others, this will result in a reduction of the value of E' from k toward 1. The formula is as follows:

$$E' = \frac{1}{1 - I}$$

where I is defined as

$$1 - \sum_{i=1}^{k} \left(\frac{O_i}{N} \right)^2$$

where O_i is the observed number of mock witnesses who choose lineup member i, N is the number of mock witnesses, and k is the number of lineup members.

Methods for using E' inferentially can be found in Tredoux (1998). These are relatively uncomplicated and can be incorporated into a spreadsheet for easy computation (download http://www.eyewitness.utep.edu/images/size-calc.xls for an example). Some authors have reported a high correlation between E' and Effective Size (Corey, Malpass, & McQuiston, 1999; Tredoux, 2002), but the relation has not been systematically investigated. In order to do so, we computed some simulation data over different numbers of mock witnesses and different sizes of lineup. Lineup frequencies were randomly generated to produce a range of values for E between 1 and nominal lineup size. Five thousand lineups were generated for each combination of nominal size and number of mock witnesses. The correlation between E' and Effective Size is shown in Table 7.3 for each of these combinations. It is clear from Table 7.3 that E' and Effective Size are very closely related, even for relatively small samples of mock witnesses.

TABLE 7.3.
Correlations between E' and Effective Size in a Series of Simulated Lineups

	$N = 20$	$N = 30$	$N = 50$	$N = 100$	$N = 1000$
$k = 6$	0.97	0.987	0.994	0.997	0.998
$k = 9$	0.986	0.996	0.998	0.999	0.999
$k = 12$	0.982	0.991	0.996	0.999	0.999

All correlations are significant at $p < 0.001$.

Are Lineup Size and Lineup Bias Independent?

There are important reasons why we should attempt to measure Effective Size as well as lineup bias when we evaluate lineups. A lineup may appear biased if the suspect is chosen at a rate higher than expected by chance, but this might not be a fair conclusion if the Effective Size of the lineup is lower than the nominal size. Consider the lineup shown in Table 7.4. The suspect is chosen by 31% of the mock witnesses, whereas chance expectation is 16.67%. This is a statistically significant difference, but is the lineup biased against the suspect? If we take into account that two other fillers are chosen at exactly the same rate as the suspect, we will probably conclude that the lineup is not biased against the suspect, as there are other fillers that receive as many mock witness choices. What is much more of a problem is that the lineup has a low Effective Size. There are only three plausible identification alternatives in the lineup: the suspect and two fillers. The real danger to the suspect is a witness who chooses randomly among the plausible lineup members: the risk of mistaken identification is not the intended 1/6, but more like 1/3.

Effective Size clearly provides information about lineups over and above that given by lineup bias, but the measures are not independent. A lineup with high bias can also be a lineup with low Effective Size. However, the converse is not true. The relation between lineup bias (when defined as proportion of mock witnesses choosing the suspect) and Effective Size (when defined as by Tredoux, 1998) is shown in Figure 7–1. Note that in the right-hand side of the figure the measures are strongly dependent, but in the left-hand side they are much less dependent.

TABLE 7.4.
Effective Size in a Series of Hypothetical Lineups

Lineup Member	1	2	3	4*	5	6	E_a	E
	1	25	2	25	2	25	3.38	3.4

E_a = Effective Size (Malpass, 1981). E' = Effective Size (Tredoux, 1998).
* = suspect

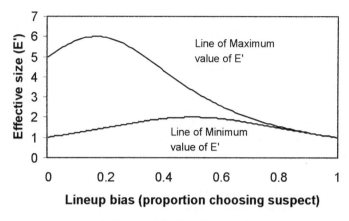

Values calculated for a six person lineup

FIGURE 7-1.   The relationship between lineup bias and lineup size.

Other Measures of Lineup Fairness

Defendant Bias.   Malpass (1981) proposed an alternative measure of lineup bias, which takes into account the Effective Size of the lineup. Ordinarily, we would consider $1/k$ to be the proportion of suspect identifications expected by chance guessing, but Malpass suggests that this might better be calculated as 1/[Effective Size]. The idea here is that the likelihood of being selected randomly by a witness is less a function of the nominal size of the lineup than a function of the number of plausible fillers present in the lineup. Then, instead of evaluating the proportion of suspect identifications against $1/k$, we evaluate it against 1/[Effective Size]. This suggestion seems very sensible to us: in most police or research lineups we have seen, Effective Size is rarely equal in value to nominal size, and testing lineup bias for significance by comparing the proportion of suspect identifications with $1/k$ would be fairly meaningless—it will nearly always be significant. In line with our discussion earlier on lineup size, it makes more sense to us to first establish the Effective Size of the lineup and then to determine whether the suspect is chosen from the remaining plausible fillers at levels greater than that of any of the other fillers.

Percentage below Expectation.   Malpass and Devine (1983) suggest a method for evaluating the suitability of individual lineup members, based on the extent to which the member is chosen below chance expectation in a mock witness task. Only those fillers that are chosen by mock witnesses above a specified proportion of chance expectation are considered to be acceptable fillers.

An alternative approach to measuring lineup fairness would then be to set a minimum number of plausible lineup members and to determine whether the lineup meets this minimum size requirement. Tredoux (1998) argued that this approach is too much at the mercy of random sampling variation and suggests that a better method may be to construct confidence intervals around the observed proportion of identifications that each filler receives and to apply the minimum criterion test to the endpoint(s) of the intervals. Assume, for example, that we set a minimum criterion of 7% of mock witness choices per lineup filler; that is, no filler should attract fewer than 7% of the mock witness choices. Now, if filler A receives 10% of the choices, but a 95% confidence interval around that point estimate of 10% is [6%–14%], then we would reject the filler because 6% falls within the confidence interval. The full interval needs to be higher than the minimum acceptable percentage of mock witness choices. This has the benefit of attaching some level of probability to decisions made about the plausibility of fillers.

VALIDITY OF MOCK WITNESS EVALUATIONS

Measures of lineup fairness are derived from mock witness evaluations of lineups. It is implicitly assumed that these measures tell us something about how eyewitnesses will perform on the same lineups. If a mock witness evaluation of a particular lineup produces a high bias estimate, this is taken to suggest that an eyewitness is more likely to choose the suspect from that lineup, even if he is innocent, than from a low-bias lineup. Is this assumption warranted? Are mock witness measures of lineup fairness valid measures? Do lineups that are unfair in either sense, size or bias, lead to the expected increases in false identification?

There are good reasons for concern, as mock witnesses and eyewitnesses differ in several important ways. Mock witnesses by definition have no direct knowledge regarding the perpetrator's (or suspect's) appearance. Eyewitnesses, on the other hand, have access to memory of the perpetrator's appearance as well as to the verbal description they gave. If an eyewitness to a particular event has given an inaccurate description of the perpetrator, or if law enforcement procedure has elicited only an impoverished description, s/he may at the same time have an intact and more differentiated memory for the perpetrator's appearance, and s/he may identify an innocent suspect who resembles the perpetrator. Because the witness's visual memory is different from the verbal description in important ways, the development of a fair lineup based on the description may not represent a fair lineup based on the witness's visual memory. This can happen even if the mock witness evaluation (based on a verbal description) suggests that the lineup is unbiased and has a reasonable number of plausible fillers. Some studies suggest that eyewitnesses are generally not good at providing accurate verbal descriptions (Meissner, Sporer, & Schooler, this volume). If lineups are constructed so that fillers match the description of the perpetrator rather than the suspect's physical appearance, we can expect this problem to be significant: a match to description strategy should ensure a favorable mock witness evaluation, but if it is based on a poor description it may not adequately test the fairness of the lineup. The lineup evaluation process needs better descriptions from the investigation process, beginning with first responder reports. And those engaging in lineup evaluation (during their initial construction as well as later evaluations) should assess the quality of available descriptions. In particular, great care should be used in deciding whether to use a match-to-description strategy in lineup construction. There is little research directly on the point of the quality of verbal descriptions of faces or the description attributes that make them useful.

The assumption that mock witness evaluations give us information about the fairness of police lineups should clearly be validated. While the number of validation studies is small, they give general support to the idea that mock witness evaluation gives us information about the fairness of police lineups.

Brigham and Brandt (1992) report a study in which overall judgments of fairness made by samples of law officers and college students were compared with estimates of Functional and Effective Size, as derived from mock witness evaluations. Twenty-three photo lineups were created, so that eight could reasonably be classified as fair, an additional eight as moderately fair, and seven as least fair. The law officers and students first assessed the overall fairness of each lineup and then evaluated each of the five fillers on a 6-point "acceptability" scale. Across the 23 lineups, two of the mock witness measures, proportion of mock witness suspect-identifications and Effective Size, were consistently related to fairness measures derived from the student and law officer samples.

Lindsay, Smith, and Pryke (2000) argued that the most important validation for lineup measures from a forensic point of view is criterion related: the measures should be able to predict the occurrence of false positive identifications (i.e., identifications of innocent suspects). Presumably, false positives are brought about by the use of biased/unfair lineups, and bias/fairness estimates—if they are valid—should be correlated with their occurrence. Lindsay et al. exposed participants to a staged crime and then conducted 18 lineups, some of which contained the perpetrator, and others of which did not. In order to generate a larger sample size than would ordinarily have been obtained for the mock witness evaluation task, Lindsay et al. treated all of the innocent lineup fillers in the perpetrator absent lineup as suspects, one at a time. They used identification rates for each filler to determine both lineup bias and Effective Size. They then correlated measures of bias and size with the rate of false-positive identification made by eyewitnesses for each of the 18 lineups. Unfortunately, because each filler is treated as a suspect replacement, their calculations of lineup size are redundant (see Tredoux, 1999, for a full version of this criticism). One lineup is turned into six lineups when each lineup member is treated as a suspect, and then the same set of mock witness choices is used to calculate effective size each time. The effective size is thus the same for each "lineup" created in this articifical way, and the resulting predictor is invalid. Lindsay et al. report a significant correlation of 0.64 ($p < 0.05$) between lineup bias (proportion of mock witnesses choosing the suspect) and the rate of false-positive identifications by eyewitnesses, and a nonsignificant correlation of 0.1 between lineup size (Effective Size) and the rate of false-positive identifications. A later study by the same authors (Smith, Lindsay, and Pryke, 1999), using much the same methodology, found a significant correlation between lineup bias and "eyewitness accuracy," albeit of considerably smaller magnitude ($r = 0.2$). They did not use a measure of lineup size as a predictor, however, and their method of calculating lineup fairness used nonindependent data in much the same manner as the earlier study.

Tredoux, Parker, and Nunez (2004), noting the statistical dependency in Lindsay et al.'s (1999) study and the similar dependency in Smith et al's (2000) study, conducted a staged crime experiment, testing the ability of lineup measures to predict eyewitness identifications of innocent suspects. Three lineups of varying degrees of fairness were created for each of two perpetrators and evaluated by mock witnesses, and were used to test eyewitness identification accuracy. Results showed a monotonically increasing (and statistically significant) relationship between lineup bias (proportion of mock witnesses choosing the suspect) and rate of false-positive identifications, as well as a monotonically increasing (and statistically significant) relationship between lineup size (E') and rate of false-positive identifications.

Mock Witness Evaluation of Sequential Lineups

The mock witness approach to lineup evaluation has generally been applied to the evaluation of simultaneously presented lineups, which is the traditional form of lineup presentation. However, sequential presentation is also used and under some circumstances may be preferable. McQuiston and Malpass (2002) investigated whether the mock witness procedure could be applied to the sequential presentation of lineup photographs and how accurately mock witnesses could detect lineup bias when the lineup was presented sequentially. They also examined the degree to which instructional manipulations affect mock witness's choices, as there is some evidence that the instruction given to mock witnesses affects their choice rates (Wells & Bradfield, 1999). Last, they examined the source(s) of information mock witnesses use when making a lineup choice.

A sample of mock witnesses read information about a robbery, along with a description of the culprit. Two instructional manipulations were included: (1) participants were told *either* that the culprit may or may not be in the lineup (unbiased instructions) *or* that the culprit was in the lineup (biased instructions); and (2) participants were told *either* that the lineup was from a real court case and that they should be absolutely certain in the lineup choice they make (high decision criterion instructions) *or* that they were only participating in a research experiment and that the lineup choice they made had trivial consequences (low decision criterion instructions). They then viewed a lineup sequentially that was constructed *a priori* to be either fair or biased. Participants were led to believe they would see 20 photographs when in fact the sequence stopped after the sixth photograph, as "backloading" the sequence of photos is standard sequential lineup administration procedure (Lindsay et al., 1991). They were asked to indicate for each photograph shown whether they thought that was or was not the culprit based on the information given.

Thirty-five percent of the participants chose one lineup member as the culprit, 49% chose two or more lineup members, and 16% chose no one. For those who made a single lineup choice or multiple lineup selections (for the multiple choice analysis, a participant's lineup choice was considered to be accurate if the target was one of the selections in the combination), the target was correctly chosen from the biased lineup significantly more often than from the fair lineup, $ps = .001$. The variation in instructions had no meaningful effect on lineup choices. Last, the majority of participants indicated that the description of the culprit was the driving force behind the lineup choice(s) they made. Based on these results, McQuiston and Malpass (2002) concluded that these data support the use of the mock witness approach to evaluate the fairness of sequentially presented lineups. They also offered several recommendations for the use of the sequential mock witness procedure, including the following: (1) mock witnesses should be instructed to make only one lineup choice, (2) they should be given a forced-choice instruction, and (3) they should be instructed to choose the lineup member who best fits the description provided.

UNEXPLORED ASPECTS OF THE MOCK WITNESS PROCEDURE

When the mock witness procedure is used to evaluate lineups in a research study, the descriptions provided to witnesses are generally contrived by experimenters or research participants and are sufficiently complete, so that there is little or no guesswork on the part of the witness. But when this procedure is used as a post hoc measurement, issues like the completeness and accuracy of descriptions become an important aspect of the procedure. As research indicates, mock witnesses rely almost solely upon the information provided to them (culprit/suspect description) as their main source of identifying information in the mock witness task (McQuiston & Malpass, 2002). Because the procedure seems to be inherently dependent upon the completeness and/or quality of the culprit's description, it becomes problematic when this information is either lacking or unclear. But we do not know what source(s) of information mock witnesses turn to in the absence of good descriptive information when attempting to make a lineup choice.

The rationale behind the use of mock witness responses as the basis for advocating for or against the fairness of a given lineup has been criticized by those in the judicial system (i.e., attorneys, law enforcement officers), based on a lack of understanding of the mock witness procedure and its rationale, and/or an unwillingness to accept this information as valid (Brigham & Pfeifer, 1994). As the influence of research on eyewitness identification continues to grow, we can also expect the use of mock witness indices as measures of lineup fairness to continue to be advocated in court. How do fact finders interpret this information? The degree to which jurors and judges perceive, understand, use, or reject this information and incorporate it into their evaluation of the evidence in a case is unknown, but it is certainly an important avenue for future research.

MAKING THE MEASURES ACCESSIBLE

There are many audiences for the concepts discussed in this chapter: researchers, law enforcement officers, judges, attorneys acting for the prosecution or the defense, and jurors, who are charged with making decisions based in part on their understanding of lineup fairness issues and their quantification. It would be useful to make these ideas and their quantification available and conceptually accessible to these constituencies.

Conceptual Accessibility. The problem is to represent the quantifications of size and bias to the various constituencies such that their meaning is easily grasped. This is less a problem for the professional participants in the criminal justice system, and much more a problem for the novices: jurors. In our experience simple graphic presentations of choice rates for lineup members against a background of chance expectation are easily understood.

Access to the Tools.   The techniques and procedures needed to implement mock witness evaluation of a lineup can be assembled from information in and cited in this chapter. For practitioners in the criminal justice system, however, constructing a complete procedure in this way would be time consuming and contain many uncertainties and disincentives. Detailed instructions do not exist in the law enforcement literature. Malpass (2004) provides detailed instructions and access to computer-based calculations of the relevant statistics. As training in lineup construction and evaluation techniques becomes more common for law enforcement personnel, access to these techniques should become more widely available.

APPENDIX

"Composing Lineups," excerpted from *Eyewitness Evidence: A Guide for Law Enforcement* (Technical Working Group, 1999).

Composing Lineups

Principle: Fair composition of a lineup enables the witness to provide a more accurate identification or nonidentification.

Policy: The investigator shall compose the lineup in such a manner that the suspect does not unduly stand out.

Procedure: *Photo Lineup:* In composing a photo lineup, the investigator should:

1.   Include only one suspect in each identification procedure.
2.   Select fillers who generally fit the witness' description of the perpetrator. When there is a limited/inadequate description of the perpetrator provided by the witness, or when the description of the perpetrator differs significantly from the appearance of the suspect, fillers should resemble the suspect in significant features.
3.   If multiple photos of the suspect are reasonably available to the investigator, select a photo that resembles the suspect description or appearance at the time of the incident.
4.   Include a *minimum* of five fillers (nonsuspects) per identification procedure.
5.   Consider that complete uniformity of features is not required. Avoid using fillers who so closely resemble the suspect that a person familiar with the suspect might find it difficult to distinguish the suspect from the fillers.
6.   Create a consistent appearance between the suspect and fillers with respect to any unique or unusual feature (e.g., scars, tattoos) used to describe the perpetrator by artificially adding or concealing that feature.

7. Consider placing suspects in different positions in each lineup, both across cases and with multiple witnesses in the same case. Position the suspect randomly in the lineup.

8. When showing a new suspect, avoid reusing fillers in lineups shown to the same witness.

9. Ensure that no writings or information concerning previous arrest(s) will be visible to the witness.

10. View the spread, once completed, to ensure that the suspect does not unduly stand out.

11. Preserve the presentation order of the photo lineup. In addition, the photos themselves should be preserved in their original condition.

REFERENCES

Brigham, J. C., & Brandt, C. C. (1992). Measuring lineup fairness: Mock witness responses versus direct evaluations of lineups. *Law and Human Behavior, 16*(5), 475–489.

Brigham, J. C., & Pfeifer, J. E. (1994). Evaluating the fairness of lineups. *Adult Eyewitness Testimony: Current Trends & Developments* (pp. 201–222). Melbourne: Cambridge University Press.

Corey, D., Malpass, R. S., & McQuiston, D. E. (1999). Parallelism in eyewitness and mock witness identifications. *Applied Cognitive Psychology, 13*, S41–S58.

Devlin, Hon. Lord Patrick. (1976). *Report to the Secretary of State for the Home Department of the Departmental Committee on Evidence of Identification in Criminal Cases*. London: Her Majesty's Stationery Office.

Doob, A. N., & Kirshenbaum, H. M. (1973). Bias in police lineups—Partial remembering. *Journal of Police Science and Administration, 18*, 287–293.

Ellison, K. W., & Buckhout, R. (1981). *Psychology and criminal justice*. New York: Harper & Row.

Laughery, K. R., Jensen, D. G., & Wogalter, M. S. (1988). Response bias with prototypic faces. In M. M. Gruneberg, P. E. Morris, & R. N. Sykes (Eds.), *Practical aspects of memory: Current research and issues* (pp. 157–162). Chichester: Wiley.

Lindsay, R. C., Lea, J. A., & Fulford, J. A. (1991). Sequential lineup presentation: Technique matters. *Journal of Applied Psychology, 76*(5), 741–745.

Lindsay, R. C. L., Smith, S. M., & Pryke, S. (1999). Measures of lineup fairness: Do they postdict identification accuracy? *Applied Cognitive Psychology, 13*, S93–S107.

Lindsay, R. C. L., & Wells, G. L. (1980). What price justice? Exploring the relationship of lineup fairness to identification accuracy. *Law & Human Behavior, 4*, 303–313.

Luus, C. A. E., & Wells, G. L. (1991). Eyewitness identification and the selection of distractors for lineups. *Law and Human Behavior, 15*, 43–57

Malpass, R. S. (1981). Effective Size and defendant bias in eyewitness identification lineups. *Law and Human Behavior, 5*(4), 299–309.

Malpass, R. S. (2004). *A lineup evaluation "do-it-yourself kit" for attorneys and law enforcement*. Retrieved from http://eyewitness.utep.edu/diy.html

Malpass, R. S., & Devine, P. G. (1983). Measuring the fairness of eyewitness identification in lineups. In S. Lloyd-Bostock & B. Clifford (Eds.), *Evaluating eyewitness evidence* (pp. 81–102). London: John Wiley & Sons.

Marwitz, D. B., & Wogalter, M. S. (1998). *Bias in photo-spreads of faces: A comparison of two lineup construction methods*. Paper presented at the Proceeding of the Human Factors Society, Santa Monica.

McQuiston, D. E., & Malpass, R. S. (2002). Validity of the mock witness paradigm: Testing the assumptions. *Law and Human Behavior, 26*(4), 439–453.

Pelwani v. S., 1963 (2) (PH) H237 (T).

Scheck, B., Neufeld, P., & Dwyer, J. (2001). *Actual innocence: When justice goes wrong and how to make it right.* New York: Doubleday.

Shepherd, J. W., & Ellis, H. (1996). Face recall—Methods and problems. In S. L. Sporer, R. S. Malpass, & G. Köhnken (Eds.), *Psychological issues in eyewitness identification* (pp. 87–115). Mahwah, NJ: Lawrence Erlbaum Associates.

Smith, S. M., Lindsay, R. C. L., & Pryke, S. (2000). Postdictors of eyewitness errors: Can false identifications be diagnosed? *Journal of Applied Psychology, 85*(4), 542–550.

Technical Working Group on Eyewitness Evidence. (1999). *Eyewitness evidence: A guide for law enforcement* (pp. i–x, 1–44). Washington, DC: National Institute of Justice. Retrieved at http://www.ojp.usdoj.gov/nij/pubs-sum/178240.htm

Topp, L. D., McQuiston, D. E., & Malpass, R. S. (2003, July). *Exploring composite production and its subsequent effects on eyewitness memory.* Poster presented at the Meetings of the Society for Applied Research in Memory and Cognition, Aberdeen, Scotland.

Tredoux, C. G. (1998). Statistical inference on measures of lineup fairness. *Law and Human Behavior, 22*(2), 217–237.

Tredoux, C. G. (1999). Statistical considerations when determining measures of lineup size and lineup bias. *Applied Cognitive Psychology, 13,* S9–S26.

Tredoux, C. G. (2002). A direct measure of facial similarity and its relation to human similarity perceptions. *Journal of Experimental Psychology: Applied, 8*(3), 180–193.

Tredoux, C. G., Parker, J. F., & Nunez, D. (2004). *Optimality of encoding and process/outcome parallelism in eyewitness and mock witness identifications.* Unpublished manuscript, University of Cape Town.

Wells, G. L. (1993). What do we know about eyewitness identification? *American Psychologist, 48*(5), 553–571.

Wells, G. L., & Bradfield, A. L. (1999). Measuring the goodness of lineups: Parameter estimation, question effects, and limits to the mock witness paradigm. *Applied Cognitive Psychology, 13,* S27–S39.

Wells, G. L., Leippe, M. R., & Ostrom, T. M. (1979). Guidelines for empirically assessing the fairness of a lineup. *Law and Human Behavior, 3*(4), 285–293.

Wells, G. L., Rydell, S. M., & Seelau, E. P. (1993). On the selection of distracters for eyewitness lineups. *Journal of Applied Psychology, 78,* 835–844.

Wells, G. L., Seelau, E. P., Rydell, S. M., & Luus, C. A. E. (1994). Recommendations for properly conducted lineup identification tasks. In D. F. Ross, J. D. Read, & M. Toglia (Eds.), *Adult eyewitness testimony: Current trends and developments* (pp. 223–244). New York: Cambridge University Press.

Wogalter, M. S., & Jensen, D. G. (1986). Response bias in lineups with prototypic faces. In *Proceedings of the Human Factors Society 30th Annual Meeting* (pp. 725–728). Santa Monica, CA: Human Factors Society.

Wogalter, M. S., Malpass, R. S., & McQuiston, D. E. (2004). A national survey of U.S. police on preparation and conduct of identification lineups. *Psychology, Crime, & Law, 10*(1), 69–82.

Wogalter, M. S., Marwitz, D. B., & Leonard, D. C. (1992). Suggestiveness in photospread lineups: Similarity induces distinctiveness. *Applied Cognitive Psychology, 6*(5), 443–453.

8

Radical Alternatives
to Traditional Lineups

Paul R. Dupuis and R. C. L. Lindsay
Queen's University, Ontario

Eyewitnesses often provide descriptions of perpetrators (Schooler, Meissner, & Sporer, this volume), create composite pictures (Davies & Valentine, this volume), and examine mug shots (McAllister, this volume) to assist police in finding suspects. Usually, an arrested suspect will be at least somewhat similar to the description given by an eyewitness. Despite matching the witness's description of the criminal, the suspect may be guilty or not guilty. Thus, when a suspect is found, the eyewitness often will be presented with a lineup to see if the witness will select the suspect. Selection from a lineup is viewed as evidence of guilt, frequently leading to further investigation, charges, prosecution, conviction, and incarceration. (Note: We use the term *selected* rather than *identified* because *selected* is neutral with regard to guilt. Witnesses clearly select lineup members. The term *identification* implies identity between the suspect and criminal and thus contains an inappropriate, linguistic presumption of guilt.)

Eyewitness evidence has been found to be highly influential, despite the fact that witnesses are often mistaken (see Beaudry, Boyce, & Lindsay, this volume). As a result, lineup procedures are needed that can help to reduce eyewitness errors to a minimum. The purpose of this chapter is to review research on lineup procedures. Research on the showup (essentially a single-person lineup) is not discussed here (but see Dysart & Lindsay, this volume). We will demonstrate that no currently used procedure reduces eyewitness errors to an acceptable level. We will conclude that, rather than just testing the limits of current police methods, more research is needed that uses radically different procedures to obtain acceptably low levels of eyewitness error.

RESEARCH METHODS

To test eyewitness selection accuracy, researchers employ staged events followed by selection procedures. Researchers simulate the real-world conditions produced when guilty suspects are arrested by including the target or perpetrator of the staged crime in their lineup procedures. To simulate the arrest of innocent suspects, some lineup procedures are employed that do not include the target or perpetrator. Lineup research explores the impact of selection procedures and other variables on the accuracy of decisions from such target-present and target-absent lineups.

Target-present lineups can result in correct selections (a choice of the target), foil selections (selection of any other lineup member), or an incorrect rejection of the lineup (choosing no one). In a target-absent situation, the correct decision is to choose no one (a correct rejection). Any choice from a target-absent lineup is an error. However, not all errors are equally dangerous. Only selection of an innocent suspect, a *false identification* in traditional terminology, will lead to prosecution and possibly to wrongful conviction. Foil choices are known errors and discredit the witness rather than the person selected (Wells, 1984).

The results of such studies are evaluated in a variety of ways. Wells (Wells & Lindsay, 1980; Wells & Turtle, 1986) discussed the "diagnosticity ratio," a Baysian likelihood ratio, as one measure of lineup effectiveness. The diagnosticity ratio is the ratio of (correct) selections of suspects from target-present lineups to (incorrect) selections of suspects from target-absent lineups. A diagnosticity ratio of 1.0 indicates that guilty and innocent suspects are equally likely to be selected from the lineup. Higher diagnosticity ratios indicate that the selection of the suspect will be more informative of a suspect's guilt. A problem with diagnosticity ratios is that some studies will obtain incorrect suspect selection rates of zero resulting in division by zero and an undefined (or infinite) diagnosticity ratio. To avoid this problem, we report data in terms of the percentage of identified suspects expected to be guilty, assuming equal numbers of target-present and target-absent lineups (Pryke, Lindsay, Dysart, & Dupuis, 2004). If the target is selected by .6 of witnesses from the target-present lineup and the innocent suspect by .2 of witnesses from the target-absent lineup, the diagnosticity ratio would be .6/.2 = 3.00. The comparable percentage guilty would be calculated as (.6/(.2 + .6) × 100) = 75%. If none of the witnesses from the target-absent lineup selected the suspect, diagnosticity would be undefined (.6/0) but the percent guilty would simply be 100% (.6/(.6 + 0) × 100). An added advantage of the percentage guilty measure is that the meaning of the statistic is transparent and thus easier to communicate to audiences without statistical training.

A piece of evidence has probative value if it provides information useful for deciding an issue before the courts. For any lineup procedure, the higher the percentage guilty, the higher is the likelihood that the selected person is guilty, and thus the greater the probative value of the evidence. Technically, the greater the deviation of a percentage guilty value from .5, the greater is the probative value, with positive deviations (values greater than .5) increasingly predicting that the suspect is guilty and negative deviations (less than .5) increasingly predicting that the suspect is innocent. In practice, percentage guilty values below .5 rarely occur. As a result, police, prosecutors, and the criminal justice system as a whole ought to prefer procedures that result in high values of the percentage guilty variable.

INNOCENT SUSPECTS

The diagnosticity ratio and percentage guilty statistics count on having estimates of the rates of selection of both innocent and guilty suspects. One of these rates is obvious; the selection of targets from target-present procedures is the estimate of the percentage of guilty suspects who would be identified under the conditions of the study. In the real world, it is clear which lineup members are suspects, but this is not the case in the research in target-absent conditions. Two approaches to this issue have been taken. One approach is to designate a specific individual in the target-absent lineup as the innocent suspect. Only selections of this individual are then treated as incorrect suspect selections. Choices of other lineup members are classified as foil selections. Often, a pilot test is conducted, and the lineup member most similar to the target is declared to be the innocent suspect. Such procedures provide a worst-case scenario for the criminal justice system. Procedures that protect innocent suspects who resemble the true criminal more than other lineup members are obviously valuable for avoiding wrongful convictions. In such studies, the percentage guilty value is easily calculated by substitution of the values for the target and designated innocent suspect into the formula.

The second approach argues that there is no reason to think that the innocent suspect will always be the lineup member most similar to the criminal in real cases. From this perspective, the worst-case scenario approach will lead to overestimates of false selections and underestimates of the accuracy of eyewitness decisions. For this reason, some studies do not designate a specific individual as the innocent suspect and confine their analyses of data from target-absent lineups to choosing (incorrect decisions) versus not choosing (correct decisions). To estimate the rate of false selection of innocent suspects for such studies, the overall false-positive selection rate is divided by the nominal size of (number of people in) the lineup to generate an average or expected false selection rate. This value is then used in the calculation of the percentage guilty statistic.

TRADITIONAL LINEUP PROCEDURES

The traditional lineup procedure places a single suspect in a set of foils (also referred to as *fillers* or *distracters*). These people may be presented live, via videotape, or as still photos. The job of the witness is to examine the lineup members to decide if one of them is a person previously seen by the witness at a particular place and time. Such procedures are referred to in the research literature as *simultaneous lineups*. (For information on lineup construction and fairness, see Malpass, Tredoux, & McQuiston, this volume. For an in-depth discussion of lineup theory see Brewer, Weber, & Semmler, this volume; Charman & Wells, this volume.) In general, witnesses are more likely to make correct decisions than incorrect decisions when confronted with an unbiased, simultaneous lineup task (Shapiro & Penrod, 1986; Steblay, Dysart, Fulero, & Lindsay, 2001).

Simultaneous lineups are subject to a number of biases. Biased instructions lead the witness to believe that the criminal (or target in experiments) is in the lineup (e.g., Malpass & Devine, 1981; see Steblay, 1997, for a review). Foil bias exists when the suspect stands out as a better match to the description provided by the eyewitness than other lineup members (e.g., Lindsay & Wells, 1980). Clothing bias exists when only the suspect is wearing clothing similar to that worn by the criminal during the crime (e.g., Lindsay, Wallbridge, & Drennan, 1987). The impact of lineup biases is clear; fair and biased lineups produce approximately the same rate of correct selections from target-present lineups. However, compared with fair lineups, biased lineups generate much higher rates of false selections from target-absent lineups. When traditional lineups are biased, they can produce extremely high rates of false selection of designated targets (e.g., Lindsay et al., 1991; Malpass & Devine, 1981). For example, the Lindsay and Wells (1980) data generate percentage guilty values of 65% for fair lineups and 50% for foil-biased lineups. Traditional lineups are thus highly prone to error and easily biased. Clearly, either lineup selection ought to be treated as weak evidence or new procedures are needed that are less likely to lead to wrongful conviction! In a subsequent section we discuss attempts to alter lineup procedures in order to increase the probative value of eyewitness selection evidence.

Questions and Instructions

Researchers tested the impact of asking witnesses various questions or giving various instructions prior to the lineup task. Malpass and Devine (1981) tested the impact of fair and biased lineup instructions with the use of simultaneous lineups and a designated innocent suspect. Fair instructions resulted in a percentage guilty value of 72% as compared with 51% with biased instructions. Steblay (1997) reviewed 18 studies of biased lineup instructions and concluded that in target-present conditions biased instructions increased the confidence of witnesses but not the likelihood that they would select the target. In target-absent conditions, biased instructions substantially increased the likelihood of falsely selecting lineup members. It is clear that instructions indicating that the guilty party may not be in the lineup are useful for reducing false-positive choices. Unfortunately, not all police then or now employ such instructions.

Dysart and Lindsay (2001) attempted to reduce incorrect lineup selections by asking witnesses a question prior to the lineup task. Witnesses to a staged crime were or were not asked prior to the lineup task if they felt they would be able to choose no one from (correctly reject) the lineup if the target was not present. They reasoned that such a question would make it more salient to the witness that the target could be absent than the instruction that the target may or may not be present. Pre-lineup instructions had minimal effect on correct selections but significantly reduced choosing from target-absent lineups. The percentage guilty in the control condition was 89%. This value increased to 95% when the pre-lineup questions were asked. If 89% seems like a high rate of accuracy, put it in the context of about 78,000 such procedures conducted by police annually in the United States (Goldstein, Chance, & Schneller, 1989) for a whopping 2,600 innocent suspect selections per year or over 7 innocent suspect selections per day from unbiased traditional lineups! (This speculation is based on expectations of 50% target-absent, six-person lineups with a 60% correct identification rate and a 40% false-positive choice rate.)

Clearly verbal manipulations (questions and instructions) prior to lineup tasks can dramatically influence the accuracy of eyewitness selections and thus the probative value of selection decisions. The Technical Working Group (1999) recommended the use of instructions reminding witnesses that the criminal need not be in the lineup, and many police forces have adopted some version of such a warning. To the best of our knowledge, no police force employs pre-lineup questions as a means of reducing incorrect selections. More research on this issue is warranted.

BLANK LINEUP

Wells (1984) argued that simultaneous lineups permitted and perhaps encouraged witnesses to use a relative judgment strategy. Such a strategy leads the witness to compare lineup members to each other and then select the lineup member most similar to their memory of the criminal. The relative judgment strategy has severe consequences when an eyewitness is viewing a target-absent lineup. When witnesses compare all of the lineup members, someone will be the best match to their memories and thus will be selected. If the lineup is fair, on average innocent suspects will be wrongly selected as the criminal at a rate of $1/N$, where N is the number of lineup members. Lineup bias may inflate the false selection rate further. Even if the suspect is not the lineup member most similar to the witness's memory, the witness may choose a foil. Foil choices discredit the witness and can interfere with the successful resolution of cases.

In an attempt to overcome problems associated with the relative judgment strategy, Wells (1984) proposed that witnesses be exposed to a "blank" lineup (i.e., a lineup composed entirely of foils and containing no suspects). Only witnesses rejecting the blank lineup would be considered "credible" as a source of recognition evidence. In effect, Wells was proposing a screening procedure such that witnesses demonstrated to be prone to selection error would be excluded from consideration as a reliable source of evidence. By selecting a member of the blank lineup before the real or "suspect-present" lineup was shown, witnesses would reveal that their selections should not be trusted. Such a screening process would shield innocent suspects from witnesses willing to choose innocent lineup members because of either poor memory or excessive zeal.

Participants were exposed to a live staged crime and then asked to provide descriptions of the criminal. Then they were presented with one of four lineup procedures, either a target-present or target-absent simultaneous lineup or a blank lineup followed by one of the same target-present or target-absent lineups. Witnesses rejecting the blank lineup were more likely to select the target from the target-present lineup (.60) than were those who made a choice from the blank lineup (.33). Witnesses rejecting the blank lineup also made fewer incorrect selections from a target-absent lineup than those who made a blank lineup choice (.23 vs. .56). Also, witnesses making no choice from a blank lineup made fewer incorrect selections from an absent lineup (.23) than did those who saw only the absent lineup (.71). There was no difference in the correct selection rates of those in the target-present condition rejecting the blank lineup (.60) versus those who saw only the target-present lineup (.60). As a result, the traditional, simultaneous lineup generated a percentage guilty value of 83%. The blank lineup produced a percentage guilty value of 94%. The blank lineup procedure would lead to about one-third the number of selections of innocent suspects. Wells demonstrated that witnesses prone to using a relative judgment strategy were less likely to make correct decisions from lineups. He also demonstrated that such witnesses could be successfully screened.

Unfortunately, blank lineups are not a viable solution to the eyewitness problem. Although blank lineups would protect innocent suspects, too many eyewitnesses would have to be discarded. Of those witnesses shown the blank lineup, 37% selected someone (Wells, 1984). The loss of so many potential witnesses would likely be unacceptable to police and prosecutors, who cannot afford to dismiss more than one-third of the potential eyewitnesses in their cases before the witnesses are given an opportunity to provide evidence against the suspects. Another serious problem for the blank lineup is that the procedure could only be used if people were not aware that it was being used (otherwise witnesses would automatically reject the first lineup).

SEQUENTIAL LINEUP

Lindsay and Wells (1985) developed the sequential lineup procedure as a means to prevent reliance on relative judgments while not discarding eyewitnesses and relying on secrecy. The sequential lineup procedure involved several important features in order to work optimally:

1. Only one lineup member is presented at a time.
2. The number of lineup members is not revealed to the witness.
3. The witness is required to make a clearly stated decision before the next member is shown (the person currently being viewed is or is not believed to be the criminal).
4. Each lineup member is viewed only once.
5. Decisions cannot be changed once they are made.
6. The lineup administrator is to be "blind" (unaware of which lineup member is the suspect).

The logic of the procedure is that witnesses who cannot compare lineup members with each other will be forced to compare each lineup member with their memory of the criminal and thus are less likely to choose a lineup member only because he looks most like the criminal. The sequential lineup procedure was designed to encourage the use of a more absolute judgment strategy. Comparing each lineup member with the memory of the criminal rather than with other lineup members was expected to reduce false selections. Because the witness really had seen the criminal, the hope was that correct selections would not be dramatically reduced. However, witnesses with a weak memory trace (poor memory for the target) are likely to find an absolute judgment more difficult than a relative judgment with target-present lineups. As a result, some loss of correct selections was likely.

Lindsay and Wells (1985) found that false selection rates of the designated innocent suspect were significantly higher for witnesses given a simultaneous lineup (.43) compared with those presented with a sequential lineup (.17). Equally important, correct selection rates from simultaneous (.58) and sequential (.50) lineups did not differ significantly. This is a critical point. If the sequential lineup reduced the correct and false selection rates equally, the importance of any reduction in false selection rates would be mitigated. When percentage guilty rates are calculated, the sequential lineup provided greater probative value (75%) than did the simultaneous lineup (57%). At the time, the sequential lineup was a dramatic departure from the simultaneous lineup both in procedure and in logic. There was a strongly held intuitive theory that allowing comparison among lineup members, a relative judgment, would aid a witness in making a correct decision. Perhaps this idea was so compelling because people were assuming that the perpetrator always would be in the lineup.

Others subsequently replicated the superiority of sequential over simultaneous lineups with regard to both reduced risk of false selection and superior probative value. In two studies, Cutler and Penrod (1988) had participants view videotaped liquor store robberies and then exposed them to target-present or target-absent lineups presented either simultaneously or sequentially. In Experiment 1, the effects of using context interviews, lineup context cues, disguise, weapon presence, and cautionary instructions were examined in both simultaneous and sequential lineups. An interaction between lineup type and context cues was found. Witnesses shown sequential or simultaneous lineups with strong context cues (use of video lineups allowing for exposure to gait, posture, and voice) or a sequential lineup with weak context cues (still face and face profile close-up photos) showed similar rates of correct decisions (.78, .80, and .84, respectively). Being shown a simultaneous lineup with weak context cues reduced the rates of correct decisions significantly (.58). Therefore, not only did strong context cues improve accuracy of decisions, so did the use of sequential lineups. When the overall rates of correct selections were examined, no difference was found between simultaneous (.76) and sequential (.80) lineups. As expected, however, the rate of false selections was significantly higher in simultaneous as compared with sequential lineups (.39 vs. .19). The overall percentage guilty value for the simultaneous lineup was 92% compared with 96% for the sequential lineup.

In Experiment 2, three levels of instructions were used: emphasizing that missing the perpetrator could result in a criminal going free, that a mistaken selection could result in the prosecution of an innocent person, or neither (control). Only those viewing a sequential lineup and made aware of the danger of identifying an innocent person had a significant reduction in the rate of false selections. Collapsing across instructions, the correct selection rates were similar for simultaneous (.47) and sequential (.41) lineups. Again the false selection rates were higher for the simultaneous (.43) as compared with the sequential lineup (.21). The resulting percentage guilty rates were 87% for the simultaneous lineup and 92% for the sequential lineup.

Sporer (1993) also used a videotaped staged crime to examine the utility of sequential and simultaneous lineups and the possibility of using confidence and decision times as proxies of eyewitness accuracy. The use of these items as proxies for accuracy is beyond the scope of this chapter and therefore is not dealt with here (but see Caputo & Dunning, this volume; Leippe & Eisenstadt, this volume; Smith, Lindsay, & Pryke, 2000). Sporer found that participants presented with sequential lineups made significantly more correct rejections of an absent lineup (.61) than did those presented with simultaneous lineups (.28). Again there was no significant difference in correct selection rates between sequential (.39) and simultaneous (.44) lineups. The sequential lineup resulted in 86% of selections being the target, compared with 79% for simultaneous lineups.

Yarmey and Morris (1998) presented a rare failure to replicate the superiority of the sequential lineup. Using only target-absent lineups, they found no difference in rates of false selections of a designated innocent suspect between simultaneous and sequential lineups. Yarmey and Morris pointed out that the false selection rates were very low in this study (.11 for sequential lineups and .08 for simultaneous lineups) and that a floor effect may have existed. Despite this, they found that the sequential lineup was superior to the simultaneous procedure because of the higher rates of correct rejections (.75 vs. .45) and the lower rates of foil selections (.14 vs. .47) obtained when a sequential versus a simultaneous lineup is used. Percentage guilty values cannot be calculated without target-present data.

Steblay, Dysart, Fulero, and Lindsay (2001) performed a meta-analysis on the sequential lineup literature. Compared with sequential lineups, simultaneous lineups generated 3 times the rate of false-positive choices of designated innocent suspects (.27 vs. .09). This pattern of fewer errors with sequential lineups is also reflected in a lower rate of correct rejections of target absent lineups presented simultaneously (.49) as compared with sequentially (.72). On the other hand, the consistent pattern of lower correct selections from sequential (.35) compared with simultaneous (.51) lineups resulted in a significant difference when the data were combined in the meta-analysis. Steblay et al. speculated that the difference in correct selection rate may not generalize. Moderator variables indicated that more realistic testing conditions resulted in smaller differences between simultaneous and sequential lineups in terms of correct selections but did not alter the superiority of sequential lineups with regard to correct rejections. Thus, the difference in correct selection rates was smaller when the staged crimes were presented live rather than on tape. Similarly, the difference was smaller when witnesses saw one event and made one selection decision than when they saw a sequence of events and made selection decisions after each. No direct test of this reasoning can be found in the literature. It would be dangerous at this point to assume that the sequential lineup produces similar correct selection rates in the real world.

Overall, these data suggest percentage guilty values of 86% for simultaneous lineups and 88% for sequential lineups, an apparently trivial difference. However, if an innocent suspect is designated, the results strongly favor sequential lineups, with the percentage guilty estimates being 65% for simultaneous lineups and 80% for sequential lineups. This pattern has important implications. In effect, estimating the false selection rate by spreading false-positive choices equally across all lineup members is the equivalent of stating that all lineups are perfectly constructed (Malpass & Lindsay, 1999; Malpass, Tredoux, & McQuiston, this volume). This is extremely unlikely in the real world. As the lineup is less perfectly constructed, the suspect will stand out more and the situation will more closely resemble the worst-case scenario represented by the designated innocent suspect. Sequential lineups are less influenced by this problem (the percentage guilty value decreased from 88% to 80%). By comparison, the simultaneous lineup suffers greatly from lineup imperfections (the percentage guilty value decreased from 86% to 65%).

Other data confirm the superiority of sequential lineups when lineup biases occur. In a series of live staged crime studies, Lindsay et al. (1991) investigated the utility of sequential lineups when different biases were introduced. In Experiment 1 witnesses viewed a target-present or target-absent "conventional" or "ideal" lineup. The conventional lineup was a simultaneous lineup, which used reasonable but not the best available foils, who were all dressed differently from the criminal and each other, and was not accompanied by a "may or may not be present" warning. The ideal lineup was a sequential lineup, which used the best available foils, who all were dressed alike, and included a "may or may not be present" warning. There was no significant difference in correct selection rates for the conventional (.67) and ideal (.77) lineups. The false selection rates (of a designated innocent suspect) were higher with the conventional lineup (.20) than with the ideal lineup (.03), resulting in percentage guilty rates of 77% for the conventional lineup and 96% for the ideal lineup. Of course, this is not a direct comparison of simultaneous to sequential lineups, because other factors were confounded in the manipulation (instructions, foil quality, and lineup attire).

Experiment 2 focused only on the effects of clothing bias. Witnesses were presented with target-present and target-absent simultaneous or sequential lineups in which either no one was dressed in clothing similar to that worn by the perpetrator or only the suspect wore similar clothing. There was no significant difference in the correct selection rates for the sequential (.47) and simultaneous (.57) lineups. False selection rates were lower for the sequential lineup, whether biased (.07) or nonbiased (.03), than for the biased (.33) and nonbiased (.20) simultaneous lineups. The percentage guilty value for the biased sequential lineup (88%) was therefore much higher than for the biased simultaneous lineup (63%) and higher than the percentage guilty value for the unbiased simultaneous lineup (74%). The best results were obtained with the unbiased sequential lineup (93%). These data reflect the same pattern as described previously. Eyewitness accuracy obtained with the sequential lineup is reduced less by a lineup bias (93% vs. 88%) than when the simultaneous lineup is used (74% versus 63%). Furthermore, the absolute level of accuracy obtained with biased simultaneous lineups is disturbingly low (63%).

Experiment 3 explored the effect of using poor foils in simultaneous and sequential lineups. Witnesses were presented with target-absent sequential or simultaneous lineups in which all of the lineup members or only the innocent suspect was close in appearance to the criminal. Overall, false selections were greater for the simultaneous lineup (.46) than for the sequential (.07). In fact, this rate was identical for the sequential lineup, regardless of the quality of the foils. For the simultaneous lineup, poor foil quality led to higher false selection rates (.53) than when better foils were used (.40), although not significantly so. In Experiment 4, Lindsay et al. (1991) looked at the use of biased or fair instructions with target-absent sequential and simultaneous lineups. Witnesses were told that the perpetrator may or may not be present in the lineup (fair instructions) or that all they had to do was pick out the perpetrator (biased instructions). Biased instructions raised the false selection rate significantly for simultaneous lineups (.33 biased vs. .13 fair) but not significantly for sequential lineups (.13 biased, .03 fair). Overall sequential lineups had a lower false selection rate than simultaneous lineups (.08 vs. .23). For Experiment 5, witnesses viewed target-absent lineups combining the previous biases. The foils did not closely resemble the perpetrator, although the innocent suspect did; witnesses were told the guilty person was present and to pick him out; and only the innocent suspect was wearing a shirt identical to that worn by the perpetrator. In this extremely biased task, the false selection rate was significantly higher when the lineup was presented simultaneously (.84) than when the lineup was presented sequentially (.25). The correct rejection rates for sequential lineups were consistently higher than for simultaneous lineups across these last three studies. Percentage guilty values cannot be calculated for these studies, because target-present conditions were not included. Across all five studies, sequential lineups provided more protection for innocent suspects than simultaneous lineups under a variety of biases by reducing the false selection rate and increasing the correct rejection rate.

Another important question regarding sequential lineups was whether all of the described aspects of the original procedure were necessary for the reduction in false selections and the increase in correct rejections. Lindsay, Lea, and Fulford (1991) examined the effects of allowing a second opportunity to view a sequential lineup and of knowing the number of members in a sequential lineup. The comparison of witnesses viewing the sequential and simultaneous lineups produced correct selection rates of .47 and .57, respectively. The false selection rates were lower for sequential (.05) than for simultaneous (.20) presentation, and the correct rejection rates were higher for sequential (.77) than for simultaneous (.43) presentation. As a result, the percentage guilty values were 90% for sequential lineups and 74% for simultaneous lineups, the standard pattern. Altering the sequential procedure reduced its effectiveness. When witnesses who initially viewed a sequential lineup were presented with a second, unexpected, simultaneous lineup, false selection rates (designated target) rose significantly from .05 to .27, and correct rejection rates fell from .77 to .55. The correct selection rates were similar for the sequential lineup (.47) and for the subsequent simultaneous lineup (.53). Allowing witnesses to view the lineup members again in a simultaneous lineup reduced the percentage guilty value from 90% to 66%.

In a second experiment by Lindsay, Lea, and Fulford (1991), the second lineup presentation was made in a simultaneous or a sequential fashion. False selection rates remained unchanged from the original sequential lineup (.25) to the second sequential presentation (.28), yet the rate was significantly larger if the second lineup was simultaneous (.69). Therefore it seems that it is the simultaneous procedure that is dangerous, whether it is the only procedure used or employed after a sequential lineup. Repeated viewing of the sequential lineup provided no advantage in that correct selections from the target-present lineup did not increase significantly. The impact of showing witnesses the same simultaneous lineup twice has not been tested. However, the procedure may suggest to the witness that the first decision was incorrect and should be reconsidered. It is difficult to believe that police would ever do this when the first decision was a suspect selection. As a result, it is likely that this procedure is highly biased and likely to lead to no better and probably much worse evidence.

In a third study, knowledge of the number of lineup members in a sequential lineup increased the false selection rate compared with a sequential lineup with the number of members hidden (.17 vs. .07). Yet the rate was still lower than for a standard simultaneous lineup (.27). When the sequential lineup procedure was not followed as outlined in Lindsay and Wells (1985), the advantage of the sequential procedure was diminished. However, the sequential lineup remained more effective than the simultaneous lineup as a means of avoiding false selections.

Phillips, McAuliff, Kovera, and Cutler (1999) tested the effect of blind testing on the accuracy of eyewitness decisions from sequential and simultaneous lineups. Some participants had viewed a staged crime and then a lineup. Other participants were asked to act as police officers. These participants presented lineups sequentially or simultaneously and did or did not know which lineup member was considered the suspect. All lineups were target-absent. Choices of the designated target were significantly increased when the lineup presenter was aware of which lineup member was the suspect and presented the lineup sequentially, particularly if an observer was in the room during the procedure. Lack of blind testing threatens to reverse the sequential lineup effect by making the number of false-positive selections higher and correct rejections lower than would be expected with simultaneous lineups.

As examples of the superiority of the sequential lineup became more frequent in the literature, researchers attempted to determine whether this superiority would hold for different populations. Although children above 6 years of age are comparable to adults in rates of correct selections, their rates of correct rejections are lower, likely because of guessing (Pozzulo, this volume; Pozzulo & Lindsay, 1998). Parker and Ryan (1993) presented target-present and target-absent simultaneous and sequential lineups to children and adults. Although not statistically significant, children's correct selection rates were lower for sequential than for simultaneous lineups (.25 vs. .42 respectively). Correct rejections were generally low with either procedure, but did occur less often for simultaneous (.17) than sequential (.33) lineups. Percentage guilty data reveal that simultaneous lineups (75%) were better than sequential lineups (69%) for child witnesses if the designated innocent suspect was ignored. Data for the designated innocent suspect produced percentage guilty estimates of 71% for the simultaneous lineup and 100% for the sequential lineup.

Lindsay, Pozzulo, Craig, Lee, and Corber (1997) examined the use of sequential lineups, simultaneous lineups, and showups with child witnesses. In Experiment 1, children (8–10 years or 11–15 years) or adults were presented with target-present or target-absent simultaneous lineups, sequential lineups, or showups. With the use of the simultaneous lineup, both younger (.71) and older (.80) children were more likely to choose the target than were adults (.55). Again, with the use of sequential lineups, both younger (.65) and older (.71) children selected the target more than the adults did (.62). This apparently superior performance is driven by a greater willingness to choose by the children. As a result, with simultaneous lineups the younger (.28) and older (.33) children were less likely than adults (.66) to correctly reject the lineup. The same pattern exists for the sequential lineups, with younger (.21) and older (.20) children less likely to correctly reject all lineup members than were adults (.75). Of greatest importance to the current discussion is the percentage guilty data. Simultaneous lineups resulted in percentage guilty estimates of 86% for younger children, 88% for older children, and 91% for adults. Sequential lineups resulted in percentage guilty estimates of 83% for younger children, 84% for older children, and 94% for adults. The adult data show the usual superiority of sequential to simultaneous lineups, whereas the data for the children do not.

A second experiment employed very young child witnesses (33 to 72 months of age). Fewer of these young children selected the target from a simultaneous (.68) than a sequential (.95) lineup. However, the data are complicated by the fact that most children selected more than one person when the lineup was presented sequentially, and some did even when the lineup was presented simultaneously. If children who chose more than one lineup member are considered inaccurate, then .53 correctly selected only the target from the simultaneous lineup and only .26 selected only the target from the sequential lineup. Target-absent lineups were not included in this study; however, the target was presented in the last position in the sequential lineup. If the data from the first five positions were used to estimate the false positive rate, the percentage guilty value would be 62%. These data suggest that sequential lineups work very poorly with young child witnesses. Of course, the data necessary to calculate the percent guilty value for the simultaneous lineups was not collected, so it is possible that no procedure will work with such young witnesses.

The failure of sequential lineups to improve children's performance may not be a serious liability. Although lineup evidence from children does appear in court (Bruck, Ceci & Hembrooke, 1998), it is not relied upon as heavily as adult evidence. On the other hand, cases involving child witnesses are not uncommon (Bala, Lee, Lindsay, & Talwar, 2001; Gray, 1993; Honts, 1994), so a selection procedure useful with child witnesses is desirable. Furthermore, there is no data indicating the age at which the sequential lineup superiority effect can be expected to start. Children up to the age of about 12 years do not exhibit the effect, whereas young adults at the age of about 18 clearly do. This leaves police, who wish to use the best available lineup procedure, in the awkward position of not knowing which procedure to use when witnesses are from 13 to 17 years of age.

Other studies fail to support a sequential lineup superiority effect in some cross-race situations. Lindsay, Brigham, Malpass, and Ross (2003) found that sequential lineups produced higher percentage guilty values than simultaneous lineups, regardless of the background of the participants, as long as the participant and lineup members were from the same background. For participants of African ancestry, the percentage guilty values were 87% for simultaneous lineups and 97% for sequential lineups. For Asian ancestry participants, the percentage guilty values were 91% for simultaneous lineups and 96% for sequential lineups. European ancestry participants produced percentage guilty values of 88% for simultaneous lineups and 92% for sequential lineups. Hispanic ancestry participants generated percentage guilty values of 95% for simultaneous lineups and 99% for sequential lineups. When witnesses of European ancestry attempted lineup tasks involving non-European targets, they continued to perform less accurately with simultaneous (85% guilty) than with sequential (90% guilty) lineups. This was not true for the other groups. People of African ancestry (92% vs. 80% guilty), Asian ancestry (88% vs. 80% guilty), and Hispanic ancestry (89% vs. 83% guilty) all performed better in the out-group conditions with simultaneous rather than sequential lineups. This limitation is much more serious than the age limitation, as many eyewitnesses of non-European ancestry will attempt to select suspects from lineups of people not of their racial/ethnic background.

Change of appearance between the time of the crime and selection procedure also may interact with lineup procedure to influence eyewitness accuracy. Pozzulo and Lindsay (1995) exposed witnesses to staged crimes committed by men who had full beards or were clean-shaven. The witnesses were shown target-present or target-absent lineups in which all lineup members were clean-shaven or bearded, but this represented a change of appearance from that of the criminal during the crime for some witnesses. The change of appearance reduced correct selections much more for sequential lineups than for simultaneous lineups.

We must conclude that the sequential lineup has serious limitations. The sequential lineup does not work well with child witnesses, particularly very young children. The sequential lineup is clearly inferior to the simultaneous lineup in some cross-race situations (see Meissner & Brigham, this volume). Nor does the sequential lineup work well when there has been a change of appearance between the crime and lineup task (Pozzulo & Lindsay, 1995). These limitations may be forgiven, because no known selection procedure deals well with the problems of young witnesses, cross-race facial memory, and change of appearance.

Other problems with the sequential lineup are more serious. The sequential lineup procedure is sensitive to relatively minor changes to lineup presentation, such as knowledge of lineup size (Lindsay, Lea, & Fulford, 1991). Major procedural errors that would be expected (and occur frequently in real cases) include allowing witnesses to change decisions after seeing all of the lineup members and setting photos aside to make a decision only after seeing all lineup members. Lack of blind testing is a particularly serious problem because it reduces (perhaps eliminates) the effectiveness of the sequential lineup procedure (Phillips, McAuliff, Kovera, & Cutler, 1999), and blind testing is resisted by police and prosecutors (Wells et al., 2000). These limitations ensure that sequential lineups are not an ideal solution to selection issues.

Some argue that an additional set of problems results from the potential for multiple selections from sequential lineups (e.g., Levi, 1998). Multiple selections (choosing more than one lineup member) can be avoided by stopping the procedure as soon as the witness selects someone. However, a witness may choose an innocent lineup member before reaching the guilty party. If the sequential procedure stops once a choice has been made, such a witness is effectively eliminated from the case. This could lead to a recommendation that the witness view all lineup members regardless of responses to earlier members of the lineup. Even if the witness continues after an early selection and selects the guilty suspect, the credibility of such a witness will be highly questionable. If the procedure continues after a selection is made until all lineup members have been seen, there also is a risk that the witness may first select the guilty suspect and then go on to impeach that choice by selecting another lineup member as well. The result of these multiple-selection problems is similar to the screening problem that contributed to rejection of blank lineups. However, multiple selection may not really be a threat to the administration of justice. In each case, the witness must have a sufficiently poor memory of the criminal or sufficiently liberal decision criteria that he or she is willing to select an innocent person (inasmuch as all of the patterns described involve selecting two lineup members from a lineup presumably containing only one suspect). Multiple selection from sequential lineups may be an appropriate way to screen witnesses unduly prone to error. Multiple selections from sequential lineups occur for only .05 or less of witnesses in laboratory studies. Unlike blank lineups, sequential lineups will eliminate relatively few witnesses because they demonstrate themselves to be too willing to choose someone.

The biggest problem with sequential lineups is not that they do not work but that they do not work well enough! Examining the data reported so far, we find that sequential lineups are associated with percentage guilty values ranging from 62% to 100%. This is better than the values for simultaneous lineups (50% to 92%) across most witnessing conditions. However, typical percentage guilty values for sequential lineups are about 90%. The rate of incorrect selection and subsequent wrongful conviction will be lower for sequential than for simultaneous lineups, but the rate will remain unacceptably high.

QUASI-SEQUENTIAL LINEUPS

Police were increasingly aware of the sequential lineup by the early 1990s. Some adopted the procedure, whereas others attempted to modify it. Modifications were motivated by a desire to avoid the blind testing recommendation due to a preference that the officer in charge of the case conduct all aspects of the investigation. To avoid blind testing, police developed a variety of techniques designed to discourage the use of relative judgments but still permit the officer in charge of the case to conduct lineup procedures. Some procedures simply informed witnesses about the distinction between relative and absolute judgments, provided instructions typical of sequential lineups ("look at only one photo at a time, decide if . . ."), and presented a standard simultaneous lineup. Other procedures arranged to have witnesses conduct sequential lineups themselves in the absence of the officer. Lindsay and Bellinger (1999) compared the original sequential procedure with a standard simultaneous lineup and four other lineup procedures that police had used in Canada. The instructed condition presented a standard simultaneous lineup with instructions similar to those for the sequential procedure. An "angled" condition presented the photos simultaneously but all at different angles. The logic of this procedure was that the witness could not effectively compare the photos so the procedure should reduce relative judgments, the stated purpose of the sequential lineup. There were also two sequential alternatives in which the witness was in control of the photos. In the stacked procedure witnesses were handed a stack of photos, given sequential lineup instructions, and then left to take themselves through the lineup. Similarly, in the album condition witnesses were given a small photo album with one lineup photo per page, were given sequential lineup instructions, and were left alone to complete the lineup task.

Lindsay and Bellinger (1999) found that the original sequential lineup procedure was significantly or marginally superior to the alternative procedures that had been developed by police officers. The correct rejection rate for the standard sequential lineup was .96, and that of the standard simultaneous lineup was .61. In the instructed simultaneous lineup condition, correct rejections were at .71 and reached only .39 for the angled simultaneous procedure. The alternative sequential procedures faired better than the simultaneous procedures, though not always significantly, resulting in .80 correct rejections for the album procedure and .75 for the stack procedure. The two self-administered sequential procedures allowed the witnesses the opportunity to ignore the sequential instructions and make comparisons among lineup members, thus facilitating a relative judgment strategy. Many witnesses were unobtrusively observed making comparisons. Thus as in the study by Lindsay, Lea, and Fulford (1991), alterations to the original sequential lineup procedure tended to reduce the effectiveness of the procedure as a means of protecting innocent people from being selected from lineups. Attempts to alter the sequential lineup procedure failed to preserve what is good (reduction of incorrect selections) and thus have not been useful.

MULTIPLE-CHOICE LARGE SEQUENTIAL LINEUP (aka MODIFIED SEQUENTIAL LINEUP)

Despite the reduction in false selections obtained with sequential lineups, several researchers have expressed appropriate concerns that these rates were still too high, especially with the real-world implications of a false selection (e.g., Levi, 1998). Because of the large number of lineup procedures conducted by police, even a very small rate of false selections could put many innocent people at risk. (Again, using the estimate of 78,000 procedures per year and 50% target-absent lineups, a 96% guilty rate still would result in more than 2.5 innocent suspects selected from lineups every day in the United States.) To counter these problems, Levi proposed two primary changes be made to the sequential lineup procedure. First he suggested increasing the size of the lineup dramatically. Provided that lineups are restricted to having only a single suspect (Technical Working Group, 1999; Wells & Turtle, 1986) and that all lineup members are selected to match the description of the criminal provided by the witness (Wells, Rydell, & Seelau, 1993), the larger the lineup, the less likely it is that an innocent suspect will be selected. However, larger lineups may make correct selection somewhat more difficult for the witness as well. To counter any such trend, Levi suggested that the witness be allowed to make multiple selections from the lineup. Allowing multiple selections may maintain the level of guilty suspect choices even in the face of larger lineups. Levi refers to the possibility of multiple selections including the suspect as "partial identifications." Levi proposed that such partial identifications would demonstrate to a judge or jury that the witness was not completely credible but at the same time provide some evidence that the suspect may be guilty, because he or she was one of the people selected by the witness. In other words, Levi argued that even partial identification should have some probative value. This was a second reason for proposing the multiple-choice feature. Partial identification should protect against over-belief in eyewitness selections because the witness obviously made at least one error of selection but may still provide evidence of some probative value.

To test the multiple-choice large sequential lineup, Levi (1998) presented witnesses with a target-present or target-absent 20-person sequential lineup. The position of the suspect (guilty or not guilty) was altered so that he or she appeared equally in the 4th, 9th, 14th, or 18th positions. Overall, in the target-present lineup .43 of witnesses chose only the suspect and .26 chose the suspect and at least one foil, that is, .26 of witnesses made partial identifications. In the target-absent lineup, no witness chose only the designated innocent suspect, and .05 of witnesses chose the innocent suspect and at least one foil. The correct rejection rate was .61. When lineup decisions were restricted to the first selection made (as would occur if the procedure was terminated after the first choice), the correct selection rate was .49. First selection only data would lead to a percentage guilty rate of 96% based on the correct rejection data. Suspect-only choices (discarding witnesses who selected more than one person) result in a percentage guilty rate of 93%. Of course, the percentage guilty rate must be 100% with choices of the designated innocent suspect, because he was never selected as the only person from the target-absent lineup. Levi points out that target-only evidence would be obtained at the expense of losing the partial identifications obtained when allowing a multiple choice, in this case reducing selections of the target from .69 to .43. As with other screening procedures, this is unlikely to be acceptable to police and prosecutors, even if the probative value of the resulting evidence is very high. Levi believes that allowing multiple choices is useful because of the gain in partial identifications obtained while correct selections and correct rejections remain similar. Examining lineup size (by considering only the first 6, 10, or 20 decisions), Levi found no evidence of a difference in target-present lineups but found fewer correct rejections in the 20-person lineup than in the 10-person lineup. Of course, increases in choices in the larger lineup are offset by the number of alternatives available to choose.

In a second examination of the multiple-choice large sequential lineup, Levi (2002) compared performance on target-present and target-absent multiple-choice large sequential lineups with the perpetrator in the 10th, 20th, or 40th positions. There were no significant differences in correct selections across suspect position. However, the correct selection rates (suspect only) were very low regardless of suspect position: .08, .11, and .11 for the 10th, 20th, and 40th positions, respectively. Even when partial identifications were allowed, the rates were still very low: .20, .16, and .14 for the respective positions. In the target-absent conditions, correct rejection rates tended to become lower as the lineup size increased: .66, .55, and .43 for 10-, 20-, and 40-person target-absent lineups, respectively. The percentage guilty rates for suspect-only choices would be 70%, 81%, and 88% for the 10-, 20-, and 40-person lineups, respectively. Allowing partial identifications, the percentage guilty rates would be 85%, 88%, and 91%.

The results indicate that increasing lineup size improves the probative value of the evidence obtained (percentage guilty increases). However, the low rates of correct selections, combined with limited data directly comparing these results with other procedures currently in use, are a problem. It is difficult to interpret some of the data from the papers as well. This leaves us unable to make any strong claims at this point about the potential usefulness of the multiple-choice, large, sequential lineup. Any strength that the procedure has may be more than offset by the problems that may exist with convincing police to use the procedure. Partial identification certainly would be a very controversial notion in court. This procedure is unlikely to be pursued further without evidence that it can provide higher percentage guilty rates without sacrificing too many correct selections. It also raises a very interesting question regarding how jurors would respond to partial identifications.

TRAINING

Parker and Ryan (1993) attempted to determine whether practice with lineups would help witnesses make better decisions. They presented target-present and target-absent simultaneous and sequential lineups to adults and children (8 to 11 years old). Although no main effect on correct selections was found, children's correct selection rates were slightly lower in the control (.33) than in the practice (.38) conditions. Correct rejections were less common in the control (.25) than the practice (.38) conditions. As a result, percentage guilty values increased from 73% without practice to 79% with practice. Compared with no practice, for adults practice also increased correct selection (.25 vs. .42) and correct rejections (.58 vs. .67), resulting in an increase in percentage guilty from 78% to 88%. All of these results suffer from very small sample size (12 per condition), and the use of stimulus materials that may have provided very poor exposure to the target.

Pozzulo and Lindsay (1997) also tested the impact of training on selection accuracy. Children (10–14 years) and adults saw a staged crime and then performed a lineup task. Performance was compared with that of a standard simultaneous lineup. One alternative lineup provided extended instructions emphasizing the importance of avoiding incorrect selections. A second procedure included the addition of a highly salient I don't know response. The other procedure provided a model (the researcher) demonstrating the correct decisions to make when a target (cartoon character) was present versus absent from the lineup (training). The experimental procedures did not influence correct rejection rates. Presenting a salient I don't know response increased overall choosing for both target-present and target-absent lineups. For reasons that are not clear, extended instructions warning of the dangers of false choices increased correct selections. None of these effects were strong, and none have been replicated. Most relevant here, training did not influence accuracy.

ELIMINATION LINEUPS

The elimination lineup was developed specifically to improve children's selection accuracy. Pozzulo and Lindsay (1999) argued that a simultaneous lineup results in a two-judgment process. The first judgment involves determining which person in a lineup is the most similar to the perpetrator, a relative judgment. The second judgment requires

deciding whether the most similar person is in fact the perpetrator, an absolute judgment. It was argued that children do not make use of the second judgment; that is, once
the child has decided who is most similar, that person is very likely to be selected,
whether he or she is guilty or innocent. Elimination lineups divided these two decisions
into distinct steps. Two procedures were used to arrive at the first judgment. The fast
elimination lineup asked witnesses to select the most similar person to the perpetrator.
In the slow elimination lineup witnesses were asked to select the least similar person,
who was removed, and to continue this process until only one person remained. Both
procedures produce a "survivor," the lineup member left at the end of the first step. The
second step is to ask the witness if the survivor is the target. Child and adult witnesses
were presented with either target-present or target-absent fast elimination, slow elimination, or simultaneous lineups. Children also received either standard lineup instructions
or modified instructions aimed at emphasizing the dangers of identifying an innocent
person and encouraging the use of an absolute judgment strategy.

Elimination lineups reduced false-positive choices by children. The resulting percentage guilty values for fast elimination lineups (92%) and slow elimination lineups
(92%) were higher than for the standard simultaneous lineup (89%). Adults performed
about equally well with the fast elimination lineup (98% guilty), the slow elimination
lineup (96% guilty), and the simultaneous lineup (97% guilty). Compared with standard instructions, the impact of the modified instructions on percentage guilty was negligible for the slow elimination lineup (92% vs. 92%) but improved performance somewhat for the fast elimination lineup (92% vs. 96%) and a little for the simultaneous
lineup (89% vs. 91%). Although some of the differences are small, it appears that elimination lineups in general and in combination with modified lineup instructions can improve selection accuracy.

Beyond the elimination procedures being effective at reducing false positives to
some extent, two new forms of selection evidence were considered. Survivor status was
shown to have some probative value as an indication of guilt. Of course, survival and selection are the same for the simultaneous lineup. For elimination lineups, being the survivor was associated with equal or higher percentage guilty values for all variations of
the procedure for both adults and children. Perhaps broadening the definition of selection evidence to include concepts such as survival status would allow for more innovative lineup techniques to be developed. The second new form of evidence was early
elimination from the lineup. Data suggested that people eliminated early rather than
late from a slow elimination lineup were unlikely to be the target. Thus, early selection
for elimination was probative of innocence.

SELECTION OF MULTIPLE FEATURES

Lindsay, Wallbridge, and Drennan (1987) proposed a method of enhancing the quality
of evidence obtained from eyewitnesses with the selection of more than just the face. In
real situations it is common for multiple features of a criminal to be presented at one
time. It would be preferable to take advantage of any information an eyewitness could

provide about the various features. In this sense, they were the first researchers to obtain independent selection of multiple features of a perpetrator, in this case, the person and his clothing. They tested the impact of clothing bias on witness accuracy by staging a crime and manipulating lineup attire. To test the effects of clothing bias, they presented witnesses with target-present or target-absent simultaneous lineups. The suspect was dressed exactly the same as the perpetrator during the crime, similar to the perpetrator during the crime (both considered biased), unlike the perpetrator and the same as the other lineup members (dressed alike), or unlike the perpetrator and different from the other lineup members (usual). They also presented witnesses with either target-present or target-absent clothing lineups. They found that witnesses who had identified the suspect clothing were more likely to identify the guilty suspect than the innocent suspect. The percentage guilty values were 93% when the eyewitness selected both the suspect and the suspect clothing, compared with 66% when the eyewitness selected the suspect but failed to select the suspect clothing. This was the first indication of the utility of using different features to obtain independent selection decisions.

Pryke, Lindsay, Dysart, and Dupuis (2004) further examined the utility of having witnesses give independent selection evidence on multiple features. In their first study, Pryke et al. exposed two classes of undergraduate psychology students to a confederate. The students attempted selections of the confederate's face, body, and voice from target-present or target-absent lineups. The authors argued that if multiple independent lineups were employed, the chances of selecting the same innocent suspect on multiple features should decrease exponentially as the number of lineups increases. Therefore, if multiple selections of independent features were made of the same person, this would indicate that he or she is more likely to be the perpetrator than an innocent suspect.

The findings supported this argument. Correct selections of the target's face were made by .74 of witnesses, and .55 selected his face and another feature. By contrast, .20 of witnesses selected the designated innocent suspect's face from the target-absent face lineup, and only .06 of witnesses picked the innocent suspect's face and at least one of his other features. If only a face was selected, the percentage guilty value was 78%. If the face and any other feature were chosen, the percentage guilty value rose to 89%. When all three features were chosen, the percentage guilty value was 92%. The data indicated that if a witness selects multiple features of the same person from independent lineups, the likelihood that the suspect is the guilty person increases as the number of features selected increases. Another interesting feature of the data was that, when examined alone, the voice and body lineups did not prove to be of much probative value. In fact, there were more false selections than correct selections in the body lineups and similar numbers of each in the voice lineups. This would be a problem if these features were used as evidence in isolation. However, an innocent suspect would only be in danger if multiple features were selected, and this did not occur very often in this study.

In their second experiment, Pryke et al. (2004) changed to a live crime staged individually, added clothing as an additional feature for selection, and all lineups were presented sequentially (in Experiment 1, the face and body lineups were presented simultaneously). Their results replicated those of Experiment 1 but were even more impressive for the sequential lineups. In this study, .70 of witnesses selected the target's face from the target-present lineup, whereas .15 of witnesses selected the designated target's face from the target-absent lineup (82% guilty). The suspect features and suspect clothing could be selected 0, 1, 2, 3, or 4 times. As expected, the percentage guilty increased dramatically as the number of suspect selections increased (26%, 63%, 91%, 100%, and 100%, respectively).

Clearly, obtaining witness evidence with sequential lineups and the selection of multiple independent features has the potential to provide highly probative evidence. The procedure has advantages over some other alternatives (e.g., multiple-choice, large, sequential lineups). The logic of the procedure is a good match to a well-established legal principle, corroboration. Rather than thinking of a multiple selection as "identification" and a single selection as failing to reach the level of "identification," Pryke et al. (2004) suggest that selection of the face is critical, as it is the most informative individual piece of selection evidence. Additional selections of the suspect, they argue, should be viewed as corroborating evidence supporting the accuracy and increasing the probative value of the face selection. As a result, face selection alone would be evidence, but weak evidence, of guilt. Selection of the face and other features from multiple independent lineups would be strong evidence of guilt and stronger as more selections of the suspect are obtained from the witness.

CONCLUSIONS

Obviously, new and, it is hoped, more effective lineup procedures are being developed. The new techniques have mainly been aimed at addressing the problem of false selection rates. The sequential lineup proved superior because of the reduction in these errors; however, the rate of false selections remains high enough with that procedure to allow for many innocent suspects to be subjected to prosecution and punishment. Being content with the improvements provided by sequential lineups is not an acceptable option for the criminal justice system. Several adaptations and extensions of the sequential procedure were examined, with varying levels of success. Even with the initial impressive results of selection from multiple independent lineups, complacency is dangerous. The procedure requires more research to examine any potential flaws or weaknesses that may be present. All new procedures will have to be tested to determine the impact on their effectiveness of known variables that influence eyewitness accuracy, such as lineup biases, cross-race situations, and age differences. Many other variables exist that may interact with lineup procedure in unknown ways (e.g., we lack studies on the impact of delay between the crime and lineup procedure on the accuracy of eyewitness decisions from the various available procedures; see Dysart & Lindsay, this volume).

Another potential shortcoming of the existing lineup research is that it may not be radical enough. Many of the new procedures were developed by adaptation of existing procedures. The development and examination of truly unique forms of gathering selection evidence may prove to be a valuable research avenue. An argument can be made that new methods of obtaining selection evidence that result in unusual forms of evidence, such as survivor status in the elimination lineups (Pozzulo & Lindsay, 1999), are not readily applicable to the criminal justice system and will not be accepted by police or the courts. Although that may be so at this time, that is not a valid reason to avoid innovative research. Any procedure that dramatically increases the probative value of eyewitness selection evidence may be considered by the justice system, regardless of conventionality. As researchers, we shouldn't worry about the difficulty of implementing new procedures. Instead, we should develop better procedures, collect the data necessary to confirm that the procedures provide better evidence of guilt and innocence, and then worry about convincing the criminal justice system to adopt them (Lindsay, 1999; Wells et al., 2000).

ACKNOWLEDGMENT

Preparation of this chapter was supported by grants to R. Lindsay from the Social Sciences and Humanities Research Council of Canada.

REFERENCES

Bala, N., Lee, K., Lindsay, R. C. L., & Talwar, V. (2001). A legal & psychological critique of the present approach to the assessment of the competence of child witnesses. *Osgoode Hall Law Journal, 38*, 409–451.

Bruck, M., Ceci, S. J., & Hembrooke, H. (1998). Reliability and credibility of young children's reports. *American Psychologist, 53*, 136–151.

Cutler, B. L., & Penrod, S. D. (1988). Improving the reliability of eyewitness selection: Lineup construction and presentation. *Journal of Applied Psychology, 73*, 281–290.

Dysart, J. E., & Lindsay, R. C. L. (2001). A pre-identification questioning effect: Serendipitously increasing correct rejections. *Law & Human Behavior, 25*, 155–165.

Goldstein, A. G., Chance, J. E., & Schneller, G. R. (1989). Frequency of eyewitness identification in criminal cases: A survey of prosecutors. *Bulletin of the Psychonomic Society, 27*, 71–74.

Gray, E. (1993). *Unequal Justice: The prosecution of child sexual abuse*. New York: Macmillan.

Honts, C. R. (1994). Assessing children's credibility: Scientific and legal issues in 1994. *North Dakota Law Review, 70*, 879–899.

Levi, A. M. (1998). Protecting innocent defendants, nailing the guilty: A modified sequential lineup. *Applied Cognitive Psychology, 12*, 265–275.

Levi, A. M. (2002). Up to forty: Lineup size, the modified sequential lineup, and the sequential lineup. *Cognitive Technology, 7*, 39–46.

Lindsay, R. C. L. (1999). Applying applied research: Selling the sequential lineup. *Applied Cognitive Psychology, 13*, 219–225.

Lindsay, R. C. L., & Bellinger, K. (1999). Alternatives to the sequential lineup: The importance of controlling the pictures. *Journal of Applied Psychology, 84*, 315–321.

Lindsay, R. C. L., Brigham, J. C., Malpass, R. S., & Ross, D. F. (2003, July). *Cross-race identification from simultaneous and sequential lineups*. Society for Applied Research in Memory and Cognition, Aberdeen, Scotland.

Lindsay, R. C. L., Lea, J. A., & Fulford, J. A. (1991). Sequential lineup presentation: Technique matters. *Journal of Applied Psychology, 76*, 741–745.

Lindsay, R. C. L., Lea, J. A., Nosworthy, G. J., Fulford, J. A., Hector, J., LeVan, V., et al. (1991). Biased lineups: Sequential presentation reduces the problem. *Journal of Applied Psychology, 76*, 796–802.

Lindsay, R. C. L., Pozzulo, J. D., Craig, W., Lee, K., & Corber, S. (1997). Simultaneous lineups, sequential lineups, and showups: Eyewitness selection decisions of adults and children. *Law and Human Behavior, 21*, 391–404.

Lindsay, R. C. L., Wallbridge, H., & Drennan, D. (1987). Do clothes make the man?: An exploration of the effect of lineup attire on eyewitness selection accuracy. *Canadian Journal of Behavioural Science, 19*, 463–478.

Lindsay, R. C. L., & Wells, G. L. (1980). What price justice? Exploring the relationship of lineup fairness to identification accuracy. *Law & Human Behavior, 4*, 303–313.

Lindsay, R. C. L., & Wells, G. L. (1985). Improving eyewitness selection from lineups: Simultaneous versus sequential lineup presentation. *Journal of Applied Psychology, 70*, 556–564.

Malpass, R. S., & Devine, P. G. (1981). Eyewitness identification. Lineup instructions & the absence of the offender. *Journal of Applied Psychology, 66*, 343–350.

Malpass, R. S., & Lindsay, R. C. L. (1999). Measuring lineup fairness. *Applied Cognitive Psychology, 13*(SI), S1–S7.

Parker, J. F., & Ryan, V. (1993). An attempt to reduce guessing behavior in children's and adult's eyewitness identification. *Law and Human Behavior, 17*, 11–26.

Phillips, M. R., McAuliff, B. D., Kovera, M. B., & Cutler, B. L. (1999). Double-blind photoarray administration as a safeguard against investigator bias. *Journal of Applied Psychology, 84*, 940–951.

Pozzulo, J. D. & Lindsay, R.C.L. (1995, June). Eyewitness identification procedures when appearance has been changed. Society for Applied Research in Memory and Cognition, Vancouver.

Pozzulo, J. D., & Lindsay, R. C. L. (1997). Conducting identifications with children: What not to do. *Expert Evidence, 5*, 126–132.

Pozzulo, J. D., & Lindsay, R. C. L. (1998). Identification accuracy of children versus adults: A meta-analysis. *Law & Human Behavior, 22*, 549–570.

Pozzulo, J. D., & Lindsay, R. C. L. (1999). Elimination lineups: An improved selection procedure for child eyewitnesses. *Journal of Applied Psychology, 84*, 167–176.

Pryke, S., Lindsay, R. C. L., Dysart, J., & Dupuis, P. (2004). Multiple independent selection decisions: A method of calibrating eyewitness selections. *Journal of Applied Psychology, 89*, 73–84.

Shapiro, P. N., & Penrod, S. (1986). Meta-analysis of facial identification studies. *Psychological Bulletin, 100*, 139–156.

Smith, S. M., Lindsay, R. C. L., & Pryke, S. (2000). Postdictors of eyewitness errors: Can false identifications be diagnosed? *Journal of Applied Psychology, 85*, 542–550.

Sporer, S. L. (1993). Eyewitness selection accuracy, confidence, and decision timesin simultaneous and sequential lineups. *Journal of Applied Psychology, 78*, 22–33.

Steblay, N. M. (1997). Social influence in eyewitness recall: A meta-analytic review of lineup instruction effects. *Law & Human Behavior, 21*, 283–297.

Steblay, N. M., Dysart, J., Fulero, S., & Lindsay, R. C. L. (2001). Eyewitness accuracy rates in sequential and simultaneous lineup presentations: A meta-analytic comparison. *Law and Human Behavior, 25*, 459–473.

Wells, G. L. (1984). The psychology of lineup selections. *Journal of Applied Social Psychology, 14*, 89–103.

Wells, G. L. (2005). Lineup theory. In R. C. L. Lindsay, D. F. Ross, J. D. Read, & M. P. Toglia (Eds.), *Handbook of eyewitness psychology: Vol. II. Memory for people.* Mahwah, NJ: Lawrence Erlbaum Associates.

Wells, G. L., & Lindsay, R. C. L. (1980). On estimating the diagnosticity of eyewitness non selections. *Psychological Bulletin, 88*, 776–784.

Wells, G. L., Malpass, R. S., Lindsay, R. C. L., Fisher, R. P., Turtle, J. W., & Fulero, S. (2000). Eyewitness research: The long road to national guidelines. *American Psychologist, 55*, 581–598.

Wells, G. L., Rydell, S. M., & Seelau, E. P. (1993). On the selection of distractors for eyewitness lineups. *Journal of Applied Psychology, 78*, 835–844.

Wells, G. L., & Turtle, J. W. (1986). Eyewitness identification: The importance of lineup models. *Psychological Bulletin, 99*, 320–329.

Yarmey, A. D., & Morris, S. (1998). The effects of discussion on eyewitness memory. *Journal of Applied Social Psychology, 28*, 1637–1648.

9

A Role for Theory in Eyewitness Identification Research

Neil Brewer, Nathan Weber,
and Carolyn Semmler
Flinders University

For 20 to 30 years eyewitness identification research has been expanding, and, increasingly, it is providing a focus for researchers in cognitive, developmental, and social psychology. By relying on carefully controlled experimentation, often guided by observations from actual criminal cases (e.g., *Kirby v. Illinois*, 1972; *People v. McDonald*, 1984; *United States v. Ash*, 1973; *United States v. Wade*, 1967), this research has advanced our understanding of eyewitness fallibility and provided many useful practical guidelines for the conduct of eyewitness identification tests (Technical Working Group for Eyewitness Evidence, 1999). Many of the advances in the field have resulted from the fact that research has directly targeted specific practical issues (e.g., the nature of instructions given to witnesses prior to the identification test, the mode of presentation of lineup members at the identification test). Much less prominent, however, has been research that has been motivated primarily by the desire to refine our theories of identification decision processes. Here we endeavor to make the case that continued and meaningful practical developments will be most likely to occur if we can provide significant theoretical insights into key aspects of the identification decision process, and that this should be a major motivating factor in future research. A problem with the purely practically motivated approach is that research studies run the risk of being haphazard or uncoordinated, leading to one-off forays into the particular field of inquiry. In contrast, a theoretically based approach, which asks fundamental questions about the nature of the processes underlying eyewitness identification behavior, can provide a structure or integrative framework that should guide research toward a more satisfying conclusion. Although the latter approach sometimes conveys the impression that researchers are merely treading water when it comes to the development of practical applications, it is our belief that, ultimately, the most useful and powerful practical claims will derive from such an approach.

Let us take one example to illustrate how theoretically motivated research is likely to lead to the most compelling practical advances. One of the most significant advances in eyewitness identification research and technology—namely, the development of the sequential lineup presentation procedure as an alternative to the simultaneous lineup (Lindsay & Wells, 1985)—clearly emerged from theorizing about the nature of the judgment task in which witnesses engage. The impetus for the development of the sequential lineup was based on the notion that witnesses are inclined to make relative judgments about the likelihood that the various members of a lineup are the offender (Wells, 1984), a decision strategy that we now know can give rise to the witness identifying the most likely-looking lineup member, even though the absolute match with the offender may be poor. This relative judgment strategy, although often leading to an accurate identification when the offender is in the lineup, has the potential to produce false identifications from a target-absent array. In response to this problem, the sequential lineup was developed to maximize the likelihood that witnesses would make an absolute, rather than relative, judgment about each lineup member. If we examine the history of research on this issue, we can see that the nature of the judgment strategy (i.e., the fundamental theoretical concern) has remained a consistent focus throughout. It is not easy to find other positions on the nature of the identification process(es) so clearly articulated, or such clear-cut and confidently held recommendations for practice.

The broad aim of this chapter is to advocate for a more prominent role for theoretically motivated research into eyewitness identification processes. At this stage we are not offering a new theory or even a modification of an old one. Rather, to illustrate our case we focus on two broad issues within the field, pointing out what seem to us to be some important and largely neglected theoretical issues, and highlighting some of the practical consequences that might flow from their resolution. The first issue is the choosing behavior of eyewitnesses, with our initial concern being to understand what governs a witness's decision to make (rather than not make) a positive identification from a lineup. Here we hope not only to demonstrate that a theory of eyewitness choosing behavior is crucial for a detailed understanding of identification performance, but also to show that achieving this understanding will be a key step in developing the most effective lineup procedures. The second issue examined is eyewitness confidence, including the origins of confidence judgments, the confidence-accuracy relation, and the malleability of eyewitness confidence. Here we try to demonstrate how a deeper theoretical understanding of identification confidence will inform our understanding of witness behavior at and subsequent to the identification test, an understanding that can translate into distinct recommendations for the practical conduct of identification tests that may take us beyond existing guidelines (e.g., Technical Working Group for Eyewitness Evidence, 1999).

EYEWITNESS CHOOSING BEHAVIOR

Why a Theory of Eyewitness Choosing Behavior?

An examination of the performance of eyewitnesses at identification tests highlights two major problems: (1) mistaken identifications of innocent suspects from perpetrator- or target-absent lineups;[1] and (2) incorrect lineup rejections—that is, failures to identify—when the perpetrator or target is actually present in the lineup. Other chapters in this volume clearly document the first problem, that of the prevalence of mistaken or false identifications in laboratory and real-world identification tests. The second problem—largely ignored by researchers—is also a problem of considerable significance. For example, a huge database (over 18,000 cases) from actual lineups in Britain reveals that only 49% of the conducted lineup procedures actually produced a positive identification (Pike, Brace, & Kynan, 2002). Obviously, some (unknown) proportion of these lineups would not have included the offender, so not all lineup rejections from these lineups can be classified as misses. We cannot know the real proportion of incorrect rejections; but the fact that laboratory experiments also find miss rates as high as 50% with target-present lineups is another indication of the extent of this second problem.

The fundamental issue that emerges from the highlighting of these two problems is why witnesses decide to make, or not make, a choice from the lineup. Clearly, from a practical perspective, the goals are to (a) stop witnesses choosing when the offender is not present in the lineup (thereby eliminating false identifications of innocent suspects) and (b) ensure witnesses do choose when the offender is present in the lineup (thereby minimizing misses, bearing in mind, of course, that the choice of known-to-be-innocent foils cannot result in miscarriages of justice, although—for target-absent lineups—such choices can be diagnostic of the suspect not being the offender; Wells & Olson, 2002). In other words, controlling choosing behavior appears to be the key to maximizing eyewitness identification performance.

Some may think it is trite to focus on the choosing behavior of witnesses, perhaps believing that variations in choosing patterns are simply the inevitable consequences of memorial images or representations that differ in quality. Here, however, we will provide three different examples to illustrate why a focus on choosing behavior is critical. First, examinations of the effect of instructional bias (warning vs. not warning witnesses about the possibility of the target's presence/absence) reveal clear differences in choosing patterns, with witnesses given biased instructions definitely more likely to choose from target-absent lineups and perhaps more likely to choose from target-present lineups (Brewer & Wells, 2006; Malpass & Devine, 1981; Steblay, 1997). Given the fact that subtle variations in lineup instructions can substantially influence witness choosing behavior, it seems quite reasonable to expect different individuals to be characterized by variations in the choosing criteria that they spontaneously adopt. A second example is provided by work on simultaneous versus sequential lineups. In a recent meta-analysis, Steblay, Dysart, Fulero, and Lindsay (2001) demonstrated that the sequential lineup produces fewer false identifications from target-absent lineups than the simultaneous procedure, but at the cost of a reduction in correct identifications from target-present lineups. Thus, the effect of the sequential procedure appears to be, at least in part, a reduction in participants' willingness to make a positive identification. Third, a similar type of outcome from a completely different context is provided by Clare and Lewandowsky

---

[1]Of course, witnesses also sometimes pick "known-to-be" innocent foils from target-present lineups.

(2004). In a set of studies on the verbal overshadowing effect—where poorer identification performance follows a witness having to provide a verbal description of the offender—they demonstrated that the verbal description manipulation produced the expected lower hit rate for a target-present lineup. However, the effect was eliminated when participants were forced to choose, and there was a higher proportion of rejections from a target-absent lineup. Clare and Lewandowsky argued that these findings are consistent with the provision of a verbal description leading witnesses to adopt a stricter criterion for making a positive identification from the lineup. Such effects on a witness's criterion for choosing from a lineup clearly have important implications for identification accuracy.

What Must a Theory of Choosing Accommodate?

Although it is not the goal of this chapter to provide a theory of choosing behavior, we will briefly highlight some of the issues that such a theory will have to address. Previous research has clearly implicated social factors in choosing behavior (Malpass & Devine, 1981; Steblay, 1997). However, we think any theory of choosing behavior will have to accommodate two other broad categories of influences: cognitive and metacognitive influences.

Cognitive Influences.   Few researchers question that a major influence on choosing patterns would have to be the quality of image, trace, or representation that the witness holds in memory. Nor would they doubt that this image quality is going to be heavily influenced by events that take place at the encoding stage. That is, a witness who had a very favorable exposure to the offender (e.g., good lighting conditions, long exposure duration, little distraction, up-close view) is more likely to hold a strong and veridical representation of the offender in memory than a witness who experiences much less favorable encoding conditions. Thus, when the former is confronted with a lineup containing the offender, a match with the image held in memory is (on average) more likely than it is for the latter witness—and subsequent choosing from the lineup is, in turn, more likely. Conversely, a lineup without the offender is more likely to result in a series of mismatches for the former witness than for the latter, and this time nonchoosing—or a rejection of the lineup—is more likely.

It is critical, however, to recognize that things are almost certainly much more complex than just outlined. For example, identification response patterns such as those outlined above are likely to be moderated by the equivalence of encoding and test stimuli, the similarity of other lineup foils (both to the target and to the image in memory), and other such variables. Consider the case of a witness who has a strong image in memory, and the target presented at test appears to be a close match to the stimulus at encoding (i.e., the person has not changed in appearance). Under these circumstances we believe it is possible to envisage several quite different choosing patterns. Perhaps the combination of a strong image and a close encoding-test match will almost guarantee that the witness will choose, regardless of any other circumstances. Alternatively, the witness's behavior may be shaped by the other stimuli in the lineup. For example, if there are a number of highly plausible stimuli in the lineup (i.e., people who are similar to the target and, more importantly, to the image in memory), witnesses may believe that the likelihood of being able to make a correct choice is low, and, consequently, they will not choose. Conversely, such a perception of the lineup (i.e., an array of what appear to be very strong possibilities) might instead persuade witnesses that the offender "must be" present in the lineup, and, therefore, the lineup member that best matches their memory must be the correct choice.

There appear to be two plausible mechanisms for resolving this issue. First, as a function of the recognition judgment processes, witnesses may consistently choose (or not choose) in these situations. Alternatively, their choosing behavior may be moderated by their metacognitive beliefs or strategies. We discuss the latter possibility in detail in the next section. Before doing that, however, let us use another example to illustrate our general point. If a witness has a relatively weak image in memory, or the target at test is not a close match to the stimulus at encoding (i.e., the person has changed in appearance or is not the offender), several possibilities again present themselves. Perhaps a weak image or a poor encoding-test match will result in the witness simply not choosing. But if there was just one lineup member who was a much more plausible match than any of the others (even though, in absolute terms, the match was not good), the witness again may be "compelled" to choose. Yet, he or she may not do so if all lineup members were similarly plausible. We suspect that, if we asked different researchers to predict which of the above outcomes are most likely, we would find considerable variability in the rated likelihood of each. And the reason for this expected variation is that, although we have acknowledged the influence of social factors on choosing, we do not yet have an understanding of the determinants of choosing that takes account of the potential interactions between other key (encoding, test, etc.) variables. In the next section, we try to address this shortcoming by developing some ideas about the potential influence of metacognitive beliefs or strategies on choosing behavior.

Metacognitive Influences. In various domains of cognitive psychology the potential contributions of metacognitive influences have become increasingly recognized. Consistent with a broader emphasis on metacognitive influences in applied cognitive psychology (see, for example, Perfect & Schwartz, 2002), some are now arguing for inclusion of such variables in discussions of eyewitness memory issues (Brewer, Weber, & Semmler, 2005; Pansky, Koriat, & Goldsmith, 2005; Perfect, 2002), although earlier research has also drawn attention to such variables (see, for example, Read, 1995). Here we suggest that a host of metacognitive variables can interact to influence the identification test choosing process and, moreover, that an understanding of these variables should facilitate our understanding and control of choosing behavior. In general, we propose that witnesses tend to assess their ability to make an identification from a lineup based not only on their image of the offender, but also on their intuitive theories of how memory works *in conjunction with* their judgments about the witnessing and testing conditions they experienced.

Consider two witnesses who have equally good memorial images of the offender's face—but one identifies the offender from a lineup and the other makes no identification. One might be tempted to explain this simply by saying that the latter had a stricter decision criterion than the former. But there are other possibilities that we believe should be considered. For example, witnesses could make decisions to attempt an identification based on their perceptions of the witnessing conditions *and* their intuitive theories— sometimes known as metacognitive beliefs or memory heuristics—about how witnessing conditions are likely to affect accuracy. For example, if a witness found that (s)he could give a very detailed description of the offender and believed that this also meant (s)he must have a good image of the offender's face, then (s)he should feel confident about attempting an identification—and choosing may be more likely. In contrast, if a witness believed (for whatever reason) that her description of the offender was inadequate, she may quite reasonably infer (despite what researchers may know about the weak relation between description and recognition accuracy) that she is unlikely to be able to make an accurate identification, thereby reducing the likelihood of choosing.

So, what we are suggesting is that decision criteria are based at least in part on this kind of metacognitive process. That is, metacognitions emerging from the witness's encounter with the crime and the lineup could well be important determinants of choosing. Furthermore, we suggest that the inferences witnesses draw from their subjective experiences will be shaped, not just by their perceptions of the event they witnessed, but also by their metamemory beliefs or heuristics. An interesting consequence of this idea is that identical memory experiences may be capable of producing quite different inferences, depending on a witness's memory heuristics or beliefs about memory (cf. Winkielman & Schwarz, 2001).

We have talked briefly here about possible investigations of cognitive and metacognitive influences on choosing. Researchers in the eyewitness identification field, to date, have not given much consideration to these types of influences, yet they seem to us to be potentially important. We believe that exploration of factors such as these is crucial to clarifying those variables that are likely to (a) increase choosing behavior when witnesses are confronted with target-present lineups, and (b) reduce choosing behavior when the target is absent. An important feature of this thrust is that it grapples not only with the issue of false identifications but also with the neglected problem of misses in target-present lineups. Specifically, the ideal lineup procedure will produce correct, positive identifications when the offender is in the lineup and correct rejections when the offender is not in the lineup (i.e., the suspect is innocent). Obviously, the development of such a procedure relies on a detailed understanding of the determinants of witness choosing behavior.

Given the potential complexity of the factors underlying a witness's decision to choose, we think a thorough understanding of choosing behavior is likely to be achieved more rapidly when research is guided by broad theoretical frameworks that take account of the influence of memorial and metamemorial (as well as social) variables on choosing behavior. The specifics of the approach outlined above may not strike a chord with everyone, but some overarching perspective that demands a consideration of the likely complex interactions between key variables in the determination of identification performance seems crucial for further advances.

It is possible that, in this endeavor, researchers might obtain some useful theoretical guidance from other areas of decision-making research. There is, for example, a large amount of research looking at the cognitive aspects of human decision making, particularly the processes that individuals engage in prior to nominating a particular choice from among several alternatives (see Brownstein, 2003, for a comprehensive review). Such models have been applied to decision-making behavior in various settings, including, for example, legal decision making, decision making in sporting contexts, and students' choices regarding their major area of study. As illustrated below, these theories usually focus on describing the way that reasoning progresses to the point at which the individual nominates an alternative (i.e., chooses) from an array of options.

Although an eyewitness identification involves deciding among several alternatives in a manner similar to that of participants in other types of decision-making studies, there are obviously important differences between this and many other decision-making contexts. Whereas the eyewitness has some standard in memory for comparison, in many decision-making contexts the information upon which the decision is based is given to participants rather than committed to memory. Furthermore, in the latter case there is rarely an objectively correct alternative (although there may be one that maximizes gains and minimizes losses). So, although decision-making theories may offer information about how individuals combine information when making a decision, together with the types of judgment heuristics they may be likely to use, the use of any theory of decision making for developing predictions regarding eyewitness decision-making behavior requires some modification. Bröder and Schiffer (2003) report several experiments contrasting the decision-making processes used by participants who have all of the information available to them when making their decision with those used by participants who have been required to learn the information and recall it when making their decision. This distinction affects the type of decision rules used by participants, with inferences from memory more likely to result in the use of "fast and frugal" decisions based on less information as cognitive resources are redistributed to the recollection of the attributes of the various decision alternatives.

The broader decision-making literature provides some interesting ideas about choosing behavior. For example, Svenson's (1992) differentiation and consolidation theory suggests that decision makers will spread their preferences for particular alternatives apart before, as well as after, making a decision. In the predecision phase the decision makers differentiate a promising alternative until it emerges as sufficiently superior, and, after choosing this alternative, they continue to consolidate the alternative's positive attributes over those of the rejected alternatives. In a similar vein, Mills and colleagues (Mills, 1965; Mills & Jellison, 1968) proposed that decision makers seek to maximize their confidence in the particular alternative they are considering and do this by spreading or adjusting their preferences for the competing alternatives so as to maximize their feelings of certainty. Specifically, they try to increase their decisional certainty by focusing on the positive attributes of the favored alternative and avoiding the negative or discrepant aspects.

Additionally, decision-making research has shown that the extent to which there are consequences attached to a decision outcome can also influence the amount and type of predecision processing that occurs. Studies by Mills and Ford (1995) and O'Neal (1971) found that evaluations of attributes for different alternatives spread apart to a significantly greater extent when the decision involved more serious consequences. Eyewitnesses of course also face a decision task that can vary in terms of the seriousness of con-sequences and involves trade-offs produced by pressures to choose and pressures to be accurate in their choice. Our reason for suggesting that researchers look for possible par-allels in other areas of decision research is to emphasize the possibility that ideas and the-ory gleaned from other decision contexts could well prove to be useful in stimulating identification research and, particularly, in developing a theory of choosing behavior.

EYEWITNESS CONFIDENCE

The second issue we use to illustrate our reasons for advocating a greater emphasis on theoretically motivated research is eyewitness confidence. Eyewitness confidence and its relationship with identification accuracy have been prominent issues in the identifica-tion literature. In the past, the predominant focus in this literature has been on the strength of the confidence-accuracy relationship and the forensic utility of confidence as an indicator of identification accuracy. As other chapters in this volume indicate, vari-ous sectors of the criminal justice system (police, lawyers, judges, jurors) have reinforced the view that confident witness identifications should be more believable than not so confident identifications, and empirical evidence from studies manipulating witness con-fidence have shown that confident witnesses certainly are more likely to be believed (Brewer & Burke, 2002; Cutler, Penrod, & Stuve, 1988). In contrast, most eyewitness researchers have consistently advocated that identification confidence is really a ques-tionable indicator of identification accuracy and certainly not one that should inform judgments about the reliability of an identification within the criminal justice system. We argue here, however, that it is premature to dismiss the utility of eyewitness identifi-cation confidence, principally because confidence is potentially informative about the underlying identification decision process(es) or cognitive mechanisms. Another reason is that findings from various laboratories indicate systematic confidence-accuracy rela-tions for choosers under a number of different conditions (Brewer, Keast, & Rishworth, 2002; Brewer & Wells, 2006; Juslin, Olsson, & Winman, 1996; Lindsay, Nilsen, & Read, 2000; Lindsay, Read, & Sharma, 1998; Olsson, 2000; Olsson, Juslin, & Winman, 1998; Read, Lindsay, & Nicholls, 1998; Weber & Brewer, 2003, 2004). Nevertheless, many re-searchers would doubtless still argue that a not infrequent pattern of eyewitness over-confidence, even if associated with good confidence-accuracy calibration, means that we cannot place any store in witnesses' confidence assessments.

It seems to us, however, that a final position on the utility of confidence as an indi-cator of identification decision processes and accuracy cannot be reached without first understanding the bases or origins of confidence judgments, and the sorts of variables that might shape the veridicality of these bases of confidence judgments and the external expression of those judgments. An understanding of these issues is crucial for resolving specific issues such as the following: (1) Can confidence judgments enhance our under-standing of identification decision processes? (2) Can we realistically expect identifica-tion confidence judgments to reliably diagnose identification accuracy? and (3) Under what conditions might confidence judgments be more or less veridical?

The Source of Confidence Judgments

Various perspectives about the origins of confidence have been advanced in signal detection and other psychophysical theories. For example, some theories suggest that confidence is directly produced by the same information that guides the recognition judgment, such as the strength or accessibility of the memory trace, or the familiarity of a probe stimulus (e.g., Gillund & Shiffrin, 1984; Hintzman, 1988). So, for example, for a witness with a very strong memory trace or for whom the stimulus appears highly familiar, confidence will be high. Another theoretical perspective from psychophysics, recently applied to recognition memory, argues that confidence is actually based on evidential discrepancies for different choices (e.g., Baranski & Petrusic, 1998; Van Zandt, 2000; Vickers, 1979). In the lineup context, a clear evidential discrepancy in favor of one lineup member over the others would thus lead to a highly confident decision. Whereas the first of the above positions would suggest high confidence given high memory strength or familiarity, regardless of the lineup composition, the latter would hold that confidence is additionally influenced by the composition of the lineup (i.e., high target-foil similarity would be associated with low confidence, even with a highly familiar target). Also, the first position suggests that confidence would always be low if there was a poor match of the memory trace to any of the lineup members, whereas the second position suggests that high confidence in an incorrect selection of a dissimilar individual may result if all other lineup members are considerably more discrepant from the memory trace than the person selected.

Yet another perspective suggests that witness confidence could also be influenced by what have been called analytic, or more consciously constructed, cues (Koriat, 1997). For example, in an interesting face recognition study by Busey, Tunnicliff, Loftus, and Loftus (2000), a mismatch between encoding and test stimuli apparently led to witnesses' confidence estimates being shaped by analytic cues. They manipulated the luminance of faces at study and test and found that confidence was largely determined by the luminance of faces at test, whereas the accuracy of recognition judgments depended on the study-test luminance match. Thus, for example, witnesses displayed greater confidence for faces shown under bright light at test, regardless of study luminance, even though they were more accurate when the brightness at test matched the brightness at study. In other words, this type of perspective suggests that witnesses may exploit a variety of sources of information, or cues, when making their confidence judgment, rather than rely solely on the memory evidence.

Not only do these perspectives say different things about the basis of confidence judgments and the relevant decision processes, but it is clearly also the case that the practical recommendations for the use of confidence vary for each of these perspectives. For example, the analytic perspective would suggest that a thorough understanding of the cues to confidence employed by witnesses would lead to interventions that encourage witnesses to use veridical cues (cf. Brewer et al., 2002). In contrast, the balance of evidence perspective would suggest that a thorough understanding of the impact of the structure of the lineup on witnesses' judgment processes is necessary to understand the situations in which confidence will be a reliable marker of identification accuracy. Yet another suggestion emerges from the signal detection perspective: quite simply, a strong confidence-accuracy relation should be present.

Factors Determining the Availability or Veridicality of These Sources of Confidence

We do not know a great deal about variables that affect the availability or veridicality of these sources of confidence or, indeed, about the factors that shape the confidence-accuracy relationship. And yet to speak knowledgably about the utility of confidence measures, we do need to resolve some of the issues we raise later in this chapter. A potentially important influence on the availability of confidence cues is the delay or interval prior to the confidence assessment—or, perhaps more importantly, the opportunity that such a delay provides for some kind of interference to occur. Clearly such a delay could affect the availability or integrity of a trace, the degree of familiarity, or the balance of evidence for different alternatives. In this particular literature we are not aware of systematic attempts to examine the effects of such delays, or interference, on witnesses' confidence assessments, although researchers have examined the effects of postidentification feedback (e.g., Semmler, Brewer, & Wells, 2004; Wells & Bradfield, 1998, 1999). We note, however, that a study in progress in our laboratory suggests more impressive confidence-accuracy calibration and less overconfidence, when the confidence assessment was obtained immediately after the identification decision rather than being delayed for as little as 5 minutes. If this finding proves to be reliable and, furthermore, the pattern becomes more pronounced as either delay or interference increases, the implications for how confidence assessments should be obtained and used are obvious. In other words, not only are confidence assessments susceptible to postidentification feedback effects (as recognized in the guidelines from the Technical Working Group for Eyewitness Evidence, 1999); they are also sensitive to other, previously unacknowledged influences.

An interesting implication of the balance of evidence perspective is that lineup structure is likely to be a crucial variable in determining confidence assessments. For example, although all lineup foils might be selected on the basis of appropriately matching the offender's description, it is not inconceivable that they can vary in subtle ways that make them much easier (or more difficult) to discriminate from the target, thereby increasing (or reducing) the balance of evidence discrepancy and altering the confidence that the person has in their choice. Thus, if the lineup choice is a 70% match to the witness's memory of the culprit and the closest foil is a 10% match, the balance of evidence would overwhelmingly favor the witness's choice and lead to high confidence. In contrast, if the lineup choice is a 90% match and the nearest foil is a 70% match, the balance of evidence may lead to lower confidence despite the superior match of the choice to the image in memory. Again, we are not aware of research that has tackled such issues.

Knowing exactly when the processing that underpins the confidence judgment takes place should also be informative about the sources of confidence. This issue has not been a primary focus of research, however, and the only suggestion in the eyewitness identification literature about when the confidence judgment takes place comes from Wells and colleagues (Wells & Bradfield, 1998, 1999), who have adopted the position that witnesses do not think about their confidence until they are explicitly asked to make a confidence judgment. This conclusion derives from their work on the effects of postidentification feedback on witnesses' confidence judgments and their perceptions of the event and lineup, and particularly from the finding that witnesses appeared to be inoculated against the postidentification feedback inflation effect by thinking about their confidence assessments before receiving feedback. In other research areas, however, there has been theorizing about the locus of confidence judgments. For example, a signal detection perspective suggests that confidence is determined when a decision is made by comparison of the decisional evidence (e.g., familiarity or trace strength) with predetermined confidence criteria (e.g., Gillund & Shiffrin, 1984; Hintzman, 1988). In contrast, the balance of evidence perspective views confidence as the result of a postdecisional interrogation of the decisional evidence (Vickers, 1979). Additionally, some research on psychophysical discriminations has used confidence latency measures to demonstrate that observers (at least those operating under an accuracy emphasis) engage in some processing of their confidence assessments prior to making their discrimination decision (Baranski & Petrusic, 1998, 2001). One possible implication of this last view is that witnesses' confidence assessments may actually play some part in regulating their identification decision. Despite the obvious face validity of this idea, again there seems to have been no serious consideration of it in eyewitness research.

Apart from answers to these questions providing some of the keys to understanding confidence-accuracy relations in eyewitness identification, there are important practical implications that would flow from the clarification of these issues. For example, if confidence assessments are only determined in response to a postdecision enquiry, then clearly these assessments are inevitably susceptible to the influence of factors that may operate in the interval between the identification and the confidence measure, including, for example, external influences such as postidentification feedback, which has been shown to exert sizable effects on confidence judgments (Bradfield, Wells, & Olson, 2002; Garrioch & Brimacombe, 2001; Luus & Wells, 1994; Semmler, Brewer, & Wells, 2004; Wells & Bradfield, 1998, 1999). So, unless confidence is assessed immediately after the identification is made, its malleability means that it is unlikely to be a reliable indicator of identification accuracy. Conversely, the signal detection and balance of evidence perspectives would suggest that confidence should be a good indicator of accuracy, provided the confidence assessment is obtained before postidentification influences can have their way with the witness. An obvious limiting condition, however, is the extent to which witnesses are able to faithfully map their internal confidence index onto the actual confidence measurement scale, an issue we discuss in more detail later. An extension of the signal detection perspective is that, if confidence is a measure of the match between a stimulus and the image in memory, then perhaps the most appropriate way to identify who best matches the witness's memory of the offender is to elicit independent confidence assessments for every person in the lineup. Of course, such a procedure would also necessitate the development of some kind of rule that determines when the best alternative should be selected as a positive identification and when the lineup should be rejected.

We also mentioned a third possibility above—namely, that confidence assessments may, in some way, regulate the identification decision process. If this proved to be the case, it not only tells us that understanding the basis of confidence judgments is crucial if we are to understand witness choosing behavior; it also will have implications for the conduct of lineups. As with the previous example, much work would need to be done to clarify the rules that would allow us to link confidence assessments to likely identification accuracy.

The preceding discussion of eyewitness confidence judgments has canvassed a number of different positions regarding the source or origins of such judgments. We do not yet have the evidence that would allow us to come down in favor of any one perspective. What is clear, however, is that resolution of such issues will not only inform our understanding of the confidence-accuracy relationship, but also that of the identification decision processes and, ultimately, the most appropriate identification test procedure.

Variables Affecting the Veridicality of the Obtained Confidence Measure

The preceding discussion drew attention to two factors that influence the confidence-accuracy relationship: (1) the scaling of confidence assessments and (2) the malleability of confidence judgments.

Confidence Scaling. Very little attention has been paid to the scaling of confidence in the eyewitness identification literature. Researchers have used a variety of different scales to measure confidence. In the real world there also seems to be no common technique used to obtain confidence estimates from witnesses. Indeed, published guidelines on the collection of eyewitness evidence simply suggest recording of "the witness's own words regarding how sure he/she is" (Technical Working Group for Eyewitness Evidence, 1999, p. 38). Thus, there has been little consideration of issues associated with the translation of internal representations of confidence onto a particular scale. Three potentially interacting factors appear likely to influence the appropriateness of the scaling of confidence. The first broadly relates to people's capacity to translate an internal representation onto the specific types of confidence scale that are typically provided in experimental research (e.g., 0–100% or 1–7). The question is whether people are able to translate their internal index or feeling of confidence onto a numerical confidence scale. There has already been research in other areas of human judgment which has questioned our ability to do this, arguing that we are generally much better suited to using a scale that is verbal rather than numerical in nature (Windschitl & Wells, 1996). A second, and obviously related, factor concerns the extent to which people can effectively use many versus few response categories. For example, confidence might be quite faithfully scaled when the response categories are few and clearly distinct rather than many or less distinct. Alternatively, any attempt to force witnesses to assign their judgment to a category rather than an unconstrained response may be problematic. Third, witnesses are confronted with lineups that can vary in size, in terms of the number of truly plausible members, and in terms of the availability of *not present* and *don't know* response options. Any eyewitness researcher, confronted with such an array of possibilities (particularly when the last two response options are also included), would find it challenging to specify the level of chance performance. This must surely mean that witnesses would find themselves similarly challenged. For example, if the internal index of confidence held by a witness was halfway between guessing and certainty, the expressed confidence value is going to vary, depending on where the witness locates guessing. These types of scaling issues are obviously not specific to this particular area of psychology, but unfortunately have received little attention in this domain. This lack of attention is particularly important, because a scaling problem could mask an otherwise strong confidence-accuracy relationship. Thus, investigations of confidence scaling and, if necessary, of methods to improve scaling are important issues for identification research.

Confidence Malleability. In contrast with the issue of confidence scaling, quite a lot of attention has been given to the issue of confidence malleability over recent years. A number of studies have shown that eyewitness identification confidence can be inflated, often quite substantially, by confirming feedback from a lineup administrator or cowitness (Bradfield et al., 2002; Garrioch & Brimacombe, 2001; Luus & Wells, 1994; Semmler et al., 2004; Wells & Bradfield, 1998, 1999). Likewise, confidence deflation has been demonstrated as a result of disconfirming feedback (Luus & Wells, 1994). Confidence inflation effects have now been demonstrated for target-present and target-absent lineups and for the various possible identification response categories. These findings have led to a general acknowledgment in the field that confidence inflation is both strong and ubiquitous. There also has been general acknowledgment that confidence estimates should not be relied upon in the judicial system if the time at which they are solicited allows for the possibility of some intervening influence by social factors.

Although researchers agree that the malleability of eyewitness confidence is a significant problem, at present we do not have a coherent and comprehensive theoretical account of this phenomenon. Various theoretical ideas have been proposed. For example, Bem's (1972) self-perception theory and Festinger's (1954) social comparison theory have both been used as a basis for suggesting that individuals (in this case eyewitnesses) are likely to defer to external cues, in the form of other people's opinions, to determine their own attitudes and opinions when the relevant internal cues are weak or inaccessible. In other words, feedback inflation is likely when witnesses have impoverished cues about the quality of their memory of the perpetrator and the event. A not dissimilar, but more cognitive account provided by Bradfield et al. (2002) suggests that feedback inflation is likely when the mnemonic cues associated with the witness's memory of the original event are impoverished. Specifically, they invoked Tulving's (1981) notion of ecphoric similarity (i.e., the degree of match between the stimulus and the memory trace) as an important internal cue upon which witnesses rely to inform their confidence judgment. These various suggestions about the origins of the postidentification feedback effect, however, have not been submitted to systematic experimental testing.

If it turns out to be the case that confidence inflation effects are truly large and ubiquitous, then it is likely to be argued that this neglect of theoretical considerations does not matter very much. But if this is not the case, then a coherent theoretical account of the phenomenon certainly will be informative about the likely occurrence and size of feedback inflation effects. Recent work in our laboratory (Semmler & Brewer, in press) suggests that the effect may vary in size. It appeared that the extent to which the feedback information contradicted people's notions of the likelihood they were correct determined whether the feedback produced a large or a small change in confidence. When there was very good evidence for a particular decision and the feedback contradicted that decision, there was a large alteration in confidence; but when there was good evidence for a decision and the feedback information did not contradict it, then the resultant change in confidence was diminished. Conversely, when there was poor evidence for a decision and the feedback contradicted that decision, there was only a small alteration in confidence, whereas when there was poor evidence for a decision and the feedback agreed with the decision, there was a large alteration in confidence. (Note that these patterns were not due to ceiling or floor effects.)

In sum, various characteristics of our data suggest that the malleability of the confidence estimate is governed not only by internal memorial cues, but also by witnesses' interpretations of their likely memory performance in light of their beliefs about how their memory operates. The data suggest that, instead of witnesses just basing their confidence assessments on feedback information because they lack insight into their own judgmental processes, they appear to engage in a quite analytical process of assessing the various sources of information on which they could base their confidence estimates. In other words, confidence is likely to be shaped both by the information upon which the recognition decision is based and the metacognitive cues invoked by the participant when attempting to interpret the recognition experience. Practical implications follow from this point. If a victim of an assault had been in close contact with the offender for an extended period of time and believed that she should be able to identify the offender, it might be expected that her initial confidence would be high, that confirming feedback would have little effect on her confidence, but the effect of disconfirming feedback may be substantial. Conversely, if—because of the exposure conditions—a witness believed that she would be unlikely to be able to identify the offender, it might be expected that her initial confidence would be low, that the effect of confirming feedback would be substantial, but disconfirming feedback would have little effect on confidence.

The important issue here, however, is not whether this particular theoretical perspective (or indeed any other account) is the correct one. Rather, our point is that only when we have a detailed theoretical understanding of the origins of the postidentification feedback effect, or the determinants of confidence malleability, can we provide unambiguous practical advice about the role factors such as postidentification feedback are likely to play in the judicial system.

SUMMARY

In this chapter we focused on two separate issues, both of which are central in the eyewitness identification literature: the choosing behavior of eyewitnesses and eyewitness confidence and its relationship to identification accuracy. We used these two issues to illustrate how the resolution of hitherto neglected theoretical issues would advance our understanding of eyewitness identification processes and provide important guides for practice. We argued that future theory development in the area of eyewitness choosing would have to accommodate not only the social factors considered in previous research but also cognitive and metacognitive influences on choosing. Such a broad approach should also enhance our understanding of some of the developmental trends in choosing behavior that have been reported (Memon, Gabbert, & Hope, 2004; Pozzulo & Lindsay, 1998). Our discussion of eyewitness confidence considered a number of different perspectives on the origins or sources of confidence judgments and on factors shaping the likely veridicality of confidence cues. We argued that answers to these basic theoretical questions are crucial for achieving a comprehensive understanding of identification decision processes, as well as, of course, for clarifying the confidence-accuracy relationship. It is worth adding at this point that theoretical development may well see the areas of choosing and confidence intersecting because of their likely reciprocal influences.

Some researchers in the eyewitness area might quibble about the applicability of theories derived from more basic areas of experimental psychology to the problems of eyewitness identification. We don't have an investment in any of the particular theories outlined. Rather, we offer them as potential starting points and would argue that, if they are not good enough, refinements or alternatives will have to be found. We also should acknowledge that the issues we have chosen to discuss are obviously quite selective and reflect our particular research directions. Although it is possible that our broad message might only apply to the investigation of these particular issues, we would be very surprised if similar types of arguments could not be developed in other areas of eyewitness identification research. Thus, we confidently expect that relevant theoretical development in those areas will also be crucial for practical advance.

ACKNOWLEDGMENTS

This research was supported by grants A00104516 and DP0556876 from the Australian Research Council.

REFERENCES

Baranski, J. V., & Petrusic, W. M. (1998). Probing the locus of confidence judgments: Experiments on the time to determine confidence. *Journal of Experimental Psychology: Human Perception & Performance, 24*, 929–945.

Baranski, J. V., & Petrusic, W. M. (2001). Testing architectures of the decision-confidence relation. *Canadian Journal of Experimental Psychology, 55*, 195–206.

Bem, D. J. (1972). Self-perception theory. In L. Berkowitz (Ed.), *Advances in experimental social psychology* (Vol. 6, pp. 1–62). New York: Academic Press.

Bradfield, A. L., Wells, G. L., & Olson, E. A. (2002). The damaging effect of confirming feedback on the relation between eyewitness certainty and identification accuracy. *Journal of Applied Psychology, 87*, 112–120.

Brewer, N., & Burke, A. (2002). Effects of testimonial inconsistencies and eyewitness confidence on mock-juror judgments. *Law & Human Behavior, 26*, 353–364.

Brewer, N., Keast, A., & Rishworth, A. (2002). The confidence-accuracy relationship in eye-witness identification: The effects of reflection and disconfirmation on correlation and calibration. *Journal of Experimental Psychology: Applied, 8,* 44–56.

Brewer, N., Weber, N., & Semmler, C. (2005). Eyewitness identification. In N. Brewer & K. D. Williams (Eds.), *Psychology and law: An empirical perspective* (pp. 177–221). New York: Guilford.

Brewer, N., & Wells, G. L. (2006). *The confidence-accuracy relationship in eyewitness identification: Effects of lineup instructions, foil similarity and target-absent base rates. Journal of Experimental Psychology: Applied, 12,* 11–30.

Bröder, A., & Schiffer, S. (2003). Take The Best versus simultaneous feature matching: Probabilistic inferences from memory and effects of representation format. *Journal of Experimental Psychology: General, 132,* 277–293.

Brownstein, A. L. (2003). Biased predecision processing. *Psychological Bulletin, 129,* 545–568.

Busey, T. A., Tunnicliff, J., Loftus, G. R., & Loftus, E. F. (2000). Accounts of the confidence-accuracy relation in recognition memory. *Psychonomic Bulletin & Review, 7,* 26–48.

Clare, J., & Lewandowsky, S. (2004). Verbalizing facial memory: Criterion effects in verbal overshadowing. *Journal of Experimental Psychology: Learning, Memory, and Cognition, 30,* 739–755.

Cutler, B. L., Penrod, S. D., & Stuve, T. E. (1988). Juror decision making in eyewitness identification cases. *Law & Human Behavior, 12,* 41–55.

Festinger, L. (1954). A theory of social comparison processes. *Human Relations, 7,* 117–140.

Garrioch, L., & Brimacombe, C. (2001). Lineup administrators' expectations: Their impact on eyewitness confidence. *Law & Human Behavior, 25,* 299–314.

Gillund, G., & Shiffrin, R. M. (1984). A retrieval model for both recognition and recall. *Psychological Review, 91,* 1–67.

Hintzman, D. L. (1988). Judgments of frequency and recognition memory in a multiple-trace memory model. *Psychological Review, 95,* 528–551.

Juslin, P., Olsson, N., & Winman, A. (1996). Calibration and diagnosticity of confidence in eyewitness identification: Comments on what can be inferred from the low confidence-accuracy correlation. *Journal of Experimental Psychology: Learning, Memory, & Cognition, 22,* 1304–1316.

Kirby v. Illinois, 406 U.S. 682 (1972).

Koriat, A. (1997). Monitoring one's own knowledge during study: A cue-utilization approach to judgments of learning. *Journal of Experimental Psychology: General, 126,* 349–370.

Lindsay, D., Nilsen, E., & Read, J. (2000). Witnessing-condition heterogeneity and witnesses' versus investigators' confidence in the accuracy of witnesses' identification decisions. *Law & Human Behavior, 24,* 685–697.

Lindsay, D., Read, J., & Sharma, K. (1998). Accuracy and confidence in person identification: The relationship is strong when witnessing conditions vary widely. *Psychological Science, 9,* 215–218.

Lindsay, R., & Wells, G. L. (1985). Improving eyewitness identifications from lineups: Simultaneous versus sequential lineup presentation. *Journal of Applied Psychology, 70,* 556–564.

Luus, C., & Wells, G. L. (1994). The malleability of eyewitness confidence: Co-witness and perseverance effects. *Journal of Applied Psychology, 79,* 714–723.

Malpass, R. S., & Devine, P. G. (1981). Eyewitness identification: Lineup instructions and the absence of the offender. *Journal of Applied Psychology, 66,* 482–489.

Memon, A., Gabbert, F., & Hope, L. (2004). The ageing eyewitness. In J. Adler (Ed.), *Forensic psychology: Debates, concepts and practice.* Devon, UK: Willan Publishing.

Mills, J. (1965). The effect of certainty on exposure to information prior to commitment. *Journal of Experimental Social Psychology, 1,* 348–355.

Mills, J., & Ford, T. E. (1995). Effects of importance of a prospective choice on private and public evaluations of the alternatives. *Personality & Social Psychology Bulletin, 21,* 256–266.

Mills, J., & Jellison, J. M. (1968). Avoidance of discrepant information prior to commitment. *Journal of Personality and Social Psychology, 8,* 59–62.

Olsson, N. (2000). A comparison of correlation, calibration, and diagnosticity as measures of the confidence-accuracy relationship in witness identification. *Journal of Applied Psychology, 85,* 504–511.

Olsson, N., Juslin, P., & Winman, A. (1998). Realism of confidence in earwitness versus eyewitness identification. *Journal of Experimental Psychology: Applied, 4,* 101–118.

O'Neal, E. (1971). Influence of future choice importance and arousal upon the halo effect. *Journal of Personality & Social Psychology, 19,* 334–340.

Pansky, A., Koriat, A., & Goldsmith, M. (2005). Eyewitness recall and testimony. In N. Brewer & K. D. Williams (Eds.), *Psychology and law: An empirical perspective* (pp. 93–50). New York: Guilford.

People v. McDonald, 37 Cal.3d 351, 690 P.2d 709, 716, 208 Cal. Rptr. 236, 245 (1984).

Perfect, T. J. (2002). When does eyewitness confidence predict performance? In T. J. Perfect & B. L. Schwartz (Eds.), *Applied metacognition* (pp. 95–120). Cambridge: Cambridge University Press.

Perfect, T. J., & Schwartz, B. L. (Eds.). (2002). *Applied metacognition.* Cambridge: Cambridge University Press.

Pike, G., Brace, N., & Kynan, S. (2002). *The visual identification of suspects: Procedures and practice* (Briefing Note 2/02). London: Home Office.

Pozzulo, J. D., & Lindsay, R. C. L. (1998). Identification accuracy of children versus adults: A meta-analysis. *Law & Human Behavior, 22,* 549–570.

Read, J. (1995). The availability heuristic in person identification: The sometimes misleading consequences of enhanced contextual information. *Applied Cognitive Psychology, 9,* 91–121.

Read, J., Lindsay, D., & Nicholls, T. (1998). The relation between confidence and accuracy in eyewitness identification studies: Is the conclusion changing? In C. P. Thompson, D. J. Herrmann, J. D. Read, D. Bruce, D. G. Payne, & M. P. Toglia (Eds.), *Eyewitness memory: Theoretical and applied perspectives* (pp. 107–130). Hillsdale, NJ: Lawrence Erlbaum Associates.

Semmler, C., & Brewer, N. (in press). Postidentification feedback effects on face recognition confidence: Evidence for metacognitive influences. *Applied Cognitive Psychology.*

Semmler, C., Brewer, N., & Wells, G. L. (2004). Effects of postidentification feedback on eyewitness identification and nonidentification confidence. *Journal of Applied Psychology, 89,* 334–346.

Steblay, N. M. (1997). Social influence in eyewitness recall: A meta-analytic review of lineup instruction effects. *Law & Human Behavior, 21,* 283–297.

Steblay, N., Dysart, J., Fulero, S., & Lindsay, R. (2001). Eyewitness accuracy rates in sequential and simultaneous lineup presentations: A meta-analytic comparison. *Law & Human Behavior, 25,* 459–473.

Svenson, O. (1992). Differentiation and consolidation theory of human decision making: A frame of reference for the study of pre- and post-decision processes. *Acta Psychologica, 80,* 143–168.

Technical Working Group for Eyewitness Evidence. (1999). *Eyewitness evidence: A guide for law enforcement.* Washington, DC: U.S. Department of Justice, Office of Justice Programs.

Tulving, E. (1981). Similarity relations in recognition. *Journal of Verbal Learning & Verbal Behavior, 20,* 479–496.

United States v. Ash, 413 U.S. 300 (1973).

United States v. Wade, 388 U.S. 218 (1967).

Van Zandt, T. (2000). ROC curves and confidence judgments in recognition memory. *Journal of Experimental Psychology: Learning, Memory, & Cognition, 26,* 582–600.

Vickers, D. (1979). *Decision processes in visual perception.* New York: Academic Press.

Weber, N., & Brewer, N. (2003). The effect of judgment type and confidence scale on confidence-accuracy calibration in face recognition. *Journal of Applied Psychology, 88,* 490–499.

Weber, N., & Brewer, N. (2004). Confidence-accuracy calibration in absolute and relative face recognition judgments. *Journal of Experimental Psychology: Applied, 10,* 156–172.

Wells, G. L. (1984). The psychology of lineup identifications. *Journal of Applied Social Psychology, 14*, 89–103.

Wells, G. L., & Bradfield, A. L. (1998). "Good, you identified the suspect": Feedback to eyewitnesses distorts their reports of the witnessing experience. *Journal of Applied Psychology, 83*, 360–376.

Wells, G. L., & Bradfield, A. L. (1999). Distortions in eyewitnesses' recollections: Can the postidentification-feedback effect be moderated? *Psychological Science, 10*, 138–144.

Wells, G. L., & Olson, E. A. (2002). Eyewitness identification: Information gain from incriminating and exonerating behaviors. *Journal of Experimental Psychology: Applied, 8*, 155–167.

Windschitl, P. D., & Wells, G. L. (1996). Measuring psychological uncertainty: Verbal versus numeric methods. *Journal of Experimental Psychology: Applied, 2*, 343–364.

Winkielman, P., & Schwarz, N. (2001). How pleasant was your childhood? Beliefs about memory shape inferences from experienced difficulty of recall. *Psychological Science, 12*, 176–179.

10

Applied Lineup Theory

Steve Charman and Gary L. Wells
Iowa State University

The notion of a theory of lineups is debatable and, in the minds of many psychological theorists, might seem peculiar. Psychological theories usually concern circumscribed psychological processes. For instance, there are theories of face recognition, theories of judgment and decision making, theories of attitude formation and change, and so on. In contrast, a lineup is a task or a procedure, and, although it involves psychological processes, it is not a psychological process per se. Nevertheless, we contend that it is possible to describe some necessary components of a theory of lineups. In particular, we propose various considerations that ought to be a part of an *applied* theory of lineups. We call it an applied theory because it is embedded in the ecology of the legal system and because it rests heavily on the applied goals of the users of lineups, principally the goal of incriminating the guilty and exculpating the innocent.

What qualities should an applied theory of lineups have? We approached this problem with the notion that an applied theory of lineups should describe the function of lineups, the structural properties of lineups and their resultant outcome distributions, and the broad psychological processes that are presumed to operate during a lineup task. In addition, in order to be useful, an applied theory ought to help illuminate gaps in our empirical knowledge, predict patterns of data not yet observed, and stimulate new research.

We thoroughly ground our lineup theory in an ecology that mimics the constraints of the real-world of police investigation and speaks to the question of courtroom probative value. These constraints have significant implications for any applied theory. Consider an example. Traditional theoretical approaches to recognition memory in psychology focus on estimating the probability of observing a particular response (e.g., positive identification) given the presentation of a particular stimulus (e.g., a previously seen stimulus or a novel stimulus). Real-world models of the lineup, on the other hand, need to inform us about the probability that a particular stimulus was presented given that a particular response was observed. As discussed in the section "Bayesian Distribution of Lineup Outcomes," this distinction between the probability of observing a response given the presence of a stimulus versus the probability that a stimulus is present given the observation of a response is critical to a practical theory of lineups. Consider another difference between traditional theoretical approaches to memory and an applied theory of lineups. In traditional psychological theorizing regarding recognition memory, the mistaken identification of a novel stimulus from a display that included the original (correct) stimulus is not fundamentally different from the identification of a novel stimulus from a display that did not include the original (correct) stimulus. As explained later in this chapter, however, there are very different types of errors in lineups that belong in different outcome categories because they can have vastly different consequences. Also, unlike traditional theorizing about recognition memory, a lineup theory must include a role for social influence and for inference processes that are not, in and of themselves, memory variables.

We begin our attempt to articulate a theory of lineups by describing the function of lineups. Why is a lineup conducted in actual cases? What is the goal? For example, is the goal to test the memory of the eyewitness? We contend that the answer is no and that the goal instead is to test a hypothesis regarding whether the suspect is the actual perpetrator. We then describe the structure of lineups. Although there are various possible structures, some elements are a necessary part of the structure, such as the perpetrator-present versus perpetrator-absent element. After establishing the function and structure of lineups, outcome categories can be meaningfully described. Here, for example, we distinguish between known errors and unknown errors. We then describe broad psychological processes that can operate to affect the ability of the lineup to serve its intended function of testing the hypothesis that the suspect is the perpetrator.

THE FUNCTION OF LINEUPS

If you asked 10 people why police conduct lineups, most would say something like "To see if the eyewitness can recognize the bad guy" or something along that line. Indeed, many eyewitness identification researchers are saying something similar when they describe a lineup as a test of the witness's memory. We could not disagree more. Although it can be the purpose of an experiment to test the ability of eyewitnesses to identify targets under particular conditions, this is not the purpose of a lineup in a criminal investigation. Instead, the purpose of a lineup in a criminal investigation is to gather evidence regarding whether the suspect in the lineup is the actual perpetrator.

The distinction between these two functions of a lineup, one testing the witness and the other testing a hypothesis regarding the suspect, is not mere semantics. Although crime investigators can and do make inferences about the reliability of an eyewitness as a function of the eyewitness's response to a lineup, their main objective is to learn something about the likely guilt of the suspect. So, if the eyewitness picks their suspect from the lineup, investigators may increase their certainty that the suspect is in fact the culprit in question. On the other hand, if the witness does not identify the suspect from the lineup, investigators may decrease their certainty that the suspect is the perpetrator. In the latter case, crime investigators could then broaden the investigation to consider other possible suspects. Whether investigators use the information from the witness appropriately is not the point. For example, it is quite possible that criminal investigators too readily dismiss nonidentifications for their exonerating qualities while readily accepting identifications of the suspect for their incriminating qualities (see Wells & Olson, 2002). But this does not negate the point that the purpose of the lineup was to test the hypothesis that the suspect is the perpetrator.

If the actual purpose of a lineup in real cases is to test the memory of the witness, then we would expect to see some things happening that are, on their face, quite absurd. For example, we would expect to have the greatest interest in conducting a lineup when there already exists definitive proof beyond all doubt that the suspect is the criminal. So, if there were a confession from the suspect, plus definitive DNA evidence and fingerprints, investigators would definitely want to conduct a lineup, because that would be the best situation for testing the memory abilities of the eyewitness. After all, that situation would be much more informative about the abilities of the eyewitness than would a situation in which there was uncertainty about whether the suspect is the perpetrator. Notice, however, that it does not make much sense to bother with a lineup under these circumstances, because the actual purpose of a lineup is not to test the memory of the witness but rather to test the hypothesis that the suspect is the perpetrator. Likewise, suppose that the case was seemingly unsolvable because there was no suspect whatsoever. Again, if the purpose of a lineup is to test the eyewitness's memory abilities, investigators would want to use a blank lineup, which is a lineup in which all members are known innocents, to see whether the eyewitness will choose someone nevertheless. After all, a lineup with no suspect would serve as a test to tell us something about whether the eyewitness is reliable. Of course, even though the memory abilities of the eyewitness are clearly relevant at some level, it is not the purpose of the lineup to test the memory abilities of the eyewitness. These examples are absurd precisely because they miss the real function of a lineup, which is to help determine whether the suspect is the perpetrator.

The test-of-witness versus test-of-suspect-guilt distinction is more important than it might first appear, as explained later in this section. At the same time, it is quite understandable that psychological researchers have commonly thought of the function of a lineup as being a test of the eyewitness. Psychological research is almost always a test of how a subject will respond to a stimulus of one type versus another type rather than a test of whether a stimulus is of one type versus another type based on the subject's response. In a signal detection task, for example, a researcher is interested in what response a subject makes to a stimulus condition (noise alone versus signal plus noise) where the stimulus condition is known with certainty. A signal detection researcher is never in the position of trying to decide what the stimulus condition was (noise alone versus signal plus noise) based on the response of the witness. In this sense, the forensic nature of the lineup task differs significantly from the nature of a signal detection experiment because the "givens" and the "unknowns" are different in criminal investigations from what they are in an eyewitness experiment. An eyewitness experiment, for example, is designed to assess the probability of a particular response from the eyewitness, given that the witness was presented with one stimulus (the actual culprit) versus a different stimulus (an innocent suspect) and the experimenter knows the status of the stimulus (i.e., whether the stimulus is the culprit or not). A real-world lineup case, in contrast, is designed to assess the probability that one stimulus (the actual culprit) versus a different stimulus (an innocent suspect) was presented to the eyewitness, given a particular response of the witness. In the language of conditional probabilities, the two situations rely on opposite conditionals: Experiments are concerned with the probability of R given S, whereas real-world eyewitness cases are concerned with the probability of S given R (where R and S mean *response* and *stimulus*, respectively).

What difference does it make to have one construal of the conditional or the other? It can make a considerable difference, and we offer some numerical examples to illustrate our point. Suppose that we conducted an experiment in which we asked people to indicate whether or not a face shown to them was a former president of the United States. We use 20 faces of former presidents and 10 of nonpresidents, for a total of 30 faces. Suppose that we obtained results like those shown in Table 10.1. As indicated in Table 10.1, of the 20 times a president's face was shown, the subject said it was a president 14 times (70% hit rate), and of the 10 times a nonpresident's face was shown, the witness said it was not a president 7 times (70% correct rejections). So, the probability of a correct response given a particular condition (i.e., saying "president" to a president's face, or saying "not president" to a nonpresident's face) is 70%. But what is the probability that a stimulus was of a particular type (president versus nonpresident), given a particular response? For example, what is the probability that the subject was looking at a president's face, given that the subject said "president"? There were 17 times that a subject said "president," during 14 of which the picture shown was of a president. Hence, the correct answer is 82.4% (14/17). And, what is the probability that a subject was looking at a nonpresident, given that the subject said "not a president"? There were 13 times in which the subject said "not president," 7 of which the picture shown was not of a president. Hence, the correct answer is 53.8% (7/13). Clearly, the probability of a response given a stimulus is not the same as the probability of a stimulus given a response. Criminal investigators and triers of fact in criminal cases are in the latter position: estimating the probability that the suspect is guilty or innocent given the response of the witness, not the probability of the witness's response given that the suspect is innocent or guilty. This directional distinction is not arbitrary but rather is necessary, given the forensic ecology under which real-world lineups are conducted.

It is important to note that our depiction of the function of lineups (to test a hypothesis regarding the innocence or guilt of the suspect) is bidirectional. When properly designed and interpreted, a lineup procedure has not only incriminating powers, but exonerating powers as well. In fact, there is clear proof using mathematical formulations that any lineup that has incriminating value from the identification of the suspect must also have exonerating value from a nonidentification (Wells & Lindsay, 1980; Wells & Olson, 2002). The magnitude of the incriminating value does not have to be mathematically

TABLE 10.1

	President	Not President	Total
Subject says "a president"	14	3	17
Subject says "not a president"	6	7	13
Total	20	10	

equal to the magnitude of the exonerating value; one can be greater than the other, depending on several factors that we discuss later in this chapter.

THE STRUCTURE AND OUTCOMES OF LINEUPS

Lineup Structure

In the most general terms, a lineup is structured so that a suspect is embedded among nonsuspects. We will call these nonsuspects *fillers*.[1] In some eyewitness identification writings, fillers are known as *foils* or *distractors*. In an episode of Seinfeld, fillers were called *decoys*. We prefer the term *fillers* because this appears to be the most common term used by law enforcement in the United States, and it seems rather neutral (*foils*, for instance, seems to imply that their purpose is to fool the witness). Whatever they are called, the important thing about fillers is that they are not suspects, but rather are known innocents. Accordingly, any identification of a filler by an eyewitness is a known error that would not result in charges against that person.

It is critical to maintain a distinction between a suspect and a perpetrator. A suspect is someone who is suspected of being the perpetrator, but there are innocent suspects and there are guilty suspects. Indeed, as discussed in the previous section, the function of a lineup is to bring evidence to bear on the question of whether the suspect and the perpetrator are the same person or are different people. Experiments on eyewitness identification represent these two types of suspects (the guilty suspect and the innocent suspect) by showing some eyewitnesses lineups that include the perpetrator and showing other eyewitnesses lineups that do not include the perpetrator. Perpetrator-present and perpetrator-absent lineups are a necessary structural feature of the design of any eyewitness identification experiment concerned with eyewitness identification accuracy precisely because they are part of the ecology of real-world lineups.

Outcomes Taxonomy

We think it is useful to depict a lineup as having eight possible outcomes. These outcomes derive from a combination of two states of truth (perpetrator present versus perpetrator absent) crossed with four possible behaviors of the eyewitness in response to the lineup. The four behaviors are the identification of the suspect, the identification of a filler, a "not present" response, and a "don't know" response.[2]

---

[1]Not all law enforcement agencies have followed this fundamental structure. In some cases, lineups have been composed entirely of suspects and no member of the lineup was a filler, even though there was only one perpetrator (Wells & Turtle, 1986). Nevertheless, our theory assumes a lineup is structured to include only one suspect and the remaining members are fillers, which is consistent with guidelines from the U.S. Department of Justice (Technical Working Group on Eyewitness Evidence, 1999).

[2]There are, of course, other possible responses that might make outcome classification difficult. For example, an eyewitness might say, "I think it is number three, but I'm not sure." Would this be an identification of number three or would this be a "don't know" response? Alternatively, an eyewitness might say, "It might be number four, but it could be number six." Our taxonomy does not itself tell us how to treat such responses.

Table 10.2 displays the eight possible outcomes. In actual cases, only the response of the witness is known with certainty, whereas in experiments the state of truth (perpetrator-present or perpetrator-absent) is also known. A miss occurs when the perpetrator is present but the eyewitness fails to identify the perpetrator. Notice that we have depicted three types of misses. A Type 1 miss occurs when the perpetrator is in the lineup and the eyewitness says that the perpetrator is "not present." A Type 2 miss occurs when the perpetrator is present and the eyewitness identifies a filler instead of the perpetrator. A Type 3 miss occurs when the perpetrator is present and the eyewitness says "don't know." A correct rejection occurs when the perpetrator is not in the lineup and the eyewitness does not identify the innocent suspect. Notice that there are three types of correct rejections. Correct Rejection Type 1 occurs when the perpetrator is absent and the eyewitness says "not present." A Correct Rejection Type 2 occurs when the perpetrator is absent and the witness identifies a filler. A Correct Rejection Type 3 occurs when the perpetrator is absent and the eyewitness says "don't know."

Undoubtedly, some readers would disagree with our characterization of Correct Rejection Types 2 and 3 as being rejections of anything. In the case of Type 2 Correct Rejection, the eyewitness clearly does not reject the lineup, but instead identifies a known-innocent filler. Nevertheless, with a Type 2 Correct Rejection, the eyewitness has correctly rejected the idea that the suspect is the perpetrator and it is in this sense that a Type 2 Correct Rejection is both correct and a rejection. Likewise, readers might find it odd to call a "don't know" response to a perpetrator-absent lineup a Correct Rejection Type 3. However, even though the eyewitness did not explicitly say that the perpetrator was not present, the eyewitness nevertheless made a correct decision to not identify the suspect.

Outcome Distributions

Outcome distributions are simply the frequencies, percentages, or probabilities associated with the eight outcome cells depicted in Table 10.2. This is the meat of the matter of eyewitness identification accuracy, because it is these distributions that define the ability of the lineup task to inform us about the hypothesis that the suspect is the perpetrator.

Note that we can partition the columns in various ways by collapsing some columns and not others. Particularly useful is collapsing the "not present," identification of filler, and "don't know" columns into a single column that we could label "non-identifications

TABLE 10.2

	Identification of Suspect	"Not Present" Response	Identification of Filler	"Don't Know" Response
Perpetrator-present lineup	Accurate identification	False rejection or Type 1 miss	Type 2 miss	Type 3 miss
Perpetrator-absent lineup	Mistaken identification	Correct rejection Type 1	Correct rejection Type	Correct rejection Type 3

of the suspect." For economy of language, we will simply call these nonidentifications, even though they include identifications of fillers. Collapsing the nonidentifications together is a useful tool for applying some simple mathematics because it leaves only two categories of response, identifications of the suspect and nonidentifications.

Consider, for example, the hypothetical distribution of responses in Table 10.3. Readers can think of these numbers as frequencies that resulted from showing a perpetrator-present lineup to 100 witnesses and a perpetrator-absent lineup to 100 witnesses in which 60 accurately identified the suspect from the perpetrator-present lineup, 40 did not, and 20 mistakenly identified the innocent suspect from the perpetrator-absent lineup, whereas 80 did not. Alternatively, readers can think of these as probabilities in which the probability was .60 that the witness would make an accurate identification of the suspect from the perpetrator-present lineup and the probability was .40 that they would not, and so on. Or, these could be construed as percentages in which 60% accurately identified the suspect from the perpetrator-present lineup, whereas 40% did not and so on. In any case, these numbers can be used to form a ratio within types of response (i.e., within the columns). Now, suppose we sample a witness at random and, as in an actual case, we do not know whether the suspect was the perpetrator or not. Suppose, instead, that all we know is that the witness identified the suspect. Given an identification of the suspect, what is the probability that the suspect is in fact the perpetrator? The answer is 75%, because 60 of the 80 who identified a suspect identified the perpetrator (i.e., were viewing a perpetrator-present lineup). What if all we knew was that the witness made a nonidentification? What is the probability now that the suspect is the perpetrator? The answer is 33.3%, because 40 of the 120 witnesses who made nonidentifications were viewing a perpetrator-absent lineup.

A somewhat preferred way of expressing the information in Table 10.3 is in the form of diagnosticity ratios. The diagnosticity ratio for a response is an indication of how much more likely one thing is than another when that response occurs. For instance, note that the identification of the suspect is three (3.0) times more likely when the suspect is the perpetrator than it is when the suspect is not the perpetrator. Likewise, the diagnosticity of a nonidentification in Table 10.3 is two (2.0) because it is twice as likely that a nonidentification response will occur when the suspect is not the perpetrator than when the suspect is the perpetrator. A diagnosticity ratio of 1.0 indicates that there is no diagnosticity at all. The higher the diagnosticity ratio, the more impact the response of the witness should have on the hypothesis that the suspect is the perpetrator.

This leads us to our first, and undoubtedly least controversial, observation about the distribution of outcomes as it relates to diagnosticity: Any lineup that has incriminating diagnosticity resulting from an identification of the suspect must also have exonerating

TABLE 10.3

	Identification of Suspect	Non-Identification
Perpetrator-present lineup	60	40
Perpetrator-absent lineup	20	80

diagnosticity from a nonidentification. The reason that this observation ought not to be controversial is that it is a mathematical necessity. The mathematical reason is simple. Because a witness must make either an identification or a nonidentification, the probability of a nonidentification has to be 1.0 minus the probability of an identification. Hence, whenever the probability of identification of a guilty suspect is greater than the probability of identification of an innocent suspect, the probability of nonidentification of an innocent suspect has to be greater than the probability of nonidentification of a guilty suspect.

The foregoing analysis tells us that nonidentifications have exonerating probative value, but it does not tell us how the exonerating value is distributed across the three types of nonidentification responses. One possibility is that exonerating diagnosticity is distributed equally across the three nonidentification responses. Another possibility is that one or two of the nonidentification response types have no exonerating value and the other one or two have exonerating value. There is nothing in the mathematics to constrain the possibilities, except that there must be exonerating value in at least one of the three nonidentification responses whenever there is incriminating value in an identification of the suspect. This is a domain in which only data collection can provide a defensible answer. Nevertheless, mere intuition and common sense would suggest that most, if not all, of the exonerating power of non-identifications resides in the "not there" response. This possibility is shown in Table 10.4. Notice in Table 10.4 that the diagnosticity ratio for "not there" responses is 3.0, but the diagnosticity ratios for filler identifications and "don't know" responses is 1.0 (no diagnosticity). This is one domain, however, where mere intuition may be wrong. Analyses of data from eyewitness identification experiments tend to show outcome distributions more like those shown in Table 10.5 in which filler identifications have some diagnostic value and even "don't know" responses have a small amount of diagnostic value (Wells & Lindsay, 1980; Wells & Olson, 2002).

PERPETRATOR-PRESENT VERSUS ABSENT LINEUPS AS A PROBABILISTIC VARIABLE

The perpetrator-present versus perpetrator-absent variable is a central and necessary aspect of any applied theory of lineups because it makes a profound difference to outcome distributions. In fact, under the assumption of a single-suspect lineup, it is impossible to have a mistaken identification of a suspect from a perpetrator-present lineup. The other reason that the perpetrator-present versus perpetrator-absent lineup variable is central and necessary to any applied theory of lineups is that it varies in actual cases.

TABLE 10.4

	Identification of Suspect	"Not Present" Response	Identification of Filler	"Don't Know" Response
Perpetrator-present lineup	60	20	10	10
Perpetrator-absent lineup	20	60	10	10

TABLE 10.5

	Identification of Suspect	"Not Present" Response	Identification of Filler	"Don't Know" Response
Perpetrator-present lineup	60	10	10	20
Perpetrator-absent lineup	20	30	25	25

In this section, we show how this variable is perhaps best represented as a probabilistic variable, and we describe the kinds of factors likely to affect the present-absent variable in actual cases.

The present-absent variable is, at one level, quite straightforward in an experiment. Because the experimenter knows who committed the "crime," it is a simple act to include this person in some lineups shown to witnesses and not include this person in other lineups shown to witnesses. In actual cases, it is not known whether the perpetrator is in the lineup or not. Indeed, the purpose of the lineup is to help make this determination based on how the witness behaves when confronted with the lineup. Hence, whereas the present-absent variable is an independent variable in an experiment, it is more like a dependent variable in actual cases. (This observation relates closely to the earlier distinction between assessing the likelihood of a witness making a particular response given the suspect is guilty, versus assessing the likelihood of guilt given that the witness makes a particular response.)

Like other dichotomous variables that are associated with uncertainty, the perpetrator-present versus perpetrator-absent variable can be construed as a probabilistic variable. In an experiment, it is common for the design to use a perpetrator-present lineup for half of the eyewitnesses and a perpetrator-absent lineup for the other half. Hence, for any given, randomly sampled lineup from the set of lineups in the experiment, the probability that the perpetrator is in the lineup (probability that the suspect is the perpetrator) is .50.

In our applied theory of lineups, in contrast, actual instances of lineups are not a random sample from some parent population of known proportions of perpetrator-present and perpetrator-absent lineups. There are several respects in which we reject the random sample from a known population idea of the present-absent variable in actual cases. First, the population of present versus absent lineups is unknown in actual cases. We acknowledge that methods might be developed to estimate the proportion of actual lineups in which the perpetrator was present versus absent. However, even if we had a large sample of past actual lineups from which we could somehow determine the proportion (base rates) of times that the perpetrator was or was not present, we would not consider this base rate to be stable across time or jurisdictions. This is due to the fact that the present-absent variable in actual cases is dynamically influenced by investigative practices and criteria that can vary dramatically over time and across jurisdictions. Wells (1993) and Wells and Olson (2002) have described hypothetical law enforcement agencies that use lax versus strict criteria for deciding whether to put a suspect in a lineup. In a strict criterion jurisdiction, investigators might require that there be probable cause, such as motive, opportunity, tools of the crime, or some other fact that would link the suspect to the crime before deciding to expose the witness to a lineup that includes that suspect. A lax criterion jurisdiction, on the other hand, might have no such requirement, and the presence of a mere hunch (or the inability to find other suspects) might be sufficient to decide to conduct a lineup with a particular suspect. Over time, the lax criterion and the strict criterion jurisdictions will run very different base rates for the present-absent variable. Because there is no legal requirement for probable cause to place a suspect in a lineup, especially with regard to the use of photographic lineups, the base rate for the present-absent factor can vary widely. Interestingly, there are times when it is possible to specify an upper limit on the present-absent base rate for a given investigation. For instance, suppose that there was one perpetrator and the eyewitness was shown two lineups, each with a different suspect. In this case, the maximum base rate across the two lineups is 50% for the witness viewing a perpetrator-present lineup. In other words, at least one of the two lineups had to be a perpetrator-absent lineup, so the 50% base rate is the upper limit.

Our applied theory of lineups cannot in itself specify a base rate for the present-absent variable, so the theory treats the present-absent factor as a continuous, probabilistic variable. Furthermore, because the present-absent factor is in fact a base rate, the present-absent factor combines with the diagnosticity factor (described in the previous section) in a manner described by Bayes' Theorem. Indeed, we are unable to imagine an applied theory of lineups that does not incorporate Bayesian parameters.

BAYESIAN DISTRIBUTIONS OF LINEUP OUTCOMES

Thus far we have laid a foundation for a Bayesian depiction of lineup outcomes. This foundation included (a) the distinction between estimating the probability of a witness response given that the suspect is or is not the perpetrator versus estimating the probability that the suspect is or is not the perpetrator given a response by the witness, (b) a description of the function of lineups as a test of the hypothesis that the suspect is the perpetrator rather than as a test of the witness's memory, (c) distinctions between various witness responses, and (d) the idea of the perpetrator-present versus absent factor as a probabilistic variable. At this point, we describe how this maps into a Bayesian model so as to see what implications can be derived for an applied theory of lineups.

Consider first a hypothetical lineup. Assume that the outcome distribution in Table 10.5 applies to the lineup. In other words, the conditions of witnessing, retention, and lineup characteristics are such that if shown a perpetrator-present lineup, we can expect a .60 probability that the witness would identify the perpetrator, a .10 probability that the witness would say "not present," and so on. Again, from Table 10.5 assume that if the perpetrator were not in the lineup, there is a .20 probability that the witness would identify the innocent suspect, a .30 probability that the witness would say "not present," and so on. Finally, assume that the nonlineup evidence against the suspect indicates a .50 probability that the suspect is the perpetrator and a .50 probability that the suspect is not the perpetrator. In other words, assume that it is equally likely based on the nonlineup evidence that the witness is observing a perpetrator-present versus a perpetrator-absent lineup. How should we revise the initial .50 probability that the suspect is the perpetrator as a function of the response of the witness? Under these conditions, if the witness identifies the suspect, the revised probability becomes .75 that the suspect is the perpetrator (i.e., 60 of 80 identifications of the suspect are of the perpetrator). If the witness says "not present," the revised probability that the suspect is the perpetrator is now only .25 (i.e., 10 of the 40 "not there" responses occur when the suspect is not the perpetrator). Similarly, if the witness picks a filler, the revised probability that the suspect is the perpetrator becomes .286 (i.e., 10 of 35 filler identifications occur when the suspect is the perpetrator). Finally, if the witness says "don't know," the revised probability that the suspect is the perpetrator becomes .444 (i.e., 20/45).

What happens, however, if the other (non-lineup) evidence against the suspect indicates a .70 probability that the suspect is the perpetrator rather than the .50 probability? This is where Bayesian statistics come into play, because they articulate a simple algebra for combining probabilistic evidence. A useful form of Bayes' Theorem links hypotheses to data with the equation

$$p(H|D) = \frac{p(D|H)\,p(H)}{p(D|H)\,p(H) + p(D|\text{notH})\,p(H)\,p}$$

where $p(H|D)$ is the probability that the hypothesis is true given the data, $p(D|H)$ is the probability of the data given that the hypothesis is true, and $p(D|\text{notH})$ is the probability of the data given that the hypothesis is not true. Now, we simply substitute lineup terms for the equation in which the data is the response of the eyewitness and the hypothesis is that the suspect is the perpetrator. To help keep this straight, we use the following terms for the witness response:

ids = witness identified suspect
idf = witness identified a filler
np = witness said "not present"
dk = witness said "don't know"

We use the following terms for the status of the hypothesis being tested:

sp = suspect is the perpetrator
s~p = suspect is not the perpetrator

We can now describe the probability that the suspect is the perpetrator, given an identification of the suspect as

$$p(sp|ids) = \frac{p(ids|sp)\,p(sp)}{p(ids|sp)\,p(sp) + p(ids|s \sim p)\,p(s \sim p)}$$

First, we apply this equation to the situation in which the non-lineup evidence indicates a .50 probability that the suspect is the perpetrator:

$$p(\text{sp}|\text{ids}) = \frac{(.60)\ (.50)}{(.60)\ (.50) + (.20)\ (.50)} = .75$$

The .75 probability is the same as the one we calculated without the aid of Bayes' Theorem. Now, however, what about the situation in which the other (non-lineup) evidence indicates a .70 probability that the suspect is the perpetrator (i.e., there is a 70% chance that the perpetrator is in the lineup)? In this case,

$$p(\text{sp}|\text{ids}) = \frac{(.60)\ (.70)}{(.60)\ (.70) + (.20)\ (.30)} = .875 \ .$$

We can then apply this analysis to the other possible witness responses:

$$p(\text{sp}|\text{np}) = \frac{(.10)\ (.70)}{(.10)\ (.70) + (.30)\ (.30)} = .438$$

$$p(\text{sp}|\text{idf}) = \frac{(.10)\ (.70)}{(.10)\ (.70) + (.25)\ (.30)} = .482$$

$$p(\text{sp}|\text{dk}) = \frac{(.20)\ (.70)}{(.20)\ (.70) + (.25)\ (.30)} = .651$$

Notice how the ultimate question that confronts the trier of fact (the probability that the suspect is the perpetrator) depends critically on the conjunction of the probability that the perpetrator is in the lineup plus the probabilistic discriminating abilities of the eyewitness.

Consider, for example, what happens when we examine the data from Table 10.5 across all possible probabilities that the lineup includes the perpetrator, which is shown in Figure 10–1. The straight diagonal line is called the *null line* and represents the hypothetical situation in which the witness response has no diagnostic value at all. Deflections from the null line indicate some degree of diagnosticity for the witness's response, and the greater the deflection the greater the diagnosticity of the response. Notice how the identification of the suspect produces a deflection above the null line (raising the probability that the suspect is the perpetrator), whereas the other three responses produce deflections below the line (lowering the probability that the suspect is the perpetrator).

There are a number of important observations to be made about Figure 10–1. First, Figure 10–1 illustrates how the judgment that triers of fact must make (the probability that the suspect is the perpetrator, given a particular response of the witness) is a complex, nonlinear interplay between the performance abilities of the eyewitness (assessed via

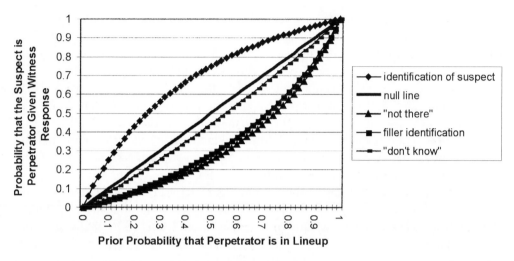

FIGURE 10–1. Probabilities that the suspect is the perpetrator as functions of witness response and prior probability that the perpetrator is in the lineup.

diagnosticity ratios) and the circumstance that the witness faced (perpetrator-present versus -absent lineup). Second, notice that all of the curves regress toward the null line when the probability that the perpetrator is in the lineup begins to approach certainty (either 1.0, which is certainty that the lineup contains the perpetrator, or 0.0, which is certainty that the suspect is not in the lineup). This makes good sense because it means that the witness response does not much matter if one is already certain that the perpetrator is or is not in the lineup. (The reader is reminded at this point that we assume only one suspect in the lineup, and, therefore, knowing that the perpetrator is or is not in the lineup is tantamount to knowing whether the suspect is or is not the perpetrator.) Notice as well that the identifications of the suspect curve and the "not there" curve are mirror images of each other, one above the null line and the other below the null line, because both responses have diagnosticity ratios of 3.0 (see Table 10.5), albeit in opposite directions (one incriminating and the other exonerating). Readers are cautioned against assuming that these two diagnosticity ratios have to be equal. They are equal in the hypothetical data of Table 10.5, but real data show a variety of patterns that depend on witnessing and testing conditions that we do not yet fully understand (see Wells & Olson, 2002). On the other hand, there are constraints on the possible patterns that can occur in Figure 10-1, and these constraints are fully free of assumptions about witnessing and testing conditions per se. The primary constraint is that any degree of upward deflection from the null line that comes from identifications of the suspect must be accompanied by a deflection below the null line for one or more of the three nonidentification responses (i.e., "not there," filler identification, or "don't know") and vice versa.

One of the useful properties of the curves in Figure 10–1 is that they specify how much "other evidence" against the suspect needs to exist in order to reach a particular level of certainty that a suspect who has been identified from the lineup is in fact the perpetrator. Suppose, for example, one needed to be 95% certain to vote guilty. Based on Figure 10–1, this means that there would have to exist other (non-lineup) evidence indicating a .86 probability that the suspect is the perpetrator in order for the identification of the suspect by the eyewitness to push the probability past 95%. Or, if one needed to be 99% certain, then there would have to exist other (non-lineup) evidence indicating a .97 probability that the suspect is the perpetrator in order for the identification of the suspect by the eyewitness to push the probability to 99% or greater. Notice as well that if the other (non-lineup) evidence in the case indicates a 95% probability that the suspect is the perpetrator, a "not present" response from the witness lowers to .84 the probability that the suspect is the perpetrator.

An alternative way to examine the data in Figure 10–1 is to graph the deflections from the null line with the use of absolute values. The result is what has been called information-gain curves (Wells & Lindsay, 1980; Wells & Turtle, 1986; Wells & Olson, 2002), and Figure 10–2 shows these curves for the data from Table 10.5. In effect, information gain is a measure of how much the witness's response changes the probability that the suspect is the perpetrator (regardless of direction). There are several observations about these information-gain curves that further illuminate our understanding of the complex interplay between witness abilities and the probability that the perpetrator is in the lineup. First, note that information gain curves are not symmetric. In particular, note that the identification of suspect curve is skewed to the right, whereas the "not present," identification of filler, and "don't know" curves are skewed to the left. Another way of describing this is to note that the identification of suspect curve peaks when the prior probability that the perpetrator is in the lineup is .37, whereas the "not present" curve peaks when the prior probability that the perpetrator is in the lineup is .63. Notice

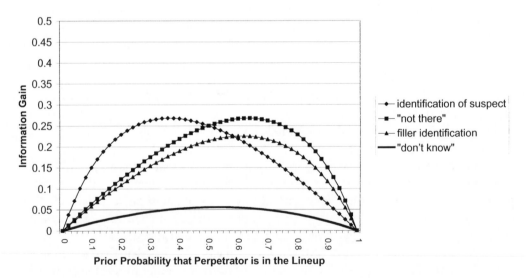

FIGURE 10–2.   Information gain as functions of witness response and prior probability that the perpetrator is in the lineup.

as well that the identification of filler and the "don't know" curves, like the "not present" curve, peak when the prior probability that the perpetrator is in the lineup is above .50. This happens because any piece of information will have more impact when it goes *against the direction* of the previously existing evidence than it will when it is in the *same direction* as the previously existing evidence. Hence, an incriminating response from the witness (an identification of the suspect) will have less informational value when the prevailing evidence indicates that the suspect is the perpetrator (i.e., $p(\text{sp}) > .50$) than when the prevailing evidence indicates that the suspect is not the perpetrator (i.e., $p(\text{sp}) < .50$). In contrast, an exonerating response from the witness (any of the three nonidentification responses) will have more informational value when the prevailing evidence is that the suspect is the perpetrator (i.e., $p(\text{sp}) > .50$) than when the prevailing evidence is that the suspect is not the perpetrator (i.e., $p(\text{sp}) < .50$). On first reflection, some readers might find this surprising. However, it simply means that new information is less informative if it agrees with what we think we already knew than if it is inconsistent with what we think we already knew.

Another observation from Figure 10–2 is that information gain diminishes and reaches 0.0 (zero) under conditions in which one already knows whether the perpetrator is in the lineup. (This is the same observation that we made about Figure 10–1, in which the curves meet the null line when $p(\text{sp}) = 1.0$ or 0.0.) This is just another way of saying that the result of the lineup (i.e., the witness response) is irrelevant if we already know with certainty from other evidence that the suspect is the perpetrator (for example, because of a DNA match).

There is one more important observation that needs to be made from Figure 10–2. In particular, we draw the reader's attention to the fact that the incriminating curve (i.e., identification of suspect) and two of the exonerating curves ("not there" curve and filler identification curve) cross at some point. For expository purposes, consider the identification of suspect curve and the filler identification curve. On average, an identification of suspect is more informative (of guilt) than is a filler identification (of innocence), as evidenced by the higher curve for identifications of suspect than for filler identifications. (This can be noted from Table 10.5 as well because the diagnosticity ratio for identifications of suspect is 3.0, whereas the diagnosticity ratio for filler identifications is only 2.5.) However, note that when the probability that the perpetrator is in the lineup exceeds .60, then a filler identification is more informative of innocence than an identification of the suspect is of guilt.

Although theories can be couched at many different levels of analysis and abstraction, we cannot imagine an adequate theory of lineups that does not provide a representation of the complex relation between the abilities of eyewitnesses (assessed via diagnosticity ratios) and the probability that the lineup includes the actual perpetrator.

PATTERNS OF RESPONDING

Clearly, there are many variables that affect eyewitness identification performance. It is not the purpose of this chapter to review all of these variables. What is important to note, however, is that eyewitness identification data tend to be patterned, and we note here the general nature of that pattern as it relates to the notion of memory strength. By memory strength, we mean the extent to which the witness has a reasonably accurate and accessible memory of the perpetrator. Clearly, memory strength is going to be determined by a host of factors at the time of encoding (e.g., distraction, arousal, distance, lighting) and during the retention interval (e.g., passage of time, post-event information, rehearsal). For our purposes, we refer simply to strong versus weak memories.

Eyewitness identification data tends to follow a predictable pattern in the literature. First, identifications of the perpetrator from the perpetrator-present lineup tend to be more probable than are identifications of the innocent suspect from the perpetrator-absent lineup. Second, "not present" responses are more probable from perpetrator-absent lineups than from perpetrator-present lineups. Third, identifications of fillers are somewhat more probable from perpetrator-absent lineups than from perpetrator-present lineups. Finally, "don't know" responses are slightly more probable from a perpetrator-absent lineup than from a perpetrator-present lineup. The first two patterns, concerning identifications of the suspect and "not present'" responses, are precisely what would be expected from above-chance performance of eyewitnesses. Indeed, Clark (2003) notes that the greater the difference obtained from perpetrator-present and perpetrator-absent lineups in identification of suspect rates, the greater the difference in "not present" responses. This pattern can easily be understood from a consideration of the role of memory strength. As memory strength increases, the rate of identification of the perpetrator from a perpetrator-present lineup should go up and the rate of identification of the innocent suspect from a perpetrator-absent lineup should go down. Conversely, as memory strength increases, the rate of correct rejections should increase and the rate of false rejections should decrease. In terms of diagnosticity, increases in the diagnosticity of identifications of the suspect are associated with increases in the diagnosticity of "not present" responses.

The pattern of filler identifications, on the other hand, is more complex. Clearly, the overall rate of filler identifications should decrease with increasing memory strength. But how does the differential rate of filler identifications in the present versus absent lineup (diagnosticity) vary as a function of changes in memory strength? We know of no data that have specifically addressed this issue, but based on Wells and Olson's (2002) notion of why filler identifications are diagnostic, we would expect the diagnosticity of filler identifications to increase with increasing memory strength. Although filler identifications themselves should become less frequent with increased memory strength, the *ratio* of filler identifications in absent versus present lineups should increase with increasing memory strength.

THE PLEADING EFFECT

The previous sections make clear one reason why it is difficult to simply go from an experiment to the real world in estimating the probability that a suspect who is identified is in fact the culprit; such estimates depend critically on the base rate proportion of lineups that contain the actual culprit. But there is another factor that also has to be considered when one is trying to generalize to trials. A trial occurs relatively late in the process. By the time of trial, various prior events are likely to have differentially affected the proportions of guilty versus innocent defendants. One especially important factor is the occurrence of guilty pleas and the striking of plea bargains (see also Penrod, 2003). Most estimates place the guilty plea (plus plea bargain) figure at 80–90% (Cole, 1986). This pretrial pleading has the effect of changing the proportions of innocent and guilty persons who choose to go to trial, an effect we call the *pleading effect*.

How does the pleading effect work, and how much could it change the probabilities that an eyewitness in a trial might have made a mistaken identification? Let us assume for purposes of exploration that 85% of guilty individuals charged with a felony plead guilty, thus choosing to not go to trial. Although we concede that false confessions occur and that innocent people can sometimes plead guilty (see Kassin, 1997), let us assume for the moment that all who plead guilty are in fact guilty. Consider now that the population of those who choose to go to trial and persist with a not guilty plea is a mix of guilty persons and innocent persons. However, when these go-to-trial proportions are compared back with the proportions of identified suspects who were mistakenly identified, the proportions are very different. Suppose, for example, out of 10,000 suspects identified from lineups, 95% (9,500) are in fact guilty and only 5% (500) are innocent. If 85% of guilty suspects plead guilty, and thereby do not proceed to trial, then 1,425 of the guilty suspects would go to trial. If none of the innocent suspects plead guilty, then all 500 of the innocent suspects would proceed to trial. This means that, among the 1,925 suspects at trial, 500 (26.0%) would be innocent. Hence, what was only a 5% rate of mistaken identification at the time of the lineup becomes a 26% rate of innocence at the trial level.

We are not suggesting that the proportion of innocent defendants in eyewitness identification cases who plead not guilty and go to trial is 26%. Obviously, this figure depends, among other things, on the original proportion of identifications of suspects that are mistaken. Although we cannot know precisely what these rates are, the pleading effect pattern can be described as a curvilinear relation between the mistaken identification rate at the lineup and the innocence rate among suspects who proceed to trial. Figure 10–3 graphs this curve for lineup identification error rates from 0.0% to a rate of 20.0%, using an 85% pleading effect. Notice how the 85% pleading effect manages to make even quite low rates of mistaken identification at the lineup result in surprisingly high rates at trial. For example, 2.0% mistaken identifications at the lineup result in 12.0% of the suspects who proceed to trial being innocent.

There are two complementary ways of looking at the pleading effect. First, the pleading effect means that even slight increases in the error rate for suspect identifications at the lineup (e.g., an increase from a 1.0% rate to a 3.0% rate) produce larger increases in the proportion of those who go to trial being innocent (an increase from a 6.3% rate to a 17.1% rate). At the same time, this means that improvements to lineups that yield seemingly small reductions in the rate of mistaken identification (e.g., a decrease from a 4.0% rate to a 2.0% rate) will yield considerable reductions in the proportion of those who go to trial being innocent (a decrease from a 21.7% rate to a 12.0% rate).

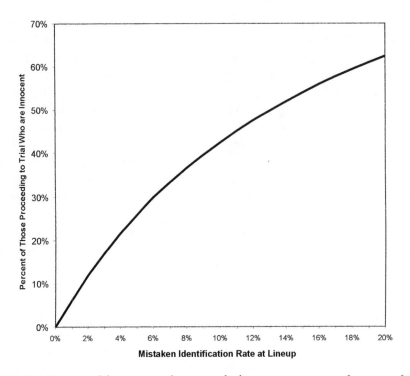

FIGURE 10–3.   Percent of those proceeding to trial who are innocent as a function of mistaken identification rates at lineup using an 85% pleading effect.

PSYCHOLOGICAL PROCESSES: A BROAD VIEW

Undoubtedly, psychological researchers will find more to quibble with in this section on psychological processes than in the previous sections (on the function of lineups, the structure of lineups, and outcome distributions). Indeed, it is here that we offer considerably more conjecture and it is here where we expect future experiments to highlight the need for revising our ideas. What we describe here are broad psychological processes that we presume operate at the time of the lineup. Critics might say that we are using the term *broad* as a euphemism for *loosely defined* or *ambiguous*. Maybe such critics would be correct in this assertion, because what we really mean is that we believe that something like these processes seems to be operating, and, although we might not be able to distinguish between subtle variations on these presumed process or their interactions, they seem to have some explanatory power.

Note as well that we are not describing a theory of memory acquisition or memory storage. For example, our lineup theory does not attempt to address such things as why cross-race identifications are less reliable than within-race identifications, the role of stress at the time of witnessing, and so on. Instead, our discussion is focused primarily on retrieval processes that operate at the time of the lineup.

AUTOMATIC VERSUS DELIBERATIVE PROCESSES

There has been relatively little empirical work investigating the psychological processes that operate at the time of lineup presentation; what has been done has generally posited a dual processing framework (e.g., Dunning & Stern, 1994). Dual-processing theories in social and cognitive psychology have proliferated, especially over the last decade (Chaiken & Trope, 1999; Sloman, 1996). Dual-processing theories posit that there are two systems by which people process information. Specific characterizations of these systems vary from one theorist to another, but they tend to argue that one system is largely effortless, rapid, and holistic, whereas the other system is relatively effortful, slow, and analytic. Shiffrin and Schneider's (1977) distinction between automatic and controlled processing is one example. Others include Petty and Cacioppo's (1981) central versus peripheral processing model, Chaiken's (1980) heuristic versus systematic processing distinction, Epstein's (1994) experiential versus rational processing distinction, and Fazio and Towles-Schwen's (1999) spontaneous versus deliberative processing distinction. Dual-processing theories vary in certain respects, such as the extent to which one type of processing is more conscious than the other, the extent to which the two processing systems are exclusive versus non-exclusive, and so on, but they all share the same basic distinction between the two processes.

Similar to these theories, Dunning and Stern (1994) originally distinguished between two processes in which witnesses may engage when presented with a lineup: automatic recognition and process of elimination. According to this conceptualization, automatic recognition judgments tend to be quick and effortless and are reached with little conscious strategy. Process of elimination judgments (otherwise known as deliberative judgments), in contrast, tend to be slow and effortful and are reached through deliberate and conscious strategies.

The automatic versus deliberative distinction can be partially appreciated by performing the two tasks shown in Figure 10–4. Task 1 is to decide whether the face is that of former President Bill Clinton. Task 2 is to decide which person is the suspect in the lineup. Consider the differences in how these two tasks are performed. In the case of deciding whether the picture was of Bill Clinton, the decision process was likely to be very rapid, effortless, and holistic. If asked how it was done, people would largely be at a loss for words, perhaps saying something like "I don't know. I just recognized him," and there would be little awareness of the complex cognitive processes that were involved. Even if a person were performing another task at the same time (e.g., talking on a phone), the Clinton task could be performed because it consumes no significant cognitive resources to perform that task. This is what is meant by an automatic process. Consider now the "which person is the suspect?" task. Compared with the Clinton task, this task took more time, involved some effort, and was performed at a particularistic level. People tend to be consciously aware of the process by which they made the judgment, and, if asked how it was done, people could probably verbally articulate some type of reasoning they used. This is what is meant by *deliberative*.

Task 1   **Task 2**

Is this Bill Clinton?

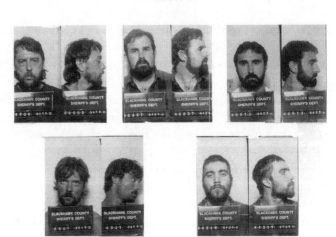

The perpetrator was in his 20s, had a moustache, brown hair, scruffy beard, and blue eyes. Which person is the suspect in this lineup?

FIGURE 10–4.   Automatic versus deliberative processing.

Dunning and Stern (1994) argued that because a lineup is basically a recognition task (an eyewitness must state whether he/she recognizes the criminal from among the members of the lineup), accurate lineup identifications should tend to be the result of automatic recognition judgments. In contrast, inaccurate identifications, which almost by definition are identifications of people the eyewitness has never seen, cannot be the result of a recognition judgment and should therefore tend to be the result of a deliberative process. Thus, by determining the strategy that eyewitnesses used to arrive at their identification decision, one should show some ability to differentiate accurate from inaccurate witnesses. Consistent with predictions, Dunning and Stern, as well as others since them (e.g., Kneller, Memon, & Stevenage, 2001; Lindsay & Bellinger, 1999), have found that when witnesses to a mock crime are asked after having made an identification about their decision processes, accurate witnesses are more likely to endorse having engaged in automatic processes (e.g., saying that the culprit's photo "popped out" from the array), whereas inaccurate witnesses are more likely to endorse having engaged in deliberative processes (e.g., saying that they compared photos with other photos or used methods of elimination).

More indirect evidence supports the automatic/deliberative judgment distinction. Identification accuracy is harmed by forcing of eyewitnesses to rely more on deliberate, verbal processes, whether by having them verbally analyze features of a criminal's face at the time of the crime (Wells & Turtle, 1988), by having them verbally give a description of a criminal prior to the lineup presentation (Schooler & Engstler-Schooler, 1990), or by having them verbally describe reasons why each person in the lineup might or might not be a good match to the criminal (Perretta & Dunning, 2001). Consistent with this, Schooler and Engstler-Schooler found that limiting the amount of time a witness had to make an identification to 5 seconds eliminated the negative effects of verbalization, presumably because those witnesses were not given enough time for the verbalization to produce its deleterious effects on accuracy.

Multiple studies also have shown that the amount of time it takes for a witness to make an identification is negatively correlated with accuracy; the quicker the decision, the more likely it is to be correct (Dunning & Stern, 1994; Smith, Lindsay, & Pryke, 2000; Sporer, 1992, 1993, 1994; Weber & Brewer, 2003). This suggests that accurate witnesses are the ones who tend to experience quick, automatic recognition experiences, as opposed to engaging in slower, deliberate processes. Finally, consistent with the idea that automatically made judgments should be less affected by contextual factors, such as array size, than are deliberately made judgments, Perretta and Dunning (2001) found that increasing the lineup size increased response latency more for inaccurate than for accurate witnesses. Thus, inaccurate witnesses seemed to be relying more on deliberative judgments than accurate witnesses.

The distinction between automatic and deliberative processes is similar to the distinction between absolute and relative judgments (Wells, 1984; Lindsay & Wells, 1985). An absolute judgment is one in which a witness compares individual members of the lineup with his or her memory of the criminal. A relative judgment, in contrast, is one in which a witness compares members of the lineup to each other in order to determine who looks most like his or her memory of the criminal. It has been found that witnesses who report engaging in an absolute judgment strategy are more accurate than witnesses who report engaging in a relative judgment strategy (Lindsay & Bellinger, 1999; Smith, Lindsay, & Pryke, 2000), and that forcing witnesses to adopt an absolute judgment strategy decreases false identifications (Lindsay & Wells, 1985). Although it has never been empirically tested whether absolute and relative judgments are automatic or deliberate processes, it has often been assumed that absolute judgments are automatic processes and relative judgments are deliberate processes; in fact, the terms have often been used interchangeably in the literature. This is, to a certain extent, understandable. Absolute judgments, like automatic judgments, are memory-dependent; both require a relatively strong memory of the criminal and should be only minimally influenced (if at all) by superficial features of the lineup. Witnesses who report having used absolute judgments, like witnesses who report having used automatic processes, tend to be more accurate in their identification decisions. In contrast, the relative judgment strategy of comparing lineup members to other lineup members is an effortful, time-consuming, and deliberate process that relies less on memory than on differences between lineup members. The tendency for witnesses to engage in relative judgments can be reduced through specific instructions (Malpass & Devine, 1981), suggesting that relative judgments are under some form of deliberate control. In fact, the similarities between absolute/relative judgments and automatic/deliberative processes can be so striking that some of the self-report questions used to determine the extent to which automatic and deliberative processes were operating during the identification procedure are the same ones used to determine the extent to which the witness used an absolute versus relative judgment strategy (e.g., the extent to which witnesses endorse the statement *I compared the pictures to each other to make my decision* is a measure of both deliberative processes and relative judgments).

It is, however, empirically tenuous to conclude that absolute judgments are necessarily automatic and relative judgments are necessarily deliberative. Absolute judgments, despite their reliance on memory, are nonetheless a process of comparison (of each lineup member to one's memory). The extent of this comparison is probably under the witness's control (how superficially the comparisons are made, the speed with which each comparison is made, whether the comparison is based on featural or holistic qualities, etc.). To the extent that absolute judgments are under the witness's control, they cannot be completely automatic. Similarly, relative judgments are not easily classifiable as deliberate judgments. One can imagine relative judgments being broken down into three parts: comparing lineup members to each other, using that comparison to determine who from the lineup looks most like the criminal, and deciding whether the person in the lineup who looks most like the criminal actually is the criminal. The first part, for reasons stated above, is probably largely deliberative. However, the next two parts are not as clearly deliberative processes. It may be, for example, that one's determination of how good a match X is to Y is an automatic process unavoidably resulting from a process of comparison. Or perhaps deciding whether the best match in the lineup actually is the criminal can be an automatic process and an unavoidable consequence of determining the best match to one's memory. Thus, although we believe that *on average* absolute judgments tend to be more automatic and relative judgments tend to be more deliberative, we urge researchers to be cautious in their assumptions as to the cognitive processes underpinning absolute and relative judgments.

Although there is evidence supporting the distinction between automatic and deliberative judgments, there also appears to be evidence that questions and challenges this simple dichotomy. Specifically, we advance the idea that automatic and deliberative judgments, instead of being dichotomous, actually lie on opposite ends of a continuum of judgment processes, and that instead of cognitive processes actually *causing* identification accuracy per se, there is a third variable—the quality of one's memory of the criminal—that drives both accuracy and judgment process and accounts for their covariation. Note that we are not rejecting the idea that automatic and deliberative processes are operating during a lineup identification; in fact, we embrace the distinction and think it has much to offer. Instead, we are suggesting potential refinements to the automatic/deliberative conceptualization that we think have solid theoretical grounding and that help explain some of the otherwise anomalous data. We will now examine the basis of our claims.

DO DECISION PROCESSES CAUSE DIFFERENCES IN ACCURACY?

The basic mechanism that is presumed to account for the correlation between self-reported cognitive process (automatic or deliberative) and accuracy is as follows: A witness is shown a lineup that either contains the actual criminal or does not contain the actual criminal. If it does contain the actual criminal, the witness should tend to undergo an immediate sense of recognition of the criminal; the criminal "pops out" of the lineup, and the witness will make a quick and accurate identification. If, however, the criminal is not in the lineup, and thus the witness does not experience that immediate sense of recognition, deliberative processes kick in. The witness will compare pictures and engage in other sorts of deliberate and cognitively effortful behaviors that will often eventually lead the witness to make a slow and necessarily inaccurate identification. Thus, quick and automatic decisions tend to be accurate, whereas slow and deliberate decisions tend to be inaccurate.

This explanation makes an easily testable prediction, namely, that interfering with a witness's ability to engage in deliberative processes and forcing witnesses to rely on automatic judgments should decrease the likelihood of that witness making a false identification. There are two ways in which this prediction has been tested. One way is by giving witnesses a cognitive task to perform while making a lineup identification, which should interfere with deliberative processes but not with automatic processes (Kahneman & Treisman, 1984). Being unable to engage in deliberative cognitive processes should force witnesses to rely on automatic judgments, and this manipulation should therefore increase witnesses' accuracy. Following this logic, Perretta and Dunning (2001) report a study in which some of their participant-witnesses were given a 9-digit number to memorize while attempting an identification from a lineup, whereas other participants were not given a number to memorize while attempting an identification. The authors predicted that the witnesses who were given the cognitive task of memorizing a number would not be able to engage in harmful, deliberative processes while viewing the lineup and should hence be more accurate than witnesses who were not given this task. Contrary to this prediction, those who were made cognitively busy were not significantly more accurate than controls.

The other way in which experimenters have interfered with deliberative processes is by limiting the amount of time witnesses have to make a lineup identification, which should necessarily limit the amount of deliberative processing in which the witnesses can engage. Thus, imposing time constraints should force eyewitnesses to rely more on automatic judgments than on deliberative judgments, which should increase their accuracy. In fact, before the automatic/deliberative judgment distinction even surfaced in the eyewitness area, Schooler and Engstler-Schooler (1990) had data that spoke to this prediction. Although they were not testing this prediction directly, one of their studies involved limiting the amount of time people had to make facial recognition judgments to 5 seconds. When witnesses gave a description of the target before viewing the lineup, which was found to impair accuracy, this time constraint eliminated the deleterious effects of giving the description. However, when witnesses did not give a description of the target before viewing the lineup, the time constraint had no significant effect on accuracy. Following similar protocols, other researchers have also failed to find significant effects of limiting decision time on accuracy rates (Brewer, Gordon, & Bond, 2000; Charman, 2004; Perretta & Dunning, 2001).

Procedures that inhibit deliberative processing do not seem to cause an increase in eyewitness accuracy. On the other hand, as previously mentioned, there is some evidence that procedures that facilitate deliberative processing cause decreases in eyewitness accuracy (e.g., Perretta & Dunning, 2001; Schooler & Engstler-Schooler, 1990; Wells & Turtle, 1988).

How can facilitating deliberative processing cause decreases in eyewitness identification accuracy, whereas inhibiting deliberative processing does not cause increases in eyewitness identification accuracy? One possibility is that past studies showing a negative effect of increased deliberation on accuracy have confounded increased deliberation with memory interference. Specifically, researchers who have attempted to increase deliberative processes have done so by giving their participants an additional task to perform, such as verbalizing some aspect of the criminal or of the lineup procedure. It may be, therefore, that it was interference of the witnesses' memories of the criminal caused by the additional task that caused the detrimental effects. For example, perhaps a witness who gives a verbal description of a criminal prior to a lineup becomes biased to retrieve only description-consistent (i.e., verbalizable) information about the criminal from memory at the time of the lineup task and to ignore other, more diagnostic information about the criminal, leading the witness to make an inaccurate identification. Thus, it might not have been the increase in deliberative processing per se that caused the detriment in accuracy, but rather the interference produced by the additional task of verbalizing the criminal's face. Therefore, deliberative processing, whether increased or decreased, may actually have no causal effects whatsoever on eyewitness accuracy; the apparent harm in accuracy caused by increased deliberative processing may actually reflect the harmful effects of interference.

QUALITY OF MEMORY AS A THIRD VARIABLE

If the type of decision process in which witnesses engage does not cause accuracy, how then can we explain the correlation between self-reported decision process and accuracy? There are two possibilities. The first is that differences in accuracy actually cause differences in self-reported decision processes. Consistent with this idea, studies have found that leading eyewitnesses to believe that they had made an accurate identification causes them to report that their process was more automatic (e.g., increase their reports that the identified person's photo "popped out" from the array; e.g., Bradfield, Wells, & Olson, 2002; Wells & Bradfield, 1998). In other words, it seems that eyewitnesses' beliefs about their accuracy influenced self-reported processes. However, this explanation seems to be lacking. It seems unlikely that identification accuracy per se is a sufficient cause of the differences in retrospective self-reports. What is the mechanism through which accuracy affects self-reports? What is different about accurate and inaccurate witnesses that would lead to the differential self-reports of cognitive decision process?

The answer to this question, and the second possible explanation of the correlation between decision process and accuracy, is that there may exist a third variable that influences both decision process and accuracy. This idea has been offered by Brewer et al.

(2000), who suggested that the quality of the memory that a witness has of the criminal may be this third variable. To examine this idea more closely, imagine that a witness who has a poor memory of the criminal is asked to attempt an identification from a lineup. It seems reasonable to assume that, because she has a poor memory of the criminal, she is less likely to make a correct decision. But how does the quality of the memory lead to differences in decision process? Let us revisit the absolute/relative judgment strategy distinction. As previously mentioned, absolute judgment strategies are more dependent on memory than relative judgment strategies because absolute judgments require comparisons between individual lineup members and the witness's memory, whereas relative judgments simply require comparisons among the various lineup members. Thus, witnesses who tend to use more absolute judgment strategies should be those who have a relatively strong memory for the criminal. Let us return to our witness who has a poor memory of the criminal. Because of her lack of a strong memory of the criminal, she may therefore be tempted to forgo an absolute judgment strategy and instead engage in a relative judgment strategy, something that witnesses readily do (Wells, 1993). Thus, because of her poor memory, she will tend to be inaccurate and will tend to engage in a relative judgment strategy. Contrast this with a witness who has a strong memory of the criminal. Because of the strength of the memory, this witness is likely to be accurate in her identification. Also because of the strength of the memory, this witness can now engage in an absolute judgment strategy to make her decision. Thus, witnesses with strong memories are more likely to be accurate witnesses and should also tend to engage in different cognitive decision processes than would inaccurate witnesses.

Can this third variable explanation account for the data? We contend that it does. First, this explanation accounts for the negative correlations found between decision time and accuracy. Imagine that decision time is a function of the number of comparisons that are made from a lineup. When using an absolute judgment strategy, witnesses compare each lineup member with their memory of the criminal; thus, the number of comparisons to make is simply equal to the number of members in the lineup. When using a relative judgment strategy, however, witnesses compare people in the lineup with other people in the lineup; thus, the number of comparisons to make can be as high as

$$\sum_{i=1}^{n} (n - i)$$

where n is equal to the number of members in the lineup. For example, with a six-person lineup, an absolute judgment strategy would take up to six comparisons, whereas a relative judgment strategy would take up to $5 + 4 + 3 + 2 + 1 = 15$ comparisons. Thus, relative judgments should tend to be slower than absolute judgments, and because relative judgments tend to indicate a poorer memory of the criminal, they should also tend to be more inaccurate than absolute judgments. Therefore, this third variable approach would predict that decision time should be negatively correlated with accuracy, without invoking the idea that automatic/deliberative processes causally determine decision time.

Second, the quality-of-memory-as-third-variable explanation accounts for both the interference explanation of the detrimental effects of having witnesses verbalize features of the criminal as well as the null effects of encouraging witnesses to rely on automatic processes. Once a witness has encoded a memory of the criminal, it is unlikely that the quality of that memory can improve, but it is very likely that the quality of the memory can be degraded by various manipulations. Experimental manipulations that lead witnesses to verbalize their memories of a criminal's face may ultimately degrade the quality of the memories that are accessed during lineups by leading witnesses to selectively retrieve features of the criminal's face that were expressed verbally and to ignore more diagnostic, nonverbally expressed features. This degraded memory would then tend to lead witnesses to engage in deliberative judgment processes and to inaccurate decisions. Thus, the observed detriment in accuracy resulting from increased deliberation about the lineup may not be a result of a change in decision process per se, but may instead originate through the quality-of-memory variable. However, because the quality of a memory of a face cannot improve over time (without additional exposure to that face), attempts to increase accuracy beyond a baseline should be doomed to fail. This would explain why limiting deliberative processing does not increase accuracy. The effects of encouraging and discouraging deliberate processing can therefore be explained without resorting to the idea that decision process differences cause changes in accuracy; rather the findings can be explained as the result of a third variable causing both decision process differences and changes in accuracy.

Finally, this explanation accounts quite easily for the differential self-reports of decision strategy between accurate and inaccurate witnesses. Because accurate witnesses tend to be those who have a good memory of the criminal, and those who have a good memory of the criminal tend to be those who use quicker and more automatic judgments, accurate witnesses should be more likely to endorse having used absolute judgment strategies. Similarly, because inaccurate witnesses tend to be those who have a poor memory of the criminal, and those who have a poor memory of the criminal tend to be those who use more relative judgment strategies, inaccurate witnesses should be more likely to endorse having used deliberative judgment strategies. Although we argued earlier that absolute and relative judgments are not necessarily automatic and deliberative processes, respectively, we nonetheless believe that an absolute judgment strategy tends to be *more* automatic than a relative judgment strategy. Thus, witnesses who use an absolute judgment strategy should be more likely to be accurate and to report having engaged in an automatic process than witnesses who use a relative judgment strategy.

A CONTINUUM OF AUTOMATICITY

The idea that the quality of memory drives both accuracy and decision processes raises an interesting conundrum. Because quality of one's memory is a continuous variable, how is it that it leads to a dichotomous automatic/deliberative decision process? Does the variability in memory quality get ignored in the automatic/deliberative distinction? We contend that the answer is no. We believe that labeling many processes as simply deliberative or automatic obfuscates finer gradations of automaticity. Instead of treating the automatic/deliberative distinction as a dichotomy, it may be more correct to think of cognitive processes as lying somewhere along an automaticity continuum, from low automaticity to high automaticity. According to this view, deliberative processes will dominate to the extent that automatic processes are toward the low end of the automaticity continuum. Thus, a lineup task may not be simply a matter of automatic versus deliberate processes, but may rather be a matter of *relatively* automatic versus *relatively* deliberate processes. Let us now examine the evidence for this assertion.

There are at least five reasons why a simple automatic/deliberative process dichotomy may be inaccurate. The first two are theoretical reasons why purely automatic recognition responses from eyewitnesses should be difficult to develop, and the subsequent three are reasons based on empirical evidence that speak against a strict dichotomy. First, from a cognitive psychology standpoint, the development of automaticity generally takes repeated and/or prolonged exposure to a stimulus (Shiffrin & Schneider, 1977). Although a prolonged exposure to a criminal is certainly possible in many cases (e.g., kidnappings, hostage situations), most real-world eyewitness probably do not receive the exposure they need to develop a purely automatic recognition response.

Second, automatic processes are very stimulus-dependent (Shiffrin & Schneider, 1977). That is, the stimulus that developed the automatic response in the first place is required to instantiate it later. Automatic responses do not generalize very well to novel or changed stimuli. Thus, an automatic recognition judgment would be dependent on the match between the physical appearance of the criminal at the time of the crime and the physical appearance of the criminal at the time of the lineup. However, there is little reason to assume that this match would be very strong. Pictures used in lineups often are not taken close to the time of the crime, and thus the criminal is likely to have changed appearance. Without a strong similarity between the criminal at the time of the crime and the criminal at the time of the lineup, purely automatic responses are unlikely.

Third, what are considered automatic judgments in the eyewitness literature often take much longer than typical cognitive automatic judgments. For example, Dunning and Perretta (2002) found across four studies that a decision time of 10–12 seconds maximally differentiated accurate from inaccurate witnesses and, by implication, those who used automatic and deliberative processes, respectively. Pure automatic recognition judgments, however, are typically much quicker. Imagine identifying a photo of your own face from a lineup; that process should be virtually instantaneous. Although it could be argued that Dunning and Perretta's participants who did experience automatic recognition all responded within, say, 2 seconds, one would then be forced to conclude that participants who took 2 to 12 seconds to respond used deliberative processing and were much more accurate than those who used deliberative processes and took longer than 12 seconds to respond. This would not only break down the dichotomy, but would also mean that deliberative processes are often highly accurate, a position antithetical to the automatic/deliberative distinction. It also could be argued that Dunning and Perretta's accurate participants did experience an automatic judgment, but looked at the other pictures to verify their experience, thus increasing their decision time. This argument is supported by the finding that accurate witnesses were more likely than inaccurate witnesses to endorse the statement *They [the pictures] helped me to confirm, reinforce my decision after I made it*. However, this only indicates that accurate witnesses actually used a combination of automatic and deliberative judgments in making their decision, a position more compatible with a continuum idea of automaticity than a strictly dichotomous view. A purely automatic response would require no comparative judgments between pictures.

Fourth, the boundary that maximally differentiates accurate from inaccurate witnesses is not stable across experimental variations and has been found to vary from as little as 5 seconds to as much as 29 seconds (Weber, Brewer, Wells, Semmler, & Keast, 2004). If accurate responses to lineups truly are a function of pure automatic responding, they should be relatively insensitive to experimental variations. The variability in the boundary that best differentiated accurate from inaccurate responses suggests that accurate decisions are not completely automatic, because automatic recognition processes should be invariant to contextual changes (Treisman & Gelade, 1980).

Fifth, an experiment by Dunning and Perretta (2002) showed that increasing lineup size increased decision time more for inaccurate than for accurate witnesses, suggesting that inaccurate witnesses, more than accurate witnesses, were engaging in deliberative processes such as comparing pictures. Although we agree with this interpretation, we do not think that this indicates that accurate witnesses were relying on *purely* automatic judgments. A purely automatic judgment should not be affected at all by an increase in array size (Schneider & Shiffrin, 1977). In fact, Dunning and Perretta found that increasing lineup size increased the time it took accurate witnesses to make a decision, suggesting that accurate identifications are not a function solely of automatic judgments. It can be argued that because accuracy is only probabilistically associated with automaticity, perhaps some accurate witnesses actually made their decisions through a deliberative process of comparing pictures, which would create an effect of lineup size on decision time for accurate witnesses. We agree that this is possible, but think it is at least as possible, if not more so, that even accurate eyewitnesses used some deliberative processing when making their decisions.

Note that a continuum of automaticity is consistent with theory and data. The degree to which a response to a lineup is automatic would be dependent on the duration of exposure a witness had to the criminal, as well as the degree to which the physical appearance of the criminal at the time of the crime matches the physical appearance of the criminal at the time of the lineup. Because these variables would not be constant across multiple experiments, different experiments should lead to differing degrees of automaticity and hence differing maximally-differentiating time boundaries. This time boundary would be longer than that for purely automatic responses, to the extent that witnesses were not using purely automatic processes. Similarly, witnesses' decision times should be influenced by lineup size to the extent that they were not using purely automatic processes. Thus, Dunning and Stern's (1994) finding that accurate witnesses endorsed having used more automatic judgment strategies than inaccurate witnesses does not necessarily indicate that accurate judgments are automatic per se, only that they are *relatively* more automatic than inaccurate judgments.

We have so far laid out two main arguments for how we think the automatic/deliberative distinction can be improved: We have argued that a third variable—quality of memory for the criminal—may be driving both accuracy and decision process, and we have argued that the automatic processes may be better thought of as a continuous variable. Is it possible to integrate these new ideas into a cohesive theory? This is the question to which we now turn.

A COMPETITION/CORROBORATION CONCEPTUALIZATION OF LINEUP IDENTIFICATION

We propose a theoretical conceptualization of lineup identification that is borrowed in part from Logan's (1988) instance theory of automatization, a popular and influential theory within the field of cognitive psychology. Because Logan's theory was developed largely within the context of other types of tasks (e.g., performing math problems), however, we needed to make certain modifications to account for the fact that lineups involve visual recognition memory rather than recall memory. Although instance theory has more recently been updated to include more general attention and memory processes (Logan, 2002), we describe the original version of the theory, which deals specifically with automatization and is thus most relevant.

Instance theory was proposed as an alternative account of the generally held ideas of the nature of automatic processes. Whereas earlier explanations of automaticity relied on the premise that the development of automaticity was equivalent to the gradual withdrawal of attention, instance theory regards the development of automaticity as a memory phenomenon that reflects a transition in reliance on cognitive processes. According to the theory, one starts out by responding to a novel stimulus with slow and tedious algorithmic responses, but with practice one accumulates discrete memories, or instances, of interacting with and responding to the stimulus. Eventually, as these instances accrue, one becomes able to respond to the stimulus on the basis of memory for those instances and abandons reliance on algorithms. Importantly, however, algorithmic responding and memory-based responding do not operate exclusively of one another; rather they always operate in parallel. Logan (1988) referred to their parallel operations as a race between the two processes, whereby the one that finishes first controls the response. Thus, as instances accumulate over time, memory-based responding is more likely to win the race over algorithmic-based responding, simply because there are more memories from which to draw. For our purposes, we consider algorithmic and memory-based processes to be roughly analogous to deliberative and automatic processes, respectively.

A number of points are important to note about this framework. First, the degree to which a lineup response is automatic or deliberative is dependent on the quality of the memory (the number of instances) that the witness has of the criminal such that the better the memory, the more automatic the response. Thus, the quality of memory not only determines accuracy, but also the cognitive process that is undertaken. Second, because automaticity is thought of as the relative quickness of memory-based judgments over algorithmic-based judgments, which in turn depends on the number of instances one has in memory, automaticity surfaces as a continuous variable. In fact, in Logan's (1988) view, no process can become completely automatic, because the addition of any single instance would increase the degree of automaticity (albeit with increasingly diminishing returns). Therefore, we can refer to cognitive processes in terms of degree of automaticity as opposed to simply automatic versus not automatic. Additionally, we can see how the degree of automaticity experienced is moderated by various factors. Anything that affects a witness's memory for the criminal (e.g., exposure time, match between criminal at the time of the crime and criminal at the time of the lineup) should affect the degree to which that witness reports experiencing a process of automaticity. Third, because strong memories are associated with both accuracy and the use of quick, memory-based processes, quick identification decisions will tend to be accurate. Fourth, memory-based and algorithmic processes are assumed to work in parallel. This is important in that eyewitness researchers have usually assumed that when automatic processes are operating, deliberative processes are not operating, and vice versa. It may be that witnesses can have an automatic process operating simultaneously with a deliberative process.

Differences between Our Competition/Corroboration Conceptualization and Instance Theory.   Our conceptualization differs from Logan's (1988) Instance Theory in a few key respects. First, instead of construing of automaticity as something that accrues as a function of discrete instances of interacting with the stimulus, our conceptualization assumes that automaticity can accrue through any number of processes that increase the quality of the eyewitness's memory for the stimulus. Although repeated instances of exposure should increase automaticity, automaticity should also increase with exposure duration within any given instance, the degree of attention paid to the stimulus, the quality of the view that the witness had during any given instance, and so on. Second, because the original exposure(s) and the lineup test are complex visual stimuli (rather than, for example, math problems), the degree of automatic response to the perpetrator in a lineup should depend not only on the quality of the original memory, but also on the extent to which the perpetrator's physical appearance in the lineup resembles the perpetrator's appearance at the time of the crime. A math problem is essentially the same whether it is presented as "$9 \times 9 = \_$?" or as "nine times nine equals $\_$?" A visual identification test, however, is heavily dependent on the extent to which the visual stimulus is a replica of the original exposure. In our conceptualization, this means that an automatic response would normally be nonexistent when the actual perpetrator is not in the lineup. We acknowledge, however, that a weak automatic response could occur if there were a person in the lineup who was highly similar to the perpetrator. Third, whereas automatic and deliberative processes are construed in Logan's theory as being involved in a race of time, our conceptualization presumes that automatic processes will always win a time race. Instead of competing in a time race, our conceptualization assumes that when an automatic response is experienced, deliberative processes are usually engaged in as well before any decision is made by the eyewitness. In other words, even when an automatic process is experienced, we propose that eyewitnesses nevertheless engage in deliberative processes in an attempt to either corroborate or call into question the validity of the automatic response. This use of a deliberative process is almost certain to occur in the absence of an automatic process and is very likely when the automatic experience is weak, but even a strong automatic response is likely to be followed by deliberation. The amount of deliberation that is needed is diminished by the strength of the automatic response (which accounts for faster decision times for accurate than for inaccurate witnesses). Nevertheless, some amount of deliberative processing is probably always involved. The use of deliberative processes when there is an automatic response stems at least in part from the importance of the decision (emanating from such considerations as the importance of not making a mistake and consequences for the witness and the accused). Furthermore, the absence of time constraints on the decisions of eyewitnesses helps guarantee that deliberative processes will almost always be engaged. Finally, we propose that the deliberative processes that follow an automatic response will generally be biased toward confirmation of the automatic response. Nevertheless, there will be circumstances in which deliberative processes conflict with automatic processes and thereby compete for the decision. For example, an automatic reaction to lineup member number 2 might be followed by the witness noting that lineup member number 4 is the only photo with a different color background, possibly leading the witness to begin reasoning that number 4 is the one that police suspect. In this case, the automatic and deliberative processes compete with each other for the final decision. In other cases, the automatic and deliberative processes might corroborate each other. It is this relation between the automatic and deliberative processes that accounts for the name we have given to our conceptualization, namely the competition/corroboration conceptualization. Agreement (corroboration) between the automatic and deliberative processes should not only make the positive identification more likely, but also increase confidence in the identification. Disagreement (competition) between the automatic and deliberative processes should make positive identification less likely and should decrease confidence in any identification that occurs.

We argue that our competition/corroboration conceptualization of automaticity explains quite a bit of the available data. Accurate identification decisions are made faster than inaccurate identification decisions because stronger automatic responses require less corroboration. At the same time, even accurate identification decisions are made surprisingly slowly (e.g., 10–12 seconds or longer) in comparison with purely automatic decisions, because some deliberative processes also are involved. Responses to target-absent lineups are slow because no appreciable automatic process is involved; it is almost all a deliberative process. Furthermore, findings showing that the manipulated addition of deliberative processes serves to reduce accuracy are consistent with our idea that deliberative processes can compete with automatic processes in terms of the final decision made by the eyewitness. The addition of certain types of deliberative processes increases the chances that the eyewitness will become aware of some deliberative information that is inconsistent with the automatic processes and, assuming the automatic processes are usually more likely to be correct, this additional deliberation will reduce decisional accuracy. The latter idea suggests that there will be special circumstances in which reducing deliberative thoughts (e.g., by requiring quick decisions or using cognitive load manipulations) will actually benefit the accuracy of eyewitness identifications, even though studies to date have not been able to demonstrate this effect. Specifically, when cues are present in the lineup task that suggest an answer that is inconsistent with the automatic response, then limiting deliberation will serve to increase reliance on the automatic process and thereby increase accuracy. Perhaps previous studies have failed to find that limiting deliberative processes increases identification accuracy because there were no cues present in the situation that would have led to inconsistencies (hence competition) between the automatic and deliberative processes.

The idea that automatic and deliberative processes do not necessarily operate exclusively is consistent with recent attempts to model eyewitness behavior mathematically (Clark, 2003). Clark's WITNESS model suggests that identification decisions by eyewitnesses are based on a fairly even combination of absolute and relative match information. To the extent that absolute and relative judgments reflect automatic and deliberative judgments, respectively (which, as we have argued above, is probably not a perfect reflection, but one that is quite likely on average), his data would suggest a nonexclusive operation of these two types of cognitive processing, consistent with the work of Logan (1988) and with our competition/corroboration conceptualization.

It may be tempting, after all this discussion, to conclude that automatic processes are necessarily desirable and deliberative processes are necessarily undesirable with respect to eyewitness identifications. We would caution against this assumption. As previously discussed, a relative judgment strategy, which tends to lead to more false identifications than an absolute judgment strategy, may operate, in part, through an automatic process. Conversely, deliberative processing may at times be beneficial. Suppose, for instance, that an eyewitness viewed a photo lineup, made no identification, and then was shown a live lineup. At the live lineup, only one person (the suspect) was also a member of the photo lineup. The result might be an automatic reaction to the suspect based merely on the fact that he is the only one who evokes familiarity. Here, we would hope that the eyewitness might deliberatively reason that, because there is only one person in common between the photo lineup and the live lineup, that person might be familiar merely because that person was previously viewed in photos. If so, then the witness might use this deliberative reasoning to avoid an identification based on mere familiarity. Deliberative thinking may thus allow witnesses to override automatic judgments that are not based on memory of the criminal.

If automatic processes are not necessarily desirable and deliberative processes are not necessarily undesirable, what value is contained in the automatic/deliberative distinction? We believe that judgments high in automaticity are desirable but only to the extent that they reflect recognition memory of the criminal. To the extent that judgments high in automaticity reflect something other than recognition memory of the criminal, they can be deleterious. It is important, therefore, to empirically develop tools to differentiate between *types* of automatic processes. Additionally, understanding the root from which automatic and deliberative processes stem (which, as we have argued, may be the quality of memory that eyewitnesses have of the criminal) may focus researchers on the development of procedures that will maximize eyewitness accuracy. Finally, understanding what processes are more deliberative and what processes are more automatic allows us to determine the extent to which witnesses can accurately report on their cognitive processes. Because people have low introspective awareness of automatic processes, the automatic/deliberative distinction allows us to learn when we can and when we cannot trust eyewitnesses' self-reports.

SUMMARY AND PROSPECTUS

We have attempted to describe an applied theory of lineups. The theory is not one of how faces are remembered or how witnessing conditions affect encoding or yet another theory of memory processes. Instead, it is a theory of the lineup task, and it is deeply embedded in the ecology of forensic evidence. We described, for instance, how the function of a lineup is not to test the witness's memory, but to test a hypothesis about whether the suspect is the perpetrator. Accordingly, the result of a lineup needs to speak to the status of the suspect given the response of the witness, not the response of the witness given the status of the suspect. This means that base rates regarding the status of the suspect (guilty or not) have a profound impact on outcomes. We also described a taxonomy of outcome distributions that distinguish sharply between false-positive identifications when the perpetrator is in the lineup and false-positive identifications of an innocent suspect when the perpetrator is not in the lineup. This distinction is required by the ecology of the lineup but is not part of any traditional theory of memory. Indeed, as we have discussed in this chapter, the lineup task involves considerations that are clearly extra-memorial, such as external influences from the lineup administrator. We also discussed the pleading effect, a factor that has largely been ignored in the eyewitness identification literature, but has profound implications for understanding how error rates at the level of the lineup might multiply in the subset of cases that go to trial. Finally, we have discussed broad psychological processes that can operate automatically, deliberatively, or both.

We stated that a good applied theory of lineups should illuminate important gaps in our knowledge about lineups. The gaps in our knowledge that would help further develop this applied theory are readily apparent. Here, we describe three important gaps. First, our analysis of outcome distributions proves that nonidentifications must have diagnostic exonerating value. But how do law enforcement and prosecutors treat nonidentifications in terms of revising their subjective probabilities that the suspect is the perpetrator? The suggestion that the legal system too readily dismisses nonidentification evidence was made over 20 years ago (Wells & Lindsay, 1980), and yet no progress has been made in finding out whether this is the case. Second, we have shown the profound role played by the perpetrator-present versus perpetrator-absent base rate variable, but we have made no progress in estimating this base rate in actual cases or in assessing practices of criminal investigators that drive this base rate. Third, we proposed a reanalysis of the distinction between automatic and deliberative processes, whereby a third variable— quality of memory for the criminal—drives both identification accuracy and decision process, and in which automatic processes may be best conceptualized as a continuous variable. Furthermore, we have suggested that deliberative processes can operate in parallel with automatic processes and can either corroborate or compete with automatic processes in terms of the final decision made by the eyewitness.

Most psychological theories confine themselves to psychological processes, and, in this sense, our sketch of an applied theory of lineups is unconventional. A conventional theorist in psychology might describe lineup identifications in terms of acquisition, storage, and retrieval processes of memory. As an applied theory, however, we posit that the relevant characteristics of lineup theory must also be steeped in an understanding of the structure of the task, the role of nonmemorial variables (such as social influence), the nature of the problem facing the trier of fact (e.g., assessing the status of the accused from the behavior of the witness, not vice versa), interactions with other types of pre-lineup evidence (which affect the base rate for the perpetrator being in the lineup), and an understanding of the role of automatic and deliberative processes (which relate to the ability of the witness to accurately testify about variables affecting his/her identification). Clearly, lineup theory must progress well beyond the sketch we have provided here, and we do not pretend that what we have written here is anything more than a beginning. Nevertheless, we believe that we have sketched some of the components that will need to be a part of an applied theory of lineups.

REFERENCES

Bradfield, A. L., Wells, G. L., & Olson, E. A. (2002). The damaging effect of confirming feedback on the relation between eyewitness certainty and identification accuracy. *Journal of Applied Psychology, 87*, 112–120.

Brewer, N., Gordon, M., & Bond, N. (2000). Effect of photoarray exposure duration on eyewitness identification accuracy and processing strategy. *Psychology, Crime & Law, 6*, 21–32.

Chaiken, S. (1980). Heuristic versus systematic information processing and the use of source versus message cues in persuasion. *Journal of Personality and Social Psychology, 39*, 752–766.

Chaiken, S., & Trope, Y. (Eds.) (1999). *Dual process theories in social psychology.* New York: Guilford Press.

Charman, S. D. (2004). *The problem with introspective eyewitnesses: Can thinking too much harm the identification process?* Unpublished manuscript, Iowa State University.

Clark, S. E. (2003). A memory and decision model for eyewitness identification. *Applied Cognitive Psychology, 17*, 629–654.

Cole, G. F. (1986). *The American system of criminal justice* (4th ed.). Monterey, CA: Brooks/Cole.

Dunning, D., & Perretta, S. (2002). Automaticity and eyewitness accuracy: A 10 to 12 second rule for distinguishing accurate from inaccurate positive identifications. *Journal of Applied Psychology, 87*, 951–962.

Dunning, D., & Stern, L. B. (1994). Distinguishing accurate from inaccurate identifications via inquiries about decision processes. *Journal of Personality and Social Psychology, 67*, 818–835.

Epstein, S. (1994). Integration of the cognitive and psychodynamic unconscious. *American Psychologist, 49*(8), 709–724.

Fazio, R. H., & Towles-Schwen, T. (1999). The MODE model of attitude-behavior processes. In Chaiken & Y. Trope (Eds.), *Dual process theories in social psychology* (pp. 97–116). New York: Guilford Press.

Kahneman, D., & Treisman, A. (1984). Changing view of attention and automaticity. In R. Parasuraman & D. R. Davies (Eds.), *Varieties of attention* (pp. 29–61). Orlando, FL: Academic Press.

Kassin, S. M. (1997). The psychology of confession evidence. *American Psychologist, 52*, 221–233.

Kneller, W., Memon, A., & Stevenage, S. (2001). Simultaneous and sequential lineups: Decision processes of accurate and inaccurate eyewitnesses. *Applied Cognitive Psychology, 15*, 659–671.

Lindsay, R. C. L., & Bellinger, K. (1999). Alternatives to sequential lineups: The importance of controlling the pictures. *Journal of Applied Psychology, 84*, 315–321.

Lindsay, R. C. L., & Wells, G. L. (1985). Improving eyewitness identification from lineups: Simultaneous versus sequential lineup presentations. *Journal of Applied Psychology, 70*, 556–564.

Logan, G. D. (1988). Toward an instance theory of automatization. *Psychological Review, 95*, 492–527.

Logan, G. D. (2002). An instance theory of attention and memory. *Psychological Review, 109*, 376–400.

Malpass, R. S., & Devine, P. G. (1981). Eyewitness identification: Lineup instructions and the absence of the offender. *Journal of Applied Psychology, 66*, 482–489.

Penrod, S. (2003). Eyewitness identification evidence: How well are witnesses and police performing? *Criminal Justice Magazine, 54*, 36–47.

Perretta, S. F., & Dunning, D. (2001). *Testing the automatic versus process of elimination distinction in differentiating accurate from inaccurate eyewitnesses.* Unpublished manuscript, Cornell University.

Petty, R. E., & Cacioppo, J. T. (1981). *Attitudes and persuasion: Classic and contemporary approaches.* Dubuque, IA: W. C. Brown.

Schooler, J. W., & Engstler-Schooler, T. Y. (1990). Verbal overshadowing of visual memories: Some things are better left unsaid. *Cognitive Psychology, 22*, 36–71.

Shiffrin, R. M., & Schneider, W. (1977). Controlled and automatic human information processing: II. Perceptual learning, automatic attending, and general theory. *Psychological Review, 84*, 127–190.

Sloman, S. A. (1996). The empirical case for two systems of reasoning. *Psychological Bulletin, 119*, 3–22.

Smith, S. M., Lindsay, R. C. L., & Pryke, S. (2000). Postdictors of eyewitness errors: Can false identification be diagnosed? *Journal of Applied Psychology, 85*, 542–550.

Sporer, S. L. (1992). Post-dicting eyewitness accuracy: Confidence, decision times and person descriptions of choosers and non-choosers. *European Journal of Social Psychology, 22*, 157–180.

Sporer, S. L. (1993). Eyewitness identification accuracy, confidence, and decision times in simultaneous and sequential lineups. *Journal of Applied Psychology, 78*, 22–33.

Sporer, S. L. (1994). Decision times and eyewitness identification accuracy in simultaneous and sequential lineups. In D. F. Ross, J. D. Read, & M. P. Toglia (Eds.), *Adult eyewitness testimony: Current trends and developments* (pp. 300–327). New York: Cambridge University Press.

Technical Working Group for Eyewitness Evidence. (1999). *Eyewitness evidence: A guide for law enforcement.* Washington, DC: United States Department of Justice, Office of Justice Programs.

Treisman, A. M., & Gelade, G. (1980). A feature-integration theory of attention. *Cognitive Psychology, 12*, 97–136.

Weber, N., & Brewer, N. (2003). The effect of judgment type and confidence scale on confidence-accuracy calibration in face recognition. *Journal of Applied Psychology, 88*, 490–499.

Weber, N., Brewer, N., Wells, G. L., Semmler, C., & Keast, A. (2004). Eyewitness identification accuracy and response latency: The unruly 10–12 second rule. *Journal of Experimental Psychology: Applied, 10*, 139–147.

Wells, G. L. (1984). The psychology of lineup identifications. *Journal of Applied Social Psychology, 14*, 89–103.

Wells, G. L. (1993). What do we know about eyewitness identification? *American Psychologist, 48*, 553–571.

Wells, G. L., & Bradfield, A. L. (1998). "Good, you identified the suspect": Feedback to eye-witnesses distorts their reports of the witnessing experience. *Journal of Applied Psychology, 83,* 360–376.

Wells, G. L., & Lindsay, R. C. L. (1980). On estimating the diagnosticity of eyewitness noniden-tifications. *Psychological Bulletin, 88,* 776–784.

Wells, G. L. & Olson, E. (2002). Eyewitness identification: Information gain from incriminating and exonerating behaviors. *Journal of Experimental Psychology: Applied, 8,* 155–167.

Wells, G. L., & Turtle, J. W. (1986). Eyewitness identification: The importance of lineup models. *Psychological Bulletin, 99,* 320–329.

Wells, G. L., & Turtle, J. W. (1988). What is the best way to encode faces? In M. M. Gruneberg & P. E. Morris (Eds.), *Practical aspects of memory: Current research and issues: Vol. 1. Memory in everyday life* (pp. 163–168). Oxford, England: John Wiley & Sons.

III

IDENTIFYING SUSPECTS:
ESTIMATOR VARIABLES

11

The Influence of Race on Eyewitness Memory

John C. Brigham and L. Brooke Bennett
Florida State University

Christian A. Meissner
University of Texas, El Paso

Tara L. Mitchell
Florida International University

One Sunday morning in May of 2000, a 15-year-old Black youth named Brenton Butler was walking to a video store to apply for a job when he was picked up by police as a possible suspect in a brutal murder that had occurred earlier that morning. Taken back to the motel where the murder had taken place, Butler was positively identified by the murder victim's husband, James Stevens, who had observed the murder from close range just two and a half hours earlier. Although he had described the murderer as 20 to 25 years old, Stevens identified Butler as the man who had demanded his wife's purse and then shot her. When asked if he was certain about his identification, he remarked that he "wouldn't send an innocent man to jail"—yet subsequent events showed that this is precisely what happened (Hattenstone, 2002; Schoettler & Treen, 2000; Schoettler & Pinkham, 2002). The misidentification and subsequent confession that was coerced from Butler were later portrayed in an Academy Award–winning documentary titled *Murder on a Sunday Morning*. Unfortunately, incidents such as this, where an innocent person is arrested or incarcerated on the basis of a cross-racial identification, may be all too common in the justice system.

The *cross-race effect* (CRE), also known as the *own-race bias* or *other-race effect*, refers to the consistent finding that adults are able to recognize individuals of their own race better than faces of another, less familiar race. Although observations involving race and face recognition have been documented since the early twentieth century (Feingold, 1914; Brigham, 2002), the past 30 years have been rich with empirical studies demonstrating the perils of witnesses attempting to identify perpetrators of another race. In a review of this research, Chance and Goldstein (1996, p. 171) observed, "The number of studies that have replicated the other-race effect is impressive. Few psychological findings are so easy to duplicate." Several surveys of research "experts" in this area have also documented wide endorsement of the CRE and its reliability (Kassin, Ellsworth, & Smith, 1989; Kassin, Tubb, Hosch, & Memon, 2001; Yarmey & Jones, 1983). In the most recent of these, Kassin and colleagues (2001) found that 90% of the experts surveyed felt that empirical evidence of the CRE was reliable enough to be presented in court.

This chapter reviews the available empirical literature on the CRE in both children and adults, reviewing the basic cognitive, social, and developmental processes believed to underlie the effect and presenting evidence of its practical influence on eyewitness identification. The parameters of the CRE are also discussed (i.e., the conditions under which the CRE is most likely to be observed), and recommendations are advanced regarding the collection of eyewitness evidence when the perpetrator is of a race or ethnic background different from that of the witness. Finally, avenues of future research in the cross-race domain are discussed.

EMPIRICAL FINDINGS ON THE CROSS-RACE EFFECT

Overall Findings: Meta-Analyses of the CRE

There have been several meta-analyses examining the CRE (Bothwell, Brigham, & Malpass, 1989; Anthony, Copper, & Mullen, 1992; Meissner & Brigham, 2001; Sporer, 2001). The largest of these, conducted by Meissner and Brigham (2001), analyzed data from almost 5,000 participants in 39 studies spread over the prior three decades. Focusing on signal detection measures of discrimination accuracy (i.e., the ability to distinguish between faces seen previously and novel faces), their analysis found a significant CRE that accounted for 15% of the variance across studies. With regard to the pattern of hits (i.e., correct identifications of previously seen faces) and false alarms (i.e., false identifications of novel faces), a "mirror effect" pattern emerged such that own-race faces were 1.40 times *more* likely to be correctly identified and 1.56 times *less* likely to be falsely identified than were other-race faces. The authors concluded that the CRE was a robust phenomenon that should be considered to have practical importance in eyewitness identifications.

The CRE across Racial Groups

Black and White Participants.   In general, the CRE is a finding that has been most often researched and demonstrated with Black and White participants. Over 85% of the participants in the meta-analysis conducted by Meissner and Brigham (2001) were from one of these two racial groups. In a moderator analysis of their data, Meissner and Brigham observed that White participants were significantly more likely to demonstrate a CRE than were Black participants. Given that the majority of studies included in the meta-analysis had been conducted in North America, the authors speculated that this pattern might be due to the "majority" race status of White participants who had participated in the studies, and the associated lower level of interracial contact experienced by these participants.

Although the majority of cross-race studies have been conducted in the United States and Canada, research with Black and White participants in parts of Africa and the United Kingdom has demonstrated that the CRE is not limited to individuals in North America (see Chiroro & Valentine, 1995; Wright, Boyd, & Tredoux, 2001; 2003). For example, using an eyewitness field study methodology, Wright and colleagues (2001) observed a significant CRE in Black and White participants from both England and South Africa. Not surprisingly, these studies have also indicated that the degree of interracial contact between group members can moderate the size of the CRE observed.

Hispanic Participants.   Only a few published studies have tested the CRE within the Hispanic population. In 1988, Platz and Hosch conducted a field study examining the performance of Mexican American, Black, and White convenience store workers in identifying customers who had interacted with them earlier in the day. A Mexican American, Black, or White customer (or "confederate") went into the store and asked for directions or made a fairly involved purchase from the clerk. Two hours after that transaction, a pair of students posing as law office interns asked the clerk for help in identifying the individual with the use of a series of lineup photos. Platz and Hosch found a significant CRE for all three of the racial groups, with clerks of each group better recognizing confederates who were of their own race than people from either of the other two races.

The performance of several racial groups (including Whites, Blacks, Latinos, and Asians) in recognizing both White and Black faces was examined by Teitelbaum and Geiselman (1997). Overall, Latino participants in their sample performed significantly better on White faces than on Black faces. In relation to the racial groups corresponding to the facial stimuli (i.e., White or Black faces), Latino participants performed no differently than White participants on White faces, but significantly more poorly than Black participants on Black faces. Given that the participants in this study were students in Los Angeles, California, the authors speculated that the Latino participants may have been perceived as less of a minority than Black participants, and that this may have encouraged social exchanges with Whites, leading to the development of perceptual skills that improved their performance in differentiating White faces.

Most recently, MacLin, MacLin, and Malpass (2001) provided a more direct test of the CRE in Hispanic participants, using a standard recognition paradigm with photographs of Hispanic and Black faces. Across two experiments, the authors found a significant CRE, with Hispanic participants showing better recognition for Hispanic faces than for Black faces. The authors also varied several factors believed to moderate the CRE, including encoding time (Experiment 1), retention interval (Experiment 1), arousal at encoding (Experiment 2), and attentional demands at encoding (Experiment 2). Of these manipulations, only the presence of attentional demands at encoding appeared to moderate the CRE, such that performance was impaired for own-race faces when attentional demand was great, but not for other-race faces. Nevertheless, participants demonstrated superior recognition for own-race faces under both attentional demand conditions.

Asian Participants. A handful of studies have examined the prevalence of the CRE with Asian faces as stimuli. In several of the earlier studies (Chance, Goldstein, & McBride, 1975; Goldstein & Chance, 1981; Chance, Turner, & Goldstein, 1982), the inclusion of Japanese facial stimuli was intended to allow for some control of the amount of contact that the White participants had with another racial group. Chance, Goldstein, and McBride (1975) showed pictures of Black, White or Japanese faces to White and Black participants and then tested for their recognition memory of these faces. Findings showed a CRE, with each racial group performing better with faces of its own race. The poorest levels of recognition were for the Japanese faces by Blacks and by Whites, who performed similarly. The second in the series of these studies (Goldstein & Chance, 1980) focused only on the facial recognition of White children in first through sixth grades and found no evidence of a CRE, whereas the third study, which included adults, found that children over the age of 11, as well as adults, showed a CRE with Japanese faces (Chance et al., 1982).

Other studies have investigated the presence of the CRE in Asian participants. Luce (1974), for example, showed Black, White, Japanese, or Chinese faces to Black, White, Japanese, and Chinese participants. He found that all four of these groups showed a CRE in facial recognition. Ng and Lindsay (1994) tested the ability of Asian (mostly Chinese) and White participants to recognize both Asian and White faces. They found a significant CRE in both false-alarm rates and measures of overall accuracy (d'), but not in hits. One interesting facet of this study was that it was conducted in Canada and Singapore, and the overall pattern of results was the same in the two countries. Thus, although the amount of contact with people of another racial group would have been different, the poorer recognition of other-race faces was present in both situations.

Sangrigoli and colleagues further investigated the issue of exposure and the CRE with Asian participants. Sangrigoli, Pallier, Argenti, Ventureyra, and de Schonen (2005) compared the facial recognition by adult Koreans who had been adopted by Caucasian families at an early age to facial recognition by adult Koreans who had been raised in Korea, and to facial recognition by adult Caucasians. The authors found that the Caucasian and adopted Korean participants exhibited a similar bias in face recognition, such that both groups were better at recognizing Caucasian faces than Asian faces. In contrast, the nonadopted Korean participants were better at recognizing Asian faces than Caucasian faces.

Other Ethnic Groups. Research on the CRE has also involved other ethnic groups. Sporer (2001), for example, reported a program of research involving Turks and Germans. Using a facial recognition paradigm, Sporer found that Germans exhibited a CRE when shown German and Turk faces, whereas Turks who were shown the same stimuli did not. Weimann, Fishman, and Rattner (1988) examined the CRE in samples of Arabs and Israeli Jews and found that whereas Arabs showed a CRE in correct identifications, Jews appeared to show a CRE in response criterion, such that they produced both more hits and more false alarms in response to Arab faces. Similar results, particularly in hit responses, were obtained by the authors in a follow-up study (Rattner, Weimann, & Fishman, 1990).

The CRE as a Function of Encoding Time and Retention Interval

In general, encoding time has been shown to influence individuals' ability to recognize previously viewed faces, such that minimizing encoding time generally reduces hits while increasing false alarms (cf. Reynolds & Pezdek, 1992). In their meta-analysis of the CRE, Meissner and Brigham (2001) observed that encoding time also appears to moderate the strength of the CRE such that, across studies, longer encoding times generally produced a decrease in the magnitude of the CRE in discrimination accuracy. This decrease appeared largely on false-alarm responses. Interestingly, a previous meta-analysis of the CRE conducted by Anthony et al. (1992) also found a moderating effect of encoding time—however, their analysis showed that the pattern observed by Meissner and Brigham held for Black participants, but was reversed for White participants (i.e., such that longer exposure times led to an *increase* in the CRE).

The only published study to vary encoding time within the CRE paradigm was conducted by MacLin et al. (2001). Using a 0.5-second versus a 5.0-second manipulation, MacLin et al. observed the expected main effect of encoding time on discrimination accuracy; however, their results failed to indicate a significant interaction between encoding time and the CRE (although the pattern of results was consistent with the predicted direction of a larger CRE in the 0.5-second encoding condition). The only other study to comment on the influence of encoding time in the CRE was that by Valentine and Bruce (1986), who conducted pilot work and found that extending the encoding time for other-race faces to 5 seconds equated participants' performance with that of own-race faces presented for 2 seconds. Taken together, it appears that encoding time does moderate the CRE, but that this effect may be small and difficult to detect in a single study. Further research in this area appears warranted.

The length of the retention interval between study and test has also been shown to influence recognition memory for faces (cf. Shepherd, Gibling, & Ellis, 1991). Retention interval appears to influence the magnitude of the CRE as well, particularly through false identifications. As noted by Meissner and Brigham (2001) in their moderator analysis across studies, longer retention intervals have been shown to increase the likelihood of false identifications for other-race faces to a greater extent than for own-race faces. However, two studies examining the relationship between retention interval and the CRE have failed to find this interaction (Barkowitz & Brigham, 1982; MacLin et al., 2001). Barkowitz and Brigham (1982) utilized a 2-day versus 7-day delay and found both a significant CRE and a main effect of retention interval, particularly with regard to participants' response criterion. Although they failed to obtain a significant interaction between delay and the CRE, the authors nonetheless noted, "The detrimental effects of time delay might be expected to be especially strong in cross-race identifications since the present study indicated that subjects of both races responded to other-race photos on the basis of a more lax criterion than they responded to same-race photos" (p. 264).

The CRE in Face Recognition versus Eyewitness Lineup Paradigms

Research on the CRE tends to utilize one of two paradigms: a facial recognition paradigm or an eyewitness lineup paradigm. The facial recognition paradigm, which is rooted in basic cognitive/memory research, involves presenting participants with a series of faces during a study phase and then testing recognition by presenting a second series of faces during a test phase. The faces presented during the test phase include some of those viewed during the study phase, as well as new faces not presented previously. This recognition framework is the most frequently utilized paradigm in the literature, in part because it allows for the calculation of signal detection theory measures of discrimination measures and response criterion (see Green & Swets, 1966). This paradigm, however, has been criticized for its lack of real-world applicability (see Lindsay & Wells, 1983). As a result, researchers concerned with the ecological validity of a facial recognition paradigm applied to the legal system have suggested the use of an eyewitness lineup paradigm, in which participants become "witnesses" to an event and a perpetrator. More specifically, participants are shown an event (either live or via film or videotape), including a target person or "perpetrator," and are subsequently asked to perform a lineup identification task in which the target person may or may not be present. In their meta-analysis across studies, Meissner and Brigham (2001) found that the CRE was observed reliably in both correct identifications and false identifications, regardless of the type of paradigm that was utilized.

The CRE in Facial Descriptions and Memory for Voice

Despite the fact that an eyewitness is likely to encode much more than simply a static face, little research has been directed at investigating the influence of the CRE on other aspects of the witness's experience, including his/her ability to verbally describe the suspect's face or to recognize the suspect's voice. The existing research suggests, however, that race may play only a minimal role in these areas. For example, Ellis, Deregowski, and Shepherd (1975) had 12 Black African and 12 White Scottish teenagers each describe a set of four faces (two faces of each race). Although they found that Black participants described more features than White participants did, and that Black faces elicited mention of a greater number of features than did White faces, they did not find a clear CRE in the verbal descriptions produced by participants. It is interesting to note, however, that participants of each race did utilize certain facial features more frequently. For example, Black participants mentioned aspects of hair position, eye size, whites of eyes, eyebrows, ears, and chin, whereas White participants more often reported iris color, hair color, and hair texture. Although Ellis and colleagues did not assess descriptions for accuracy or discriminability, they did note that White participants often reported rather "redundant" descriptions of Black faces (e.g., "he has black skin, black, kinky hair and brown eyes") that would likely be indiscriminant upon later assessment (p. 123).

In his review of the voice identification literature, Yarmey (1995) noted that several studies have demonstrated that individuals are less accurate in identifying voices of an unfamiliar accent or racial background. For example, Thompson (1987) found that English speakers' recognition of voice was significantly impaired when the voice sample was in English but contained a notable Spanish accent or when the voice sample was in Spanish (see also Goggin, Thompson, Strube, & Simental, 1991). A research study conducted by Doty (1998) involving cross-national voice recognition found similar results, such that participants were better able to recognize voices from their own country (even if those voices were of a different race) than they were able to recognize voices from other countries.

The CRE in Children versus Adults

Although much of the research on the CRE has involved adult participants, researchers have also attempted to understand the extent to which the CRE is present in children. The first researchers to examine the CRE specifically in children were Cross, Cross, and Daly (1971), who studied the recognition memory of Black and White participants in three age groups (ages 7, 12, and 17). The authors found an overall CRE but did not provide enough additional information to break the effect down by age or race of participant. In another early study, Feinman and Entwisle (1976) also found a significant CRE for children (first, second, third, and sixth graders), with the White children showing a larger effect than Black children (consistent with what is often seen in adults; cf. Meissner & Brigham, 2001). In addition, Feinman and Entwisle also reported that the accuracy of children's recognition increased with age, although age failed to interact with the CRE.

Other studies have found a CRE at some ages but not at others. Thus, when Chance, Turner, and Goldstein (1982) looked at children in grades one through eight, as well as a comparison group of college students, they found a CRE that interacted with age, such that larger effects were observed as age increased. Unfortunately, research with children has not always found this developmental interaction or the CRE. For example, a study by Goldstein and Chance (1980) examined White children in first through sixth grades who viewed faces of White and Japanese individuals and were later tested for their recognition of these individuals. Although the authors found an overall increase in accuracy across age, there was neither a CRE nor an interaction between the CRE and age.

Several more recent studies have also found mixed results. Pezdek, Blandon-Gitlin, and Moore (2003) found evidence of the CRE in children. Using several modified videotaped lineups, Pezdek and colleagues found that overall accuracy increased with age, but the magnitude of the CRE did not vary with age. Lee and Goodman (2000) examined the ability of Asian and White children ages 5 to 6, 9 to 10, 12 to 13, as well as undergraduates, to recognize Asian, White, and Black faces. The researchers found that the size of the CRE varied at different ages and across different races. In particular, they found no evidence of the CRE in either the youngest (age 5 to 6) or the oldest (undergraduate) age groups. (This was somewhat surprising, given that the oldest group would have been expected to perform similarly to adults in previous studies.) However, White children in the 9 to 10 and 12 to 13 age groups and Asian children in the 12 to 13 age group did display a significant CRE. The authors speculated that the unusual pattern could have occurred because of a cohort effect caused by the increasingly multicultural area (southern California) where the study had been conducted. In contrast to these findings, another recent study of Whites and Blacks in the Southeast (Bennett & Brigham, 2005) found evidence of a CRE in Whites at each of four grade levels (grades 2, 6, 10, and college), but not in Black respondents at any grade level.

Efforts to explain these inconsistencies have focused on the developmental aspects of facial processing. In particular, research has shown that children's facial recognition performance tends to increase with age, except for a small "dip" between the ages of 10 and 12 (e.g., Carey et al., 1980). Several researchers have argued that, before the age of 10, children encode and recognize faces via a featural encoding strategy (also known as piecemeal encoding) that focuses on isolated, salient features of individual faces (Carey, 1981; Carey et al., 1980; Chung & Thomson, 1995; Thomson, 1986; 1989). Older children, in contrast, utilize configural information relative to the global appearance of a face (also known as holistic encoding), which takes into consideration the relationship between various facial features. For featural encoding, as age and experience increase, children are able to scan faces in a more systematic and organized manner, thereby encoding more features that are relevant. The dip in performance around ages 10 to 12 could be due to difficulties in making the shift from the earlier featural encoding strategy to the utilization of configural information. From this perspective, the dip may represent a "growth error" or an "intermediate effect." Studies of the development of expertise in complex tasks, such as making medical diagnoses, have found similar temporary plateaus or dips in performance that are associated with acquiring new skills or knowledge (Patel, Arocha, & Kaufman, 1994; Schmidt & Boshuizen, 1993).

In contrast, other researchers have argued that there is not an age-related shift from one strategy to the other. Such studies indicate that young children do not engage in a qualitatively different kind of process for recognizing faces than do older children and adults (e.g., Baenninger, 1994); rather, older children and adults are simply able to encode more information of all types than are younger children (Flin, 1985; Flin & Dziurawiec, 1989; Thomson, 1986). Several reviews of this research have concluded that the most parsimonious explanation of the accumulated findings is that the manner of encoding facial information does not change with age; older children simply encode more facial information of all types, both featural and configural (Baenninger, 1994; Chung & Thomson, 1995; Flin & Dziurawiec, 1989).

One finding in the face memory literature has involved research on the face inversion effect—the phenomenon that inverted (upside-down) photos of faces are identified more poorly than inverted photos of other objects (e.g., houses, cars, etc.) (see Yin, 1969). Researchers have used this effect to investigate configural and featural processing. It has been argued that inverted faces are encoded in a featural manner, whereas upright faces are encoded with regard to their configural properties (Diamond & Carey, 1986). Research on the inversion effect in children has shown that children do not show as large an inversion effect as adults, perhaps because of their reliance on featural processing. Sangrigoli and de Shonen (2004a; 2004b) found that whereas young children (age 3) showed neither the CRE nor an inversion effect, older children (age 4 and 5) showed both the CRE and an inversion effect. Furthermore, these effects interacted such that older children were better able to recognize upright faces of their own race and inverted faces of another race. Sangrigoli and de Shonen concluded that the CRE may begin to develop some time during early childhood, perhaps between 3 and 4 years of age.

The CRE in Elderly Adults

Little work has been conducted on older adults and the CRE. Eyewitness memory research has generally shown that older adults perform worse than younger adults on identification tasks (see Memon, Bartlett, Rose, & Gray, 2003). The only study to examine the CRE in older adults was conducted by Brigham and Williamson (1979). The authors had older adults (age 60 to 84) and younger adults (college students) take part in a recognition paradigm in which they viewed a series of own- and other-race faces and later attempt to recognize these individuals from a series of novel faces. Brigham and Williamson found that although the older adults performed significantly more poorly than the younger adults, they showed the same pattern of CRE as the younger participants.

The Diagnostic Value of Confidence in the CRE

In general, people tend to be less confident overall when making other-race identifications than when making same-race identifications (cf. Smith, Stinson, & Prosser, 2004). Research examining the utility of confidence as a postdictor of eyewitness identification accuracy has generally demonstrated a weak positive relationship (see meta-analyses by Bothwell, Deffenbacher, & Brigham, 1987; Sporer, Penrod, Read, & Cutler, 1995). Yet there appear to be some conditions in which a stronger relationship may exist. For example, when conditions vary widely across witnesses, greater confidence has been shown to be associated with greater identification accuracy (cf. Lindsay, Nilsen, & Read, 2000). Furthermore, initial judgments made with very high confidence under unbiased conditions have been shown to be quite diagnostic of witness accuracy (Juslin, Olsson, & Winman, 1996). Research suggests that the confidence-accuracy relationship is significantly *weaker* for other-race than for own-race identifications (Wright, Boyd, & Tredoux, 2001). Meissner, Brigham, and Butz (2005) found that individuals experienced a greater proportion of *false recollections* for other-race faces—namely, incorrect identifications made with high confidence. An awareness of this differential rate of false recollections and the lack of diagnosticity for other-race confidence ratings would seem to be useful for those who must evaluate a disputed cross-racial identification.

COGNITIVE AND SOCIAL PROCESSES THAT MAY AFFECT THE CRE

Given the prevalence of the CRE in eyewitness identifications, what cognitive, perceptual, or social processes might be responsible for the phenomenon? Several possibilities have been suggested in recent years, including: (1) that individuals may have *less contact* with members of other races, resulting in an inability to recognize other-race faces; (2) that individuals may pay *less attention* to other-race persons and may *"cognitively disregard"* them, resulting in a *categorization response* that leads to poor encoding; (3) that individuals may focus their attention on *characteristics that are less useful* for distinguishing among other-race persons than for distinguishing among same-race persons; (4) that individuals may use a *different cognitive processes* for evaluating other-race faces than for same-race faces (e.g., shallower processing or a featural strategy); and/or (5) that individuals may have a *representational system that is optimized for the encoding of own-race faces rather than other-race faces*, thereby leading to the CRE. These possible mechanisms are reviewed below.

The Role of Interracial Contact and Attitudes in the CRE

Many theorists have asserted that the amount of contact one has with members of a group will affect recognition ability, such that more experience and contact should lead to better recognition. One of the earliest theorists to mention the possible involvement of contact in the CRE was Feingold (1914), who asserted "all other things being equal, individuals of a given race are distinguishable from each other in proportion to our familiarity, to our contact with the race as a whole" (p. 50). This theory seemed fairly promising with regard to the CRE and was proposed by several other researchers within the area (e.g., Brigham & Malpass, 1985; Chance & Goldstein, 1996; Ng & Lindsay, 1994).

A number of studies with adults have attempted to identify the role of contact in the CRE, with varying levels of success. Some studies have found a smaller CRE in individuals who reported more interracial contact (Brigham, Maass, Snyder, & Spaulding, 1982; Carroo, 1986, 1987; Cross, Cross, & Daly, 1971; Lavrakas, Buri, & Mayzner, 1976). For example, an eyewitness field study conducted by Brigham and colleagues (1982) indicated that self-reported interracial experience was significantly related to cross-racial identification accuracy for White convenience store clerks. Other studies, however, have not found any relationship between contact and the CRE (Brigham & Barkowitz, 1978; Malpass & Kravitz, 1969; Ng & Lindsay, 1994; Swope, 1994), and still other studies have yielded mixed results (Chiroro & Valentine, 1995; Platz & Hosch, 1988). In their meta-analysis of the CRE, Meissner and Brigham (2001) identified 29 studies that measured self-reported interracial contact and found that it accounted for "a small but reliable" amount of variability, approximately 2%. Interestingly, a moderator analysis of this relationship showed that the influence of interracial contact on the CRE has increased over the years, such that more recent studies have yielded larger correlations (see Meissner & Brigham, 2001). This effect over time may be due to a cohort effect, in which individuals have had more opportunity for interracial contact in recent years, or to improvements in the precision of estimating interracial contact in more recent studies.

Rather than using questionnaires to assess contact, other researchers have attempted to study groups that are presumed to have limited contact with one another. Chance, Goldstein, and McBride (1975) found that Japanese faces (as compared with Black or White faces) were most poorly recognized by both White and Black participants, presumably because these participants had the least amount of contact with Japanese individuals. A study by Galper (1973) found that White students in a Black studies class displayed less of a CRE than did other White students in a psychology class, and a study by Li, Dunning, and Malpass (1998) found that White individuals who said they frequently watched NBA basketball showed less of a CRE than individuals who rated themselves as basketball novices (see also MacLin, Van Sickler, MacLin, & Li, 2004). Shepherd, Deregowski, and Ellis (1974) used African and European participants who had little or no contact with other-race individuals and found a significant CRE for both races, leading them to conclude that "the results are consistent with the hypothesis that people learn to discriminate among faces of the members of their own group as a result of frequent experience with them" (p. 210). Several other investigators have found similar results with African and British participants (Chiroro & Valentine, 1995; Wright, Boyd, & Tredoux, 2001).

The contact perspective suggests that positive attitudes toward other racial groups, which hypothetically should be associated with greater levels of (positive) intergroup contact, should be positively correlated with ability to recognize members of that group (see Meissner & Brigham, 2001). Furthermore, one could speculate that negative intergroup attitudes could motivate one to avoid contact with members of the disliked group, or to limit contact to very superficial interactions, thereby constraining the opportunity to develop expertise in distinguishing between other-race faces (Chance & Goldstein, 1996). In addition, one could speculate that negative attitudes toward another race could lead people to cease processing a face once it has been categorized as belonging to the disliked group (Brigham & Malpass, 1985). However, several studies that directly measured racial attitudes in adults have failed to find a relationship between attitudes and the CRE, casting doubt upon this explanation (Brigham & Barkowitz, 1978; Lavrakas et al., 1976; Platz & Hosch, 1988; Slone, Brigham, & Meissner, 2000). Across studies, Meissner and Brigham (2001) found that racial attitudes were not significantly related to the CRE.

As noted earlier, several studies have found the predicted relationship between negative attitudes toward a group and less self-reported contact with members of the disliked group (e.g., Brigham, 1993; Slone et al., 2000), as more prejudiced Whites and African Americans generally reported less interracial contact, both in the past and in present-day interactions, than did less-prejudiced persons. Reflecting these findings, the Meissner and Brigham (2001) meta-analysis found that racial attitudes and amount of interracial contact were significantly related to one another, suggesting that perhaps racial attitudes can play an *indirect* role in the CRE by influencing the amount and quality of contact that people have with other-race individuals.

Overall, it appears that although contact plays a small role in the CRE, it may be the *quality* of the contact, rather than the quality, that is related to the CRE. Although attitudes do not appear to have a direct effect on the size of the CRE, there is evidence that attitudes may indirectly influence the CRE by influencing both the quantity and quality of contact with members of other races.

Differential Attention and "Cognitive Disregard" for Other-Race Faces

Many observers have noted how in-group members may behave as if out-group members are "invisible" to them, perhaps by a process that Rodin (1987) labeled "cognitive disregard." She proposed that people conserve their cognitive resources by using a strategy in which some strangers (e.g., out-group members) are recognized and categorized only at a superficial level and no individual or individuating information is sought or stored. Rodin (1987) proposed that people may try to conserve their resources by paying more attention to those individuals who are part of their in-group. If this is the case, then we would expect that out-group members might be categorized and later recognized at a very superficial level. Although the labels of in-group versus out-group are not limited to distinctions of race, in the case of the CRE this theory would assume that people would pay more attention to individuals of their own race, as they might feel on some level that recognizing those people would be of the most importance to them.

Research on the CRE has found that when encoding faces of another race, individuals appear to focus upon "race" as a preeminent feature. Levin (1996, 2000) termed this a "facilitated classification process" in which individuals automatically categorize faces in a race-specific manner and ignore other individuating information (quite consistent with Rodin's [1987] notion of cognitive disregard). If this occurs, Levin suggested that it should interfere with later recognition of other-race faces and result in a tendency to respond "seen before" at recognition. In support of this theory, Levin has found that participants who performed more poorly when attempting to recognize Black faces were paradoxically quick to detect or classify them as racial out-group members. Utilizing a set of "ambiguous race faces," MacLin and Malpass (2001, 2003) similarly demonstrated that racial categorization may drive the perceptual encoding process and thereby hinder the encoding (and subsequent recognition) of other-race faces.

How does contact enter into the equation? Levin (2000) asserted, "The failure of the contact hypothesis [note that the Meissner and Brigham (2001) meta-analytic results indicate that failure is too strong a term] is mysterious because at some level it has to be true unless one points to an innate inability to accurately code CR [other-race] faces." Perhaps, as Levin (1996, 2000), MacLin and Malpass (2001, 2003), and others (e.g., Shepard, 1981; Valentine, Chiroro, & Dixon, 1995) have suggested, recognition of other-race faces will be improved only by contact that involves processing those faces with the goal of individuation—a notion quite related to that of "social utility" put forth by Malpass (1990). As a result, Levin pointed out that a categorization response should only operate when the other race is a numerical minority in the population (e.g., Blacks in the United States). Meissner and Brigham's (2001) meta-analysis provided some support for this prediction, as the magnitude of the CRE, as measured by false alarms or by a measure of discrimination (d' or A'), was found to be significantly greater for White perceivers than for Black perceivers or other "minority" groups.

Encoding of Features That Are Less Diagnostic for Other-Race Faces

An alternative reason for the CRE is that the phenomenon might result from attention being paid to facial features that are useful and informative for faces of one's own race but are relatively uninformative for distinguishing among persons of another race. If certain facial features or characteristics are useful in aiding one to discriminate between members of one's own race, one might continue to focus on those features when evaluating other-race faces, even if a different set of features might be more informative. In support of this hypothesis, Ellis, Deregowski, and Shepherd (1975) found that British Whites and African Blacks tended to focus on somewhat different characteristics when describing faces. Consistent with this study, Shepherd and Deregowski (1981) found that White participants considered several characteristics of hair (color, texture, and length) that did not seem to be as important to the Black participants, who were more likely to consider nose breadth and skin tone.

In an early expression of the idea that encoding systems can be more useful for some sets of faces (e.g., same-race faces) than other sets, Goldstein and Chance (1980) and Chance, Turner, and Goldstein (1982) proposed that developmental differences in the CRE could be explained by schema theory. According to the theory, schemas develop through experience and interactions with stimuli, in this case faces. The "schemata function by producing expectations, by determining which aspects of the stimuli will be attended to, by reducing necessity for conscious, voluntary processing to a minimum, by making attending and encoding automatic yet accurate and exceptionally quick" (Goldstein & Chance, 1980, p. 48). Facial processing is assumed to improve as the frequency of exposure to a specific class of stimuli increases; however, facial rigidity may also occur, which is a reduction of flexibility due to overlearning of a class of stimuli (Goldstein & Chance, 1980). Schema theory predicts that schemas develop with age and aid recognition of faces of the familiar class. Therefore, as children get older and have more experience with faces, they become increasingly tuned to faces of their own race and are better able to discriminate between members of that class. They are also less able to discriminate between members of other, less familiar, classes. Therefore the difference between own- and other-race recognition ability should increase with age.

Differential Cognitive Processing of Own- and Other-Race Faces

An early candidate for a cognitive process that might affect the CRE was differential *depth of processing*. Researchers proposed that same-race faces would be cognitively processed at a deeper level, leading to better subsequent recognition (Chance & Goldstein, 1981); however, research findings have not generally supported the depth-of-processing hypothesis. Several studies that attempted to manipulate depth of processing, via instructions to make superficial (e.g., size of facial features; racial classification) or deep (e.g., friendliness or intelligence) judgments, did not find that deeper-processing instructions significantly affected the CRE (Chance & Goldstein, 1981; Devine & Malpass, 1985;

Sporer, 1991). The most consistent finding appears to be that shallow-processing instructions impair memory for all faces, regardless of race (Chance & Goldstein, 1996).

It is possible, however, that individuals might use different encoding processes when
viewing own- and other-race faces. In a series of studies, Diamond and Carey (1986)
showed that the previously discussed inversion effect was not unique to faces, but rather
occurred when participants had a great deal of experience with the stimulus materials.
In particular, inversion appeared to disrupt the effectiveness with which individuals were
able to encode stimuli that were highly familiar to them. Diamond and Carey believed
that this effect stemmed from experienced participants' reliance upon *configural* (or rela-
tional) properties of the stimulus. Novice participants, on the other hand, relied upon
only the *featural* (or isolated) aspects of the face that were less influenced by inversion. A
number of subsequent studies have supported this general configural-featural hypothesis
(see Farah, Wilson, Drain, & Tanaka, 1998).

The notion that expertise leads to configural processing has also been applied to the
CRE. Rhodes, Brake, Taylor, and Tan (1989) proposed that greater experience with own-
race faces would lead to a larger inversion effect, because of an increased reliance upon
configural information. The encoding of other-race faces, on the other hand, should not
be as inhibited by inversion, because of a focus on featural aspects. As hypothesized,
Rhodes and colleagues observed that own-race faces were significantly more susceptible
to inversion than were other-race faces for measures of both reaction time and accuracy
(see also Fallshore & Schooler, 1995; MacLin et al., 2004). It should be noted, however,
that other studies have failed to observe this interaction of inversion with the CRE (Buckhout & Regan, 1988; Burgess, 1988).

Different Representational Systems
for Own- and Other-Race Faces

A final possibility, one quite related to the two previous theories, concerns the way that
own- and other-race faces may be stored in memory. Valentine's (1991) "multidimensional face space model" is an "exemplar-based" model that assumes that specific faces
are stored as category exemplars. The model proposes that both own- and other-race
faces are encoded as locations (points, nodes) in a multidimensional space, and that
these representations are distributed from a central exemplar with respect to their typical or distinctive aspects. Familiar individual faces are represented as points, and face
categories (such as race) are represented as different clusters or "clouds" of points
(Levin, 1996). When one is identifying a previously seen face, the nearest and therefore
most active node will be chosen as the correct one for that face. This model generally accounts quite well for the empirical recognition findings without involving the storage
and abstraction of a face-related norm.

Because "the dimensions of the space are *based on experience with faces of predominantly one race*, the feature dimensions underlying the multidimensional space will be
those that are appropriate for discriminating one particular race of faces" (Valentine,
1991, p. 190, italics added). Representations of other-race faces are more densely clus-

tered in the multidimensional space because the dimensions of the space are most appropriate for own-race faces. Recognition is thus impaired for other-race faces because an other-race face activates many neighboring nodes in the dense cluster of representations for other-race faces (Byatt & Rhodes, 1998; Valentine & Endo, 1992). There are two minimum requirements for the type of contact that would be necessary to learn the statistical structure of a new group of other-race faces. First, one must have a need to recognize other-race individuals, and second, "contact must require the individual to recognize a sufficient number of other-race faces to *enable* the statistical structure of the population of other-race faces in the face space to be abstracted and to *require* that the structure is abstracted in order to be able to recognize the necessary individuals" (Valentine et al., 1995, p. 87, italics in original).

Sporer's (2001) In-Group/Out-Group Model

In his In-Group/Out-Group Model (IOM) of the CRE, Sporer (2001) attempted to bring together these varied social-cognitive explanations. Sporer's IOM assumes that a default or automatic process occurs when an individual encounters an own-race (or in-group) face, such that encoding involves deeper level processing with the individual focused upon relevant, configural properties, or dimensions of the face that are useful for distinguishing it from other, similar faces in memory (consistent with Valentine's, 1991, face space model). In contrast, when an individual encounters an other-race (or out-group) face, racial characteristics first signal an automatic categorization response. This categorization response may then be linked to other cues to cognitively disregard such faces and may result in attentional processes being allocated elsewhere. This categorization may also signal that less effort should be extended in the encoding process, thereby leading to shallow (or feature-based) encoding of the face, and may signal stereotyping processes that lead to improper inferences regarding salient characteristics of the face in memory. Given the greater homogeneity in the representation of other-race faces resulting from the lack of distinctiveness effects, Sporer's IOM also predicts an effect on response bias such that individuals will be more liberal in responding to other race faces (consistent with the general empirical literature; see Meissner & Brigham, 2001). The model also proposes to account for other in-group/out-group phenomena in the facial memory literature, such as the effects of age (Wright & Stroud, 2002) and gender (Slone et al., 2000).

RECOMMENDATIONS FOR COLLECTING CROSS-RACIAL EYEWITNESS EVIDENCE

In the late 1990s, a subcommittee formed by the American Psychology-Law Society proposed a set of recommendations to be used in eyewitness identification procedures (Wells et al., 1998). Although these recommendations do not specifically deal with cross-race situations, they can be considered a starting point for the best possible outcome in all eyewitness procedures. Wells and colleagues presented four rules that they felt would decrease the risk of false identifications. First, a *double-blind* procedure should be used when eyewitness identifications are conducted, in which the lineup administrator is unaware of the position or presence of the suspect in the lineup. This would prevent any influence (intentional or not) that the administrator might have on the choice of the eyewitness. Second, eyewitnesses should be given *unbiased instructions* that warn that the suspect *may or may not* be part of the lineup. Including this simple instruction may serve to decrease the number of false identifications made by eyewitnesses. Of course, false identifications are most prominent in the CRE, and any lineup instructions that might heighten the criterion of other-race witnesses may reduce the possibility of bias at identification.

Third, Wells et al. (1998) suggested that the suspect in the lineup should *not stand out in any way* from the other individuals used as foils (or distractors). In practice this means that the suspect should not have his or her picture taken from a different angle, or be the only one wearing a prison jumpsuit, or the only person with a certain hairstyle named in the description. Potential lineups can be tested by showing them to mock witnesses who have read the description of the suspect but did not witness the crime. In a well-constructed lineup the suspect will not be identified by the mock witness at more than chance levels (see Brigham, Meissner, & Wasserman, 1999, for more information on this procedure).

Research by Brigham and Ready (1985) demonstrated that the CRE effect also shows up in the construction of lineups. Blacks and Whites in their study were given a target photo and asked to go through a stack of facial photos (of persons of the same race as the target person) until they had picked out five photos that were "similar in appearance" to the target photo. This is the same task that a lineup constructor might carry out in selecting foils for a photo lineup. Both Blacks and Whites went through more photos when looking at own-race persons—that is, they had a stricter criterion for "similarity" than when viewing photos of other-race persons. Hence, the lineups that would result would be fairer (higher similarity between suspect/target person and foils) when the lineup constructor was of the same race as the lineup members. Several other studies have demonstrated similar effects of race on the assessment of lineup "fairness" (Brigham, Ready, & Spier, 1990; Lindsay, Ross, Smith, & Flanigan, 1999). Taken together, we recommend that lineups be constructed and assessed by investigators who are of the same race as the suspect.

The fourth recommendation put forth by Wells et al. (1998) was that the eyewitness should be asked about his or her *confidence* in the identification choice (either a positive identification or a nonidentification). Although confidence has been shown to be only minimally related to accuracy (e.g., see Bothwell, Deffenbacher, & Brigham, 1987), it is often very influential at trial. Between the initial identification and trial an eyewitness may experience an inflation of confidence, sometimes referred to as "confidence hardening," which can be due to many factors, such as learning about other evidence, being prepped by prosecution attorneys, wanting to be forceful on the witness stand, and so forth. It would thus be useful to have a statement of the initial confidence level reported by the eyewitness. Given the research, discussed previously, regarding the nondiagnostic nature of confidence in other-race identifications (Meissner et al., 2005; Smith et al., 2004; Wright et al., 2001), we recommend additional caution in relying upon postidentification confidence statements provided by other-race witnesses.

One final issue that appears particularly pertinent to cross-racial identification situations regards the initial *person description* that is provided by the witness. Although no differences in the accuracy of own- versus other-race descriptions has been shown, research has shown that own-race observers are particularly sensitive to characteristics that differentiate between members of their own race, such as skin tone and hair styles for African Americans (Shepherd & Deregowski, 1981). Therefore, it would seem desirable for the initial descriptions to be garnered by an investigator who is of the same race as the perpetrator, because this individual would be better able to inquire about characteristics that are particularly diagnostic in differentiating between persons of the perpetrator's (and investigator's) race.

IMPORTANT REMAINING RESEARCH QUESTIONS

In our view, there are two major areas where a host of important research questions remain. The first area concerns the origin of the CRE and its developmental course through childhood. The second critical area is whether the CRE is reduced or eliminated by practice or training.

As reviewed above, only a handful of studies have investigated the CRE in childhood, and even these few studies have yielded inconsistent results. One can make different predictions about this issue, depending on whether the CRE is seen as biologically based or as resulting from experience (e.g., cross-racial contact). Some scientists have proposed that face recognition is a unique perceptual/cognitive process involving a face-specific "module" in the brain (see Brigham, 2002, for a brief review). A module has been defined as a mandatory, domain-specific, hardwired input system that performs innately determined operations (Fodor, 1983). There are two ways in which modularity can be conceived: as the existence of a specific part of the brain (a processing system) that processes faces in a way similar to that of other systems (specificity), or in terms of a process of recognizing faces that is qualitatively different from recognizing other stimuli (uniqueness) (Hay & Young, 1982). These concepts are theoretically independent of one another, and both have been invoked as evidence for modularity (Tanaka & Gauthier, 1997). From this perspective, face recognition is seen as "special," a unique process mediated by a separate face-specific module in the brain that is biologically endowed and relatively unaffected by experience. If one accepts the modularity position, a logical extension could posit that such modules may be *race-specific*, just as they are species-specific. From this perspective, the CRE could be seen as a natural outcome of a race-specific face-recognition module that is present throughout life.

In contrast, the skill (or expertise) hypothesis asserts that the recognition of faces is not a unique process, but rather occurs in the same way as recognition of other objects. Both hypotheses assert that face recognition will improve through childhood, but for different reasons. The modularity hypothesis attributes improvement largely to the maturation of the face-recognition module, whereas the skill position attributes improvement with age to extensive experience with faces. Forensically, these theories have different implications for face recognition (e.g., identifications from lineups) of children. If face recognition is an innate skill, then perhaps the experiences of the child are not relevant to the likelihood that the child can make an accurate identification decision. In contrast, if face recognition is a learned skill, then the amount of experience that the child has had in recognizing faces of strangers could be seen as important for determining how much confidence one should have in the accuracy of the child's identification decision.

If the second position is more accurate, and contact/experience plays a key role in face-recognition ability, then an important question is: How and when does this effect become strong? Will very young children who have had little experience with recognizing strangers' faces (of either race) show no CRE in face recognition? That is, might the overall contribution of experience to creating the cognitive conditions for the CRE in recognition memory be less in these younger children, who have fewer experiences overall? Alternatively, if the CRE is biologically based (e.g., a race-based face-recognition module), or if it can be created by very early experiences with same-race faces (e.g., parents, siblings), might the CRE be stronger in very young children who as yet have had virtually no experience in distinguishing between other-race faces?

Several interesting research questions remain concerning the development of the CRE in children: (1) Is there an own-race bias in children's recognition memory for faces of adults? (2) Does the magnitude of the CRE differ for children of different ages? (3) Is the magnitude of the CRE in children related to the degree of contact/experiences with other-race persons? (4) Is the CRE of comparable magnitude among children from different ethnic groups or in different societies? (5) Do children of mixed racial ancestry show the CRE for both, one, or neither race?

Several different patterns for the development of the CRE can be postulated. If the CRE is present early in childhood, perhaps because of a face/race-specific module, and remains consistent into adulthood, then no age-related changes in magnitude would be visible. In contrast, if the CRE develops as a consequence of differential contact/experience with own- and other-race individuals, then there would be no CRE in early childhood, but it would develop later on, as more experiences accrue with own- than with other-race people. Finally, one could posit that both of these effects occur, producing a relatively small CRE effect in early childhood that grows in size with age. These developmental trends might be made more complex by a leveling off or decrease in performance at ages 10–14 due to the dip in performance at this age that has been observed in some previous studies. So, although the CRE has been a consistent finding with adults (Meissner & Brigham, 2001), there is simply not enough evidence with children's memory for other-race faces to come to conclusions as to its appearance in children or the origins of the effect in general.

One thing that is not known, for children or for adults, is whether there is a CRE for *descriptions*, as well as for identifications. If a child is describing a person of his or her own race, is that description more likely to be accurate than might a description of an other-race person? This might seem to be a logical extension of the other-race effect in recognition memory, but it may not be so simple. Description memory, unlike recognition memory, may benefit from featural encoding processing. And, as noted, there is some reason to believe that cognitive processing of other-race faces is more likely to involve featural processing than is the processing of same-race faces (cf. Fallshore & Schooler, 1995). If so, this could produce *better* descriptions of other-race faces than of same-race faces, because descriptions mainly involve features. This is purely conjecture at this point, because not much pertinent research addressing this possibility has been carried out. One preliminary study on this issue found no evidence of a CRE in descriptions given by White or Black adult perceivers (Dore, Brigham, & Buck, 2004).

The second major issue is whether adults can be trained to become better at other-race identifications. There are a number of mechanisms by which training or experience could improve memory performance by improving their cognitive strategies or by acquiring relevant knowledge (Kuhn, 1992). More specifically, these include improving processing efficiency, improving encoding and representation, improving strategy selection and regulation, improving the execution of strategies, improving processing capacity, and increasing domain-specific knowledge (Klahr, 1992; Poole & Lamb, 1998). A handful of studies in the 1970s and early 1980s investigated training adults in cross-race recognition, with mixed results. Elliott, Wills, and Goldstein (1973) found that Whites trained on a paired associates task with White and Japanese faces showed improved performance on Japanese faces immediately after training. Goldstein and Chance (1985) used a similar training technique and found that improved performance for Japanese faces persisted up to 5 months after the training. Other training studies, however, found that training had no effect on memory for other-race faces (Malpass, 1981; Woodhead, Baddeley, & Simmonds, 1979) or found that the effects of training were inconsistent and temporary (Lavrakas, Buri, & Mayzner, 1976; Malpass, Lavigueur, & Weldon, 1973). Hence, it is unclear at this juncture whether or not systematic training can reduce or eliminate the CRE, and the temporal nature of any change that occurs is also unclear. Indeed, it appears that investigators in the past two decades have not even found this to be an interesting empirical question, given the paucity of recent published studies.

Given that there have been no published studies of training with children, we (Brigham, Bennett, & Butz, 2005) carried out a series of studies designed to provide participants with experience in distinguishing between other-race faces in a user-friendly, game-like situation. Our goal was to see if this can improve their ability to make cross-race identifications and thereby reduce or eliminate the CRE. We developed a modification of a memory game that provides practice in making distinctions between faces as well as immediate feedback on accuracy. In each game, participants view a 4 by 5 grid of 20 face-down cards on a computer screen, with a head-and-shoulders photo of an adult on the other side of each. The participant turns over any two cards by mouse clicks; if there is a match (i.e., the identical photos, or two different photos of the same person) the selected cards disappear from the board; otherwise they are turned face-down again. The participant's task is to remember where the various types of cards are for future trials and to remove all the cards in as few trials as possible. Each participant plays the game six times, either with sets of same-race faces, with six sets of other-race faces, with nonface objects, or a control game is played that does not involve face memory (pinball). After a short distractor task, all get a standard face recognition memory task in which they see 24 faces (of the same race as in the memory game, but none of the same persons). After a short break, they are shown 48 new faces, which include different photos of the 24 seen previously. Their task is to say whether each face is new or old (seen previously).

Prior to using this new paradigm with children, we conducted two initial studies with college students, Blacks and Whites. The first study, involving 42 Blacks and 55 Whites, was designed as above, and in the second study, 25 Blacks and 59 Whites had the additional task of verbalizing the reasons for their card choice in each trial of the last three memory games. As predicted, in both studies we found a significant three-way interaction [race of participant X race of face (indicative of the CRE) X training condition] on both mean accuracy scores (A') and on a measure of response criterion. However, examination of the means indicated that it was *not* the cross-race training that accounted for the effect. Rather, the own-race training produced a more liberal response criterion (i.e., responding "seen before" in the recognition task) for own-race faces, similar to what is typically seen for other-race faces. Because this produced too many "seen before" responses, it led to poorer recognition scores for own-race faces. Hence, the CRE was not present for those in the own-race training conditions in either study, but it was still present for those in the other-race training conditions, as well as those in the control conditions. Verbalization had no significant impact on accuracy or response criterion.

These findings are provocative, indicating that the memory game paradigm can affect subsequent memory performance, in terms of both accuracy and response criterion. However, the direction of this effect was not as predicted, at least when college students were studied. Studies are currently under way that employ this paradigm with children of both races in grades 2, 6, and 10, to see whether the training may affect them differently. Our preliminary results illustrate the complexity of this area, and the possible effect of training is an issue about which much remains to be discovered.

ACKNOWLEDGMENTS

Support for the writing of this chapter was provided by grants from the National Science Foundation to John C. Brigham and to Christian A. Meissner.

REFERENCES

Anthony, T., Copper, C., & Mullen, B. (1992). Cross-racial identification: A social cognitive integration. *Personality and Social Psychological Bulletin, 18*, 296–301.
Baenninger, M. (1994). The development of face recognition: Featural or configurational processing? *Journal of Experimental Child Psychology, 57*, 377–396.
Barkowitz, P., & Brigham, J. C. (1982). Recognition of faces: Own-race bias, incentive, and time delay. *Journal of Applied Social Psychology, 12*, 255–268.
Bennett, L. B., & Brigham, J. C. (2005). *The development of the "cross-race effect" in children's face recognition memory.* Unpublished manuscript, Florida State University.
Bothwell, R. K., Brigham, J. C., & Malpass, R. S. (1989). Cross-racial identification of faces. *Personality and Social Psychology Bulletin, 15*, 19–25.

Bothwell, R. K., Deffenbacher, K. A., & Brigham, J. C. (1987). Correlation of eyewitness accuracy and confidence: Optimality hypothesis revisited. *Journal of Applied Psychology, 72,* 691–695.

Brigham, J. C. (1993). College students' racial attitudes. *Journal of Applied Social Psychology, 23,* 1993–1967.

Brigham, J. C. (2002). Face identification: Basic processes and developmental changes. In M. L. Eisen, J. A. Quas, & G. S. Goodman (Eds.), *Memory and suggestibility in the forensic interview* (pp. 115–140). Mahwah, NJ: Lawrence Erlbaum Associates.

Brigham, J. C., & Barkowitz, P. (1978). Do "They all look alike"? The effect of race, sex, experience, and attitudes on the ability to recognize faces. *Journal of Applied Social Psychology, 8,* 384–386.

Brigham, J. C., Bennett, L. B., & Butz, D. (2005). *The effect of training in face recognition: When practice does not make perfect.* Symposium presentation, American Psychology-Law Society, La Jolla, CA.

Brigham, J. C., Maass, A., Snyder, L. D., & Spaulding, K. (1982). Accuracy of eyewitness identification in a field setting. *Journal of Personality and Social Psychology, 42,* 673–681.

Brigham, J. C., & Malpass, R. S. (1985). The role of experience and contact in the recognition of faces of own- and other-race persons. *Journal of Social Issues, 41,* 139–155.

Brigham, J. C., Meissner, C. A., & Wasserman, A. W. (1999). Applied issues in the construction and expert assessment of photo lineups. *Applied Cognitive Psychology, 13,* S73–S92.

Brigham, J. C., & Ready, D. R. (1985). Own-race bias in lineup construction. *Law and Human Behavior, 9,* 415–424.

Brigham, J. C., Ready, D. J., & Spier, S. A. (1990). Standards for evaluating the fairness of photograph lineups. *Basic & Applied Social Psychology, 11,* 149–163.

Brigham, J. C., & Williamson, N. L. (1979). Cross-racial recognition and age: When you're over 60 do they still "all look alike"? *Personality and Social Psychology Bulletin, 5,* 218–222.

Buckhout, R., & Regan, S. (1988). Explorations in research on the other-race effect in face recognition. In M. M. Gruneberg, P. E. Morris, & R. N. Sykes (Eds.), *Practical aspects of memory: Current research and issues: Vol. 1. Memory in everyday life* (pp. 40–46). New York: John Wiley & Sons.

Burgess, M. C. R. (1988). The cross-race effect in facial recognition: A function of expertise? *Dissertation Abstracts, International Section B: The Sciences and Engineering, 58*(12-B), 6850.

Byatt, G., & Rhodes, G. (1998). Recognition of own-race and other-race caricatures: Implications for models of face recognition. *Vision Research, 38,* 2455–2468.

Carey, S. (1981). The development of face perception: In G. Davies, H. Ellis, & J. Shepherd (Eds.), *Perceiving and remembering faces* (pp. 9–38). New York: Academic Press.

Carey, S., Diamond, R., & Woods, B. (1980). The development of face recognition—A maturational component? *Developmental Psychology, 16,* 257–269.

Carroo, A. W. (1986). Other race recognition: A comparison of Black Americans and African subjects. *Perceptual and Motor Skills, 62,* 135–138.

Carroo, A. W. (1987). Recognition of faces as a function of race, attitudes, and reported cross-racial friendships. *Perceptual and Motor Skills, 64,* 319–325.

Chance, J. E., & Goldstein, A. G. (1981). Depth of processing in response to own and other race faces. *Personality and Social Psychology Bulletin, 7,* 475–480.

Chance, J., & Goldstein, A. (1996). The other-race effect and eyewitness identification. In S. L. Sporer, R. Malpass, & G. Koehnken (Eds.), *Psychological issues in eyewitness identification* (pp. 153–176). Mahwah, NJ: Lawrence Erlbaum Associates.

Chance, J., Goldstein, A. G., & McBride, L. (1975). Differential experience and recognition memory for faces. *Journal of Social Psychology, 97,* 243–253.

Chance, J. E., Turner, A. L., & Goldstein, A. G. (1982). Development of face recognition for own- and other-race faces. *Journal of Psychology, 112,* 29–37.

Chiroro, P., & Valentine, T. (1995). An investigation of the contact hypothesis of the own-race bias in face recognition. *The Quarterly Journal of Experimental Psychology, 48A,* 879–894.

Chung, M. S., & Thomson, D. (1995). Development of face recognition. *British Journal of Psychology, 86*, 55–87.

Cross, J. F., Cross, J., & Daly, J. (1971). Sex, race, age, and beauty as factors in recognition of faces. *Perception and Psychophysics, 10*, 393–396.

Devine, P. G., & Malpass, R. S. (1985). Orienting strategies in differential face recognition. *Personality and Social Psychology Bulletin, 11*, 33–40.

Diamond, R., & Carey, S. (1986). Why faces are and are not special: An effect of expertise. *Journal of Experimental Psychology: General, 115*, 107–117.

Dore, H. A., Brigham, J. C., & Buck, J. (2005). *Is there an "other-race effect" in the accuracy of descriptions of people?* Unpublished manuscript, Florida State University.

Doty, N. D. (1998). The influence of nationality on the accuracy of face and voice recognition. *American Journal of Psychology, 111*, 191–215.

Elliott, E. S., Wills, E. J., & Goldstein, A. G. (1973). The effects of discriminationtraining on the recognition of white and oriental faces. *Bulletin of the Psychonomic Society, 2*, 71–71.

Ellis, H. D., Deregowski, J. B., & Shepherd, J. W. (1975). Descriptions of white and black faces by white and black subjects. *International Journal of Psychology, 10*, 119–123.

Fallshore, M., & Schooler, J. W. (1995). The verbal vulnerability of perceptual expertise. *Journal of Experimental Psychology: Learning, Memory, and Cognition, 21*, 1608–1623.

Farah, M. J., Wilson, K. D., Drain, M., & Tanaka, J. W. (1998). What is "special" about face perception? *Psychological Review, 105*, 482–498.

Feingold, G. A. (1914). The influence of environment on the identification of persons and things. *Journal of Criminal Law and Political Science, 5*, 39–51.

Feinman, S., & Entwisle, D. R. (1976). Children's ability to recognize other children's faces. *Child Development, 47*, 506–510.

Flin, R. H. (1985). Development of face recognition: An encoding switch? *British Journal of Psychology, 76*, 123–134.

Flin, R. H., & Dziurawiec, S. (1989) Developmental factors. In A. Young & H. Ellis (Eds.), *Handbook of research on face Processing.* Amsterdam: North Holland.

Fodor, J. (1983). *The modularity of the mind.* Cambridge: MIT Press.

Galper, R. E. (1973). Functional race membership and recognition of faces. *Perceptual and Motor Skills, 37*, 455–462.

Goggin, J., Thompson, C., Strube, G., & Simental, L. (1991). The role of language familiarity in voice identification. *Memory and Cognition, 19*, 448–458.

Goldstein, A. G., & Chance, J. E. (1980). Memory for faces and schema theory. *Journal of Psychology, 105*, 47–59.

Goldstein, A. G., & Chance, J. E. (1985). Effects of training on Japanese face recognition: Reduction of the other-race effect. *Bulletin of the Psychonomic Society, 23*, 211–214.

Green, D., & Swets, J. (1966). *Signal detection theory and psychophysics.* New York: Wiley.

Hattenstone, S. (2002, October 18). Angry young man. *Guardian.*

Hay, D. C., & Young, A.W. (1982). The human face. In A.W. Ellis (Ed.), *Normality and pathology in cognitive functions* (pp. 173–202). New York: Academic Press.

Juslin, P., Olsson, N., & Winman, A. (1996). Calibration and diagnosticity of confidence in eyewitness identifications: Comments on what can be inferred from the low confidence-accuracy relationship. *Journal of Experimental Psychology: Learning, Memory, and Cognition, 22*, 1304–1316.

Kassin, S. M., Ellsworth, P. C., & Smith, V. L. (1989). The "General Acceptance" of psychological research on eyewitness testimony: A survey of the experts. *American Psychologist, 44*, 1089–1098.

Kassin, S. M., Tubb, V. A., Hosch, H. M., & Memon, A. (2001). On the "General Acceptance" of eyewitness testimony research: A new survey of the experts. *American Psychologist, 56*, 405–416.

Klahr, D. (1992). Information-processing approaches to cognitive development. In M. H. Bornstein & M. E. Lamb (Eds.), *Developmental psychology: An advanced textbook* (3rd ed., pp. 273–336). Hillsdale, NJ: Lawrence Erlbaum Associates.

Kuhn, D. (1992). Cognitive development. In M. H. Bornstein & M. E. Lamb (Eds.), *Developmental psychology: An advanced textbook* (3rd ed., pp. 211–272). Hillsdale, NJ: Lawrence Erlbaum Associates.

Lavrakas, P. J., Buri, J. R., & Mayzner, M. S. (1976). A perspective of the recognition of other race faces. *Perception and Psychophysics, 20*, 475–481.

Lee, J. S., & Goodman, G. (2000). *The development of memory for own- and other-racial/ethnic faces.* Unpublished manuscript, University of California at Davis.

Levin, D. T. (1996). Classifying faces by race: The structure of face categories. *Journal of Experimental Psychology: Learning, Memory, and Cognition, 22*, 1364–1382.

Levin, D. T. (2000). Race as a visual feature: Using visual search and perceptual discrimination tasks to understand face categories and the cross race recognition deficit. *Journal of Experimental Psychology: General, 129*, 559–574.

Li, J. C., Dunning, D., & Malpass, R. S. (1998, March). *Cross-racial identification among European-Americans: Basketball fandom and the contact hypothesis.* Paper presented at the American Psychology–Law Society, Redondo Beach, CA.

Lindsay, D. S., Nilsen, E., & Read, J. D. (2000). Witnessing-condition heterogeneity and witnesses' versus investigators' confidence in the accuracy of witnesses' identification decisions. *Law & Human Behavior, 24*, 685–697.

Lindsay, R. C. L., Ross, D. F., Smith, S. M., & Flanigan, S. (1999). Does race influence measures of lineup fairness? *Applied Cognitive Psychology, 13*, S109–S119.

Lindsay, R. C. L., & Wells, G. L. (1983). What do we really know about cross-race identification? In S. M. A. Lloyd-Bostock & B. R. Clifford (Eds.), *Evaluating witness evidence.* Chichester: Wiley.

Luce, T. S. (1974). The role of experience in inter-racial recognition. *Personality & Social Psychology Bulletin, 1*, 39–41.

MacLin, O. H., MacLin, M. K., & Malpass, R. S. (2001). Race, arousal, attention, exposure and delay: An examination of factors moderating face recognition. *Psychology, Public Policy, and Law, 7*, 134–152.

MacLin, O. H., & Malpass, R. S. (2001). Racial categorization of faces: The ambiguous race face effect. *Psychology, Public Policy, and Law, 7*, 98–118.

MacLin, O. H., & Malpass, R. S. (2003). The ambiguous race face illusion. *Perception, 32*, 249–252.

MacLin, O. H., Van Sickler, B. R., MacLin, M. K., & Li, A. (2004). A re-examination of the cross-race effect: The role of race, inversion, and basketball trivia. *North American Journal of Psychology, 6*, 189–204.

Malpass, R. S. (1981). Training in face recognition. In G. Davies, H. Ellis, & J. Shepherd (Eds.), *Perceiving and remembering faces* (pp. 271–285). London: Academic Press.

Malpass, R. S. (1990). An excursion into utilitarian analyses, with side trips. *Behavior Science Research, 24*, 1–15.

Malpass, R. S., & Kravitz, J. (1969). Recognition for faces of own and other race. *Journal of Personality and Social Psychology, 13*, 330–334.

Malpass, R. S., & Lavigueur, H., & Weldon, D. E. (1973). Verbal and visual training in face recognition. *Perception and Psychophysics, 14*, 330–334.

Meissner, C. A., & Brigham, J. C. (2001). Thirty years of investigating the other-race effect in memory for faces: A meta-analytic review. *Psychology, Public Policy, and Law, 7*, 3–35.

Meissner, C. A., Brigham, J. C., & Butz, D. (2005). Memory for own- and other-race faces: A dual-process approach. *Applied Cognitive Psychology, 19*, 545–567.

Memon, A., Bartlett, J. C., Rose, R., & Gray, C. (2003). The aging eyewitness: The effects of face-age and delay upon younger and older observers. *British Journal of Gerontology, 58*, 338–345.

Neil versus Biggers, 409 U.S. 188 (1972).

Ng, W., & Lindsay, R. C. L. (1994). Cross-race facial recognition: Failure of the contact hypothesis. *Journal of Cross-Cultural Psychology, 25,* 217–232.

Patel, V. L., Arocha, J. F., & Kaufman, D. R. (1994). Diagnostic reasoning and medical expertise. *Psychology of Learning and Motivation, 31,* 187–254.

Pezdek, K., Blandon-Gitlin, I., & Moore, C. (2003). Children's face recognition memory: More evidence for the cross-race effect. *Journal of Applied Psychology, 88,* 760–763.

Platz, S. J., & Hosch, H. M. (1988). Cross-racial ethnic eyewitness identification: A field study. *Journal of Applied Social Psychology, 18,* 972–984.

Poole, D. A., & Lamb, M. E. (1998). *Investigative interviews of children: A guide for helping professionals.* Washington, DC: American Psychological Association.

Rattner, A., Weimann, G., & Fishman, G. (1990). Cross ethnic identification and misidentification. *Sociology and Social Research, 74,* 73–79.

Reynolds, J. K., & Pezdek, K. (1992). Face recognition memory: The effects of exposure duration and encoding instruction. *Applied Cognitive Psychology, 6,* 279–292.

Rhodes, G., Brake, S., Taylor, K., & Tan, S. (1989). Expertise and configural coding in face recognition. *British Journal of Psychology, 80,* 313–331.

Rodin, M. J. (1987). Who is memorable to whom? A study of cognitive disregard. *Social Cognition, 5,* 144–165.

Sangrigoli, S., Pallier, C., Argenti, A.-M., Ventureyra, V. A. G., & de Schonen, S. (2005). Reversibility of the other-race effect in face recognition during childhood. *Psychological Science, 16,* 440–444.

Schmidt, H. G., & Boshuizen, H. P. A. (1993). On acquiring expertise in medicine. *Educational Psychology Review, 5,* 1–17.

Schoettler, J., & Pinkham, P. (2002, April 29). Falsely accused teen settles for $775,000. *Jacksonville Times-Union.*

Schoettler, J., & Treen, D. (2000, May 8). Boy, 15, held in slaying. *Jacksonville Times-Union.*

Shepherd, J. (1981). Social factors in face recognition. In G. Davies, H. Ellis, & J. Shepherd (Eds.), *Perceiving and remembering faces* (pp. 55–79). San Diego: Academic Press.

Shepherd, J. W., & Deregowski, J. B. (1981). Races and faces—A comparison of the responses of Africans and Europeans to faces of the same and different races. *British Journal of Psychology, 20,* 125–133.

Shepherd, J. W., Deregowski, J. B., & Ellis, H. D. (1974). A cross-cultural study of recognition memory for faces. *International Journal of Psychology, 9,* 205–211.

Shepherd, J. W., Gibling, F., & Ellis, H. D. (1991). The effects of distinctiveness, presentation time and delay on face recognition. *European Journal of Cognitive Psychology, 3,* 137–145.

Slone, A., Brigham, J. C., & Meissner, C. A. (2000). Social and cognitive factors affecting the own-race bias in whites. *Basic and Applied Social Psychology, 22,* 71–84.

Smith, S. M., Stinson, V., & Prosser, M. A. (2004). Do they all look alike? An exploration of decision-making strategies in the cross-race facial identifications. *Canadian Journal of Behavioural Science, 36,* 146–154.

Sporer, S. L. (1991). Deep—Deeper—Deepest? Encoding strategies and the recognition of human faces. *Journal of Experimental Psychology: Learning, Memory, and Cognition, 17,* 323–333.

Sporer, S. L. (2001). Recognizing faces of other ethnic groups: An integration of theories. *Psychology, Public Policy, and Law, 7,* 36–97.

Sporer, S. L., Penrod, S., Read, D., & Cutler, B. (1995). Choosing, confidence, and accuracy: A meta-analysis of the confidence-accuracy relation in eyewitness identification studies. *Psychological Bulletin, 118,* 315–327.

Swope, T. (1994). *Social experience, illusory correlation, and facial recognition ability.* Unpublished master's thesis, Florida State University.

Tanaka, J. W, & Gauthier, I. (1997). Expertise in object and face recognition. *Psychology of Learning and Motivation, 36,* 83–125.

Teitelbaum, S., & Geiselman, R. E. (1997). Observer mood and cross-racial recognition of faces. *Journal of Cross-Cultural Psychology, 28,* 93–106.

Thompson, C. (1987). A language effect in voice identification. *Applied Cognitive Psychology, 25,* 121–131.

Thomson, D. M. (1986). Face recognition: More than a feeling of familiarity? In H. D. Ellis, M. A. Jeeves, F. Newcombe, & A. Young (Eds.), *Aspects of face processing* (pp. 391–399). Amsterdam: Elsevier.

Thomson, D. M. (1989). Issues posed by developmental research. In A. W. Young & H. D. Ellis (Eds.), *Handbook of research on face processing* (pp. 391–399). Amsterdam: Elsevier.

Valentine, T. (1991). A unified account of the effects of distinctiveness, inversion and race on face recognition. *Quarterly Journal of Experimental Psychology, 43A,* 161–204.

Valentine, T., & Bruce, V. (1986). The effect of race, inversion, and encoding activity upon face recognition. *Acta Psychologica, 61,* 259–273.

Valentine, T., Chiroro, P., & Dixon, R. (1995). An account of the other-race effect and the contact hypothesis based on a 'face space' model of face recognition. In T. Valentine (Ed.), *Cognitive and computational aspects of face recognition: Exploration of face space* (pp. 69–94). London: Routledge.

Valentine, T., & Endo, M. (1992). Towards and exemplar model of face processing: The effects of race and distinctiveness. *Quarterly Journal of Experimental Psychology, 44,* 671–703.

Weimann, G., Fishman, G., & Rattner, A. (1988). Social distance and misidentification. *International Journal of Comparative Sociology, 27,* 217–225.

Wells, G. L., Small, M., Penrod, S., Malpass, R. S., Fulero, S. M., & Brimacombe, C. A. E. (1998). Eyewitness identification procdures: Recommendations for lineups and photospreads. *Law and Human Behavior, 22,* 603–647.

Woodhead, M. M., Baddeley, A. D., & Simmonds, D. C. V. (1979). On training people to recognize faces. *Ergonomics, 22,* 333–343.

Wright, D. B., Boyd, C. E., &, Tredoux, C. G. (2001). A field study of own-race bias in South Africa and England. *Psychology, Public Policy and Law, 7,* 119–133.

Wright, D. B., Boyd, C. E., & Tredoux, C. G. (2003). Inter-racial contact and the own-race bias for face recognition in South Africa and England. *Applied Cognitive Psychology, 17,* 365–373.

Wright, D. B., & Stroud, J. N. (2002). Age differences in lineup identification accuracy: People are better with their own age. *Law & Human Behavior, 26,* 641–654.

Yarmey, A. D. (1995). Earwitness speaker identification. *Psychology, Public Policy, & Law, 1,* 792–818.

Yarmey, A. D., & Jones, H. P. T. (1983). Is the psychology of eyewitness identification a matter of common sense? In S. Lloyd-Bostock & B. R. Clifford (Eds.), *Evaluating witness evidence* (pp. 13–40). Chichester, England: Wiley.

12

Person Description and Identification by Child Witnesses

Joanna D. Pozzulo
Carleton University, Ontario

When children witness crime, they may be asked to describe and identify the persons involved in the event. The information provided by the child witnesses may be used to narrow the search for the suspect and eventually to select foils for the lineup identification task (Luus & Wells 1991). Foils are innocent people placed in the lineup as distractors. Children's abilities to describe and identify persons are reviewed in this chapter and are contrasted with comparable abilities of adults.

DESCRIBING CULPRITS

Quantity of Descriptors

News reports alert the public to culprits who remain at large, usually offering descriptions provided by witnesses. Unfortunately, the descriptions are often vague and apply to many persons. An example description may be: Caucasian, medium height and build, short brown hair, clean shaven, wearing a white t-shirt and blue jeans. Descriptions provided by adult witnesses have been examined by researchers via archival reviews and laboratory studies (Schooler, Meissner, & Sporer, this volume).

Archival reviews consist of researchers examining descriptions provided by witnesses to real crime. Accuracy is estimated by comparing the description provided by the witness(es) with the appearance of the arrested/convicted offender. Laboratory studies entail exposing participants to an unfamiliar individual(s) or face(s). Participants are unaware they will need to describe the individual or face once it is no longer in view. With the "target" out of sight, the participant is asked to describe the target, using an open-ended format, and/or the participant might be asked a series of questions about the target's appearance. For example, the participant might be asked if the target had facial hair; to rate the target's skin tone, using a scale from light to dark; or to state how much the target weighed.

In an archival review, Kuehn (1974) found that adult witnesses to real crime reported an average of 7.20 descriptors. In a laboratory study, Ellis, Shepherd, and Davies (1980) found that adult participants reported an average of 9.38 descriptors following a 1-hour delay between viewing the target and having to describe the target. Lindsay, Martin, and Webber (Exp. 1, 1994) examined descriptions provided by adults to staged and real crimes. Witnesses to staged crimes reported an average of 7.35 descriptors. In contrast, witnesses to real crime reported an average of 3.94 descriptors. Adults appear to report few descriptors, in the range of 4 to 9 descriptors for an unfamiliar target.

A few studies have examined the ability of children to describe unfamiliar targets. Unfortunately for the criminal justice system, children provided fewer person descriptors than adults. In one study, Davies, Tarrant, and Flin (1989) asked younger (6- to 7-year-olds) and older children (10- to 11-year-olds) to describe a stranger with the use of a free recall format. Younger children recalled fewer items (M = 1.00 descriptor) than older children (M = 2.21 descriptors). Dent and Stephenson (1979) found that few children provided descriptions of the target at all (0 descriptors) when they used a free recall format. However, it is necessary to compare child and adult witnesses in the same study to determine the difference or similarity in their descriptors.

Pozzulo and Warren (2003) conducted two studies comparing free recall descriptions provided by youths (10- to 14-year-olds) and adults. In study one, Pozzulo and Warren (2003) found that youths provided significantly fewer descriptors (M = 7.61) than adults (M = 9.85) overall. More specifically, youths reported significantly fewer descriptors than adults across three descriptor categories: exterior face, such as hair items (M = 1.71 vs. M = 2.22); interior face, such as eye color (M = 1.00 vs. M = 2.38); and body, such as weight (M = .97 vs. M = 1.35). Conversely, adults reported significantly fewer accessories such as belts and necklaces (M = .05) compared with youths (M = .16), though neither reported many items in this category. Youths and adults reported a similar number of clothing descriptors (M = 2.73 vs. M = 2.67). In study two, Pozzulo and Warren (2003) also found that youths provided significantly fewer descriptors (M = 3.64) than adults (M = 8.09) overall. Youths reported significantly fewer descriptors than adults across five categories: exterior face (M = 1.58 vs. M = 2.66), interior face (M = .24 vs. M = .82), body (M = .49 vs. M = 1.23), clothing (M = 1.03 vs. M = 2.66), and accessories (M = .13 vs. M = .34).

Why do children provide fewer descriptors than adults, even when adults seem to provide so few descriptors? Providing a free recall description is a verbal task that may be hindered by children's less developed linguistic ability compared with that of adults. Children may have fewer words to describe people. Alternatively, children may use an encoding strategy that is different from that of adults, in which children encode fewer individual items, thus limiting the number of descriptors that could be recalled.

Nature and Accuracy of Descriptors Reported

Frequent descriptors by "real" adult witnesses include sex, age, height, build, race, weight, complexion, and hair color (Kuehn, 1974). Lindsay et al. (1994) found that clothing, hair color, and height were reported frequently by adult witnesses. In a study by Ellis et al. (1980) and in a study by Sporer (1996), hair was the most common feature reported by adult participants. Similar to the results with adult witnesses, King and Yuille (as cited in Davies, 1996) found that hair descriptors, presence of facial hair, and glasses were likely to be reported by children. Davies, Tarrant, and Flin (1989) also found that hair was the feature most frequently mentioned by both younger and older children. The exterior feature of hair seems to be a dominant descriptor focused on by both children and adults (Ellis, Shepherd, & Davies, 1980; Sporer, 1996). Pozzulo and Warren (2003) found that exterior facial descriptors (e.g., hair items) were predominant and were accurately reported by youths and adults. It is important to note, however, that often both the target and most of the participants are Caucasian, which may suggest a possible race issue. It is likely that with non-Caucasians, whose hair is almost always darkbrown/black, less attention may be paid to hair.

Some studies suggest that younger children, under 9 years of age, are better at recognizing exterior facial features (e.g., hair, face shape) than interior features (e.g., eyes, ears, nose) of familiar persons (Campbell, Walker, & Baron-Cohen, 1995). Davies, Tarrant, and Flin (1989) found that in describing unfamiliar persons, younger children recalled fewer interior facial features than older children. Pozzulo and Warren (2003) found that accuracy was significantly lower for youths than adults when they reported interior facial features (e.g., nose shape) versus exterior facial features (e.g., hair).

Although interior features are less likely to change and may be unique in helping facilitate narrowing of the suspect search, these features may not be accurately reported by children or youths. Various explanations are possible for youths' difficulty with interior facial features. For example, a developmental trend may be present where initially exterior features may be more salient and, hence, focused on. With increasing age, interior facial features are observed, encoded, and recalled, along with exterior facial features. Alternatively, interior features may be more difficult to describe, requiring a richer vocabulary (e.g., stating that she had a turned-up nose may be more accurate than stating that her nose was small). Furthermore, in order to describe interior features, one may need to consider a relation between features (e.g., eyes may appear large on a small face) that may only occur later in childhood (e.g., Carey & Diamond, 1977).

Other descriptors such as height, weight, and age often seem to be reported and, if not reported, are descriptors police may ask about specifically. Unfortunately, height, weight, and age appear to be particularly problematic for children and youths. Davies, Stevenson-Robb, and Flin (1988) found that children/youths (7- to 12-year-olds) were inaccurate when asked to report the height, weight, and age of an unfamiliar visitor. Also, Goetze (as cited in Davies, 1996) found that the accuracy of height, weight, and age estimates increased with the age of the participants (8-year-olds vs. 11-year-olds vs. 13-year-olds). Janssen and Horowski (as cited in Sporer, 1996) examined height estimates by participants aged 10–18 years and found that the accuracy of these descriptors increased with age. Brigham, Van Verst, and Bothwell (1986) found that children had difficulty with weight estimates. Dent (1982) found that age was the most inaccurate descriptor provided by children. Flin and Shepherd (1986) reported that a participant's height (adult participants) was related to height estimates of others. Furthermore, it has been suggested that a witness's self characteristics may influence reports of others (Clifford & Bull, 1978). Pozzulo and Warren (2003) found that youths had greater difficulty accurately reporting body descriptors, such as height and weight, than adults. They also found that age was unlikely to be reported by youths or adults using a free recall format.

Children and youth may be inaccurate with height and weight estimates because of a lack of knowledge and/or experience with these descriptors. Understanding the relation between height and weight is necessary to provide accurate body estimates. For example, taller people are heavier than shorter people with a similar girth. The development of these relations may not occur until the middle teen years, when youths become more interested in body image and health. Children's and youths' difficulty with age estimates may be due to an ingroup age bias, such that people are more accurate when reporting the ages of others who are similar in age to themselves and have difficulty with estimating ages of those who are younger or older. The studies reviewed here have used adult targets. Ongoing research in my laboratory is examining whether a cross-age effect occurs in descriptions of unfamiliar targets.

Policy Implications and Police Recommendations

Children report fewer person descriptors than adults. Accuracy of the descriptors varies. Hair items are commonly reported by both children and adults and appear to be fairly accurately reported by both groups of witnesses. Aside from interior facial features and body descriptors such as weight and height, police can interpret children's and adult's person descriptions in a similar manner.

Of greater concern to police may be child witnesses' limited descriptions rather than accuracy. Children report very few person descriptors when asked to recall what the "stranger" looked like. It is unlikely that the few descriptors that children provide would be successful at narrowing the suspect search. In addition, with so few descriptors available, it is unclear whether these items would be sufficient to aid in foil selection for the lineup identification task. Efforts should be concentrated on developing procedures that increase the number of descriptors children report. Moreover, it is important to establish the extent of the descriptors children are able to report without losing accuracy. Interview type (e.g., cognitive interview) may help increase the amount of information reported (e.g., Comparo, Wagner, & Saywitz, 2001). Certainly, the research examining suggestive and misleading questions will be useful for revealing the effects of asking direct questions about person description (Ceci & Bruck, 1993; Saywitz & Camparo, 1998).

IDENTIFYING CULPRITS

Far more attention has been paid to children's ability to identify culprits or unfamiliar faces than their ability to describe them. There are two lines of research, differing in their approach and the questions they ask, that have been undertaken to address issues of identification by children.

Methodology for the Study of Children's
Recognition versus Identification Abilities

Two subdisciplines of psychology have been involved in investigating children's recognition/identification abilities: cognitive psychology and social psychology. The task of face recognition typically falls under the domain of cognitive psychology using cognitive psychology terminology and methodology. Conducted in the laboratory, the face recognition paradigm is initiated with participants being presented with numerous slides (e.g., 20) of faces for encoding. Background and clothing information may be removed from the slides, leaving only the hair and face intact. Faces are displayed serially for a short period of time (e.g., 5 seconds). Participants may or may not be told that they should try to remember the faces for a later recognition task. Moreover, a time delay may or may not be imposed between display of the slides for encoding and the recognition task. Past research has employed one of two methods to examine recognition memory. In one method, previously seen faces are interspersed among new faces (e.g., an additional 20). All faces then are shown serially to participants, who must determine which faces had previously been displayed for encoding. The second method requires the participant to choose from sets of faces (i.e., sets of two faces shown simultaneously) which faces were previously seen.

Recognition accuracy is most often measured by examination of the proportion of faces participants correctly recognized as previously seen, termed the *hit rate*. Accuracy can also be measured by examination of the proportion of faces participants correctly labeled as not previously seen, termed the *true negative* or *correct rejection rate*. However, the true negative rate is rarely discussed in the literature. Errors can be measured by examination of the proportion of faces participants incorrectly recognized as previously seen, termed the *false-alarm rate*, or by examination of the proportion of faces participants failed to classify as previously seen, termed the *miss rate*.

Until the mid-1980s assumptions about a child witness's identification abilities in a forensic context were drawn primarily from face recognition studies. However, the criminal justice system and some researchers noted the numerous discrepancies between the face recognition methodology and the applied situation. The issue of ecological validity was raised.

Partly in response to the criticisms levelled against those who used results from the face recognition literature in an applied eyewitness context, social and cognitive psychologists developed a more ecologically valid paradigm to study eyewitness identification. These studies used different terminology and methodology. The identification studies could be conducted in the laboratory or in the field. Unsuspecting participants are exposed to an event (e.g., crime) containing a target person (e.g., culprit). The event and target may be shown to participants via a slide sequence, in a staged event that is videotaped, or in a live staging. To simulate the unexpectedness of real-life crime, participants are unaware of the true nature of the study (e.g., to test their identification ability). Following the event, participants (now witnesses) are informed of the true nature of the study, and they are asked to describe who and what they saw. A time delay could be imposed between the event exposure and the identification task. In the identification phase, witnesses are given a lineup task to test their ability to identify the target. Note that usually witnesses are exposed to only one target. Most often, the lineup task consists of a set of photographs (e.g., six) and the target may or may not be included in the lineup. Thus, target-present lineups as well as target-absent lineups are constructed. The lineup photos typically are selected to have some resemblance to the target (Luus & Wells, 1991).

Two measures of accuracy are used, one for target-present lineups and one for target-absent lineups. When participants are shown a target-present lineup, accuracy is measured by examination of the proportion of witnesses who correctly identified the target, termed the *correct identification rate*. When participants are shown a target-absent lineup, accuracy is measured by examination of the proportion of witnesses who correctly rejected the lineup as not containing the target, termed the *correct rejection rate*. There are two errors that witnesses can make with target-present lineups and two errors that witnesses can make with target-absent lineups. With target-present lineups, witnesses may incorrectly identify a foil as being the target, generating a foil identification rate. Also with target-present lineups, witnesses may incorrectly reject the lineup, termed the *false rejection rate*. As with target-present lineups, with target-absent lineups witnesses may incorrectly identify a foil, also termed a foil identification. The most serious error a witness can make is to incorrectly identify an innocent suspect. In many studies, there is an individual in the target-absent lineup who the experimenter has deemed to be the innocent suspect, generating a false identification rate. Recently, researchers in the field are combining false identifications and foil identifications from target-absent lineups and referring to them as the false-positive rate (Lindsay, Pozzulo, Craig, Lee, & Corber, 1997).

There are many differences between the face recognition and the eyewitness identification research paradigms. First, the number of targets presented differs. Face recognition studies use a relatively large number of targets (e.g., 20) for the participant to recognize, whereas identification studies usually use one target for recognition. Second, in face recognition studies, the same photographs are used for encoding and for recognition. Eyewitness identification uses different presentations: video or live or slide for encoding and photographs for recognition. Also, the target in identification studies is viewed from different perspectives (e.g., profile/side view) at encoding than for identification (full face, frontal). Finally, with face recognition research, the participant is always presented with the targets during the recognition task. In other words, a target-present arrangement is used at all times. Although a target-present lineup may be used in identification research, a target-absent lineup also is used. A target-absent lineup is necessary to assess false identification rates. It is not possible to determine the rate at which a witness will identify an innocent suspect from a target-present lineup because the suspect in a target-present lineup is guilty.

Theoretical issues such as how faces are encoded and recognized and how these abilities change over time often are addressed by face recognition studies. Applied questions such as the best identification procedures to use with children often are addressed by eyewitness identification studies.

Face Recognition Studies

The Development of Face Recognition.   A consistent finding in the face recognition literature is that with increasing age comes increased recognition accuracy of unfamiliar faces. Face recognition studies have generally found that the proportion of hits, and thus the level of accuracy, increases with participants' age (Blaney & Winograd, 1978; Carey, Diamond, & Woods, 1980; Chance, Turner, & Goldstein, 1982; Cross, Cross, & Daly, 1971; Ellis, Shepherd, & Bruce, 1973; Feinman & Entwistle, 1976; Flin, 1980). A significant increase in recognizing unfamiliar faces is observed between the ages of 5 and 12 years (Blaney & Winograd, 1978; Carey, 1981; Carey, Diamond, & Woods, 1980; Flin, 1980; Goldstein & Chance, 1964). In a review of the face recognition literature, Chance and Goldstein (1984) reported hit rates between 35% and 40% for children at a kindergarten level (4- to 5-year-olds), between 50% and 58% for 6- to 8-year-olds, between 60% and 70% for 9- to 11-year-olds, and between 70% and 80% for 12- to 14-year-olds. Adult performance has been found to be similar to that of 12- to 14-year-olds (Goldstein, 1977). In a meta-analysis by Shapiro and Penrod (1986), age was found to yield a large effect size for hits.

As important as it is for a witness to be able to identify the culprit (i.e., make a correct identification), it is also important for a witness to be able to correctly reject a lineup when the culprit is not present (i.e., when an innocent suspect has been arrested). In face recognition studies, we can only assess the rate at which participants make correct rejections if false-alarm rates are reported. Some, but not all, face recognition studies report false-alarm rates. Not surprisingly, as hits increase with age, false alarms have been found to decrease with age (Chance et al., 1982; Cross et al., 1971; Ellis et al., 1973; Flin, 1980). In their meta-analysis, Shapiro and Penrod (1986) found that age yielded one of the largest effect sizes for false alarms. Chance and Goldstein (1979) reported that adolescents 13 years old and older produce false-alarm rates similar to those of adults. Cross et al. (1971) reported that false-alarm rates of 12-year-olds, 17-year-olds, and adults (M = 36 years) were comparable (11%, 9%, and 7%, respectively).

Face Processing: Featural versus Holistic Debate.   Some researchers have attempted to explain the increasing trend for hits and the decreasing trend for false alarms by examining how faces are encoded or processed. Faces may be encoded featurally or holistically, or by a combination of both strategies. Featural encoding involves focusing on facial features such as the eyes or nose. In contrast, holistic encoding involves representing the entire face, not just its parts (Farah, Wilson, Drain, & Tanaka, 1998). For example, although specific facial features are noted, the face is encoded as a configuration of these features, such as the distance from the forehead to the eyes (Schwarzer, 2000). Being able to consider the relations between features rather than merely the features greatly increases participants' ability to accurately discriminate between faces (Bartlett & Searcy, 1993; Bradshaw & Wallace, 1971; Diamond & Carey, 1986; Farah, Tanaka, & Drain, 1995; Rhodes, 1988; Sergent, 1984).

In a seminal study, Carey and Diamond (1977) suggested that in later childhood, children shift from an emphasis on featural encoding to a more holistic approach. To demonstrate their proposition, Carey and Diamond (1977; also Carey, Diamond, & Woods, 1980) used a face inversion paradigm. This paradigm involves presenting faces in an upright position for encoding and then presenting the faces inverted for recognition. The logic behind the face inversion paradigm is that if faces are represented by features, inverting the face should not influence recognition. On the other hand, if faces are represented holistically, inverting the face would distort the pattern of the face and thus make recognition more difficult. Adults are believed to process faces holistically and are found to have more difficulty recognizing inverted than upright faces (Hochberg & Galper, 1967; Scapinello & Yarmey, 1970; Yin, 1969). Carey and Diamond (1977) found that although children's recognition accuracy with upright faces increased from age 6 to 10 years, their accuracy in recognizing inverted faces remained uniform. These results suggested that younger children were not distracted with the pattern of the face when the face was inverted. With feature encoding, the inverted face did not pose difficulty for recognition, whereas, with holistic encoding, the face is seen as a whole and inversion disrupts accurate recognition.

Using a paraphernalia manipulation, Baenninger (1994) found that having a target face wear paraphernalia (e.g., a hat) at both the encoding stage and the recognition stage aided children in their recognition. When the targets were not wearing their paraphernalia at the recognition stage, children believed that the target was absent (when in fact the target was present). To further support the view that younger children process faces featurally, Hay and Cox (2000) found that 6- to 7-year-olds were better at recognizing individual features of faces, specifically the eyes, compared with 9- to 10-year-olds.

In two studies, Ellis and Flin (1990) attempted to determine whether children's face recognition abilities were effected by delay and exposure duration. Recognition accuracy by 7-year-olds was not effected by delay. In contrast, recognition accuracy decreased for 10-year-olds with a 1-week delay between encoding and recognition. Ellis and Flin suggested that younger children may only encode a few features to begin with, making them less susceptible to forgetting. In the second study Ellis and Flin (1990) conducted, exposure duration of the face stimuli at encoding was varied. Recognition accuracy did not vary as a function of exposure duration for 7-year-olds. Again, 10-year-olds were more accurate at the longer exposure duration, when the exposure duration increased from 2 seconds to 6 seconds. Ellis and Flin suggested that the older children may have benefited from the extra exposure duration because their encoding capabilities are more advanced. Thus, older children may be able to encode more information during a given time period, or they may have better strategies to help them integrate this newly encoded information while still presented with the stimulus. Alternatively, the few features that younger children will encode may not require as much time to process as the more complicated configural information used by older children and adults.

These three lines of research, inversion, paraphernalia, and delay, led to the conclusion that between the ages of 10 and 12 years, children attain the capability of processing faces holistically. Prior to the age of 10 years, children encode faces featurally. However, there is a tendency for some of the developmental increases in recognition to decrease or plateau around the ages of 10, 12, and 14 years. Carey et al. (1980) observed that overall performance in face encoding declined slightly after the age of 10 years and improved again until the age of 16 years. Chung and Thomson (1995) demonstrated an inferior performance in face recognition with 12 to 14 year olds compared with 6-, 8-, 10-, and 16-year-olds. On the other hand, Diamond and Carey (1977) found that at the age of 10 years and until the age of 16 years, accuracy in recognition tended to remain constant rather than decline. Researchers disagree as to whether this decline occurs and, if so, the age at which it occurs. Moreover, an adequate explanation for this effect has yet to be provided.

Although most researchers agree that the ability to process faces improves with age, there is a great disagreement concerning the processing abilities of children (Tanaka, Kay, Grinnell, Stansfield, & Szechter, 1998). For example, it has been argued that even though children may not process faces holistically, with holistic encoding instructions they may improve their recognition accuracy, approximating the performance of adults (Chung & Thomson, 1995). Thus, one alternative view to children's processing abilities is that they *can* encode faces holistically but prefer to use a featural approach until later childhood. An experiment by Blaney and Winograd (1978) examined the effect of holistic versus featural encoding instructions on children's memory for unfamiliar faces. Children in grades 1, 3, and 5 were presented with 20 male faces. One-third of the children were asked (for each picture) if the man had a big nose (i.e., featural instruction), one-third were asked if the man looked nice (i.e., holistic instruction), and the final third were told to look carefully at the faces and try to remember them (i.e., use their "normal" strategy). Holistic instructions improved recognition for each age group. Thus, even young children seem able to encode faces holistically.

Tanaka et al. (1998) examined 6-year-olds, 8-year-olds, and 10-year-olds when they were presented with parts of a face that were either placed within the whole face or placed in isolation for the recognition phase. Consistent with the notion that children are capable of holistic encoding, all three age groups of children recognized the parts of a face more accurately when they were presented within the whole. To follow-up these results, Tanaka et al. (1998) added inverted faces at the recognition phase. They found that the whole-face advantage was only present when the face was upright for recognition.

Furthermore, Baenniger (1994) compared the recognition of intact faces versus scrambled faces in 8- and 11-year-olds and adults. Baenniger hypothesized that if children processed faces featurally, then recognition accuracy should not differ across conditions. This hypothesis was not supported. All groups were less accurate at recognizing faces when they were scrambled versus intact. Friere and Lee (2001) found that 4-year-olds were able to recognize target faces that had the same features but whose spacing differed, suggesting that children were processing faces as a whole. In a study by Tanaka, Kay, Grinnell, Stansfield, and Szechter (1998; also Tanaka & Farah, 1993), a target face was presented and identified by name for encoding (e.g., This is Tom). For recognition, some children were shown the target face and a foil face that differed from the target by only one feature (eyes, nose) and asked which face was Tom (holistic condition). Other children were presented with one feature from the target face and one feature from the foil face and asked which one was Tom's nose, for example (feature condition). The inversion paradigm also was employed. Six- 8- and 10-year-olds were each increasingly more accurate with whole faces that were presented upright compared with features. This effect was not present for inverted faces. Thus, given upright faces were more accurately recognized than features for each age group, it is suggestive that even young children can and do encode faces holistically.

Conclusions

Although the debate continues regarding the face-processing abilities of children, there are some generally accepted conclusions regarding the development of face recognition. First, children's ability to accurately recognize unfamiliar faces increases with age between 5 and 10 years old (e.g., Goldstein & Chance, 1964; Carey et al., 1980; Baenninger, 1994). Second, younger children have greater difficulty with recognizing faces when they do not match their appearance from encoding (e.g., Diamond & Carey, 1977; Ellis, 1992). There also are a number of questions that have yet to reach an accepted conclusion. For example, do young children naturally use holistic processing with unfamiliar faces? At what age do children reach an adult level of face recognition accuracy? Does a decrease in face recognition occur before adult-level accuracy is reached and, if so, why?

What Would Our Conclusions of Child Witnesses Be, Based on Face Recognition Studies?

Based on the research reviewed above, we may conclude that children would be more accurate witnesses with increasing age. When presented with a lineup (identification task), we would expect 6-year-olds to be less accurate at identifying the culprit than 8-year-olds or adults. Moreover, we would expect 10- to 12-year-olds to have an adult level of identification accuracy. Studies using a more ecologically valid methodology, however, suggest a different picture of children's identification abilities.

Identification Task

To mirror real-life lineup identification procedures, identification studies often use the simultaneous lineup procedure, where witnesses are shown all of the lineup members at the same time. The witness might choose one of the lineup members or reject the lineup as not containing the culprit. It has been suggested that witnesses use a relative strategy to make their identification decision with a simultaneous lineup (Wells, 1993). That is, the witness chooses the lineup member that is most similar in physical appearance to the culprit. Provided the culprit is in the lineup, a relative strategy is effective because the culprit will, most likely, look most like himself/herself. However, it is possible that the culprit is not in the lineup, as when police have arrested an innocent person. In this situation, a relative strategy would lead to high false identification or false-positive rates.

To decrease false positives, an alternative to the simultaneous lineup procedure was developed by Lindsay and Wells (1985). They created the sequential lineup procedure, in which lineup members are shown serially to witnesses. Once a lineup member is shown, the witness must decide whether that lineup member is the culprit. Witnesses are not allowed to reexamine previously shown lineup members or to proceed in the sequence until they have made a decision about the lineup member currently being shown. Essentially, witnesses are not allowed to examine more than one lineup member at a time. Lindsay and Wells (1985) suggested that witnesses are likely to use an absolute strategy with the sequential lineup. That is, the witness compares each lineup member with his/her memory of the culprit, and only if there is a match will the lineup member be identified as the culprit.

The third identification procedure that can be used with witnesses is known as a *show-up*. The witness is shown one person, the suspect. This procedure has been criticized for increasing pressure on the witness to make an identification because it is clear who the police suspect. Very few studies have used the show-up procedure with children.

Identification Studies

The early identification studies used only target-present lineups. For example, Marin, Holmes, Guth, and Kovac (1979) published one of the first studies examining children's identification abilities with the use of a live staged event. Children (5- to 6-year-olds, 8- to 9-year-olds, 12- to 13-year-olds) and adults were exposed to a live target who they would later have to identify from a simultaneous lineup. A significant increase in the correct identification rate was not observed across the different age groupings. Even the youngest children were as accurate as adults at identifying the target. In another early study, Goodman and Reed (1986) examined children (3- to 4-year-olds, 6- to 7-year-olds) and adults who were exposed to an unfamiliar individual. Shown a simultaneous lineup, 6- to 7-year-olds and adults produced a similar correct identification rate (.94 vs. .75, respectively). The younger children (3- to 4-year-olds) had a significantly lower correct identification rate (.38) than the older children and adults. Producing a somewhat different pattern of results, Brigham, Van Verst, and Bothwell (1986) exposed 4th, 8th, and 11th graders to a live staged theft. A six-person simultaneous lineup was used to test identification accuracy. Fourth graders produced a significantly lower correct identification rate than 8th and 11th graders (68% vs. 93% vs. 88%, respectively). Eighth and 11th graders did not differ in their correct identification rates.

Target-absent lineups provide a fuller picture of children's abilities. For example, Parker and Carranza (1989) examined the abilities of 9- to 10-year-olds and adults. Participants were exposed to a slide sequence. A six-person target-present or target-absent simultaneous lineup was used. Shown a target-present lineup, children produced a higher correct identification rate than adults (.33 vs. .08). Shown a target-absent lineup, children produced a lower correct rejection rate than adults (.42 vs. .67). In another study by Parker and Ryan (1993), children (9-year-olds) and adults were exposed to a slide sequence. The identification task in this study consisted of a target-present or target-absent simultaneous or sequential lineup. The typical pattern with the target-present, simultaneous lineup occurred. That is, children produced a correct identification rate similar to that of adults. Children had difficulty with the sequential lineup, however, producing a lower correct identification rate compared with adults. Children produced a lower correct rejection rate compared with adults, regardless of the type of lineup procedure used.

In an attempt to clarify children's identification abilities compared with adults, Pozzulo and Lindsay (1998) conducted a meta-analysis. The identification abilities of four groups of children (4-year-olds, 5–6-year-olds, 9–10-year-olds, and 12–13-year-olds) were compared with those of adults. In addition, moderator variables that may differentially influence the identification accuracy of children and adults were examined (e.g., presence vs. absence of target; method of lineup presentation). Pozzulo and Lindsay (1998) found that preschoolers (M = 4 years) produced a significantly lower correct identification rate than adults (.47 vs. .67, respectively). With studies contrasting the performance of children between 5 and 6 years of age and adults, correct identification rates differed, but not in the expected direction (.71 vs. .54, respectively). Children made significantly more correct identifications than adults. In a comparison of older children (9 to 10 years) with adults, similar correct identification rates were observed between the two groups (.47 vs. .48, respectively). Adolescents (12 to 13 years of age) also maintained adult-level performance in terms of correct identification. Thus, children over 5 years old produced correct identification rates comparable to those of adults. Preschoolers had more difficulty than adults at picking out the target from a lineup that contained the target.

In terms of correct rejections, children of all ages were less likely than adults to correctly reject lineups that did not contain the target (Pozzulo & Lindsay, 1998). More specifically, preschoolers were significantly less likely to correctly reject a target-absent lineup (.39 vs. .98). Although not significant, young children (5- to 6-year-old) made fewer correct rejections than adults (.57 vs. .65, respectively). Older children were significantly less likely to correctly reject a target-absent lineup compared with adults (.41 vs. .70, respectively). Adolescents also were significantly less likely to correctly reject target-absent lineups (.48 vs. .74, respectively). Thus, all children had difficulty with target-absent lineups, choosing to select a lineup member as the target rather than reject the lineup as not containing the target.

In terms of identification procedures, compared with simultaneous lineup presentation, sequential lineups increased the child–adult gap for correct rejections (Pozzulo & Lindsay, 1998). The sequential lineup, a procedure that aids adults in correctly rejecting target-absent lineups over simultaneous presentation, seems particularly challenging for children. The sequential lineup produced higher false positives than the simultaneous lineup for children. It is important to note that the sequential lineup procedures used in the studies reviewed in the meta-analysis (Pozzulo & Lindsay, 1998) differed from the recommended practice outlined by Lindsay and Wells (1985). For example, the participants should be unaware of the number of photographs to be shown. This element can be critical to the sequential procedure, because once witnesses are aware that they are running out of pictures, they are likely to identify someone (Lindsay, Lea, & Fulford, 1991). The sequential procedures used in some of the child studies did not conceal the number of pictures to be shown. Although this procedural modification did not seem to hinder adult performance, it may have had a greater impact on child performance. That is, assuming that children perceive a greater pressure than adults that they should identify someone (Ceci, Toglia, & Ross, 1987), knowing there are few pictures left may increase this pressure and thus increase choosing. See subsequent sections for a further discussion of how pressure may influence children's responding.

Explaining Differences in Recognition versus Identification Studies

Face recognition studies suggest that an adult hit rate is reached by children around 10 to 12 years of age (Chance & Goldstein, 1984). However, children in identification studies reach an adult level of correct identification at a much earlier age. Children as young as 5 years old are able to correctly pick out the target from a lineup. It might be possible to explain this later onset of adult hit rates in face recognition studies compared with identification studies by examining the methodology used in both. Face recognition studies use a greater number of targets than identification studies: 20 targets versus 1 target, respectively. Consequently, face recognition studies may be demonstrating a developmental trend in memory load capacity rather than recognition/identification per se. With memory load relatively low in identification studies, and likely in some real cases, strains on encoding, storage, and retrieval that are relevant in face recognition studies may be less of a concern in the applied context for child witnesses over 5 years of age.

    Also different between the two types of studies is the false-alarm rate and correct rejection rate. As children get older, their false-alarm rate decreases and approaches adult level around 10 to 12 years of age. In the identification literature, a less optimistic picture emerges when children's correct rejection rates are compared with those of adults. Even the oldest group of children examined in Pozzulo and Lindsay's (1998) meta-analysis produced a correct rejection rate that was significantly lower than that of adults. Moreover, the rate of correct rejection did not appear to increase substantially from the time children were 9 to 10 years old to the time they were 12 to 13 years old. Identification studies have not yet determined the age at which adolescents reach adult correct rejection rates. But it does seem that this age differs from that found in the face recognition literature. Furthermore, the age at which correct identifications are made at an adult rate is not the same age at which adult-level performance is reached with regard to correct rejections. In contrast, the age that children's hits and false-alarm rates reach adult levels in face recognition studies seem to be the same. The different ages for adult performance across correct identification and correct rejection may be suggestive of performance being driven by different processes in the eyewitness context. Correct identification rates may be predominately determined by cognitive memory processes, such as encoding, whereas correct rejection rates (and thus false-positive rates) may be highly influenced by social factors, such as an expectation to make an identification, as well as cognitive factors.

Children's Identification Abilities: The Challenge for the Criminal Justice System

Although children as young as 5 years are as accurate as adults at picking out a target from a target-present lineup, their higher false-positive rate poses a number of difficulties for the criminal justice system. Two types of false-positive lineup decisions are possible, with varying consequences for the person identified and the witness (Wells, 1984). A false positive may be an identification of either an innocent suspect (false identification) or a known-to-be-innocent lineup member (foil identification). An innocent suspect who is identified may be prosecuted while the culprit remains at large, possibly committing further crimes. Although foils are not prosecuted because such identifications are known errors, foil identifications damage the credibility of the witness. Maintaining witness credibility may be important for two reasons. First, other testimony by the witness may be less credible after a known identification error, because such errors suggest both that the witness' memory is faulty and that the witness is willing to report inaccurate memories. Second, if police find another suspect they wish to place in a lineup, an identification decision from a witness who has made a known error in a previous lineup is unlikely to be considered reliable.

An identification procedure is needed that increases children's correct rejection rates, ideally to a level reached by adults when a sequential lineup is used, and maintains a high level of correct identification. One potential guide for increasing children's correct rejection rates is to determine why accuracy differs in target-present versus target-absent lineups. Speculations on various possibilities for differential identification performance between children and adults across target-present versus target-absent lineups are described below.

Why Do Children Produce More False Positives Than Adults (with Target-Absent Lineups)?

Demand. The lineup task itself may exert pressure on the witness to make an identification, to select someone (Ceci et al., 1987). The pressure is further increased given it is presented by an authority figure such as a police officer or experimenter. Moreover, the authority figure is an adult. Children may be more susceptible than adults to adults' questions, and children may be more willing to please than adults. Thus, children may be more likely than adults to provide the answers they think the adults want. Once a witness is asked if the target is among the photographs shown, a child may infer the task is to select one of them. Children may perceive that not selecting a lineup member is an undesirable response. A target-present lineup elicits a correct response because children see the target, select the target, and make an identification. A target-absent lineup elicits an incorrect response because children think they need to make an identification and consequently select a lineup member. The perceived pressure to pick someone may be lower for adults, or adults may be better able to resist such pressure. Thus, adults are less likely to make an identification than children when shown a target-absent lineup. On the other hand, adults' higher choosing rate with simultaneous lineups compared with sequential presentation suggests that adults are not immune from the pressure to make an identification.

If the feeling of pressure explains children's higher false-positive rate compared with adults, identification procedures should be geared toward reducing children's expectation to make an identification. Some researchers have used practice lineup trials in an attempt to decrease children's expectations to make an identification (Davies, Stevenson-Robb, & Flin, 1988; Parker & Ryan, 1993; Pozzulo & Lindsay, 1999). These studies and their success rate are reviewed later in the chapter.

Processing Strategy.   Face recognition studies suggest that children may encode faces with the use of a a strategy that is different from that of adults: featural versus holistic, respectively. As stated above, a higher recognition accuracy for faces is found when participants use a holistic rather than a featural strategy (Bower & Karlin, 1974; Wells & Hryciw, 1984; Winograd, 1976). Some data from the face recognition literature suggests that children under 10 years are more likely to use a featural strategy to encode unfamiliar faces, whereas adults are more likely to use a holistic strategy (Carey & Diamond, 1977; Diamond & Carey, 1977). A featural strategy may explain the difference in identification rates for children and adults across target-present and target-absent lineups.

If a face is encoded via one or a few features, this feature(s) may be sufficient to produce a correct identification with a target-present lineup. For example, a child may have focused on and encoded a target's hairstyle. When examining a target-present lineup, the child matches his/her memory of the hairstyle with the target's hairstyle in the lineup, resulting in a correct identification, provided the lineup does not consist of lineup members who are overly similar to the target (clones). Relative to the other lineup members, it is likely that the target would have the hairstyle most similar to the child's memory. With a target-absent lineup, holistic processing is necessary for correctly rejecting the lineup. It is not sufficient to match one feature when examining a target-absent lineup. A lineup member may have a similar or even the same hairstyle as the target but not be the target. Thus, other facial information is necessary to make a correct decision. If children are not using a holistic approach, it is likely that they will reach an erroneous decision with a target-absent lineup.

Memory Trace.   Differences in encoding also may lead to differences in memory strength such that memory strength increases with age (and declines in later years, as seen in the elderly). A weaker memory trace may lower the threshold for a match between memory and lineup member. A lineup member who resembles the target somewhat is selected and identified. An innocent lineup member is selected in a target-absent lineup because he or she provides a sufficient level of similarity to the child's, but not the adult's, memory of the target.

Research specifically designed to examine the causes of higher false-positive responses in children compared with adults with a target-absent lineup is necessary before definitive conclusions can be reached regarding the specific causes of this effect.

Attempts at Increasing Children's Identification Accuracy

The Role of Training.   In an attempt to increase children's identification accuracy and more specifically children's correct rejection rate, a number of researchers have examined the use of practice lineups and identification training (Davies, Stevenson-Robb, & Flin, 1988; Goodman, Bottoms, Schwartz-Kenney, & Rudy, 1991; Parker & Myers, 2001; Parker & Ryan, 1993; Pozzulo & Lindsay, 1997). Training has typically consisted of exposing participants to an event, as in typical identification studies, and, prior to the identification task, participants are shown an unrelated lineup and are given practice with feedback. The identification decision made on the practice lineups may be that of the child participant or may be modeled by another child, possibly via videotape.

Davies et al. (1988) showed children two three-person simultaneous lineups: a target-present lineup for practice, followed by a target-absent lineup for the actual identification test. For the practice identification, children were asked to pick out the photo of the experimenter. During examination of the accuracy of the actual identification task, practice was not helpful at increasing correct rejections. Using different forms of practice, Pozzulo and Lindsay (1997) attempted to determine whether a demonstration video of accurate decision making with a six-person, simultaneous lineup or a handout illustrating accurate decision making with a six-animal, simultaneous lineup would increase identification accuracy. Surprisingly, the correct identification rate increased for children, but no increase in correct rejections was observed. In contrast to these findings, using three practice lineups, two target-present and one target-absent, Goodman et al. (1991) found a reduction in false positives from target-absent lineups.

Much of the training with children has been done with simultaneous lineups. However, Parker and Ryan (1993) used practice in an attempt to improve identification accuracy from simultaneous and sequential lineups. They used two three-person practice lineups (a target-present lineup followed by a target-absent lineup) in a simultaneous or sequential format. If practice would be helpful with the sequential lineup for children, the criminal justice system could use sequential lineups for both child and adult witnesses. Parker and Ryan (1993) found an increase in correct rejections following practice, but only for simultaneous lineups. Practice was not helpful with sequential presentation. In another study, Parker and Myers (2001) tried practice to increase identification accuracy from sequential lineups with children. In an elaborate design, either participants practiced themselves or practice was modeled. These conditions were crossed with the content of the practice lineups. That is, practice lineups consisted of either two target-absent sequential lineups or a target-absent and a target-present sequential lineup. Moreover, data were divided by gender. As was the case with Pozzulo and Lindsay (1997), practice improved the correct identification rate, but only for females. Practice did not improve the correct rejection rates for females or males.

In their meta-analysis, Pozzulo and Lindsay (1998) reviewed the identification studies that used training to increase children's identification accuracy. Children (9 to 14 years old) who were given practice were not more likely to correctly reject target-absent lineups than children (of the same age group) who were not given practice. Intriguingly, 9- to 10-year-olds who received training were more likely to make a correct identification than children who did not receive training. The effect size was small, however ($d = .29$).

Although practice may not be effective at increasing children's correct rejection rates, it may have some positive effects for increasing correct identification rates. Further research should more clearly delineate the type of practice that may be beneficial for increasing correct identification rates and the mechanisms that are involved. Once again, these results may suggest that correct identifications and correct rejections are driven by different processes. Greater understanding of these mechanisms may explain why practice is not effective at increasing correct rejections.

A New Identification Procedure.   Given the limited positive effects of training on increasing correct rejections, Pozzulo and Lindsay (1999) sought to develop an identification procedure specifically geared toward child witnesses. The researchers hypothesized a two-judgment theory of identification accuracy. They postulated that first, witnesses use a relative judgment to narrow down the lineup members to the one person who looks most like the culprit. Once this judgment is made, witnesses use an absolute judgment to decide whether that most similar person is in fact the culprit. Pozzulo and Lindsay (1999) reasoned that children may be less likely to make the second, absolute judgment, than adults, thus leading to higher rates of false-positive responding. They proposed that children may not be using an absolute judgment because of a feeling of pressure to make a selection/identification (why else would I be shown a lineup if not to pick someone out?). With a target-present lineup, a differential in correct identification rates between children and adults is not observed, because children feel pressure to make an identification, see the culprit, and identify the culprit. With a target-absent lineup, children feel greater pressure than adults to make an identification, so an innocent lineup member is selected, thus producing a lower correct rejection rate than adults.

Based on the two-judgment theory and the notion of an increased feeling of pressure to make an identification, Pozzulo and Lindsay (1999) developed an identification procedure whereby the simultaneous lineup explicitly required two judgments from the child witness. First the witness is asked to make a relative judgment and select the lineup member who looks most like the culprit. Once that person is selected, the remaining lineup members are removed, and the witness is asked to make an absolute judgment, that is, to compare his/her memory of the culprit with the selected lineup member to decide whether that lineup member is in fact the culprit. The lineup procedure was termed the "elimination lineup."

Pozzulo and Lindsay (1999) developed various versions of the elimination procedure by altering how the instructions were phrased. They compared these elimination procedures with the simultaneous procedure using both child and adult participants. The elimination procedure was shown to be effective at increasing the correct rejection rate while maintaining the correct identification rate compared with the simultaneous procedure for child witnesses. This pattern of identification rates, however, was not observed for adult witnesses. The simultaneous and elimination procedures produced comparable correct identification and rejection rates for adult witnesses.

The elimination procedure presents a promising procedure for increasing children's identification accuracy. One major difficulty with having different procedures for child and adult witnesses is determining the age at which a child ceases performing as a child. The criminal justice system would require knowing age ranges for identification procedures, so that witnesses would be presented with the age-appropriate lineup procedure. Future research may wish to explore these developmental ranges.

A Note on Methodology and Generalizability of Identification Studies

Although identification studies use more ecologically valid methodology than face recognition studies, a number of differences remain between the experiences of a "real" witness and a witness in a laboratory study. Researchers test children's identification abilities following exposure to slides or videotapes or personally experienced events. The major criticism against using slides or a videotape exposure relates to whether these exposures parallel experienced stressful events (Lindberg, Jones, Collard, & Thomas, 2001).

Steward and Steward (1996) have proposed that the results of bystander eyewitness research may underestimate a child's ability at recall and identification compared with victims. Some studies have demonstrated that compared with bystanders, those who experience the event have improved memory (e.g., Baker-Ward, Hess, & Flannagan, 1990; Jones, Swift, & Johnson, 1988; Rudy & Goodman, 1991; Tobey & Goodman, 1992). To compare the differences between watching a stressful event and experiencing a stressful event, Lindberg, Jones, Collard, and Thomas (2001) followed 5-year-olds with a video camera as they received their inoculations. Each child was matched to a similar child who was to merely watch the videotape. Children were tested at different intervals (20 minutes after the event versus 1 month later). Stress and direct experience affected the memory of items congruent with the stressor, such as the identification of the nurses. Results indicated that children in the videotape condition may underestimate accuracy for items congruent with the stressor after longer delays. In Pozzulo and Lindsay's meta-analysis (1998), they also found that videotape or slide sequence exposure underestimated children's ability to make a correct rejection compared with live exposure. That is, a smaller child-adult gap for correct rejections was observed when a live exposure was used than when a slide exposure was used. This point is important methodologically, given that most identification studies use a videotape or slide sequence to expose participants to a target.

These results need to be reconciled with other literature that finds high anxiety leading to lower face recognition accuracy (Shapiro & Penrod, 1986). In one study by Peters (1991), children's ability to accurately recognize the dentist following a dental visit was examined. He found that children who were highly anxious were less accurate at recognizing the dentist than less anxious children.

The relation between stress/anxiety and identification is complicated. Although direct experience may increase identification accuracy, stress may lower it. When applying identification results to the real world, it is important to consider the role of stress and experience (see Pickel, this volume).

Future Directions for Identification Research

Theoretical. At this point, the processes engaged in by children and adults making an identification decision are unclear. We need to understand how these processes are similar and different across target-present and target-absent lineups and for different ages. Both cognitive (e.g., encoding) and social (e.g., expectations, pressure) factors should be examined to provide a more adequate explanation of witnesses' performance. Research has yet to tackle whether errors (or accurate decisions) made by children and adults occur for the same reasons.

Methodological.   The methods used in face recognition and identification studies should be examined to better explain the differing pattern of results. The reliance on videotape and slide sequence in both face recognition and identification studies should be more closely examined. More studies should employ live targets. Videotape and slide paradigms may obscure the age at which children produce adult correct rejection rates.

Application of the Child Witness Literature.   If courts are to accept child identification evidence, it is imperative to know the age at which children's performance approximates that of adults and to be able to estimate accuracy rates for children of all ages. A number of age groups have been neglected in identification research: preschoolers and children under 8 years, and children over 12 years and adolescents. We are uncertain about the age at which children are too young to provide reliable identification evidence and the age at which children/adolescents have reached adult-level performance.

Some research has provided impetus for alternative identification procedures to be used with children. Further research in this direction may increase children's identification accuracy. Moreover, a procedure may be developed that is suitable for all age ranges.

RELATION BETWEEN AGE, IDENTIFYING, AND DESCRIBING

As mentioned at the beginning of this chapter, descriptions tend to be limited and vague. These types of descriptions may suggest that the witness did not get a good look at the culprit or has a poor memory of the culprit. Unfortunately, briefer descriptions are characteristic of children and youths. The criminal justice system may perceive children and youth as bad witnesses who should not attempt an identification. However, the relation between description and identification may be tenuous for a variety of reasons (for both youths and adults).

Providing a description is a recall task dependent on verbal ability, whereas identification is a recognition task that is almost independent of linguistic demands (other than being able to understand the task instructions). Wells (1984) has suggested that recall and recognition tasks may be driven by different processes. Ellis (1984) suggests that verbal processes may be irrelevant to encoding and the recognition of faces (also, Chance & Goldstein, 1976; Goldstein, Johnson, & Chance, 1979; Malpass, Lavigueur, & Weldon, 1973). Also, it has been suggested that retrieval cues for recall tasks may differ from those for recognition tasks (Flexser & Tulving, 1978). In examination of the relation between description accuracy and identification accuracy for adults, a significant relation has not been found (Cutler, Penrod, & Martens, 1987; Pigott & Brigham, 1985; Pigott, Brigham, & Bothwell, 1990). However, Sporer (1996) reported a significant relationship between description length (number of descriptors) and correct identification decisions for adults.

Witnesses who made a correct decision reported more descriptors (M = 6.52) than witnesses who made an incorrect decision (M = 5.16).

Pozzulo and Warren (2003) found that youths (10 to 14 years old) provided fewer descriptors than adults, regardless of identification accuracy. Description length did not predict the identification accuracy from a youth witness. Description length also did not appear to be a good marker for identification accuracy from adults.

Policy Implications and Police Recommendations

Children may be witnesses to a variety of crimes, such as theft, vandalism, and murder. In some cases the children also are the victims of crime, as is the case with physical or sexual abuse. When the crime witnessed or experienced by the child occurs at the hands of someone known to the child such as a parent, description and identification are less of an issue. Identifying a familiar person is more about the issue of whether the child is telling the truth. This chapter focused on children's abilities to identify an unfamiliar target. It should be noted that there are no known published *identification* studies of familiar targets. Some face recognition literature has examined how children process features of a familiar versus an unfamiliar face, however.

It is most likely that the criminal justice system is concerned with children's abilities to accurately identify unfamiliar persons in a lineup identification task. On a positive note, children as young as 5 years old can accurately identify a guilty suspect from a simultaneous lineup at the same rate as adults. Unfortunately, in those cases where police have arrested an innocent suspect, children, even over 12 years of age, are more likely than adults to make an identification of an innocent person. Of course, police have no way of knowing whether they have arrested a guilty or innocent suspect—thus the main reason for seeking a lineup identification. Not all identifications from target-absent lineups will be of the suspect. Foil identifications are known errors. Police can easily disregard foil identifications from both children and adults. Foil identifications, however, jeopardize the credibility of the witness, perhaps making his or her testimony about other crime details less believable.

There may be methods for increasing children's accuracy with target-absent lineups. For example, a new identification procedure, the elimination lineup, provides a promising alternative to the simultaneous lineup. Further research should be conducted with this procedure to determine its usefulness in real cases. Moreover, it may be possible to modify the procedure further to increase children's and adults' identification accuracy.

In the absence of alternative identification procedures, it may be possible to increase lineup size to reduce false identifications. Consider that the estimated false identification rate of a given lineup is 1 divided by the number of lineup members. With increasing lineup size, the false identification rate decreases. Research may be directed at examining how large lineups can be before children's correct identification rates begin to decline.

A dilemma arises in considering the trade-off between children's adult level performance for correct identifications and lower correct rejections. This decision may need to be made in light of the circumstances in each case, rather than have a general policy for all child witness identification evidence. For example, the justice system may want to seriously consider child identification when there is additional circumstantial evidence such as fingerprints. In contrast, in cases where there is only a child identification of the suspect and absolutely no other evidence linking the suspect to the crime, other suspects may be examined. This type of case may be more challenging to prosecute, given the data we currently have. It is critical that child identification research is continued, given its persuasiveness in the criminal justice system. That is, adult misidentification has been found to be the leading cause of wrongful convictions (Wells et al., 1998). Ultimately, procedures need to be improved to increase children's accuracy.

REFERENCES

Baenninger, M. (1994). The development of face recognition: Featural or configurational processing? *Journal of Experimental Child Psychology, 57,* 377–396.

Baker-Ward, L., Hess, T. M., & Flannagan, D. A. (1990). The effects of involvement on children's memory for events. *Cognitive Development, 5,* 55–70.

Bartlett, J. C., & Searcy, J. (1993). Inversion and configuration of faces. *Cognitive Psychology, 25,* 281–316.

Blaney, R. L., & Winograd, E. (1978). Developmental differences in children's recognition memory for faces. *Developmental Psychology, 14,* 441–442.

Bower, G. H., & Karlin, M. B. (1974). Levels of processing: A framework for memory research. *Journal of Verbal Learning and Verbal Behavior, 11,* 671–684.

Bradshaw, J. L., & Wallace, G. (1971). Models for the processing and identification of faces. *Perception & Psychophysics, 9,* 443–448.

Brigham, J. C., Van Verst, M., & Bothwell, R. K. (1986). Accuracy of children's eyewitness identifications in a field setting. *Basic and Applied Social Psychology, 7,* 295–306.

Campbell, R., Walker, J., & Baron-Cohen, S. (1995). The development of differential use of inner and outer face features in familiar face identification. *Journal of Experimental Child Psychology, 59,* 196–210.

Carey, S. (1981). The development of face perception. In G. Davies, H. Ellis, & J. Shepherd (Eds.), *Perceiving and remembering faces* (pp. 9–38). New York: Academic Press.

Carey, S., & Diamond, R. (1977). From piecemeal to configurational representation of faces. *Science, 195,* 312–314.

Carey, S., Diamond, R., & Woods, B. (1980). Development of face recognition: A maturational component? *Developmental Psychology, 16,* 257–269.

Ceci, S. J., & Bruck, M. (1993). Suggestibility of the child witness: A historical review and synthesis. *Psychological Bulletin, 113,* 403–439.

Ceci, S. J., Toglia, M. P., & Ross, D. F. (1987). *Children's eyewitness memory.* New York: Springer-Verlag.

Chance, J., & Goldstein, A. (1976). Recognition of faces and verbal labels. *Bulletin of the Psychonomic Society, 7,* 384–387.

Chance, J. E., & Goldstein, A. G. (1979). Reliability of face recognition performance. *Bulletin of the Psychonomic Society, 14,* 115–117.

Chance, J. E., & Goldstein, A. G. (1984). Face-recognition memory: Implications for children's eyewitness testimony. *Journal of Social Issues, 40,* 69–85.

Chance, J. E., Turner, A. L., & Goldstein, A. G. (1982). Development of differential recognition of own- and other-race faces. *Journal of Psychology, 112,* 29–37.

Chung, M., & Thomson, D. M. (1995). Development of face recognition. *British Journal of Psychology, 86,* 55–87.

Clifford, B. R., & Bull, R. (1978). *The psychology of person identification.* London: Routledge & Kegan Paul.

Comparo, L. B., Wagner, J. T., & Saywitz, K. J. (2001). Interviewing children about real and fictitious events: Revisiting the narrative elaboration procedure. *Law and Human Behavior, 25,* 63–80.

Cross, J. F., Cross, J., & Daly, J. (1971). Sex, race, age, and beauty as factors in recognition of faces. *Perception and Psychophysics, 10,* 393–396.

Cutler, B. L., Penrod, S. D., & Martens, T. K. (1987). Improving the reliability of eyewitness identifications: Putting context into context. *Journal of Applied Psychology, 72,* 629–637.

Davies, G. (1996). Children's identification evidence. In S. Sporer, R. Malpass, & G. Koehnken (Eds.), *Psychological issues in eyewitness identification* (pp. 233–258). Mahwah, NJ: Lawrence Erlbaum Associates.

Davies, G. M., Stevenson-Robb, Y., & Flin, R. (1988). Tales out of school: Children's memory for a simulated health inspection. In M. Gruneberg, P. Morris, & R. Sykes (Eds.), *Practical aspects of memory: Current research and issues: Vol. 1. Memory in everyday life* (pp. 122–127). Chichester, England: Wiley.

Davies, G., Tarrant, A., & Flin, R. (1989). Close encounters of the witness kind: Children's memory for a simulated health inspection. *British Journal of Psychology, 80,* 415–429.

Dent, H. (1982). The effects of interviewing strategies on the results of interviews with child witnesses. In A. Trankell (Ed.), *Reconstructing the past* (pp. 279–298). Dordrecht, the Netherlands: Kluwer.

Dent, H., & Stephenson, G. (1979). An experimental study of the effectiveness of different techniques of questioning child witnesses. *British Journal of Social and Clinical Psychology, 18,* 41–51.

Diamond, R., & Carey, S. (1977). Developmental changes in the recognition of faces. *Journal of Experimental Child Psychology, 23,* 1–22.

Diamond, R., & Carey, S. (1986). Why faces are and are not special: An effect of expertise. *Journal of Experimental Psychology: General, 115,* 107–117.

Ellis, H. D. (1984). Practical aspects of face memory. In G. L. Wells & E. F. Loftus (Eds.), *Eyewitness testimony: Psychological perspectives* (pp. 12–37). New York: Cambridge University Press.

Ellis, H. D. (1992).The development of face processing skills. *Proceedings of the Royal Society, Series B, 335,* 105–111.

Ellis, H. D., & Flin, R. H. (1990). Encoding and storage effects in 7-year-olds' and 10-year-olds' memory for faces. *British Journal of Developmental Psychology, 8,* 77–92.

Ellis, H. D., Shepherd, J., & Bruce, A. (1973). The effects of age and sex upon adolescents' recognition of faces. *Journal of Genetic Psychology, 123,* 173–174.

Ellis, H. D., Shepherd, J. W., & Davies, G. M. (1980). The deterioration of verbal descriptions of faces over different delay intervals. *Journal of Police Science and Administration, 8,* 101–106.

Farah, M. J., Tanaka, J. W., & Drain, H. M. (1995). What causes the face inversion effect? *Journal of Experimental Psychology: Human Perception and Performance, 21,* 628–634.

Farah, M. J., Wilson, K. D., Drain, H. M., & Tanaka, J. W. (1998). What is "special" about face perception? *Psychological Review, 105,* 482–498.

Feinman, S., & Entwistle, D. R. (1976). Children's ability to recognize other children's faces. *Child Development, 47,* 506–510.

Flexser, A. J., & Tulving, E. (1978). Retrieval independence in recognition and recall. *Psychological Review, 85,* 153–171.

Flin, R. H. (1980). Age effects in children's memory for unfamiliar faces. *Developmental Psychology, 16*, 373–374.

Flin, R. H., & Shepherd, J.W. (1986). Tall stories: Eyewitnesses' ability to estimate height and weight characteristics. *Human Learning, 5*, 29–38.

Friere, A., & Lee, K. (2001). Face recognition in 4- to 7-year-olds: Processing of Configural, featural, and paraphernalia information. *Journal of Experimental Child Psychology, 80*, 347–371.

Goldstein, A. G. (1977). The fallibility of the eyewitness: Psychological evidence. In B. D. Sales (Ed.), *Psychology in the legal process*. New York: Spectrum.

Goldstein, A. G., & Chance, J. F. (1964). Recognition of children's faces. *Child Development, 35*, 129–136.

Goldstein, A. G., Johnson, K. S., & Chance, J. E. (1979). Does fluency of face description imply superior face recognition? *Bulletin of the Psychonomic Society, 13*, 15–18.

Goodman, G. S., Bottoms, B. L., Schwartz-Kenney, B., & Rudy, L. (1991). Children's memory for a stressful event: Improving children's reports. *Journal of Narrative and Life History, 1*, 69–99.

Goodman, G., & Reed, R. (1986). Age differences in eyewitness testimony. *Law and Human Behavior, 10*, 317–332.

Hay, D. C., & Cox, R. (2000). Developmental changes in the recognition of faces and facial features. *Infant and Child Development, 9*, 199–212.

Hochberg, J., & Galper, E. (1967). Recognition of faces: 1. An exploratory study. *Psychonomic Society, 9*, 619–620.

Jones, D. C., Swift, D. J., & Johnson, M. A. (1988). Nondeliberate memory for a novel event among preschoolers. *Developmental Psychology, 24*, 641–645.

Kuehn, L. L. (1974). Looking down a gun barrel: Person perception and violent crime. *Perceptual and Motor Skills, 39*, 1159–1164.

Lindberg, M. A., Jones, S., Collard, L. M., & Thomas, S. W. (2001). Similarities and differences in eyewitness testimonies of children who directly versus vicariously experience stress. *The Journal of Genetic Psychology, 162*, 314–333.

Lindsay, R. C. L., Lea, J. A., & Fulford, J. A. (1991). Sequential lineup presentation: Technique matters. *Journal of Applied Psychology, 76*, 741–745.

Lindsay, R. C. L., Martin, R., & Webber, L. (1994). Default values in eyewitness descriptions. *Law and Human Behavior, 18*, 527–541.

Lindsay, R. C. L., Pozzulo, J. D., Craig, W., Lee, K., & Corber, S. (1997). Simultaneous lineups, sequential lineups, and showups: Eyewitness identification decisions of adults and children. *Law and Human Behavior, 21*, 391–404.

Lindsay, R. C. L., & Wells, G. L. (1985). Improving eyewitness identifications from lineups: Simultaneous versus sequential lineup presentations. *Journal of Applied Psychology, 70*, 556–564.

Luus, C. A. E., & Wells, G. L. (1991). Eyewitness identification and the selection of distracters for lineups. *Law and Human Behavior, 15*, 43–57.

Malpass, R. S., Lavigueur, H., & Weldon, D. E. (1973). Verbal and visual training in face recognition. *Perception and Psychophysics, 14*, 285–292.

Marin, B. V., Holmes, D. L., Guth, M., & Kovac, P. (1979). The potential of children as eyewitnesses. *Law and Human Behavior, 3*, 295–305.

Parker, J. F., & Carranza, L. E. (1989). Eyewitness testimony of children in target-present and target-absent lineups. *Law and Human Behavior, 13*, 133–149.

Parker, J. F., & Myers, A. (2001). Attempts to improve children's identifications from sequential-presentation lineups. *Journal of Applied Social Psychology, 21*, 796–815.

Parker, J. F., & Ryan, V. (1993). An attempt to reduce guessing behavior in children's and adults' eyewitness identifications. *Law and Human Behavior, 17*, 11–26.

Peters, D. P. (1991). The influence of stress and arousal on the child witness. In J. L. Doris (Ed.), *The suggestibility of children's recollections* (pp. 60–76). Washington, DC: American Psychological Association.

Pigott, M. A., & Brigham, J. C. (1985). Relationship between accuracy of prior description and facial recognition. *Journal of Applied Psychology, 70*, 547–555.

Pigott, M. A., Brigham, J. C., & Bothwell, R. K. (1990). A field study on the relationship between quality of eyewitnesses' descriptions and identification accuracy. *Journal of Police Science and Administration, 17*, 84–88.

Pozzulo, J. D., & Lindsay, R. C. L. (1997). Increasing correct identifications by children. *Expert Evidence, 5*, 126–132.

Pozzulo, J. D., & Lindsay, R. C. L. (1998). Identification accuracy of children versus adults: A meta-analysis. *Law and Human Behavior, 22*, 549–570.

Pozzulo, J. D., & Lindsay, R. C. L. (1999). Elimination lineups: An improved identification procedure for child eyewitnesses. *Journal of Applied Psychology, 84*, 167–176.

Pozzulo, J. D., & Warren, K. L. (2003). Descriptions and identifications of strangers by child and adult witnesses. *Journal of Applied Psychology, 88*, 315–323.

Rhodes, G. (1988). Looking at face: First-order and second-order features as determinants of facial appearance. *Perception, 17*, 43–63.

Rudy, L. & Goodman, G. S. (1991). Effects of participation on children's report: Implications for children testimony. *Developmental Psychology, 27*, 527–538.

Saywitz, K., & Camparo, L. (1998). Interviewing child witnesses: A developmental perspective. *Child Abuse and Neglect, 22*, 825–843.

Scapinello, K. F., & Yarmey, A. D. (1970). The role of familiarity and orientation in immediate and delayed recall of pictorial stimuli. *Psychonomic Science, 21*, 329–330.

Schwarzer, G. (2000). Development of face processing: The effect of face inversion. *Child Development, 71*, 391–401.

Sergent, J. (1984). An investigation into component and configural processes underlying face perception. *The British Journal of Psychology, 75*, 221–242.

Shapiro, P. N., & Penrod, S. (1986). Meta-analysis of facial identification studies. *Psychological Bulletin, 100*, 139–156.

Sporer, S. L. (1996). Psychological aspects of person descriptions. In S. Sporer, R. Malpass, & G. Koehnken (Eds.), *Psychological issues in eyewitness identification* (pp. 53–86). Mahwah, NJ: Lawrence Erlbaum Associates.

Steward, M. S., & Steward, D. S. (1996). Interviewing young children about body touch and handling. *Monographs of the Society for Research in Child Development, 61*, 4–5.

Tanaka, J. W., & Farah, M. J. (1993). Parts and wholes in face recognition. *Quarterly Journal of Experimental Psychology, 46*, 225–245.

Tanaka, J. W., Kay, J. B., Grinnell, E., Stansfield, B., & Szechter, L. (1998). Face recognition in young children: When the whole is greater than the sum of its parts. *Visual Cognition, 5*, 479–496.

Tobey, A., & Goodman, G. S. (1992). Children's eyewitness memory: Effects of participation and forensic context. *Child Abuse and Neglect, 16*, 779–796.

Wells, G. L. (1984). The psychology of lineup identifications. *Journal of Applied Social Psychology, 14*, 89–103.

Wells, G. L. (1993). What do we know about eyewitness identification? *American Psychologist, 48*, 553–571.

Wells, G. L., & Hryciw, B. (1984). Memory for faces: Encoding and retrieval operations. *Memory & Cognition, 12*, 338–344.

Wells, G. L., Small, M., Penrod, S., Malpass, R. S., Fulero, S. M., & Brimacombe, C. A. E. (1998). Eyewitness identification procedures: Recommendations for lineups and photospreads. *Law and Human Behavior, 22*, 603–647.

Winograd, E. (1976). Recognition memory for faces following nine different judgements. *Bulletin of the Psychonomic Society, 8*, 419–421.

Yin, R. K. (1969). Looking at upside-down faces. *Journal of Experimental Psychology, 81*, 141–145.

13

Eyewitness Memory in Young and Older Adults

James C. Bartlett
University of Texas at Dallas

Amina Memon
University of Aberdeen

Why study performance by the older eyewitness? As one of us wrote recently in another context, "If sheer neglect of a topic can justify its being studied, then surely our question is answered" (Halpern & Bartlett, 2002). The voluminous literature on eyewitness testimony includes many thousands of studies assessing young-adult performance and a growing number of studies (certainly several hundred) assessing performance by children. By contrast, the major journals for work on aging and cognition (e.g., *Psychology and Aging, Journal of Gerontology*), contain only a sprinkling of articles on aging and eyewitness performance, and the major journals publishing eyewitness research (e.g., *Law and Human Behavior, Legal and Criminological Psychology, Applied Cognitive Psychology*) contain fewer still.

This situation needs changing for at least three different reasons. The first is simply the need to establish the generality and ecological validity—and forensic applicability—of our research findings. Young adults like those used in most eyewitness studies are not the only witnesses to crime in real life. Middle-aged and older adults are more likely to witness crimes (Bornstein, 1995) and often are asked to view identification lineups (Rothmans, Dunlop, & Entzel, 2000) and testify in other ways. We clearly need to know if the conclusions we have reached in assessing young adults and children apply to other age groups.

The second reason pertains to recent evidence (e.g., Yarmey, Jones, & Rashid, 1984; 1984: Ross, Dunning, Toglia, & Ceci, 1990; Kwong See, Hoffman, & Wood, 2001) that, although older eyewitnesses are perceived by mock jurors as honest and valuable, by some measures they appear to be regarded as less accurate in their testimony, as well as less persuasive, than are young adults. Although this result is not always obtained (see Brima-

combe, Jung, Garrioch, & Allison, 2003), there is cause for suggesting that, in some conditions, an age stereotype might reduce the credibility of the older eyewitness.

An age stereotype applied to the older eyewitness might be viewed as justified based
on much evidence for age-related deficits in memory performance (see, e.g., Anderson
& Craik, 2000; Salthouse, 2004). However, if the literature on aging and memory tells us
anything at all, it tells us that age-related deficits are not found across the board. Rather,
they vary across different subsets of seniors, being larger, for example, among seniors
with less formal education and lower verbal skill (particularly verbal memory; see Rice
& Meyer, 1986) and among seniors with signs of mild deficits in frontally mediated
controlled processes and/or medial-temporal mnemonic processes (Glisky, Polster, &
Routhieaux, 1995; Glisky, Rubin, & Davidson, 2001; Henkel, Johnson, & De Leonardis,
1998; Butler, McDaniel, Dornburg, Roediger, & Price, 2004). These deficits also vary
across different variants of memory tasks, often increasing in situations that place controlled processes such as conscious recollection in opposition to more automatic memory
processes (Balota, Dolan, & Duchek, 2000), and diminishing with provision of "environmental support" for the processes that are needed for successful performance (Craik, 1986;
Anderson & Craik, 2000).

Environmental support is a concept of great relevance to eyewitness memory, and it
comes up several times in the course of this chapter. It is a broad concept, referring to a
variety of conditions that might provide information or trigger a process that is useful in
a task. When the task involves memory, one important type of environmental support is
a good retrieval cue: When memory is probed with strong retrieval cues (e.g., exact
copies of previously studied words in a test of verbal recognition memory), age differences are smaller than with weak cues (e.g., the simple instruction to recall a list of previously studied words in a test of verbal recall memory). The concept is important in the
eyewitness situation, where retrieval cues are often weak. Verbal testimony regarding
the details of a prior crime event is based on the most impoverished of cues (e.g., *Can
you tell me what you saw that night?*). The lineup task might be viewed as providing a
much better cue—the actual face of a person seen previously at the crime. However, the
appearance of the face will nearly always have changed, and there is very strong evidence that even minor changes in a face's appearance impair recognition (Bruce, 1982;
Davies, & Milne, 1982; Memon & Gabbert, 2003a) and even perceptual matching
when there is no memory load (Bruce et al., 1999).[1] Consider also that the foils in the
lineup can be quite similar to the perpetrator, and we arrive at the conclusion that the
cue in a lineup is not only far from perfect in an absolute sense, but in a relative sense as
well (it may not be any stronger as a reminder than one or more foils). These considerations suggest that age-related deficits in eyewitness testimony are likely to be found, but
not in all conditions. There are many different forms of environmental support, and
some of these may compensate for poor retrieval cues or even work to transform a poor

---

[1]This is not true of well-known faces that can be recognized despite great changes in appearance. However, recognition of a face seen only one time before (as is often required in the lineup situation) is highly
sensitive to even minor alterations.

external cue into a better internal cue. Indeed, the well-known cognitive interview technique (Fisher & Geiselman, 1992) was designed, in part, to accomplish just that.

In view of the evidence that environmental support and other factors are moderators of age differences in memory, it is critical to examine how these various factors work in eyewitness situations. We need to know the conditions in which older witnesses will perform with lower accuracy, as well as the conditions in which they will acquit themselves as well as, or perhaps even better than, young adults. College-educated older people outperform young adults in tests of vocabulary and other types of verbal knowledge (see Salthouse, 2004),[2] and it therefore is possible that, where accurate testimony depends more on verbal knowledge than on attentional resources and processing speed (Anderson & Craik, 2000), age-related improvements in performance will be found.

Perhaps the most important reason to conduct more research on the aging eyewitness is that such research is likely to spawn advances in theory that will illuminate the processes underlying performance in eyewitness tasks. Our understanding of the processes used in standard laboratory tasks such as free recall and old-new recognition has benefited enormously from work on age differences. Indeed, today, seniors often are included in experiments on memory at least partly to address theoretical issues concerning the role of attentional resources and conscious recollection (both known to show age-related reductions) in memory performance (see, e.g., theoretical reviews by Yonelinas, 2002; and Kelley & Jacoby, 2000). The use of older persons in eyewitness research will have a similar positive effect in improving our theories, and this will make possible more and better predictions about the behavior of eyewitnesses in real-life contexts (Memon & Wright, 2000).

We hope to make the case in this chapter that, although research on the older eyewitness is in its infancy, we have already made some important observations, and the stage is well set for further advances that will produce payoffs in cognitive theory and forensic practice. Our review is focused on the best established findings and their implications, but we also discuss issues on which the evidence is scant or mixed but which have, in our opinion, important implications. We start by clarifying what we mean by defining the terms we use to describe individuals in different age groups (*young, middle-aged, old,* etc.). We turn next to research on verbal recall and recognition, treating the currently mixed evidence on misinformation effects in young and older adults. Next we turn to lineup research, focusing on comparisons of young and older eyewitnesses in correct identifications from target-present lineups and correct rejections of target-absent lineups. In the course of this discussion, we examine several factors that appear to moderate age differences, along with other factors that apparently do not. The conclusion section raises some methodological issues and points to areas where new research is needed.

YOUNG, MIDDLE-AGED, AND OLD ADULTS

To the best of our knowledge, no precise definitions of *young, middle-aged,* and *old* or *senior* enjoy wide and formally acknowledged agreement (see Bäckman, Small, & Wahlin, 2000).

---

[2]At least to a point. Salthouse's (2004) data suggest a rise in vocabulary from 20 to 60 years of age, but a mild drop-off after that.

However, the literature on cognitive aging offers some guidance in this area, as the vast majority of studies use an extreme-group design in which "young adults" aged from 18 to no more than 40 years are compared with "old" or "senior" adults aged from 60 to not more than 80 years (see Salthouse, 2000). The prevailing meaning of *middle-aged* is harder to pin down, as relatively few studies include middle-aged participants. However, it seems reasonable at this stage in research to employ that term to refer to persons falling between the young and old age ranges. Hence, in this chapter, we use the words *young* for persons between 20 and 40 years old, *middle-aged* for those between 40 and 60, and *old* and *senior* for those between 60 and 80 (except where explicitly noted). When describing studies comparing "young-old" and "old-old" adults, we note the authors' operational definitions.

VERBAL RECALL AND RECOGNITION

Where straightforward comparisons have been made between different age groups, young adults have been found to be significantly superior to old adults in their accuracy of recall for perpetrator characteristics, environmental details, and details of actions and events (see Yarmey, 2001, for an overview of the literature). This applies to both free recall (where the witness provides a narrative account from his or her own perspective) and to cued recall (where the witness responds to interviewer questions; see Yarmey & Kent, 1980; Yarmey, Jones, & Rashid, 1984). Yarmey averaged the results across three studies (Yarmey, 1982; Yarmey & Kent, 1980; Yarmey et al., 1984) to explore age differences further and found that young adults (mean age of 21 years) were 20% more accurate in free recall, 13% more accurate in cued recall, and 15% more complete in their descriptions of a suspect as compared with old adults (mean age of 70 years). Other studies have shown that old-adult witnesses provide fewer descriptions of the perpetrator (physical and clothing characteristics) than young-adult witnesses (Brimacombe, Quinton, Nance, & Garrioch, 1997). This finding resembles that found in a recent comparison of children with young adults (Pozzulo & Warren, 2003).

Exceptions to this finding of age-related deficits in verbal recall may occur when education and/or verbal skills are uncontrolled, as in a study by Mello and Fisher (1996). These investigators compared standard interview procedures with the cognitive interview (CI) developed by Fisher and Geiselman (1992; Memon, 1999) as well as a variant of the CI developed specifically for old eyewitnesses. The CI increased the amount of information recalled without affecting accuracy in young adults and seniors, but the two groups did not differ in overall performance. Indeed, the positive effects of the CI were stronger among seniors, and the consequence was that the seniors' recall exceeded that of young adults when the CI was employed (the version did not matter).

These are important findings, but, as Mello and Fisher noted, the lack of an age-related deficit in this study may reflect a confounding of age and verbal intelligence: The seniors scored much higher than the young adults on a vocabulary test. A similar confounding may also explain why Adams-Price (1992) found no age differences in verbal recall of two crime videos. Although the young and old subjects in this investigation did not differ reliably in years of education (12.4 and 13.7 years for the young adults and se-niors, respectively), the education level for the seniors was high for their cohort (almost 2 years of college). As noted previously, college-educated seniors often exceed college-educated young adults in vocabulary (Salthouse, 2004).

In a more recent study, we examined long-term (1-month delayed) verbal recall of a previous encounter with a young-adult experimenter (Searcy, Bartlett, Memon, & Swan-son, 2001). We tested 45 young adults ($M = 22$ years) and 49 seniors ($M = 71$ years) who differed neither in vocabulary nor in years of education. Half of the subjects were tested with the CI, and the remainder received a modified CI that omitted context-reinstatement techniques. Regardless of interview type (which had no effects), the young adults re-called over twice as many details as the seniors ($M = 48.7$ versus 24.2, respectively) and were accurate more often in their recall of these details. Of all of the details recalled, the proportion correct averaged .89 and .77 for young adults and seniors, respectively. The large age difference may be partly attributable to the long retention interval used in this study (see below), and so we need more information on how verbal ability and education might moderate performance by the old eyewitness with long and short retention inter-vals. For the present, we can say that age-related deficits in verbal recall appear to be well established in a range of forensically relevant tasks, but that verbal ability is impor-tant as well (see, e.g., Rice & Meyer, 1986, for supporting evidence from laboratory tasks of verbal memory). Indeed, it is vital for police and jurors to know that although verbal recall can be reduced in old age, a verbally skilled and well-educated senior can be a more reliable witness than a young adult with less verbal skill and/or education. More re-search is needed to test the generality of Mello and Fisher's (1996) intriguing observa-tion that the cognitive interview can improve recall by seniors even more than it can im-prove recall by young adults. If this finding can be established, it too will be important for police and jurors to know.

Misinformation Effects

One of the best-established cases of eyewitness error is when witnesses' memory becomes contaminated by information they have acquired after they witnessed the event (Wright & Loftus, 1998). When this post-event information is misleading or errant, it is referred to as *misinformation*. In studies of the misinformation effect, participants are exposed to an event (e.g., a simulated crime) and then later misinformed about some aspect of it (e.g., an erroneous newspaper report about the crime). The typical finding is that partic-ipants exposed to misinformation will often incorporate misleading details into their memory reports (e.g., Wright & Loftus, 1998).

Research in the field of cognitive aging suggests that old adults *should* be more prone to misinformation effects. For example, research indicates that old adults often have deficits in source monitoring (Johnson, Hashtroudi, & Lindsay, 1993; Schacter, Kaszniak, Kihlstrom, & Valdiserri, 1991). As compared with young adults, seniors have more diffi-culty in distinguishing information they have experienced themselves from information they may have received from someone else (i.e., a problem identifying the precise *source* of the information). Source confusion has been shown to play a major role in susceptibility to post-event misinformation (Zaragoza, Lane, Ackil, & Chambers, 1997), and seniors are particularly prone to making this kind of error (Schacter et al., 1993). A typical consequence of source confusion is that the suggested information is erroneously reported as if it were part of the original memory (Johnson et al., 1993; Wegesin, Jacobs, Zubin, Ventura, & Stern, 2000; Zaragoza et al., 1997).

Mitchell, Johnson, and Mather (2003) explored age differences in source monitoring performance with the use of a standard misinformation paradigm and found that old adults were more likely than young adults to say that they saw information that was actually only suggested to them. They were also more confident in their source misattributions than were younger adults. Similarly, Karpel, Hoyer, & Toglia (2001) found that old adults were more likely to falsely report items that had only been suggested. Again it was found that old adults were more confident about the falsely recognized items. Cohen and Faulkner (1989) and Loftus, Levidow, and Duensing (1992) have also demonstrated that old adults are more likely to retrieve misinformation than younger adults.

There are, however, exceptions to the finding that old adults show larger misinformation effects. One is reported by Coxon and Valentine (1997), who had young adults and seniors (as well as a group of children) view a short video, followed by 17 questions about the video. In the misinformed condition, four of the questions contained misleading information, and in the control condition, none of them did. Fifteen minutes later, the participants answered 20 new questions, four of which were "critical." These critical questions tested acceptance of the misinformation that had previously been presented in the misinformation condition (though not in the control condition). Among young adults, the critical questions were answered with misleading information at a rate of .39 in the misinformation condition but only .14 in the control condition. Among seniors, the comparable rates were 39 and .24, respectively. The data show a misinformation effect, but this effect was no larger (indeed it may have been smaller) in the older age group.

The Coxon and Valentine (1997) study can be criticized on the grounds that the senior adults were less highly educated than were the young adults (the young adults appear to have been high school graduates, whereas the seniors were, on average, only 14 years old when they terminated their formal education). It is possible that the seniors' verbal skills (which were not assessed) were lower than those of the young-adult participants, and that, for this reason, the seniors were less likely to encode the misleading information at the time it was presented.

Such an account cannot be applied to a more recent finding of no age differences in misleading information effects. Gabbert, Memon, and Allan (2003) compared a group of young (18- to 30-year-old) adults with a group of (60- to 80-year-old) seniors who were superior in verbal skills as measured by a vocabulary test. In each experimental session, two same-age participants were led to believe that they would see the same video of a crime scene. Although the two video clips contained exactly the same sequence of events, they were filmed from different angles to simulate different witness perspectives. Critically, this manipulation allowed different features of the event to be observed for each participant. After viewing the event, participants were asked to discuss the event alone or in (same-age) pairs. The key feature of the discuss-in-pairs condition is that each of two eyewitnesses had an opportunity to (unintentionally) introduce items that he or she correctly observed, but which constituted misinformation from the other eye-witness's perspective. An individual recall test was then administered to each eyewitness separately to examine the effects of the discussion on subsequent memory reports. A significant proportion (71%) of witnesses in the discuss-together condition reported erroneous details acquired during the discussion (i.e., details they simply could not have seen from their perspective). Age differences emerged in the amount of information correctly recalled from the video (means = 18.00 and 15.95 for the young and old age-groups, respectively). However, the recall of items of misinformation was the same in the two age groups.

It is not yet clear why misinformation effects sometimes appear stronger among senior witnesses and sometimes they do not. In discussing their finding of no age differences in such effects, Gabbert et al. (2003) argue that the process of actively discussing memories provides old adults with additional memory cues about event details and helps them focus their attention on the event. Such discussion might function as *environmental support* for memorial processes that distinguish what was seen from what was talked about. As mentioned earlier in this chapter, incrementing the level of environmental support reduces age differences in a range of situations (see Anderson & Craik, 2000), and so this account is plausible.

Another possible explanation for the Gabbert et al. (2003) findings is focused on the way in which the misinformation was presented to the participants. In the discuss-together condition, the co-witnesses were matched for age group (young/old). Thus, both young and old witnesses in this condition were receiving misinformation from their own peer group. One possibility entertained by the authors is that the young adults differed from senior adults in feeling greater pressure to go along with their peer group (see Borsari and Carey, 2001, for relevant literature) and hence were more influenced by misinformation.

In closing this section on misinformation effects in young and old adults, we note that progress in this area is likely to depend on our solving two methodological problems that plague many of the relevant studies. First, the appearance of misinformation effects depends on the initial encoding and acceptance of the misinformation when it is first presented (Weingardt, Loftus, & Lindsay, 1995). Thus, to interpret age differences (or age invariances) in misinformation effects, we need to know if there were age differences in misinformation encoding and acceptance. Yet, the published studies provide no evidence that bears on such age differences.

The second methodological problem is that, in most cases, old adults are more subject to false recall and recognition *even in the control conditions* (or with noncritical questions). Hence, to evaluate the hypothesis that misinformation effects are increased in old age, investigators attempt to determine if the age-related differences found in the misinformation condition are still larger than they are in the control condition. The interaction, if obtained, is generally not of the crossover type. Rather, senior participants have higher error rates than young adults in the misinformation condition (e.g., means = .58 and .28, respectively, in Cohen & Faulkner, 1989) and in the control condition (means = .28 and .13, respectively, in that same study). Although the age difference might be larger in the first case than in the second, and although this pattern may produce a reliable interaction in an analysis of variance, its interpretation is equivocal because it might be attributable to scaling artifacts. Future studies should attempt to match the performance of young and old subjects in the control conditions (perhaps, for example, by increasing study time for the old subjects) and then examine whether age differences emerge in the misinformation conditions (see, e.g., Schacter, Kaszniak, Kihlstrom, & Valdiserri, 1991).

LINEUP IDENTIFICATION

One of the best-known claims about aging and memory—one frequently encountered in introductory texts—is that age-related deficits are stronger in recall than recognition. Indeed, the claim has been supported in numerous studies, and it fits the general principle that environmental support reduces age differences in memory (Anderson & Craik, 2000). These points notwithstanding, there are many observations of *robust* age differences in recognition memory, including recognition memory for faces. Moreover, the age differences found in face recognition tasks show a particular pattern that is provocative for theories of aging and memory as well as forensic psychology: The hit rate of recognizing old (i.e., seen before) faces as old is often as high among seniors as among young adults. By contrast, the false-alarm rate of recognizing new faces as old is usually increased among old adults (e.g., Bartlett, 1993; Bartlett & Fulton, 1991; Bartlett & Leslie, 1986; Bartlett, Leslie, Tubbs, & Fulton, 1989; Fulton & Bartlett, 1991; Mason, 1986; Smith & Winograd, 1978). Searcy, Bartlett, and Memon (1999) examined the data from 10 published articles comprising 12 different experiments and found that the average hit rates for young and old adults were virtually identical (.82 and .81, respectively). By contrast, the false-alarm rate for young adults was only half that of seniors (.20 and .40, respectively). When these findings are cited by us and others (e.g., Bornstein, 1995), it is frequently suggested that they may carry forensic implications: although young adults are notoriously prone to false identifications in the lineup task, seniors might be even more dangerous.

Is this implication valid? We should note first of all that an answer of yes cannot be viewed as a foregone conclusion because of many differences between laboratory tests of face recognition and the lineup task. Perhaps the most critical of these differences is that the standard crime video includes only one face or a handful of faces, while most laboratory paradigms involve the presentation of many faces, usually 24 or more, followed by a lengthy test. The faces used in laboratory tasks are usually homogeneous in nature (often all young adult Caucasian), producing what can be viewed as a large set of instances of a basic-level category (Rosch, Mervis, Gray, Johnson, & Boyes-Braem, 1976). Research on age differences in object recognition (Koutstaal & Schacter, 1997; Koutstaal, Schacter, Galluccio, & Stofer, 1999) has shown that homogeneous stimulus sets of this type (e.g., 18 photographs of ladies' shoes) will produce a constant-hits/increased-false-alarms pattern like that found with faces. By contrast, pictures appearing within smaller sets do not show this pattern. Koutstaal and Schacter (1997) argue that, with larger sets, seniors base their recognition judgments on the goodness of match between a test item and gist-level representation of the set of stimuli from which it came. This coping strategy supports high hit rates but tends to increase false alarms in response to new gist-matching lures. If this reasoning is valid, we might *not* expect to observe the constant-hits/increased-false-alarm pattern in typical lineup identification studies in which only one or a handful of faces are shown.

What do the data show? Table 13.1 summarizes the results from 10 studies comparing young and old adults with respect to (a) proportions of correct target identifications in target-present lineups (TP hits) and (b) proportions of correct rejections of target-absent lineups (TA correct rejections). We show correct-rejection rates instead of false-alarm rates, so that high proportions represent good performance in both TP and TA lineups (the correct-rejection rate = 1 − the false-alarm rate). Table 13.1 includes only studies with standard lineups in which there is only one target (TP lineups) or no targets at all (TA lineups), and in which the foil faces are completely unfamiliar (i.e., no foils pre-exposed as mugshots or as innocent bystanders). When a study had two delay conditions, two exposure-time conditions, or two lineup-format conditions (simultaneous and sequential), the data from each of the two conditions is shown (an exception is lineup 3 of Searcy et al., 1999, in which lineup structure was manipulated but had no effects). There are a total of 17 young-senior comparisons with target-absent lineups and 15 with target-present lineups.

A first point to note in Table 13.1 is that, averaging over all available data sets, there is a close approximation to the constant-hits/reduced-correct-rejections (increased-false-alarms) pattern found in laboratory studies of face recognition. Whereas the average proportion of TP hits is similar for young adults and seniors (.41 and .37, respectively), the average proportion of TA correct rejections shows a drop of .22 (.53 − .31). This is not to say, however, that the pattern is apparent in every case. In fact, two data sets showed a correct-rejection-age-deficit of .08 or less (Pierce et al., 2004; and the simultaneous condition of Searcy et al., 2000), and one showed a reversal (the short exposure condition of Memon, Hope, & Bull, 2003). Note in addition that, in two of these cases (Pierce et al. and Memon et al.), there was near age invariance in TP hits as well.

How can the variable outcomes be explained? A perusal of the table suggests one factor to consider: young adults' performance level. Where young-adult performance is low, senior performance appears not much if any lower. This point is made graphically in Figure 13–1, which shows the TP hit data (upper graph) and the TA-correct-rejection data (lower graph) ordered by young-adult performance (the numbers along the abscissas represent data sets as numbered in Table 13.1). TP hit rates by young adults and seniors are usually quite similar and are strongly correlated across the 15 data sets ($r = .80$, $df = 13$, $p < .01$). This point notwithstanding, young-minus-senior differences are robust in a few cases. A key point to note is that the young-minus-senior differences are +.09 or less, *except* for the three data sets where the TP hit rates are high (.68 or greater). In these three cases, the age differences are +.35 (Searcy et al., 2000), +.29 (Lineup 3 of Searcy et al., 1999), and +.10 (long-exposure condition of Memon et al., 2003). And in the last of these three cases, ceiling effects may have artifactually reduced the age difference. To statistically evaluate these observations, we computed the correlation

TABLE 13.1.

Study, Participant, Condition, and Experiment Information with Mean Proportion Hits in Target-Present (TP) Lineups and Correct Rejections in Target-Absent (TA) Lineups Across 19 Data Sets from 12 Studies of Age Differences in Lineup Performance

Data Set	Young n's (mean age)	Senior n's (mean age)	Lineup Delay	Condition or Exp.[a]	TP Hits Young	TP Hits Senior	TA Correct Rejections Young	TA Correct Rejections Senior
1. Yarmey et al., 1984 (victim)	128 (21)	128 (71)	30 min.*	Lineup 1	0.25	0.18	0.77	0.33
2. Searcy et al., 1999	77 (24)	75 (70)	15 min.	Lineup 1	0.26	0.19	0.36	0.19
3. "			1 hr.	Lineup 3	0.68	0.39	0.58	0.20
4. Searcy et al., 2000	97 (24)	98 (69)	1 hr.	Sim			0.22	0.14
5. "			1 hr.	Seq			0.62	0.46
6. Searcy et al., 2001	45 (23)	49 (71)	1 month		0.68	0.33	0.40	0.28
7. Memon & Bartlett, 2002	57 (21)	67 (70)	1 hr.	Sim	0.28	0.42		
8. "				Seq	0.13	0.13		
9. Memon et al., 2002 (Ctrl)	20 (23)	20 (68)	48 hrs.				0.80	0.50
10. Pierce et al., 2002	73 (19)	73 (74)	48 hrs.		0.46	0.47	0.26	0.19
11. Memon et al., 2003	84 (19)	80 (68)	38 min	Short exp	0.29	0.35	0.10	0.20
12. "			38 min.	Long exp	0.95	0.85	0.59	0.50
13. Memon, Bartlett, et al., 2003	84 (19)	88 (72)	35 min		0.41	0.45	0.43	0.21
14. "			1 week		0.35	0.26	0.62	0.08
15. Memon et al., 2004	32 (19)	31 (69)	1 week	Study 2	0.48	0.46	0.66	0.55
16. Bartlett et al., 2003	49 (23)	47 (70)	1 hr.	Exp 1	0.34	0.43	0.57	0.32
17. "	39 (20)	80 (69)	1 hr.	Exp 2	0.47	0.48	0.72	0.50
18. Memon & Gabbert, 2003b	120 (20)	120 (69)	1 hr.	Sim	0.17	0.21	0.47	0.10
19. "			1 hr.	Seq			0.90	0.60
Mean					0.41	0.37	0.53	0.31

*Estimate; lineup delay not directly stated.

[a]Sim. and Seq. = simultaneous and sequential lineup presentation, respectively. All lineups were simultaneous except for those designated as sequential and for lineup 3 in Searcy et al. (1999), which was sequential for half of the participants (lineup structure had no effect there). Short exp = 12-second perpetrator presentation and long exp = 45-second perpetrator presentation.

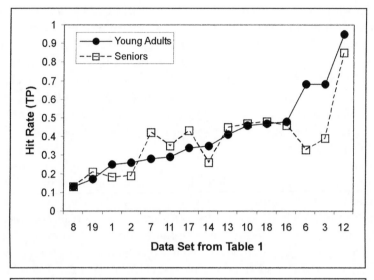

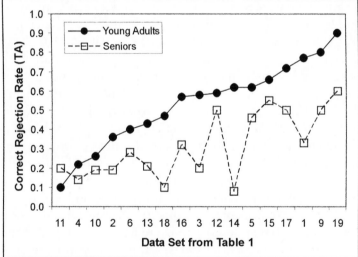

FIGURE 13–1. Hit rates for target-present lineups (top) and correct rejection rates for target-absent lineups (bottom) for data sets listed in Table 13.1.

between TP hit rates by young adults and the young-minus-senior *differences* in hit rates. The r was $+.58$ ($df = 13$, $p < .05$), supporting the conclusion that age differences are larger when young adults do well.

Comparing the upper and lower graphs in Figure 13.1, it is clear that age differences are more frequently observed in TA-correct-rejections (lower graph) than in TP hits (upper graph). However, as in the case of hits, correct rejections by young adults and seniors are reliably correlated across the 17 data sets ($r = .69$, $df = 15$, $p < .01$), and young adults' performance level shows a correlation with the age-related deficit ($r = .63$, $df = 15$, $p < .01$). Thus, although age-related differences are generally stronger with correct rejections than with hits, age-related differences with either measure are more likely in conditions where young adults do well. How can we interpret this pattern?

One possible explanation of the TA-correct-rejection data is that the pattern reflects a scaling artifact. It might be, for example, that correct rejections from TA lineups have an effective floor of about .20; perhaps at least 1/5 of eyewitnesses will reject a target-absent lineup, no matter the situation. Thus, if young adults are performing at this level, it is simply not possible that seniors will do worse. This account is less workable for the TP hit data, where age-related deficits are minimal or absent, as young-adult performance varies from .13 to .50.

An alternative account holds that, because of our procedures for constructing fair lineups, the lineup task is *intrinsically* difficult and demanding of cognitive resources and attentional control (Anderson & Craik; 2000; Balota, Dolan, & Duchek, 2000). High levels of performance on lineup tasks are likely to depend on effortful, strategic, processes of retrieval, decision-making, and monitoring the products of retrieval (e.g., a witness might reject a lineup face despite the fact that it seems familiar because she recalls a face seen on the street that same day that resembles this face, and she attributes familiarity to this source). There is much emerging evidence that these processes involve frontal brain systems that are known to show deficits in many old persons (Schacter, Koutstaal, & Norman, 1997; Glisky et al., 1995; Henkel et al., 1998; Balota et al., 2000). Hence, if high performance on lineups depends on cognitive resources and attentional control, high performance should be rarer among seniors than among young adults.

By this strategic-processing account, age-related differences in the lineup task appear in those conditions where young adults are able to marshal their strategic processing resources to perform reasonably well. All too often, however, the task is so difficult that not even young adults can improve their performance through strategic processing. In these cases, both young and old persons will perform rather poorly. Note that the strategic-processing hypothesis is directly opposed to the intuitive notion that the deficits suffered by senior adults are larger in more difficult tasks than in less difficult tasks. The latter idea, despite its appeal, has not been supported in eyewitness studies (see Yarmey, 2001). The reason might be that, in eyewitness studies, accurate performance is rarely achieved through easy or "automatic" processes. It may depend more often on attentional and executive processes that are subject to age differences.

Test Delay and Age of Seniors as Moderators of Age Differences

Regardless of how we might explain the general pattern of age differences across performance level, another problem remains: How can we account for those instances where age differences are larger than would be expected based on the performance of young adults? As shown in Figure 13.1, one clear case is the study by Memon, Bartlett et al. (2003), where rates of TA-correct rejections showed a moderate difference between young adults and seniors with a short (35-minute) retention interval (.43 and .21, respectively) but a very large age difference with a long (1-week) retention interval (.62 and .08, respectively). TP hits showed a similar albeit weaker pattern: no age-related deficit with the short retention interval (.41 and .45 for young adults and seniors, respectively), but a trend for such a deficit with the long retention interval (.35 and .26, respectively).

Can we conclude that age differences in eyewitness accuracy are increased at long delays? Mixed support for this conclusion comes from Searcy et al. (2001), who used a 1-month retention interval and found that the rates of TP hits were .66 and .33, respectively, for young adults and seniors. This is certainly a substantial age difference, and there was a sizable age difference in verbal recall as well (see above). However, it must be noted that rates of TA correct rejections in the same study were .40 and .28 for young adults and seniors, a moderate age difference at most. Moreover, study 2 of Memon, Gabbert, and Hope (2004) employed a 1-week retention interval and found an even smaller age difference in TA correct rejections (.66 versus .55, respectively) that did not attain significance. Additionally, Memon and Gabbert (2003) found robust age differences in TA correct rejections with simultaneous and sequential lineups, and their retention interval was only 1 hour. We must conclude that if a long test delay is particularly detrimental to the senior eyewitness, delay is not the only moderating variable we need to consider.

Another good candidate for a moderating variable is age of the senior eyewitness. When Memon et al. (2004, study 2) divided their seniors into a young-old group (68 years and under) and an old-old group (69 years and above), they found that TA correct rejections (with a 1-week test delay) were significantly (and dramatically) more probable in the young-old group (.87) than in the old-old group (.25). The pattern requires replication, but it suggests that the combination of a long test delay and an eyewitness over 70 is associated with a high probability of a false identification.

Face Age as a Moderator of Age Differences

Another strong candidate for a variable that moderates lineup performance differences between young adults and seniors is that of *face* age. With just one exception, all of the studies covered thus far have used young faces as stimuli (the exception is Memon, Bartlett, et al., 2003, which we discuss below). This can be viewed as a confounding factor, because young adults were tested with same-age faces, whereas seniors were tested with other-age faces. An other-race effect in face recognition memory has been known for some time (Bothwell, Brigham, & Malpass, 1989; Shapiro & Penrod, 1986): people are better at recognizing faces of their own ethnic group than those of other ethnic groups. The analogous effect with age as the variable—what we will term the *other-age effect* in face recognition—was examined by Bartlett and Leslie (1986). In each of two experiments, they found a subject-age X face-age interaction in a criterion-free measure of discrimination (A′) between previously viewed faces and new items. The interaction was asymmetric: younger subjects performed better with young than old faces, whereas seniors showed no reliable difference. The consequence was that discrimination scores for young and old subjects differed with younger faces (mean A′ = .87 and .80, respectively, in Experiment 1, and .88 and .76 in Experiment 2), but not with old faces (mean A′ = .79 and .81 in Experiment 1, and .82 and .79 in Experiment 2). A subsequent study by Fulton and Bartlett (1991) replicated this pattern with the use of a between-subject design. Half of their young-adult and senior subjects received a study list and tests containing young and middle-aged faces, and the remainder received a study list and test containing middle-aged and old faces. Discrimination between previously viewed faces and new items (measured by d') was highest for young faces, lower for middle-aged faces (averaging over lists), and lowest for old faces. However, this trend was largely restricted to the young subjects (mean d' = 2.08, 1.75, and 1.43, respectively, for young adults, versus 1.38, 1.17, and 1.22 for seniors). As a result, discrimination scores were reliably higher for young subjects than for seniors with young faces and middle-aged faces, but not with old faces.

Broadly consistent data come from Mason (1986), Rodin (1987), and Bäckman (1991). Mason had young women (mean age = 20) and senior women (mean age = 75) study a set of 40 face-name pairs and then take a test in which each of 80 faces was presented with two names, and the participants judged each face as seen before or new, and circled the name they thought was correct for each face judged to be seen before. Half of the faces were 20 years old and the remainder were 70 years old, and the d' scores for face recognition showed a marginally reliable interaction between face age and participant age, with the young adults showing a marginally reliable advantage of young faces over old faces (3.47 and 3.13, respectively), and the seniors showing a smaller and nonsignificant trend in the opposite direction (1.05 and 1.20, respectively). Rodin had her young and senior subjects view an array of 10 young, 10 middle-aged, and 10 old faces, followed (after 25 minutes) by a test array containing the 30 target faces intermixed with 30 distractors. In general agreement with Fulton and Bartlett (1991), the young adults recognized the young, middle-aged, and old faces at rates of .63, .49, and .47, respectively. And as would be expected based on the Fulton and Bartlett findings, the seniors showed approximately equivalent recognition of the young and old faces (.59 and .57, respectively). Puzzlingly, the seniors performed quite poorly with the middle-aged faces (mean = .37), perhaps because these faces were not very distinctive. In any event, the data suggested a young-subject advantage with young and middle-aged faces (mean differences = .04 and .14, respectively), but not with old faces, with which the old subjects actually scored higher (mean difference = .10). The pattern is similar to that observed by Fulton and Bartlett (1991), except that the age-related deficit in Fulton and Bartlett's study was merely reduced (not reversed) when older faces were employed.

In the study by Bäckman (1991), young adults and three different groups of seniors viewed a study list containing famous faces along with nonfamous young and nonfamous old faces. Looking at the nonfamous faces, a comparison of young participants with the youngest group of seniors (mean age = 69 years) produced a symmetric interaction between subject age and face age: whereas young adults performed better with young than with old faces (d' = 2.74 and 1.98, respectively), the young seniors performed more poorly with young than with old faces (d' = 1.27 and 2.04, respectively). The other two groups of seniors in Bäckman's (1991) study were aged 76 years and 85 years, respectively. Performance in these two groups resembled that in prior studies; there was no difference between young and old faces (d' = 1.21 and 1.23, respectively, in the 76-year-old group, and .87 and .83, respectively, in the 85-year-old group). Hence, comparing either of these older-old groups with the young adult group produced the asymmetric pattern found in prior studies (i.e., a face-age effect with young adults but not seniors).

It is noteworthy that the ages of seniors averaged 74.2 and 66.5 in Bartlett and Leslie's (1986), Experiments 1 and 2, and 71.4 in the Fulton and Bartlett (1991) study. Thus, two of these three samples resembled Bäckman's 76-year-old sample in (a) being over 70 years old (on average) and (b) showing no effect of face age. Arguably, the anomalous sample is the senior group of Bartlett and Leslie's Experiment 2. This sample was similar in age to Bäckman's young-old sample, and yet it differed from that sample in failing to show a reliable face-age effect. We note, however, that a trend was present, and it just missed significance by a one-tailed test (mean $A' = .76$ versus $.79$ for young and older faces, respectively, t (17) $= 1.70$). Thus, the data in hand are largely consistent with Bäckman's conclusion that whereas young adults perform better with young-adult faces, younger seniors perform better with old faces and older seniors show no face-age effect.

Face-age X subject-age interactions are not restricted to face recognition. They have been found as well in verbal recognition memory for actions performed by actresses in shoplifting videos (List, 1986) and in verbal recall of descriptive characteristics (hair color, jewelry) of photographs of persons (Lindholm, 2003). The ages of the seniors in the List and Lindholm studies averaged 68 and 74 years, respectively, approximating the ages of Bäckman's (1991) 69- and 76-year-old groups. And it is interesting to note that, as in Bäckman's study, the younger seniors (those in List's study) showed an old-actress advantage in action recall, whereas the older seniors (those in Lindholm's study) showed no old-face advantage in facial-characteristic recall. It must be noted, however, that List's older actresses were middle-aged rather than old, and this may have affected the results.

We conclude that young adults show better memory for young faces (or persons and their actions) than older faces, whereas seniors show either no effect or the opposite effect, depending, apparently, on how old the seniors are. In any case, it appears well established that age-related deficits in face (and person) memory are at least relatively smaller and are sometimes eliminated when older faces are employed. This point notwithstanding, two studies we reviewed (Rodin, 1987; Fulton & Bartlett, 1991) suggest that middle-aged faces produce an age-related deficit that is about as large as, or larger than, that found with young faces. More research is needed on this point, particularly in view of List's (1986) finding that seniors performed as well as young adults in remembering actions performed by young versus middle-aged actresses. Nonetheless, the available data on face recognition suggest it is only with faces aged 60 years and older that age-related deficits are significantly reduced.

Do these data imply that age-related deficits in the lineup task—especially age-related deficits in rejecting TA lineups—are reduced or eliminated when the suspects are seniors? Evidence bearing on this question comes from laboratory studies that examined false-alarm rates separately from hits. When Fulton and Bartlett (1991) made separate analyses of hits and false alarms, they found that the subject-age X face-age interaction was restricted to hits. False-alarm rates were lower (i.e., correct rejection rates were higher) for young adults than for seniors with old faces (mean false-alarm rates = .35 and .50, respectively) as well as younger faces (means = .25 and .41, respectively). Similarly, Bäckman (1991) found that false-alarm rates with young adult faces averaged

.04, .18, .20, and .24 for young-adult participants, young-old participants, 76-year-old participants, and 85-year-old participants, respectively. The comparable false-alarm rates with old faces averaged .10, .08, .20, and .26. Note that the older-old subjects showed inflated false-alarm rates with both old and young faces.

Three recent studies using the lineup paradigm also speak to our question. Although all three studies, summarized in Table 13.2, represent a worthwhile move toward ecological validity, each made a compromise with the attainment of that goal in pursuit of statistical power. Specifically, all three studies had subjects view either two or four faces followed by lineups. Wright and Stroud's (2002) young and middle-aged subjects viewed four videos, two of a car theft and two of a television theft, using a young (23-year-old) and middle-aged (51-year-old) perpetrator in each crime scenario. Subjects viewed all four videos in a random sequence, and, either 1 day or 1 week later, they were given a lineup test for each one. In Experiment 1, all lineups were target present (TP), whereas in Experiment 2, half of the lineups were target absent (TA). The results were in line with the Fulton and Bartlett (1991) and Bäckman (1991) studies in that subject-age X face-age interactions were found in TP hits, but not in TA–correct rejections (the complete lack of age differences with TA correct rejections is attributable to the fact that the "older" subjects in the Wright and Stroud study were middle-aged rather than old).

In the Memon, Bartlett, et al. (2003) study, each young and old subject viewed only two videos, one depicting a 22-year-old man looking around and then entering a house, and the other depicting a 60-year-old man doing the same thing. Both subsequent lineups were administered after a 35-minute or 1-week delay, and both were TP for half of the subjects and both were TA for the remainder. In contrast to Wright and Stroud (2002), TP hits showed absolutely no evidence for the standard other-age effect. In fact, the young subjects showed no face-age effect, whereas the seniors showed a trend for a *young*-face advantage. The TA correct rejections showed a less surprising pattern: there was a young-face advantage among young adults and an old-face advantage among seniors, so the age-related deficit in correct rejections was reduced with the old lineup. This pattern was especially clear with the longer (1-week) retention interval.

Perfect and Harris's (2003) Experiment 3 did not use videos, but rather had subjects view still photographs of a 21-year-old male, a 21-year-old female, a 71-year-old male and a 71-year-old female. These photographs were followed (after 20–25 minutes) by 16 mugshots, including four faces that resembled each of the four original faces. One week later, the subjects were administered two TP and two TA lineups. Both TP lineups included a face from the first set shown, and both TA lineups included a face from the mugshots. In this study, both TP hits and TA correct rejections showed an other-age effect, and age-related deficits with both measures were large with young faces and reduced with old faces. Indeed, the age-related deficit in TP hits disappeared with old faces.

Although the TP hit data from the Perfect and Harris (2003) study clearly differ from those of Memon, Bartlett et al. (2003), the TA correct rejection data are much more consistent. With a 1-week delay, both studies showed a strong age-related deficit in TA correct rejections with young adult faces that was reduced with old faces. The pattern departs from Fulton and Bartlett's (1991) hypothesis that whereas hit rates show a face-age effect, false-alarm rates are higher (and correct rejection rates are lower) among se-

TABLE 13.2

Lineup Delay and Subject Information with Mean Proportion Hits in Target-Present (TP) Lineups and Correct Rejections in Target-Absent (TA) Lineups in Three Studies of Lineup Performance with Young and Older Subjects and Faces

Experiment & Delay	n's (mean age)		TP Hits			TA Correct Rejections		
	Young Ss	Older Ss	Young Ss	Older Ss	Diff.	Young Ss	Older Ss	Diff.
Wright & Stroud, 2002								
Exp.1	56 (22*)	57 (45*)						
24 hr.								
Young faces			0.47	0.24	0.23			
Older faces			0.37	0.47	-0.10			
1 week								
Young faces			0.29	0.20	0.09			
Older faces			0.21	0.23	-0.02			
Exp. 2 (24 hr.)	90 (26*)	90 (48*)						
Young faces			0.49	0.32	0.17	0.36	0.33	0.03
Older faces			0.36	0.43	-0.07	0.33	0.36	-0.03
Memon et al., 2003	84 (19)	88 (72)						
35 min								
Young faces			0.41	0.45	-0.04	0.48	0.21	0.27
Older faces			0.41	0.36	0.05	0.38	0.26	0.12
1 week								
Young faces			0.35	0.26	0.09	0.62	0.08	0.54
Older faces			0.35	0.04	0.31	0.48	0.29	0.19
Perfect & Harris, 2003	30 (20)	30 (67)						
Exp. 3 (1 week)								
Young faces			0.73	0.37	0.36	0.90	0.33	0.57
Older faces			0.80	0.83	-0.03	0.67	0.50	0.17

*Estimate; mean age not directly stated.

niors regardless of face age. Note, however, that the subject-age effects in the studies by Perfect and Harris and Memon, Bartlett et al. were only reduced with old faces; they did not appear to be eliminated entirely.

Apart from the issue of face age as a moderator of subject-age effects, the assembled research has important implications when it comes to understanding how young-adult eyewitnesses perform with lineups in real life. Every single study using face-age as a variable has found that young subjects do better with young than with old faces. For example, the young-adult data summarized in Table 13.2 show a young-face superiority with TP hits (Wright & Stroud, 2002), TA correct rejections (Memon et al., 2003), or both (Perfect & Harris, 2003). This finding is striking in view of the fact that most prior research on lineup performance has examined young subjects viewing young lineups. Such research is likely to overestimate performance by young subjects viewing old-face lineups. When a crime suspect is a senior, it may well be the case that the real-world performance of young-adult eyewitnesses is even worse than we have been led to believe.

The path forward from this point is likely to require advances in theoretical accounts of other-age effects. In the existing literature, these effects have been attributed to (a) young-adults' lack of expertise in distinguishing among older adult faces than young-adult faces (Fulton & Bartlett, 1991), (b) "cognitive disregard" for the details of faces from social classes deemed less relevant or personally important to an observer (Rodin, 1987), (c) less elaborate semantic and/or self-referential processing of faces from age groups different from one's own (List, 1986), (d) less available schemata or prototypes that aid the encoding of the physical characteristics of other-age faces (Bäckman, 1991), and (e) different social attributions for different-aged persons with subsequent effects on decision criteria (e.g., a senior might view a behavior as more suspicious if it is performed by a young adult than if it is performed by a senior, and later feel more motivated to "get him" in a subsequent lineup (Memon, Bartlett et al., 2003)). These ideas must be tested: If we understood the reasons why other-age faces are more poorly recognized, we would be better able to specify the conditions in which an eyewitness of a certain age is most prone to error. We also might be in a position to improve performance in lineup tasks through changes in instructions or procedure.

Other Possible Moderators of Age Differences

Several studies in the literature have included standardized neuropsychological and personality tests in an effort to determine if age-related deficits in lineup performance are linked to problems in perceptual face-matching, executive function, and various personality variables. Of these various tests, the Benton Face Recognition Test (BFRT)—a test of perceptual face-matching used in diagnosis of posterior brain damage—has shown the most consistent correlations with lineup performance (see Benton, Sivan, Hamsher, Varney, & Spreen, 1994, for a description of this test). Reliable lineup-accuracy/BFRT correlations were reported by Searcy et al. (1999); Searcy, Bartlett, and Memon (2000); Searcy et al. (2001); and Seipel et al. (2000). However, the relevant correlations have been small (gammas or Pearson $r < .30$), except in the case of Seipel et al., where BFRT scores and lineup identification accuracy showed a .40 correlation. Moreover, Memon and Bartlett (2002) failed to replicate a reliable correlation. We have assessed executive function by examining preservative errors on the Wisconsin Card Sorting task (see Benton et al., 1994), as well as performance on the self-ordered pointing task (Shimamura & Jurica, 1994). As compared with the BFRT, these executive-function measures have been less consistent predictors of performance, and various personality measures included in some studies have been less consistent still.

There are some intriguing indications that verbal recall ability and/or education may be *negatively* related to lineup performance, perhaps especially among seniors. Using a multiple-regression approach, Adams-Price (1992) found that years of education were *positively* related to verbal recall of a prior video but were *negatively* related to performance on a lineup task in which subjects attempted to identify three characters seen in that video. Adams-Price did not examine the education/lineup performance relation separately for young and senior eyewitnesses. However, we have observed in two different studies that, among senior eyewitnesses, correct rejections of target-absent lineups were negatively related to verbal recall measures (Searcy et al., 2000, 2001). These findings may be linked to the "verbal overshadowing effect" (see, e.g., Dodson, Johnson, & Schooler, 1997: Schooler, Fiore, & Brandimonte, 1997), which is a negative effect of verbal recall on a subsequent test of recognition of faces or other nonverbal stimuli (e.g., colors, music, wines). Indeed, limited support for this conjecture was provided by Memon and Bartlett (2002), who found that (a) verbal recall prior to a TP lineup was linked to reported use of features in performing the lineup task, and (b) the use of features in performing the task was linked to poor performance. These effects were restricted to the senior eyewitnesses, implying that verbal recall of facial features can harm lineup performance in this age group. Such an effect might explain why verbal recall and education (plausibly correlated with verbal recall) can show negative correlations with lineup performance. However, the standard overshadowing effect was not statistically reliable in the Memon and Bartlett study (a not infrequent finding; see Meissner & Brigham 2001), which somewhat undermines the argument.

An interesting new candidate for a predictor of lineup performance is context- or source-memory ability. Memory for context is particularly important in the lineup task, as the question being put to the eyewitness is *not* whether a face has been seem somewhere before, but whether this face was seen performing a specified action (e.g., committing a crime) at a certain time and place. Recollection of context or circumstances of encounter is impaired in old age (see preceding discussion), but no one would propose that all seniors suffer deficits in context or source memory. Indeed, there is evidence that source memory in seniors is linked to their performance on tests of frontal-lobe function (Glisky et al., 1995, 2001). For that matter, even young adults might vary considerably in context recollection.

With these considerations in mind, Memon, Bartlett et al. (2003) tested the hypothesis that a measure of context recollection would predict performance in the lineup task. Their approach was to include within their design a laboratory test of face recognition designed to involve source memory. Specifically, at the end of the first of two experimental sessions (after the viewing of two crime videos and several other tasks), a lengthy study list of faces was presented. Furthermore, at the end of the second experimental session (after the two lineup tasks), a recognition test for the faces in the study list was given. Following a paradigm developed by Jennings and Jacoby (1997), the test included old and new faces, with most of the new faces repeated within the test. The task was to identify truly old faces (those from the study list), rejecting new faces both times they appeared. False-alarm rates in response to new faces increased from their first to their second presentation, an effect that is suggestive of context-recollection failures (Jennings & Jacoby, 1997). The effect was stronger in the senior group than in the young-adult group, and a measure of source memory (hit rates for old faces minus false-alarm rates for repeated new faces) showed a strong age deficit. Most importantly, the source memory measure was positively (and reliably) correlated with lineup accuracy among both young adults and seniors in the TP condition. These correlations were respectably strong (gammas = .50 and .35 for young adults and seniors, respectively, with $n = 28$ and 42, and $p < .002$ and .01. respectively), and they indicate that accurate identifications in TP lineups were linked to our participants' source memory ability. Correct rejections of TA lineups were not correlated with our source memory measure, which suggests that although source memory might be important for correct identifications from TP lineups, the deficits shown by seniors with TA lineups (Figure 13.1) might not be due to their source-memory problems. This clearly is an area where more research is warranted.

We suspect that one reason for the mixed state of evidence linking lineup performance to neuropsychological and verbal-recall measures is that the lineup task, with only one or a handful of responses per subject, is a very poor instrument for identifying stable individual differences. Another reason is that measures of abstract constructs such as executive function and source memory need to be based on multiple tests that converge on the construct of interest. Glisky and her colleagues (Glisky et al., 1995, 2001) have developed a multitest battery for frontal-lobe function that has successfully distinguished high-performing seniors from low-performing seniors in verbal memory tasks, and recent evidence suggests that this battery may prove useful in predicting false memory effects in seniors (see Butler et al., 2004). The use of this battery in eyewitness research would appear to be timely.

In view of these considerations, we now believe that the individual-difference approach will have limited utility in the examination of age differences unless and until we have multiple measures and/or trials-on-task to converge on the constructs of interest. However, a recent dissertation conducted in our laboratories explored a new approach to the problem (Seipel, 2002; Seipel & Bartlett, 2002). Rather than examining correlations between performance on lineups and other tasks, Seipel asked whether training on a face-matching task that requires attention to configural and featural information might be effective in improving lineup performance. The results (with young subjects) have been promising thus far, and Macrae and Lewis (2002) have reported related findings (also with young-adult eyewitnesses). A training approach holds the promise of leading to advances in theory as well as application. The prospect that a brief training regimen given prior to a lineup might improve the performance of an old (or young) eyewitness is exciting indeed.

Nonmoderators of Age Differences: Variables That Work Similarly with Young and Old Adults

Although it is critical to determine those factors that have differential effects on lineup performance by young and old witnesses, it is equally important to know about factors that have constant effects across age groups. In fact, an important study by O'Rourke, Penrod, Cutler, and Stuve (1989) found that adult age differences in lineup performance were not reliably altered by (a) disguise of the perpetrator (hat covering hair versus no hat), (b) weapon visibility (a gun openly brandished versus hidden), (c) use (versus nonuse) of a pre-lineup context-reinstatement interview, (d) suggestive (versus unbiased) lineup instructions, or (e) the presence (versus absence) of test information (about gait, posture, voice, or facial appearance). This negative outcome is impressive in that several of these variables produced main effects (weapon visibility and interview) and/or were involved in interactions with factors besides age (interview, disguise, instructions).

More recent studies have suggested that some additional variables have age-invariant effects, and, in some cases, this outcome is surprising from the standpoint of theory. One such factor is misinformation, which we considered previously in our review of verbal recall and recognition performance. To the best of our knowledge, only one study has examined the misinformation effects on lineup performance by young and old adults. This was the study by Searcy et al. (2000), whose young and old adults viewed a videotape of a simulated crime and then received misinformation about the criminal's physical features in the form of a post-event narrative. In line with the previously described studies of verbal memory by Coxon and Valentine (1997) and Gabbert et al. (2003), young and old subjects were more likely to choose a lineup foil who had a chipped tooth if the post-event narrative referred to a chipped tooth than if it referred to another physical feature. Another study by Bornstein, Witt, Cherry, and Greene (2000) failed to find age differences in misinformation effects in a test of memory for slides depicting an automobile-pedestrian incident. More research is needed on this issue, as, theoretically and empirically, there are grounds for predicting that misinformation effects should be strengthened in old age.

Another factor working in defiance of theory to produce age-invariant effects is the exposure to faces prior to their appearance as foils in a lineup. Under some conditions, prior exposure to a face can increase the chances it will be chosen in a lineup despite the fact that it is not the face of the perpetrator. One example is the "innocent bystander" or "unconscious transference" effect, whereby a face seen near the time of a crime, or even during the crime itself, is falsely identified as the perpetrator when in fact it is not. Another example is the "mugshot exposure effect," whereby a face seen previously in a mugshot book is wrongly chosen from a lineup as the perpetrator of a crime. Our interest in prior-exposure effects derived from laboratory studies showing that seniors, as compared with young adults, are more likely to recognize faces based on generalized feelings of perceived familiarity as opposed to recollection of more diagnostic information (Bartlett, 1993; Bartlett & Fulton, 1991; Bartlett et al., 1991). Based on this research, we predicted that old eyewitnesses will be more prone to prior exposure effects in the lineup task. That is, although we expected young adults might show such effects, we expected old adults would show them more strongly.

Searcy et al. (1999) first tested this prediction using the innocent-bystander paradigm. They had their young and old participants take three lineup tasks, one of which was ostensibly for the accomplice of the perpetrator in a crime video. The accomplice did not appear in the lineup, but an innocent bystander (a salesman) was present for half of the participants but not for the others. We did not find an innocent bystander effect, but our old participants showed what appeared to be a related phenomenon: the presence of the salesman in the lineup increased the probability that one of the *other* lineup faces was (incorrectly) chosen. Such an effect is potentially important, and so we tried to replicate it in a subsequent experiment with additional controls (Seipel et al., 2000). In fact, the result did not replicate, and so we are inclined to view it as a fluke. There is some controversy in the literature pertaining to the unconscious transference effect. Earlier studies (Ross, Ceci, Dunning, & Toglia, 1994) showed unconscious transference in young adults but used bystanders who bore a strong resemblance to the culprit. Hence participants may have believed the bystander and culprit were the same person in the video (a case of mistaken identity). Later studies have not found reliable effects, and some researchers have concluded that the bystander effect is ephemeral at best (e.g., Read, 1994). Indeed, our own findings are in line with this view.

In a more recent study of prior exposure effects, we switched from the innocent-bystander paradigm to the mugshot-exposure paradigm (Brown, Deffenbacher, & Sturgill, 1977). Memon et al. (2002) showed a crime video that was followed either by a mugshot identification task that did not include the target (mugshot condition) or by unrelated activities (control condition). Two days later, the participants viewed a target-absent lineup including one of the mugshot faces along with five additional foils (across subgroups of participants, two different mugshot faces appeared in the lineup as a check for generality). We found that seniors, as compared with young adults, made more false identifications in both the mugshot test and the subsequent lineup test, and we also found that, in both age groups, mugshot-foil choices were more frequent in the mugshot-exposure condition than in the control condition. Importantly, the age X condition interaction was not reliable.

Broadly consistent findings have been reported by Perfect and Harris (2003). In each of three experiments, young and senior subjects viewed four photographs of faces, followed (after 30 minutes of intervening activity) by eight additional faces (the "mugshots"). One week later, the participants viewed target-absent lineups, each of which contained a mugshot face along with four or five other foils (in Experiment 3 the participants took two target-present lineups as well). A key independent variable in this study was that of face age, and, as discussed previously, with the old-face lineups, age differences were small. In the case of young lineups, seniors exceeded young adults in two types of error to about the same extent: (a) choices of the mugshot included in the lineups (termed "transference errors") and (b) choices of other foils ("other identification errors"). In Experiment 1 (which used only young lineups), the percentage of subjects making one or more transference errors averaged 10 and 26 for young adults and seniors, respectively, whereas the percentage of subjects making one or more other-identification errors aver-

aged 20 and 34, respectively. In the young-lineup condition of Experiment 3, the percentage of transference errors averaged 10 and 40, respectively, whereas the percentage
of other-identification errors averaged 0 and 27, respectively. This outcome does not
support our hypothesis (Bartlett, 1993; Searcy et al., 1999) that seniors, as compared
with young adults, place more reliance on perceived familiarity in making lineup decisions. A familiarity hypothesis would predict larger age differences in transference errors
(false identifications of familiarized foils) than in other identification errors (false alarms
to entirely new faces). In fact, however, age differences in the two types of error were approximately the same. Looking at the findings of Perfect and Harris alongside those of
Memon et al. (2002) and Searcy et al. (1999), we see no evidence that seniors as a group
rely more on familiarity as compared with young adults in the lineup task.

This is not to say, however, that feelings of familiarity are never the basis for lineup
decisions. An important finding from the Memon et al. (2002) study emerged from a
comparison of two classes of eyewitnesses; those who chose a mugshot face as the likely
perpetrator ("mugshot-choosers") and those who did not ("mugshot-nonchoosers"). The
mugshot-choosers exceeded mugshot-nonchoosers in selecting the familiarized mugshot
foil in the subsequent lineup task. Specifically, the mugshot foil was picked by 40% of
the mughot-choosers, as compared with only 16% of the mugshot-nonchoosers and 13%
of the control participants who saw no mugshots. In interpreting this finding, it is important to note that mugshot-choosers and nonchoosers did not differ in their tendency to
pick other lineup foils (i.e., the foils who were not familiarized). Thus, mugshot-choosers
differed from nonchoosers *only* in their choices of familiarized foils. This outcome indicates that the mugshot-choosers differed from the nonchoosers in using general feelings
of familiarity as a basis for responding in the lineup task.

In line with this interpretation, mugshot-choosers' tendency to pick mugshot foils did
not depend on which mugshot they chose. The faces that were chosen on the mugshot
test were only occasionally the mugshot foil faces that appeared in the lineup. Moreover,
our findings were unchanged when we discarded the data from those mugshot-choosers
who initially picked the face that reappeared as a foil in the lineup. We conclude, therefore, that a witness who makes a mugshot choice is relatively more likely to use familiarity as a basis for responding in a subsequent lineup task. This puts him or her at risk for
a false identification if a mugshot face (either the initially chosen face or some other
mugshot face) is included in a lineup. Perfect and Harris (2003) also found evidence that
choosing a face in the mugshot task is linked to high rates of "transference errors" (i.e.,
identifications of the mugshot) in a subsequent lineup task. However, following a different analytical logic than Memon et al. (2002), they looked only at choices of "critical"
mugshots (those that subsequently appeared in the lineup) when assessing this relation.
Hence, the Perfect and Harris finding might be due to a "commitment effect," whereby
a witness who once has chosen a face (e.g., in a mugshot book) is likely to choose that
face again (see Dysart, Lindsay, Hammond, & Dupuis, 2001). The commitment effect
undoubtedly occurs, but it does not appear to capture the Memon et al. findings.

Some practical implications of these findings are clear. It is dangerous to administer
a lineup built around a suspect whose face was shown previously to an eyewitness, and
this practice is especially dangerous if the witness has previously picked a face. Judging

from the findings of Memon et al. (2002), a danger exists even when the witness previously picked a face other than that of the current suspect. At the level of theory, a mugshot choice appears to be diagnostic of a familiarity strategy for making identification decisions, and the use of this strategy is likely to lead to a false identification (if the suspect is innocent). Contrary to our previous view that only (or primarily) old adults use a familiarity strategy, it appears that a subset of healthy young adults use this strategy as well.

A final factor that appears to produce age-invariant effects is that of lineup structure. Since the classic study by Lindsay and Wells (1985), we have known that sequential presentation reduces false identifications of faces in target-absent lineups. Whether it can do so without also reducing correct identifications in target-present lineups is somewhat controversial. Early studies suggested that it could, supporting the view that witnesses use a better decision strategy with sequential lineups than with simultaneous lineups (i.e., an absolute decision strategy versus the inferior, relative strategy by which a witness simply picks that suspect who looks most similar to his or her image of the target face). However, more recent studies suggest that sequential presentation often reduces hits as well as false alarms, in line with the view that it leads to stricter criteria for identifying a suspect than does simultaneous presentation (Ebbesen & Flowe, 2002; Steblay, Dysart, Fulero, & Lindsay, 2001). Three of the studies in Table 13.1 included a simultaneous-sequential comparison, and, taken as a group, they appear to be in line with the latter conclusion: Searcy et al. (2000) found that sequential presentation of target-absent lineups increased correct rejections (i.e., it reduced false alarms), whereas Memon and Bartlett (2002) found that sequential presentation of target-present lineups reduced hits. Memon and Gabbert (2003b) used both target-present and target-absent lineups and found that sequential presentation both increased correct rejections and reduced hits. The simultaneous-sequential differences were observed with both young adults and seniors, and there was no support for age X lineup-structure interactions. Thus, if it is viewed as desirable that both young and old witnesses use a stringent criterion in the lineup task, sequential presentation may be a good option. One can only hope that future research will better characterize those conditions in which sequential presentation improves correct rejections without reducing hits (see Steblay et al., 2001). As such conditions are identified, it will become important to determine if young adults and seniors enjoy equal benefits from sequential presentation.

SUMMARY AND CONCLUSIONS

The small body of research on the older eyewitness has supported several important conclusions, taught us several methodological lessons, and raised a host of interesting questions for theory and application that new research should address. One well-supported conclusion is that memory for crime-relevant information—including memory for a perpetrator's face as tested in a lineup—is generally impaired in senior witnesses if education and verbal ability are controlled, if the seniors are over 70 years of age, and if the perpetrator is young. With highly educated and verbally skilled seniors, or seniors who are less than 70 years old, age deficits may be absent or even reversed. This appears to be true with older perpetrators too, though subject-age X face-age interactions are currently much better established in standard laboratory paradigms than in more forensically relevant tasks. What can be concluded from the evidence in hand is that young-adult witnesses perform better with young-adult faces than with old faces. The rather perpetrators, young-adult eyewitnesses may be even less reliable than prior evidence suggests.

Within the lineup task, age-related deficits in correct rejections of target-absent lineups are larger and more consistent than age-related deficits in correct identifications from target-present lineups, a finding in line with a good deal of evidence from standard laboratory paradigms. Additionally, age-related deficits with either type of lineup are more likely to appear in conditions where young-adult performance is high. Lineup performance by young adults and seniors appears to be related to face-matching ability, efficiency of executive functioning, and source memory ability, although the mixed state and/or paucity of evidence calls for more research on these points.

Four methodological points arise from this review. First, education level and verbal skills of the participants in different age groups should always be reported and, where appropriate, controlled. Second, where investigators are assessing interactions between age and an independent variable (e.g., mugshot presentation), they should take steps to match the performance of young adults and seniors in at least one test condition. Otherwise, the interactions will be subject to scaling artifacts that will plague interpretation. Third, future researchers working on predictors of individuals' performance in eyewitness tasks should consider using multiple measures to converge on each construct of interest (e.g., multiple measures of executive function if that is the construct of interest). Fourth, when stimulus variables (e.g., face age) are being examined, it is important to examine generality over stimuli. The mixed evidence on face-age effects in lineup tasks is quite likely to be due, at least in part, to use of a small set of young and old faces that might vary in distinctiveness and other characteristics that can affect performance apart from face age.

More evidence is needed on almost every issue discussed in this review. However, there are certain issues where the need for new research is particularly pressing. One of these issues is how retention interval affects young and old eyewitnesses. A handful of studies suggest that senior eyewitnesses—at least those over 70—are particularly impaired at longer retention intervals, a finding of enormous forensic importance if it generalizes widely. Another pressing issue is whether a brief regimen of training prior to a lineup (or verbal interview) can improve the performance of an old (or young) eyewitness. A third important issue is how mugshot viewing and mugshot choosing are related to lineup performance by both young adults and seniors.

No doubt the reader can add to the list, but perhaps we should close with an appeal for research that is guided by theory. Put simply, we do not understand the nature and causes of age differences in eyewitness testimony. We previously have advanced the hypothesis that, because of problems in memory for source, older individuals place more reliance on perceived familiarity in making lineup decisions. This hypothesis has been partly supported by Memon, Bartlett et al. (2003), who found a substantial age deficit in a source memory measure and who showed that this measure was reliably correlated with successful identifications in a lineup task. However, we and others have failed to find evidence that seniors' problems with false identifications occur because they rely more heavily on perceived familiarity than do young adults. The field is in need of additional hypotheses and experiments that test them.

ACKNOWLEDGMENTS

Research reported in this paper was supported by National Science Foundation grants SBR 9515231 to the first author and SBR 9809977 and an Economic & Social Research Council grant to both authors.

REFERENCES

Adams-Price, C. (1992). Eyewitness memory and aging: Predictors of accuracy in recall and person recognition. *Psychology and Aging, 7*, 602–608.

Anderson, N. D., & Craik, F. I. M. (2000). Memory in the aging brain. In E. Tulving & F. I. M. Craik (Eds), *The Oxford handbook of memory* (pp. 411–426). Oxford: New York.

Bäckman, L. (1991). Recognition memory across the adult lifespan: The role of prior knowledge. *Memory & Cognition, 19*, 63–71.

Bäckman, L., Small, B. J., & Wahlin, Å (2000). Cognitive functioning in very old age. In F. I. M. Craik & T. A. Salthouse (Eds.), *The handbook of aging and cognition* (pp. 499–558). Mahwah, NJ: Lawrence Erlbaum Associates.

Balota, D. A., Dolan, P., & Duchek, J. (2000). Memory changes in healthy older adults. In E. Tulving & F. I. M. Craik (Eds), *The Oxford handbook of memory* (pp. 395–410). Oxford: New York.

Bartlett, J. C. (1993). Limits on losses in face recognition. In J. Cerella, J. Rybash, W. Hoyer, & M. L. Commons (Eds.), *Adult information processing: Limits on loss* (pp. 352–379). New York: Academic Press.

Bartlett, J. C., & Fulton, A. (1991). Familiarity and recognition of faces: The factor of age. *Memory & Cognition, 19*, 229–23.

Bartlett, J. C., & Leslie, J. E. (1986). Aging and memory for faces versus pictures of faces. *Memory & Cognition, 14*, 371–381.

Bartlett, J. C., Leslie, J. E., Tubbs, A., & Fulton, A. (1989). Aging and memory for pictures of faces. *Psychology and Aging, 4*, 276–283.

Bartlett, J. C., Strater, L., & Fulton, A. (1991). False recency and false fame of faces in young adulthood and old age. *Memory & Cognition, 19*, 177–188.

Benton, A. L., Sivan, A., Hamsher, K., Varney, N. R., & Spreen, O. (1994). *Facial recognition: stimulus and multiple choice pictures: Contributions to neuropsychological assessment* (pp. 35–52). New York: Oxford University Press.

Bornstein, B. H. (1995). Memory processes in elderly eyewitnesses: What we know and what we don't know. *Behavioral Sciences and the Law, 13*, 337–348.

Bornstein, B. H., Witt, C. J., Cherry, K. E., & Greene, E. (2000). The suggestibility of older witnesses. In M. B. Rothman, B. D. Dunlop, & P. Entzel (Eds.), *Elders, crime, and the criminal justice system* (pp. 149–161). New York: Springer.

Borsari, B., & Carey, K. B. (2001). Peer influences on college drinking: A review of research. *Journal of Susbstance Abuse, 13*, 391–424.

Bothwell, R. K., Brigham, J. C., & Malpass, R. S. (1989). Cross-racial identification. *Personality and Social Psychology Bulletin, 15*, 19–25.

Brimacombe, C. A. E., Jung, S., Garrioch, L., & Allison, M. (2003). Perceptions of older adult witnesses: Will you believe me when I am 64? *Law & Human Behavior, 27*, 507–523.

Brimacombe, C. A. E., Quinton, N., Nance, N., & Garrioch (1997). Is age irrelevant? Perceptions of young and old eyewitnesses. *Law and Human Behavior, 21*, 619–634.

Brown, E., Deffenbacher, K., & Sturgill, W. (1977). Memory for faces and the circumstances of encounter. *Journal of Applied Psychology, 62*, 311–318.

Bruce, V. (1982). Changing faces: Visual and nonvisual coding processes in face recognition. *British Journal of Psychology, 73*, 105–116.

Bruce, V, Henderson, Z., Greenwood, K., Hancock, P. J. B., Burton, A. M., & Miller, P. (1999). Verification of face identities from images captured on video. *Journal of Experimental Psychology: Applied, 5*, 339–360.

Butler, K. M., McDaniel, M. A., Dornburg, C. C., Roediger, H. L., & Price, A. L. (2004). Age differences in veridical and false recall are not inevitable: The role of frontal lobe function. *Psychological Bulletin and Review.*

Cohen, G., & Faulkner, D. (1989). Age differences in source forgetting: Effects on reality monitoring and on eyewitness testimony. *Psychology and Aging, 4*, 10–17.

Coxon, P., & Valentine, T. (1997). The effects of the age of eyewitnesses on the accuracy and suggestibility of their testimony. *Applied Cognitive Psychology, 11*, 415–430.

Craik, F. I. M. (1986). A functional account of age differences in memory. In F. Klix & H. Hagendorf (Eds.), *Human memory and cognitive capabilities* (pp. 409–422). Amsterdam: Elsevier.

Davies, G. M., & Milne, A. (1982). Recognizing faces in and out of context. *Current Psychological Research, 2*, 235–246.

Dodson, C. S., Johnson, M. K., & Schooler, J. W. (1997). The verbal overshadowing effect: Source confusion or strategy shift? *Memory & Cognition, 25*, 129–139.

Dysart, J., Lindsay, R. C. L., Hammond, R., & Dupuis, P. (2001). Mugshot exposure prior to lineup identification: Interference, transference and commitment effects. *Journal of Applied Psychology, 86*, 1280–1284.

Ebbesen, E., & Flowe, H. (2002). *Simultaneous v. sequential lineups: What do we really know?* Unpublished manuscript.

Fisher, R. P., & Geiselman, R. E. (1992). *Memory-enhancing techniques for investigative interviewing: The cognitive interview.* Springfield, IL: Charles C. Thomas.

Fulton, A., & Bartlett, J. C. (1991). Young and old faces in young and old heads: The factor of age in face recognition. *Psychology and Aging, 6*, 623–30.

Gabbert, F., Memon, A., & Allan, K. (2003). Memory conformity: Can eyewitnesses influence each other's memories for an event? *Applied Cognitive Psychology, 17*, 533–544.

Glisky, E. L., Polster, M. R., & Routhieaux, B. C. (1995). Double dissociation between item and source memory. *Neuropsychology, 9*, 229–235.

Glisky, E. L., Rubin, S. R., & Davidson, S. R. (2001). Source memory in older adults: An encoding or retrieval problem? *Journal of Experimental Psychology: Learning, Memory and Cognition, 27*, 1131–1146.

Halpern, A. R., & Bartlett, J. C. (2002). Aging and memory for music: A review. *Psychomusicology, 18*, 10–27.

Henkel, L. A., Johnson, M. K., & De Leonardis, D. M. (1998). Aging and source monitoring: Cognitive processes and neuropsychological correlates. *Journal of Experimental Psychology: General, 127*, 251–268.

Jennings, J. M., & Jacoby, L. L. (1997). An opposition procedure for detecting age related deficits in repetition: The telling effects of repetition. *Psychology and Aging, 12*, 352–361.

Johnson, M. K., Hashtroudi, S., & Lindsay, D. S. (1993). Source monitoring. *Psychological Bulletin, 114*, 3–28.

Karpel, M. E., Hoyer, W. J., & Toglia, M. P. (2001). Accuracy and qualities of real and suggested memories: Nonspecific age differences. *Journal of Gerontology: Psychological Sciences and Social Sciences, 56*, 103–110.

Kelley, W. M., & Jacoby, L. L. (2000). Recollection and familiarity: Process-dissociation. In E. Tulving & F. I. M. Craik (Eds.), *The Oxford handbook of memory* (pp. 215–228). Oxford: New York.

Koutstaal, W., & Schacter, D. (1997). Gist based false recognition of pictures in older and younger adults. *Journal of Memory and Language, 37,* 555–583.

Koutstaal, W., Schacter, D. L., Galluccio, L., & Stofer, K. A. (1999). Reducing gist-based false recognition in older adults: Encoding and retrieval manipulations. *Psychology and Aging, 14,* 220–237.

Kwong See, S. T., Hoffman, H. G., & Wood, T. L. (2001). Perceptions of an old female eyewitness: Is the older eyewitness believable? *Psychology and Aging, 16,* 346–350.

Lindholm, T. (2003). *Own-age bias in verbal person memory.* Paper presented at the SARMAC Conference, University of Aberdeen, Scotland, July, 2003.

Lindsay, R. C. L., & Wells, G. L. (1985). Improving eyewitness identifications from lineups: Simultaneous versus sequential lineup presentation. *Journal of Applied Psychology, 70,* 556–564.

Loftus, E. F., Levidow, B., & Duensing, S. (1992). Who remembers best? Individual differences in memory for events that occurred in a science museum. *Applied Cognitive Psychology, 6,* 93–107.

Macrae, C. N., & Lewis, H. L. (2002). Do I know you? Processing orientation and face recognition. *Psychological Science, 13,* 194–196.

Mason, S. E. (1986). Age and gender as factors in facial recognition and identification. *Experimental Aging Research, 12,* 151–154.

Meissner, C. A., & Brigham, J. C. (2001). A meta-analysis of the verbal overshadowing effect in face identification. *Applied Cognitive Psychology, 15,* 603–616.

Mello, E. W., & Fisher, R. P. (1996). Enhancing older adult eyewitness memory with the cognitive interview. *Applied Cognitive Psychology, 10,* 403–417.

Memon, A. (1999). Cognitive Interviewing. In A. Memon & R. Bull (Eds.), *Handbook of the psychology of interviewing.* Chichester: Wiley.

Memon, A., & Bartlett, J. C. (2002). The effects of verbalization on face recognition in young and older adults. *Applied Cognitive Psychology, 16,* 635–650.

Memon, A., Bartlett, J. C., Rose, R., & Gray, C. (2003). The aging eyewitness: The effects of face-age and delay upon younger and older observers. *Journal of Gerontology: Psychological Sciences and Social Sciences, 58,* P338–P345.

Memon, A., & Gabbert, F. (2003a). Unravelling the effects of a sequential lineup. *Applied Cognitive Psychology, 6,* 703–714.

Memon, A., & Gabbert, F. (2003b). Improving the identification accuracy of senior witnesses: Do pre-lineup questions and sequential testing help? *Journal of Applied Psychology, 88,* 341–347.

Memon, A., Gabbert, F., & Hope, L. (2004). The ageing eyewitness. In J. Adler (Ed.), *Forensic psychology: Debates, concepts and Practice* (pp. 96–112). Willan, Forensic Psychology Series: Ufcolme Devon.

Memon, A., Hope, L., Bartlett, J. C., & Bull, R. (2002). Eyewitness recognition errors: The effects of mugshot viewing and choosing in young and old adults. *Memory & Cognition, 30,* 1219–1227.

Memon, A., Hope, L., & Bull, R. H. C. (2003). Exposure duration: Effects on eyewitness accuracy and confidence. *British Journal of Psychology, 94,* 339–354.

Memon, A., & Wright, D. (2000). Eyewitness testimony: Theoretical and practical issues. In J. McGuire, T. Mason, & A. O'Kane (Eds.), *Behaviour, crime and legal process.* Chichester: John Wiley & Sons.

Mitchell, K. J., Johnson, M. K., & Mather, M. (2003). Source monitoring and suggestibility to misinformation: Adult age-related differences. *Applied Cognitive Psychology, 17,* 107–119.

O'Rourke, T. E., Penrod, S. D., Cutler, B. L., & Stuve, T. E. (1989). The external validity of eye-witness identification research: Generalizing across subject populations. *Law and Human Behavior, 13,* 385–395.

Perfect, T. J., & Harris, L. J. (2003). Adult age differences in unconscious transference: Source confusion or identity blending? *Memory and Cognition, 31,* 570–580.

Pierce, B. H., Smith, S. M., & Bartlett, J. C. (2004). Age differences in environmental context-dependent eyewitness recognition. Unpublished manuscript.

Pozzulo, J. D., & Warren, K. L. (2003). Descriptions and identifications of strangers by youth and adult eyewitnesses. *Journal of Applied Psychology, 88,* 315–323.

Read, J. D. (1994). Understanding bystander misidentifications: The role of familiarity and contextual knowledge. In D. F. Ross, J. D. Read, & M. P. Toglia (Eds.), *Adult eyewitness testimony: Current trends and developments* (pp. 56–79). New York: Cambridge University Press.

Rice, G. E., & Meyer, B. J. F. (1986). Reading behavior and prose recall performance of young and older adults with high and average verbal ability. *Educational Gerontology, 11,* 57–72.

Rodin, M. J. (1987). Who is memorable to whom: A study of cognitive disregard. *Social Cognition, 5,* 144–165.

Rosch, E., Mervis, C. B., Gray, W., Johnson, D., & Boyes-Braem, P. (1976). Basic objects in natural categories. *Cognitive Psychology, 8,* 382–439.

Ross, D. F., Ceci, S. J., Dunning, D., & Toglia, M. P. (1994). Unconscious transference and mistaken identity: When a witness misidentifies a familiar but innocent person. *Journal of Applied Psychology, 79,* 918–930.

Ross, D. F., Dunning, D., Toglia, M. P., & Ceci, S. J. (1990). The child in the eyes of the jury: Assessing mock jurors' perceptions of the child witness. *Law and Human Behavior, 14,* 5–23.

Rothmans, M. B., Dunlop, B. D., & Entzel, P. (2000). *Elders, crime and the criminal justice system: Myth, perceptions and reality in the 21st century.* Springer Series on Life Styles and Issues in Aging. New York: Springer.

Salthouse, T. A. (2000). Methodological assumptions in cognitive aging research. In F. I. M. Craik & T. A. Salthouse (Eds.), *The handbook of aging and cognition* (pp. 467–498). Mahwah, NJ: Lawrence Erlbaum Associates.

Salthouse, T. A. (2004). What and when of cognitive aging. *Current Directions in Psychological Science, 13,* 140–144.

Schacter, D. L., Kihlstrom, J. F., Kaszniak, A. W., & Valdiserri, M. (1993). Preserved and impaired memory functions in elderly adults. In J. Cerella, J. M. Rybash, W. Hoyer, M. L. Commons (Eds.), Adult information processing: Limits on loss (pp. 327–350). San Diego: Academic Press.

Schacter, D. L., Kaszniak, A. W., Kihlstrom, J. F., & Valdiserri, M. (1991). The relation between source memory and aging. *Psychology and Aging, 6,* 559–568.

Schacter, D. L., Koutstaal, W., & Norman, K. A. (1997). False memories and aging. *Trends in Cognitive Sciences, 1,* 229–236.

Schooler, J. W., Fiore, S. M., & Brandimonte, M. A. (1997). At a loss for words: Verbal overshadowing of perceptual memories. In D. L. Medin (Ed.), *The psychology of learning and motivation* (pp. 292–334). San Diego: Academic Press.

Searcy, J. H., Bartlett, J. C., & Memon, A. (1999). Age differences in accuracy and choosing rates on face recognition and eyewitness identification tasks. *Memory & Cognition, 27,* 538–552.

Searcy, J. H., Bartlett, J. C., & Memon, A. (2000). Influence of post-event narratives, line-up conditions and individual differences on false identification by young and older eyewitnesses. *Legal and Criminological Psychology, 5,* 219–235.

Searcy, J. H., Bartlett, J. C., Memon, A., & Swanson, K (2001). Aging and lineup performance at long retention intervals: Effects of metamemory and context reinstatement. *Journal of Applied Psychology, 86*(2), 207–214.

Seipel, A. H. (2002). *Face-processing practice: A new tool for improving eyewitness identification.* Doctoral dissertation, University of Texas at Dallas, 2002.

Seipel, A. H., & Bartlett, J. C. (2002). *Whole-face processing practice and improved eyewitness testimony.* "Hot Topic" talk presented at the Meeting of the American Psychological Society, New Orleans, June, 2002.

Seipel, A. H., Bartlett, J. C., Searcy, J. H., & Memon, A. (2000). *The role of familiarity and cognitive performance in predicting the accuracy of young and old eyewitnesses in a lineup identification task.* Poster presented at the American Psychology and Law Society Conference, New Orleans, 2000.

Shapiro, P. N., & Penrod, S. (1986). Meta-analysis of facial identification studies. *Psychological Bulletin, 100,* 139–156.

Shimamura, A. P., & Jurica, P. J. (1994). Memory interference effects and aging: Findings from a test of frontal lobe function. *Neuropsychology, 8,* 408–412.

Smith, A. D., & Winograd, E. (1978). Adult age differences in remembering faces. *Developmental Psychology, 14,* 443–444.

Steblay, N. M., Dysart, J., Fulero, S., & Lindsay, R. C. L. (2001). Eyewitness accuracy rates in sequential and simultaneous lineup presentations: A meta-analytic comparison. *Law and Human Behavior, 25,* 459–474.

Wegesin, D. J., Jacobs, D. M., Zubin, N. R., Ventura, P. R., & Stern, Y. (2000). Source memory and encoding strategy in normal aging. *Journal of Clinical and Experimental Neuropsychology, 22,* 455–464.

Weingardt, K., Loftus, E., & Lindsay, D. S. (1995). Misinformation revisited: New evidence on the suggestibility of memory. *Memory & Cognition, 23,* 72–82.

Wright, D. B., & Loftus, E. F. (1998). How misinformation alters memories. *Journal of Experimental Child Psychology, 71,* 155–164.

Wright, D. B., & Stroud, J. (2002). Age differences in lineup identification accuracy: People are better with their own age. *Law and Human Behavior, 26,* 641–54.

Yarmey, A. D. (1982). Eyewitness identification and stereotypes of criminals. In A. Trankell (Ed.), *Reconstructing the past: The role of psychologists in criminal trials* (pp. 205–225). Stockholm: Norstedt & Soners.

Yarmey, A. D. (2001). The Older Eyewitness. In M. B. Rothman, B. D. Dunlop, & P. Entzel (Eds.), *Elders, crime and the criminal justice system* (pp. 127–147). New York: Springer.

Yarmey, A. D., Jones, H. T., & Rashid, S. (1984). Eyewitness memory of elderly and young adults. In D. J. Muller, D. E. Blackman, & A. J. Chapman (Eds.), *Psychology and law* (pp. 215–228). Chichester, England: John Wiley & Sons.

Yarmey, A. D., & Kent, J. (1980). Eyewitness identification by elderly and young adults. *Law and Human Behavior, 4,* 359–371.

Yonelinas, A. P. (2002). The nature of recollection and familiarity: A review of 30 years of research. *Journal of Memory and Language, 46,* 441–517.

Zaragoza, M. S., Lane, S. M., Ackil, J. K., & Chambers, K. L. (1997). Confusing real and suggested memories: Source monitoring and eyewitness suggestibility. In N. L. Stein, P. A. Ornstein, B. Tversky, & C. Brainerd (Eds.), *Memory for everyday and emotional events* (pp. 401–425). Mahwah, NJ: Lawrence Erlbaum Associates.

14

Remembering and Identifying Menacing Perpetrators: Exposure to Violence and the Weapon Focus Effect

Kerri L. Pickel
Ball State University

On the morning of March 5, 2001, 17-year-old John Schardt watched from a classroom at Santana High School near San Diego as a younger boy with a .22-caliber revolver emerged from the restroom across the hall and began firing at other students, who tried to scramble out of harm's way. Wounded students who could not escape fell to the floor, screaming. It was total chaos, John later told a reporter. The perpetrator fired more than 30 rounds in all, striking 15 people, two of whom died. Short, scrawny, and often ignored or picked on by other teens, he seemed to want some sort of revenge for being mistreated, but many of the students in the hallway apparently did not know him. John noticed that the boy was smiling as he fired the pistol (Finz, Kim, & Fagan, 2001; Finz, Kim, Fagan, & Brazil, 2001).

WITNESSING VIOLENCE

Unfortunately, incidents like this one, along with gang violence, convenience store robberies, street muggings, and drug deals gone bad, occur all too frequently. Police often look to witnesses to help them create a list of suspects, so it is important for researchers to discover how witnesses remember violent events.

Accuracy of Witnesses' Reports

Some studies have compared the accuracy of witnesses' memory for violent versus neutral events. For example, Clifford and Scott's (1978) participants watched either a violent or a nonviolent version of a black-and-white video of an interaction between two police officers and a civilian. In the nonviolent scene, the officers ask a reluctant civilian to help locate a crime suspect. In the violent version, the man's reluctance leads to an exchange of physical blows. The witnesses who saw the nonviolent scene provided more accurate descriptions of the characters than did those who saw the violent scene, regardless of whether they responded with free recall or by answering specific questions.

Loftus and Burns (1982) obtained similar results when they asked participants to view a film depicting a robbery that was created for training bank employees. One version ends in violence when the robber, fleeing through a parking lot, fires a gunshot that hits one of two young boys who had been playing in the area. The wounded boy falls, bleeding from the face. The control version ends with the bank manager calming the employees and customers. After watching the film, witnesses answered several questions, including some about the robber's appearance and one "critical item" that asked for the number on the football jersey of one of the boys. Witnesses who saw the nonviolent version were much more likely to recall the jersey number than were witnesses who saw the violent ending, and they also answered most of the other questions more accurately.

Although these two lab studies imply that violence reduces accuracy, some field research points to a different conclusion. Yuille and Cutshall (1986) interviewed 13 witnesses to an actual shooting 4 to 5 months after the incident, in which a gun shop owner chased a robber from his store into the street and exchanged shots with him, resulting in serious injury to the shopkeeper and the death of the robber. In order to analyze witness accuracy, the researchers endeavored to reconstruct what actually happened by referring to police reports and photographs, medical reports, and other information and by integrating the statements of all of the witnesses. Yuille and Cutshall judged that the descriptions of the persons and objects involved, as well as the actions that occurred, were mostly accurate, even after several months had passed, and their attempt to mislead the witnesses about the appearance of a car at the scene was unsuccessful. These conclusions should be tempered, however, by the fact that certain kinds of errors were common, notably in connection with physical descriptions. For example, estimates of height, age, and weight were about as likely to be wrong as they were to be correct. Clothing colors were also frequently misreported (see Cutshall & Yuille, 1989, for additional, similar data).

In another field study, Woolnough and MacLeod (2001) evaluated the accuracy of statements to police by witnesses to eight incidents of assault that had been captured on closed-circuit television (CCTV) surveillance systems in a Scottish town. All of the incidents involved a physical attack, though apparently not all resulted in serious injury. In only one case was a weapon used. The authors argued that their access to the CCTV tapes allowed them to overcome a common limitation of field studies, which is the difficulty of verifying the details in witnesses' reports. The authors found a high accuracy rate for recall of action details and physical descriptions, and accuracy did not vary as a function of the degree of violence. However, these results must be viewed cautiously, because (a) some details (e.g., clothing color) could not be verified because the CCTV tapes were monochrome or because the camera did not capture parts of certain incidents; (b) the police failed to question some witnesses in depth, possibly because they knew that the CCTV tapes were available; and (c) it is unclear whether some witnesses may have personally known some of the perpetrators they described, which could have increased accuracy for certain details.

Central versus Peripheral Details.   Rather than measure witness accuracy for all details combined, some researchers have found it helpful to distinguish between central and peripheral details in a scene. Generally, "central" details are defined as those that are thematically related to the gist of the event (e.g., the color of a bank robber's gun), whereas "peripheral" details are irrelevant (e.g., the color of a bystander's coat), or perhaps less relevant, as centrality is actually a continuous variable. Christianson (1992) pointed out that it can be difficult to ascertain in advance which details are central and which are peripheral, especially in field studies. However, in lab studies researchers can gather norms for this purpose.

Many studies have indicated that, compared with control participants, those exposed to a negative emotional event tend to exhibit improved recall for central details and worse recall for peripheral details (e.g., Brown, 2003; Christianson & Loftus, 1987, 1991). However, in most of this research the stimulus event was not specifically a violent crime but instead was a traumatic injury, such as a car accident or a scene of the aftermath of a crime, such as a slide of a woman lying on the ground with her throat cut. Nevertheless, it seems reasonable to expect that memory for the details of a violent crime may be consistent with the usually obtained pattern, such that physical details about the perpetrator should be well retained (at least if he or she is unarmed), whereas peripheral details such as information relating to bystanders might be poorly remembered.

Other Variables That May Affect Accuracy

Degree of Involvement.   The "involvement" of a witness could be defined as close proximity to the perpetrator or as being personally affected by the event. Either way, there are some reasons to predict that more involved witnesses would provide more accurate reports (Woolnough & MacLeod, 2001; Yuille & Cutshall, 1986). First, they might have a better opportunity to observe than would other witnesses. Second, they might be more motivated to encode and remember their observations so that they can protect themselves during the event or in order to bring the perpetrator to justice afterward. Finally, involved witnesses' active participation in an event could naturally lead to more elaborate encoding. In support of this prediction, Yuille and Cutshall classified the witnesses to the shooting they studied according to whether or not they had direct contact with the robber, shopkeeper, or weapon, and they discovered that the more involved witnesses were significantly more accurate in the police interview (though not in the research interview) than the other witnesses. The authors noted, however, that in this analysis involvement was confounded with stress.

Other data dispute the involvement hypothesis. When Yuille and Cutshall conducted an analysis using a slightly different definition of involvement and divided the witnesses into two groups (one that watched the event from a central location and one that remained at the periphery of the scene), they found that, although the "central" witnesses provided more details, they were not more accurate.

Similarly, Stanny and Johnson (2000) manipulated involvement while controlling the vantage point. In their Experiment 1, police officers watched realistic training videos that allowed trainees to interact with the characters. One version requires the officer to shoot at the perpetrator after the perpetrator fires his own weapon at the officer. The participants were tested in pairs such that one actually interacted with the video while the other merely watched, but both were positioned in locations that allowed an adequate opportunity to observe. The researchers reported no difference between the two groups in terms of the number of correct details remembered about the perpetrator, victim, weapon, and the characters' actions.

Although not about violence per se, lab studies of nonviolent robberies and thefts may be informative because some deal with the effects of experiencing a personal loss at the hands of a potentially threatening perpetrator. These studies yield mixed findings. Some have demonstrated no significant differences between the accuracy of victims and bystander witnesses (Behrman & Davey, 2001;[1] Hosch & Cooper, 1982; Hosch, Leippe, Marchioni, & Cooper, 1984). Others have found that victims are more accurate than bystanders when describing the perpetrator but not when making a lineup identification (Hosch & Bothwell, 1990). Similarly, Christianson and Hübinette (1993) reported that bank robbery victims (tellers) remembered details (including physical information about the perpetrators) more accurately than did bystander witnesses, but they were unsure about the cause of this difference. It may have occurred because of the victims' personal engagement with the robbers, perhaps accompanied by high levels of motivation to see them arrested, but it may instead have resulted from the victims' vantage point (facing the robbers across the bank counter), which allowed them to see details the bystanders could not. Alternatively, the difference could be attributed to the training that the tellers may have received to prepare them for possible robberies; in support of this hypothesis, the employee bystanders provided more accurate information than did the customer bystanders. In summary, it is at present unclear whether more involvement leads to better memory and, if so, why it does so.

Male versus Female Witnesses. Some data (e.g., Clifford & Scott, 1978; Kuehn, 1974; McLeod & Shepherd, 1986) suggest that male witnesses and victims can report more details or more accurate details concerning violent crimes than females can, possibly because women are socialized to feel more fearful or helpless in such situations than men are (Kuehn, 1974). However, Lindholm and Christianson (1998) noted that these findings may simply reflect a same-gender bias, as most perpetrators in previous studies were probably male. These researchers showed participants a video of a stabbing in which the genders of both the victim and perpetrator were manipulated. Their results showed, in addition to a same-gender bias, a tendency for females to recall the perpetrator more accurately than males. The authors proposed that females might have more elaborate person categories (as other research has shown), which might help them encode more detailed information about the perpetrator. As these results conflict with those of earlier studies, more investigation is clearly needed.

---

[1]Behrman and Davey included a few violent crimes (e.g., assaults) in their analysis.

Attributions About Victims and Perpetrators.   Gender differences may also play a role in the attributions witnesses make about victims and perpetrators. In their study, in which witnesses viewed a video of a stabbing that occurred in the kitchen of an apartment during a party, Lindholm and Christianson (1998) reported that witnesses saw male perpetrators as more culpable than female perpetrators and male victims as more responsible than female victims. The witnesses also thought the perpetrator of either gender was more responsible when the victim was female rather than male. The authors interpreted their results as evidence that witnesses are influenced by the social stereotypes that men are agentic whereas women are submissive.

Other forms of stereotypes can similarly affect observers' inferences. Lindholm, Christianson, and Karlsson (1997) showed Swedish university students, police recruits, and police officers a video in which a man robs a grocery store and cuts the cashier with a knife. The researchers manipulated the apparent ethnicity of the perpetrator so that he seemed to be either a native Swede with fair skin and blonde hair or an immigrant with dark hair and skin. The students and recruits rated the perpetrator as more culpable if they saw the immigrant rather than the native Swede, but the pattern was reversed for police witnesses. Lindholm et al. thought that the students and recruits were simply displaying an anti-outgroup bias that reflected Swedish citizens' concerns about the overrepresentation of immigrants in crime statistics in Sweden. They also suggested two reasons that the police officers failed to show this bias: (a) their training might allow them to watch a violent incident without increased stress, which in turn leaves them with a relatively large amount of cognitive resources to devote to perceiving the perpetrator as an individual; and (b) the police organization and/or the citizenry may exert pressure on the officers to avoid ethnocentrism, so they may try to inhibit prejudiced behavior, at least publicly.

Witnesses of any social group might be influenced by the stereotypes known to them as they encode and retrieve information about others at the scene. Moreover, witnesses might be affected by prejudiced beliefs regarding not only a perpetrator's gender and ethnicity, but also his or her age, socioeconomic status, and, as in the case of certain terrorist attacks, religion. Future research could identify the ways in which these stereotypes distort witnesses' perceptions as well as the limits of such effects.

Police versus Civilian Witnesses.   Some researchers have investigated the possible effects of police training on the ability to remember crime details. Both police officers and citizens believe that officers can notice and remember events happening around them better than others (Yarmey, 1986). There are several reasons to expect that police personnel might display a better memory for violent incidents than would civilians. For example, police training may give officers detailed knowledge about criminal behavior, which would help them attend to relevant details and avoid distraction. Moreover, having learned about variables that affect witness accuracy, they might be able to adopt techniques that take advantage of the beneficial influence of certain ones while minimizing the negative impact of others. Police officers might also have figured out how to control stress reactions to the extent that they would perform better than civilians (Stanny & Johnson, 2000). Although police training might produce the benefits described above, an alternative reason to predict that officers should show superior eyewitness memory is that the profession might attract individuals who already possess good observational skills and/or an ability to manage stress reactions (Christianson, Karlsson, & Persson, 1998; Stanny & Johnson, 2000).

Many studies have compared police versus civilian eyewitness memory with the use of neutral or emotional but nonviolent stimuli, but few have explicitly looked at memory within the context of a violent crime. In one such study (Stanny & Johnson, 2000), citizens (students) and officers watched two interactive training videos, the first enacting a domestic disturbance in which the perpetrator relinquishes a gun without threatening to shoot and the second portraying an attempted abduction in which the perpetrator fires at participants. Witnesses answered questions about the perpetrator, victim, weapon, and other details. The results showed similar levels of accuracy in police and citizen witnesses.

In contrast, two other studies yielded different findings. Lindholm et al. (1997) asked university students, police recruits, and police officers to watch a video of a robbery and stabbing. Compared with the recruits and students, the officers remembered more information about the perpetrator and were better at selecting his knife in a photo lineup. However, the groups did not vary in their ability to identify the perpetrator.

In the second study (Christianson et al., 1998), university students, high school teachers, police recruits, and police officers viewed a slide sequence in which a man stabs a woman walking through a park. The witnesses attempted to recall information about the crime, including the perpetrator's appearance and actions, before answering multiple-choice questions about the same details. Finally, they tried to identify the perpetrator in a photo lineup. On the recall task, the officers and students remembered a higher proportion of correct details about the perpetrator than did the teachers, with the recruits' performance not varying from any other group's. The officers also reported more information about the victim than did the recruits and teachers, but not more than the students. On the recognition task, the officers remembered more about the perpetrator than did the teachers, with no other comparisons reaching significance, but memory for the victim did not vary across groups. There were also no differences in rates of identification of the perpetrator.

In additional analyses, Christianson et al. discovered that, among police officers, memory performance was predicted by years of service on the job. They took this correlation as evidence that police training can improve one's ability to encode and retain relevant details and/or control stress reactions over that of civilian witnesses. The results offer less support for the hypothesis that high-performing individuals are attracted to law enforcement careers, as the recruits did not respond exactly like the officers.

Repeated Attempts to Remember Information.   Most studies involve testing memory at only a single point in time. An interesting question is whether witnesses tested repeatedly at different delay intervals might exhibit *hypermnesia*, defined as "increases in net recall on successive trials" (Turtle & Yuille, 1994, p. 261). This question is particularly pertinent because real witnesses are commonly asked to describe what they saw more than once; they will probably give an initial statement to the responding police officer, another days later to a detective, and perhaps others to lawyers, to a victim services agency, and at trial (Turtle & Yuille).

Although the phenomenon of hypermnesia itself has been well documented, little research has explored whether it will occur after a person witnesses a violent and perhaps upsetting crime. In one study (Scrivner & Safer, 1988), participants watched a police training video depicting a break-in during which the burglar shoots three people. The witnesses completed three separate 7-minute attempts to recall information from the video (including the burglar's appearance) during the next hour, followed by a fourth attempt 48 hours later. Hypermnesia occurred across the four trials for details of all types, with only a slight increase in the number of errors. Scrivner and Safer suggested that successful recall of any specific crime detail increases the likelihood of later recalling related details as well as that same detail. They also cautioned that typical eyewitness memory studies that use only one recall test "may seriously underestimate what a witness can report about events" (p. 375).

Scrivner and Safer's procedure was criticized by Turtle and Yuille (1994), who argued that it is unrealistic to limit the amount of time witnesses can spend on each recall attempt and to use brief intertrial intervals ranging from a few minutes to 48 hours. Therefore, Turtle and Yuille's witnesses were allowed to take as long as they wanted to complete each trial, and the four recall trials were separated by 1-week periods. The stimulus event was a video of a shooting of two people during an attempted robbery. The authors found no gain in the *net* number of details reported over successive attempts (i.e., hypermnesia did not occur). However, they did obtain a *reminiscence* effect; there was an increase in *gross* recall, such that new details were provided across attempts, but witnesses did not reiterate previously reported details. Increases in errors across trials were minimal. Turtle and Yuille concluded that, although hypermnesia is unlikely to occur in actual criminal investigations, the fact that reminiscence can occur makes it worthwhile to question witnesses multiple times, although they acknowledged that a reminiscence pattern could be interpreted by jurors or judges as inconsistency, which opposing counsel could try to exploit in the courtroom. The authors conceive of memory retrieval as an example of stimulus sampling and argue that successive attempts to recall the same event retrieve different samples from a population of potential details. This conceptualization seems to imply that different samples are independent of one another, which might not be true if the intertrial interval is small or if witnesses rehearse the previous attempt before beginning the next. Future investigation is needed to determine which situations will produce hypermnesia or reminiscence.

Underlying Mechanisms Regarding the Impact of Violence on Memory

Researchers have presumed that the mechanisms involved when people witness violence are the same as when they experience any negative emotional event, such as a traumatic accident or disaster (see Reisberg & Heuer, other volume). A commonly invoked account based on Easterbrook's (1959) cue utilization hypothesis states that a traumatic event elevates witnesses' levels of psychological and physiological arousal,[2] which causes an automatic narrowing of attention such that witnesses tend to focus on central details (those most related to the source of the arousal) instead of peripheral ones (Safer, Christianson, Autry, & Österland, 1998). Post-stimulus elaboration also occurs; witnesses will spend time and effort rehearsing central information because "emotional materials are, by their nature, often worth thinking about" (Heuer & Reisberg, 1992, p. 171). Through this combination of attentional and elaborative mechanisms, witnessing a traumatic event rather than a neutral episode will lead to better memory for central details and worse memory for peripheral details.

An example of an experiment that lends support to the Easterbrook hypothesis is one conducted by Safer et al. (1998) in which participants watched a slide sequence that contained either a scene of a woman with her throat slashed or a neutral scene. Witnesses in the traumatic condition exhibited "tunnel memory," in that they remembered the emotion-arousing details on the slide as being more spatially focused than they actually were. In contrast, control witnesses showed "boundary extension," incorrectly remembering that a presented slide had included certain details that were not actually visible but were likely to exist just outside the slide's frame. Safer et al. proposed that elaboration as well as attentional narrowing caused these effects, no doubt because other research has demonstrated that attentional processes alone are probably insufficient to explain the central/peripheral findings. Christianson, Loftus, Hoffman, and Loftus (1991) obtained the usual difference between memories for central and peripheral details, even when witnesses' allocation of attention to the details (operationally defined as eye fixations) was controlled.

The biological underpinnings of the processes described in the Easterbrook hypothesis could be the activity of β-adrenergic hormones in the amygdala (see McGaugh, 2004), which is a structure within the brain's limbic system that is involved in emotional processing. Cahill, Prins, Weber, and McGaugh (1994) reported that propanolol (a β-adrenergic blocker) selectively impaired participants' memory for emotional but not neutral details from a story, which implies that the adrenergic hormones are involved when witnesses to emotional events remember central details relatively well and peripheral details relatively poorly. Furthermore, Cahill, Babinsky, Markowitsch, and McGaugh (1995) found that a participant with bilateral damage to the amygdaloid complex failed to show the usual central/peripheral pattern when asked to remember details of a slide sequence depicting a traumatic injury.

Yuille and colleagues (Cutshall & Yuille, 1989; Tollestrup et al., 1994; Yuille & Cutshall, 1986; Yuille & Tollestrup, 1992) have argued that lab results may not generalize to

---

[2]As used in the literature to describe Easterbrook's hypothesis, *arousal* seems synonymous with *anxiety* (an unpleasant experience of tension or fearfulness) or Christianson's (1992, p. 285) term, *emotional stress* (a feeling of "stress or distress with concurrent autonomic-hormonal changes" that occurs as "a consequence of [witnessing] a negative emotional event"). Arousal can range along a continuum from mild to overwhelming. Except when paraphrasing authors who prefer the term *arousal*, I use the word *anxiety*, because it clearly describes the emotional and physiological state in question and differentiates it from alternative definitions of *arousal*, such as an orienting response toward a stimulus.

real eyewitness situations because lab participants do not feel nearly as anxious as actual witnesses do. In response, Schooler and Eich (2000) have pointed out that "the success of Cahill and his associates in documenting the unique role of emotion in eyewitness memories in the lab suggests that memorial processes observed in the lab may not be qualitatively different from those induced in more extreme situations" (p. 381). An additional rebuttal, by Christianson (1992), is that "horror film makers have known . . . for decades" that it is possible for people to be frightened by stimuli they know are simulated (p. 294). Finally, it is interesting that some witnesses to actual crimes, even violent ones, report feeling low or moderate levels of fear during the event. In Christianson and Hübinette's (1993) study, customers who had been present at nonviolent bank robberies 4 to 5 months earlier rated their fear of injury, fear of death, and overall level of fear below the midpoint of the scale, and the ratings of bank employees (including victim-tellers) were near the midpoint. Even some of Yuille and Cutshall's (1986) witnesses to a shooting felt less than terrified. Among those whom the authors classified as less directly involved, stress ratings ranged from 1 to 5 on a 7-point scale, with one witness reporting no stress at all. None in this group had experienced troubles such as sleeping difficulties in the months since the incident. In sum, it seems reasonable to extend lab findings to real-world situations.

Some of the variables described in the previous sections that seem to affect memory for details of violent events may be related to anxiety, and future research could explicitly investigate this possibility. For example, one effect of police officers' training might be to allow them to avoid significant increases in anxiety. In addition, more involved witnesses may experience higher anxiety than others, which in turn could enhance the usual central/peripheral pattern.

THREATENING INCIDENTS: THE WEAPON FOCUS EFFECT

The preceding section deals with events in which actual violence occurs. Sometimes, however, perpetrators threaten violence by brandishing weapons, but the incident ends without injury to anyone. The following section reviews research on memory for scenes that include weapons.

Definition and Typical Findings

The weapon focus effect is one in which witnesses who observe a criminal with a visible weapon tend to remember less about the criminal's physical features and clothing than do witnesses who see the criminal either empty-handed or with a neutral object. In one of the first rigorous studies of the effect, Loftus, Loftus, and Messo (1987) showed participants an 18-slide sequence depicting customers moving through the order line at a fast-food restaurant. On four critical slides the male target character extends either a gun or a personal check toward the cashier, who hands him some money. Compared with the witnesses who saw the check, fewer of those in the weapon condition successfully identified the target in a photo lineup (in two experiments), and they provided poorer descriptions of him (in one experiment). A corneal reflection device revealed that eye fixations on the gun were more frequent and lasted longer than fixations on the check, and the ability to answer questions about details that appeared on slides preceding the critical slides was not affected by the weapon's presence. These latter results suggest that the weapon attracted the witnesses' visual attention to the extent that their capacity to encode other details that appeared simultaneously with the weapon was impaired.

Loftus et al. used a slide sequence as a stimulus, but others have obtained the effect using videos (e.g., Cutler, Penrod, & Martens, 1987b; Pickel, 1998, 1999) and live events (e.g., Maass & Köhnken, 1989). Various kinds of weapons can produce the effect, including guns (e.g., Cutler et al., 1987b; Loftus et al., 1987; Pickel, 1999), knives (e.g., Pickel, 1998), a meat cleaver (Kramer, Buckhout, & Eugenio, 1990), a liquor bottle (Kramer et al., 1990), and a syringe (Maass & Köhnken, 1989). Furthermore, the same results have been found with a community sample as with college student participants (O'Rourke, Penrod, Cutler, & Stuve, 1989).

The strength of the effect appears to depend in part on whether accuracy is measured with respect to lineup identifications or descriptions of the perpetrator. In her meta-analysis, Steblay (1992) calculated a moderate effect size (.55) for descriptive accuracy but only a small effect size (.13) for identification accuracy, probably because the former variable is a more sensitive measure of witnesses' memory. In fact, not all studies have found better identification rates for control than for weapon condition witnesses (Cutler & Penrod, 1988; Cutler, Penrod, & Martens, 1987a; Shaw & Skolnick, 1994), though some have (e.g., Cutler et al., 1987b; Loftus et al., 1987; O'Rourke et al., 1989; Tollestrup, Turtle, & Yuille, 1994; Tooley, Brigham, Maass, & Bothwell, 1987). Although several additional studies have been conducted since the publication of Steblay's article, recent data seem to support her conclusion about effect sizes.

In most weapon focus studies, researchers have compared weapon-present with weapon-absent conditions. In some, however, the manipulation actually involves the degree to which the weapon is visible. For example, Kramer et al.'s (1990, Experiment 1) participants viewed the weapon (a liquor bottle) for either 12 or 4 seconds. In other studies, the weapon is "implied" or assumed to be present in both conditions but is held in the perpetrator's pocket or under his coat in the "low-visibility" condition (Cutler & Penrod, 1988; Cutler et al., 1987a, 1987b; O'Rourke et al., 1989; Tollestrup et al., 1994). Although some of the latter studies have demonstrated weapon focus effects (and they represent worthwhile investigations in their own right), it seems inappropriate to equate a condition in which the witness believes that a weapon is present, but hidden, with a truly weapon-absent condition. If a witness believes that a perpetrator has a gun that he or she might draw at any moment from a pocket, that expectation could cause the witness to gaze repeatedly at the pocket (though possibly not as much as at a visible weapon), which in turn could impair encoding of other visual details.

Over time eyewitness memory experts have become more convinced of the reliability of the weapon focus effect, as shown by two surveys conducted by Kassin and colleagues. In the first, collected in 1989 before much relevant data had been compiled, 57% of the experts said that they would be willing to testify in court that the effect is reliable (Kassin, Ellsworth, & Smith, 1989). Twelve years later, the proportion of willing experts had risen significantly, to 87% (Kassin, Tubb, Hosch, & Memon, 2001).

Field Studies Investigating Weapon Focus

Although the findings described in the previous section, most of which were obtained in lab settings, provide strong evidence for the weapon focus effect, the results of some field studies contradict them. For example, some archival studies show no weapon effect, at least with certain measures. In an analysis of a set of crimes (mostly armed robberies) committed in California from 1987 to 1998, Behrman and Davey (2001) compared witnesses to crimes in which a weapon was used ($n = 240$) and witnesses to weaponless crimes ($n = 49$) and found similar rates of identification of the police suspect. In a second study, using crimes of robbery, rape, and assault, Wagstaff et al. (2003) looked at the accuracy of the descriptions of perpetrators in witnesses' statements to police. Because a suspect had been convicted in each case, the researchers assessed the accuracy of the statements by comparing them with descriptions of the suspects compiled by the arresting officers. They discovered no effect of weapon presence. In a final example, although Tollestrup et al. (1994) reported a higher rate of identifications among witnesses to armed than to unarmed robberies (as noted in the previous section), they reported no difference in terms of the accuracy of descriptions.

Taking another approach, Cooper, Kennedy, Hervé, and Yuille (2002) interviewed 24 female prostitutes, asking them to describe a previous experience of sexual assault. Eight women had been victimized by an armed perpetrator, and 16 were attacked without a weapon. Cooper et al. reported that the two groups provided about the same total number of details of six types: person, object, action, relation, subjective, and conversational details.

Field studies obviously have the advantage of greater ecological validity when compared with lab studies. One could argue that the lab results might not generalize to actual eyewitness situations because of certain dissimilarities between lab simulations and real incidents, such as the level of anxiety and engagement witnesses feel and the knowledge that their testimony will have genuine consequences (Cutshall & Yuille, 1989). Furthermore, the police might question witnesses differently than researchers do (Tollestrup et al., 1994), and actual witnesses are not instructed beforehand to pay close attention (Cooper et al., 2002). However, field research is troubled by a number of problems that can be avoided in the lab, as discussed in the following sections.

Defining the "Presence" and "Absence" of a Weapon.   Tollestrup et al. (1994) included in their "weapon present" category some robberies committed with an "implied" weapon. It was noted in a previous section that an implied weapon is not the same as an absent weapon, but neither is it really "present." It is unreasonable to expect that a hidden weapon can duplicate the effect of a visible one.

Measuring Accuracy and Number of Details Reported.   A major disadvantage of studies of actual crimes is the extreme difficulty of determining what really happened, which of course is necessary if the goal is to analyze witness accuracy. Researchers may try to reconstruct the crime by using evidence other than witness statements (e.g., blood stains or ballistics), but such evidence sheds little light on the perpetrator's appearance. In some cases a suspect is arrested and convicted, and perhaps even confesses, so researchers may feel that they know what the perpetrator looked like (e.g., Wagstaff et al., 2003). Problems still remain, however. First, it is not necessarily true that a convicted suspect, even one who confessed, is guilty (see Kassin, this volume). Second, even if the guilty person is caught, it is difficult to determine exactly how he or she looked at the time of the crime. Although some physical characteristics (e.g., height) are stable, others (e.g., hair style and color, facial hair, clothing) may change. A surveillance tape of the crime in progress may help considerably, although it might not if the tape is black and white or of poor quality.

If the dependent variable is the amount of information reported rather than accuracy, researchers should count only details about the perpetrator's appearance. The presence of a weapon will not necessarily impair memory for actions, objects, or other people, especially if these items were visible before or after the time that the weapon was part of the visual scene. Unfortunately, Cooper et al. (2002) included various types of information in addition to those relevant to the perpetrator's appearance when tallying the number of details their witnesses reported.

Whatever the dependent variable, researchers who examine witnesses' statements to police must face the possibility that the police failed to question witnesses in much depth. For example, police officers might not ask about the perpetrator's appearance in cases where they arrived and apprehended the perpetrator before he or she could get away (Cutshall & Yuille, 1989).

Possible Confounding Variables.   There are several variables that can be controlled in lab studies but might be naturally confounded with weapon presence in actual crimes. First, possessing a weapon might make a criminal feel bold. Therefore, during crimes in which the perpetrator does not make physical contact with the witness, an armed perpetrator might get closer than an unarmed one, which could give the witness a better viewing opportunity. Armed criminals might also feel less hurried, so they might stay at the scene longer. Moreover, they might actually call attention to themselves. For example, a robber might take up a position in a central location and brandish a gun in an attempt to get the customers and employees to notice him or her, see the gun, and decide to cooperate. In contrast, an unarmed robber might try to blend in with other customers or at least behave in a more low-key manner, and he or she might even go unnoticed by some witnesses (Cutshall & Yuille, 1989).

Differences in the police investigations could also be confounds. Because crimes committed with weapons could be seen as more serious than weaponless ones, witnesses might contact the police more promptly after the incident ends and/or officers might arrive more quickly in the former cases, which would result in a shorter retention interval for witnesses, and perhaps improved reports as well. Similarly, the police might question witnesses in more depth, thus eliciting more details, if a weapon was used. Furthermore, witnesses who observed a weapon might take the investigation more seriously and feel more motivated to help bring the perpetrator to justice, so that they try harder to provide more details and more accurate information.

Researchers could try to take these variables into account, but it may be difficult to measure some of them after the fact. For example, witnesses may be unable to estimate correctly the amount of time that the perpetrator was in their presence (Loftus, Greene, & Doyle, 1989).

Other Uncontrolled Variables.   There are a number of variables that are typically not discussed by field researchers, so that it is impossible to tell whether they are confounds or not. At the least, they are uncontrolled and add noise to the data. One example of this is vantage point. Some witnesses might be in front of the perpetrator while others are behind him or her. During a bank robbery, the teller behind the counter might be unable to see the robber's shoes but, having a good view of his or her face, might notice eye color. For a witness standing in the lobby, the reverse might be true (Christianson & Hübinette, 1993). Relatedly, different witnesses might be exposed to different information, for example if some arrived on the scene later than others or did something that gave them unique access to certain details, as when one witness in Yuille and Cutshall's (1986) field study handled the shop owner's gun, possibly discovering how many rounds he had fired.

Witnesses to dramatic incidents surely rehearse them, either by thinking privately about what happened or by telling the story to friends and relatives. Nevertheless, none of the archival studies of weapon focus reviewed here addressed rehearsal (Behrman & Davey, 2001; Tollestrup et al., 1994; Wagstaff et al., 2003). Cooper et al. (2002) did ask the prostitutes they interviewed whether they had previously told someone about their assault experience. However, the researchers ignored the extent to which the victims had thought privately about it.

Although Cooper et al. did not say, it is likely that few, if any, of their participants reported their assaults to police, as most prostitutes do not (McKeganey & Barnard, 1996). However, if researchers question the witnesses after the police interview them, it is impossible to know what effect the police interview had on the data collected by the researchers.

Cooper et al. also did not specify whether any of the prostitutes were attacked by persons who were known to them. Chances are that some were, as many prostitutes are sexually assaulted by clients (Farley & Barkan, 1998) who may have engaged their services previously. Obviously, witnesses should be able to describe familiar individuals better than strangers. Like Cooper et al., Wagstaff et al. (2003) did not say whether the victims and witnesses they studied knew the perpetrators. Most of their robbery witnesses probably did not know the perpetrators, but based on data presented by Yuille and Tollestrup (1992), one would predict that about half of the assault witnesses/victims and most of the rape witnesses/victims did.

A final variable that is uncontrolled in field studies is the sobriety of the witnesses or victims. Many sexual assault victims are intoxicated at the time of the attack (Ullman, Karabatsos, & Koss, 1999), as are victims and witnesses in nonsexual assaults (Yuille & Tollestrup, 1990), as in the case of a bar fight. Cooper et al. (2002) wisely dropped some of the data they collected because their participants were under the influence of drugs or alcohol at the time of the interview or because they failed to follow instructions to describe a sexual assault that occurred when they were sober. However, one cannot be sure that the researchers were successful in identifying all of the assaults that should be excluded. Moreover, memory data obtained from habitual drug users (which most of the prostitutes were) might not generalize to other witnesses.

Methodological Problems.   Some field studies are marred by flaws that might be avoidable. One problem is that some researchers have included crimes of various types in the same study, even though they may differ in seriousness (from a legal standpoint) or level of violence. Crime type could even be confounded with the likelihood of a weapon being present, and, at minimum, noise is introduced by allowing it to vary.

Second, some studies involve only a small number of witnesses, which limits the generalizability of the results. After dropping more than half of their data, Cooper et al. (2002) had only 24 participants left, and some of the cell sizes in Tollestrup et al.'s (1994) study were small. A related problem is that excluded data may differ in important ways from those that remain in the analyses.

A third problem is that some studies include situations in which the weapon focus effect is unlikely to emerge. The weapon is presumed to impair memory for other information that is *simultaneously* present. Additionally, if the weapon is outside the witness's visual field, it cannot exert its influence. During certain crimes, such as the sexual assaults studied by Cooper et al. (2002) and Wagstaff et al. (2003), the weapon might disappear from the victim's visual field for part of the time. The attacker may cover the victim's eyes, or the victim may decide on her own to close them. Or, he may press the gun to the side of her head or hold the knife against her throat so that she cannot see it.

Recommendations.   Because lab studies are limited in their ecological validity, some research should be conducted in field settings. However, poorly controlled field studies add little scientific knowledge because it is difficult to interpret their results. As Roediger (1991) noted in his commentary on Banaji and Crowder's (1989) criticism of "everyday memory," researchers should prefer situations high in both ecological validity and generalizability, but ecological validity should be sacrificed before generalizability (which is dependent on experimental control).

Therefore, field researchers must go to great lengths to control as many variables as they can. For example, they should not group together crimes of different types. They should also find out whether their witnesses knew the perpetrator, rehearsed the experience in any way, arrived at the scene late, or were intoxicated, and they must either exclude some of the data in order to hold variables constant or else find a way to figure out what effects those variables have. Perhaps some confounds can be eliminated by working closely with the police (e.g., to find out how much time elapsed between the crime and the police interview) or by using high-quality surveillance videos to establish the accuracy of witness reports and to determine the positions of various witnesses.

Researchers should also take care to avoid methodological problems. They should obtain large enough sample sizes and should compare conditions in which a weapon was clearly visible with those in which there is no evidence that a weapon was present.

It is interesting that, of the field results that do not show the weapon focus effect, most reveal null results rather than an effect in the unexpected direction. If researchers could exert more control and reduce noise, the findings might turn out to be consistent with those from lab settings.

Possible Explanations for the Weapon Focus Effect

One approach to explaining the effect is to apply Easterbrook's (1959) hypothesis and to see it as a consequence of arousal or anxiety (Steblay, 1992). The reasoning is that the sight of a weapon causes arousal, especially for victims who are threatened directly with injury, but perhaps also for bystander witnesses. This arousal ultimately leads to good memory for central details (i.e., the weapon, which is the source of the arousal) and poor memory for peripheral details (e.g., the criminal's clothing). This approach is appealing because it seems intuitive that the presence of a weapon will frighten witnesses because of its threatening nature.

However, there are several problems with this explanation. First, as noted in a previous section, witnesses who see armed perpetrators may not report feeling extremely afraid (e.g., Christianson & Hübinette, 1993). Also, a number of studies that have in some way examined the effect of weapon-produced anxiety have failed to find any effect. For example, Kramer et al. (1990) showed participants a slide sequence that depicted an assault and robbery during a card game. In the high-visibility weapon condition, the perpetrator enters the scene brandishing a liquor bottle, which can be seen for 12 seconds. In the low-visibility condition the perpetrator initially hides the bottle behind his back, and it can be seen for only 4 seconds in total. Witnesses in the high-visibility condition did not describe the perpetrator as well as those in the low-visibility condition. Although witnesses in the former condition also reported feeling more anxious, Kramer et al. demonstrated in a series of follow-up experiments that the weapon focus effect can be obtained even with the use of nonemotional, nonviolent slides to which witnesses responded with low self-reported anxiety.

Other studies have manipulated threat or anxiety without obtaining the results predicted by the Easterbrook hypothesis. Maass and Köhnken (1989) used a live event in which participants saw a confederate holding either a syringe (the "weapon") or a pen. They told some randomly selected participants that they would receive an injection as part of the experiment. Later, the participants tried to describe and identify the confederate. The authors predicted that, if the Easterbrook hypothesis is correct, the anxiety-producing threat of injection should interact with the weapon's presence, but it did not.

Instead of the anxiety explanation, an alternative, suggested by Kramer et al. (1990) and Loftus et al. (1987), is that weapons seem unusual within most contexts in which they appear, and this unusualness attracts attention. Customers in a bank or convenience store, for example, undoubtedly realize that armed robberies sometimes occur, but most people are fortunate to have escaped ever having to witness one. Even among those who have seen them, the number of times in which a robbery has occurred while they were in a business establishment is surely a small proportion of their total number of visits. Thus, a weapon in such a context would seem unusual. Furthermore, research has shown that unusual items attract attention. For example, participants in Henderson,

Weeks, and Hollingworth's (1999) study looked more often and for longer durations at unexpected (i.e., semantically inconsistent) rather than predicted objects in line drawings of complex scenes (see also Loftus & Mackworth, 1978). Loftus et al.'s finding that witnesses made significantly more and longer eye fixations on the gun but not the check in their slide sequence fits nicely with this result.

In direct comparisons of the two hypotheses, the unusualness explanation has emerged as stronger than the one based on Easterbrook's hypothesis. In two experiments conducted by Mitchell, Livosky, and Mather (1998), participants watched a videotape of an interaction between two men. They remembered the target character less accurately if he held an unusual or "novel" item (a stalk of celery) rather than no object. Performance in the celery condition was about the same as in a condition in which the target threatened the other man with a gun.

I obtained similar results (Pickel, 1998). In a pair of experiments, witnesses watched a video shot at a business (e.g., a hair salon). Unusualness and threat were manipulated independently by varying the object carried by a male character who enters the business. Some objects (e.g., a gun or scissors used for cutting hair) were threatening in the sense that the man could use them to hurt or kill another person, and therefore they should cause more anxiety than nonthreatening objects if the Easterbrook hypothesis is correct. In addition, some objects (e.g., the gun or a raw chicken) were unusual or out of place given the context, whereas others (e.g., scissors, a wallet) were not. Witnesses described the man less accurately if they saw unusual rather than expected objects, but the threat associated with the objects had no effect.

Another way to test the unusualness explanation is to inquire whether a weapon might fail to produce the usual weapon focus effect if it is expected within the context in which it appears. In the first of two experiments exploring this question (Pickel, 1999), I defined "context" as the location where the scene occurs. In one version of a video, the story that was depicted takes place at a shooting range, where one would expect to see a gun. The other version is set at a baseball field, where a gun would seem unusual. When the witnesses tried to describe the man's features, a weapon focus effect emerged only with the second version, and the level of threat in the man's behavior did not matter. *Context* could alternatively be defined as the target character's apparent occupation, as revealed by his clothing. In the second experiment, the target was dressed either as a police officer (who should have a gun) or as a Catholic priest (who is not expected to be armed). The weapon's presence affected witnesses' descriptions of the man only if they saw the priest and not the officer.

Thus, although witnesses are probably sometimes frightened at seeing a weapon, several experiments suggest that unusualness, not increased anxiety produced by the threat that weapons represent, causes the weapon focus effect by attracting witnesses' attention (see also Shaw & Skolnick, 1999). The unusualness hypothesis leads to several interesting questions. For instance, if a weapon's presence consumes attentional resources, is it possible for it to impair memory for auditory as well as visual information? Multiple resource models of attention (Navon & Gopher, 1979; Wickens, 1984) postulate that there are separate "pools" of perceptual and cognitive resources that can be allocated to various tasks. The extent to which two tasks interfere with one another depends in part on whether they draw resources from the same pool. Because two different pools are devoted to the auditory and visual modalities, people should usually be able to perform auditory and visual tasks simultaneously, with little interference. However, the modality-specific pools are nested inside a general pool from which all tasks consume resources to some extent, and significant resources can be drawn from the general pool if the modality-specific resources become depleted (Wickens, 1984). Therefore, an attention-demanding weapon may consume a large quantity of resources not only from the visual pool but also from the general one. In this way, the weapon's presence might interfere with an auditory task that, because of its difficulty, also needs significant resources from the general pool. On the other hand, the weapon should not interfere with an easy auditory task that can be performed with the use of only the resources from the auditory-specific pool. In support of this prediction, witnesses who watched a video of a man threatening a woman with a gun could perform an easy auditory task (describing the acoustic characteristics of his speech, such as pitch and rate) as well as witnesses who saw the man with a neutral object, but they were less able to perform a difficult auditory task (reporting the semantic content of a hard-to-comprehend statement; Pickel, French, & Betts, 2003).

Other predictions based on the unusualness hypothesis are currently untested. For example, Mitchell et al. (1998) proposed that there might be individual differences in susceptibility to the weapon focus effect because some people, such as gang members, may be exposed to guns so much that they no longer consider them novel or unusual, even in contexts in which guns are rarely seen. Therefore, the effect might not occur with these individuals. The same authors also suggested that viewing a weapon for a long period of time during a single episode (as in a hostage situation, perhaps) might reduce its novelty and thus attenuate or cancel the effect of the weapon's presence.

Just as differences between witnesses might be important, perpetrators' characteristics could matter as well. For example, witnesses may believe that Black perpetrators are more likely to be armed than White ones (Greenwald, Oakes, & Hoffman, 2003). If so, a weapon's presence could have a weaker effect when the perpetrator is Black, because in that case the weapon seems less unusual to witnesses.

Another question that remains is whether witnesses' visual fixations are under their control or whether weapons capture attention automatically, meaning that the fixations are involuntary and unavoidable, occurring without any corresponding intent on the part of the witnesses and perhaps without their awareness (Yantis & Egeth, 1999). Obviously, this question is theoretically important, as it could help researchers develop a model of the attentional mechanisms that operate when an observer notices a weapon, but there are practical considerations as well. If attentional capture does not occur, then individuals who are most at risk to observe a crime committed by an armed perpetrator (e.g., bank tellers and convenience store workers) could possibly be trained so that they would be prepared to perform better as witnesses. My colleagues Steve Ross and Ron Truelove and I have collected preliminary data indicating that witnesses instructed to look at the perpetrator more than at a weapon can do so, which suggests that weapons do not capture attention automatically (Pickel, Ross, & Truelove, in press). However, more testing is needed.

INTEGRATING EXPOSURE TO VIOLENCE
AND WEAPON FOCUS

What cognitive mechanisms engage when people witness a violent shooting, as did the students at Santana High School whose classmate killed two people and injured 13? If the witness's initial processing of the scene involves noticing the weapon, as teenager John Schardt apparently did as the perpetrator came out of the boys' restroom, then its unusualness or unexpectedness might attract attention, so that the witness looks at it longer and more often than he or she would have if the perpetrator had been holding a common object. The witness will probably also fail to look at the perpetrator's physical features and clothing as much as he or she otherwise would, so that these details are remembered less accurately later, although some details will no doubt be correctly reported. The one physical detail that John Schardt emphasized was that the Santana shooter smiled during the attack. It is unknown whether he could remember other information, such as the perpetrator's hair style, the color of his shirt, or what kind of pants he wore.

It makes sense to ask about anxiety at this point. Even though the Easterbrook explanation for weapon focus has received little support, shouldn't one expect the witness to feel fear upon noticing the weapon, and wouldn't this fear have some effect on memory? The answer to the first part of the question is that the witness might not feel intense fear at first, before any actual violence has occurred. Recall that Christianson and Hübinette (1993) found that bystander witnesses to a nonviolent crime rated their fear on the lower half of the scale, and some (though not all) of Yuille and Cutshall's (1986) witnesses to a shooting indicated moderate or low levels of stress.

The second part of the question asks about the effect of anxiety. Existing data indicate that, although many witnesses who see a weapon, especially if the perpetrator begins using it to commit violence, will probably become frightened, their fear is not necessary to produce the weapon focus effect. Still, elevated anxiety might lead to other results, such as the tendency to recall central rather than peripheral details because of a narrowing of attentional focus and increased elaboration of central information. What Austin Floyd, a student who survived the Santana shooting, seems to remember most is his position on a bench in the school's hallway relative to the perpetrator's position. "I was too close," he told a reporter after the incident (Finz, Kim, & Fagan, 2001, p. A1). "I was right next to the bathroom. If he took two more steps toward me, I might not be here." The experience clearly scared Austin; he went on to say that he was still too upset, 2 days later, to return to classes. It is impossible to know exactly what he could and could not recall after the attack, but research suggests that he probably could not remember some of the peripheral information that was around him when the shooting erupted, such as details about other students or objects in the hallway. In sum, it seems likely, as Heuer and Reisberg (1992) speculated, that both anxiety and a weapon's unusualness influence the processing of a violent scene, with the two variables leading to different results. In any event, future research should continue to explore the memorial consequences of observing weapons and violence, as well as the causes of these effects.

REFERENCES

Banaji, M. R., & Crowder, R. G. (1989). The bankruptcy of everyday memory. *American Psychologist, 44,* 1185–1193.

Behrman, B. W., & Davey, S. L. (2001). Eyewitness identification in actual criminal cases: An archival analysis. *Law and Human Behavior, 25,* 475–491.

Brown, J. M. (2003). Eyewitness memory for arousing events: Putting things into context. *Applied Cognitive Psychology, 17,* 93–106.

Cahill, L., Babinsky, R., Markowitsch, H. J., & McGaugh, J. L. (1995). The amygdala and emotional memory. *Nature, 377,* 295–296.

Cahill, L., Prins, B., Weber, M., & McGaugh, J. L. (1994). Beta-adrenergic activation and memory for emotional events. *Nature, 371,* 702–704.

Christianson, S.-Å. (1992). Emotional stress and eyewitness memory: A critical review. *Psychological Bulletin, 112*(2), 284–309.

Christianson, S.-Å., & Hübinette, B. (1993). Hands up! A study of witnesses' emotional reactions and memories associated with bank robberies. *Applied Cognitive Psychology, 7*(5), 365–379.

Christianson, S.-Å., Karlsson, I., & Persson, L. G. W. (1998). Police personnel as eyewitnesses to a violent crime. *Legal and Criminological Psychology, 3,* 59–72.

Christianson, S.-Å., & Loftus, E. F. (1987). Memory for traumatic events. *Applied Cognitive Psychology, 1,* 225–239.

Christianson, S.-Å., & Loftus, E. F. (1991). Remembering emotional events: The fate of detailed information. *Cognition and Emotion, 5,* 81–108.

Christianson, S.-Å., Loftus, E. F., Hoffman, H., & Loftus, G. R. (1991). Eye fixations and memory for emotional events. *Journal of Experimental Psychology: Learning, Memory, and Cognition, 17*(4), 693–701.

Clifford, B. R., & Scott, J. (1978). Individual and situational factors in eyewitness testimony. *Journal of Applied Psychology, 65*(3), 352–359.

Cooper, B. S., Kennedy, M. A., Hervé, H. F., & Yuille, J. C. (2002). Weapon focus in sexual assault memories of prostitutes. *International Journal of Law and Psychiatry, 25,* 181–191.

Cutler, B. L., & Penrod, S. D. (1988). Improving the reliability of eyewitness identification: Lineup construction and presentation. *Journal of Applied Psychology, 73,* 281–290.

Cutler, B. L., Penrod, S. D., & Martens, T. K. (1987a). Improving the reliability of eyewitness identification: Putting context into context. *Journal of Applied Psychology, 72,* 629–637.

Cutler, B. L., Penrod, S. D., & Martens, T. K. (1987b). The reliability of eyewitness identification: The role of system and estimator variables. *Law and Human Behavior, 11,* 233–258.

Cutshall, J., & Yuille, J. C. (1989). Field studies of eyewitness memory of actual crimes. In D. C. Raskin (Ed.), *Psychological methods in criminal investigation and evidence* (pp. 97–124). New York: Springer.

Easterbrook, J. A. (1959). The effect of emotion on cue utilization and the organization of behavior. *Psychological Review, 66,* 183–201.

Farley, M., & Barkan, H. (1998). Prostitution, violence, and posttraumatic stress disorder. *Women and Health, 27,* 37–49.

Finz, S., Kim, R., & Fagan, K. (2001, March 7). School gunman shows little remorse, police say: Motive for fatal rampage remains a mystery [electronic version]. *San Francisco Chronicle,* p. A-1.

Finz, S., Kim, R., Fagan, K., & Brazil, E. (2001, March 6). Rampage at school—Two students slain: 15-year-old boy arrested after shootings near San Diego wound 13 [electronic version]. *San Francisco Chronicle,* p. A–1.

Greenwald, A. G., Oakes, M. A., & Hoffman, H. G. (2003). Targets of discrimination: Effects of race on responses to weapons holders. *Journal of Experimental Social Psychology, 39,* 399–405.

Henderson, J. M., Weeks, P. A., & Hollingworth, A. (1999). The effects of semantic consistency on eye movements during complex scene viewing. *Journal of Experimental Psychology: Human Perception and Performance, 25*(1), 210–228.

Heuer, F., & Reisberg, D. (1992). Emotion, arousal, and memory for detail. In S.-Å. Christianson (Ed.), *The handbook of emotion and memory: Research and theory* (pp. 151–180). Hillsdale, NJ: Lawrence Erlbaum Associates.

Hosch, H. M., & Bothwell, R. K. (1990). Arousal, description, and identification accuracy of victims and bystanders. *Journal of Social Behavior and Personality, 5,* 481–488.

Hosch, H. M., & Cooper, D. S. (1982). Victimization as a determinant of eyewitness accuracy. *Journal of Applied Psychology, 67,* 649–652.

Hosch, H. M., Leippe, M. R., Marchioni, P. M., & Cooper, D. S. (1984). Victimization, self-monitoring, and eyewitness identification. *Journal of Applied Psychology, 69,* 280–288.

Kassin, S. M., Ellsworth, P. C., & Smith, V. L. (1989). The "general acceptance" of psychological research on eyewitness testimony: A survey of the experts. *American Psychologist, 44,* 1089–1098.

Kassin, S. M., Tubb, V. A., Hosch, H. M., & Memon, A. (2001). On the "general acceptance" of eyewitness testimony research. *American Psychologist, 56*(5), 405–416.

Kramer, T. H., Buckhout, R., & Eugenio P. (1990). Weapon focus, arousal, and eyewitness memory: Attention must be paid. *Law and Human Behavior, 14,* 167–184.

Kuehn, L. L. (1974). Looking down a gun barrel: Person perception and violent crime. *Perceptual and Motor Skills, 39,* 1159–1164.

Lindholm, T., & Christianson, S.-Å. (1998). Gender effects in eyewitness accounts of violent crime. *Psychology, Crime, and Law, 4,* 323–339.

Lindholm, T., Christianson, S.-Å., & Karlsson, I. (1997). Police officers and civilians as witnesses: Intergroup biases and memory performance. *Applied Cognitive Psychology, 11,* 445–455.

Loftus, E. F., & Burns, T. E. (1982). Mental shock can produce retrograde amnesia. *Memory & Cognition, 10*(4), 318–323.

Loftus, E. F., Greene, E. L., & Doyle, J. M. (1989). The psychology of eyewitness testimony. In D. C. Raskin (Ed.), *Psychological methods in criminal investigation and evidence* (pp. 3–45). New York: Springer.

Loftus, E. F., Loftus, G. R., & Messo, J. (1987). Some facts about "weapon focus." *Law and Human Behavior, 11,* 55–62.

Loftus, G. R., & Mackworth, N. H. (1978). Cognitive determinants of fixation location during picture viewing. *Journal of Experimental Psychology: Human Perception and Performance, 4*(4), 565–572.

Maass, A., & Köhnken, G. (1989). Eyewitness identification: Simulating the "weapon effect." *Law and Human Behavior, 13,* 397–408.

MacLeod, M. D., & Shepherd, J. W. (1986). Sex differences in eyewitness reports of criminal assaults. *Medical Science Law, 26*(4), 311–318.

McGaugh, J. L. (2004). The amygdala modulates the consolidation of memories of emotionally arousing experiences. *Annual Review of Neuroscience, 27,* 1–28.

McKeganey, N., & Barnard, M. (1996). *Sex work on the streets: Prostitutes and their clients.* Philadelphia: Open University Press.

Mitchell, K. J., Livosky, M., & Mather, M. (1998). The weapon focus effect revisited: The role of novelty. *Legal and Criminological Psychology, 3,* 287–303.

Navon, D., & Gopher, D. (1979). On the economy of the human processing system. *Psychological Review, 86,* 214–255.

O'Rourke, T. E., Penrod, S. D., Cutler, B. L., & Stuve, T. E. (1989). The external validity of eyewitness identification research: Generalizing across subject populations. *Law and Human Behavior, 13*(4), 385–395.

Pickel, K. L. (1998). Unusualness and threat as possible causes of "weapon focus." *Memory*, 6(3), 277–295.

Pickel, K. L. (1999). The influence of context on the "weapon focus" effect. *Law and Human Behavior*, 23(3), 299–311.

Pickel, K. L., French, T. A., & Betts, J. M. (2003). A cross-modal weapon focus effect: The influence of a weapon's presence on memory for auditory information. *Memory*, 11(3), 277–292.

Pickel, K. L., Ross S. J., & Truelove, R. S. (in press). Do weapons automatically capture attention? *Applied Cognitive Psychology*.

Roediger, H. L. (1991). They read an article? A commentary on the everyday memory controversy. *American Psychologist*, 46, 37–40.

Safer, M. A., Christianson, S.-Å., Autry, M. W., & Österland, K. (1998). Tunnel memory for traumatic events. *Applied Cognitive Psychology*, 12, 99–117.

Schooler, J. W., & Eich, E. (2000). Memory for emotional events. In E. Tulving & F. I. M. Craik (Eds.), *The Oxford handbook of memory* (pp. 379–392). Oxford, UK: Oxford University Press.

Scrivner, E., & Safer, M. A. (1988). Eyewitnesses show hypermnesia for details about a violent event. *Journal of Applied Psychology*, 73(3), 371–377.

Shaw, J. I., & Skolnick, P. (1994). Sex differences, weapon focus, and eyewitness reliability. *The Journal of Social Psychology*, 134, 413–420.

Shaw, J. I., & Skolnick, P. (1999). Weapon focus and gender differences in eyewitness accuracy: Arousal versus salience. *Journal of Applied Social Psychology*, 29, 2328–2341.

Stanny, C. J., & Johnson, T. C. (2000). Effects of stress induced by a simulated shooting on recall by police and citizen witnesses. *American Journal of Psychology*, 113(3), 359–386.

Steblay, N. M. (1992). A meta-analytic review of the weapon focus effect. *Law and Human Behavior*, 16(4), 413–424.

Tollestrup, P. A., Turtle, J. W., & Yuille, J. C. (1994). Actual victims and witnesses to robbery and fraud: An archival analysis. In D. F. Ross, J. D. Read, & M. P. Toglia (Eds.), *Adult eyewitness testimony: Current trends and developments* (pp. 144–160). Cambridge, UK: Cambridge University Press.

Tooley, V., Brigham, J. C., Maass, A., & Bothwell, R. K. (1987). Facial recognition: Weapon effect and attentional focus. *Journal of Applied Social Psychology*, 17, 845–859.

Turtle, J. W., & Yuille, J. C. (1994). Lost but not forgotten details: Repeated eyewitness recall leads to reminiscence but not hypermnesia. *Journal of Applied Psychology*, 79(2), 260–271.

Ullman, S. E., Karabatsos, G. E., & Koss, M. P. (1999). Alcohol and sexual assault in a national sample of college women. *Journal of Interpersonal Violence*, 14(6), 603–625.

Wagstaff, G. F., MacVeigh, J., Boston, R., Scott, L., Brunas-Wagstaff, J., & Cole, J. (2003). Can laboratory findings on eyewitness testimony be generalized to the real world? An archival analysis of the influence of violence, weapon presence, and age on eyewitness accuracy. *Journal of Psychology*, 137, 17–28.

Wickens, C. D. (1984). Processing resources in attention. In R. Parasuraman & D. R. Davies (Eds.), *Varieties of attention* (pp. 63–102). Orlando, FL: Academic Press.

Woolnough, P. S., & MacLeod, M. D. (2001). Watching the birdie watching you: Eyewitness memory for actions using CCTV recordings of actual crimes. *Applied Cognitive Psychology*, 15, 395–411.

Yantis, S., & Egeth, H. E. (1999). On the distinction between visual salience and stimulus-driven attentional capture. *Journal of Experimental Psychology: Human Perception and Performance*, 25(3), 661–676.

Yarmey, A. D. (1986). Perceived expertness and credibility of police officers as eyewitnesses. *Canadian Police College Journal*, 10, 36–58.

Yuille, J. C., & Cutshall, J. L. (1986). A case study of eyewitness memory of a crime. *Journal of Applied Psychology, 71*(2), 291–301.

Yuille, J. C., & Tollestrup, P. A. (1990). Some effects of alcohol on eyewitness memory. *Journal of Applied Psychology, 75*(3), 268–273.

Yuille, J. C., & Tollestrup, P. A. (1992). A model of the diverse effects of emotion on memory. In S.-Å Christianson (Ed.), *The handbook of emotion and memory: Research and theory* (pp. 201–215). Hillsdale, NJ: Lawrence Erlbaum Associates.

15

The Effects of Delay on Eyewitness Identification Accuracy: Should We Be Concerned?

Jennifer E. Dysart
John Jay College of Criminal Justice CUNY

R. C. L. Lindsay
Queen's University, Ontario

The current chapter discusses the research literature on the effects of delay on eyewitness identification accuracy. Delay, as it is defined in this chapter, is the amount of time that elapses between encoding (seeing) of the original event (the crime) and the identification attempt from a line-up, show-up, or mug shots. We begin with a discussion of why the delay issue is legally important. Next we describe the various methods that have been used to measure the impact of delay. The delay research then is discussed from the perspective of the methods used: archival evidence, studies in which delay was manipulated, and studies in which delay varied haphazardly. After discussing the eyewitness literature, we provide a brief discussion of other research on delay in regard to memory for faces but conclude that it is difficult to generalize from that research to the eyewitness situation. After a discussion of future research that is desperately needed on this topic, we conclude that it is risky to assume that we currently know what impact delay actually has on the accuracy of eyewitness identification.

LEGAL EVIDENCE THAT DELAY MAY BE IMPORTANT

When discussing any issue related to eyewitness identification, it is important to keep in mind the legal context in which we hope to apply our research findings. In a landmark decision (*Neil v. Biggers*, 1972), the U.S. Supreme Court declared that there are five characteristics of a case involving eyewitnesses that should be taken into consideration when evaluating the potential accuracy of eyewitness identification. One of those factors was the amount of time that elapses between an event and the identification procedure, in other words, delay. The precise amount of delay was not specified by the Supreme Court, and, therefore, this criterion is ambiguous. In addition, in their decision, the court discounted the fact that the identification of Biggers occurred 7 months after the initial event, stating that, although a delay of this magnitude would normally be detrimental, the circumstances of the Biggers case (long exposure and the witness was highly confident) made it likely that the identification was accurate. Although the delay criterion seems logical and intuitive, at the time this decision was made, little empirical evidence existed to suggest that delay did or did not have a significant impact on eyewitness identification accuracy.

Other judicial decisions of that time have indicated that delay is an important factor. In *Commonwealth v. Bumpus* (1968), the Supreme Judicial Court of Massachusetts found that a show-up identification (where only one person is presented to the witness for identification; see Dysart & Lindsay, this volume) did not violate due process because it was conducted quickly after the criminal event. The court reasoned that the witness's memory was still fresh, and therefore the show-up procedure increased the likelihood that the witness had made a correct identification decision (as compared with forcing the witness to wait until a line-up could be conducted). Consistent with this ruling, in *Wright v. United States* (1968), Judge Bazelon stated that the preservation of memory is key in being able to justify a show-up procedure. In fact, Bazelon stated the value of conducting a show-up within minutes of the crime should arguably outweigh the potential suggestiveness of the procedure. Bazelon reasoned that if police have detained a suspect soon after the crime, and it normally takes 24 hours to arrange a lineup, then a show-up should be the preferred method of identification. However, if the suspect is detained several weeks after the crime, then the benefit of using a show-up would no longer apply. In sum, the courts have generally concluded that the show-up procedure can yield more accurate identifications than lineups because they are (usually) conducted sooner after the crime.

A question raised by the courts' attitude toward delay is whether it is reflected in the common sense reasoning of prospective jurors. Bradfield and Wells (2000, study 2) examined whether mock jurors are sensitive to the Biggers criteria when choosing a verdict. Mock jurors read a transcript of a case in which the eyewitness identification was made the night of the crime versus 6 months later. They found no significant main effects of delay on willingness to convict or in the believability of the eyewitness' accuracy. Therefore, the mock jurors in this study seemed to disagree with the Supreme Court's belief that identifications made quickly after an event are more likely to be accurate. Similarly, Cutler, Penrod, and Dexter (1990) found that mock jurors were just as willing to convict a defendant if an eyewitness testified that the identification decision was made 14 days after the crime as they were if the identification had occurred 2 days after the crime. The results of these studies may seem to suggest that, although the courts have decided that delay is an important factor to consider, mock jurors fail to take this information into account when choosing a verdict. Alternatively, people may believe that delay matters but that 6 months is not a sufficient delay to reduce eyewitness accuracy, though this seems unlikely.

Ironically, although the courts have declared delay between event and identification procedure to be an important consideration, it may not actually influence judicial decisions. Brief delays are used as justification for believing eyewitness identification evidence (e.g., *Commonwealth v. Bumpus*), but long delays are readily dismissed based on other factors in the case (e.g., Biggers). Mock jurors do not appear to be persuaded that delay matters either. These findings support Lindsay's (1994) contention that triers of fact may use evidence to support or justify their decisions (verdicts) rather than to determine them. The question that we address in the remainder of this chapter is whether this situation is a problem, because delay is an important determinant of eyewitness accuracy that is being inappropriately ignored. Of course, the failure to be influenced by delay may be serendipitously helpful, because an irrelevant but court touted factor is not influential.

METHODOLOGICAL ISSUES

Before we begin the review of the research literature, a short discussion is warranted concerning the distinction among archival data, investigating delay as an independent variable, examining the effects of haphazardly different delay periods, and simply investigating how participants perform across different periods of delay.

Archival data on delay are available from cases varying in delay between the crime and identification attempt. As is always the case with archival data, the advantage is that the data are directly relevant to the context in which we wish to apply our knowledge; that is, there is no issue of ecological validity. The problem with archival data is that one can rarely be certain of the accuracy of the identification evidence. Even if stringent screening procedures are used to ensure a high probability that the accuracy of identification is known, it is possible that cases that fail to pass the screening procedure are significantly different from those that do pass, and thus the data may not generalize to all cases. Archival studies can provide excellent evidence of the impact of delay on choosing in particular and perhaps of foil selections but are unable to provide unambiguous evidence about the accuracy of suspect selections.

To test the hypothesis that delay between an event and an identification attempt has a causal impact on identification accuracy, delay must be manipulated as an independent variable with at least two levels. The values of the levels of delay are not critical (at least to demonstrate the mere existence of a delay effect), as long as two or more delay periods are used. For example, it is not necessary to test one group immediately after the exposure to the target and the other group(s) at a later time. Of course, researchers may want an immediate identification condition to serve as a baseline or best performance comparison for the longer delay conditions, but such a condition is not logically necessary to demonstrate effects of delay. If delay is not treated as an independent variable with at least two levels, then it is impossible to draw a causal conclusion that a change in identification accuracy was due to the amount of delay between the event and the identification attempt.

Some studies are conducted in such a way that witnesses will experience differences in delay as part of the procedure, but the delay will not have been intentionally created and controlled by the researcher. For example, a research technique we have been using for some years involves sending two people into shopping malls (e.g., Dysart, Lindsay, & Dupuis, 2005). One person (the recruiter) approaches employees and asks if the employee would be willing to participate in a brief experiment later in the day. Later, the second person approaches the employee and requests that the employee attempt to describe and identify the recruiter. By recording the times of initial contact and attempted identification, delay periods can be established. Just as in the archival studies, causal inferences are not warranted. Poor identification performance and long delays could be spuriously related to a third variable, such as how busy the mall was on the day the data were collected.

A fourth possibility is that researchers collect all of the data after a relatively long delay (e.g., weeks or months) and note that they obtained a very low accuracy rate or a pattern of results that is different from those reported in studies with different delays. Again, many factors other than delay (including the quality of the viewing conditions, distinctiveness of the targets, lineup quality, etc.) could be responsible for the identification accuracy rates obtained. These examples are, of course, nothing more than illustrations of the importance of proper control conditions in research if causal inferences are to be entertained.

ARCHIVAL EVIDENCE OF DELAY EFFECTS

Several published studies have examined delay and identification responses from witnesses in real criminal cases (Behrman & Davey, 2001; Tollestrup, Turtle, & Yuille, 1994; Valentine, Pickering, & Darling, 2003; Wright & McDaid, 1996). Again, the identity of the actual perpetrators is unknown, and therefore it is difficult (or impossible) to determine if suspect identifications made by witnesses are accurate or inaccurate. Nonetheless, this type of research is valuable for examining the choosing behavior of real witnesses.

In the first study to examine real witness behavior, Tollestrup et al. (1994) examined 98 fraud and robbery cases. They found that both robbery and fraud witnesses were most likely to choose the suspect when he was presented after shorter delay periods. Robbery witnesses chose the suspect 78% of the time after 0–1 days, 46% after 4 days, 33% after 19 days, and 14% after 120 days. Fraud witnesses chose the suspect 78% of the time after 33 days, 5% after 74 days, 20% after 132 days, and 17% after 200 days. Tollestrup et al. do not report any statistical analyses of the delay effect; however, given their sample size and the large differences obtained, it seems likely that significant effects of delay of suspect selection were occurring.

Behrman and Davey (2001) analyzed the data from 271 cases and 689 identification attempts in California (258 field show-ups, 284 photographic line-ups, and 58 live line-ups). The delay results were broken down into two categories: delays of 0 to 7 and 8 or more days. Overall, the results showed a significant decrease in suspect identifications when the identification occurred after 7 days (45%) rather than within 7 days (55%) of the crime. The results were further broken down into cases where there was versus cases where there was not additional information (independent evidence) about the potential guilt of the suspect. When additional evidence existed, 64% of witnesses in the 0–7-day delay and 33% in the longer delay conditions made suspect identifications. In cases where there was no additional evidence, there was no difference in suspect identifications over the delay periods (49% and 47%). Unlike Tollestrup et al., Behrman and Davey did not find a significant decrease in suspect identifications after 2 days, but did find a drop after 1 week.

Most recently, Valentine et al. (2003) examined several factors relating to eyewitness identification performance in real lineups, including delay. Delay was categorized into eight levels, from less than 1 week to over 6 months. The results showed that across the delay levels, there were no significant differences in suspect identifications, foil identifications, or "no identification" responses. Valentine et al., however, did report that suspect identifications were more likely if the line-up had been presented within a week of the crime, although the statistical analysis was not reported. These results are consistent with those of Behrman and Davey (2001).

Wright and McDaid (1996) examined 1561 witness decisions viewing 623 suspects in real criminal cases. Their results showed a positive relationship between the length of delay and the number of foils chosen from the lineups. These data clearly imply a decrease in accuracy with increased delay because foil choices are known to be in error (Wells, 1984, 1993). As a result, we may not be able to conclude that correct identification rates suffer with delay, but identification errors do appear to be more likely.

In sum, the archival research that has been conducted with delay and real police cases suggests that there likely is a drop in suspect identifications after a period of 1 week. As Behrman and Davey (2001) and others have aptly noted, however, this does not necessarily reflect a decline in either the witnesses' memory or the accuracy of the witnesses' decisions. Instead, decreased choosing could be a function of many other factors. A lower likelihood of apprehending the criminal after longer delays may result in fewer criminal-present line-ups and show-ups, which in turn result in fewer choices overall and fewer suspect selections in particular. Alternatively, the rate of suspect presence could remain constant, but witnesses may become more cautious in their decisions as delay increases, thus again reducing selections in general and selections of suspects (whether innocent or guilty) in particular. Nonetheless, these archival studies are informative only as to the choosing behavior of witnesses in real cases after periods of delay. We turn now to the experimental evidence of delay effects.

EXPERIMENTAL EVIDENCE OF DELAY EFFECTS

A summary of the empirical literature on delay will now be presented. First, the results from three meta-analyses that examined delay are presented. Then, individual studies that used delay as an independent variable, allowed delay to vary haphazardly, or used unusual delays are described, followed by a discussion of apparent patterns in these studies and their implications. Unfortunately, many studies fail to provide the data on the impact of delay when delay effects were not significant. It is impossible to determine whether the failure to find delay effects in these studies is the result of floor effects. If accuracy is at or near chance after the shortest delay, longer delays cannot reasonably be expected to reduce accuracy further. Percentage correct is reported where available.

META-ANALYSES AND DELAY

Three recent meta-analyses, Steblay, Dysart, Fulero, and Lindsay (2001, 2003) and Shapiro and Penrod (1986), have examined the issue of delay and its relation to eyewitness identification accuracy. The two Steblay et al. meta-analyses suffer because delay was considered only as a moderator variable, and thus the results tell us only whether delay interacted with other variables to influence identification accuracy. Of course, such interactions are important to know about. Shapiro and Penrod's research differs slightly from the other two meta-analyses in that their research included both facial memory and eyewitness identification studies, whereas the other meta-analyses examined only eyewitness identification studies. Steblay et al. (2001) explored identification accuracy from simultaneous line-ups (when the line-up members are presented all at the same time) and sequential line-ups (when the line-up members are presented one at a time; Lindsay & Wells, 1985). Although the purpose of the meta-analysis was to explore whether sequential lineups yield higher accuracy rates over simultaneous line-ups, several potential moderator variables, including delay, also were coded. The analyses compared simultaneous and sequential line-ups at immediate test and when there was a delay of 1 hour or more after the event. Therefore, the analyses did not examine delay as an independent variable; that is, this was not a meta-analysis of the impact of delay across multiple studies in which delay was manipulated. For target-present lineups, the results favored simultaneous line-ups regardless of whether the procedure was conducted immediately ($r = .15, p < .001$) or after 1 hour or more ($r = .13, p < .001$). For target-absent conditions, sequential lineups produced higher rates of correct rejection regardless of whether the test occurred immediately ($r = .25, p < .001$) or after 1 hour or more ($r = .32, p < .001$). Overall, the results from Steblay et al. suggest that, regardless of the delay period, simultaneous lineups produce a higher rate of correct identifications of the criminal, and sequential line-ups are more likely to result in correct rejections of target-absent lineups. Although the delay results for both target-present and target-absent conditions were significant, only a small number of studies were available for these analyses (4 and 1, respectively). Therefore, the results should be interpreted with caution. Furthermore, the results do not directly address the issue of interest. The analyses described do not test whether a delay effect exists, but rather whether delay interacts with identification procedure, which it apparently does not.

Steblay et al. (2003) analyzed studies that compared line-up accuracy with that obtained with show-ups. Although delay was not considered as an independent variable, it was analyzed as a potential moderator variable. In target-present show-ups, there was no significant difference in the rate of correct identifications between line-ups and show-ups in the immediate ($r = .03, N = 8$) or the 2-day to 1-week condition ($r = .10, N =$

3). There was a significant increase in correct rejections of target-absent conditions for show-ups over line-ups, regardless of whether the identification took place immediately ($r = .33$, $N = 7$) or after 2 days to 1 week ($r = .34$, $N = 3$). Although the results show that show-ups yield higher correct rejections regardless of whether they are used immediately or after a delay of up to 1 week, the same concern exists as for Steblay et al.'s (2001) results regarding the interpretation of the results due to a small number of studies in the delay conditions and that the tests are tests of interactions, not the main effect of delay.

As stated earlier, Shapiro and Penrod (1986) examined the direct impact of delay on identification accuracy. The results of their meta-analysis showed a significant effect of delay on both correct identifications (effect size 0.43) and false identifications (effect size 0.33) with an average delay of 4.5 days.

All of the meta-analytic results suffer from the need to collapse over large blocks of time. Generally, the small number of available data sets leads researchers to divide delay into categories in such a way as to ensure some data points in each category (short versus long delay). Thus, the failure to find apparent effects of delay could be due to the fact that immediate (or less than 24-hour) delays were compared with delays ranging from 24 hours to several months. If delay effects only begin to appear after several days or weeks, then the longer delay condition may contain a small number of data points past the critical time and a great number before it, thus masking the delay effect. This is a strong argument for studies that manipulate rather than measure delay.

STUDIES WITH DELAY AS AN INDEPENDENT VARIABLE

Fortunately, some researchers have systematically manipulated delay, and these studies provide the best available evidence of the likely impact of delay on identification accuracy. On the other hand, it will become apparent that delay as an issue has not been investigated systematically within the eyewitness literature. The delay periods employed in studies often are unique to the individual studies, delay generally was not the only or even the primary variable of interest, and, as a result, interpretation of the results can be difficult.

One of the earliest studies to investigate delay as an independent variable was that by Egan, Pittner, and Goldstein (1977). After a delay of 2 days, 21 days, or 56 days, participants were asked to make an identification of two targets that they had viewed during a live exposure. Egan et al. found no significant decrease in correct identifications over the delay; however, the rate of false alarms increased from 2 days (48%) to 21 days (62%) to 56 days (93%). Shepherd (1983) has conducted the most extensive investigation of delay on identification accuracy, using delay periods from 1 week to 11 months. After viewing a live event, participants were asked to return at a later time (1 week, 1 month, 3 months, or 11 months) to view a target-present line-up. Participants were not aware that they were witnesses to an event until after they returned to the laboratory. The results showed no significant decrease in correct identifications from the 1-week

(65%) to the 1-month (55%) to the 3-month (50%) intervals; however, there was a significant decrease in correct identifications between the 11-month delay (10%) and the other three conditions. There was no significant increase in false alarms across the four delay conditions. In a second study, Shepherd again found no significant decrease in correct identifications or foil identifications between a 1-month and a 4-month delay.

Other researchers (Cutler, Penrod, & Martens, 1987; Cutler, Penrod, O'Rourke, & Martens, 1986; Dysart, 1999; Dysart, Lindsay, & Dupuis, 2005; Krafka & Penrod, 1985; Laughery, Fessler, Lenorovitz, & Yoblick, 1974; Mauldin & Laughery, 1981; Memon, Bartlett, Rose & Gray, 2003; Read, Hammersley, Cross-Calvert, & McFadzen, 1989; Turtle & Yuille, 1994; Yarmey, 2004; Yarmey, Yarmey, & Yarmey, 1996) have also explored delay as an independent variable in eyewitness identification studies. Cutler et al. (1986) examined identification accuracy from target-present and target-absent lineups 7 or 28 days after viewing a videotaped crime. They found a significant main effect of delay on identification accuracy, where participants were significantly more likely to make a correct decision after 7 days than after 28 days. In addition, Cutler et al. found a significant interaction between delay and whether the participant was asked to read the description they had provided of the target. When participants were asked to read the description, the effects of delay were eliminated, and participants performed equally well after 7 or 28 days. However, if participants were not asked to read their description, there was a significant decrease in correct decisions over a period of 28 days. Cutler et al. did not find a significant interaction between retention interval and type of lineup (target-present and target-absent lineups), which suggests that the delay period did not have a differential effect on correct identifications or false identifications of innocent suspects.

In another study, Cutler et al. (1987) examined the effects of 10 independent variables on identification accuracy from target-present and target-absent lineups following a videotaped event, including context reinstatement and delay intervals of 2 days and 2 weeks. Overall, there was no significant main effect of delay on identification accuracy, but there was a significant interaction between delay and the type of context reinstatement procedure used. Participants were more accurate in their identification after 2 weeks' delay if they had received context reinstatement, but context cues had no effect after the 2-day delay. Cutler et al. concluded that, together with other research on the effects of context reinstatement on identification accuracy, there must be some delay period or impairment of memory for context reinstatement to be effective.

Participants in the study by Laughery et al. (1974) viewed either a 1-minute video clip or four slides depicting the target person. Then, following a 4-minute, 30-minute, 1-hour, 4-hour, 1-day, or 1-week delay, participants were asked to identify the target from 149 photographs (the target appeared in position 104). There was no significant effect of delay on identification accuracy over the six time intervals.[1] In the study by Mauldin and Laughery (1981), participants were exposed to a target for either 4 or 15 seconds and were then asked to look through 130 photographs to see if there was a photo

---

[1]The data for each time interval was not presented in the original publication, and therefore floor or ceiling effects cannot be ruled out as potential explanations for the lack of delay effects.

of the target (which always appeared in position 125). No effect of delay was found between the 30-minute and 2-day delay groups.[2] In addition, Mauldin and Laughery investigated whether producing a composite of the target would interact with the delay period. No significant interaction between composite production and delay was found.

Krafka and Penrod (1985) conducted a field study where they explored 2-hour and 24-hour delays, using target-present and target-absent lineups. In the target-present conditions, they found no significant effect of delay on correct identification accuracy over the two time periods. They did find, however, a significant increase in foil identifications over time from 8.3% to 35.7%. In the target-absent conditions, a significant decrease in correct rejections of the lineup was found from 2 hours (85%) to 24 hours (48%).

Read, Hammersley, Cross-Calvert, and McFadzen (1989) examined the effects of delay on identification accuracy from target-present and target-absent lineups after a delay of 20 minutes or 1 week (Experiment 2). After viewing a videotaped event, participants were asked either to rehearse the event in their mind or to complete a filler task. Then, participants were shown a line-up or asked to return 1 week later to view a line-up. Although the statistical analysis for overall delay effects is not reported, the results appear to indicate that there was no overall effect of delay on identification accuracy. There was a significant interaction between the timing of the rehearsal (first 3 minutes after event or 10 minutes after event) and the delay period.

Dysart (1999), in her unpublished master's thesis, examined identification accuracy rates from simultaneous and sequential, target-present and target-absent line-ups immediately after a staged event or 3 weeks later. Results showed no significant effects of correct identifications (47.2% and 51.7%, respectively) or correct rejections (89.8% and 81.0%, respectively) over the delay period. In addition, there was no significant interaction between type of line-up and delay period on identification accuracy. The accuracy of participants who viewed a line-up immediately or 3 weeks later was not affected by whether they had viewed a simultaneous (71.2% and 62.1%, respectively) or sequential (64.0% and 70.1%, respectively) line-up.

Memon et al. (2003) tested identification accuracy between young adults (M age = 19.4 years) and older adults (M age = 71.7 years) after a 35-minute or a 1-week delay. There was no significant effect of age on overall correct decisions in the 35-minute delay conditions; however, there was a significant difference in accuracy between young adults (90%) and older adults (35%) after the 1-week delay period. Yarmey (2004), in a recent field study, investigated the effects of an immediate versus a 4-hour delay on identification accuracy from target-present and target-absent lineups. The results showed no significant main effect of delay on identification accuracy from either type of line-up.

Two studies have investigated the effects of delay with the show-up identification procedure. Yarmey et al. (1996) conducted a field study where participants were asked to view target-present or target-absent show-ups and line-ups immediately after the exposure, 30 minutes later, 2 hours later, or 24 hours later. For the target-present condi-

---

[2]The data for each time interval was not presented in the original publication, and therefore floor or ceiling effects cannot be ruled out as potential explanations for the lack of delay effects.

tions, correct identifications of the target decreased by approximately 15% after 24 hours. In the target-absent conditions, there was little decrease in correct rejections for line-ups (11%) and a large decrease in accuracy for show-ups (35%). In contrast to these findings, Dysart, Lindsay, and Dupuis (2005) found no significant decrease in identification accuracy from a field study using target-present and target-absent show-ups; however, no delay exceeded 24 hours.

ACCURACY AFTER A PERIOD OF DELAY

Dozens of identification studies have been conducted where the identification test was not completed immediately following the exposure to the criminal. A complete review of these studies is not appropriate for this chapter because delay did not vary within the studies, but a brief review of three frequently cited papers will be used to illustrate the nature of such studies, the sort of data they generate, and the difficulty of interpreting their results as demonstrating effects of delay. The difficulty in interpretation is not a result of these studies being flawed. They were not designed as tests of delay effects. On the other hand, people sometimes do inappropriately interpret the results of these studies as demonstrating delay effects.

A study by Malpass and Devine (1981b) is often cited as demonstrating the deleterious effects of delay. Malpass and Devine were interested in examining whether, 5 months after viewing of an event, a guided memory task would increase correct identifications from a target-present lineup. Low correct decision rates were obtained and are attributed by some to the lengthy delay. Turtle and Yuille (1994) examined identification accuracy after 3 weeks of repeated recall of a criminal event. Searcy, Bartlett, Memon, and Swanson (2001) explored differences in identification accuracy between seniors and young adults after a 1-month delay. The results of these studies are not important in the current context. Regardless of whether identification accuracy was high or low, regardless of whether differences in identification accuracy across manipulated conditions were similar to or different from those described in studies with brief or no delay, it is not possible to conclude that these studies demonstrate delay effects. The absence of early and later testing makes results such as those obtained by Malpass and Devine suggestive and interesting but not informative with regard to delay.

PATTERNS

There are some interesting patterns in these data. Show-up studies revealed significant effects on accuracy in terms of both decreased correct identifications and increased false identifications after 24 hours (Yarmey et al., 1996). Another study reported no delay effects with variations in delay of less than 24 hours (Dysart et al., 2002). These results provide some support for the concern that show-ups, if they are to be used, should be used within a short period after the crime, perhaps a maximum of 24 hours. On the other hand, such a conclusion is highly speculative, given the minimal amount of data available on the issue. If police are determined to continue using show-ups, it is imperative that more data be collected on the impact of delay (and other factors) on the accuracy of identification decisions from show-ups (Dysart & Lindsay, this volume).

If we consider the impact of delay only on correct identification of targets from lineups, delay has surprisingly little effect. Of 12 opportunities for delay to decrease correct identification from lineups, only three significant effects were obtained, and each of these is interesting. In one study, the effect occurred only for elderly witnesses (Memon et al., 2003). In another study, the effect disappeared if the witnesses reviewed their original descriptions of the perpetrator before attempting the identification (Cutler et al., 1987). In the third study, the effect appeared only after a very long delay of 11 months (Shepherd, 1983). Collectively, these data suggest that, in general, there is little risk of loss of correct identification from line-ups unless delays become very large.

One implication of this pattern in the data is that the argument that show-ups can be justified by the need to protect witnesses from decay of their memories for perpetrators is highly questionable. Show-ups generate fewer correct identifications and more false identifications than line-ups (Dysart & Lindsay, this volume; Gonzalez, Ellsworth, & Pembroke, 1993; Lindsay, Pozzulo, Craig, Lee, & Corber, 1997; Steblay, Dysart, Fulero, & Lindsay, 2003). They may suffer from delay effects to a greater extent and much sooner than do line-ups. The only justifications for their use would appear to be that they permit quick exoneration of the innocent and that they are less work for police. Neither justification seems sufficient, given the risks. If suspects were correctly informed that they are at greater risk of false identification from a show-up and given the option of an immediate show-up or a delayed line-up, many may opt for the line-up. For police to unilaterally make this decision for people seems inappropriate. The greater work required of police would be in the form of more thorough investigation before any identification procedure was attempted. Given multiple suspects, investigation to determine the most probable culprit (if any) would be required before conducting a line-up (if show-ups were banned). The alternative is to expose a sequence of individuals, most of whom are innocent, to the risk of misidentification in show-ups. Given a single suspect, it is difficult to see how some investigation prior to an identification attempt (such as attempting to verify an alibi) could lead to increased miscarriages of justice.

Only four data sets provide clear comparisons for target-absent lineups (some studies unfortunately collapse across target-present and target-absent lineups and simply report overall accuracy). Two of the studies generated significantly and substantially lower correct rejection rates as delay increased (Egan et al., 1977; Krafka & Penrod, 1985). In one case, the effect occurred with a difference between 2 and 24 hours of delay (Krafka & Penrod, 1985). One study failing to find delay effects involved differences in delay of 0 to 3 weeks (Dysart, 1999).

Mug shot research found no decline in participant ability to recognize targets as a result of delays up to 7 days (Laughery et al., 1974; Mauldin & Laughery, 1981). Longer delays have yet to be tested. The lack of data for longer delays is problematic as long delays do occur with mug shot searches in real cases. Police and the courts need to know if longer delays result in declines in correct selections or catastrophic increases in false positive choices from mug shots.

DELAY AND MEMORY IN GENERAL

Psychological research on the deleterious effects of delay on the strength of memory traces has been conducted for over a century (Ebbinghaus, 1885/1913). Based on the results of hundreds of studies, the general conclusion is that the accuracy of performance on memory tasks decreases with the passage of time. However, the majority of information about memory and delay from early studies may not be applicable to eyewitness identification situations. For example, Ebbinghaus (1885/1913) explored the effects of delay on forgetting lists of nonsense syllables or words and found that there is a rapid decrease in forgetting up to 24 hours, after which there is a leveling-off period where forgetting occurs but at a very slow rate over extended periods of time. Researchers later questioned whether Ebbinghaus's forgetting curve applied to real-life events. For example, Linton (1978) tested the likelihood of remembering both trivial and significant events in a person's life and found that forgetting was less rapid than the forgetting curve would have predicted.

As researchers became more concerned with everyday events rather than with abstract symbols or words, discussion turned to autobiographic memories (Rubin, 1996). Certainly, many autobiographic memories last for a very long time. For example, Burt, Kemp, and Conway (2001) reported that some aspects of autobiographic memory were unchanged after a delay of over 10 years, and Bluck (2001) reported maintenance of autobiographic memories decades after they were formed. On the other hand, Walls, Sperling, and Weber (2001) reported a great deal of variability in the amount and nature of undergraduates' memories of elementary school experiences. Clearly, eyewitness memories are autobiographic, may be maintained over extended periods of time, but also do suffer from "forgetting." Furthermore, the fact that a person has a memory for an event or person long after exposure is no guarantee that the memory is accurate (Loftus, 2001). The autobiographic memory literature tells us that delay may, but does not automatically, result in decreased accuracy on memory tasks. The most important reason for not reviewing the large literature on autobiographic memory is that it generally does not address sufficiently or directly the issues we are interested in, because memory for faces is rarely examined.

Of course, many studies have been conducted that explicitly tested memory for faces. Research on the effects of delay on face memory has been conducted at least since the 1960s. However, most of this research used the old-new face memory paradigm. Researchers showed participants a large number of faces, one at a time, and usually for a short period of time (1–5 seconds). Then, following a delay period from minutes to months, participants were shown another set of faces, some of which were seen before (old faces) and some of which were not (new faces). This type of experiment allows researchers to collect many data points for each participant (reducing the number of participants required) and to use analyses (e.g., signal detection) that are not available with standard eyewitness identification tasks that provide a single data point per participant.

Although facial recognition research is extremely useful, there are factors related to eyewitness identification accuracy that cannot be (or at least generally are not) tested with the use of the traditional old-new paradigm (Wells, 1993; Wells & Olson, 2001). Compared with eyewitness study participants, participants in facial memory studies are presented with different tasks and information at both encoding and test, including knowledge of the purpose of the study before encoding and (often) the number of target faces to be encoded. The ecological validity or mundane realism of the old-new recognition paradigm is suspect for eyewitness purposes. For example, it is not clear that we encode, store, and retrieve faces in the same way when they are presented as to-be-remembered photos as we do when we meet people live in social situations and only realize during or after exposure that we may want to remember the face. This and many other factors may lead to differences in the difficulty of the recognition task for traditional facial memory versus eyewitness tasks.

Shapiro and Penrod (1986), in their meta-analysis of facial recognition and eyewitness identification studies, acknowledged that the two types of studies are indeed different. Although Shapiro and Penrod collapsed across the variable "type of study" for the majority of their analyses, they did find that recognition accuracy for traditional (old-new) face recognition studies was higher than that for eyewitness identification studies. Even using the old-new facial memory paradigm, some researchers have failed to find significant, deleterious effects of delay between encoding and test on the accuracy of memory for faces (e.g., Chance & Goldstein, 1987; Chance, Goldstein, & McBride, 1975; MacLin, MacLin, & Malpass, 2001). Other researchers have found significant delay effects (e.g., Barkowitz & Brigham, 1982; Krouse, 1981; Shepherd, Gibling, & Ellis, 1991). For the reasons cited above, the current chapter focused only on delay in the eyewitness identification paradigm.

Preparation of this chapter was supported by grants to R. Lindsay from the Social Sciences and Humanities Research Council of Canada.

CONCLUSIONS

The research on the impact of delay on identification accuracy presents a complex picture. The most that can be said at this point is that delay *probably* increases errors from both target-present and target-absent lineups and show-ups and probably increases such errors only in some circumstances, and that we have insufficient data to determine when to expect such increases to occur.

The evidence suggests that show-ups may be dangerous to use after as little as 24 hours (and possibly less, but we have no data systematically testing intervals shorter than 2 hours). Furthermore, the claim that show-ups provide a means of safely and quickly screening out innocent suspects appears to be false; though again, the amount of data available precludes any strong conclusions.

Clearly, a great deal of research is required on delay effects. Studies are needed that systematically address the impact of length of delay on identification accuracy from lineups, show-ups, and mug shot searches. As with many aspects of eyewitness research, progress is slowed by the lack of theory. We need to think about the reasons that delay may be more disruptive to memory in some situations or for some witnesses. We particularly need to think about the reasons that delay effects may differ across identification procedures (line-ups, show-ups, mug shots). Finally, we need to be restrained in our statements to the courts because, quite simply put, at this point in time we do not know much about the impact of delay on eyewitness identification accuracy.

ACKNOWLEDGMENT

Preparation of this chapter was supported by grants to R. Lindsay from the Social Sciences and Humanities Research Council of Canada.

REFERENCES

Barkowitz, P., & Brigham, J. C. (1982). Recognition of faces: Own-race bias, incentive, and time delay. *Journal of Applied Social Psychology, 12*, 255–268.

Behrman, B. W., & Davey, S. L. (2001). Eyewitness identification in actual criminal cases: An archival analysis. *Law and Human Behavior, 25*, 475–491.

Bluck, S. (2001). Autobiographical memories: A building block of life narratives. In G. M. Kenyon, P. G. Clark, & B. deVries (Eds), *Narrative gerontology: Theory, research, and practice* (pp. 67–89). New York: Springer.

Bradfield, A. L., & Wells, G. L. (2000). The perceived validity of eyewitness identification testimony: A test of the five Biggers criteria. *Law and Human Behavior, 24*, 581–594.

Burt, C. D. B., Kemp, S., & Conway, M. (2001). What happens if you retest autobiographical memory 10 years on? *Memory & Cognition, 29*, 127–136.

Chance, J. E. & Goldstein, A. G. (1987). Retention interval and face recognition: Response latency measures. *Bulletin of the Psychonomic Society, 25*, 415–418.

Chance, J., Goldstein, A. G., & McBride, L. (1975). Differential experience and recognition memory for faces. *Journal of Social Psychology, 97*, 243–253.

Commonwealth v. Bumpus, Mass, 238 N.E.2d 343, 347 (1968).

Cutler, B. L., Penrod, S., & Dexter, H. R. (1990). Juror sensitivity to eyewitness identification evidence. *Law and Human Behavior, 14*, 185–191.

Cutler, B. L., Penrod, S. D., & Martens, T. K. (1987). Improving the reliability of eyewitness identification: Putting context into context. *Journal of Applied Psychology, 72*, 629–637.

Cutler, B. L., Penrod, S., O'Rourke, T. E., & Martens, T. K. (1986). Unconfounding the effects of contextual cues on eyewitness identification accuracy, *Social Behavior, 1*, 113–134.

Dysart, J. E. (1999). *The effects of delay on eyewitness identification accuracy.* Unpublished master's thesis, Queen's University, Kingston, Ontario, Canada.

Dysart, J. E., Lindsay, R. C. L., & Dupuis, P. R. (2005). *Clothing matters: The effects of clothing bias on identification accuracy from show-ups.* Unpublished manuscript.

Dysart, J. E., Lindsay, R. C. L., MacDonald, T. K., & Wicke, C. (2002). The intoxicated witness: Effects of alcohol on identification accuracy from show-ups. *Journal of Applied Psychology, 87*, 170–175.

Ebbinghaus, H. M. (1885/1913). *Memory: A contribution to experimental psychology* (H. A. Ruger & C. E. Bussenius, trans.). New York: Teachers College Press, Columbia University.

Egan, D., Pittner, M., & Goldstein, A. G. (1977). Eyewitness identification: Photographs vs. live models. *Journal of Law and Human Behavior, 1*, 199–206.

Gonzalez, R., Ellsworth, P. C., & Pembroke, M. (1993). Response biases in line-ups and show-ups. *Journal of Personality and Social Psychology, 64*, 525–537.

Krafka, C., & Penrod, S. (1985). Reinstatement of context in a field experiment on eyewitness identification. *Journal of Personality and Social Psychology, 49*, 58–69.

Krouse, F. L. (1981). Effects of pose, pose change, and delay on face recognition performance. *Journal of Applied Psychology, 66*, 651–654.

Laughery, K. R., Fessler, P. K., Lenorovitz, D. R., & Yoblick, D. A. (1974). Time delay and similarity effects in facial recognition. *Journal of Applied Psychology, 59*, 490–496.

Lindsay, R. C. L. (1994). Expectations of eyewitness performance. In D. Ross, D. Read, & M. Toglia (Eds), *Adult eyewitness testimony: Current trends and developments* (pp. 362–384). New York: Cambridge University Press.

Lindsay, R. C. L., Pozzulo, J. D., Craig, W., Lee, K., & Corber, S. (1997). Simultaneous lineups, sequential lineups, and showups: Eyewitness identification decisions of adults and children. *Law and Human Behavior, 21,* 219–225.

Lindsay, R. C. L., & Wells, G. L. (1985). Improving eyewitness identifications from lineups: Simultaneous versus sequential lineup presentation. *Journal of Applied Psychology, 70,* 556–564.

Linton, M. (1978). Real-world memory after six years: An in vivo study of very long-term memory. In M. M. Gruneberg, P. E. Morris, & R. N. Sykes (Eds.), *Practical aspects of memory.* London: Academic Press.

Loftus, E. F. (2001). Imagining the past. *Psychologist, 14,* 584–587.

MacLin, O. H., MacLin, M. K. & Malpass, R. S. (2001). Race, arousal, attention, exposure and delay: An examination of factors moderating face recognition. *Psychology, Public, and Law, 7,* 134–152.

Malpass, R. S., & Devine, P. G. (1981). Guided memory in eyewitness identification. *Journal of Applied Psychology, 66,* 343–350.

Mauldin, M. A., & Laughery, K. R. (1981). Composite production effects of subsequent facial recognition. *Journal of Applied Psychology, 66,* 351–357.

Memon, A., Bartlett, J., Rose, R., & Gray, C. (2003). The aging eyewitness: Effects of age on face, delay, and source-memory ability. *Journal of Gerontology: Psychological Sciences, 58B,* 338–345.

Neil v. Biggers, 409 U.S. 188 (1972).

Read, J. D., Hammersley, R., Cross-Calvert, S., & McFadzen, E. (1989). Rehearsal of faces and details in action events. *Applied Cognitive Psychology, 3,* 295–311.

Rubin, D. C. (Ed.). (1996). *Remembering our past: Studies in autobiographical memory.* New York: Cambridge University Press.

Searcy, J. H., Bartlett, J. C., Memon, A., & Swanson, K. (2001). Aging and lineup performance at long retention intervals: Effects of metamemory and context reinstatement. *Journal of Applied Psychology, 86,* 207–214.

Shapiro, P. N., & Penrod, S. (1986). Meta-analysis of facial identification studies. *Psychological Bulletin, 100,* 139–156.

Shepherd, J. (1983). Identification after long delays. In S. Lloyd-Bostock & B. R. Clifford (Eds.), *Evaluating witness evidence: Recent psychological research and new perspectives* (pp. 173–188). Chichester, New York: John Wiley & Sons.

Shepherd, J. W., Gibling, F., & Ellis, H. D. (1991). The effects of distinctiveness, presentation time and delay on face recognition. *European Journal of Cognitive Psychology, 3,* 137–145.

Steblay, N. M., Dysart, J., Fulero, S., & Lindsay, R. C. L. (2001). Eyewitness accuracy rates in sequential and simultaneous lineup presentations: A meta-analytic comparison. *Law and Human Behavior, 25,* 459–474.

Steblay, N., Dysart, J. E., Fulero, S., & Lindsay, R. C. L. (2003). Eyewitness accuracy rates in police show-up and lineup presentations: A meta-analytic comparison. *Law and Human Behavior, 27,* 523–540.

Tollestrup, P. A., Turtle, J. W., & Yuille, J. C. (1994). Actual victim and witnesses to robbery and fraud: an archival analysis. In D. F. Ross, J. D. Read, & M. P. Toglia (Eds.), *Adult eyewitness testimony: Current trends and developments* (pp. 144–160). Cambridge: Cambridge University Press.

Turtle, J. W., & Yuille, J. C. (1994). Lost but not forgotten details: Repeated eyewitness recall leads to reminiscence but not hypermnesia. *Journal of Applied Psychology, 79,* 260–271.

Valentine, T., Pickering, A., & Darling, S. (2003). Characteristics of eyewitness identification that predict the outcome of real lineups. *Applied Cognitive Psychology, 17,* 969–993.

Walls, R. T., Sperling, R. A., & Weber, K. D. (2001). Autobiographical memory of school. *Journal of Educational Research, 95,* 116–127.

Wells, G. L. (1984). The psychology of line-up identifications. *Journal of Applied Social Psychology, 14,* 89–103.

Wells, G. L. (1993). What do we know about eyewitness identification? *American Psychologist, 48,* 553–571.

Wells, G. L., & Olson, E. A. (2001). The other-race effect in eyewitness identification: What do we do about it? *Psychology, Public Policy, and Law, 7*, 230–246.

Wright, D. B., & McDaid, A. T. (1996). Comparing system and estimator variables using data from real line-ups. *Applied Cognitive Psychology, 10*, 75–84.

Wright v. United States. 404 F.2d 1256 (D.C. Cir) (1968).

Yarmey, A. D. (2004). Eyewitness recall and photo identification: A field experiment. *Psychology, Crime & Law, 10*, 53–68.

Yarmey, A. D., Yarmey, M. J., & Yarmey, A. L. (1996). Accuracy of eyewitness identifications in show-ups and lineups. *Law and Human Behavior, 20*, 459–477.

16

Eyewitness Confidence and the Confidence-Accuracy Relationship in Memory for People

Michael R. Leippe and Donna Eisenstadt
Saint Louis University

I was certain, but I was wrong.

—*Jennifer Thompson*, New York Times, 6/18/00

Police officers routinely follow up a positive identification of their suspect with the question, *Are you sure?* If the case and the eyewitness make it into the courtroom, the prosecuting attorney is almost certain to ask a similar question, inviting the witness to tell the jury that they are certain—100% confident—that the defendant was the person they saw commit the crime. Such was the case with Jennifer Thompson. She was raped with a knife to her throat, pinned down and facing her attacker. She made it a point to study her assailant's face, because she wanted "to make sure that he was put in prison and he was going to rot." Several days later, Jennifer identified a man as her attacker from a photo spread and later identified the same man from a live lineup. On both occasions, she was "completely confident" she had "picked the right guy" (Thompson, 2000). Except he wasn't the right guy. The man Jennifer identified was convicted based on her sworn courtroom testimony and sentenced to two life sentences. A year later an appellate court overturned the conviction because another man admitted to being her attacker. Yet when this man was brought into court at the second trial of the man she had originally accused, Jennifer answered passionately that "I have never seen him in my life" (Thompson, 2000). So the accused was convicted and sentenced again. Eleven years later, DNA tests proved that the man who raped her was the man she fervently believed she had never seen, and that the man she had so absolutely confidently identified as the rapist was, in fact, innocent.

Setting aside for the moment Jennifer Thompson's story—and other cases of mistaken identification that have resulted in wrongful convictions that have been uncovered through DNA testing and other means (Loftus & Ketcham, 1991; Scheck, Neufeld, & Dwyer, 2000)—consider why eyewitnesses' confidence statements are considered so important by police investigators and fact finders. Intuitively, it would seem that memories about which we feel certain should more likely be accurate than less certain memories. Indeed, surveys have shown that adults commonly believe in a strong relationship between memory accuracy and confidence in that memory (Wells, 1984; Yarmey & Jones, 1983). In studies in which mock jurors watch and judge the testimony of eyewitnesses to staged crimes and other events, mock jurors' ratings of witness confidence are highly positively correlated with their perceptions of the accuracy of witnesses' line-up identifications (Wells & Murray, 1984) and accuracy of recall memory (Leippe, Manion, & Romanczyk, 1992). And in trial simulations, mock jurors more readily believe courtroom eyewitnesses who assert high (vs. low) confidence (Whitley & Greenberg, 1986). Finally, a positive confidence-accuracy (CA) relationship is assumed by the courts. In *Neil v. Biggers* (1972), the U.S. Supreme Court identified witness confidence as one of five valid criteria for evaluating eyewitness evidence.

Police investigators, of course, make the same assumption that confidence is indicative of memory accuracy. Accordingly, one motive behind their eagerness to ask the confidence question is to find out how confident *they* can be that they have apprehended the correct person. But there is likely a second police motive as well. The police understandably should want their evidence to be persuasive to district attorneys, judges, and, ultimately, to jurors. They know that the most persuasive eyewitnesses are confident eyewitnesses.

Eyewitness confidence, then, is clearly a player variable in criminal justice. Its status rests squarely on the assumption that expressed confidence in memory is indicative of the likely accuracy of the memory and on the related assumption that confidence is primarily determined by the accuracy of the memory—the strength of the memory trace. Research findings over the past 30 years, however, often have been at odds with these assumptions, in suggesting that confidence, as in Jennifer Thompson's case, is a poor indicator of accuracy. At the same time, researchers have learned a great deal about the psychology of eyewitness confidence. The picture, as we shall see, is much more complex than the assumptions shared by parties in the criminal justice system, and specifically the Supreme Court of the United States in *Neil v. Biggers* (1972). The emerging picture of eyewitness confidence is not as optimistic as those assumptions. Nor, however, is the picture as pessimistic about the usefulness of confidence as some researchers, and their findings, have suggested (cf. Read, Lindsay, & Nicholls, 1998).

In this chapter, we examine the history of research and theory on eyewitness confidence and develop a perspective on confidence that integrates the accumulated knowledge. The main focus is on the confidence-accuracy relationship, particularly in the realm of memory for people. Face identifications from lineups and photo spreads, as well as (less often) descriptions of a culprit's face, body, and clothing, constitute the objects of memory. After reviewing the findings of three decades of research, we present a conceptual model of the intrapsychic and interpersonal sources and psychological nature of memory confidence. In turn, using this model as an interpretive and integrative framework, we examine the factors that moderate the confidence-accuracy (CA) relationship, sometimes by directly influencing confidence. We also look at how confidence itself may be both a result of and a cause of memory responses. Our ultimate aim is to suggest some scientific answers about *how*, *how well*, and *when* confidence in memory relates to the accuracy of memory for once- or briefly seen people.

CONFIDENCE DEFINED AND MEASURED

The focus here is on *verbally expressed confidence*—an oral or written assertion by the witness of his or her confidence or certainty on some quantitative dimension. To be sure, confidence may be communicated, consciously or unconsciously, in other ways, such as in paralinguistic, facial, and bodily expressions, which may be correlated with verbal statements (cf. Leippe, 1994). But, like police and lawyers, our concern is with what eyewitnesses *consciously believe* about their memory and are willing to convey to fact finders. In this sense, eyewitness confidence indeed can be seen as a belief, akin to beliefs about physical and social objects (Wells, Olson, & Charman, 2002). Even more aptly, confidence in memory may be thought of as an evaluative belief or, more simply, as an *evaluation* of the memory on a validity dimension (see Petty, Brinol, & Tormala, 2002, for a similar characterization of confidence in thoughts about objects of persuasion). Importantly, like other evaluations and beliefs, confidence can be influenced by internal and external forces (Leippe, 1980; Wells et al., 2002).

Police investigators routinely assess confidence rather informally, sometimes before and very often after an eyewitness attempts to identify a culprit from a live or photo lineup. It is not uncommon for investigators to finish their initial questioning of the witness by a probe such as *Do you think you'd be able to recognize this guy?* The witness's response is not likely to be recorded or elaborated in terms of a scale of certainty, but the investigator obtains a sense of just how useful the witness will be in the apprehension and arrest of a suspect. Based on cases in which the authors and some of their colleagues have served as consultants and expert witnesses, it appears more common, if not commonplace, for lineup administrators to follow up a lineup identification with a query such as *Are you sure?* or *How certain are you?* It is not common for a scale to be described or provided on which witnesses can define their responses. But some police jurisdictions do use a scale. For example, Behrman and Davey (2001) report that the Sacramento, California, police ask witnesses to check one of three options: "I'm sure number __ was the person . . .," "I'm not positive, but I think number __ was the person . . .," and "I did not recognize anyone as being the person. . . ." This scale illustrates an important quality of the typical police confidence probe to which we will return later: For witnesses who make a positive identification, the confidence dimension, in terms of police and prosecution interest, shrinks into two categories, 100% certain ("sure") and any level of confidence that is less than certain.

More formal and careful assessments of eyewitness confidence are made in scientific studies of eyewitness behavior in which participants witness a stranger engaging in a crime or crime-like activity or have an interaction with a stranger, and then, at some later point, attempt to identify the stranger from a lineup. Typically, the confidence question is asked only after witnesses make a lineup decision (although a few studies also have asked it before the identification), and witnesses are asked to record their rating of their confidence by marking a scale that appears on a sheet of paper or a computer screen. The rating scales represent a quantitative dimension in which higher numbers represent increasing certainty that the person identified is the culprit or target person witnessed earlier, or, in the case of a lineup rejection (i.e., admitting to recognizing no one in the lineup as the target), increasing certainty that the target is not in the lineup.

Scales that have been used have been remarkably similar over three decades. They include scales anchored at the poles by the uncertain and certain extremes: 5-point scales ("not at all sure" to "very certain"; e.g., Read, 1995), 7-point scales ("completely uncertain" to "certain enough to testify in court"; e.g., Fleet, Brigham, & Bothwell, 1987; "not at all confident" to "extremely confident"; e.g., Memon, Hope, & Bull, 2003), 9-point scales ("not very certain" to "absolutely certain"; e.g., Wells, Lindsay, & Ferguson, 1979), and 10-point scales ("not at all confident" to "very confident"; e.g., Kassin, Rigby, & Castillo, 1991; Luus & Wells, 1994). Another form of confidence scale asks for certainty in percentage or probability terms. Leippe, Wells, and Ostrom (1978) presented witnesses with a scale that ranged from 0.0 to 1.0, with the endpoint and midpoints labeled according to their logical meaning (0.0 = completely certain he was not the thief; 0.5 = uncertain; 1.0 = completely certain he was the thief). More recently, percentage scales have been used, which correspond to the form of expression that actual witnesses often use or are asked to use (e.g., "I'm 90% sure that's the person I saw point the gun"), with an 11-point scale ranging from 0% to 100% and anchored by "not at all certain" and "totally certain" (e.g., Bradfield, Wells, & Olson, 2002; Juslin, Olsson, & Winman, 1996; Leippe, Eisenstadt, Rauch, & Stambush, 2006; Weber & Brewer, 2003).

In the vast majority of studies, the CA relationship is assessed by computation, across and/or within experimental conditions, of the point-biserial correlation (r_{pb}, or simply r hereafter) between the continuous, scaled measure of confidence and the dichotomous measure of eyewitness accuracy (accurate, inaccurate).[1] Although it is by far the most common measure of the CA relationship, r is not, as we shall see, the only one.

There is little basis for preferring one single-item confidence measure over others. There has been no research reporting a failure of participant-witnesses to understand the

---

[1] A witness can be accurate by correctly identifying a *guilty suspect* (the culprit or target) from a lineup that includes the culprit (target-present lineup) or by correctly rejecting the lineup by identifying no one from a lineup that does not include the culprit (target-absent lineup). A witness can be inaccurate by incorrectly identifying a foil (a lineup member known to be innocent) from a target-present or target-absent lineup or by identifying an *innocent suspect* from a target-absent lineup. Wells and Lindsay (1985) argued that inaccuracies of the first type—foil identifications—have no forensic relevance because they are "known errors" in actual cases, and knowledge that they are made equally or less confidently than an accurate identification of the culprit is not useful to the police. What is more forensically useful is information about whether identifications of an innocent suspect from a target-absent lineup are made equally or less confidently than accurate identifications of the culprit from a target-present lineup. Because the latter CA relationship cannot be determined in a study that uses only a target-present lineup, Wells and Lindsay (1985) recommended that eyewitness studies include both a target-present lineup and a target-absent lineup in which the culprit is replaced by an innocent look-alike. In turn the CA correlation should be computed only for witnesses who viewed a target-present lineup and chose the culprit (accurate) or viewed a target-absent lineup and chose the look-alike (inaccurate).

rating task posed by any of the items. The scales seem equally face valid in directly asking for a rating of a feeling or belief about a memory that is readily understood. And a cursory review of the literature reveals no systematic differences in CA correlations obtained with different single-item measures. If one measure is most preferable it is the percentage scale, because it resembles how people sometimes spontaneously express their confidence and provides the ability to frame questions of CA calibration, as described below, straightforwardly in terms of obtained and predicted (e.g., the confidence rating) percentages of accuracy.

A potential problem with research on confidence is that it is usually assessed with only a single item, leaving confidence scores prone to measurement error (unreliability). Unreliability in one of the variables may artificially depress CA correlations, leading to underestimation of the degree to which confidence is indicative of accuracy. Reliability worries, however, are somewhat assuaged by evidence that single-item confidence measures have good test-retest reliability and correlate moderately with parallel single-item measures (e.g., degree-of-certainty rating and degree of stated willingness to sign a sworn statement that the identified person is the culprit; Wells & Murray, 1984). Still, the only-moderate parallel-forms reliability suggests that multiple-item measures of confidence may be desirable in research that studies confidence theoretically. One possibility is the approach used in research on confidence in thoughts about one's attitudes (e.g., Petty, Brinol, & Tormala, 2002). Participants rate their confidence in their thoughts on up to five semantic differential scales anchored by *not at all* and *extremely*. They may rate such confidence-related qualities as *certain, valid, confident, convincing,* and *clear.* In turn, these ratings, which are typically moderately to highly correlated, are averaged to create a composite measure of confidence. In eyewitness research, witnesses might rate some of these perceived attributes of their identification, as well as attributes uniquely relevant

---

Wells and Lindsay (1985) also suggested that CA correlations that are based only on target-present line-ups and include foil identifications might overestimate the CA relationship, because those who identify a foil even when the culprit is present may be especially unconfident (and more so than witnesses who identify an innocent suspect from a target-absent lineup).

We agree to an extent with the forensic-usefulness argument and endorse the inclusion of target-absent lineup conditions in eyewitness research. However, in this chapter we include in our review estimates of the CA relationship (of which there are many more) based on target-present-only data along with estimates (of which there are far fewer) based on data from target-present and target-absent lineups and excluding foil identifications. Although the latter estimates of the CA relationship may be more forensically useful, they are not necessarily more theoretically useful when the issue, as it is in this chapter, is the question of whether accurate memories are reported more confidently than inaccurate memories of any sort. Indeed, Wells and Lindsay (1985) themselves suggested that CA relations calculated with foils included can be used for theoretical reasons. Both contemporary eyewitness (e.g., Lindsay, Read, & Sharma, 1998; Perfect, Hollins, & Hunt, 2000; Smith, Lindsay, & Pryke, 2000) and more basic memory (e.g., Clark, 1997; Dobbins, Kroll, & Liu, 1998) research that tests theory about CA relationships has typically included the equivalent of foil identifications (e.g., choosing the "distractor" [previously unseen item] instead of the previously seen item in a two-item "lineup") in computation of the relationship. In addition, little support has been reported for the idea that the CA relationship is overestimated when foil identifications are included as inaccuracies. The most recent meta-analysis of the CA relationship found that excluding from the computations foil identifications in target-present line-ups did not change the size of the aggregate CA correlation from 24 studies (Sporer, Penrod, Read, & Cutler, 1995). Accordingly, we do not distinguish between CA relationships computed with or without foil and/or target-absence data in this chapter.

to a memory (e.g., *strong*). In addition, a basic single-item rating (e.g., overall confidence on a 0–100%, 11-point scale) might also be obtained, and an average taken of a standard score of this rating and a standard score of the semantic-differential composite. The reliability and precision of confidence measured from so many angles are likely to be very high.

Single-item ratings of confidence arguably have high external validity. This is evident in the fact that police typically ask about confidence with a single question much like the research versions. As discussed later, however, research and police investigators may use the explicit or implicit scale much differently in defining what is high and low confidence.

IN SEARCH OF THE TYPICAL CONFIDENCE-ACCURACY RELATIONSHIP: THE RESEARCH

Two Illustrative Studies

To illustrate a typical eyewitness setting in which identification accuracy, confidence, and the CA relationship are studied, consider two early experiments co-investigated by the senior author. Leippe et al. (1978) staged the same theft for small groups of unwitting students waiting in a reception room for a study to begin. The thief posed as a fellow waiting student. After sitting for several minutes, the thief jumped up, grabbed, dropped, and finally ran off with a bag containing an object the experimenter had previously identified as the property of a previous participant. Later, after several intervening tasks, the experimenter divulged to participants individually that the theft had been staged and administered a photo-lineup identification test and a post-lineup confidence rating scale (described earlier) to each one. Only 31% of 65 student-witnesses (more when the stolen object was known to be expensive, less when it was not) accurately identified the thief from the six-person lineup. Among the 43 who made a positive identification, the accuracy rate was 47%, and the CA *r* was a nonsignificant .16.

Hosch, Leippe, Marchioni, and Cooper (1984) staged a theft in a campus laboratory and carried the ruse through until after the identification test, which was administered by a campus police detective. Eyewitnesses had either seen their own (a wristwatch) or the university's (a laboratory computer) property stolen in one of an apparent rash of thefts. Regardless of what the thief stole, identification accuracy and confidence were unrelated. The 36 (out of 80) witnesses who correctly identified the thief gave an average confidence rating of 4.6 on a 9-point scale. The 21 witnesses who made a false identification (of a foil) gave an average confidence rating of 5.1.

These two studies give a flavor for one important kind of research setting—the laboratory staged crime—from which evidence about the CA relationship has emerged over the years. There have been other paradigms, as well, as we will see. The two studies also illustrate the research outcome—a nil or very small CA *r*—that led to much additional research and a consensus of worry among experts that confidence may have little to do with eyewitness accuracy (Kassin, Ellsworth, & Smith, 1989; Kassin, Tubb, Hosch, & Memon, 2001). Let us look at the larger body of research.

Comprehensive Surveys of the Confidence-Accuracy Correlation

Research findings regarding the eyewitness CA relationship were systematically reviewed at least five times in the published literature between 1980 and 1995. In all cases, the focus was on the CA r. Two reviews employed formal meta-analytic methods (Bothwell, Deffenbacher, & Brigham, 1987; Sporer, Penrod, Read, & Cutler, 1995), two aggregated and classified confidence-accuracy correlations across studies in various ways that yielded average correlations across certain research conditions (Deffenbacher, 1980; Wells & Murray, 1984), and one was primarily a narrative review (Penrod & Cutler, 1995). It is instructive to examine these reviews, as they identify some of the conceptual issues and psychological factors that comprise an integrative understanding of the confidence-accuracy relationship. Perhaps more significantly, the reviews share a critical commonality in that they all converged on the same conclusion that, although not *unrelated* to accuracy as the illustrative studies found, eyewitness confidence is, at best, only modestly predictive of eyewitness identification accuracy.

Deffenbacher's (1980) review sounded the first clarion call of distrust in eyewitness confidence. A review of 22 studies reporting 40 assessments of the CA r revealed that only 21 of the 40 correlations were significant. A number of the studies, however, involved memory tasks that are quite dissimilar to the task of identifying a single target from a lineup. Others involved recall of events or qualities of targets within those events, rather than recognition of a face. For the more relevant studies, the relative frequency of significant correlations was, if anything, worse than the overall rate. Deffenbacher concluded that eyewitness confidence was not reliably related to accuracy, and should not be used by the police.

Wells and Murray (1984) reached the same conclusion after examining "a relatively complete summary of the relevant modern studies" (p. 160) on eyewitness identification. The CA r was statistically significant in only 13 of the 31 (42%) investigations, and the average correlation across all 31 studies was $r = .08$. Even the statistically reliable relationships were relatively weak, averaging $r = .31$.

Like Deffenbacher (1980), Wells and Murray included in their review a number of studies that assessed something other than recognition of an unfamiliar in a lineup task. The next review, by Bothwell et al. (1987), focused exclusively on studies that "met the joint criteria of testing recognition memory for unfamiliar faces seen live only once during a staged presentation, of using post-decision confidence rating scales, and of computing interindividual accuracy-confidence correlations (p. 692)." The authors subjected the CA r computed for the full samples of 35 staged-event studies to a formal meta-analysis. The weighted average r turned out to be .25, which was significantly different from zero (the 95% confidence interval was from $-.08$ to $.42$). Two subsamples of 17 studies were created by division of the studies by a median split into those for which the duration of visual exposure to the to-be-recognized target was greater than 74 seconds (long duration) and those for which it was less than 74 seconds (short duration). Separate meta-analyses revealed an average r of .31 and .19 for the long- and short-duration study sets, respectively.

Sporer et al. (1995) conducted a meta-analysis of 30 staged-event studies that included both target-present and target-absent lineup conditions. All of these studies were reported between 1985 and 1994, and only about 10% of them were also included in the 1987 meta-analysis of Bothwell et al. Looking at the overall correlations, the average correlation was .27—statistically significant and very close in magnitude to the .25 reported by Bothwell et al. However, another analysis was conducted in which correlations for each investigation were computed only for "choosers"—participant-witnesses who made a positive identification (i.e., chose the target from a target-present lineup or an innocent person from the target-absent or target-present lineup). This yielded an average correlation of .41, the highest estimate to date of the CA r based on aggregating studies. Sporer et al. argued that this CA relationship is substantial enough to advise the legal system that witness confidence is a valid although "far from perfect, indicator of witness accuracy" (p. 324) that should be considered along with other factors, at least when it is assessed before exposure to extra-memorial factors that can reshape confidence (e.g., coaching or information about other witnesses' identifications).

A second 1995 piece was a narrative review by Penrod and Cutler (1995). These authors took note of the earlier reviews and examined some of the situational and person factors that moderate the CA relationship. Penrod and Cutler were more negative in their conclusions here than they were in the study by Sporer et al. (where they are co-authors), concluding that the eyewitness CA relationship, in likely forensic situations, is too small to warrant its use as an accuracy indicator. Their argument, in essence, is that the best-case scenario of perhaps $r = .41$ is not an especially close correspondence of accuracy and confidence, and the reality in actual cases is likely to be even less correspondence, given the likely presence of witnessing and testing factors (which we will soon review) that make it more difficult for witnesses to track their accuracy and the likelihood that confidence will be altered by social influence and learning following the identification (also to be reviewed).

Recent Empirical Observations of the CA Correlation

Eyewitness studies since the major reviews have not found CA r values that are much different, on average, from those reported in earlier studies. For example, Yarmey, Yarmey, and Yarmey (1994) administered target-present or target-absent pictorial lineups to individuals who had interacted briefly with the target just minutes earlier and found CA r values ranging from .16 to .29. In two studies involving a videotaped theft of a personal computer, Leippe, Eisenstadt et al. (2006) observed CA correlations among choosers of .18 and .21. At the higher end, in an experiment involving videotape viewing of a male target engaged in a series of behaviors over 3 minutes, Bradfield et al. (2002) observed an r of .58 when all accurate identifications were made from a target-present lineup and all inaccurate identifications were false identifications of a look-alike in a target-absent lineup. D. S. Lindsay, Read, and Sharma (1998) observed within-condition rs that ranged from .24 to .53 across four conditions that varied in the quality of witnessing conditions (e.g., duration of exposure to the target, study instructions, retention interval) and produced large differences in accuracy rates and confidence ratings. When the CA *r* was computed with data collapsed across conditions and thereby contained wide variability, especially in accuracy scores, the result was a correlation of .59. In a similar study by D. S. Lindsay, Nilson and Read (2000), the across-condition *r* was .68. Finally, Smith, Lindsay, and Pryke (2000) presented one of three videotaped staged crimes to student-witnesses and later had them attempt a lineup identification from a target-present or target-absent lineup. Among choosers, the overall CA *r* was a significant .34.

The Bottom Line—So Far—About the CA Correlation

We now know, after dozens of studies and several comprehensive reviews, that the relationship between eyewitness confidence and accuracy is certainly not nil. Rather, it is positive, albeit modest in magnitude. A reasonable extrapolation from the mass of reported correlations is that, averaging across many different sets of witnessing and testing conditions, and excluding situations involving substantial postidentification nonmemorial influences on confidence, the typical "correlation may be as high as +.40 when the analysis is restricted to individuals who make an identification" (Wells et al., 2002, p. 152). At such a level of correspondence with accuracy, eyewitness confidence can be useful in attempting to gauge trust in an eyewitness identification. For example, if eyewitnesses are likely to be accurate about 50% of the time—which seems an appropriate figure to use based on the large body of eyewitness research (cf. Haber & Haber, 2001)—70% of witnesses with above-average confidence will be accurate, compared with only 30% of witnesses with below-average confidence (Penrod & Cutler, 1995; Wells et al., 2002). Or, to use another example presented by Wells et al. (2002), .40 is very close to the *r* between gender and height in the adult population. High confidence, then, should increase belief in the accuracy of the witness about as much as knowing that an unseen person is very tall would increase belief that the person is male.

This conclusion that stated confidence can be a useful, but imperfect, guide to accuracy is not the entire or most precise story, however. It is only a broad generalization at this point. A more complete picture of the usefulness of confidence can only emerge through consideration of what conditions are required for the CA relationship to be as strong as or stronger than .40 and why these conditions are necessary. Conversely, the conditions or factors that reduce the relationship, and why they do so, need to be understood. The moderators of the CA relationship will be discussed presently, after an examination of an alternative way of looking at the relationship that suggests that, if the best confidence question is asked, the answer may be especially useful for estimating accuracy.

Research on Calibration, an Alternative Look at the CA Relationship

Some researchers (e.g., Juslin et al., 1996; Olson, 2000; Weber & Brewer, 2003) have argued that the usual measure of the CA relationship, the point-biserial correlation, may not be the most informative measure of the relationship. A better measure is *calibration*, which is "the extent to which participants' judgments of confidence in their decision (made on a percentile scale) correspond with the actual probability that their decision was correct" (Weber & Brewer, 2003, p. 490). To compute this measure, participant-witnesses are asked to indicate their confidence that their identification decision was correct in percentage terms, typically in 10% increments (e.g., *I am 80% confident in my identification choice.*). In turn, witnesses are grouped according to their confidence level (i.e., all witnesses who indicated 10% confidence, all who indicated 20% confidence, and so on), and the percentage of witnesses who made an accurate identification choice in each grouping is discerned. Perfect calibration is found if the percentage correct in each grouping equals the group's confidence level (e.g., 80% of the witnesses in the 80% confidence group made the correct decision). Calibration level can be expressed with calibration curves that plot accuracy rates as a function of confidence grouping. A calibration index (CI) can also be computed, which is the average (across witnesses) squared discrepancy for each witness of the confidence level and actual proportion of witnesses who were correct in the witness's confidence group. A related statistic is over/underconfidence (O/U), computed by subtraction of mean accuracy from mean confidence for the entire witness sample (hence, O/U ranges from -1 to $+1$, with negative scores indicative of underconfidence and positive scores of overconfidence).

Juslin et al. (1996) demonstrated that good calibration might exist even when the same data yield a low r, because calibration and correlation tap into relatively independent aspects of a relationship. Whereas correlation measures how well confidence scores allow one to discriminate between accurate and inaccurate identifications, calibration concerns how much agreement there is between subjective and objective probabilities of accuracy, when both are expressed on a scale of multiple points. As an illustration of this point, Juslin et al. asked 256 college students to watch a videotape of a staged crime that was said to include subliminal stimuli (to discourage intentional learning) and then attempt to identify the two actor-culprits from photo-lineups and give confidence judgments on an 11-point, 0–100% scale. The point-biserial r values within experimental conditions (that are not of interest here) ranged from .42 to .49—higher than average. But the calibration curves were even more impressive. One of these curves is shown in part A of Figure 16–1; it is associated with an r of .49 and an O/U of $-.06$ (slight underconfidence). Olsson (2000) examined the r, CI, and O/U values of several studies (including Juslin et al., 1996) and found that, among the studies that used full-range confidence scales (i.e., 0–100%), totaling 16 separate data sets, the correlations ranged (95% confidence interval) from .35 to .49 and averaged .42. The CI and O/U (where smaller is better) ranges were .05 to .08 and $-.02$ to .04, respectively—indicative of good calibration. Moreover, across the data sets, r and CI were not significantly correlated, $r =$ .11. Finally, Brewer, Keast, and Rishworth (2002) found CI and O/U values of .05 and $-.058$ in the baseline eyewitness condition of a study involving a videotaped theft, which translate into the calibration curve depicted in part B of Figure 16–1. The CA r in this condition was .14. Part C shows even stronger calibration in another experimental condition of Brewer et al., to be discussed later.

In sum, although still limited in number, studies that have examined calibration suggest that the CA relationship is stronger when expressed in terms of calibration than when expressed in terms of r, and that, in fact, CA calibration might typically be strong

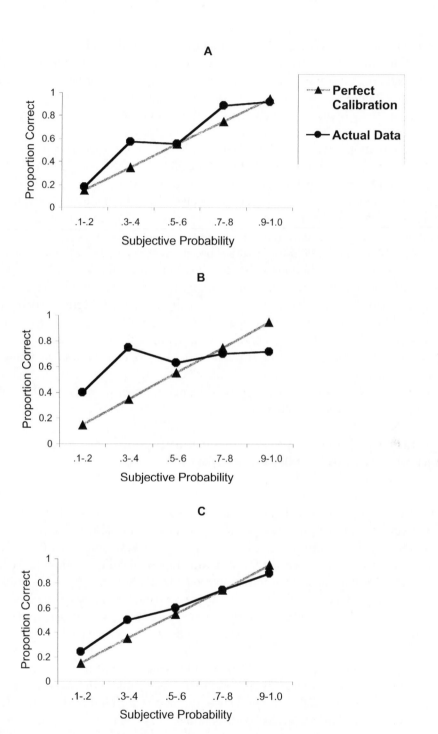

FIGURE 16–1. Calibration curves obtained in two eyewitness studies. A: Calibration in the culprit-description condition of a study by Juslin et al. (1996). B and C: Calibration among choosers in control and reflection conditions, respectively, in a study by Brewer et al. (2002). Redrawn estimates from originals.

in absolute terms. As a result, it can be argued that expressed confidence can have substantial forensic usefulness. Because subjective certainty ratings calibrate well with the actual probability of accuracy, having an eyewitness express his or her confidence in a lineup identification on a subjective certainty scale should provide police investigators with a realistic sense of just how likely it is that the chosen suspect is, indeed, the culprit.

On the other hand, there are reasons to take a more tempered view about the usefulness of calibration. First, among the few eyewitness studies that have measured CA calibration, not all have found especially good calibration (see, e.g., Cutler & Penrod, 1989a; Granhag, 1997). Second, looking at CI's in one way reveals some of the same problems with diagnosticity of accuracy that characterizes modest CA r values. For example, a CI of .05 means that, on average, a witness's subjective probability of accuracy differed by .22 (the square root of .05) from the actual accuracy rate of his or her confidence group. Third, calibration studies use the percentage scale. Police do not. We do not know that good calibration with the use of that scale reflects even reasonable calibration with the use of open-ended responses typical of police requests for confidence estimates. Fourth, there is still the problem, to which we will turn shortly, that confidence is influenced by social factors, so that regardless of the procedure used to calculate the CA relationship, there is always the problem that confidence is highly malleable. Finally, as we will note later, realistic subjective probabilities may not go over well in actual cases in which the parties want to know if the witness is completely certain. Nevertheless, the calibration studies suggest an encouragingly higher level of correspondence between confidence and accuracy than do results focused on the CA r.

Type and Content of Memory Questioning, Confidence, and the CA Relationship

The vast majority of studies of confidence and the CA relationship have examined face recognition memory, as revealed in lineup identifications. Eyewitnesses, however, usually do more than attempt identifications by face recognition. They also are asked to describe what they saw and the person they saw commit the crime. These descriptions may be made in a variety of ways in terms of the structure imposed by the questioning, including free, narrative recall, guided or interrogative recall, and statements of recognition of possible event and target details posed by the investigator. A brief look at some of the relatively scant studies of confidence in these reports suggests that, for descriptive recall, the CA relationship is about as modest and variable as it is for face recognition.

Recall of Personal Attributes.   Ebbesen and Rienick (1998) had pairs of strangers recruited in public places interact briefly and then answer questions about the personal attributes (e.g., eye color, hair color and style, ethnicity, clothing) of the other, 1, 7, or 28 days later. Participants also rated their confidence in their recall responses to each question on a 5-point scale (*not at all* to *absolutely* confident). The average confidence rating per person did not vary with retention interval: it was 3.51, 3.88, and 3.46 for participants in the 1-, 7-, and 28-day conditions, respectively. The CA r was computed as a correlation between average confidence ratings and number of recall errors. It was a significant $-.36$ at the first recall attempt and $-.40$ after 28 days. These correlations are similar to those typically obtained for lineup identifications. Ebbeson and Rienick also examined the CA relationship at the level of single questions and found that the likelihood of an answer being correct increased monotonically with confidence in the answer. After 28 days, the slope of this function was not particularly steep for confidence ratings 1 through 4, however, as percentage correct climbed from about 31% to about 54%. But it jumped to about 85% for "absolutely confident" answers.

Free vs. Interrogative Recall.   In another field study, Yarmey and Yarmey (1997) studied memory of passers-by for the physical appearance and clothing of a female target who had approached them minutes before and requested some minor assistance. Half of the participants were given an interrogative test (15 cued-recall questions) and half were asked to freely describe the target. Consistent with other research (cf. Deffenbacher, 1991), interrogative reports were more complete, but free recall reports were more accurate in terms of fewer errors. Participants seemed intuitively aware of this latter fact— confidence in the overall memory report was significantly greater for free recall than for interrogative reports (5.12 vs. 4.51 on a 7-point scale). On the other hand, when correct and incorrect responses were factored into an overall accuracy score, the CA relationship was nil for both free and interrogative recall.

Central and Peripheral Details.   Using interrogative questions in the form of true-or-false statements of what was seen, Migueles and Garcia-Bajos (1999) probed the memory and confidence of witnesses to a videotaped kidnapping seen minutes earlier. Witnesses were more confident in their memory responses regarding central details of various targets' appearance and actions, compared with more peripheral details. The CA relationship was positive and significant, except in the case of *central actions*. It appears that confidence in memory about the critical actions seen in a stirring event such as the kidnapping is high whether the memory is accurate (agreeing with a true statement) or inaccurate (agreeing with a false statement).

Conceptualizing Confidence and the CA Relationship: The Cognition of Correspondence

Although the CA relationship is commonly a moderate one when expressed as a correlation, we have seen that, across studies, it may range from nil to moderately strong. Some of this variability in observed CA relationships is due to measurement error, restricted range in one or both of the measured variables, and other artifacts. But the CA relationship is also influenced by a number of situational factors associated with the conditions of witnessing and memory testing, as well as by factors associated with the psychological states of witnesses. These moderator variables are critical both to a conceptual understanding of how and when eyewitness confidence tracks memory accuracy and to any practical or forensic usefulness eyewitness confidence might have. We will consider the factors that influence both the CA relationship and confidence in subsequent sections. First, however, it is important to understand the determinants of eyewitness confidence, the psychology of how confidence is linked to memory accuracy, and the reasons why the CA link can be strong or weak.

Direct Trace Access

If confidence in the accuracy of one's memory is an evaluative belief, what are the sources of such a belief? One likely source is the object of the belief itself—the memory trace. According to trace access theory, when making a confidence judgment about a reported memory, people often have *direct access to the contents of memory* and are able to sense or assess the strength of the memory trace (see, e.g., Burke, MacKay, Worthley, & Wade, 1991; Clark, 1997; Hintzman, 1988). As a result, the stronger the memory trace, or the greater the number of stimulus attributes encoded to form a memorial representation of the stimulus (Bower, 1967), the more likely the stimulus (e.g., a face) is to be both correctly and confidently recognized from a stimulus array (e.g., a lineup). Trace access theory and related models that view both memory decisions and confidence in those decisions as based on stimulus familiarity are supported by a great deal of memory research (Busey, Tunnicliff, Loftus, & Loftus, 2000; Clark, 1997).

Optimality and Trace Access. In the eyewitness realm, direct access to the memory trace is a basic assumption of the optimality hypothesis proposed by Deffenbacher (1980). In this early review of research measuring the CA relationship, Deffenbacher divided the studies into those in which the witnessing and testing conditions were poor (e.g., included multiple memory-unfriendly factors such as very brief exposure to the target, long interval between exposure and recognition test, biased testing instructions, high similarity of lineup foils, etc.) and those in which they were better or more "optimal." A statistically significant CA r was far more likely to be found in the studies that had more optimal conditions. Deffenbacher (1980) proposed that, "under more ideal processing conditions a witness is more able to track accurately the adequacy of his/her memory performance in overtly expressed confidence ratings" (p. 246). In essence, the argument is that more optimal memory-processing conditions make it more likely that the memory trace is strong enough to be accessed in a clear fashion amenable to scrutiny.

There has been little articulation in the research literature of *how* high optimality favors a stronger CA relationship (cf. Leippe, 1980). Clearly, under optimal conditions, witnesses will have generally stronger memory traces, and thus more witnesses will have correct recognition. But how does this serve to enhance the CA relationship, when, in fact, one might even expect the relationship to be reduced, owing to restricted range of accuracy at the correct end? The answer may lie in two additional probable consequences of high-optimal eyewitness conditions. First, not all of those who have strong memory traces will have accurate recognition, but the better access to evaluating the memory trace will allow the inaccurate witnesses to appropriately downgrade their confidence. Second, among witnesses who have weaker memory despite the optimal processing conditions, the memory traces will not only be weaker—leading to more inaccurate recognition—but will also be less accessible for scrutiny. These witnesses may be more likely to rely on other sources of information to decide their confidence, including their inability to access the memory trace. Both cases of inaccurate recognition, it would seem, would favor lower confidence ratings compared with the strong-trace/accurate-recognition case; hence, a decent-sized positive CA relationship is obtained.

Metamemory

What about the low-optimal eyewitness situation? Consideration of this raises the more general question of what other sources of confidence may exist besides the information derived from direct access to the memory trace. Witnesses' metamemory, or beliefs and assumptions about memory processes and abilities, may serve as an additional source of information that helps gauge confidence, especially—but not exclusively—when direct access to the memory trace is limited. Cues to accuracy rooted in metamemory may be divided into three categories: *intrinsic cues* based on reflection on the memory process, *extrinsic or heuristic cues* based on reflection on the conditions surrounding memory formation and retrieval, and *self-credibility cues* based on reflection on one's memory skills and experience.

Intrinsic Cues.   The act of remembering may contain information that people have learned to associate with good or bad memory (Busey et al., 2000; Kelley & Lindsay, 1993; Koriat, 1997; Shaw, 1996). In face recognition, it may be the *speed* with which the sense of recognition emerges that serves as an accuracy cue. In attempts to recall or describe a target, the *number* of qualities that come to mind or the *ease* with which they are retrieved may serve a similar function. A number of studies outside the eyewitness realm have found that speed of memory responses and the confidence with which they are given are reliably negatively correlated—the less time given to answer a memory question, the greater the confidence (see, e.g., Robinson, Johnson, & Herndon, 1997, for a review and an empirical demonstration). This relationship also has been observed when witnesses answer multiple-choice questions about the culprit in a staged crime (e.g., Shaw, 1996) and attempt to identify the culprit from a lineup (e.g., Sporer, 1992).

In the case of ease of retrieval, Kebbel, Wagstaff, and Covey (1996), for example, found that confidence was lower in correct answers to difficult (i.e., hard to retrieve) memory questions about the people and objects in a videotaped scene than it was in correct answers to easy (i.e., easy to retrieve) questions. The availability heuristic (Tversky & Kahneman, 1973) also may be relevant here. This refers to the tendency for people to make belief judgments and assessments of their internal states based on what readily comes to mind—that is, what is most available in memory. Consistent with this, confidence in the accuracy of answers to general-knowledge questions has been found to be higher when supportive information is made more available through prior repeated exposure to it (Kelley & Lindsay, 1993). Read (1995) used the availability heuristic to predict and explain the finding that witnesses who had longer prior interactive exposure to a target were more likely to confidently identify a look-alike from a target-absent lineup 2 days later than were witnesses who had considerably shorter prior exposure. Because the longer exposure allowed encoding of more features of the target, these features were more available in memory, and thus more feature matches to the look-alike were retrieved during the recognition test, increasing confidence that the sense of familiarity of the look-alike was an accurate memory. Finally, in the social cognition realm, people's confidence that they possess a personal attribute can be increased or decreased by making the subjective sense of ease of retrieval of supporting information high (e.g., *List three examples of when you behaved assertively*) or low (*List 12 examples . . .*; e.g., Schwarz et al., 1991). It is reasonable to assume that eyewitness confidence likewise varies as a function of how easily memories come to mind.

Extrinsic Cues. Just as they have beliefs about what their experience of remembering suggests about the accuracy of their memories, witnesses also have beliefs about how situational factors associated with witnessing and testing conditions affect memory (Busey et al., 2000; Koriat, 1997). For example, people appear to assume that the accuracy of their memory for a target's face is positively related to the duration of their visual exposure to the face (Read, 1995); hence confidence is apt to be higher, the more prolonged the exposure is. Similarly, the beliefs that one studied an object (Busey et al., 2000) and that one put great effort into retrieving a memory (Shaw & Zerr, 2003) serve to enhance confidence in the memory. Confidence, theoretically, could also be shaped by prior beliefs about the difficulty of the memory task (Cutler & Penrod, 1989a).

Finally, research has established that cues made available in the testing situation can shape memory responses. For example, biased lineup instructions that fail to explicitly provide a "none of them" option increase false identifications (e.g., Malpass & Devine, 1981), and lineups in which the suspect distinctively sticks out create an increased likelihood that the suspect will be chosen (Lindsay, Wallbridge, & Drennan, 1987). One likely reason for these effects on memory responses is that witnesses draw metacognitive conclusions from the suggestive cues in the situation that push their confidence in a positive identification (e.g., *That guy really sticks out, so my memory must be correct.*). Consistent with the use of extrinsic cues in determining confidence, witness confidence is readily altered by knowledge that a co-witness made the same or a different identification choice (Luus & Wells, 1994).

Self-credibility. A third set of metamemory cues derives from how individuals construe their own memory skills, either in general or with respect to a specific memory event. Some individuals believe they have better-than-average memories and assign themselves high credibility as memory sources; others believe they lack memory ability and so have low self-credibility (see, e.g., Olsson & Juslin, 1999; Woodhead & Baddeley, 1981). It is plausible that overall self-credibility exerts some influence on confidence in the accuracy of responses in specific memory tasks, and indeed there is evidence in the eyewitness literature that it does (Olsson & Juslin, 1999; Leippe, Eisenstadt et al., 2006).

Confidence Cues, Accuracy Cues, and the CA Relationship: Congruence and Incongruence

The idea that the sources of eyewitness memory may emanate from either the memory trace itself or from cues and beliefs about memory that are extra-memorial, or independent of the memory trace itself, is critically important to understanding not only the causes of confidence, but also the CA relationship and the extent to which confidence can be used to diagnose or postdict accuracy. When confidence is determined mainly through direct access to the memory trace, and therefore is based on the same sources or cues as is the memory response itself, there is likely to be a reasonably strong CA relationship (unless an undetected change in the memory trace itself occurs or the wrong memory trace is accessed). This memorial scenario is consistent with what has traditionally been observed in multiple-stimulus face recognition studies (Dobbins, Kroll, & Liu, 1998; Murdock & Duffy, 1972; Wickelgren, 1970), and it is precisely the thrust of the optimality hypothesis. Unlike the optimality hypothesis, however, the present view locates the causes of divergence from a strong CA relationship not in a reduction in information-processing optimality *per se*, but in the extent to which metamemory confidence cues are (1) present and (2) incongruent with trace-strength determinants of the memory response. The fewer the extra-memorial confidence cues, the more likely it is that confidence will be significantly calibrated with accuracy, with the limit of the CA relationship determined by the degree of direct access to the memory trace. Cues that trigger metamemory beliefs are almost always present to some degree, so cases in which confidence judgments draw exclusively from the memory trace are probably rare.

Importantly, this analysis also points to the possibility that extra-memorial confidence cues may increase the CA relationship. *Valid* cues, or cues that are congruent with information stemming from the memory trace, will push confidence ratings in the direction of actual accuracy, creating a stronger correlation and tighter calibration. For example, duration of exposure to the target is likely to be positively related to the strength of the memory trace for that target. In addition, witnesses may employ a "length (of exposure) is strength" heuristic in deciding their confidence. Accordingly, among witnesses who had *varying* durations of exposure to the target, the CA r in identifications from a target-present lineup might be especially high (cf. Lindsay et al., 1998).

In addition to the optimality hypothesis, this cue-congruence perspective is related to the analysis presented a number of years ago by Leippe (1980), which views eyewitness memory and confidence as susceptible to influence from different social and cognitive variables. Memory, but not confidence, for example, might be altered by suggestive questioning when the suggestiveness of the questions goes unnoticed. Confidence, but not memory, might be influenced by the psychological pull of commitment to a lineup choice. From the present perspective, this latter case of a change in confidence but not memory is readily understood in terms of cue congruence. The witness takes his or her choosing behavior as a cue to credibility, which, of course, can have no effect on memory itself (the report of which, in this case, has already occurred). In the case of undetected changes in memory, the CA relationship is dampened by leaving the witness reliant on the same, unaltered confidence cues, including intrinsic ones like ease of retrieval. The memory may come to mind easily—maybe even more easily, given that the suggestive questioning occurred more recently than the exposure to the original event—but the memory would more likely be inaccurate. If the actual memory trace has changed, been overwritten, or blended with the suggestive information (e.g., Loftus, 1981; Hall, Loftus, & Tousignant, 1984), accuracy and confidence might disconnect, even when the confidence judgment is informed by direct trace access. This happens because individuals have only limited ability to distinguish between equally strong memory traces that are real versus constructed (Schooler, Gerhard, & Loftus, 1986; Roediger & McDermott, 1995).

Looking through the lens provided by the cue-congruence analysis, we can now review the research on moderators of the CA relationship.

MODERATORS OF THE CA RELATIONSHIP: THE HIGHS AND LOWS OF CALIBRATION

The CA relationship varies systematically as a function of situational variables that can impinge on memory or confidence decisions at several points in the experience of eyewitnesses. We examine here moderator variables that might be in play during each of the following occasions: witnessing of an event, the witnessing-to-memory-test interval, the memory test, and the immediate aftermath of a memory test. In addition, we look at qualities of the eyewitness that appear to moderate the CA relationship.

Factors During Witnessing

The optimality hypothesis suggests that as conditions of witnessing improve, the within-condition CA r should increase. The same prediction has also been made for primarily a statistical reason, namely that variability in memory accuracy will be greater with better conditions, because there is more opportunity for individual differences in memory skills and attention to exert an impact (D. S. Lindsay et al., 1998). R. C. L. Lindsay, Wells, and Rumpel (1981) found no support for this prediction, however, in a study in which the optimality of witnessing conditions was manipulated in an omnibus way. By varying duration of exposure to the culprit in a staged crime, along with how full a view of his face witnesses had, R. C. L. Lindsay et al. created three situations in which the percentages of accurate identifications were 33%, 50%, and 74%. Despite the clear differences in optimality, the CA r values were equivalently weak in all three conditions (Wells & Murray, 1984). In a more recent study in which participant-witnesses viewed non-crime videotapes of two targets, D. S. Lindsay et al. (1998) varied overall optimality by improving both witnessing conditions (exposure duration, instructions about what to pay attention to) and the witnessing-to-lineup-test retention interval over four levels. Identification accuracy increased more or less linearly as conditions improved (11%, 44%, 78%, and 86%). Although statistically significant in 5 of 8 cases (2 targets × 4 conditions), the within-condition CA r values did not differ significantly from each other and were not ordered in size in a fashion that corresponded to optimality. The CA r values were on the higher side of the typical range, ranging from .24 to .42 for one target, and from .33 to .53 for the other. At least when the manipulation of optimality is multifaceted, the CA relationship does not appear to be enhanced by greater optimality.

Duration of Exposure to the Target's Face.   Examination of how variation in single facets of the witnessing situation affects the CA relationship paints a somewhat different and more complicated picture, one that is conducive to the cue-congruence perspective. Let us begin with duration of exposure to a culprit's face. Longer duration is generally associated with greater recognition accuracy (Shapiro & Penrod, 1986). Confidence in memory also increases as exposure duration lengthens (D. S. Lindsay et al., 1998; Menon et al., 2003). Computing the CA relationship across several exposure duration conditions, therefore, should result in a substantial correlation. What about within duration conditions? It can be recalled that Bothwell et al. (1987) found in their meta-analysis that the average CA r in studies in which exposure to the face exceeded 74 seconds was somewhat higher than the average CA r in studies with shorter exposure. But since the Bothwell et al. review, at least two studies have found evidence that the CA relationship may be weaker when exposure duration is longer (vs. shorter). Menon et al. (2003) had college students and older community residents view a videotaped reenactment of an actual robbery in which the robber's face was exposed for either 12 or 45 seconds. In the 12-second condition, a positive CA relationship was found in identifications from a robber-present lineup. Accurate witnesses were significantly more confident on average than were inaccurate witnesses. In the 45-second condition, however, this difference disappeared—the confidence ratings of accurate and inaccurate witnesses did not reliably differ. This finding is reminiscent of Read's (1995) finding noted earlier, that convenience store clerks made more false-but-confident identifications of a look-alike from a target-absent lineup following a long interaction than they did following a short interaction. Although more research is needed, longer exposure durations may at least sometimes lead to a weaker CA relationship because witnesses use exposure duration as an extrinsic cue to accuracy, and the cue is used even by inaccurate witnesses, overriding any direct-access evidence they have to distrust their memory.

How can the results showing a weaker CA r with longer durations be reconciled with Bothwell et al.'s meta-analytic finding of just the opposite? First, it can be noted that, at least in Memon et al.'s study, both the long and short exposure durations would be classified as short according to Bothwell et al.'s cutoff. Perhaps the relationship is curvilinear, with stronger CA relationships found at very short and very long exposures. Second, Read's (1995) results required a target-absent lineup from which a look-alike to the target stood out somewhat. This feature itself—essentially a biased lineup—is itself a source of accuracy cues, as we shall see later, and may be required to "trick" the witness with long exposure into both a false identification and false confidence. Finally, the Bothwell et al. result comes from a summary of numerous studies. It is not clear what other factors might have co-varied with exposure duration across studies. At this point, then, we cannot be confident that exposure duration reliably moderates the CA relationship. But it does seem to combine with other variables to moderate the relationship. Perhaps quality, not quantity, of exposure matters more.

Disguise and Quality of Exposure. Exposure to the culprit's face may vary in quality as well as quantity. What happens when the ability to get a good or complete view of a face is impeded? In a study reported by O'Rourke, Penrod, Cutler, and Stuve (1989), community residents and college students viewed a videotaped robbery in which the robber either wore no hat or wore a hat that completely covered his hair. In the no-hat condition, the CA r was significant and, at .40, moderate in size. In the hat-

disguise condition, the CA r was significantly lower, a nonsignificant .11. The hat disguise was associated with a nonsignificant reduction in identification accuracy (50% vs.
43%) but had no effect on confidence. The hat-disguise effect on the CA r was replicated in a multiple-face slideshow study, yielding remarkably similar CA r values of .41
(no hat) and .12 (hat). Calibration measures of the CA relationship were similarly affected, including in one telling manner: overconfidence was greater in the hat-disguise
condition. Thus, one interpretation of the elimination of the CA relationship is that the
hat disguise contributed to a weaker memory trace but had little meta-memorial cue
value. A conceptually similar finding was obtained in a study in which faces with or without eyeglasses were slide-projected either upright or inverted. Although neither eyeglasses nor inversion affected confidence, they each hindered accuracy and wiped out
the significant CA relationship found in a baseline (no eyeglasses or inversion) condition (McKelvie, 1993).

Attention.   A more optimal witnessing situation exists when witnesses have a mindset that encourages paying careful attention to the culprit. Two experiments manipulated attention by varying whether a target was viewed by herself versus in a group among
distracting others (Maass & Brigham, 1982) or by having participant-witnesses make
judgments of a target that either required (e.g., honesty) or did not require (e.g., height)
elaborate processing (Pigott & Brigham, 1985). The gist of the findings is that attention promotes more accuracy and more confidence, which contributes to a substantial
across-conditions CA r of about .50. The Pigott and Brigham study reported separate r
values *within* low- and high-attention conditions and found that the CA r (among lineup
choosers) was higher in the high-attention case (.64 vs. .41). It is noteworthy that studies involving interactions that require paying considerable attention to the target, such
as those involving complex interactions with convenience store clerks, generally find
higher CA correlations than do laboratory, live-staged, or videotaped event studies (cf.
Brigham, Maass, Snyder, & Spaulding, 1982). Possibly, greater attention within a given
time frame facilitates formation of a clear and accessible memory trace but occurs subtly,
without arousing strong metamemorial cues.

Violence and Fear-arousing Qualities.   Under some circumstances, formation of a
strong memory trace may be inhibited when the witnessing experience evokes great
stress and anxious arousal (Christiansen, 1992; Deffenbacher, Bornstein, Penrod, & Mc-
Gorty, 2004; Pickel, this volume; Yuille & Daylen, 1998). Presumably, a violent assault
should arouse greater stress and anxiety during witnessing than a nonviolent incident,
and memory for the former may thus be inhibited. Consistent with this reasoning, Clifford and Hollin (1981) had participants watch on videotape either a graphically violent
crime or a wholly innocuous interaction, while controlling for exposure duration and
view across the two scenes. Indeed, accuracy of memory for the perpetrator was better in
the nonviolent condition. In addition, whereas a significant positive relationship between identification accuracy and confidence was observed in the nonviolent condition,
the CA relationship was nil in the violent condition.

Factors During the Retention Interval

The major threat to the correspondence of confidence and accuracy during the interval between witnessing and a memory test is the receipt of information that weakens or alters the memory trace without influencing confidence. The classic example of such a process is the well-known misinformation effect (Loftus, 1981; Weingardt, Toland, & Loftus, 1994). In a demonstration of this effect, since replicated in various forms many times, Loftus, Miller, and Burns (1978) presented participant-witnesses with a series of slides depicting a car accident in which the car was seen at a yellow yield sign. During questioning, some witnesses were asked whether another vehicle had passed the car while it was stopped at the yield sign. Others were asked the same question, except that "stop sign" replaced "yield sign" in the question. More participants in this latter, misled condition than in a no-prior-question control condition later mistakenly reported seeing a stop sign. A number of studies have demonstrated that the misinformation effect can involve genuine changes in the memory trace (Loftus, 1981), or at least in which memory trace (that formed by the original event or by the misleading question) is retrieved and thought accurate (D. S. Lindsay, 1994). In addition, the effect occurs for remembered details about people (e.g., Wright & Stroud, 1998). Most importantly for present purposes, witnesses often report as much confidence in misled, incorrect memories as in non-misled, correct memories (Loftus, Donders, Hoffman, & Schooler, 1989).

In two misinformation studies using the classic paradigm but adding confidence questions designed to assess calibration, Wiengardt, Leonesio, and Loftus (1995) found that misleading questions led to a virtual elimination of what was a strong CA calibration in the no-misleading questions condition, primarily because misled witnesses failed to adjust downward their confidence in their incorrect memory responses.

Face recognition from a lineup also has been found to be adversely influenced by misleading information. Jenkins and Davies (1985) had adults drawn from the community watch a videotape of a shoplifting. Either minutes or several days later, some witnesses were shown a Photofit composite picture of the shoplifter supposedly made through consultation with another witness. This composite either did or did not include misleading information in the form of a feature (e.g., added moustache or different hairstyle) the shoplifter did not possess. Not surprisingly, accuracy on a later photo-lineup test was lower among witnesses who examined the misleading composite relative to those who saw an accurate or no composite. Identification confidence, however, was largely unaffected by composite condition. And the CA r? It went from significant and positive in the accurate (.27) and no composite (.47) conditions to nil in the two inaccurate composite conditions (.15 and .06).

A somewhat different form of facial misinformation was studied by Schooler and Engstler-Schooler (1990)—self-generated misinformation. Based on the well-documented notion (see, e.g., Paivio, 1986) that some visual experiences and mental representations are difficult to describe in words, these researchers hypothesized that verbally describing a visual memory would impair memory for a stimulus such as a face by biasing a recoding of the stimulus in the direction of verbal descriptions that have incomplete fidelity to the original memory trace. And, indeed, compared with those who did not do so, witnesses to a videotaped target who spent 5 minutes writing a detailed description of the target's face later were less likely to correctly recognize the target in an eight-face photo-lineup. Moreover, whereas a significant positive CA relationship was found among nonverbalizers, the CA relationship was absolutely nil for verbalizers.

All of these misinformation effects can be understood, at least in part, as examples of confidence judgments being (mis)informed by direct access to a memory trace that has either been altered or is the wrong memory trace.

Factors in Testing for Identification Memory

The factors present in the testing of eyewitness memory (as well as in the retention interval we have just examined) are probably the most important in an applications sense, because they are controllable by police investigators. They are system variables (Wells, 1978), as opposed to estimator variables like most witnessing conditions, the influence of which can only be estimated after the fact. Theoretically, factors that are discovered to moderate the CA relationship during testing could be controlled before, during, and after an identification test to maximize the degree to which confidence in identification can be considered diagnostic of identification accuracy.

(Not) Encouraging Choosing. The fact that the CA relationship is stronger when computed only for choosers is now well established (cf. Wells & Olson, 2003). One likely reason for this is that there are multiple potential reasons for the failure to make an identification (i.e., *I know he's not there* vs. *They look equally familiar* vs. *I don't recognize anyone*), and therefore the confidence ratings of nonchoosers may vary widely and for different reasons. Removing nonchoosers removes the accuracy-unrelated variance from the equation, allowing a stronger and presumably truer CA *r* to emerge among the choosers that remain (and are more forensically relevant, in any event). But this does not imply that witnesses should be deliberately encouraged to choose. Indeed, factors that have the effect of increasing the likelihood of making a positive identification appear to be unhelpful, indeed destructive, to the CA *r*. In their meta-analysis of the CA relationship, Sporer et al. (1995) included as one moderator variable the choosing rate observed in each study (i.e. the percentage of witnesses who made a positive identification of someone in the lineup). They found that the CA *r* among choosers was negatively related to choosing rate. The CA *r* generally was lower in studies in which a larger percentage of the witnesses made a positive identification, even after controlling for overall effects of choosing rates on confidence and accuracy. These results suggest that factors such as biased lineup instructions (Malpass & Devine, 1981) and the extent to which the suspect stands out from the foils in a lineup (Wells, Rydell, & Seelau, 1993), which are known to increase the choosing rate and, in turn, the false identification rate, have the additional effect of reducing the diagnosticity of confidence.

Why might this be? The answer lies in the nature of the additional witnesses who are pulled into the chooser category by suggestive biases in lineups. These witnesses are likely to have rejected the lineup in the absence of situational pressures, and they are thus more likely to be both incorrect and less confident than other choosers. This concurs with correlational trends across studies observed by Sporer et al. (1995). On the surface, this would seem to bode well for a strengthened CA relationship. But consider the various sources of confidence in relation to likely memory accuracy for these situationally recruited choosers—which should differ from the sources for what we might refer to as *choosers-anyway*. *Recruited choosers* should have weaker memory traces, which reduces the appropriate impact of actual memory strength on confidence and increases the impact of extrinsic cues. Biased instructions, for example, have been found to bolster confidence in an inaccurate choice (Leippe, Rauch, & Eisenstadt, 2006), apparently by serving as an extrinsic cue to suggest that "the culprit must be there, and therefore my choice of the closest looking person must be the culprit." Or some recruited choosers with depressed confidence will, by chance or because of a biased lineup in which a guilty suspect sticks out, accurately identify the culprit. In short, confidence and accuracy will more readily disconnect among recruited choosers.

Pre- versus Post-lineup Confidence Assessment. An obvious testing factor is the timing of the confidence question. Research has demonstrated relatively conclusively that witnesses' statements of confidence that they will be able to identify the culprit before a lineup is presented are utterly unrelated to the accuracy of their subsequent identification choices. Cutler and Penrod (1989b) reviewed nine studies that assessed prelineup confidence; in none of the studies did the (pre)CA r exceed .20, and it averaged less than .10 across studies. Moreover, in seven of the studies, it was possible to compare correlations of pre- and post-lineup confidence and accuracy. In six of severn studies, the (pre)CA r was significantly smaller than the (post)CA r, which ranged from .28 to .45. Sporer (1992) found essentially the same results in a study in which confidence and identification measures occurred a week after student witnesses had viewed a staged intrusion in a laboratory, but before witnesses were made aware that the intrusion was staged. The (pre)CA r was .06 for all witnesses and .03 for choosers only, whereas the comparable (post)CA r values were .45 and .57, respectively. The nil relationship between pre-identification confidence and identification accuracy is consistent with findings that, following an initial failure at recall, individuals' predictions that they can recognize a stimulus are unrelated to subsequent accuracy of recognition (Perfect & Hollins, 1999).

In a cue-congruence analysis, the most compelling explanation for this nil relationship involving pre-lineup confidence is not that witnesses have misleading cues to their memory accuracy, but that they have too few cues and too little information. A preliminary confidence assessment resembles a recall (as opposed to a recognition) test in that individuals are asked to access their memory trace without the cues and partial information gained from a visually presented to-be-recognized stimulus. Recall often fails to be accurate where recognition might be correct, precisely because of its dearth of cues that trigger a sense of familiarity (cf. Raaijmakers & Shiffrin, 1992). In recall, witnesses are left with intrinsic cues such as ease of retrieval (e.g., Robinson & Johnson, 1996), but, in the recall-like case of pre-identification confidence assessments, it is not clear that ease of retrieval varies much between conjuring up a more versus a less accurate image. Thus, witnesses are left with the less reliable cues of self-credibility and general beliefs about eyewitness memory as sources by which to gauge their confidence. The practical implication, of course, is that pre-lineup confidence should not really factor into decisions regarding the pursuit of a criminal investigation. At the same time, as Penrod and Cutler (1995) observed, police officers should not rule out administering an identification test to a witness who asserts a lack of confidence in advance of the test.

Similarity of Lineup Foils.   By accident or design, lineups can vary in terms of how much the suspect "sticks out." Non-suspect lineup members may look more or less like the suspect, and/or match more or less the eyewitness's verbal description of the culprit than does the suspect. In general, the diagnosticity of a confidence statement will be less, the more the suspect sticks out in either of these ways. This happens because confidence should be informed by such accuracy cues as (a) the greater attention the suspect will receive through being visually salient (cf. Taylor & Fiske, 1978), (b) the impression based on a relative comparison of faces that the suspect most resembles the memory trace of the culprit, and (c) the ease and speed of making this resemblance decision. As a result, compared with when similarity to foils is greater, confidence in identifications of the suspect who stands out as dissimilar (especially in terms of greater resemblance to the culprit) will likely be higher whether the identification is correct (i.e., the suspect is guilty) or incorrect (i.e., the suspect is innocent). There has been surprisingly scant empirical testing of this proposed moderating role of foil similarity, but both conceptual analyses of foil selection and similarity and what data there are point strongly to this conclusion (cf. R. C. L. Lindsay, 1985; Wells, Rydell, & Seelau, 1993).

Similarity of Target at Witnessing and Testing.   The appearance of a culprit may change between the time of the crime and the time of an identification test. When there is a lengthy time interval (e.g., 2 years) between the witnessed event and apprehension of a suspect, aging, weight gain or loss, changes in hair length and style, and other transformations may occur. Even short retention intervals may involve fairly substantial changes in facial appearance. To test the influence of target similarity at witnessing and at test, Read, Vokey, and Hammersley (1990) presented 10th-grade yearbook photos and then tested recognition memory and confidence in memory for the faces depicted in the photos by using as test stimuli the 12th-grade yearbook photos of the same people (interspersed, of course, with filler, never-seen faces). The 10th–12th photo pairs had been carefully rated for similarity, and low-, medium-, and high-similarity pairs were tested. In two experiments, Read et al. found that the within-participant CA r values decreased monotonically as similarity decreased. At the lowest level of similarity, the correlations were seldom significant, and it seems clear why this should be so. When similarity is low, the sense of recognition is likely the result of partial matches of the presented face and the memory traces. If confidence judgments result from information coming directly from the memory trace, they must involve some algebra for deciding on the basis of a mixed bag of familiar and unfamiliar features. Under circumstances of low similarity, compared with when similarity is high, instances of confidence-accuracy inversions are more likely, such as an accurate identification accompanied by a confidence judgment tempered by worries about what seems unfamiliar, or an inaccurate identification accompanied by high certainty because one feature seems exceedingly familiar.

Read et al. (1990) did not report confidence ratings, but it seems likely that confidence decreases as similarity decreases. Some evidence for this was found by Maass and Brigham (1982). In this study, either the stimulus and test photos of a target were highly similar (indeed, identical) in terms of hairstyle, clothing, background color, and the absence of eyeglasses, or they differed on all counts. Confidence (and accuracy) in recognition decisions was significantly higher in the similar condition.

Retrospective Self-awareness and Reflection.   Drawing partly from a self-perception hypothesis introduced by Leippe (1980), Kassin (1985) reasoned that confidence judgments would track accuracy better if eyewitnesses viewed themselves as they made a lineup decision. In a series of studies, Kassin and his colleagues (Kassin, 1985; Kassin, Rigby, & Castillo, 1991) provided this opportunity for what they refer to as retrospective self-awareness (RSA) to subsets of witnesses to videotaped staged crimes of vandalism, burglary, and theft, by having them watch a videotape of their lineup decision immediately after making the decision. In the videotape, they saw and heard themselves from the time the photo lineup was presented until they pointed to their choice (or orally rejected the lineup). After this, witnesses rendered a confidence judgment. Across studies, the CA *r* was consistently higher in RSA conditions than in no-RSA conditions. Kassin (1985) found an average CA *r* of .48 in the RSA conditions of four experiments, compared with an average of .04 in control conditions. Kassin et al. (1991) observed similar *r* values of .40 and −.03 in RSA and control conditions, respectively.

According to Kassin et al. (1991), the opportunity to watch oneself increases the extent to which a witness takes note of overt, yet subtle, behaviors during his or her identification efforts, such as speed in making an identification and the number of times each photo was looked at. These behaviors reflect speed and ease of retrieval, which, as we have seen, are generally valid intrinsic cues to accuracy. To the extent that RSA increases awareness of these cues and people recognize them as indicative of their memory accuracy, resultant confidence judgments should correspond better to identification accuracy. Two additional findings of Kassin et al. lend strong support to this interpretation. First, those RSA witnesses who showed a strong CA correspondence were considerably more likely to notice these aspects of their behavior while watching themselves than were RSA witnesses who, despite RSA, showed no CA correspondence. Second, the RSA effect was especially likely to occur among witnesses who would most likely focus on their public behavior and appearance, namely, individuals who tested high on public self-consciousness (Fenigstein, Scheier, & Buss, 1975).

This account of the RSA effect, of course, is entirely compatible with the cue-congruence analysis. RSA provides more information on which to make a confidence judgment, and that information—behavioral cues about retrieval speed and ease—influences confidence ratings in the same direction as information from the memory trace itself, because speed and ease of retrieval are, in fact, correlated with memory trace strength.

A finding conceptually similar to the RSA effect was observed in a calibration study by Brewer et al. (2002). In a study that involved exposure to a videotaped theft of a credit card at a restaurant, calibration was appreciably improved by having witnesses reflect on their just-made identification by completing a questionnaire that asked about witnessing conditions and the ease, speed, and process of making the identification. In this reflection condition, the calibration index (CI) was .022, very close to zero, and considerably smaller than in a no-reflection control condition (CI = .05; see Figure 16.1). To the extent that reflection on identification contributed to the effect, the same process of better recognizing and using intrinsic accuracy cues seems to have been at work.

In a third condition of the Brewer et al. (2002) study, before providing a confidence response, witnesses contemplated why their lineup decision might be wrong. This also served to improve calibration (CI = .017). Perhaps examining one's memory response in terms of how it might be in error also has the effect of compelling better recognition and analysis of internal—and even external (e.g., the lineup)—accuracy cues.

Accountability. In addition to RSA, Kassin et al. (1991) found that the CA relationship was moderated by a second testing factor: post-identification instructions regarding the confidence judgment that emphasized *accountability* led to a stronger CA *r*. In the social judgment and decision-making literatures, accountability is defined as the belief that one's actions require explanation (Tetlock, 1983) and is manipulated in terms of such factors as the publicity of one's action or decision, the personal consequences of a decision, and the requirement of discussing it with another. When accountability is high, decisions tend to be more carefully thought out, more integrative of available information, and more evaluatively balanced (cf. Leippe & Elkin, 1987; Tetlock, 1983). In Kassin et al.'s (1991) high-accountability conditions, the experimenter told witnesses that their already videotaped identification decision would be shown in a class and that they should "think carefully before answering because I will then ask you to announce your rating and explain it to me" (p. 702). Presumably, witnesses viewing the lineup under this accountable mindset were more careful in examining the faces against each other and the memory image and used and integrated more systematically the available internal and external cues to memory accuracy.

Robinson and Johnson (1998) included a high-accountability condition in a study in which participants watched a videotape of a crime and then attempted to identify the culprit under varying instructional sets. Compared with the no-instructions control condition, the accountability condition was not associated with a higher CA relationship. However, unlike in the Kassin et al. (1991) study, accountability instructions were given *before* instead of after the identification attempt and, indeed, were framed in terms of being accountable for making an accurate identification decision instead of being accountable, as in Kassin et al.'s (1991) study, for making a confidence judgment that was sensitive to the likely accuracy of a decision already made. Thus, it is possible that Robinson and Johnson's (1998) accountable witnesses did not have an accountable mindset as they contemplated their confidence, that accountability influenced identification decisions in ways that negated its influence on confidence ratings, or both.

Consequences and Realism. Some of the factors that enhance accountability, including instructions to be careful, the expectation of public disclosure of the lineup decision, and, especially, the awareness that an identification will have important consequences, are normally prevalent in actual cases. This implies that the CA relationship in actual cases may typically be more at the higher level found in Kassin et al.'s high-accountability condition ($r = .44$) than at the lower level found in their low-accountability condition ($r = -.03$). Brigham et al. (1982) made a similar argument upon finding that in a field study in which the eyewitnesses (convenience store clerks) reasonably could have expected their decisions to have important consequences, the CA r was .50. Of course, given that the accountability effect to date only has been found when accountability centers on the confidence judgment, and not the identification, the conclusion that the CA relationship will be stronger in real cases is questionable, at least if it relies on accountability as the critical variable. The police are likely to emphasize the consequences of the identification, not the confidence statement. In addition, research on consequences and realism is mixed. Murray and Wells (1982) manipulated whether student-witnesses to a staged theft attempted a photo-lineup identification before or after being informed that the crime had been staged. That is, unlike witnesses in most staged-crime studies, witnesses in the informed-after condition believed their identification and confidence judgments—delivered to a police officer—would have real consequences in a real case. Yet, whereas significant CA r values were observed for two confidence measures in the standard informed-before condition ($r = .28$ and .50), the CA r values in the condition with consequences were smaller and insignificant ($-.09$ and .32). In another study in which witnesses believed the crime was real as they attempted an identification, Hosch et al. (1984) obtained a nil CA correlation.

On the other hand, Behrman and Davey (2001) were able to examine archival records of 58 live lineup identifications in which, based on other evidence, it was deemed very likely that the suspect in the lineup was guilty and that, therefore, identification of the suspect was likely to be an accurate decision and failure to identify the suspect (by selecting either a foil or no one) was likely to be an inaccurate decision. The investigators compared witnesses who chose ("accurate") and did not choose ("inaccurate") the suspect on their ratings on a 2-point confidence scale (*I'm sure it's number* X vs. *Although I'm not positive, I think . . .*) given to the police administrator of the lineup. They obtained a biserial r between confidence and "accuracy" of .47. Thus, if one accepts the possibly questionable assumption that the suspects were indeed guilty in all of these cases, this archival field study, unlike the laboratory studies, suggests that eyewitness identifications that have real consequences might indeed promote confidence judgments that are moderately diagnostic of accuracy.

Incentives. Shaw and Zerr (2003) found that the offer of a monetary prize for good memory—a positive personal consequence—significantly *reduced* the CA relationship in responses to multiple-choice questions about a person witnessed 5 days earlier. On the surface, this result seems to be the opposite of what we would expect, given the observed and theoretically sensible role of accountability. However, accountability was actually quite low in this study. The memory test was group-administered and anonymous and was a forced choice, verbal task, not a face recognition task replete with cues to accuracy. Under these circumstances, the merely personal incentive appears to have increased self-perceived effort at remembering among a subset of witnesses, and the self-perception of effort itself served as an extrinsic cue to accuracy (*I racked my brains to remember, so I must be correct*), which led to increased confidence but not increased accuracy. Alternatively, because effort unaccompanied by success (i.e., accuracy) would arouse cognitive dissonance (Festinger, 1957), witnesses may have justified their effort by becoming more confident (cf. Blanton, Pelham, DeHart, & Carvallo, 2001). Thus, factors that increase how hard witnesses try to remember do not necessarily increase the predictive value of confidence judgments—they may actually decrease it. It depends on whether sensitivity to valid accuracy cues is enhanced by greater remembering efforts.

Sequential versus Simultaneous Lineups.   In most real cases, and most research studies, *simultaneous lineups* are used, in which the suspect and all foils are presented at the same time. An alternative is to use a *sequential lineup*, in which faces are presented one at a time, and the witness gives a yes/no response to each one. Research suggests that the risk of false identifications is less with sequential lineups (see, e.g., Steblay, Dysart, Fulero, & Lindsay, 2001). This is due primarily to the fact that sequential presentation compels witnesses to use an absolute judgment strategy of comparing the single face with their memory trace, because they cannot readily use a relative judgment strategy of comparing faces and making an identification on the basis of which one looks most familiar (Kneller, Memon, & Stevenage, 2001; Wells, 1984). Absolute memory judgments would seem to be more likely than relative judgments to be characterized by a stronger CA relationship, because more, possibly invalid accuracy cues are available when a relative judgment is possible (e.g., how much one lineup member stands out). It is surprising, then, that, in studies that have measured it, the CA relationship has not generally been found to differ between sequential and simultaneous lineup conditions (e.g., Lindsay & Wells, 1985; Sporer, 1993). However, in a recent calibration study using a multiple-face recognition paradigm instead of an eyewitness paradigm, Weber and Brewer (2003) found better calibration when participants made absolute decisions (old or new?) about single faces (a sequential-like task) than when they made relative decisions (which face is old?) about two faces (a simultaneous-like task). More research is needed on whether lineup type moderates the CA *r*.

Witness Factors

The condition of the eyewitness at the time of the identification test may influence the degree to which her or his self-reported confidence is a good indicator of accuracy. Indeed, a number of witness characteristics, mostly acute ones, have been found to moderate the CA relationship.

Anxiety.   An attempt to describe or to identify a criminal from a lineup can be more anxiety-provoking for some witnesses than for others. People who are highly test-anxious tend to become self-preoccupied with worry, doubtful of their ability, and acutely conscious of possible negative consequences in evaluative situations (Sarason, 1972). Interestingly, such individuals may evince better confidence-accuracy correspondence than those who can approach an identification test less nervously. Nolan and Markham (1998) exposed high-anxiety and low-anxiety college students to a videotaped restaurant holdup and, 1 week later, administered to them cued- and free-recall memory questions focused partly on descriptions of the culprits. The CA relationship was measured as the correlation between the proportion of questions answered correctly and the mean of the confidence ratings given to each answer. Among high-anxiety witnesses, r was a significant and impressive .60, whereas among low-anxiety witnesses, it was a nonsignificant .28. This finding is conceptually similar to a finding by Bothwell, Brigham, and Pigott (1987) of a higher CA r among witnesses higher (vs. lower) in neuroticism, a component of which is high anxiety. The moderating role of anxiety may involve tendencies of high-anxiety individuals to be less overconfident and more likely to be self-aware and monitor their memory performance in an on-line variant of RSA.

Fatigue and Sleeplessness. The eyewitness who enters the police station exhausted and deprived of sleep is at risk of providing an especially uninformative confidence statement, judging from a careful study by Blagrove and Akehurst (2000). These authors compared the accuracy and confidence of memory reports about audiotaped stories of complex events given by adults who were were not sleep-deprived or had been sleep-deprived under controlled conditions for 29–50 hours. The CA relationship regarding various indices of accuracy was consistently lowest among the most sleep-deprived witnesses, in part because these witnesses were most suggestible in response to leading questions, leading to less accuracy, yet to no decreases in confidence. The authors suggest that the "cognitive slowing effect of sleep loss" (p. 69) reduces the ability to use intrinsic cues such as retrieval times of elements of correct memories. In other words, access to cues congruent with memory trace strength is blocked.

Expectations and Self-Credibility. Expectations about the difficulty of a memory task are potential extrinsic accuracy cues. For example, the belief that most identifications under the encountered witnessing circumstances are likely to be accurate may serve to increase identification confidence regardless of accuracy, whereas a belief that identifications tend to be false may push confidence down. Interestingly, however, this was not what was found in a multiple-face recognition study. Cutler and Penrod (1989a) informed participants that a low (20–40), moderate (40–60), or high (60–80) percentage of the faces they would see in a recognition test phase had in fact been presented to them previously. Although this base-rate information influenced the tendency to report recognizing a face (i.e., a positive identification), it had no effect on either confidence or CA calibration.

Cutler and Penrod (1989a) speculated that this lack of base-rate impact might be due to the absence of incentive to be sensitive to base rate in an uninvolving task characterized by the slide-projected presentation of countless faces. And, indeed, an effect of expectation on confidence and the CA relationship was found in an eyewitness identification paradigm in which expectations were manipulated in a very different way. In two experiments, Leippe, Eisenstadt et al. (2006) led some witnesses to a videotaped theft to believe they had either good memory or poor memory for the theft and the thief, based on their initial memory reports. Compared with a no-feedback condition, good-memory feedback increased post-identification confidence in a subsequent lineup identification, whereas poor-memory feedback decreased identification confidence. No parallel effects on identification accuracy were observed. It appears, then, that memory expectations in the form of witnesses' acute self-credibility as a memory source can contribute to disconnecting confidence and accuracy by serving as an invalid cue to accuracy.

Experience and Practice.   Eyewitnesses' expectations about their identification accuracy also might be based on their personal experiences with remembering faces. Perfect, Hollins, and Hunt (2000) conducted two studies in which witnesses were given from 0 to 2 trials of practice making memory responses similar to a final eyewitness memory test. In one study, the stimuli were videotaped crimes, and cued recall for details of the crime and criminal was assessed; in the other study, the stimuli were briefly seen faces, and lineup identification accuracy was assessed. In both studies, the CA r increased linearly as practice increased, but only when the practice included feedback about both witness and normative accuracy. In a related vein, Bornstein and Zickafoose (1999) found that feedback that one has been overconfident in previous eyewitness decisions decreased witnesses' tendency to be overconfident but did not improve CA calibration. Practice-with-feedback effects may occur because individuals get a more realistic sense of their skill within a memory domain and how their accuracy tends to covary with various witnessing conditions. As a result, the information derived from beliefs about their memory in a given case becomes more likely to be congruent—or at least not incongruent—with trace strength and intrinsic cues. In addition, as Perfect et al. (2000) suggest, practice with feedback may teach people to rely less on their beliefs and more on intrinsic cues to accuracy.

It is not unreasonable to expect eyewitnesses to vary in their experience or practice in eyewitness-like situations. Investigators might gain information relevant to interpreting confidence judgments by inquiring about such experience. It would be crucial, however, to confirm that the practice experiences included trustworthy feedback.

Self-reported Identification Strategy and Recognition Skill.   There is recent evidence that investigators would do well to inquire even further about witnesses' memory experiences. In a large-scale study involving nearly 400 student-witnesses to a videotaped staged theft, Olsson and Juslin (1999) asked (post-identification) witnesses to rate their skill at recognition and to indicate whether they used primarily a holistic (i.e., formed an overall impression of the face as a whole) or analytic (i.e., examined the face feature by feature) strategy in identifying the culprit from a photo lineup. Holistic encoding is known to yield superior memory (e.g., Sporer, 1991). Higher self-rated recognition skill and a more holistic identification strategy were each associated with both higher identification accuracy *and* stronger CA calibration.

DIRECT INFLUENCES ON CONFIDENCE DURING AND FOLLOWING THE MEMORY REPORT

Many of the numerous moderators of the CA relationship we have reviewed work by altering witness confidence without having corresponding effects on accuracy (e.g., incentive-driven effort at retrieval heightens confidence even though it is unsuccessful) or by altering the memory trace without having corresponding effects on confidence (e.g., disguise at exposure yields an impoverished memory trace but has little impact on confidence). In other cases (e.g., duration of exposure during an interaction), the impact on confidence is greater or less than that justified by the size of the impact on the memory trace. In still other cases, the moderator pushes confidence and accuracy in opposite directions (e.g., an innocent suspect stands out as uniquely different in a lineup). All of these moderating variables appear to work mainly at the metacognitive level of providing or distorting the memory cues to accuracy that inform a confidence judgment. And they mainly impose their influence before or during the memory test. We now shift our attention to another class of factors—variables that may be introduced *following* the eyewitness's initial memory statement but usually before the initial (post-report) confidence statement. These factors directly influence confidence without having any effect on accuracy or the memory trace in general, because they work less at the metacognitive level and more at the level of adjusting the overall belief that one's memory is accurate or inaccurate. Invariably, because they affect only confidence, these factors indeed moderate the CA relationship by reducing or utterly destroying it. But our focus here also will be on the direction of influence. Is confidence increased or decreased?

Briefing. An early demonstration of the post-identification alteration of eyewitness confidence was provided by Wells, Ferguson, and Lindsay (1981). In their experiment, college students, sitting alone in laboratory cubicles, witnessed a staged theft and then attempted to identify the thief from a photo lineup. Immediately after their identification, those witnesses who chose the thief from a target-present lineup (accurate) or a similar-looking replacement from a target-absent lineup (inaccurate) were either briefed or not briefed about the nature of the "cross-examination" they would soon face. The briefing consisted of warnings that the cross-examiner would ask questions about the thief and would try to antagonize and discredit the witness, as well as suggestions to rehearse answers and avoid inconsistencies. In turn, witnesses responded to cross-examination questions, the last of which asked them to rate their confidence. When there had been no briefing, there was a positive CA relationship—accurate witnesses were significantly more confident than inaccurate witnesses. There was no CA relationship when there had been briefing, however, because briefing served to increase confidence, especially among inaccurate witnesses. Wells et al. offered a self-persuasion interpretation of the briefing effect, suggesting that "witnesses seem to convince themselves of their accuracy, perhaps because rehearsal involves a biased search for consistent supporting evidence" (p. 694).

Thinking about One's Identification.   The biased-search interpretation is consistent with the effects of private contemplation of one's attitudes and beliefs. For example, merely thinking about a stimulus previously rated as somewhat likeable leads to polarization of attitude (Tesser, 1978). The thought-about stimulus becomes liked even more, apparently because the initial attitude serves as a mental theory that directs access to memories and evaluations of the stimulus in a way that activates primarily evaluatively consistent cognitions during thinking. In the realm of beliefs, similar biased processing has been observed. For example, the task of generating reasons for why a certain belief is correct causes the belief to become stronger (Anderson, Lepper, & Ross, 1980), and reading mixed evidence regarding an already held belief strengthens belief, presumably because belief-consistent information is more readily assimilated and less counterargued than is belief-inconsistent information (Lord, Lepper, & Ross, 1979; Munro & Ditto, 1997). Given these effects of contemplation, it is not surprising that rehearsing one's memory in order to defend it leads to the escalation in confidence observed by Wells et al. (1981). Indeed, in a more recent study, Wells and Bradfield (1999) found that confidence in false identifications was increased merely by asking witnesses to a videotaped crime enactment, in the 6 minutes between the identification and the confidence measure, "to spend time thinking privately" (p. 140) about such things as how clearly they could see the gunman's face, how easy it was to make their identification, how good they are at remembering faces, and how confident they are in their identification. When witnesses freely make an identification, we can assume they have at least some belief that it is correct. Thus, thinking about their identification primarily yields thoughts that support the veracity of the identification and strengthen confidence in it.

Co-witness Information.   A powerful influence on identification confidence is information about the identification made by a co-witness to the event. Luus and Wells (1994) used biased lineup instructions and a suggestive perpetrator-absent photo spread to induce eyewitnesses to a staged crime to make false identifications. Some eyewitnesses learned immediately after their identifications about a co-witness's identification. Confidence was raised an average of 2 points on a 10-point scale if the co-witness had identified the same person, and lowered by 2 points if the co-witness chose someone else. Moreover, the changes in confidence were not reversible by later telling witnesses that the investigator had been mistaken about the co-witness's identification and actually did not know the co-witness's choice. This perseverance of feedback-altered confidence resembles the belief perseverance observed in thought-induced belief change studies (cf. Anderson et al., 1980) and suggests that confidence changes occur because co-witness feedback guides thoughts about one's memory that become internalized.

It is important to note that, although the primary focus here is on variables that enter the scene after a memory test, co-witness information might also be introduced beforehand. In this case, we might expect it to affect both confidence and the memory response itself. We are not aware of any study that provided a co-witness's lineup identification to witnesses before they attempted the identification themselves. However, Shaw, Garven, and Wood (1997) varied whether, before the witness answered, a co-witness gave a correct or incorrect answer, or no answer, to cued-recall questions concerning the people and events in a videotaped crime. Relative to no co-witness information, correct co-witness information increased response accuracy, whereas incorrect co-witness information decreased it. Confidence was assessed in one of three experiments and, interestingly, was not influenced by co-witness information. This absence of effects on confidence in light of robust effects on memory accuracy renders confidence an untrustworthy guide to accuracy. That is, although Shaw et al. (1997) found strong within-condition CA *r* values, the between-condition patterns show that witnesses led astray by an incorrect co-witness were less often accurate but just as confident as witnesses who received no co-witness information. Witnesses who received no co-witness information, in turn, were no less confident but less often accurate than those who received correct co-witness information.

Information or Feedback from the Test Administrator.   Returning to the post-identification moment, studies have found that besides information about a co-witness, the test administrator during this moment can provide other information that affects confidence in identifications. Using a procedure similar to that of Luus and Wells (1994), Wells and colleagues (Bradfield, Wells, & Olson, 2002; Wells & Bradfield, 1998; 1999) have shown that confidence in a false identification can be dramatically altered by a statement from the lineup administrator that indicates the witness chose the suspect (e.g., *Good, you identified the suspect*) or a foil (e.g., *Actually, the suspect is number __*). The confidence inflation created by confirming that the suspect was chosen is particularly problematic because confirmation can easily be communicated, either deliberately or inadvertently, and sends the case against the accused into prosecution with the eyewitness evidence strengthened by hyped-up confidence. Highlighting the ease with which administrators can communicate who is the suspect, Garrioch and Brimacombe (2001) found that an innocent suspect (i.e., a lineup substitute for the culprit in a staged crime) was more likely to be identified when administrators knew which lineup member was the suspect than when they were kept blind to this.

The damaging effect of confirming feedback to the CA relationship was demonstrated by Bradfield et al. (2002). In this study, accurate identifications from an easy culprit-present lineup and inaccurate identifications from a difficult culprit-absent lineup were compared. Under these circumstances, much higher confidence was associated with the accurate identifications than the inaccurate ones when no feedback was provided before the confidence rating; the CA *r* was .59. However, the accurate-inaccurate difference in confidence was considerably smaller when witnesses received confirming feedback, primarily because confirming feedback served to inflate the confidence of inaccurate witnesses. The CA *r* in the confirming feedback condition was .37—significantly lower than .59.

Confirming or disconfirming feedback regarding a lineup identification not only alters confidence. The studies just described also reveal that feedback influences witnesses' retrospective reports of the formation and quality of their memories. For example, following their confidence ratings, compared with no-feedback controls, witnesses who received confirming feedback reported that they had a better look at the culprit, paid greater attention, and found it easier to make an identification, whereas witnesses who received disconfirming feedback reported less attention and greater difficulty in making an identification. These effects on retrospective reports of the memory experience have been interpreted as involving a self-perception process (e.g., Bem, 1972). According to this account (Wells & Bradfield, 1999), witnesses do not evaluate their view of the culprit, the attention they paid, the speed of their identification, or, indeed, their confidence "on-line" during memory formation and testing. Rather, when asked about these factors, witnesses use the information about their memories contained in the current feedback—what we would refer to as an external cue—to infer how good a memory they formed and so on. This analysis points up the importance of external cues during and after testing in forming the confidence belief. It also suggests that an external cue can have an additional influence on confidence because it distorts beliefs about the memory experience in ways that serve as additional evidence that the memory is good or bad.

Repeated Questioning.   Under certain circumstances, repeated open-ended questioning of witnesses can lead to an increase in the number of details of an incident or a person that are accurately recalled, an increase in cumulative accuracy known as hypermnesia (Dunning and Stern, 1992; Scrivner & Safer, 1988). Repeated asking of questions to which witnesses have already supplied answers, on the other hand, can only lead to greater accuracy if witnesses somehow remember some things differently and switch from incorrect to correct memory responses. It seems likely that witnesses most of the time will stick to their original answers, whether they are accurate or not. But will confidence in the memory change with repeated questioning, even when accuracy remains relatively constant? This is exactly the question that Shaw (1996; Shaw & McClure, 1996) addressed. For example, Shaw and McClure (1996) staged a classroom interruption (a stranger arguing with the professor) and then asked a series of questions about the event and the people involved in it. These questions involved a question (e.g., *What color was the woman's shirt?*) followed by two response options (e.g., *Blue* and *Green*). Some of the questions were repeated as many as four times over about a month (Experiment 1) or twice over 5 days (Experiment 2). The results: Confidence, but not accuracy, increased as the frequency of questioning increased. Of particular interest here, the staged interruption in one experiment involved two culprits. Witnesses were questioned about one once and about the other twice (with the same questions) and ultimately had significantly greater confidence (but equal accuracy) in their descriptive memories of the culprit they were twice questioned about. This repeated-questioning effect appears to result from processes we are familiar with. Repeatedly retrieving a memory increases what Shaw (1996) refers to as retrieval fluency. Retrieval becomes easier, and this ease of retrieval serves as an internal cue to accuracy. In addition, the sense of familiarity with the memory image may become stronger, not because the image is accurate, but because it is repeatedly conjured up. Social-psychological factors may also be at work, such as heightened commitment to one's freely stated responses (see, e.g., Cialdini, 1987).

CONFIDENCE AS A CAUSE OF MEMORY CHANGE

We have concentrated on factors that have separate or incongruent influences on eyewitness confidence and on the memory referents of that confidence. Confidence is readily malleable by certain forces, but, ironically, it is insensitive to some factors that have subtle but sure impact on memory. But confidence is not only an object of influence. Confidence and changes in confidence can also be a *cause* of changes in other facets of cognition and memory. Although research into the consequences of confidence is in an early stage, it is instructive to examine briefly the prospect of confidence changes triggering other changes in the memory system.

The post-identification feedback studies (e.g., Wells & Bradfield, 1998), as described in the previous section, have shown that confirming and disconfirming feedback about an identification not only causes witnesses to adjust their confidence, but also causes changes in retrospective reports of the witnessing and testing experience. In effect, feedback influences eyewitnesses' memory about their memory processes as well as, apparently, their sense of memory trace strength (e.g., recipients of confirming feedback describe their memory image of the target as clearer). It has not been established whether change in confidence causes, results from, or merely coincides with changes in retrospective memory reports. It seems likely, however, that feedback-driven change in confidence is at least partly a causal agent in the chain of redefining the quality of memory. One argument for this comes from viewing confidence as the bottom-line belief about the relevant memory's accuracy. Beliefs are directly influenced by feedback that is viewed as authoritative (e.g., Hovland & Weiss, 1951; Smith & Ellsworth, 1987) and by consensus information (e.g., co-witness agreement with one's identification; see, e.g., Cialdini, 1987). There is thus no reason to expect that memory confidence is not directly affected by such information. As we have seen, people also have metacognitive beliefs about how memory works, and these likely include notions such as *good memories of a face are formed when we have a good view of the face* and *if someone has a good memory for a face, he or she will recognize that face immediately*. Accordingly, upon being asked retrospective questions about their memory, witnesses should make adjustments to what their memory—and the conditions under which it was formed and tested—"must" be like, especially if impressions about memory were not formed on-line. In addition, a change in confidence may also compel changes in memory about memory through the evaluatively consistent thought processes we described earlier.

In contrast to the effects on retrospective impressions of the memory experience, Leippe, Eisenstadt et al. (2006) have shown that feedback-driven changes in confidence can have *prospective* effects on memory responses. As described previously, this research showed that feedback about the accuracy of a descriptive memory report given before an identification test affected confidence in the subsequent lineup decision. Beyond this outcome, feedback also affected the speed with which witnesses made the identification as well as susceptibility to the misinformation effect. Witnesses who received positive feedback made their subsequent lineup choices more confidently *and* more quickly than witnesses who received no prior feedback. Also, in a cued-recall test, witnesses who received either positive or negative (vs. no) feedback were more likely to give in-correct answers that had previously been suggested by misleading questions. Presumably, negative feedback made witnesses less sure of which source—their original memory or the suggested information—was true, whereas positive feedback lulled witnesses into low-effort heuristic processing, which would give the more recent information (the mis-leading information) a retrieval advantage. These results suggest that confidence altered by feedback about memory for one aspect of an event generalizes to other aspects of memory for the event. Because individuals see memory as organized and connected, memory self-credibility for the entire event is altered.

DECISION TIME AS AN ALTERNATIVE INDICATOR OF IDENTIFICATION ACCURACY

A number of studies (e.g., Dunning & Stern, 1994; Dunning & Perretta, 2002; Sporer, 1993) have found that accurate lineup identifications tend to be made spontaneously in a matter of seconds, with witnesses reporting that the face "jumped out at them" (sug-gesting an immediate match of the face to the memory trace). In contrast, inaccurate identifications tend to be made more deliberately and slowly, with witnesses reporting they employed a feature-by-feature analysis of the faces and a "relative comparison process" of comparing array faces with each other to discern which one most resembles their memory image. Decision time has been found to be negatively correlated with the accuracy of lineup choosers, typically in the range of $-.30$ to $-.40$ (Dunning & Stern, 1994; Leippe, Eisenstadt et al., 2006; Sporer, 1992, 1993).

Decision time and confidence are also related. In Sporer's (1992) study, for example, the r among choosers was $-.61$. This relationship is sensible, given that decision time is akin to speed of retrieval, an internal accuracy cue that can inform confidence judg-ments. There is some evidence that, as a more automatic response than a reflective con-fidence judgment, decision time may better and more consistently correspond to accu-racy than does confidence. Smith et al. (2000) conducted a study involving more than 300 student-witnesses and replications with three different videotaped crimes that sug-gests that confidence is, in fact, less diagnostic of false identifications than is decision time. After witnesses watched the crime, they attempted to identify the criminal from a criminal-present or criminal-absent lineup that was either fair (all lineup foils matched the description of the criminal) or moderately unfair (all foils looked only "somewhat" like the criminal). Lineup decision accuracy, time, and confidence were assessed, as were witnesses' retrospective ratings of witnessing/testing conditions and of whether they made their identifications via absolute or relative judgments. For present purposes, the main results involve the contributions of confidence and decision time in postdicting accuracy. The CA r among choosers was a significant .34, and a discriminant function analysis in which confidence was the only predictor variable indicated that, using confi-dence alone, 62.3% of the witness identification choice could be correctly classified as accurate or inaccurate. However, when all of the predictor variables were entered into a multiple regression, confidence did not emerge as a significant predictor. Only decision time and lineup fairness (and witnesses' estimate of the distance between the criminal and the video camera) did so. And when only these variables were entered into a discriminant function analysis, the correct classification of witnesses into accurate and inaccurate groups was 75.2%. Decision time was more useful in postdicting accuracy than was confidence.

In general, decision time may be a superior indicator of accuracy, compared with self-reported confidence (cf. Wells & Olson, 2003). The decision-time/accuracy relationship, that is, may be more consistently reliable across situations, and less prone to being weakened, than is the CA relationship. Decision time is independent of accuracy cues that inappropriately affect confidence judgments, such as the conclusion from a relative comparison of lineup faces about which one best matches the memory image. Decision time is itself a usually valid internal accuracy cue, whereas confidence involves a less direct contemplative process that requires accessing this cue information. Most generally, decision time is more automatic and therefore less influenced by variables that require deliberative processing.

Because decision time is more behavioral, automatic, and less contemplative, it has been argued that the decision-time/accuracy relationship is not readily damaged by the manipulation of confidence (Wells et al., 2002). This may indeed be true when confidence is altered after the identification. However, as noted previously, Leippe, Eisenstadt et al. (2006) found that pre-identification memory feedback influenced identification decision time. As a result, it also reduced the decision-time/accuracy r to nonsignificance. In addition, virtually none of the many variables that moderate the CA relationship or generally affect confidence have been studied in terms of their impact on identification decision time. Nor has *time pressure* been studied for its impact on the decision-time/accuracy relationship. If decision time becomes a criterion of accuracy in court, police (or witnesses themselves) are likely to put pressure on witnesses to choose quickly. Research needs to be done on what influence time pressure might have.

CONCLUSIONS, IMPLICATIONS, AND DIRECTIONS FOR RESEARCH AND APPLICATION

There is now little question that the CA relationship is positive and, on average, small to moderate in magnitude. A reasonable conclusion is that, *in the absence of conditions that reduce it*, the typical CA r when confidence is measured immediately following a positive identification is about .40 and has been observed to be as high as .55 to .60. As we have seen, according to some calculations (e.g., Wells et al., 2002), if r = .40 and witnessing conditions are such that the identification accuracy rate is likely to be only 50%, the witness who reports above-average confidence has a 70% chance of being accurate. If r = .60, the chance is 80%. Using calibration measures that ask witnesses for their subjective probabilities of accuracy and testing large samples of witnesses, the relationship can look even better. Under good conditions, the actual probability that the identification is accurate may correspond to the witness's subjective probability within a 10–20% range.

It is also clear from our review and the metamemorial cue-congruence analysis that eyewitness research has led to important advances in understanding theoretically *how*, psychologically, confidence is related to accuracy. Although there is still much to learn, it appears that confidence is an evaluative belief about memory that is informed by a number of sources, including the memory trace itself, internal cues emanating from the process of remembering, external cues in the witnessing and testing situations, and beliefs about one's credibility as a rememberer. Confidence disconnects from accuracy when these sources provide information that is incongruent with the accuracy status of the memory trace. Perhaps the most common form of CA disconnection occurs when the memory is wrong but some sources suggest otherwise, leading to, by definition, *overconfidence*.

Is the CA relationship, and what we know about how it works, of any practical use to the criminal justice system? There is not a simple or single answer to this question. Rather, there are a number of possibilities for application, which depend on what criminal investigators need from a confidence assessment and on what they can do when making the assessment. In addition, some of the possible usefulness of confidence judgments cannot yet be judged, because the critical research has not yet been done. In the following, final, sections of this chapter, we consider practical usefulness on various dimensions (and, along the way, point out where more research is needed).

Confidence Is Useful When Conditions for a Positive CA Relationship Have Prevailed, and Investigators Should Consider These Before They Consider Confidence

Confidence appears to track accuracy better when certain conditions of witnessing, retention interval, *and* testing are met. On the witnessing side, duration of exposure to the perpetrator has a mixed record in terms of the CA relationship, probably because it potentially can be a misleading external accuracy cue and can serve to increase the familiarity of a stand-out innocent suspect. What does seem important are witnessing conditions associated with the emotional and attentional states of the witness and the ability of the witness to get a clear look at a perpetrator whose appearance is not likely to have changed much since being witnessed. The police can reasonably estimate these conditions. In turn, they can control the system variables to create the additional conditions necessary to trust identification confidence. Specifically, police investigators must avoid questioning of witnesses that involves misleading information, gratuitous repetition, and instructions that lead witnesses to overly verbalize about the perpetrator's face. Most important, the police must conduct a proper lineup. Lineup instructions should be unbiased, the lineup should be fair in terms of high similarity of foils based on resemblance to the description of the perpetrator, and communication with the witness should be minimal during identification until after a confidence judgment has been recorded. If and only if all of these conditions have been met, the confidence rating may be considered as one (imperfect and only suggestive) indicator of identification accuracy. Otherwise, it is unwise to consider confidence at all.

Usefulness Depends on How the Confidence
Question Is Asked and Answered

Eyewitness research has relied almost exclusively on the use of confidence ratings scales, and, in most instances, the numerical scales have not even been tied to percentage or probability terms. In stark contrast, police investigators seldom use any scale at all. Indeed, federal guidelines published in 1999 by the Department of Justice in a manual titled *Eyewitness Evidence: A Guide for Law Enforcement*, and based on scientific research and the deliberations of research psychologists, attorneys, and police officers (Wells et al., 2000), recommend that the eyewitness be asked to describe his/her level of confidence "in his/her own words" (p. 32). This is a major disconnect between research and practice and begs for research on the questions of (1) how verbal descriptions of confidence can be decoded into some quantitative and/or comparative (with other confidence statements) estimate and (2) the extent to which these verbal descriptions correspond to likely eyewitness accuracy.

Even if police investigators were to use numerical scales, there may be difficulties in applying what we now know about the CA relationship to the kinds of responses eyewitnesses to actual crimes provide. Consider the question used in calibration, which closely resembles the percentage scales used increasingly in eyewitness research in general. In essence, the witness needs only to fill in the blank in the following statement: *I am ___% confident that my identification choice is accurate*. There is a need for research on how real witnesses interpret and understand it, but, on the face of it, the question seems quite straightforward. It is the criterion side, the estimate predicted by the response to the question that may be more problematic. Suppose a witness claims 80% certainty. If the police believe that good conditions for confidence to track accuracy exist, and therefore that the witness is well calibrated, they can conclude that, in crime circumstances similar to the present one, about 80% of the witnesses would be accurate. That is a pretty high percentage. Yet can the number itself be useful any way? It suggests a 1 in 5 chance that the witness is inaccurate. In the justice system, such a statement will raise the red flag of reasonable doubt.

In the authors' experience with police reports, there is a tendency in the criminal justice system to define *confident* in absolute terms. *Confident* connotes "certain" and "sure," which imply the magical number 100%. The police investigator may not be wholly comfortable with the fact that the major eyewitness is 80% or even 90% certain in his or identification of the suspect. The departure from complete certainty may raise concerns about the suspect's guilt. (*Why isn't the witness completely sure? Maybe we've got the wrong guy.*) Of course, the police may be convinced themselves that they do have the right guy. In this case, the 80% statement is even more problematic to them. It potentially weakens the case they are trying to make for the district attorney and opens the door for a defense attorney to play the reasonable doubt card. For these reasons, lineup administrators may be disinclined to ask for confidence in probability, calibration-relevant terms. If they do, nothing less than 100% certain may suffice to bolster their belief in the witness's accuracy. More likely than a probability question, the confidence question asked by the police will be *Are you sure?*

Eyewitness research has not reported many findings that speak to the diagnosticity of eyewitness confidence when it is classified dichotomously as *completely certain* versus *less than completely certain*. What percentage of witnesses who claim very high confidence (i.e., 90% or 100% certain or 9 or 10 on a 10-point scale) are accurate? Such data have almost never been reported in eyewitness studies. We were able to pull this information from one of our earliest studies and two very recent studies. In the staged crime experiment reported by Leippe et al. (1978), 3 of the 5 (60%) witnesses who reported 100% certainty made an accurate identification, but only 2 of the 7 (29%) witnesses who reported 90% certainty did so. In Leippe, Eisenstadt et al.'s (2006) two videotape experiments, the accuracy rates for the 100% and 90% confident witnesses (choosers only) were 50% and 33%, and 46% and 62%, respectively. The accuracy rate of highly confident witnesses can be extracted from calibration curves reported in some studies. In creating the curves, the categories are normally collapsed into five categories (i.e., 10–20%, 30–40%, etc.). In the baseline condition of Brewer et al.'s (2002) study, about 70% of the choosers who were 90% or 100% certain they made the correct lineup choice were actually accurate; this figured jumped to about 85% in the reflection condition. The figures in Olsson and Juslin's (1999) study were about 80% to 87% across conditions. Some of these accuracy rates are quite high, but none are perfect, and some are quite low.

Absolute Certainty Is No Guarantee of Accuracy

When they have gone beyond simply reporting r, most investigations of the CA relationship have described confidence as a function of accuracy, reporting, for example, that mean confidence was, say, 5.5 on a 7-point scale among accurate witnesses and 4.8 among inaccurate witnesses. What would be more useful to application is to study and report accuracy as a function of confidence (e.g., Lindsay, 1985). This is essentially what is reported in calibration studies. A wider use of expressing the CA relationship in this way would allow researchers to study the *slope* and *intercept* of the confidence-accuracy function. Within some limits, the same CA r could describe a flatter or steeper climb in likely accuracy as confidence increases. Slope estimates, expressed in intuitive terms, of course, would be enormously helpful in conveying the meaning and usefulness of confidence in postdicting accuracy. Consider, for example, the functions relating lineup identification accuracy to confidence ratings on a 7-point scale in Figure 16–2, both illustrating a CA r of .45. For the relationship characterized by a steeper slope, the decrease in the proportion of witnesses who are accurate is appreciably greater as confidence decreases from 7 ("absolutely sure") to 6 than it is in the case of the flatter slope. If a steep slope involving a precipitous drop in accuracy as confidence departs from certainty proved to be the rule across research studies, this would be important for both application and theory. Absolute certainty would have special and greater diagnostic status, and we would be curious about how this works metacognitively. Moreover, the diagnostic status of absolute certainty would be enhanced by the fact that the steeper the slope, the greater the accuracy hit rate (see Figure 16–2). If the slope was less inclined, investigators could legitimately be more inclined to treat "highly" and "completely" certain

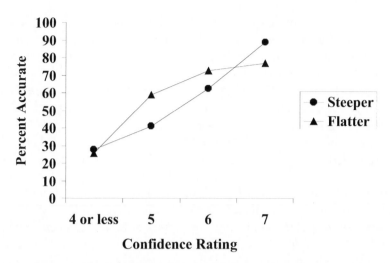

FIGURE 16–2. Percentage of identifications that are accurate at different levels of confidence for two hypothetical witness samples. In each case, $n = 100$, 50% of the identifications are accurate overall, and $r = .45$.

confidence statements more or less equivalently—an important option, given the reluctance of some people to report absolute certainty about anything.

The intercept of the confidence-accuracy function is also important to study. There is applied value in knowing the point on a confidence scale below which the majority of witnesses will have made an incorrect identification choice.

Supplemental Measures and Better Methods Show Promise for Practice

Confidence statements can be made better accuracy indicators by providing stronger congruent cues to accuracy through directed introspection techniques based on retrospective self-awareness, reflecting on encoding, and contemplation of how one's memory might be wrong (cf. Wells & Olson, 2003). In addition, decision time and retrospective reports of identification strategy might provide supplemental information in the estimation of accuracy. It is not clear whether and how these procedures can be incorporated into the police process of obtaining identifications, but the possibility of richer confidence data collection like this is certainly worth pursuing.

Post-Identification Influences on Confidence Likely Render Anything but an Immediate Post-Identification Confidence Judgment Un-useful

The ready malleability of confidence by feedback, co-witness information, deliberate or inadvertent communication by police investigators, repeated questioning, lawyer briefings, and other events make it clear that confidence statements made following an immediate post-identification confidence judgment will inevitably be hopelessly undiagnostic of memory accuracy. Short of being restricted to a hermetically sealed room until the trial, it is hard to imagine an eyewitness not being subjected to manipulative influences on his or her confidence. Even the isolated witness might experience confidence escalation in the service of justifying the effort of isolation! This is mainly a jest, of course, but it serves as a reminder that, in addition to the active situational variables that will change confidence, there is a normal social-cognitive course over time of bringing one's behavior (e.g., past identification and a possible future stint on a witness stand) and beliefs (e.g., confidence that one's identification is correct) into a consistent line with one another.

Eyewitness confidence is a mixed bag. Properly assessed, it should not be ignored as a potential indicator of identification accuracy. On the other hand, it is overrated by the criminal justice system and by people in general. And, at its worst, it can be what Leippe (1995) referred to as a "miscue" that can cause miscarriages of justice. Eyewitness confidence needs to be understood and used in proper perspective, under the proper conditions. Psycho-legal researchers have learned quite a bit about that perspective and those conditions, as we have attempted to demonstrate, using the cue-congruence model as an interpretive framework for organizing and integrating this knowledge. But much remains to be learned through energetic research. Research energy can be drawn from two observations, one about theory and one about application. First, we note that solving the mysteries of the CA relationship is at the very heart of understanding human self-understanding in the memory domain. Second, practically speaking, the better we understand the CA relationship, the better the legal system can become at using eyewitness confidence as a tool for separating true from false, yet incriminating, memories like Jennifer Thompson's, thereby serving the cause of justice.

REFERENCES

Anderson, C. A., Lepper, M. R., & Ross, L. (1980). Perseverance of social theories: The role of explanation in the persistence of discredited information. *Journal of Personality and Social Psychology, 39*, 1037–1049.

Behrman, B. W., & Davey, S. L. (2001). Eyewitness identification in actual criminal cases: An archival analysis. *Law and Human Behavior, 25*, 475–491.

Bem, D. J. (1972). Self-perception theory. In L. Berkowitz (Ed.), *Advances in experimental social psychology* (Vol. 6, pp. 1–62). New York: Academic Press.

Blagrove, M., & Akehurst, L. (2000). Effects of sleep loss on confidence-accuracy relationships for reasoning and eyewitness memory. *Journal of Experimental Psychology: Applied, 6*, 59–73.

Blanton, H., Pelham, B. W., DeHart, T., & Carvallo, M. (2001). Overconfidence as dissonance reduction. *Journal of Experimental Social Psychology, 37*, 373–385.

Bornstein, B. H., & Zickafoose, D. J. (1999). "I know it I know it, I know I saw it": The stability of the confidence-accuracy relationship across domains. *Journal of Experimental Psychology: Applied, 5*, 76–88.

Bothwell, R. K., Brigham, J. C., & Pigott, M. A. (1987). An exploratory study of personality differences in eyewitness memory. *Journal of Social Behavior and Personality, 2*, 335–343.

Bothwell, R. K., Deffenbacher, K. A., & Brigham, J. C. (1987). Correlation of eyewitness accuracy and confidence: The optimality hypothesis revisited. *Journal of Applied Psychology, 72*, 691–695.

Bower, G. H. (1967). A multicomponent theory of the memory trace. In K. W. Spence & J. T. Spence (Eds.), *The psychology of learning and motivation: Advances in theory and research* (Vol. 1). New York: Academic Press.

Bradfield, A. L., Wells, G. L., & Olson, E. A. (2002). The damaging effect of confirming feedback on the relation between eyewitness certainty and identification accuracy. *Journal of Applied Psychology, 87*, 112–120.

Brewer, N., Keast, A., & Rishworth, A. (2002). The confidence-accuracy relationship in eyewitness identification: The effects of reflection and disconfirmation on correlation and calibration. *Journal of Experimental Psychology: Applied, 1*, 44–56.

Brigham, J. C., Maass, A., Snyder, L. D., & Spaulding, K. (1982). Accuracy of eyewitness identification in a field setting. *Journal of Personality and Social Psychology, 42*, 673–681.

Burke, D. M., MacKay, D. G., Worthley, J. S., & Wade, E. (1991). On the tip of the tongue: What causes word finding failures in young and old adults? *Journal of Verbal Learning and Verbal Behavior, 6*, 325–337.

Busey, T. A., Tunnicliff, J., Loftus, G. R., & Loftus, E. F. (2000). Accounts of the confidence-accuracy relation in recognition memory. *Psychonomic Bulletin & Review, 7*, 26–48.

Christiansen, S.-Å. (1992). Emotional stress and eyewitness memory: A critical review. *Psychological Bulletin, 25*, 284–309.

Cialdini, R. B. (1987). Compliance principles of compliance professionals: Psychologists of necessity. In M. P. Zanna, J. M. Olson, & C. P. Herman (Eds.), *Social influence: The Ontario symposium* (Vol. 5, pp. 165–184). Hillsdale, NJ: Lawrence Erlbaum Associates.

Clark, S. E. (1997). A familiarity-based account of confidence-accuracy inversions in recognition memory. *Journal of Experimental Psychology: Learning, Memory, and Cognition, 23*, 232–238.

Clifford, B. R., & Hollin, C. R. (1981). Effects of type of incident and the number of perpetrators on eyewitness memory. *Journal of Applied Psychology, 66*, 364–370.

Cutler, B. L., & Penrod, S. D. (1989a). Moderators of the confidence-accuracy correlation in face-recognition: The role of information-processing and base-rates. *Applied Cognitive Psychology, 3*, 95–107.

Cutler, B. L., & Penrod, S. D. (1989b). Forensically relevant moderators of the relation between eyewitness identification accuracy and confidence. *Journal of Applied Psychology, 74*, 650–652.

Deffenbacher, K. A. (1980). Eyewitness accuracy and confidence: Can we infer anything about their relationship? *Law and Human Behavior, 4*, 243–260.

Deffenbacher, K. A. (1991). A maturing of research on the behaviour of eyewitnesses. *Applied Cognitive Psychology, 5*, 377–402.

Deffenbacher, K. A., Bornstein, B. H., Penrod, S. D., & McGorty, E. K. (2004). A meta-analytic review of the effects of high stress on eyewitness memory. *Law and Human Behavior, 28*, 687–706.

Dobbins, I. G., Kroll, N. E. A., & Liu, Q. (1998). Confidence-accuracy inversions in scene recognition: A remember-know analysis. *Journal of Experimental Psychology: Learning, Memory, and Cognition, 24*, 1306–1315.

Dunning, D., & Perretta, S. (2002). Automaticity and eyewitness accuracy: A 10- to 12 second rule for distinguishing accurate from inaccurate positive identifications. *Journal of Applied Psychology, 87*, 951–962.

Dunning, D., & Stern, L. (1992). Examining the generality of eyewitness hypermnesia: A close look at time delay and question type. *Applied Cognitive Psychology, 6*, 643–657.

Dunning, D., & Stern, L. B. (1994). Distinguishing accurate from inaccurate eyewitness identifications via inquiries about decision processes. *Journal of Personality and Social Psychology, 67*, 818–835.

Ebbesen, E. B., & Rienick, C. B. (1998). Retention interval and eyewitness memory for events and personal identifying attributes. *Journal of Applied Psychology, 83*, 745–762.

Fenigstein, A., Scheier, M. F., & Buss, A. H. (1975). Public and private self-consciousness: Assessment and theory. *Journal of Consulting and Clinical Psychology, 43*, 522–527.

Festinger, L. (1957). *A theory of cognitive dissonance.* Stanford, CA: Stanford University Press.

Fleet, M. L., Brigham, J. C., & Bothwell, R. K. (1987). The confidence-accuracy relationship: The effects of confidence assessment and choosing. *Journal of Applied Social Psychology, 17*, 171–187.

Garrioch, L., & Brimacombe, C. A. E. (2001). Lineup administrators' expectations: Their impact on eyewitness confidence. *Law and Human Behavior, 25*, 299–315.

Granhag, P. A. (1997). Realism in eyewitness confidence as a function of type of event witnessed and repeated recall. *Journal of Applied Psychology, 82*, 599–613.

Haber, R. N., & Haber, L. (2001, November). *A meta-analysis of research on eyewitness lineup identification accuracy.* Paper presented at the annual meeting of the Psychonomics Society, Orlando, FL.

Hall, D. F., Loftus, E. F., & Tousignant, J. P. (1984). Postevent information and changes in recollection for a natural event. In G. L. Wells & E. L. Loftus (Eds.), *Eyewitness testimony: Psychological perspectives* (pp. 124–141). New York: Cambridge.

Hintzman, D. L. (1988). Judgments of frequency and recognition memory in a multiple-trace memory model. *Psychological Review, 95*, 528–551.

Hosch, H. M., Leippe, M. R., Marchioni, P. M., & Cooper, D. S. (1984). Victimization, self-monitoring, and eyewitness identification. *Journal of Applied Psychology, 69*, 280–288.

Hovland, C. I., & Weiss, W. (1951). The influence of source credibility on communication effectiveness. *Public Opinion Quarterly, 15*, 635–650.

Jenkins, F., & Davies, G. (1985). Contamination of facial memory through exposure to misleading composite pictures. *Journal of Applied Psychology, 70*, 164–176.

Juslin, P., Olsson, N., & Winman, A. (1996). Calibration and diagnosticity of confidence in eyewitness identification: Comments on what can be inferred from the low confidence-accuracy correlation. *Journal of Experimental Psychology: Learning, Memory, and Cognition, 22*, 1304–1316.

Kassin, S. M. (1985). Eyewitness identification: Retrospective self-awareness and the accuracy-confidence correlation. *Journal of Personality and Social Psychology, 49*, 878–893.

Kassin, S. M., Ellsworth, P. C., & Smith, V. L. (1989). The "general acceptance" of psychological research on eyewitness testimony: A survey of the experts. *American Psychologist, 44*, 1089–1098.

Kassin, S. M., Rigby, S., & Castillo, S. R. (1991). The accuracy-confidence correlation in eyewitness testimony: Limits and extensions of the retrospective self-awareness effect. *Journal of Personality and Social Psychology, 61*, 698–707.

Kassin, S. M., Tubb, V. A. Hosch, H. M., & Memon, A. (2001). On the "general acceptance" of eyewitness testimony research: A new survey of the experts. *American Psychologist, 56*, 405–416.

Kebbel, M. R., Wagstaff, G. F., & Covey, J. A. (1996). The influence of item difficulty on the relationship between eyewitness confidence and accuracy. *British Journal of Psychology, 87*, 653–662.

Kelley, C. M., & Lindsay, D. S. (1993). Remembering mistaken for knowing: Ease of retrieval as a basis for confidence in answers to general knowledge questions. *Journal of Memory and Language, 32*, 1–24.

Kneller, W., Memon, A., & Stevenage, S. (2001). Simultaneous and sequential lineups: Decision processes of accurate and inaccurate witnesses. *Applied Cognitive Psychology, 15*, 659–671.

Koriat, A. (1997). Monitoring one's own knowledge during study: A cue-utilization approach to judgments of learning. *Journal of Experimental Psychology: General, 126*, 349–370.

Leippe, M. R. (1980). Effects of integrative memorial and cognitive processes on the correspondence of eyewitness accuracy and confidence. *Law and Human Behavior, 4*, 261–274.

Leippe, M. R. (1994). The appraisal of eyewitness testimony. In D. F. Ross, J. D. Read, & M. P. Toglia (Eds.), *Adult eyewitness testimony: Current trends and developments* (pp. 385–417). New York: Cambridge University Press.

Leippe, M. R. (1995). The case for expert testimony about eyewitness memory. *Psychology, Public Policy, and Law, 1*, 909–959.

Leippe, M. R., Eisenstadt, D., Rauch, S. M., & Stambush, M. A. (2006). Effects of social-comparative memory feedback on eyewitnesses' identification confidence, suggestibility, and retrospective memory reports. *Basic and Applied Social Psychology, 28*, 201–220.

Leippe, M. R., & Elkin, R. A. (1987). When motives clash: Issue involvement and response involvement as determinants of persuasion. *Journal of Personality and Social Psychology, 52*, 269–278.

Leippe, M. R., Rauch, S. M., & Eisenstadt, D. (2006). *Cueing confidence in eyewitness identifications: The roles of lineup instructions and presumed memory for the witnessed event.* Manuscript under review, Saint Louis University.

Leippe, M. R., Manion, A. P., & Romanczyk, A. (1992). Eyewitness persuasion: How and how well do factfinders judge the accuracy of adults' and children's memory reports? *Journal of Personality and Social Psychology, 63*, 181–197.

Leippe, M. R., Wells, G. L., & Ostrom, T. M. (1978). Crime seriousness as a determinant of accuracy in eyewitness identification. *Journal of Applied Psychology, 63*, 345–351.

Lindsay, D. S. (1994). Memory source monitoring and eyewitness testimony. In D. F. Ross, J. D. Read, & M. P. Toglia (Eds.), *Adult eyewitness testimony: Current trends and developments* (pp. 27–55). New York: Cambridge University Press.

Lindsay, D. S., Nilson, E., & Read, J. D. (2000). Witnessing-condition heterogeneity and witnesses' versus investigators' confidence in the accuracy of witnesses' identification decisions. *Law and Human Behavior, 24*, 685–697.

Lindsay, D. S., Read, J. D., & Sharma, K. (1998). Accuracy and confidence in person identitifcation: The relationship is strong when witnessing conditions vary widely. *Psychological Science, 9*, 215–218.

Lindsay, R. C. L. (1985). Confidence and accuracy of eyewitness identification from lineups. *Law and Human Behavior, 10*, 229–239.

Lindsay, R. C. L., Wallbridge, H., & Drennan, D. (1987). Do clothes make the man? An exploration of the effect of lineup attire on eyewitness identification accuracy. *Canadian Journal of Behavioral Science, 19*, 463–478.

Lindsay, R. C. L., & Wells, G. L. (1985). Improving eyewitness identifications from lineups: Simultaneous versus sequential lineup presentation. *Journal of Applied Psychology, 70*, 556–564.

Lindsay, R. C. L., Wells, G. L., & Rumpel, C. (1981). Can people detect eyewitness identification accuracy within and between situations? *Journal of Applied Psychology, 66*, 79–89.

Loftus, E. F. (1981). Mentalmorphosis: Alterations in memory produced by the mental bonding of new information to old. In J. Long & A. Baddeley (Eds.), *Attention and performance: IX* (pp. 417–434). Hillsdale, NJ: Lawrence Erlbaum Associates.

Loftus, E. F., Donders, K., Hoffman, H. G., & Schooler, J. W. (1989). Creating new memories that are quickly accessed and confidently held. *Memory & Cognition, 17*, 607–616.

Loftus, E. F., & Ketcham, K. (1991). *Witness for the defense: The accused, the eyewitness, and the expert who puts memory on trial.* New York: St. Martin's Press.

Loftus, E. F., Miller, D. G., & Burns, H. J. (1978). Semantic integration of verbal information into a visual memory. *Journal of Experimental Psychology: Human Learning and Memory, 4*, 19–31.

Lord, C. G., Ross, L., & Lepper, M. R. (1979). Biased assimilation and attitude polarization: The effects of prior theories on subsequently considered evidence. *Journal of Personality and Social Psychology, 37*, 2098–2109.

Luus, C. A. E., & Wells, G. L. (1994). The malleability of eyewitness confidence: Co-witness and perseverance effects. *Journal of Applied Psychology, 79*, 714–723.

Maass, A., & Brigham, J. C. (1982). Eyewitness identification: The role of attention and encoding specificity. *Personality and Social Psychology Bulletin, 8*, 54–59.

Malpass, R. S., & Devine, P. G. (1981). Eyewitness identification: Lineup instructions and the absence of the offender. *Journal of Applied Psychology, 66*, 345–351.

McKelvie, S. J. (1993). Confidence and accuracy in facial memory: Further evidence for the optimality hypothesis. *Perceptual and Motor Skills, 76*, 1257–1258.

Memon, A., Hope, L., & Bull, R. (2003). Exposure duration: Effects on eyewitness accuracy and confidence. *British Journal of Psychology, 94*, 339–354.

Migueles, M., & Garcia-Bajos, E. (1999). Recall, recognition, and confidence patterns in eyewitness testimony. *Applied Cognitive Psychology, 13*, 257–268.

Murdock, B. B., & Duffy, P. O. (1972). Strength theory and recognition memory. *Journal of Experimental Psychology, 94*, 284–290.

Murray, D. M., and Wells, G. L. (1982). Does knowledge that a crime was staged affect eyewitness performance. *Journal of Applied Social Psychology, 12*, 42–53.

Neil v. Biggers, 409 U.S. 188 (1972).

Nolan, J., & Markham, R. (1998). The accuracy-confidence relationship in an eyewitness task: Anxiety as a modifier. *Applied Cognitive Psychology, 12*, 43–54.

Olsson, N. (2000). A comparison of correlation, calibration, and diagnosticity as Measures of the confidence-accuracy relationship in witness identification. *Journal of Applied Psychology, 85*, 504–511.

Olsson, N., & Juslin, P. (1999). Can self-reported encoding strategy and recognition skill be diagnostic of performance in eyewitness identifications. *Journal of Applied Psychology, 84*, 42–49.

O'Rourke, T. E., Penrod, S. D., Cutler, B. L., & Stuve, T. E. (1989). The external validity of eyewitness identification research: Generalizing across subject populations. *Law and Human Behavior, 13*, 385–395.

Paivio, A. (1986). *Mental representations: A dual coding approach*. New York: Oxford University Press.

Penrod, S., & Cutler, B. (1995). Witness confidence and witness accuracy: Assessing their forensic relation. *Psychology, Public Policy, and Law, 1*, 817–845.

Perfect, T. J., & Hollins, T. S. (1999). Feeling-of-knowing judgments do not predict subsequent recognition performance for eyewitness memory. *Journal of Experimental Psychology: Applied, 5*, 250–264.

Perfect, T. J., Hollins, T. S., & Hunt, A. L. R. (2000). Practice and feedback effects on the confidence-accuracy relation in eyewitness memory. *Memory, 4*, 235–244.

Petty, R. E., Brinol, P., & Tormala, Z. L. (2002). Thought confidence as determinant of persuasion: The self-validation hypothesis. *Journal of Personality and Social Psychology, 82*, 722–741.

Pigott, M., & Brigham, J. C. (1985). Relationship between accuracy of prior description and facial recognition. *Journal of Applied Psychology, 70*, 547–555.

Raaijmakers, J. G. W., & Shiffrin, R. M. (1992). Models for recall and recognition. *Annual Review of Psychology, 43*, 205–234.

Read, J. D. (1995). The availability heuristic in person identification: The sometimes misleading consequences of enhanced contextual information. *Applied Cognitive Psychology, 9*, 91–121.

Read, J. D., Lindsay, D. S., & Nicholls, T. (1998). The relationship between confidence and accuracy in eyewitness identification studies: Is the conclusion changing? In C. P. Thompson, D. Bruce, J. D. Read, D. Hermann, D. Payne, & M. P. Toglia (Eds.), *Eyewitness memory: Theoretical and Applied Perspectives* (pp. 107–130). Mahwah, NJ: Lawrence Erlbaum Associates.

Read, J. D., Vokey, J. R., & Hammersley, M. (1990). Changing photos of faces: Effects of exposure duration and photo similarity on recognition and the accuracy-confidence relationship. *Journal of Experimental Psychology: Learning, Memory, and Cognition, 16*, 870–882.

Robinson, M. D., & Johnson, J. T. (1996). Recall memory, recognition memory, and the eyewitness confidence-accuracy correlation. *Journal of Applied Psychology, 81*, 587–594.

Robinson, M. D., & Johnson, J. T. (1998). How not to enhance the confidence-accuracy. Relation: The detrimental effects of attention to the identification process. *Law and Human Behavior, 22,* 409–428.

Robinson, M. D., Johnson, J. T., & Herndon, F. (1997). Reactions time and assessment of cognitive effort as predictors of eyewitness memory accuracy and confidence. *Journal of Applied Psychology, 82,* 416–425.

Roediger, H. L., III, & McDermott, K. B. (1995). Creating false memories: Remembering words not presented in lists. *Journal of Experimental Psychology: Learning, Memory, and Cognition, 21,* 803–814.

Sarason, I. G. (1972). Experimental approaches to test anxiety: Attention and the uses of information. In C. D. Spielberger (Ed.), *Anxiety: Current trends in theory and research* (Vol. 2). New York: Academic Press.

Scheck, B., Neufeld, P., & Dwyer, J. (2000). *Actual innocence: Five days to execution and other dispatches from the wrongly convicted.* New York: Cambridge University Press.

Schooler, J. W., & Engstler-Schooler, T. Y. (1990). Verbal overshadowing of visual memories: Some things are better left unsaid. *Cognitive Psychology, 22,* 36–71.

Schooler, J. W., Gerard, D., & Loftus, E. F. (1986). Qualities of the unreal. *Journal of Experimental Psychology: Learning, Memory, and Cognition, 12,* 171–181.

Schwarz, N., Bless, H., Strack, F., Klumpp, G., Rittenauer-Schatka, H., & Simons, A. (1991). Ease of retrieval as information: Another look at the availability hypothesis. *Journal of Personality and Social Psychology, 61,* 195–202.

Scrivner, E., & Safer, M. A. (1988). Eyewitnesses show hypermnesia for details about a a violent event. *Journal of Applied Psychology, 73,* 371–377.

Shapiro, P. N., & Penrod, S. D. (1986). Meta-analysis of facial identification studies. *Psychological Bulletin, 100,* 139–156.

Shaw, J. S., III. (1996) Increases in eyewitness confidence resulting from postevent questioning. *Journal of Experimental Psychology: Applied, 2,* 126–146.

Shaw, J. S., III, Garven, S., & Wood, J. M. (1997). Co-witness information can have immediate effects on eyewitness memory reports. *Law & Human Behavior, 21,* 503–523.

Shaw, J. S., III, & McClure, K. A. (1996). Repeated postevent questioning can lead to elevated levels of eyewitness confidence. *Law and Human Behavior, 20,* 629–653.

Shaw, J. S., III, & Zerr, T. K. (2003). Extra effort during memory retrieval may be associated with increases in eyewitness confidence. *Law and Human Behavior, 27,* 315–329.

Smith, S. M., Lindsay, R. C. L., & Pryke, S. (2000). Postdictors of eyewitness errors: Can false identifications be diagnosed? *Journal of Applied Psychology, 85,* 542–550.

Smith, V. L., & Ellsworth, P. C. (1987). The social psychology of eyewitness accuracy: Misleading questions and communicator expertise. *Journal of Applied Psychology, 72,* 294–300.

Sporer, S. L. (1991). Deep-deeper-deepest: Encoding strategies and the recognition of human faces. *Journal of Experimental Psychology: Learning, Memory, and Cognition, 17,* 323–333.

Sporer, S. L. (1992). Post-dicting eyewitness accuracy: Confidence, decision-times, and Person descriptions of choosers and non-choosers. *European Journal of Social Psychology, 22,* 157–180.

Sporer, S. L. (1993). Eyewitness identification accuracy, confidence, and decision times in simultaneous and sequential lineups. *Journal of Applied Psychology, 78,* 22–33.

Sporer, S. L., Penrod, S. D., Read, J. D., & Cutler, B. L. (1995). Choosing, confidence, and accuracy: A meta-analysis of the confidence-accuracy relationship in eyewitness identification studies. *Psychological Bulletin, 118,* 315–327.

Steblay, N., Dysart, J., Fulero, S., & Lindsay, R. C. L. (2001). Eyewitness accuracy rates in sequential and simultaneous lineup presentations: A meta-analytic comparison. *Law and Human Behavior, 25,* 459–473.

Taylor, S. E., & Fiske, S. T. (1978). Salience, attention, and attribution: Top of the head phenomena. In L. Berkowitz (Ed.), *Advances in experimental social psychology* (Vol. 11, pp. 249–287). New York: Academic Press.

Tesser, A. (1978). Self-generated attitude change. In L. Berkowitz (Ed.), *Advances in experimental social psychology* (Vol. 11, pp. 288–338). New York: Academic Press.

Tetlock, P. E. (1983). Accountability and complexity of thought. *Journal of Personality and Social Psychology, 45,* 74–83.

Thompson, J. (2000, June 18). I was certain, but I was wrong. *The New York Times,* Section 4, p. 15.

Tversky, A., & Kahneman, A. (1973). Availability: A heuristic for judging frequency and probability. *Cognitive Psychology, 5,* 207–232.

Weber, N., & Brewer, N. (2003). The effect of judgment type and confidence scale on confidence-accuracy calibration in face recognition. *Journal of Applied Psychology, 88,* 490–499.

Weingardt, K. R., Leonesio, R. J., & Loftus, E. F. (1995). Viewing eyewitness research from a metacognitive perspective. In J. Metcalfe & A. P. Shimamura (Eds.), *Metacognition: Knowing about memory* (pp. 157–184). Cambridge, MA: MIT Press.

Weingardt, K. R., Toland, H. K., & Loftus, E. F. (1994). Reports of suggested memories: Do people truly believe them? In D. F. Ross, J. D. Read, & M. P. Toglia (Eds.), *Adult eyewitness testimony: Current trends and developments* (pp. 3–26). New York: Cambridge University Press.

Wells, G. L. (1978). Applied eyewitness testimony research: System variables and estimator variables. *Journal of Personality and Social Psychology, 36,* 1546–1557.

Wells, G. L. (1984). How adequate is human intuition for judging eyewitness testimony. In G. L. Wells & E. L. Loftus (Eds.), *Eyewitness testimony: Psychological perspectives* (pp. 256–272). New York: Cambridge University Press.

Wells, G. L., & Bradfield, A. L. (1998). "Good, you identified the suspect": Feedback to witnesses distorts their reports of the witnessing experience. *Journal of Applied Psychology, 83,* 360–376.

Wells, G. L., & Bradfield, A. L. (1999). Distortions in eyewitnesses' recollections: Can the post-identification-feedback effect be moderated? *Psychological Science, 10,* 138–144.

Wells, G. L., Ferguson, T. J., & Lindsay, R. C. L. (1981). The tractability of eyewitness confidence and its implications for triers of fact. *Journal of Applied Psychology, 66,* 688–696.

Wells, G. L., & Lindsay, R. C. L. (1985). Methodological notes on the accuracy-confidence relation in eyewitness identifications. *Journal of Applied Psychology, 70,* 413–419.

Wells, G. L., Lindsay, R. C. L., & Ferguson, T. J. (1979). Accuracy, confidence, and juror perceptions in eyewitness identification. *Journal of Applied Psychology, 64,* 440–448.

Wells, G. L., Malpass, R. S., Lindsay, R. C. L., Fisher, R. P., Turtle, J. W., & Fulero, S. M. (2000). From the lab to the police station: A successful application of eyewitness research. *American Psychologist, 55,* 581–598.

Wells, G. L., & Murray, D. M. (1984). Eyewitness confidence. In G. L. Wells & E. L. Loftus (Eds.), *Eyewitness testimony: Psychological perspectives* (pp. 155–170). New York: Cambridge University Press.

Wells, G. L., & Olson, E. A. (2003). Eyewitness testimony. *Annual Review of Psychology, 54,* 277–295.

Wells, G. L., Olson, E. A., & Charman, S. D. (2002). The confidence of eyewitnesses in their identifications from lineups. *Current Directions in Psychological Science, 11,* 151–154.

Wells, G. L., Rydell, S, M., & Seelau, E. P. (1993). The selection of distractors for eyewitness lineups. *Journal of Applied Psychology, 78,* 835–844.

Whitley, B. E., Jr., & Greenberg, M. S. (1986). The role of eyewitness confidence in juror perceptions of credibility. *Journal of Applied Social Psychology, 16,* 387–409.

Wickelgren, W. A. (1970). Multitrace strength theory. In D. A. Norman (Ed.), *Models of human memory.* New York: Academic Press.

Woodhead, M. M., & Baddeley, A. D. (1981). Individual differences and memory for faces, pictures, and words. *Memory & Cognition, 9,* 368–370.

Wright, D. B., & Stroud, J. N. (1998). Memory quality and misinformation for peripheral and central objects. *Legal and Criminological Psychology, 3,* 273–286.

Yarmey, A. D., & Jones, H. P. T. (1983). Is the psychology of eyewitness identification a matter of common sense? In S. M. A. Lloyd-Bostock, & B. R. Clifford (Eds.), *Evaluating witness evidence: Recent psychological research and new perspectives* (pp. 13–40). Chichester, England: Wiley.

Yarmey, A. D., & Yarmey, M. J. (1997). Eyewitness recall and duration estimates in field settings. *Journal of Applied Social Psychology, 27,* 330–344.

Yarmey, A. D., Yarmey, A. L., and Yarmey, M. J. (1994). Face and voice identification in showups and lineups. *Applied Cognitive Psychology, 8,* 453–464.

Yuille, J. C., & Daylen, J. (1998). The impact of traumatic events on eyewitness memory. In C. P. Thompson, D. Bruce, J. D. Read, D. Hermann, D. Payne, & M. P. Toglia (Eds.), *Eyewitness memory: Theoretical and applied perspectives* (pp. 155–176). Mahwah, NJ: Lawrence Erlbaum Associates.

17

Distinguishing Accurate Eyewitness Identifications from Erroneous Ones: Post-dictive Indicators of Eyewitness Accuracy

Deanna D. Caputo and David Dunning
Cornell University

An eyewitness has just looked up from the lineup to disclose to the criminal investigator what her decision is. She may have incriminated the suspect as the person who committed the crime. Or, she may have concluded that the culprit is not in the lineup. The criminal investigator now faces the question that is the central issue discussed in this chapter: how to tell whether the witness's decision is an accurate one or one that is wrong. What signs in the eyewitness's behavior does the investigator look for? What questions should be asked of the witness? What circumstances surrounding the crime or the identification procedure should be noted? In a sense, the critical task facing the investigator is one of *post-diction*: The investigator must now look back on all of the information available to determine whether that eyewitness's decision is likely to be an accurate one.

In this chapter we review what the psychological research literature suggests the criminal investigator should do in this situation. We discuss *post-dictive* indicators that help to distinguish accurate from inaccurate eyewitnesses. We begin by talking about historical perspectives on post-dicting eyewitness accuracy, starting with the information the Supreme Court suggested investigators should look for in the case of *Neil v. Biggers*. We continue by discussing newer research suggesting that investigators should query witnesses about how they reached their identification, or at least observe how long it takes them to reach an identification.

We also examine how various eyewitness decisions can be used to inform criminal investigators as to whether they have the culprit in hand. Finally, we discuss outstanding issues still left open by all of this research. And, along the way, we offer a few recommendations about how criminal investigators can diagnose eyewitness accuracy and avoid eyewitness error.

HISTORICAL OVERVIEW:
THE *NEIL V. BIGGERS* CRITERIA

In 1972, in the case of *Neil v. Biggers*, the U.S. Supreme Court took an official position about how to evaluate the accuracy of eyewitness identification evidence. The issue before the Court centered on which procedures for pretrial eyewitness identifications violated due process of the suspect. Prior to this case, due process concerns focused on the suggestiveness on the part of criminal investigators. In *Neil v. Biggers*, the Court downplayed the importance of police procedures and proposed that the crucial issue was the competence of the witness. Did the witness show characteristics associated with accurate eyewitness identifications? If so, the witness was presumed to be resistant to whatever suggestive procedures the criminal investigators may have used. The Court then used its intuition and experience to specify five factors that it believed are correlated with eyewitness identification accuracy and that could be used to post-dict whether an eyewitness was accurate. Those five factors were:

a.   The opportunity of the witness to view the criminal, at the time of the crime,
b.   the witness's degree of attention,
c.   the accuracy of the witness' prior description of the criminal,
d.   the level of certainty demonstrated by the witness at the time of confrontation,
e.   the length of time between the crime and the confrontation (*Neil v. Biggers*, p. 199).

After the *Neil v. Biggers* criteria (henceforth referred to as the *Biggers* criteria) were identified, judges and jurors were told to pay particular attention to these five variables when assessing the credibility of eyewitness evidence, a practice that is still standard today. Thus, assessing the actual post-dictive value of these criteria is crucial, especially since survey data indicate that people genuinely do believe that all five criteria are important determinants of identification accuracy (Lindsay, 1994). Over the years since the *Biggers* decision, a voluminous amount of empirical research has focused on these criteria and provides a comprehensive and nuanced assessment of the value of the five indicators specified in the case.

Opportunity to View the Criminal

The first of the *Biggers* criteria is the opportunity of the witness to view the criminal at the time of the crime. This post-dictor concerns both quantity and quality of view. Intuitively, jurors should be confident in eyewitnesses who had long and unobstructed views of the criminals. Much work in facial recognition has shown that one aspect of the opportunity to view the criminal, namely, increasing the amount of time a person views another individual's face, leads to boosts in recognition accuracy (Ellis, Davies, & Shepherd, 1978; for a review see Shapiro & Penrod, 1986). However, two caveats apply to these findings. First, facial recognition studies have tended to assess memory with the exact same photographs that the person originally studied. More recent experiments have shown that using different and dissimilar photographs reduces the impact of exposure time on recognition accuracy (Read, Vokey, & Hammersley, 1990).

Second, at times, the only way to gauge how much time a witness had to view the culprit is to ask the witness to estimate it. People, unfortunately, tend to overestimate the duration of events (Munsterberg, 1908; Buckhout, Alper, Chern, Silverberg, & Slomovits, 1974; Shiffman & Bobko, 1974). This temporal bias was reliably found, unless the witness was specifically attending to some other external source of temporal duration (i.e., a clock). In one illustrative study (Wells & Murray, 1983), participants who had only 1 minute of actual exposure to an individual on a video estimated having 4.5 minutes of unobstructed exposure, with participants on average estimating that the 5-minute video had lasted for over 9 minutes. Other research has found that witnesses' verbal descriptions are influenced by the amount of light present at the time of the crime (Yarmey, 1986), as well as by positive feedback. After being told that they had successfully identified a suspect out of a lineup, witnesses inflated their judgments of how good a view of the criminal they had (Wells & Bradfield, 1998).

In sum, there is no question that the opportunity to view the assailant will influence the witness's ability to identify that person later on. There are, however, variables that affect the relationship between this criterion and eyewitness accuracy that need more empirical work. Future work needs to further address other conditions, including obstructions of view and witness's distance from the perpetrator, that influence opportunity to view. More importantly, future work needs to be conducted on how well people's self-reports of these different witnessing conditions predict their actual witnessing conditions and their recognition accuracy.

Degree of Attention

Some argue that eyewitness accuracy rests less on the opportunity to view the criminal and more on the amount and *type* of attention the witness gives the perpetrator. Did the witness give the culprit only a passing glance? Did the witness study the culprit's face? Did the witness focus on individual facial features or try to ascertain the specific motives of the culprit? There are many different ways that witnesses can attend to a culprit, and the seriousness and depth of this attention can influence identification accuracy in significant ways. Indeed, a meta-analysis of facial recognition studies found that "quality of viewing," which focused centrally on the type of attention that participants paid to the face (as well as knowledge of future recognition task and the mode of presentation at study) was the most important determinant of facial identification performance (Shapiro & Penrod, 1986).

Several factors influence an eyewitness's attention to the crime and criminal. Eyewitnesses often do not realize that they have witnessed a crime until after the criminal has fled the scene, or until police arrive on the scene. These witnesses may have had a significant opportunity to view the perpetrator, yet they probably had little reason to pay great attention. In one study, researchers showed that when people were aware of the value of an item before a surprise staged theft, they were significantly more accurate in their identification than those who were told the value afterward, were told that the item was trivial before, or were told that the item was trivial afterward (Leippe, Wells, & Ostrom, 1978). All conditions had the same opportunity to view the criminal, but crime seriousness (presumable acting via motivation) affected their degree of attention (i.e., amount of attention) and, ultimately, their ability to accurately identify the thief.

The type of thoughts eyewitnesses have while viewing the culprit also potentially influences their accuracy. As found in work on "depth" of processing (Craik & Lockhart, 1972), people making "deep," abstract, and meaningful inferences about another person while they view them, such as assessing the personality of the individual, later show greater recognition accuracy than those processing the face in a superficial, concrete, and detail-oriented manner, such as concentrating on the person's facial features (Wells & Hryciw, 1984). Why would more abstract inferences (i.e., personality inferences) produce greater identification accuracy than physical feature judgments? Perhaps because abstract inferences require holistic processing of the face, whereas the physical judgments require only processing of peripheral details, and holistic processing has been associated with successful facial recognition (Diamond & Carey, 1986; Rhodes, Tan, Brake, & Taylor, 1989; Sergent, 1984).

In sum, degree of attention does seem to affect eyewitness accuracy and is a reasonable criterion for triers of fact. However, its use is problematic. Once again, assessing a witness's degree of attention means asking him or her to report it, and such reports might be open to errors and biases in memory, or be influenced by feedback from criminal investigators. Thus, although research shows that certain types of attention (e.g., knowing that a crime is in progress, thinking about the face deeply) enhance eyewitness performance, researchers do not know whether *self-reports* about attention to the crime predict eyewitness performance. The question then remains whether self-reports of attention predict accuracy. Can investigators frame questions for eyewitnesses that will accurately determine what kind of attention they were paying to the criminal (Wells & Murray, 1983)? Future research should focus on determining these questions.

Accuracy of Prior Description

The Court stated that "accuracy of the witness' prior description of the criminal" is the third criterion that triers of fact should consider as an indicator of subsequent lineup identification accuracy (Neil v. Biggers, p. 199). However, Wells and Murray (1983) were quick to point out that the criterion, as it is written, requires the assumption that the suspect is guilty. Otherwise, how would one assess the accuracy of the description if one does not presume that the suspect is actually the culprit to be described? In retrospect, one could presume that the Court was really interested in the degree of similarity or congruence between the witness's description of the criminal and the defendant's physical characteristics. This interpretation of the *Biggers* criteria is, of course, the same as determining accuracy if the defendant is guilty—but the guilt or innocence of the defendant cannot be assumed until a jury trial is complete, if even then. In any event, most researchers have found witness or participant descriptions not to be diagnostic of identification accuracy (Bothwell, Deffenbacher, & Brigham, 1987; Deffenbacher, 1991; Geiselman, Schroppel, Tubridy, Konishi, & Rodriquez, 2000; Goldstein, Johnson, & Chance, 1979; Pigott & Brigham, 1985). Further research has shown that the completeness of a witness's description also fails to correlate with identification accuracy (Wells, 1985; van Koppen & Lochun, 1997; Geiselman et al., 2000; Pozzulo & Warren, 2003). Indeed, only one study has found a modest positive correlation. In this study, Wells (1985) sought to determine whether the correlation was due to (a) good describers being good identifiers or (b) faces that were easier to describe being easier to identify. After pairing one participant's description with another participant's identification, of the same face, he found an equivalent correlation between description and accuracy. Thus, he concluded that the description-identification accuracy correlation had to be due to the characteristics of the target faces (i.e., some faces were easy to describe and identify, whereas others were more difficult).

Taken together, these findings appear to cast doubt on the U.S. Supreme Court's endorsement of accuracy of description as a good predictor of the value of any subsequent identification. Although at an intuitive level the match of eyewitnesses' descriptions to their identifications should be meaningful, there are also other possible reasons for such a relationship to arise. Most significant, the witness's prior description often determines the content of the lineup. Hence, if there is an error in the description there is a good chance that it will carry over into the lineup identification. However, the Wells (1985) study suggests a correlation between description accuracy and identification success due to "target factors" (i.e., whether the culprit's face is easy to describe and identify), and further work could examine what influences those target factors.

Witness Certainty

The *Biggers* criterion for assessing eyewitness evidence that has received the most attention by researchers is the confidence with which witnesses make their eyewitness judgments. This is probably due to the fact that jurors commonly believe that eyewitness confidence is a valid sign of accuracy (Brigham & Bothwell, 1983; Wells, Lindsay, & Ferguson, 1979). Despite the power of the intuition that confidence is closely linked to accuracy, research into the relationship paints a difficult and complicated portrait (Deffenbacher, 1980; Leippe, 1980; Wells & Murray, 1983, 1984). Overall, the relationship is weak to modest, at best, and depends on a number of circumstances. The magnitude of the accuracy-confidence relationship was influenced by exposure duration to target faces (Bothwell, Deffenbacher, & Brigham, 1987), completeness and distinctiveness of those features (Cutler & Penrod, 1988), and similarity between initial target photograph and identification photograph (Read, Vokey, & Hammersley, 1990). Greater exposure, more complete faces, and greater similarity of photos allowed for greater predictability of accuracy from confidence. Most important, a meta-analysis combining data from 30 studies indicates that the correlation between accuracy and confidence exists to a modest extent only among those who choose someone out of a lineup: Witnesses accurately choosing the culprit tend to be moderately more confident than those who make a false-positive identification.

Among those rejecting the lineup (i.e., saying the culprit is not present), confidence and accuracy are unrelated (Sporer, Penrod, Read, & Cutler, 1995). Eyewitness confidence can also be contaminated. It is not uncommon for an eyewitness to be asked multiple times by police officers and lawyers to describe the perpetrator they saw and to be asked to look at mugshots or create a composite. Research has demonstrated that repeated post-event questioning, involving recall or recognition practice, can lead to higher witness confidence ratings without affecting accuracy (Shaw & McClure, 1996), thus obscuring any confidence-accuracy relationship that might be there initially. Furthermore, positive feedback to eyewitnesses (e.g., telling them they chose the suspect) can raise confidence with no impact on accuracy (Wells & Bradfield, 1998, 1999), again reducing any confidence-accuracy relationship. Because of this and other issues, most researchers to date have concluded that the courts should not rely solely on certainty to infer accuracy (for a complete review of these issues, see Leippe and Eisenstadt, this volume).

Time Between Crime and Identification

This final criterion from the *Biggers* case reflects the basic understanding that forgetting increases with time. Studies looking at memory decay over time have shown that memory for unfamiliar faces does decrease over time (Chance, Goldstein, & McBride, 1975; Davies, Ellis, & Shepherd, 1978; Laughery, Fessler, Lenorovitz, & Yoblick, 1974; Shapiro & Penrod, 1986). Indeed, the amount of decay tends to be far greater than people expect (Wells & Murray, 1983). As a consequence, identifications after a significant delay can be quite problematic. Future work needs to determine the degree of decay at tremendous, but not uncommon, time delays of 6 months or a year. These delays may lead to significant decreases in eyewitness memory and accuracy. At some point in time, time delay between crime and identification may even lead to such profound memory decay that it could be considered a central post-dicting variable.

Time delay presents other dangers beyond simple decay. The longer the interval between the crime and attempts to provide eyewitness evidence, the greater likelihood that the witness will experience events that will contaminate and distort their memory. They might be exposed to misinformation, and a tremendous amount of research has documented the profound impact that misleading information might have on memory (see Loftus, 1997). The witness might be exposed to other stimuli that interfere with their memory for the crime and the perpetrator, such as mugshots, composite sketches, media descriptions, or pictures, that could become incorporated into their memory for the culprit (for a more thorough discussion of the time delay issues, see Dysart and Lindsay, this volume).

Summary

Of course, all of the research described above did not exist at the time the Supreme Court proposed the criteria criminal investigators and triers of fact should evaluate eyewitnesses on when deciding whether they were accurate. As a consequence, the Court was compelled to rely on intuition and the reactions of jurors in selecting what aspects of eyewitness testimony triers of fact should pay particular attention to in determining the validity of eyewitness evidence. However, years later, researchers know quite a bit about the criteria set forth in *Biggers* (e.g., Bradfield & Wells, 2000). In some ways, the proposals of the Court have been found to have some validity. In other ways, the Court has been found to have erred in its intuition. In yet other ways, the links between the criteria and eyewitness accuracy have turned out to be complex.

The *Biggers* criteria, however, present another layer of complication beyond their validity, in that it is sometimes difficult to determine how they can be applied to individual eyewitness cases. At times, the criteria are difficult to define and to quantify. Opportunity to view the culprit is one such criterion, in that it is tricky to list and then to measure all of the factors that influence a witness's chances to observe the culprit. The length of time the culprit is in view can be assessed, although problematically, but what about the witness's eyesight, his or her distance from the perpetrator, whether the perpetrator turned his or her face full-on toward the witness, whether there were any obstructions to view, or whether the lighting conditions at the locale were optimal? All of these factors matter, but it is difficult if not impossible to measure them, much less to determine their impact. Indeed, one aspect of opportunity to view, the length of time the witness saw the perpetrator, may not be easy to establish. If a surveillance camera records the crime, one can obtain an accurate sense of how long the perpetrator was in view. However, if no camera is present, the witness's self-report can be quite faulty.

As a consequence, although some of the *Biggers* criteria are useful in that they are indicative of accuracy, at times they are not practical to use with exactitude with any specific eyewitness. What would be more practical would be assessments closer to the eyewitness decision itself, assessments that could be taken just after an eyewitness has reached a judgment after viewing a lineup. Such criteria could be more precisely defined and measured, and because they are derived directly from the eyewitness decision itself, they hold much promise to help resolve whether a witness has decided correctly. Of all the *Biggers* criteria, only witness certainty fits this description. One can measure witness confidence right after the identification, and confidence, if properly handled, does distinguish accurate from inaccurate eyewitnesses—but only in some circumstances and only to a partial degree (Sporer et al., 1995).

DECISION PROCESSES

Given the difficulties in using the criteria discussed above, particularly confidence, more recent research has turned toward identifying other indicators of eyewitness accuracy and error. Over the last decade, researchers have increasingly discovered that asking eyewitnesses how they reached their identification decisions is a fruitful way to distinguish accurate eyewitness identifications from erroneous ones, at least when it comes to witnesses who choose an individual from a lineup. Accurate and inaccurate eyewitnesses reach their decisions via different cognitive routes.

How Decision Processes Differ

Decisions by accurate eyewitnesses tend to be *automatic* and *absolute* (Dunning & Stern, 1994; Dunning & Perretta, 2002). By *automatic* we mean that accurate eyewitnesses reach their decisions swiftly, with little or no conscious strategy or effort. They often have little awareness of what leads them to know that the person they chose was the culprit, describing their decisions not so much as something they authored but rather as something that came to them. By *absolute* we mean that accurate witnesses reach their identifications by comparing the culprit's appearance with the image in their memory. If the match between the culprit's appearance and their memory reaches some adequate absolute standard, they identify the culprit, without any consideration of other lineup members.

Decisions by inaccurate eyewitnesses, in contrast, tend to be *conscious, effortful*, and *relative*. Eyewitnesses making false-positive identifications tend to think their way into an identification. They employ a deliberative and effortful strategy to determine which of the people in the lineup they will pick. Usually, their conscious strategy is to compare the individuals in the lineup to each other, eliminating individuals until they narrow their choice to the best option available. In doing so, they practice a *relative judgment strategy*, in that they choose the most likely individual relative to all the others.

The reasons for these distinctions between accurate and inaccurate eyewitnesses are rather clear. Facial recognition is a task that tends to be over-learned and over-practiced across a lifetime, which means that people are expert at it. With such expertise, the cognitive mechanisms underlying facial recognition become rapid, and witnesses complete their task without any conscious monitoring or awareness (Bahrick, Bahrick, & Wittlinger, 1975; Ellis, 1981). For example, suppose the reader looked up from reading this chapter to find that Harrison Ford or Cameron Diaz had walked into the room. The act of recognizing such celebrity faces is automatic—the recognition occurs immediately without conscious intervention. Indeed, Hay, Young, and Ellis (1986) discovered that people recognized the faces of well-known celebrities out of lineups rather quickly and were not influenced by the number of distracting faces also included in the lineup.

Extending this observation that facial recognition is an expert process to the eyewitness situation explains potential differences in the decision processes of accurate and inaccurate eyewitnesses. If the eyewitness has a good memory of the perpetrator, this will lead to a rapid and accurate identification. However, if the eyewitness does not have such an automatic experience, he or she still has the option of effortfully comparing the lineup choices to arrive at the best decision, given an imperfect memory.

A growing body of empirical evidence supports this automatic/absolute versus effortful/relative distinction between witnesses making accurate and false-positive identifications. Dunning and Stern (1994) exposed college students to a videotape of a staged crime and later asked them to identify the culprit out of a photo spread. They were then given several options of how they could describe the process that led to their identification. Those choosing accurately were more likely to say that *I just recognized him, I cannot explain why* and *His face just popped out at me*. They further stated that the other photographs had had little influence over their decision and that their decision had been a product of their memory, not the photographs they were shown. Inaccurate eyewitnesses were more likely to state that *I compared the photos to each other in order to narrow the choices, I first eliminated the ones not him, then chose among the rest*, and *He was the closest person to what I remember, but not exact*. They were also more likely to say that their decision had been a product of the photographs they were shown and not their memory. Other studies, using the same or similar probes for automatic versus deliberative decision processes, have revealed the same differences between accurate and inaccurate eyewitnesses (Dunning & Perretta, 2002; Smith, Lindsay, & Pryke, 2000; Stern & Dunning, 1994). The distinction has also been shown to be useful beyond the lineup identification task. When witnesses are asked to describe the details of a crime, they are more likely to provide information effortlessly and quickly when they are accurate than when they are in error (Robinson & Johnson, 1998; Robinson, Johnson, & Herndon, 1997).

Using other methods, researchers have shown that inaccurate eyewitnesses make their decisions in an effortful relative judgment strategy more often than do accurate witnesses. Lindsay and Wells (1980) studied how eyewitnesses made identifications when the culprit was absent from the lineup, thus making any positive identification erroneous. One innocent individual was chosen for study because he shared some superficial resemblance to the perpetrator. His photograph was placed in one of two lineups—one in which all of the other individuals were rather similar to the original perpetrator and one in which they were quite dissimilar. Only 31% of participants chose the person superficially resembling the perpetrator when other lineup choices were similar, but 70% chose the person when other choices were dissimilar (see also Wells, 1984, for related data).

In addition, Lindsay and Bellinger (1999) asked participants to make identifications in a variety of eyewitness formats, including variations of the simultaneous and sequential lineup procedure. Afterward, witnesses were asked to describe how absolute versus relative their decisions had been. Witnesses making false-positive identifications described their decisions as more relative than those choosing correctly. Additionally, participants in some conditions had been instructed to use an absolute decision strategy when making an identification and thus avoid comparing the photographs to each other. The experimenter then left the room so that participants could make their identifications in private, but surreptitiously watched participants through a crack in the door while they looked over the photographs. Some participants disobeyed their instructions and compared the photographs to each other—and these participants made up the bulk of those who made false-positive identifications.

Decision Time

Although the research above suggests that witness's reports of their decision processes are valuable for separating accurate eyewitness identifications from erroneous ones, it is likely to do so only imperfectly. It has long been known that people are notoriously unskilled at accurately describing how they reach their decisions (Nisbett & Wilson, 1977). In the eyewitness context, researchers have observed participants comparing photographs, only to be told by participants later that no comparison had occurred (Lindsay & Bellinger, 1999). If people fail to have accurate access to internal mental events, or if they are prone to lie on occasion, then the worth of their self-reports in distinguishing eyewitness accuracy from error will be diminished.

Given the imperfect nature of witness self-reports, researchers have also recently been looking for objective indicators of decision processes that might distinguish accurate identifications from erroneous ones, indicators that can be independently measured and that do not depend on witness self-reports. Luckily, there is one simple and easily measured indicator of decision processes: how quickly eyewitnesses make their identifications.

Recent research has shown that accurate witnesses reach their identifications far more quickly than inaccurate eyewitnesses. For example, Sporer (1993) asked witnesses to make identifications from either simultaneous or sequential lineups. Whichever type of lineup witnesses were shown, accurate witnesses took less time than their inaccurate counterparts to reach their decisions. However, this difference arose, again, only for witnesses making positive identifications and did not extend to those who rejected the lineup (i.e., decided the culprit was not present). Other research labs have replicated these findings for memory of faces and details of the crime (Dunning & Stern, 1994; Kassin, 1985; Robinson et al., 1997; Sporer, 1992, 1994). For example, Smith et al. (2000) found that 69% of witnesses who made their identification within 15 seconds were likely to be accurate, but that only 18% of those taking longer than 30 seconds were correct. However, work on decision time produces both a mystery and an opportunity. The mystery centers on how fast an eyewitness must be for a criminal investigator to be confident that the witness has reached a correct identification. Often, an investigator has only one eyewitness to a crime who makes one identification. If that witness takes 20 seconds to make a positive identification, should that be considered fast, and thus the witness accurate, or should it be considered slow, and the witness inaccurate? Comparing the speeds of accurate and inaccurate eyewitnesses does not address this issue, although it suggests that speed of the witness is a crucial indicator of eyewitness accuracy.

To resolve the mystery faced by the criminal investigator, one would have to determine some absolute time standard or boundary to use to differentiate the quick and the correct from the slow and inaccurate. However, gathering data on eyewitness speed offers an opportunity to determine whether such an absolute standard exists. Using data from Dunning and Stern (1994), as well as some additional studies, Dunning and Perretta (2002) attempted to determine whether there was some reliable time boundary that separated accurate from inaccurate witnesses. In all, Dunning and Perretta examined data from four different studies. In each study, they examined the time boundary that best differentiated accurate witnesses from inaccurate ones and then looked to see if similar boundaries emerged across all studies. They found that a boundary of between 10 and 12 seconds did the best job of separating accurate witnesses from inaccurate ones. Witnesses making their identification within 10 seconds made accurate identifications 87% of the time. Accuracy rates plunged to 50% for witnesses even taking only slightly longer than 10 to 12 seconds to make their choice and stayed at that level all along the rest of the time continuum. From this Dunning and Perretta concluded that a quick identification (i.e., taking place within 10 to 12 seconds) was very likely to be accurate, but that the accuracy of an identification taking longer could not be diagnosed (although see Weber, Brewer, Wells, Semmler, & Keast, 2004, for an example that is not consistent with this conclusion).

IDENTIFICATION OF LINEUP DISTRACTORS

Recent research also suggests that criminal investigators may already typically have information in hand that can be used to assess eyewitness accuracy—if they shift somewhat how they look at the issue. In their *information gain approach* to eyewitness accuracy, Wells and Olson (2002) shift their attention away from asking whether an eyewitness decided accurately. Instead, they emphasize whether an eyewitness has been presented a culprit-present or -absent lineup. In doing so, they then explore what a witness's decision (i.e., choosing the suspect, choosing another person, stating the culprit is not present, or refusing to reach a decision) says about the likelihood that the culprit is, indeed, present in the lineup. In particular, they focus on how much information is gained from the witness's decision.

Wells and Olsen (2002) begin with the premise that criminal investigators often approach the lineup with some suspicions about the likely guilt of the suspect. These suspicions can be converted to probabilities that can range from 0% to 100%. Wells and Olsen then ask how much investigators should shift these probability estimates once they learn of the witness's decision. Obviously, if the witness chooses the culprit, the investigator's probability estimate should rise; if the witness claims the culprit is not in the lineup, the investigator should lower that estimate. But by how much?

Wells and Olsen (2002), reanalyzing past data, discover that how much investigators should shift their probability level depends on a variety of circumstances. First, it depends on the investigator's initial probability estimate, taken before the lineup, that the suspect is guilty. If the investigator thinks that the suspect is not very likely to be guilty, then a positive identification should serve to move that impression more than if the investigator thought the chances were high for the suspect to be guilty. However, we do note, as do the authors, that often the *true* probability that the suspect is guilty is something that can only be guessed or estimated—it is rarely known with certainty. That is, the investigator may have some notion of the probable guilt of the culprit, based on other evidence and circumstances, before an identification, but that notion does not necessarily match the true probability.

Information gain, however, depends importantly on other circumstances. Information gain for sequential lineups is typically higher than it is for simultaneous lineups, because sequential lineups avoid false-positive identification errors. Information gain is also greater when the lineup is fair rather than when it is biased (Wells & Olson, 2002). But, importantly, an information gain analysis reveals that a decision by the eyewitness to incriminate someone other than the suspect in the lineup—in other words, a distracting choice—can be quite informative. Depending on the circumstances (e.g., is the lineup fair, would the investigator harbor heavy suspicions about the suspect), positive identification of a distractor provides substantial evidence that the suspect is innocent. When people identify a filler lineup choice, it is usually indicative that the lineup does not contain the actual culprit. Because of this, identifications of filler individuals should not be ignored by criminal investigators—such choices may successfully post-dict that the suspect is not guilty.

RECOMMENDATIONS FOR RESEARCHERS

The last 10 years of research have been spent identifying potentially valuable indicators of eyewitness accuracy, as well as how those indicators combine, compare, and contrast with previously identified indicators. However, research on these post-dictive indicators is far from complete. Indeed, three particularly crucial research avenues, among many possible, stand out as crucial. First, the indicators that researchers have identified work only for choosers (i.e., people who correctly or incorrectly choose a face out of a lineup) but not for non-choosers. Second, more work is needed on how these indicators can be practically used in the police station to diagnose eyewitness accuracy with individual witnesses. Third, we need to know how well those indicators of accuracy work across a variety of circumstances, particularly those involving cross-race identifications or alternative lineup procedures. Are post-dictors robust in their ability to tell accurate witnesses from inaccurate ones, or are there times in which they are likely to fail?

Non-Choosers

First, although research to date has demonstrated ways to differentiate accurate from inaccurate judgments when dealing with positive identifications (i.e., choosers), it has yet to identify indicators that could distinguish correct rejections of the lineup from incorrect ones. When witnesses decide not to choose someone from the lineup, proclaiming instead that the culprit is not present, how is the criminal investigator to know whether the witness is right or wrong? Such a question has obvious legal importance and clear everyday implications: Knowing when one can conclusively exonerate a suspect is just as important as, if not more important than, knowing when the suspect has been decisively incriminated. However, in research focusing on non-choosers, confidence, decision time, and decision process measures tend not to help investigators discriminate correct from incorrect witnesses (e.g., Dunning & Stern, 1994; Sporer et al., 1995). However, this is only the current state of affairs, and perhaps a more careful examination of the processes by which witnesses reject lineups may give rise to clues to accuracy that could be of use to criminal investigators.

Creating Profiles of the Accurate versus Inaccurate Eyewitness

Second, it may be profitable to create a standard set of post-diction measures that could be used by criminal investigators to categorize individual witnesses as accurate or inaccurate. So far, most of the research has not been conducted with the goal of handing a criminal investigator a checklist and a decision rule to help classify the witness's identification as right or wrong. Instead, the focus has been on testing more general principles (e.g., faster witnesses are more likely to be accurate) that are helpful to investigators in an abstract way but not directly applicable to individual witnesses. Is there any way to combine post-diction information to create decision rules that investigators can use to classify individual witnesses as accurate or not?

Research suggests that this task might be feasible. Smith et al. (2001) used confidence, decision time, and judgment processes to statistically distinguish correct eyewitness identifications from false-positive ones and found that they could successfully classify 67% of eyewitnesses making own-race identifications. Stirring function size of the lineup into the mix, this classification rate rose to 76% (Smith et al., 2000). However, these exercises were statistical in nature and were not designed to provide criminal investigators with a concrete "how-to" for diagnosing accuracy among eyewitnesses they were dealing with. More specifically, they did not describe the boundaries along these variables that separated accurate witnesses from inaccurate ones. To create a how-to, researchers would have to describe those borders. They would have to repeat with multiple variables what Dunning and Perretta (2002) did with the single variable of decision time, showing that a border of 10 to 12 seconds best separated accurate positive identifications from the rest. Researchers would have to take multiple variables and determine the boundaries that best separated accurate from inaccurate identifications or show how the variables could be combined to define a reliable boundary.

Exploring the Generality of Post-dictor Usefulness

Third, it is essential to explore how well post-dicting measures work across a wide variety of circumstances. How well do currently identified indicators work when optimal lineup procedures are not followed, such as when a lineup is biased? How well do they work with children, or the elderly? In any situation where existing decision measures fail, are there alternative measures that do a better job? In particular, we believe future research aiming to explore the generality of eyewitness post-dictors should examine three specific sets of circumstances.

Cross-Racial Identifications

First, a good deal of research has established that cross-race identifications differ significantly from own-race identifications. In particular, people make many more errors trying to identify people of races and ethnicities different from their own. Indeed, in a meta-analysis of the cross-race effect literature, Meissner and Brigham (2001) reported that the chance of a mistaken identification is 1.56 times greater in other-race than in same-race conditions. If this is the case in real investigations, then an African American innocent suspect has a 56% greater chance of being misidentified by a European American eyewitness than by an African American eyewitness.

A good deal of scholarship suggests why people find it more difficult to identify someone of a different race different from their own. The issue is not one of racial attitudes or stereotypes—but one of cognitive expertise. People just tend to spend more time with others of their own race, leading them to process and remember own-race faces in a more complex, configural, and expert way, which leads to more accurate memory (for a review of relevant research, as well as other accounts of cross-race deficits, see Sporer, 2001). But this difference leads to a potential problem for post-dictors of eyewitness accuracy. These post-dictors rely on successful facial recognition being a quick and expert process, as it is with own-race faces. People identify faces more rapidly and automatically to the extent that they remember those faces in a complex and configural way. If they fail to possess these types of memories for the culprit's face, which is typically more common in the cross-race situation, then they may not be quick and automatic in their identification.

It is important, therefore, to know how well post-dictive indicators of eyewitness accuracy (e.g., decision time, judgment processes, as well as more historical indicators such as the *Biggers* criteria) distinguish accuracy and error in cross-race situations. To date, only one study has looked at post-dicting eyewitness accuracy in cross-race circumstances. In that study, researchers looked at how well confidence, decision time, and decision-making strategy could post-dict accuracy in same-race versus cross-race situations (Smith et al., 2001). With same-race identifications, the post-dictors correctly classified the accuracy of the participant 67% of the time. However, in the cross-race situation these same post-dictors were not at all effective at classifying the accuracy of participants. This research highlights the observation that the cross-race effect significantly affects our ability to post-dict eyewitness accuracy and suggests that future research could profitably focus on the cross-race situation. Do these indicators reliably fail to diagnose eyewitness accuracy for cross-race identifications? Do alternative indicators exist that would help distinguish accuracy from error when dealing with cross-race judgments?

Alternative Lineup Procedures

Second, future research must explore how well post-dictive indicators perform when investigators use alternatives to the traditional lineup. One such alternative is the sequential lineup procedure. In this procedure, eyewitnesses are presented with lineup choices (whether photo or live) one at a time in a sequence and must decide for each choice whether or not that person is the perpetrator before being allowed to view the next person. Although eyewitnesses can decide when viewing one person that they are a relatively better match to the perpetrator than the previous person, the eyewitness cannot be sure that the next person (not yet viewed) will not look even more like the perpetrator. This sequential procedure stands in contrast to the traditional simultaneous method, in which all choices are shown at once, and is thought to be an improvement over the simultaneous method because it precludes witnesses from pursuing the relative judgment strategy associated with false-positive identifications. Consistent with this reasoning, witnesses making choices out of a sequential lineup make significantly fewer false-positive judgments, whereas the rate at which they correctly pick the culprit remains relatively unchanged (Lindsay & Wells, 1985).

Results from a recent meta-analysis found that, overall, odds of guilt from identification from a sequential procedure will be twice that of the simultaneous lineup—even considering the slight decrease in correct identifications (Steblay, Dysart, Fulero, & Lindsay, 2001). The sequential lineup also prevents false identifications in situations that push for them, such as when investigators use biased instructions (Lindsay et al., 1991; for a more complete discussion of the sequential versus simultaneous lineups, see Lindsay & Dupuis, this volume). However, the sequential lineup is not perfect. Although false identifications are reduced, they are not eliminated. Thus, the issue of distinguishing accurate identifications from erroneous ones still remains. There are, however, only a few scattered studies looking at how to diagnose eyewitness accuracy when sequential lineups are used. Sporer (1993), for example, found that witnesses accurately choosing the culprit took less time viewing his face than did those who chose an incorrect face. In our lab, we are currently looking at the decision processes of accurate and inaccurate eyewitnesses facing a sequential lineup to see if they can be distinguished (Caputo, 2004). In the case of a sequential lineup, the usual route to inaccuracy for erroneous witnesses—use of a relative judgment strategy—is unavailable to them. However, inaccurate eyewitnesses still show signs of conscious effort in their identifications, mentioning that they consciously compare lineup photographs with their memory of the culprit, and that their choice is not an exact match to their memory. Accurate witnesses, in contrast, describe their decision as a simple match between the image they have in their head of the culprit and the photograph they chose, and they state that the other photographs have little influence on their decision (Caputo, 2004). These results, as well as those of Sporer, provide a good start at determining what post-dictive information would be useful to obtain when witnesses confront sequential lineups.

Future research could also explore ways to post-dict eyewitness accuracy in show-up procedures. A showup is a procedure in which only one person, the suspect, is presented to the eyewitness, either in a picture or in a live viewing, and the witness is asked to indicate if the suspect is the criminal. Although quite common in everyday criminal investigation, show-up procedures have proved to be quite controversial within the research community, with some favoring the procedure over traditional lineups and others opposing. On the favorable side, one could presume that show-ups should act much like the sequential lineup, in that showing the witness only one choice prevents a relative judgment strategy and thus also a bias toward choosing (Gonzalez, Ellsworth, & Pembroke, 1993). As well, show-ups can be conducted soon after the crime while the witness's memory is fresh. However, on the negative side, one could argue that witnesses want to be helpful, and thus may be biased to implicate anyone that the police suspect could have committed the crime (Wells & Lindsay, 1980; Yarmey, Yarmey, & Yarmey, 1996; Behrman & Davey, 2001). Each side of the debate has data supporting their arguments (see Dysart & Lindsay, this volume).

Given this state of affairs, and the fact that showups continue to be conducted in police stations and on street corners every day, future research could profitably explore post-dictors that detect eyewitness accuracy and error for witnesses making show-up judgments. One might presume, although future data is needed, that accurate witnesses will identify culprits quickly and automatically and that inaccurate witnesses will require more cognitive effort to reach a judgment, but what form will that cognitive effort take? Will it express itself in the amount of time it takes to reach a judgment?

RECOMMENDATIONS FOR INVESTIGATORS

"The police lineup is both the critical means of presenting eyewitness identification in court and one of the most dangerous tools of justice" (Brooks, 1983, p. 45). There are a number of things that police investigators can do to assist in the successful post-diction of eyewitness accuracy. These include collecting and recording post-dicting information throughout an investigation and discouraging eyewitnesses from using relative judgments, which includes protecting innocent suspects through procedural safeguards. We recommend that investigators follow researchers' lead in using modern procedures for creating and implementing diagnostic and unbiased lineups.

Collecting and Recording More Information

Through the collection of additional information, that may seem invaluable at the time, investigators and jurors will be able to better assess the accuracy of each eyewitness's package of information. That package includes their description of culprit, details of the event, decision processes, decision time, and confidence during an identification, as well as any feedback they are given after the fact. Whether or not any eyewitnesses have chosen a lineup distractor could be noted, in that identifications of distractors can indicate that the defendant is innocent (Wells & Olson, 2002). The research suggests that providing triers of fact with information about witnesses' decision processes, decision time, and confidence would help them better determine the eyewitness's accuracy. For example, educating people about decision-processing differences helped them to assess an eyewitness's identification, particularly when the witness was wrong. Dunning and Stern (1994, Study 5) provided a set of participants with information about how 20 witnesses had reached their decisions. The researchers then asked participants to separate the accurate witnesses from the inaccurate ones. Participants showed some facility at this task, achieving an accuracy rate of 61% (where chance accuracy was 50%), a rate that rose to 66% after participants were given a mini-lecture on how decision processes differentiate accurate from inaccurate witnesses. That increase in accuracy arose because the lecture corrected participants' faulty understanding of inaccurate witnesses. Although they properly suspected, without any intervention from the researchers, that accurate witnesses would reach their decisions automatically, they did not realize until told that inaccurate witnesses tended to work their way to an identification through a process of elimination strategy. Once told, they were much better at spotting when a witness had chosen incorrectly, with their accuracy rates rising from 58% to 67% in this circumstance.

Educating triers of fact about the ambivalent research on eyewitness confidence will lead them to put less emphasis on how confident the eyewitness seems on the stand. Eyewitnesses are well prepped for trial, and by the time they get to sit on the stand they need to be confident in their identification and do feel like they were confident during the identification decision as well (Wells & Bradfield, 1998, 1999). In addition, response time is a promising indicator of eyewitness accuracy that triers of fact have never had the opportunity to explore because it is most often unrecorded. It is important that judges and jurors have an opportunity to know all of the eyewitness events that occurred before trial, in order for them to assess accuracy.

Managing Witness Decision Processes

However, one might be tempted to go even further. If people are more accurate when they are automatic, then we can force people to be more automatic when they look over a lineup. They should be forced not to think, perhaps to make their identification as quickly as possible, in a matter of seconds. This is a tempting idea, but we and others have found that it is not a worthwhile one. In our lab, we have tried to force eyewitnesses to be more automatic through making their decisions quickly, or by distracting them while they view the lineup, and have found that these interventions have either no effect or a deleterious one on eyewitness accuracy (Perretta, 1998). Other researchers have tried similar tactics, with similar lackluster results (Brewer, Gordon, & Bond, 2000).

At first blush, these failures would appear to present a paradox. How can an automatic decision process indicate eyewitness accuracy, but forcing witnesses to rely on such processes not promote accuracy? The resolution of this paradox is a simple one, and it rests on the causal connection between automatic decision processes and eyewitness accuracy. It is not the case that automatic processes cause eyewitness accuracy. A witness either has a good memory of the perpetrator's appearance or not, and there is nothing forcing that witness to think automatically to improve that memory. Rather, a good memory (which usually leads to an accurate identification) causes the eyewitness to have an automatic experience when the perpetrator is presented to them. If the witness has a good and complete memory of a perpetrator's face, then that witness will recognize the perpetrator rapidly and without conscious deliberation. As such, although automatic decision processes are reflective of eyewitness accuracy, they are not responsible for that accuracy.

That said, the research suggests what criminal investigators and witnesses should avoid doing if they wish to stay away from making false-positive identifications. Criminal investigators should prevent witnesses from pursuing an effortful relative judgment strategy in which they consciously and analytically compare lineup choices with each other. Such a strategy can override or alter a good memory and thus induce witnesses to make erroneous positive identifications. For example, in our lab, we have found that forcing participants to analytically compare lineup choices to each other damages their accuracy. After such comparison, participants are significantly less likely to choose the culprit than they would have been without making comparisons (Perretta & Dunning, 2003). In addition, Lindsay and others have suggested that the primary reason why sequential lineup procedures prevent false-positive identifications is that those procedures preclude witnesses from making comparisons among lineup choices (Lindsay & Wells, 1985; Lindsay & Bellinger, 1999).

There is an additional reason why criminal investigators should be sure not to prompt eyewitnesses toward effortful and conscious deliberation over a lineup. Conscious and analytical processes tend to be verbal. People verbalize, at least in their heads, what they are doing as they reach a deliberative decision—and such articulation might have negative consequences for eyewitness memory. Faces in memory are stored in ways that defy verbalization. As an example, the reader is invited to describe the face of his or her friend—and to note how difficult it is to provide any satisfactory description. Memories for faces defy verbalization because they are represented as holistic configurations, not as a laundry list of facial features. People remember faces according to the relation and proportion of facial features to each other, as well as noting the general shape and size of the face (Diamond & Carey, 1986; Rhodes et al., 1980; Sergent, 1984). Such relations and proportions are difficult if not impossible to describe, and thus asking people to describe a face causes them to distort or supplant their original memory, leading to impaired eyewitness accuracy—a phenomenon known as *verbal overshadowing* of visual information (Fallshore & Schooler, 1995; Schooler & Engstler-Schooler, 1990). Thus, to the extent that witnesses can avoid conscious verbal thoughts about a face, the more their original—and hopefully accurate—memory will stay intact.

Preventing Use of Relative Judgments

Police investigators have the ability to help eyewitnesses not fall prey to relative judgments that stem from eyewitness's belief that their responsibility or job is to merely select the person who best resembles the perpetrator and the closest match wins out, or perhaps loses in many cases. They can do this by educating eyewitnesses and warning them that the culprit may not be present, by creating unbiased lineups that contain enough good distractors and by using sequential lineups.

Researchers have proposed that one simple verbal manipulation can help reduce the witness's reliance on relative judgments. Malpass and Devine (1981) believed that making it clear to eyewitnesses that the actual offender might *not* be present would help. They staged an incident of vandalism, had eyewitnesses attempt identifications of target-present or target-absent lineups, and told half that the eyewitness "may or may not be present." They found a significant decrease in the likelihood of false identifications (78% to 33%), and they also found no significant loss in accurate identifications (83% to 75%) with the use of the verbal manipulation. Because accurate identifications were unaffected, the manipulation did not simply make witnesses more cautious. Instead, it increased the likelihood of a no-choice response in the target-absent condition and perhaps led to reliance on a more absolute judgment match that had a higher threshold of match re-quired before selection (i.e., decreasing the choosing rate). A recent study used an addi-tional pre-lineup question to witnesses: "How confident are you that you will realize that the guilty person is *not* in the lineup if you are shown a lineup with only innocent people in it?" (Dysart & Lindsay, 2001, p. 160). They found that having a witness answer this question prior to viewing the lineup led to significantly more correct rejections of target-absent simultaneous lineups.

Criminal investigators should also be mindful of any bias in their lineup. A *biased* lineup is defined as "one where a person who was not a witness to the crime is more likely to pick the suspect out of the lineup than we would expect by chance" (Doob & Kirshen-baum, 1973, p. 288). Functioning under the assumption that eyewitnesses are motivated to pick some one, whether or not they select an innocent person can depend greatly on how good the distractors are and how many distractors there are. When the relative judgment process biases eyewitnesses, the choice they make in a lineup containing an in-nocent suspect should more likely be spread across the lineup, toward distractors, and away from the innocent suspect if the distractors look similar to the criminal (Lindsay & Wells, 1980). This is only successful if the distractors match the description given by the eyewitness, instead of selecting people who look like the suspect. In addition, a distinc-tion has been made between the nominal size and functional size of a lineup (Wells, Leippe, & Ostrom, 1979). Nominal size is the mere count of how many people are in the lineup, and functional size reflects the number of feasible lineup choices. If triers of fact find that the functional size of the lineup is less than the number of distractors in the lineup, then they should be concerned about the eyewitness's accuracy.

In conclusion, researchers recommended that police investigators pay particular atten-tion to designing and implementing bias-free lineups that protect innocent suspects but allow the actual perpetrator to stand out in a lineup. For a more complete discussion of lineup construction and fairness see, Malpass, Tredoux, and McQuiston (this volume).

CONCLUSION

Since the time of *Neil v. Biggers*, the courts have highlighted the importance of using post-dictors to assess the accuracy of eyewitnesses. The review of the literature provided in this chapter points to two seemingly contradictory conclusions. First, researchers now know a good deal about indicators of eyewitness accuracy and error. They know which indicators one can lean on to evaluate an eyewitness's decision—but more important, they know quite a bit about the limits and complications associated with those indica-tors. Researchers know, for example, that confidence can indicate eyewitness accuracy—but only modestly, and only when the witness chooses someone out of a lineup (Sporer et al., 1995). They know that a delay before viewing a lineup detracts from a witness's performance—but much more so if the witness has been exposed to misleading informa-tion (Davis & Loftus, volume 1) or distracting stimuli (Dysart & Lindsay, this volume). Depending on the circumstances, a positive identification of an irrelevant distractor in a lineup might actually be worthwhile evidence that the suspect is innocent (Wells & Olson, 2002). And measures of decision time and decision processes may help to distinguish accurate witnesses from erroneous ones (Dunning & Stern, 1994; Smith et al., 2000).

That all said, the contradiction is that there is still much work to be done. In particular, researchers have identified a number of post-dictors closely tied to the eyewitness's decision—such as judgment process, decision time, and confidence, that help to discriminate accurate judgments from inaccurate ones—but have only begun to explore how these criteria can be used and combined in a practical way in the police station to classify witnesses as accurate or inaccurate (e.g., Dunning & Perretta, 2002; Smith et al., 2000). Further work on turning these criteria into practical instruments that criminal investigators can use would be valuable. Further research exploring the strengths and weaknesses of these criteria would be mandatory (e.g., Smith et al., 2001). And exploring situations that still vex researchers, such as discriminating accurate from inaccurate non-choosers, would be profitable.

Until that work is done, however, there is much that criminal investigators can use to promote eyewitness accuracy, or at least to avoid eyewitness error. One continuing theme in this chapter is that a thinking, deliberative witness, one who is comparing lineup choices in a relative way, is a witness who is most likely to make a mistake. Taking steps to avoid this process would potentially go a long way toward avoiding the wrongful incrimination of innocent individuals.

ACKNOWLEDGMENTS

The writing of this chapter was supported financially by National Institute of Mental Health grant RO1 56072, awarded to David Dunning.

REFERENCES

Bahrick, H. P., Bahrick, P. L., & Wittlinger, R. P. (1975). Fifty years of memory for names and faces: A cross-sectional approach. *Journal of Experimental Psychology: General, 104,* 54–75.

Behrman, B. W., & Davey, S. L. (2001). Eyewitness identification in actual criminal cases: An archival analysis. *Law & Human Behavior, 25,* 475–491.

Bothwell, R. K., Deffenbacher, K., & Brigham, J. C. (1987). Correlation of eyewitness accuracy and confidence: Optimality hypothesis revisited. *Journal of Applied Psychology, 72,* 691–695.

Bradfield, A. L., & Wells, G. L. (2000). The perceived validity of eyewitness identification testimony: A test of the five Biggers criteria. *Law and Human Behavior, 24,* 581–594.

Brewer, N., Gordon, M., & Bond, N. (2000). Effect of photoarray exposure duration on eyewitness identification accuracy and processing strategy. *Psychology, Crime & Law, 6,* 21–32.

Brigham, J. C., & Bothwell, R. K. (1983). The ability of prospective jurors to estimate the accuracy of eyewitness identifications. *Law and Human Behavior, 7,* 19–30.

Brooks, N. (1983). *Pretrial eyewitness identification procedures.* Ottawa: Law Reform Commission of Canada.

Buckhout, R., Alper, A., Chern, S., Silverberg, G., & Slomovits, M. (1974). Determinants of eyewitness performance on a line up. *Bulletin of the Psychonomic Society, 6,* 71–74.

Caputo, D. D. (2004). *Got Perp? Eyewitness accuracy, decision processes, and presentation procedures using sequential lineups.* Unpublished doctoral dissertation, Cornell University.

Chance, J. E., Goldstein, A. G., & McBride, L. (1975). Differential experience and recognition memory for faces. *Journal of Social Psychology, 97,* 243–253.

Craik, F., & Lockhart, R. (1972). Levels of processing: A framework for memory research. *Journal of Verbal Reasoning and Verbal Behaviour, 11,* 671–684.

Cutler, B. L., & Penrod, S. D. (1988). Improving the reliability of eyewitness identification lineup construction and presentation. *Journal of Applied Psychology, 72,* 281–290.

Davies, G., Ellis, H. D., & Shepherd, J. W. (1978). Face recognition accuracy as a function of mode of representation. *Journal of Applied Psychology, 63,* 180–187.

Deffenbacher, K. (1980). Eyewitness and confidence: Can we infer anything about their relationship? *Law and Human Behavior, 4,* 261–274.

Deffenbacher, K. A. (1991). A maturing of research on the behaviour of eyewitnesses. *Applied Cognitive Psychology, 5,* 377–402.

Diamond, R., & Carey, S. (1986). Why faces are and are not special: An effect of expertise. *Journal of Experimental Psychology: General, 115,* 107–117.

Doob, A. N., & Kirshenbaum, H. M. (1973). Bias in police lineups-partial remembering. *Journal of Police Science and Administration, 1,* 287–293.

Dunning, D., & Perretta, S. (2002). Automaticity and eyewitness accuracy: A ten to twelve second rule for distinguishing accurate from inaccurate positive identifications. *Journal of Applied Psychology, 87,* 951–962.

Dunning, D., & Stern, L. B. (1994). Distinguishing accurate from inaccurate eyewitness identifications via inquiries about decision processes. *Journal of Personality and Social Psychology, 67,* 818–835.

Dysart, J., & Lindsay, R. C. L. (2001). A preidentification questioning effect: Serendipitously increasing correct rejections. *Law and Human Behavior, 25,* 155–165.

Ellis, H. D. (1981). Theoretical aspects of face recognition. In G. Davies, H. Ellis, & J. Shepherd (Eds.), *Perceiving and remembering faces* (pp. 171–200). San Diego: Academic Press.

Ellis, H. D., Davies, G. M., & Shepherd, J. W. (1978). Remembering pictures of real and unreal faces: Some practical and theoretical considerations. *British Journal of Psychology, 69,* 467–474.

Fallshore, M., & Schooler, J. W. (1995). The verbal vulnerability of perceptual expertise. *Journal of Experimental Psychology: Learning, Memory, and Cognition, 21,* 1608–1623.

Geiselman, R. E., Schroppel, T., Tubridy, A., Konishi, T., & Rodriguez, V. (2000). Objectivity bias in eyewitness performance. *Applied Cognitive Psychology, 14,* 323–332.

Goldstein, A. G., Johnson, K. S., & Chance, J. E. (1979). Does fluency of face description imply superior face recognition? *Bulletin of the Psychonomic Society, 13,* 15–18.

Gonzalez, R., Ellsworth, P., & Pembroke, M. (1993). Response biases in lineups and showups. *Journal of Personality and Social Psychology, 64,* 525–537.

Hay, D. C., Young, A. W., & Ellis, H. D. (1986). What happens when a face rings a bell? The automatic processing of famous faces. In H. D. Ellis, M. A. Jeeves, F. Newcombe, & A. Young (Eds.), *Aspects of face processing* (pp. 136–144). Dordrecht, the Netherlands: Martinus Nijhoff.

Kassin, S. M. (1985). Eyewitness identification: Retrospective self-awareness and the accuracy-confidence correlation. *Journal of Personality and Social Psychology, 49,* 878–893.

Laughery, K. R., Fessler, P. K., Lenorovitz, D. R., & Yoblick, D. A. (1974). Time delay and similarity effects in face recognition. *Journal of Applied Psychology, 59,* 490–496.

Leippe, M. R. (1980). Effects of integrative and memorial and cognitive processes on the correspondence of eyewitness accuracy and confidence. *Law and Human Behavior, 4,* 261–274.

Leippe, M. R., Wells, G. L., & Ostrom, T. M. (1978). Crime seriousness as a determinant of accuracy in eyewitness identification. *Journal of Applied Psychology, 63,* 345–351.

Lindsay, R. C. L. (1994). Expectations of eyewitness performance. In D. Ross, D. Read, & M. Toglia (Eds), *Adult eyewitness testimony: Current trends and developments* (pp. 362–384). New York: Cambridge University Press.

Lindsay, R. C. L., & Bellinger, K. (1999). Alternatives to the sequential lineup: The importance of controlling the pictures. *Journal of Applied Psychology, 84,* 315–321.

Lindsay, R. C. L., Lea, J. A., Nosworthy, G. J., Fulford, J. A., Hector, J., Levan, V., et al. (1991). Biased lineups: Sequential presentation reduces the problem. *Journal of Applied Psychology, 76*, 796–802.

Lindsay, R. C. L., & Wells, G. L. (1980). What price justice? Exploring the relationship of lineup fairness to identification accuracy. *Law and Human Behavior, 4*, 303–314.

Lindsay, R. C. L., & Wells, G. L. (1985). Improving eyewitness identification from lineups: Simultaneous vs. sequential lineup presentation. *Journal of Applied Psychology, 70*, 556–564.

Loftus, E. F. (1997). Creating false memories. *Scientific American, 277*, 70–75.

Malpass, R. S., & Devine, P. G. (1981). Eyewitness identification: Lineup instructions and the absence of the offender. *Journal of Applied Psychology, 66*, 482–489.

Meissner, C. A., & Brigham, J. C. (2001). Thirty years of investigating the own-race bias in memory for faces: A meta analytic review. *Psychology, Public Policy and Law, 7*, 3–35.

Munsterberg, H. (1908). *On the witness stand: Essays on psychology and crime.* New York: The McClure Company.

Neil v. Biggers, 409 U.S. 188 (1972).

Nisbett, R. E., & Wilson, T. D. (1977). Telling more than we can know: Verbal reports on mental processes. *Psychological Review, 84*, 231–259.

Perretta, S. F. (1998). *Whodunnit? Eyewitness accuracy, decision time, and decision processes.* Unpublished doctoral dissertation, Cornell University.

Perretta, S. F., & Dunning, D. (2003). *Testing the automatic versus process of elimination distinction in differentiating accurate from inaccurate eyewitnesses.* Unpublished manuscript, Cornell University.

Pigott, M. A., & Brigham, J. C. (1985). Relationship between accuracy of prior description and facial recognition. *Journal of Applied Psychology, 7*, 547–555.

Pozzulo, J. D., & Warren, K. L. (2003). Descriptions and identifications of strangers by youth and adult eyewitnesses. *Journal of Applied Psychology, 88*, 315–323.

Read, J. D., Vokey, J. R., & Hammersley, R. (1990). Changing photos of faces: Effects of exposure duration and similarity on recognition and the accuracy-confidence relationship. *Journal of Experimental Psychology: Learning, Memory and Cognition, 16*, 870–882.

Rhodes, G., Tan, S., Brake, S., & Taylor, K. (1989). Expertise and configural coding in face recognition. *British Journal of Psychology, 80*, 313–331.

Robinson, M. D., & Johnson, J. T. (1998). How not to enhance the confidence-accuracy relation: The detrimental effects of attention to the identification process. *Law & Human Behavior, 22*, 409–422.

Robinson, M. D., Johnson, J. T., & Herndon, F. (1997). Reaction time and assessments of cognitive effort as predictors of eyewitness memory accuracy and confidence. *Journal of Applied Psychology, 82*, 416–425.

Schooler, J. W., & Engstler-Schooler, T. Y. (1990). Verbal overshadowing of visual memories: Some things are better left unsaid. *Cognitive Psychology, 22*, 36–71.

Sergent, J. (1984). An investigation into component and configural processes underlying face perception. *British Journal of Psychology, 75*, 221–242.

Shapiro, P., & Penrod, S. D. (1986). Meta-analysis of facial identification studies. *Psychological Bulletin, 100*, 139–156.

Shaw, J. S. & McClure, K. A. (1996). Repeated postevent questioning can lead to elevated levels of eyewitness confidence. *Law and Human Behavior, 20*, 629–653.

Shiffman, H. R., & Bobko, D. J. (1974). Effects of stimulus complexity on the perception of brief temporal intervals. *Journal of Experimental Psychology, 103*, 156–159.

Smith, S. M., Lindsay, R. C. L., & Pryke, S. (2000). Postdictors of eyewitness errors: Can false identifications be diagnosed? *Journal of Applied Psychology, 85*, 542–550.

Smith, S. M., Lindsay, R. C. L., Pryke, S., & Dysart, J. (2001). Predictors of eyewitness errors: Can false identifications be diagnosed in the cross-race situation? *Psychology, Public Policy and Law, 7*, 153–169.

Sporer, S. L. (1992). Post-dicting eyewitness accuracy: Confidence, decision-times and person descriptions of choosers and non-choosers. *European Journal of Social Psychology, 22*, 157–180.

Sporer, S. L. (1993). Eyewitness identification accuracy, confidence, and decision times in simultaneous and sequential lineups. *Journal of Applied Psychology, 78,* 22–33.

Sporer, S. L. (1994). Decision-times and eyewitness identification accuracy in simultaneous and
sequential lineups. In D. F. Ross, J. D. Read, & M. P. Toglia (Eds.), *Adult eyewitness testimony:
Current trends and developments* (pp. 300–327). New York: Cambridge University Press.

Sporer, S. L. (2001). Recognizing faces of other ethnic groups: An integration of theories. *Psychology, Public Policy, and Law, 7,* 36–97.

Sporer, S. L., Penrod, S. D., Read, D., & Cutler, B. L. (1995). Choosing confidence and accuracy:
A meta-analysis of the confidence-accuracy relation in eyewitness identification studies. *Psychological Bulletin, 118,* 315–327.

Steblay, N., Dysart, J., Fulero, S., & Lindsay, R. C. L. (2001). Eyewitness accuracy rates in
sequential and simultaneous lineup presentations: A meta analytic comparison. *Law and
Human Behavior, 25,* 459–473.

Stern, L. B., & Dunning, D. (1994). Distinguishing accurate from inaccurate eyewitness identifications: A reality monitoring approach. In D. F. Ross, J. D. Read, & M. P. Toglia (Eds.),
Adult eyewitness testimony: Current trends and developments (pp. 273–299). New York: Cambridge University Press.

Van Koppen, P. J., & Lochun, S. K. (1997). Portraying perpetrators: The validity of offender
descriptions by witnesses. *Law and Human Behavior, 21,* 663–687.

Weber, N., Brewer, N., Wells, G. L., Semmler, C., & Keast, A. (2004). Eyewitness identification
accuracy and response latency: The unruly 10–12 second rule. *Journal of Experimental Psychology: Applied.*

Wells, G. L. (1984). The psychology of lineup identifications. *Journal of Applied Social Psychology,
14,* 89–103.

Wells, G. L. (1985). Verbal descriptions of faces from memory: Are they diagnostic of identification accuracy? *Journal of Applied Psychology, 70,* 619–626.

Wells, G. L., & Bradfield, A. L. (1998). "Good, you identified the suspect": Feedback to eyewitnesses
distorts their reports of the witnessing experience. *Journal of Applied Psychology, 83,* 360–376.

Wells, G. L., & Bradfield, A. L. (1999). Distortions in eyewitness' recollections: Can the post-
identification-feedback effect be moderated? *Psychological Science, 10,* 138–144.

Wells, G. L., & Hryciw, B. (1984). Memory for faces: Encoding and retrieval operations. *Memory
and Cognition, 12,* 338–344.

Wells, G. L., Leippe, M. R., & Ostrom, T. M. (1979). Guidelines for empirically assessing the fairness of a lineup. *Law and Human Behavior, 3,* 285–293.

Wells, G. L., & Lindsay, R. C. L. (1980). On estimating the diagnosticity of eyewitness nonidentifications. *Psychological Bulletin, 88,* 776–786.

Wells, G. L., Lindsay, R. C. L., & Ferguson, T. J. (1979). Accuracy, confidence, and juror perceptions in eyewitness identification. *Journal of Applied Psychology, 64,* 440–448.

Wells, G. L., & Murray, D. M. (1983). What can psychology say about the *Neil v. Biggers* criteria
for judging eyewitness accuracy? *Journal of Applied Psychology, 68,* 347–362.

Wells, G. L., & Murray, D. M. (1984). Eyewitness confidence. In G. L. Wells & E. F. Loftus
(Eds.), *Eyewitness testimony: Psychological perspectives* (pp. 155–170). Cambridge: Cambridge
University Press.

Wells, G. L., & Olson, E. A. (2002). Eyewitness identification: Information gain from incriminating and exonerating behaviors. *Journal of Experimental Psychology: Applied, 8,* 155–167.

Yarmey, A. D. (1986). Verbal, visual, and voice identification of a rape suspect under different
levels of illumination. *Journal of Applied Psychology, 71,* 363–370.

Yarmey, A. D., Yarmey, M. J., & Yarmey, A. L. (1996). Accuracy of eyewitness identifications in
showups and lineups. *Law and Human Behavior, 20,* 459–477.

IV

BELIEF OF EYEWITNESS IDENTIFICATION

18

Has Eyewitness Testimony Research Penetrated the American Legal System? A Synthesis of Case History, Juror Knowledge, and Expert Testimony

Tanja Rapus Benton, Stephanie McDonnell
and David F. Ross
University of Tennessee, Chattanooga

Honorable W. Neil Thomas, III
Circuit Court of Tennessee, Chattanooga

Emily Bradshaw
University of Kentucky

Historically, there has been an ebb and flow in the willingness of the American judicial system to admit testimony from experts in eyewitness memory. Some judges have indicated that eyewitness testimony is fallible and that experts can offer valuable information that will assist the trier of fact. Over 30 years ago, Justice Bazelon, in a concurring opinion in *United States v. Brown*, 461 F.2d 134 (D.C. Cir. 1972), commented on how crucial eyewitness identifications are to the fairness and reliability of convictions, which speaks directly to the need for eyewitness experts:

> One critical problem [of eyewitness identifications] concerns their reliability, yet courts regularly protest their lack of interest in the reliability of identifications, as opposed to the suggestivity that may have prompted them, arguing that reliability is simply a question of fact for the jury. There already exists, however, great doubts—if not firm evidence—about the adequacy and accuracy of

the process. . . . We need more information about the reliability of the identification process and about the jury's ability to cope with its responsibility. For it should be obvious that we cannot strike a reasonable and intelligent balance if we take pains to remain in ignorance of the pitfalls of the identification process. The empirical data now available indicates that the problem is far from fanciful. But for a variety of reasons we have been unwilling to face up to the doubts to which this data gives rise. . . . We have developed a reluctance that is almost a taboo against even acknowledging the question, much less providing the jury with all of the available information. . . . More information is needed to assist the jury's resolution of identification issues, [and] our doubts will not disappear merely because we run away from the problem. (461 F.2d at 146, n.1)

In sharp contrast, some courts reject eyewitness experts and research on eyewitness memory for a variety of reasons. In *Criglow v. State*, 183 Ark. 407, 36 S.W.2d 400 (1931), one of the first cases where the defense attempted to admit the testimony of an eyewitness expert, the testimony was rejected by the court. In that case the defendant called upon E. E. Brooks to testify as an expert about the "powers of observation and recollection" and to question the accuracy of the eyewitness identification evidence. In rejecting the testimony, the court explained:

The court properly excluded this testimony. There was no contention that these witnesses were of unsound mind . . . [T]he question whether these witnesses were mistaken in their identification, whether from fright or other cause, was one which the jury, and not the expert witness, should answer. This was a question which one man as well as another might form an opinion, and the function of passing upon the credibility and weight of testimony should not be taken from the jury. (36 S.W.2d at 409–410)

Nearly 70 years later, the conclusions reached in *Criglow* were echoed in *State v. Coley*, 32 S.W.3d 831 (Tenn. 2000), where the Tennessee Supreme Court adopted a *per se* exclusionary rule prohibiting the admissibility of eyewitness expert testimony. Under *Coley, supra,* the court determined that eyewitness experts have nothing to offer the trier of fact because their testimony has no scientific or technical underpinnings, that it would only confuse the jury, and that it has nothing to offer that would be outside the common knowledge of jurors. Furthermore, if problems exist with the testimony of an eyewitness, the court held that the jury would detect it from the cross-examination of the witnesses, closing argument, and jury instructions:

To admit such testimony in effect would permit the proponent's witness to comment on the weight and credibility of opponents' witnesses and open the door to a barrage of marginally relevant psychological evidence. Moreover, we conclude, as did the trial judge, that the problems of perception and memory can be adequately addressed in cross-examination and that the jury can adequately weigh these problems through common sense evaluation. (Coley, *supra*, 32 S.W. 3d at 836)

The *Coley* opinion is in direct contrast to the published finding that error in eyewitness identification is the single most common reason for wrongful convictions. If eyewitness memory is common sense to jurors, and problematic eyewitness testimony is detected by juries during cross-examination, it is difficult to understand how misidentification errors by eyewitnesses are the leading cause of wrongful convictions in the United

States (Huff, Rattner, & Sagarin, 1986), with an estimated 4,500 innocent people convicted each year (Cutler & Penrod, 1995). The magnitude of the problem was also recently documented by a National Institute of Justice (NIJ) study that reported 28 cases in which DNA testing exonerated the accused, finding that 90% of the wrongful convictions were due to errors in eyewitness identification (Connors, Lundregan, Miller, & McEwen, 1996). Subsequent studies reported by Wells et al. (1998) that included 12 additional cases demonstrate the same result. Collectively, these exonerations included five individuals who were wrongly convicted of capital crimes and were on death row waiting to be executed. While eyewitness errors and wrongful convictions may appear to be a recent problem to some, this finding can be observed in studies that date back to the 1930s (Borchard, 1932; Brandon & Davies, 1973; Frank & Frank, 1957; Huff et al., 1986).

One recent attempt to correct this problem has been to focus attention, not on the jury, but on the police procedures used to collect the identification evidence. If proper police procedures are used, perhaps then jurors would not be presented with eyewitness testimony that is fraught with problems. The result of the DNA exoneration study was the formation by then Attorney General Janet Reno of a commission of 34 individuals to serve as a technical working group and included law enforcement personnel, research psychologists, investigators, and attorneys. The group's mission was to develop a set of guidelines to be used by police as a standard for the collection of identification evidence. The product was a 1999 NIJ publication titled *Eyewitness Evidence: A Guide for Law Enforcement*. According to our recent interactions with the Department of Justice personnel, 44,000 copies of this publication were distributed across the country to law enforcement agencies and personnel, investigators, court personnel, and others involved in the collection of identification evidence. In September of 2003 the NIJ published a follow-up training manual designed for instructors to teach law enforcement personnel how to properly conduct interviews and construct lineups and photo spreads. Approximately 3,000 copies of this publication were distributed across the country to law enforcement agencies, including police training academies.

The development and distribution of the DOJ training manual is yet further evidence that eyewitness memory is not common sense to the police and investigators who collect and handle the identification evidence, much less to jurors. Consequently, the admissibility of eyewitness experts is a critical issue facing the judicial system. The basis for acceptance of expert testimony is that such testimony serves to inform the court and jury about affairs not within the full understanding of the average person. Accordingly, proffered expert testimony should only be excluded if it does not assist the jury, or if it unnecessarily diverts the jury's attention from the relevant issues. Thus, could an expert educate the jury on proper procedures that should be used to collect identification evidence? Could an expert provide information to a jury that would increase its ability to differentiate accurate from inaccurate eyewitnesses?

This chapter has five interlocking sections that address different aspects of this problem. First, we explore the decision process a judge must use to evaluate an eyewitness expert and review the literature on judges' ability to evaluate scientific research in general, and specifically their knowledge of eyewitness issues. Second, we report the results of an analysis of the admissibility of eyewitness testimony in state and federal courts in the

United States in order to provide a measure of the extent to which eyewitness research has penetrated the legal system. If courts are issuing *per se* exclusionary rulings, as seen in Tennessee, then the door is shut on the ability of eyewitness research to affect the courts. But if courts are admitting experts, under what circumstances are they admitted and how many states allow such testimony? Third, we explore one of the most commonly cited reasons used by trial courts for excluding the testimony of eyewitness experts, namely that the information the experts have to offer is common sense to the average juror. That reason raises the question of what exactly jurors know. We review the extant literature and attempt to link what jurors know with the knowledge professed by experts as a measure of the gap between the two. Additionally we provide a review of the literature on what judges, police investigators, and lawyers know about eyewitness testimony, because these are the individuals who deal directly with the eyewitness and are involved in decisions of admissibility and how the eyewitness is examined by the prosecution and the defense. Fourth, the safeguards currently in the legal system protecting against errors in eyewitness memory that can result in wrongful convictions are examined. Specifically, we explore the effectiveness of the jury, judicial instructions, and cross-examination as safeguards in the evaluation of eyewitness testimony. Finally, we finish with an overall analysis of the issue regarding whether or not eyewitness testimony research has penetrated the legal system and, if so, how and what can be done to foster the relationship between eyewitness research and judicial decisions regarding the admissibility of eyewitness experts.

JUDICIAL EVALUATION OF EYEWITNESS EXPERTS IN A POST-DAUBERT WORLD

Judges are given broad discretion in the admission of expert testimony. The standards by which that discretion is exercised are set forth in Rules 401 and 702 of the Federal Rules of Evidence and the landmark decision of *Daubert v. Merrill Dow Pharmaceuticals, Inc.* [509 U.S. 579, 125 L.Ed.2d 469, 113 S. Ct. 2786 (1993)]. Rule 401 permits only relevant evidence to be admitted, where relevant evidence is defined as evidence that has "any tendency to make the existence of any fact that is of consequence to the determination of the action more probable or less probable than it would without the evidence." (Fed. R. Evid. 401). This rule allows trial judges to exclude the expert testimony if it is simply not relevant to an issue in the case (Gross, 1999). In addition, Rule 403 provides an exception to the admissibility of relevant evidence and states, "Although relevant, evidence may be excluded if its probative value is substantially outweighed by the danger of unfair prejudice, confusion of the issues, or misleading the jury, or by considerations of undue delay, waste of time, or needless presentation of cumulative evidence." Finally, Rule 702 states that an expert can testify "if scientific, technical, or other specialized knowledge will assist the trier of fact to understand the evidence or to determine a fact in issue."[1]

---

[1]It should be noted that Tennessee Rule 702 is actually more restrictive than the Federal Rule on this issue, because of the addition of the word "substantially," inserted before "assist the trier of fact."

With respect to the admissibility of expert testimony, a trial judge must determine if the testimony is reliable and valid, and whether five nonexclusive factors have been satisfied in order to determine scientific integrity. These factors include whether the content of the scientific testimony is falsifiable or testable, whether it was subjected to peer review or publication, whether the evidence has been generally accepted in the scientific community, and whether there was a known or potential error rate [*Daubert v. Merrill Dow Pharmaceuticals, Inc.*, 509 U.S. 579, 125 L.Ed.2d 469,113 S. Ct. 2786 (1993)].

These rules and guidelines place an enormous responsibility on trial judges because they are forced to become scientists who must evaluate scientific testimony, and they must perform this task across a variety of content areas. There is, however, a serious question concerning how qualified judges are to evaluate science in general and, specifically, eyewitness memory issues. Recent findings indicate that judges are often not given adequate training in scientific methodology to perform this task effectively. For example, Gatowski et al. (2001) gave a national sample of state court judges a questionnaire measuring their knowledge of the *Daubert* factors used to evaluate expert testimony (falsifiability, peer review, error rate, and general acceptance), and the results provide cause for serious concern. The judges had considerable difficulty understanding these basic concepts. Only 4% of the judges were able to define falsifiability, 4% were able to define error rate, and there was considerable variability among the judges in terms of which of the factors they felt were most important in evaluating expert testimony. Similar results are reported in a study by Kovera and McAuliff (2000), who presented judges with expert testimony that varied in terms of the presence or absence of methodological problems and whether or not the research was peer reviewed. The quality of the expert's testimony had no impact on the evaluations given by the judges. When judges were given training in scientific methodology, their evaluations were more accurate than their untrained peers, although they too made serious errors in evaluating the expert testimony.

Not only do judges appear to have considerable difficulty in comprehending and applying the *Daubert* standard in the evaluation of scientific testimony, they also appear to have limited knowledge of eyewitness memory. This was evidenced in a study by Wise and Safer (2004), who examined judicial knowledge about a wide range of factors that affect eyewitness accuracy. One hundred sixty judges completed a questionnaire and responded to 14 statements about eyewitness memory. Across the 14 items, the mean accuracy rate was 55%, which is comparable to accuracy rates obtained from lay jurors, whose performance across similar questionnaire surveys has ranged from 35% to 61% (with a mean accuracy rate of 44%). Clearly, judges are not outperforming laypeople.

Judges in this study were also surveyed about their perceptions concerning the reliability of eyewitness testimony and its relation to wrongful convictions. Specifically, in response to the statement, "Only in exceptional circumstances should a defendant be convicted of a crime solely on the basis of eyewitness testimony," 48% of judges disagreed, 23% agreed, and 29% neither agreed nor disagreed. Less than half of the judges (43%) indicated that eyewitness error contributes to at least half of all wrongful convictions, and 19% did not respond to this question. Furthermore, judges who did provide a response were more knowledgeable about eyewitness factors, in general, based on their performance on the survey items, and greater knowledge was also associated with a more critical attitude toward eyewitness testimony. This finding is extremely important in light of the fact that eyewitness misidentification errors, as reviewed above, are one of the leading causes of erroneous convictions in the United States and that in recent cases of exoneration based on DNA evidence, 90% of the wrongful convictions were based on eyewitness errors (Conners et al., 1996). Clearly, these results indicate that judges are underestimating the role that eyewitness errors play in wrongful convictions.

With judges being forced to use the *Daubert* standard to evaluate scientific evidence in the absence of appropriate scientific training, with insufficient knowledge of scientific principles and eyewitness issues, and the extent to which errors in eyewitness memory contribute to wrongful convictions, a serious concern is raised as to whether judges are qualified to evaluate eyewitness testimony itself or experts in eyewitness testimony. Therefore, one hypothesis is that this lack of knowledge would cause judicial reasoning and decisions for including or excluding eyewitness experts to be very inconsistent across jurisdictions. This inconsistency becomes apparent in a comparison of the various approaches taken by courts regarding the admissibility of eyewitness experts. The analysis of state and federal cases reveals two broad approaches. First is the discretionary approach, which leaves the admissibility and limits of expert testimony to the sound discretion of the trial court. This category is the broadest, because it can include admitting the testimony, not admitting the testimony while using language to suggest an almost *per se* exclusionary rule, or not admitting the testimony but recognizing that it could be admissible under different circumstances. Under the discretionary approach, which has been adopted by a majority of the courts, judges are able to rationalize on a case-by-case basis their reasons for including or excluding expert testimony.

A second approach is prohibitory. This is a *per se* rule of exclusion, prohibiting the exercise of discretion and the admission of expert eyewitness testimony under any circumstances. While it seems that courts are turning away from this approach to adopt the approach of the majority in a discretionary view, our analysis reveals that many courts are basically still operating in a manner that is nearly *per se* exclusionary.

The problem of variability in judicial decision-making on this topic largely lies in the discretionary approach. As the review will show, the rationales that fall within this category constitute most of the inconsistency found in judicial review of the admissibility of the eyewitness expert. Furthermore, courts rarely overrule a trial court's exercise of discretion. If the defendant chooses to appeal a trial court's decision, the appellate court will only review the lower court decision under an "abuse of discretion" rule, which means that even though the evidence may be otherwise admissible, the trial court decision will be overturned only if the court has abused its discretion in refusing to admit the evidence or if the exclusion was not harmless to the outcome of the case. With this type of review, trial court decisions are rarely overturned, which aids in keeping expert identification testimony out of the court.

We now turn to an analysis of the state and federal courts to determine which approach the courts have adopted when evaluating eyewitness experts and to examine and compare the judicial rationale given in each case.

ON THE ADMISSIBILITY OF EXPERTS IN EYEWITNESS TESTIMONY: AN ANALYSIS OF STATE AND FEDERAL COURTS

This section reports the results of a comprehensive survey conducted to examine how courts are treating expert testimony on eyewitness memory. Although the most recent authoritative cases on the issue are presented, it should be recognized that they may or may not constitute cases in which the rule is established. There will, however, be some discussion of prior precedent. To ensure that each case analyzed was representative of the current view held by each state and circuit, LexisNexis legal research database and a procedure known as *shephardizing* was utilized. In doing so, one can be certain that no subsequent case law has overturned that ruling. The cases were content analyzed and sorted according to the ruling made by the court. The cases analyzed were specific to that state or circuit and represent the thinking of each under the principle of *stare decisis*. No attempt was made to focus on any particular jurisdiction. This section sets forth the assumptions made by the courts in admitting the evidence, excluding the evidence as a matter of law, or deferring to the discretion of the trial judge. Within the two broad approaches taken by the courts, five categories of decisions exist. In reaching its decision, the reviewing court can (1) admit the testimony and declare that the trial court did not abuse its discretion in admitting the evidence, (2) admit the testimony and declare that the trial court *did* abuse its discretion in excluding the testimony, (3) not admit the testimony and declare that the trial court did not abuse its discretion, (4) not admit the testimony but claim that in general, the testimony could be admissible under other circumstances, (5) not admit the testimony under a *per se* rule of inadmissibility, or (6) remand the case to the trial court for further review. Table 18.1 provides further clarification of this categorization.

State Analysis

The state-by-state analysis revealed that the issue of expert eyewitness identification evidence has not been addressed in a published opinion in five states: Hawaii, Montana, New Hampshire, New Mexico, and the District of Columbia. Therefore, the following review is based on case holdings in 46 states and 11 federal circuits. Table 18.2 displays each case reviewed and the decision in that case, and Table 18.3 consists of a summary of our analysis. The review of decisions is intended to provide a snapshot of how states are currently ruling on this issue. It is clear, however, that this is an evolving issue, and the most recent decision may not predict rulings in the future.

As seen in Table 18.2, only one state, Tennessee (constituting 2%), takes a *per se* prohibitory approach. In its most recent pronouncement, the court was very stringent and forceful in its logic that such testimony not be allowed. In *State v. McKinney* [74 S.W.3d 291, 302 (Tenn. 2002)], the court held that "The State is correct that a majority of this Court has ruled that expert testimony on the issue of eyewitness identifications is *per se* inadmissible under Tenn. R. Evid. 702." Timothy McKinney, who was on trial for premeditated first-degree murder and attempted second-degree murder, was sentenced to death.

TABLE 18.1
Judicial Admissibility Decisions on Eyewitness Expert Testimony

Approach	Decision type	Result	Explanation
Inadmissible	Per se inadmissible	Testimony not admitted	The testimony will be excluded under all circumstances.
Inadmissible	Discretion not abused in excluding	Testimony not admitted	The trial court did not abuse its discretionary powers in excluding the evidence; strong language suggests per se inadmissibility.
May be admissible	Discretion not abused in excluding	Testimony not admitted	Although the testimony is admissible in general, it was not admitted in this case; rationale suggests admissibility of testimony is possible but not probable. This category can also include cases in which some testimony was admitted but the defendant appealed the exclusion of the remaining testimony.
May be admissible	Discretion not abused in admitting	Testimony admitted	The trial court did not abuse its discretionary powers in admitting the testimony.
May be admissible	Discretion abused in excluding	Testimony admitted	The trial court abused its discretionary powers in excluding the testimony when it should have been admitted.
May be admissible	Discretion may or may not have been abused	Case Remanded	The reviewing court finds that the trial court did not properly review the expert testimony and remands it back to the trial court to conduct the proper analysis.

In reaching its decision, the court referred to its own ruling in *State v. Coley* [32 S.W. 3d 831 (Tenn. 2000)], in which the court reasoned:

> Eyewitness testimony has no scientific or technical underpinnings which would be outside the common understanding of the jury; therefore, expert testimony is not necessary to help jurors "understand" the eyewitness's testimony. Moreover, expert testimony about the eyewitness's accuracy does not aid the jury in determining a fact in issue because the question whether an eyewitness should be believed is not a "fact in issue" but rather a credibility determination. (32 S.W. 3d at 833–834)

In opposition to this view, 98% of the states take a discretionary approach. The first decision type within this approach, inadmissible, was held by 15 states (33%) in their most recent cases. The analysis of the rationales used in these cases reveals that, although the courts do not actually declare a rule of *per se* inadmissibility of expert identification testimony, they use language that nearly suggests a *per se* rule. For example, in the most recent

TABLE 18.2
State Rulings

State	Most recent case	Ruling
Alabama	*Ex parte Williams* 594 So. 2d 1225 (Ala. 1992)	Discretionary—may be admissible. Discretion not abused in refusing to admit. Expert not familiar with facts of case, had no personal contact with victim or knowledge of event.
Alaska	*Skamarocius v. State* 731 P.2d 63 (Alaska App. 1987)	Discretionary—may be admissible. Discretion abused in refusing to admit. Trial court ruling overturned, testimony should have been admitted. Trial court abused its discretion in excluding the expert testimony because the identification of defendant as the assailant by the witness was weak and uncorroborated.
Arizona	*State v. Nordstrum* 200 Ariz. 229; 25 P.3d 717 (Ariz. 2001)	Discretionary—may be admissible. Discretion not abused in refusing to admit. The expert was permitted to testify at length about a variety of eyewitness variables, but was not permitted to express any opinion about the accuracy of the defendant's eyewitness testimony or to address the specifics of this case.
Arkansas	*Utley v. State* 308 Ark. 622; 826 S.W.2d 268 (Ark. 1992)	Discretionary—inadmissible. The question whether these witnesses were mistaken in their identification, whether from fright or other cause, was one which the jury, and not an expert witness, should answer. The experts testimony was a matter of common understanding and would not assist the trier of fact.
California	*People v. McDonald* 37 Cal. 3rd 351, 690 P.2d 709 (Cal. 1984)	Discretionary—may be admissible. Discretion abused in refusing to admit. Trial court judgment reversed. The exclusion the eyewitness expert was not harmless error. The court found it reasonably probable that a result more favorable to the defendant would have been reached in absence of this error, and the judgment must be reversed.
Colorado	*Campbell v. People* 847 P.2d 228 (Colo. App. 1992)	Discretionary—may be admissible. Case remanded. The trial court erred in relying on Frye as a basis for excluding the proffered testimony. This error was not harmless, and the case was remanded to vacate judgment and reevaluate the admissibility of the expert's testimony.
Connecticut	*State v. McClendon* 248 Conn. 572; 730 A.2d 1107 (Conn. 1999)	Discretionary—may be admissible. Discretion not abused in refusing to admit. The general principles should come as no surprise to the average juror. He was unable to state his opinion to a reasonable degree of scientific certainty.
Delaware	*Garden v. State* 815 A.2d 327; (Del. 2003)	Discretionary—may be admissible. Discretion abused in refusing to admit but was harmless error. Partial testimony allowed. Expert testified on a variety of estimator variables but was not permitted to testify on the confidence/accuracy relationship. The exclusion was ruled an abuse of discretion but found to be harmless error.
District of Columbia		No cases found.

(continued)

TABLE 18.2 (*Continued*)

State	Most recent case	Ruling
Florida	*Johnson v. State* 438 So. 2d 774 (Fla. 1983)	Discretionary—inadmissible. Held that a jury is capable of assessing a witness' ability to perceive and remember, given assistance of cross-examination and cautionary instruction.
Georgia	*Johnson v. State* 272 Ga. 254; 526 S.E.2d 549 (Ga. 2000)	Discretionary—may be admissible. Discretion not abused in refusing to admit. Abundance of corroborating evidence.
Hawaii	No cases found	No cases found.
Idaho	*State v. Pacheco* 134 Idaho 367; 2 P.3d 752 (Idaho Ct. App. 2000) *See also 657 P.2d 17 (1983)	Discretionary—may be admissible, discretion not abused in refusing to admit. Court refused to allow expert to testify on the memory or perceptions of witnesses relative to the presence of a firearm on the ground that such testimony would not assist the trier of fact. This court does recognize, however, that in certain circumstances such testimony may be of assistance to the jury.
Illinois	*State v. Tisdel* 338 Ill. App. 3d 465; 788 N.E.2d 1149 (Ill. App. Ct. 2003)	Discretionary—may be admissible, discretion not abused in refusing to admit. The record shows that the judge considered the reliability and potential helpfulness of the testimony, balanced the proffered testimony against cases in which this court has upheld the exclusion of such evidence, and found that the testimony would not assist the jury. The court notes, however, that had the trial court allowed the testimony, it would not have been an abuse of discretion.
Indiana	*Cook v. State* 734 N.E.2d 563; (Ind. 2000)	Discretionary—may be admissible, discretion not abused in refusing to admit. Defendant failed to establish the factual predicate upon which his expert's testimony would have rested. The number of witnesses identifying defendant as the shooter supports the view that expert testimony in this case would not have assisted the jury in understanding the evidence or determining any fact in issue.
Iowa	*State v. Schutz* 579 N.W.2d 317 (Iowa 1998)	Discretionary—may be admissible. Discretion abused in refusing to admit, case remanded. Per se exclusionary rule overturned. The exclusion of expert testimony is a matter committed to the sound discretion of the trial court, and it was error to apply the per se rule of exclusion. Case remanded to the district court for a new trial.
Kansas	*State v. Gaines* 260 Kan. 752; 926 P.2d 641; (Kan. 1996)	Discretionary—inadmissible. Reliability of eyewitness identification is within the realm of jurors' knowledge and experience. We continue to follow the previous line of cases and hold that expert testimony regarding eyewitness identification should not be admitted.
Kentucky	*Commonwealth v. Christie* 98 S.W.3d 485 (Ky. 2002)	Discretionary—may be admissible. Discretion abused in refusing to admit, case remanded. Per se exclusionary rule overturned. Lack of direct evidence against defendant so expert testimony should have been admitted. Blanket exclusion of expert testimony was due to the trial court's incorrect belief that that the testimony was inadmissible

(*continued*)

TABLE 18.2 (Continued)

State	Most recent case	Ruling
Kentucky (continued)		per se. Case remanded for new trial to determine the relevancy and reliability of the testimony under a proper analysis.
Louisiana	State v. Gurley 565 So. 2d 1055 (La. App. 4 Cir. 1990)	Discretionary—inadmissible. Prejudicial effect outweighs its probative value and usurps jury's function. The testimony would not have been an aid to the jury.
Maine	State v. Kelley 2000 ME 107; 752 A.2d 188 (Sup. Jud. Ct. of Maine, 2000) *See 549 A.2d 742 (1988)	Discretionary—inadmissible. The trial court found that the testimony would not be helpful to the jury, and the court did instruct the jury. Therefore, the court's conclusion that the expert's testimony would not be helpful is not clearly erroneous, and its decision to deny funds for that reason was within its broad discretion.
Maryland	Bloodsworth v. Maryland 307 Md. 164; 512 A.2d 1056 (Md. App.1986)	Discretionary—inadmissible. Reliability of the witnesses and the identification is better tested by cross-examination than by the opinion of an expert. Defendant failed to make a case for the use of an expert by failing to persuade the court that the technique has general acceptance in the relevant scientific community, and the proffer is not sufficient to persuade exactly what is even being offered to the jury other than some generalized explanation of the studies that have been made. Nothing that has been proffered suggests that it will be helpful.
Massachusetts	Commonwealth v. Santoli, Jr. 424 Mass. 837; 680 N.E.2d 1116; (Mass. 1997)	Discretionary—may be admissible, discretion not abused in refusing to admit. No error in excluding the testimony where the physical evidence and other facts provided significant corroboration of the victim's identification.
Michigan	People v. Hill 84 Mich. App. 90, 269 N.W. 2d 492 (Mich. 1978)	Discretionary—inadmissible. The court rejected defendant's assertion that the trial court erred in excluding expert testimony on the process by which people perceive and remember events and how pretrial identification procedures could affect this process. The expert did not interview the eyewitnesses about whom he was to testify and only observed them in the courtroom. Also, the trial court offered to let defendant pursue the matter in closing argument.
Minnesota	State v. Miles 585 N.W.2d 368; (Minn. 1998)	Discretionary—may be admissible, discretion not abused in refusing to admit. There is nothing to suggest that expert testimony on the accuracy of eyewitness identification in general would be particularly helpful to the jury in evaluating the specific eyewitness testimony. Numerous safeguards are in place, and there was other corroborating evidence.
Mississippi	White v. Mississippi 847 So. 2d 886 (Miss. Ct. App. 2002)	Discretionary—inadmissible. Evidence did not rely on proven scientific principles and Court held that they had been shown nothing to suggest that the science about which the expert was to testify is generally accepted.

(continued)

TABLE 18.2 (*Continued*)

State	Most recent case	Ruling
Missouri	*State v. Whitmill* 780 S.W.2d 45; (Mo. 1989)	Discretionary—inadmissible. Relates to the credibility of witnesses and constitutes an invasion of the province of the jury.
Montana		No cases found.
Nebraska	*State v. George* 264 Neb. 26; 645 N.W.2d 777; (Neb. 2002) *See also 305 N.W.2d 812 (1981)	Discretionary—inadmissible. Expert testimony on reliability of eyewitness identifications is unnecessary.
Nevada	*White v. State* 112 Nev. 1261; 926 P.2d 291; (Nev. 1996) *See also 839 P.2d 589 (1992)	Discretionary—may be admissible; discretion not abused in refusing to admit. There was corroborating evidence of identification.
New Hampshire	No cases found	No cases found.
New Jersey	*State v. Gunter* 231 N.J. Super. 34; 554 A.2d 1356; (N.J. 1989)	Discretionary—may be admissible. Case remanded. Because there was no preliminary hearing, we cannot say with any assurance whether the proffered testimony would have actually assisted the jury. Nor can we begin to consider the reliability issue. Case remanded to hold preliminary hearing to determine scientific reliability of expert's testimony.
New Mexico	No cases found	No cases found.
New York	*People v. Lee* 96 N.Y.2d 157; 750 N.E.2d 63 (N.Y. 2001)	Discretionary—may be admissible; discretion not abused in refusing to admit. The trial court was aware of corroborating evidence in addition to the identification testimony. Given the particular facts and circumstances, we cannot say the trial court's denial constituted an abuse of discretion.
North Carolina	*State v. Lee* 154 N.C. App. 410; 572 S.E.2d 170; (N.C. 2002)	Discretionary—may be admissible; discretion not abused in refusing to admit. Testimony not case specific and lacked probative value.
North Dakota	*State v. Fontaine* 382 N.W. 2d 374; (N.D. 1986)	Discretionary—may be admissible. Discretion not abused in refusing to admit. Partial testimony allowed. Expert testified on several estimator variables, but was not allowed to answer a hypothetical question concerning accuracy. The court did not abuse its discretion.
Ohio	*State v. Buell* 22 Ohio St. 3d 124; 489 N.E.2d 795; (Ohio 1986)	Discretionary—may be admissible; discretion not abused in refusing to admit. Expert testimony regarding the credibility of a *typical* witness is admissible, but testimony regarding the credibility of a *particular* witness is not.
Oklahoma	*Torres v. State* 1998 OK CR 40;	Discretionary—may be admissible; discretion not abused in refusing to admit. While it might be that expert testimony

(*continued*)

TABLE 18.2 (*Continued*)

State	Most recent case	Ruling
Oklahoma (*continued*)	962 P.2d 3 (Okla. 1998)	regarding eyewitness identification would have been admissible in this case, defendant did not present any evidence to show what that expert testimony would have revealed or how the failure to present such expert evidence prejudiced him.
Oregon	*State v. Goldsby* 59 Ore. App. 66; 650 P.2d 952 (Ore. 1982)	Discretionary—inadmissible. Although eyewitness identification evidence has a built-in potential for error, the law does not deal with that by allowing experts to debate the quality of evidence for the jury.
Pennsylvania	*Commonwealth v. Abdul-Salaam* 544 Pa. 514; 678 A.2d 342 (Pa. 1996)	Prohibitory—inadmissible. Testimony would give unwarranted appearance of authority as to the subject of credibility, a subject which an ordinary juror can assess.
Rhode Island	*State v. Martinez* 774 A.2d 15 (R.I. 2001)	Discretionary—inadmissible. In general, the jury does not need assistance in determining the trustworthiness of an eyewitness.
South Carolina	*State v. Whaley* 305 S.C. 138; 406 S.E.2d 369 (S.C. 1991)	Discretionary—may be admissible. Discretion abused in refusing to admit. Trial court ruling reversed and case remanded. It was an abuse of discretion to exclude the expert's testimony concerning eyewitness reliability because the main issue in this case was the identity of the assailant, the only evidence establishing the defendant as the assailant was the testimony of the two eyewitnesses, and other factors existed which could have affected the identification.
South Dakota	*State v. McCord* 505 N.W.2d 388 (S.D. 1993)	Discretionary—may be admissible. Discretion not abused in admitting. The only case in which the prosecution called an identification expert. The Court ruled that jurors do not possess an expert's comprehensive training in assessing the reliability of identification. The court found that the trial court did not abuse its discretion in finding this testimony as relevant.
Tennessee	*State v. McKinney* 74 S.W.3d 291 (Tenn. 2002) *See also 32 S.W.3d 831 (2000)	Prohibitory. Per se exclusionary rule. Expert testimony regarding eyewitness identification is inadmissible and the exclusion of such testimony does not violate a defendant's due process right to present a defense.
Texas	*Weatherred v. State* 15 S.W.d 540 (Tex. Crim. App. 2000)	Discretionary—inadmissible. Appellant failed to carry his burden of showing that the proffered testimony was scientifically reliable or relevant.
Utah	*State v. Maestas* 63 P.3d 621 (Utah 2002)	Discretionary—may be admissible, discretion not abused in refusing to admit. The trial court is in the best position to balance the probative value of proffered testimony against

(*continued*)

TABLE 18.2 (*Continued*)

State	Most recent case	Ruling
Utah (*continued*)		the risk of intrusion upon the fact-finding functions of the jury. The trial court acted within its discretion in excluding the testimony.
Vermont	*State v. Percy* 156 Vt. 468; 595 A.2d 248; (Vt. 1990)	Discretionary—inadmissible. Juries may be made to understand psychological factors which affect accuracy of an identification through cross-examination and closing arguments.
Virginia	*Currie v. Commonwealth* 30 Va. App. 58; 515 S.E.2d 335 (Va. 1999)	Discretionary—may be admissible. Discretion not abused in refusing to admit. Partial testimony allowed. It was not error to limit expert witness's testimony concerning the correlation between eyewitness certainty and accuracy, and those other areas of witness's proffered testimony which were within the common knowledge and experience of the jurors.
Washington	*State v. Nordlund* 2002 Wash. App (Wash. 2002)	Discretionary—may be admissible, discretion not abused in refusing to admit. During voir dire, the trial court found that the potential jurors' answers demonstrated that they already understood each of the factors the expert wanted to explain.
West Virginia	*State v. Taylor* 200 W. Va. 661; 490 S.E.2d 748; (W.Va. 1997)	Discretionary—may be admissible, discretion not abused in refusing to admit. The testimony would not have affected the overall outcome of the case. Fees to hire an expert were denied.
Wisconsin	*State v. Blair* 164 Wis. 2d 64; 473 N.W.2d 566; (Wis. 1991)	Discretionary—may be admissible, discretion not abused in refusing to admit. All topics proffered were within the common knowledge and sense and perception of the jury.
Wyoming	*Engberg, v. Meyer* 820 P.2d 70; (Wyo. 1991)	Discretionary—may be admissible, discretion not abused in refusing to admit. The court recognizes the modern trend more favorable to the admission of expert testimony relating to eyewitness identification, but holds that their consistent rule is that the admission of expert testimony is within the discretion of the trial court.

case in Kansas, the court ruled: "Reliability of eyewitness identification is within the realm of jurors' knowledge and experience. We continue to follow the previous line of cases and hold that expert testimony regarding eyewitness identification should not be admitted into trial" (*State v. Gaines*, 926 P.2d at 649). This type of reasoning suggests that the court renders this type of testimony unnecessary and implies that the court would be highly unlikely to admit it. Another example of such a rationale can be found in *State v. Percy* [156 Vt. 468, 475 (Vt. 1990)], in which the court stated: "There is ample authority holding that juries may be made to understand psychological factors which affect the accuracy of an identification when these factors are brought to light at cross-examination and during closing argument." It should be noted, however, that Vermont has held that it may be an error *not* to admit the testimony under certain circumstances (595 A.2d 248, 253). In *Weatherred v. State of Texas* [15 S.W.3d 540 (Tex. 2000)], the Texas Court

TABLE 18.3
Admissibility Approaches by State

	Type of approach	Percentage of states	States in each category	
PROHIBITORY	*Prohibitory*: Court explicitly declares a *per se* inadmissibility rule.	2% (1 state)	Tennessee	
DISCRETIONARY	*Inadmissible*: Under discretionary view, these courts find that discretion was not abused in excluding the testimony. These decisions use strong language which suggests a *per se* rule of inadmissibility.	33% (15 states)	Arkansas Florida Kansas Louisiana Maine Maryland Michigan Mississippi	Missouri Nebraska Oregon Pennsylvania Rhode Island Texas Vermont
	May be admissible, but not admitted in this case: Under discretionary view, although the testimony is admissible in general, the court found that discretion was not abused in refusing to admit, and rationale often suggests admissibility of testimony is possible but not probable. *Partial testimony was admitted in these cases	48% (22 states)	Alabama Arizona* Connecticut Delaware* Georgia Idaho Illinois Indiana Massachusetts Minnesota Nevada New York	North Carolina North Dakota* Ohio Oklahoma Utah Virginia* Washington West Virginia Wisconsin Wyoming
	May be admissible: Discretion abused in refusing to admit the testimony.	7% (3 states)	Alaska California	South Carolina
	May be admissible: Discretion not abused in admitting testimony.	2% (1 state)	South Dakota	
	May be admissible: Case remanded for further review.	9% (4 states)	Colorado Iowa	Kentucky New Jersey

of Criminal Appeals held that the appellant had the burden of proving that the eyewitness expert testimony was not mere "junk science" and had failed to do so by failing to show that the proffered testimony was scientifically reliable. These examples are representative of the type of language currently being used by courts in their exclusion of expert identification testimony. The type of reasoning and the language used by these judges in their analysis can be construed as holding that the testimony is *per se* inadmissible.

As shown in Table 18.1, the most common ruling, which falls under the discretionary approach, occurs when the court rules that the type of testimony is generally considered admissible, although in this instance it was not found to be so. Nearly half (48%) of the most recent cases involving this issue fall within this category, holding that it was not an abuse of discretion for the trial court to exclude the testimony. The court is essentially suggesting that it is open to such testimony; however, for some reason it was not admissible in that particular case. An example of this type of rationale is found in Alabama in *Ex parte Williams* [594 So. 2d 1225, 1227 (Ala. 1992)], in which the court held: "It appears that the trial court's ruling was based upon the fact that [the expert] was not familiar with facts of case and had no personal contact with victim. Therefore, we conclude that the trial court did not abuse its discretion in ruling [the expert] testimony inadmissible." Another example can be found in *Johnson v. State* [272 Ga. 254, 260 (Ga. 2000)], in which the court held: "We find that while the testimony of [the expert] might have been helpful to some degree, under the circumstances in this case there was no clear abuse of discretion in the trial court's refusal to admit [the expert's] testimony." A review of the rationale employed in these cases quickly reveals that the courts are using a variety of reasons to exclude the testimony, which vary to such an extent that it causes one to wonder when it *ever* would be admitted. In these states the rulings appear to suggest that although admissibility of expert testimony is possible, it is not probable. One should note, however, that in four of these cases partial testimony from the expert *was* admitted: 25 P.3d 717 (Ariz. 2001), 815 A.2d 327 (Del. 2003), 382 N.W. 2d 374 (N.D. 1986), and 515 S.E.2d 335 (Va. 1999). These states are placed in this category, however, because the defendant appealed the court's decision in excluding any testimony that was not initially admitted. In all four cases, the reviewing court held that the trial court did not abuse its discretion in excluding some of the expert's testimony.

The analysis further reveals that expert identification testimony was admitted in only 17% of the most recent cases involving this type of testimony. This percentage does include the four cases in which some of the testimony was admitted and some of it was excluded. As Table 18.2 depicts, a distinction is drawn between the type of rationale used in admitting the testimony. One state (2%) falls in the category in which the appellate court found no abuse in the trial court's decision to admit the testimony. What is important to point out in this lone instance is that this was the only case in which the prosecution, not the defense, introduced the eyewitness expert. The expert was actually a police officer, who was brought in to inform the jury as to why an eyewitness may not give a completely accurate description. He was actually permitted to give his opinion with respect to the similarities and dissimilarities of the facial features of the person depicted in the composite sketch and the defendant's photograph and to give a similar opinion with respect to the composite sketch and the defendant in the courtroom. This opinion is in direct contradiction to the more common ruling that experts are not permitted to testify as to the specifics of the case. Three states (7%) fall in the category in which the appellate court *did* find an abuse of discretion in the trial court's decision to exclude the testimony. In these instances, the appellate court ruled that the testimony should have been admitted and, therefore, overturned the trial court's decision. These decisions hold great weight on the admissibility of expert eyewitness testimony because these are the holdings in which the appellate court finds that the trial court's exclusion of the testimony was arbitrary. The rationales used by judges who admitted the eyewitness expert are in direct opposition to the rationale previously mentioned in the cases where an expert was not admitted. An example can be found in *Commonwealth v. Christie* [98 S.W.3d 485, 491 (Ky.2002)]:

> Where identity is a crucial and closely contested issue, however, and where critical testimony is given by people who did not know the perpetrator and had only a short time to see him or were limited or distracted by other factors, expert testimony seems more clearly warranted. Thus, the particular facts of this case—that (1) eyewitness identification by strangers of a different race was the main and most compelling evidence against [the defendant], (2) there was no other direct evidence against [the defendant], and (3) the circumstantial evidence against [the defendant] was weak—make exclusion of [the expert's] testimony under KRE 403 an abuse of discretion. Further, the error was not harmless.

This example portrays the variability in judicial rationale, where in some case evaluations the testimony of the expert was within the common knowledge of the jury, and in the decisions within this category, it was not. Furthermore, in *People v. McDonald* [690 P.2d 709, 720–721 (Cal. 1984)], the court reasoned:

> It appears from the professional literature, however, that other factors bearing on eyewitness identification may be known only to some jurors, or may be imperfectly understood by many, or may be contrary to the intuitive beliefs of most. . . . We conclude that although jurors may not be totally unaware of the foregoing psychological factors bearing on eyewitness identification, the body of information now available on these matters is "sufficiently beyond common experience" that in appropriate cases expert opinion thereon could at least "assist the trier of fact."

Additionally, in Alaska in *Skamarocius v. State* [731 P.2d 63, 66–67 (Alaska App. 1987)], the court found an abuse of discretion in excluding the testimony, and reasoned: "We are also satisfied that the testimony was germane to the main issue in the case: the accuracy of [the] identification of [the defendant] as her assailant. . . . [The expert's] testimony would have been helpful to the jury in this regard. We cannot conclude that exclusion of the defendant's expert testimony was harmless. [The defendant] is therefore entitled to a new trial." In *State v. Whaley* [406 S.E.2d 369, 372 (S.C. 1991)], the court similarly reasoned: "Accordingly, we hold that it was an abuse of discretion to exclude [the expert's] testimony concerning eyewitness reliability because the main issue in this case was the identity of the assailant, the only evidence establishing Whaley as the assailant was the testimony of the two eyewitnesses, and other factors existed which could have affected the identification." In addition to the cases found that admit expert identification testimony, it should be noted that two other courts actually recently overturned a *per se* rule of inadmissibility of this type of testimony. In *State v. Schutz* [579

N.W.2d 317, 320 (Iowa 1998)], the Supreme Court of Iowa overturned the *per se* exclusionary rule that had been adopted almost 20 years earlier in *State v. Galloway* [275 N.W.2d 736 (Iowa 1979)], holding, "We conclude the *per se* rule adopted by *Galloway* must be reversed. The exclusion of expert testimony is a matter committed to the sound discretion of the trial court and we will reverse only for an abuse of that discretion. Although the district court could not have anticipated our holding in this matter, it was error to apply the per se rule of exclusion." Furthermore, in *Commonwealth v. Christie* [98 S.W. 3d 485 (Ky. 2002)], the trial court initially excluded the expert testimony based upon the *per se* exclusionary rule established in *Pankey v. Commonwealth* [485 S.W.2d 513 (Ky.1972)] and *Gibbs v. Commonwealth* [723 S.W.2d 871 (Ky.1986)]. These prior rulings were overturned, however, with the court holding that "there was no direct evidence against [the defendant] other than the eyewitness identifications. Further, the circumstantial evidence against [the defendant], standing alone, would not have been sufficient to sustain a conviction. Thus, the eyewitness identifications of [defendant] were central to [the defendant's] conviction" (98 S.W. 3d at 491). The court reversed the ruling and remanded the case to the trial court to consider the expert testimony. As these cases show, the rationales used by the judges in admitting the testimony directly contradict those rationales used when they exclude the testimony.

Federal Analysis

At the federal level, a case from each of the 12 circuits was content analyzed and sorted in the same manner as the state cases. As previously mentioned, no case directly regarding the admission of expert eyewitness testimony was found in the U.S. Court of Appeals for the District of Columbia. The analysis of the 11 remaining circuits reveals that expert identification testimony was excluded in all circuits. The decisions found in these cases can be categorized in the same way as the state cases: (1) may be admissible, discretion not abused in admitting; (2) may be admissible, discretion abused in exclusion; (3) may be admissible, but discretion not abused in exclusion; (4) inadmissible, discretion not abused in excluding; and (5) *per se* inadmissible. The frequencies are reported in Table 18.4, and the case-by-case decisions are listed in Table 18.5.

As seen in Table 18.4, none of the circuits has a rule of *per se* inadmissibility. Three circuits (25%) found the testimony inadmissible, using language to suggest a rule of *per se* inadmissibility. The standard utilized in these cases can be construed as a *per se* exclusion. In *United States v. Kime* [99 F.3d 870, 883 (8th Cir. 1996)], the court, noting that the district court gave a jury instruction on eyewitness identification, held that the "proffered expert eyewitness identification testimony fails to qualify as 'scientific knowledge' under Daubert's first prong." This view is also found in the Eleventh Circuit. In *United States v. Smith* [122 F.3d 1355, 1359 (11th Cir. 1997)], the court reasoned, "Defendants who want to attack the reliability of eyewitness recollections are free to use the powerful tool of cross-examination to do so. They may also request jury instructions that highlight particular problems in eyewitness recollection." Without declaring a rule of *per se* inadmissibility, the logic and reasoning used in these decisions suggest that this type of testimony would never be admissible.

TABLE 18.4
Federal Categorization

	Type of approach	Percentage of circuits	Circuits in each category
PROHIBITORY	*Prohibitory*: Court explicitly declares a *per se* inadmissibility rule.	0	0
DISCRETIONARY	*Inadmissible. Discretion not abused in excluding.*: Under discretionary view, these courts find that discretion was not abused in excluding the testimony. These decisions use strong language which suggests a *per se* rule of inadmissibility.	27%	8th, 9th, 11th
DISCRETIONARY	*May be admissible. Discretion not abused in exclusion.* Under discretionary view, although the testimony is admissible in general, it was not admitted in this case, and rationale suggests admissibility of of testimony is possible but not probably.	64%	1st, 2nd, 4th, 5th, 6th, 7th, 10th
DISCRETIONARY	*May be admissible. Discretion abused in exclusion.*	9%	3rd
DISCRETIONARY	*May be admissible. Discretion not abused in admitting.*	0	0

Over half of the circuits (64%), however, although suggesting that such testimony might be admissible, affirm the trial court's exclusion of the testimony. For example, in *United States v. Crotteau* [218 F.3d 826 (7th Cir. 2000)], the court found that the instructions given by the trial judge and the substantial corroborating evidence were sufficient and referred to its previous holding in *United States v. Hall* (165 F.3d 1095, 1107) that "any weaknesses in eyewitness identification testimony ordinarily can be exposed through careful cross-examination of the eyewitnesses."

TABLE 18.5
Federal Rulings

First Circuit Maine Massachusetts New Hampshire Rhode Island	*U.S. v. Brien* 59 F.3d 274 (1st Cir. 1995)	May be admissible. Discretion not abused in exclusion. The Court of Appeals sustained the district court's ruling not to admit the testimony on the ground that the defense offered practically nothing as far as a proffer of data or literature underlying the expert's assumptions and conclusions, despite being asked for it repeatedly. There is no reason it couldn't be supplied, and it was necessary since the expert's testimony "did not concern a single long-established scientific principle."
Second Circuit Connecticut New York Vermont	*U.S. v. Lumpkin* 192 F.3d 280 (2nd Cir. 1999)	May be admissible. Discretion not abused in exclusion. The Court of Appeals upheld the district court's ruling that the expert could not testify on the confidence-accuracy relationship. It "would have confused the jury's assessment of the officers' credibility, thereby usurping their role."
Third Circuit Delaware New Jersey Pennsylvania	*U.S. v. Mathis* 264 F.3d 321 (3rd Cir. 2001)	May be admissible. Discretion aAbused in exclusion. Despite finding that the government abused its discretion in not admitting several pieces of the proffered testimony, the Court of Appeals ultimately decided that had the testimony been admitted, the outcome of the case would not have been different. Harmless error.
Fourth Circuit Maryland North Carolina South Carolina Virginia West Virginia	*U.S. v. Harris* 995 F.2d 532 (4th Cir. 1993)	May be admissible. Discretion not abused in exclusion. The court affirmed the district court's judgment, finding that none of the limited circumstances under which courts allow expert testimony on eyewitness identification were present in this case.
Fifth Circuit Louisiana Mississippi Texas	*U.S. v. Moore* 786 F.2d 1308 (5th Cir. 1986)	Not admitted: admissible, but discretion not abused in exclusion. The decision whether to admit this testimony is squarely within the discretion of the trial judge and properly so. This is not a case in which the eyewitness identification testimony is critical. Even if the identifications of the defendants are completely disregarded, the other evidence of guilt are overwhelming.
Sixth Circuit Kentucky Michigan Ohio Tennessee	*U.S. v. Langan* 263 F.3d 613 (6th Cir. 2001)	Not admitted: admissible, but discretion not abused in exclusion. The Court of Appeals affirmed the judgment of the district court in that it agreed that the testimony failed to meet the second prong of *Daubert*, which requires that the proposed testimony fit the issue to which the expert is testifying. The court agreed that the "hazards of eyewitness identification are within the ordinary knowledge of most lay jurors."

(continued)

TABLE 18.5 (*Continued*)

Seventh Circuit Illinois Indiana Wisconsin	*U.S. v. Crotteau* 218 F.3d 826 (7th Cir. 2000)	Not admitted: admissible, but discretion not abused in exclusion. The court denies the defendant's motion for the appointment of an eyewitness identification expert because "the facts of the case do not create an unusual or compelling situation in which the aid of an expert witness is required" and "as the Seventh Circuit has stated, cross examination, cautionary instructions, and corroborating evidence can obviate the need for expert testimony on eyewitness identification."
Eighth Circuit Arkansas Iowa Minnesota Nebraska North Dakota South Dakota	*U.S. v. Kime* 99 F.3d 870 (8th Cir. 1996)	Inadmissible. The court agrees with the district's court ruling to not admit the testimony for several reasons: the testimony fails to qualify as "scientific knowledge" under *Daubert's* first prong; it fails under the second prong because it would not assist the trier of fact since the evaluation of eyewitness testimony is for the jury alone and the testimony would intrude the jury's domain; the minimal probative value is outweighed by the danger of juror confusion; the concerns were adequately addressed in jury instruction; and the testimony was supported by several other witnesses.
Ninth Circuit Alaska Arizona California Hawaii Idaho Montana Nevada Oregon Washington	*U.S. v. Labansat* 94 F.3d 527 (9th Cir. 1996)	Inadmissible. The court upheld the district court's denial of the defendants request for funds to hire an expert on eyewitness identification because "as we have previously explained, 'the admissibility of this type of expert is strongly disfavored in most courts' and any weaknesses . . . can ordinarily be revealed by counsel's careful cross-examination." The defendant has not shown by clear and convincing evidence that he was prejudiced by the lack of expert assistance.
Tenth Circuit Colorado Kansas New Mexico Oklahoma Utah Wyoming	*U.S. v. Smith* 156 F.3d 1046 (10th Cir. 1998)	Not admitted: admissible, but discretion not abused in exclusion. The district court did not abuse its discretion in excluding the testimony. The district court considered the matter in detail, conducting a lengthy *Daubert* hearing. There were five eyewitnesses identifications, not one.
Eleventh Circuit Alabama Florida Georgia	*U.S. v. Smith* 122 F.3d 1355 (11th Cir. 1997)	Inadmissible. The court explains that, under the prior panel precedent rule, it is bound by earlier panel holdings. Expert testimony not needed because the jury could determine reliability under the tools of cross-examination and jury instruction to highlight particular problems in eyewitness recollection. The defendant was successful in this case in getting the district court to instruct the jury about cross-racial identification, potential bias in earlier identification, delay between even and time of identification, and stress. Therefore expert testimony not needed.
D.C. circuit		No cases found.

The Third Circuit stands apart from the rest, as depicted in its decision in *United States v. Mathis* [264 F.3d 321 (3rd Cir. 2001)]. In that case the court held that it was an abuse of discretion to refuse to admit the expert testimony. The court reasoned:

> We find it difficult to accord the customary degree of deference to the District Court's discretion in this case because the District Court explained its ruling with little more than a series of conclusions. . . . In short, we see no reason to believe [the expert's] aura of reliability reflected anything other than his actual reliability as an expert witness. With respect to the District Court's concern with "confusing or misleading the jury" or "unfair prejudice" we are unable to discern from these references, any more than from our own review of the record, how such problems might arise . . . we believe that testimony of this sort, with its accompanying level of scientific detail, would not simply duplicate juror's intuitions or common sense, and such principles seem difficult to establish indirectly through cross-examination. (264 F.3d at 338)

However, after this optimistic line of reasoning, the court proceeded to determine, in its final step of review, that the exclusion of the testimony was harmless error, and as such affirmed the District Court's conviction of the defendant: "Although we believe that portions of [the expert's] proffered testimony should have been admitted, we also find that, in the context of the record as a whole, his testimony was highly unlikely to have caused a different result" (264 F.3d at 343).

Based on an analysis of 47 of the most recent state cases and 11 of the most recent federal cases that have appeared in court across the nation, ranging in date from 1986 to 2004, it is clear that criteria for admissibility of the testimony varies widely at the state level, with the majority (48%) of states claiming that although the testimony is admissible, it was not found to be so in these cases. It can be inferred from the rationales used in these cases that although the admission of the testimony is possible, it is not probable. Two percent (one state) hold a *per se* rule of inadmissibility, whereas 33% hold the testimony inadmissible while using such strong language to indicate a *per se* rule of inadmissibility. Seventeen percent of the states found the testimony admissible, with all but one finding that the testimony should have been admitted and that the trial court abused its discretion in excluding the testimony.

At the federal level, 7 of the 11 circuits (64%) found the testimony may be admissible, but they found that it was not an abuse of discretion for the trial court to exclude it. One circuit found that the district court abused its discretion in excluding the testimony, but ultimately decided that this exclusion constituted a harmless error. Three circuits (27%) found the evidence inadmissible, using strong language to imply a *per se* rule of inadmissibility.

Whether this variation in admissibility decisions can be attributed to the characteristics of the jurisdiction, the personal views of the judge, the wide discretion granted to the judge, or the ambiguity of admission criteria, it is clearly problematic that the decisions are not based primarily on the specific characteristics of the case. In search of an explanation as to why the rationale used by courts varies to such a wide degree, some suggest that this may be due to the judicial system's overall skepticism of the field of social science. Although the research in the field is sometimes ignored, some make decisions that contradict established findings. Collins (2003) points out that the system has failed to integrate procedures recommended by leading social science researchers, thereby making the courts an ineffective solution to a serious problem. Research indicates that courts look unfavorably upon this type of testimony. Groscup and Penrod (2003) conducted a study to determine how courts evaluate different types of testimony. Specifically, testimony from police officers was compared with testimony from psychologists. Of the experts testifying in their sample of criminal cases, 265 were police officers and 376 were psychologists. Sixty-eight of the psychologists were experimental psychologists, and the vast majority testified about issues relating to eyewitness reliability. Overall, psychologists were admitted only 50% of the time, compared with the 86% admissibility rate for police officers. It was further determined that courts differentially treated clinical psychologists and experimental psychologists, with testimony from experimental psychologists being the type of testimony least likely to be admitted, with only a 22% admissibility rate. These findings indicate that courts are more critical of psychologists as experts, particularly experimental psychologists who testify as eyewitness experts. Answers to questionnaires also indicated that overall, judges were "disinterested or hostile toward social science" (p. 2003). Analysis of their results brought them to the conclusion that "courts may be making decisions that are inconsistent with the informational needs of the fact finder, the opinions of the experts on the need for their testimony, and the extent of our knowledge about the reliability of their respective testimonies" (Groscup & Penrod, 2003, p. 1160). Furthermore, Findley (2002) states, "Courts have created rules or followed procedures that ignore or even contradict what the empirical evidence shows." He continues on the topic of expert testimony, saying:

> Hard evidence shows that jurors do not understand the psychological processes at work in eyewitness identification and tend to rely an unwarranted extent on such identifications. Nonetheless, courts in many jurisdictions routinely continue to exclude expert testimony designed to educate jurors on these matters, often on the ground that such information is within the common knowledge of jurors. (p. 334)

Judges (2000) comments, "Despite the years of research that social scientists have devoted to the study of eyewitness identification evidence, experts within the legal community remain 'skeptical.' The law's generic skepticism of social science risks deteriorating into a counterproductive bias if the legal system fails to recognize the genuine strides that social science has made in recent decades" (p. 232).

It is this skepticism and lack of knowledge on the topic that lead courts to the misguided conclusion that the factors that affect eyewitness identification evidence are common sense to the average juror.

IS EYEWITNESS MEMORY COMMON SENSE TO JURORS?

One of the most commonly cited reasons for excluding the testimony of eyewitness experts is that factors that may affect eyewitness identification are merely common sense to jurors, and thus an expert has nothing to offer the jury. The ability to assess the credibility of a witness is thought to be so commonplace that if the eyewitness testimony is not accurate, most courts believe that it will be detected by the jury during cross-examination of the witness or as a result of following instructions given to them. To provide a flavor for this assumption, Table 18.6 displays excerpts taken directly from some of the most recent cases in which the defense sought to admit expert eyewitness testimony but was denied. As will be shown from the review of the social science literature, these citations, in fact, stand in direct opposition to the research that has been conducted on whether eyewitness issues are common sense to jurors.

There are two general approaches to determining whether eyewitness memory is common sense to jurors. One includes surveys of individuals' knowledge, and the other includes experimental studies investigating how people evaluate and use eyewitness identification evidence in mock jury decision-making. This includes studies that have manipulated dimensions of eyewitness evidence to examine the effect on guilty verdicts, studies that have examined people's ability to predict the results of eyewitness identification experiments, and studies that assessed whether mock jurors can differentiate accurate from inaccurate witnesses. Both the survey and experimental studies converge on the finding that there is widespread variability among individuals' beliefs about eyewitness testimony, and that individuals do not possess accurate knowledge concerning the factors that affect eyewitness evidence. As can be seen from the following sections, these findings cause serious concern about whether jurors are able to adequately evaluate the accuracy and credibility of eyewitness testimony.

HOW ACCURATE IS "COMMON SENSE"? SURVEY STUDIES OF LAY KNOWLEDGE

This section provides a general chronological review of the research that has directly examined laypeople's knowledge of eyewitness issues. The first systematic studies of this kind employed the Knowledge of Eyewitness Behavior Questionnaire (KEBQ) to assess lay knowledge of eyewitness factors in samples of college students as well as jury-eligible citizens (Deffenbacher & Loftus, 1982; Loftus, 1979). This 14-item multiple-choice questionnaire was designed to assess knowledge of several factors that affect eyewitness accuracy, including cross-racial identification; confidence; witness training; the effects of stress, violence, and delay; and interview factors. For example, for one item designed to measure knowledge of cross-race identification, respondents are asked: "Appropriate to the situation where people of one racial group view those of another, you may have heard the expression, 'They all look alike.' Which of the following best reflects your personal view of this expression?" Respondents are provided the following response options: (a) It is true, (b) It is a myth, (c) It is more applicable to whites viewing nonwhites than the reverse, and (d) It is more applicable to nonwhites viewing whites than the reverse. Across samples, the typical respondent performed significantly above chance, but overall accuracy levels were low, with responses to many items not achieving above-chance levels. In the 5-item version of the questionnaire, 54% of a college sample provided correct responses (Loftus, 1979). In the extended 14-item version used by Deffenbacher and Loftus (1982), 46% of respondents across two college samples provided correct responses, and college respondents performed marginally better than community members,

TABLE 18.6
Judicial Reasoning on Eyewitness Memory as Common Sense to Jurors

State	Quotation
Connecticut *State v. McClendon* 730 A.2d 1107 (Conn. 1999)	"These general principles should not come as a surprise to the average juror. It is common knowledge that eyewitnesses may make mistakes and may forget what they have seen." (Id at 1115)
Florida *Johnson v. State* 438 So. 2d 774 (Fla. 1983)	"We hold that a jury is fully capable of assessing a witness' ability to perceive and remember, given the assistance of cross-examination and cautionary instructions, without the aid of expert testimony." (Id at 777)
Kansas *State v. Warren* 635 P.2d 1236 (Kan. 1981)	"The reliability of the eyewitness identification was within the realm of the jurors' knowledge and experience. . . Requiring trial courts to admit this type of expert evidence is not the answer to the eyewitness identification problem." (Id at 394–395)
Maine *State v. Rich* 549 A.2d 742 (1988)	"Expert testimony must be concerned with a matter beyond common knowledge so that the untrained layman will not be able to determine it intelligently without expert help; and the expert's testimony must be helpful to the jury's understanding. If it offers no advantage over the general knowledge of jurors it is irrelevant." (Id at 743–744)
Nebraska *State v. Ammons,* 208 Neb. 812 (Neb. 1981)	". . .The accuracy or inaccuracy of eyewitness observation is a common experience of daily life. Such testimony would invade the province of the jury." (Id at 814)
Pennsylvania *Commonwealth v. Simmons,* 541 Pa. 211 (Pa. 1995)	". . .testimony concerning the reliability of eyewitness identification would give an unwarranted appearance of authority as to the subject of credibility, a subject which an ordinary juror can assess." (Id at 230)
Rhode Island *State v. Martinez* 774 A.2d 15 (R.I. 2001)	". . . in general, the jury does not need assistance in determining the trustworthiness of an eyewitness. Specifically, we held that 'a jury is perfectly capable of assessing the witness' credibility by weighting the inconsistencies and deficiencies elicited in cross-examination. We have also held that testimony concerning the reliability or unreliability of an eyewitness would serve only to confuse and mislead the jury. . .'" (Id at 19)
Tennessee *State v. Coley* 32 S.W. 3d 831 (Tenn. 2000)	"Eyewitness testimony has no scientific or technical underpinnings which would be outside the common understanding of the jury; therefore, expert testimony is not necessary to help jurors understand the eyewitness's testimony." (Id at 833–834)
Virginia *Currie v. Commonwealth* 515 S.E.2d 335 (Va. 1999)	"The trustworthiness of eyewitness observations is not generally beyond the common knowledge and experience of the average juror and is, therefore, not a proper subject for expert testimony." (Id at 338)
Wisconsin *State v. Blair* 473 N.W.2d 566 (Wis. 1991)	"The trial court reviewed the offer-of-proof at length . . . and concluded 'that everything that the expert would testify to in essence is within the common knowledge and sense and perception of the jury' and would overly emphasize a particular school of thought 'as to exactly what memory is.'" (Id at 572)

who averaged 35% correct. Furthermore, respondents with jury experience performed better than those without jury experience, but only by a very small margin (36% versus 34%, respectively). Rahaim and Brodsky (1982) used a 10-item questionnaire to test the knowledge of a community sample of potential jurors on three aspects of eyewitness memory: the effects of race and stress on identification accuracy, and the relationship between confidence and accuracy. The level of accuracy obtained across these topics was 34%, which was lower than that observed in previous investigations with college student samples but similar to that found in Deffenbacher and Loftus's (1982) community-based sample.

Using a similar multiple-choice format, Yarmey and Jones (1983) assessed knowledge of eyewitness factors in different samples of mainly Canadian respondents. They found a level of performance in a college sample of potential jurors comparable to that reported by Deffenbacher and Loftus (1982). Specifically, only 42% of the students provided correct responses, which is comparable to the 46% level obtained by Deffenbacher and Loftus. In contrast, this study revealed no significant difference in performance between the college sample and a sample of jury-eligible citizens. Furthermore, the average rate of responding correctly for these two samples combined was 41%, which stands in sharp contrast to the 77% of a sample of 16 experts, who were also surveyed, who gave correct responses in this study.

Noon and Hollin (1987) also used the KEBQ with several samples of British respondents. No difference in accuracy was found between student samples and older eligible voters, and the average accuracy level across these groups was 44%. Furthermore, this level of accuracy is higher than the 34% found by Rahaim and Brodsky (1982) but consistent with the 46% accuracy rate found with the KEBQ in American samples (e.g., Deffenbacher and Loftus, 1982). Although there was no overall significant difference between the American and British samples, there were some differences in the pattern of correct responding between the two groups. As Noon and Hollin (1987) report, the British sample was more accurate about the effects of race and age on eyewitness identification, whereas the American sample was more knowledgeable about the relationship between accuracy and confidence, the accuracy of time estimation, and the effects of stress and violence on eyewitness memory. Expanding upon international comparisons in lay knowledge, McConkey and Roche (1989) surveyed samples of college students in New South Wales, Australia. With the KEBQ, the performance of advanced psychology students was found to exceed that of introductory students. The level of accuracy reached by the advanced sample was 61%. In contrast, the mean level of accuracy for introductory students was 44%, which is once again consistent with the performance observed in both American and British samples, which obtained an accuracy rate of 46% and 44%, respectively, on the KEBQ (e.g., Deffenbacher & Loftus, 1982; Noon & Hollin, 1987). The almost identical levels of accuracy obtained across international samples provide compelling evidence that the limitation in lay knowledge of eyewitness factors is widespread and that training is likely one pivotal factor enhancing lay knowledge, given that advanced psychology students were more accurate than their introductory and non-student counterparts. Once again there were some differences in response patterns among the international samples. Specifically, the American sample performed better with respect to the effects of stress on memory, and the British and Australian samples were more accurate about cross-racial effects.

Thus far, the survey studies conducted to assess lay knowledge have utilized samples of potential jurors, either jury-eligible college students or jury-eligible members of the public. To date, the work of Seltzer, Lopes, and Venuti (1990) is the only published study that has examined the knowledge of actual jurors. Post-trial interviews were conducted with 190 individuals who had just completed jury service. Five questions were derived from the KEBQ and modified to be more comprehensible to a non-college sample, and the number of response options was reduced from four to three. These items assessed juror knowledge about the effects of violence, stress, training, cross-race identifications, and viewing conditions on memory. Overall, jurors demonstrated an accuracy rate approximating 36%, which, unfortunately, is not different from what would be observed on the basis of random responding. Only 13% of jurors were accurate about the effects of violence on eyewitness memory, 54% accurately responded that extreme stress can impede eyewitness memory, 42% correctly responded that training is not necessarily effective in enhancing recall, 33% of jurors accurately endorsed the difficulty that cross-race identifications pose for eyewitnesses, and 33% correctly stated that when viewing conditions are poor the relation between witness confidence and accuracy is drastically diminished. With respect to these eyewitness issues, jurors were most accurate about the effects of stress on memory, which is consistent with previous findings where respondents also showed an increase in accuracy concerning the effects of stress (e.g., Noon & Hollin, 1987). Although the overall accuracy rates are very low, the findings indicate that there are stronger and weaker points of correspondence between people's intuitive eyewitness psychology and scientific evidence.

One aspect of the study by Seltzer et al. (1990) that may be of particular value is the assessment of whether juror experience with eyewitness identification issues in their trial experience, such as challenges and disputes over accuracy, enhanced juror knowledge. That is, when these issues were made salient for jurors, were they more likely to recognize the difficulties associated with eyewitness testimony in general? Does this kind of exposure help sensitize jurors to eyewitness issues? In this sample, 46% of jurors sat on cases where there was an issue over eyewitness identification. Although there were no significant differences in responding on four of the five questions, jurors with this experience were *less* likely to be accurate about the relation between eyewitness confidence and identification accuracy than other jurors (27% versus 42%, respectively). Unfortunately, this finding suggests that actual experience may serve to galvanize certain preexisting, yet incorrect, assumptions about eyewitness issues, particularly in the absence of any contradictory factual information. In all of these cases, expert testimony about eyewitness issues was *not* presented, and there was no evidence that such testimony was requested (Seltzer et al., 1990). The implication of this finding, which supports the use of expert testimony on eyewitness memory, is that mere exposure to eyewitness issues, even when identifications are disputed in trial, does not necessarily prompt jurors to think skeptically and recognize that there are problems inherent in eyewitness testimony.

Kassin and Barndollar (1992) assessed lay knowledge of eyewitness testimony and compared these beliefs with those of expert psychologists. College- and community-based respondents were required to endorse the general truth or falsity of 21 statements concerning eyewitness issues derived from empirical studies. This study differs in an important way from most past investigations in that lay responses were compared with the responses of experts, as measured by Kassin, Ellsworth, and Smith (1989). In the study by Kassin et al. (1989), 63 experts were surveyed about the reliability of these 21 items, and they found that 13 of these items were viewed as reliable enough to be presented in court by at least 70% of the experts. With this baseline in place, the *correspondence* of beliefs between laypeople and experts was measured, whereas previous studies have measured the *accuracy* of lay responses to questionnaire items summarizing research findings.

One notable problem associated with the multiple-choice instruments used in earlier studies was determining a consistent standard for *accuracy*, given that experts sometimes disagreed on the correct responses to the items (Lindsay, 1994). For example, Yarmey and Jones (1983), in their survey of a small sample of experts, found that the percentage of experts endorsing the response considered correct ranged from 44% to 100%, with experts selecting the appropriate response at an overall rate of 77%. Furthermore, only one item was endorsed unanimously, and it was the item concerning the effect of prior mugshot exposure on subsequent line-up identifications. Kassin and Barndollar's methodology, however, permits the level of agreement or correspondence between lay and expert beliefs to be measured, rather than the difference between accuracy rates as such. In assessment of the level of agreement, several relationships can be distinguished, including eyewitness issues that are generally accepted by experts but less so by laypeople, issues that are generally rejected by experts but believed by laypeople, issues accepted by both groups, and issues that are rejected by both groups.

Consistent with prior research, Kassin and Barndollar found that the college and non-student samples provided similar responses. Of the 21 items presented, there were 13 items where lay responses differed significantly from expert opinion. In contrast to the experts, fewer laypeople demonstrated an understanding of line-up fairness, the effects of line-up instructions, show-ups, exposure time, the forgetting curve, cross-race bias, hypnotic suggestibility, and color perception under monochromatic light. However, significantly more laypeople than experts believed that eyewitness confidence is positively related to accuracy, that women are better at facial recognition than men, and that hypnosis facilitates the retrieval of an eyewitness's memory. There were also some points of correspondence between lay and expert opinion. Specifically, there was agreement on the effects, or lack thereof, of attitudes and expectations on memory, the wording of questions, unconscious transference, weapon focus, event violence, and the tendency for eyewitnesses to overestimate the duration of events. More recent research by Kassin, Tubb, Hosch, and Memon (2001) provides further evidence for the consensus among experts on what factors reliably affect eyewitness memory, where the following factors achieved an 80% agreement rate or higher: wording of questions, line-up instructions, confidence malleability (where an eyewitness's confidence can be influenced by factors unrelated to identification accuracy), mug-shot-induced bias, the effect of post-event information, child witness suggestibility, alcoholic intoxication, cross-race bias, weapon focus, accuracy-confidence correlation, exposure time, line-up presentation format, and unconscious transference (where eyewitnesses sometimes identify as a culprit someone seen in a different context).

Furthermore, recent data demonstrates that the discrepancy between expert knowledge and that of actual jurors is still large (Dunlap, Ross, Bradshaw, & Thomas, 2003). These results help further delineate what correspondence does exist between lay and expert knowledge and can help identify where jurors are likely to require assistance in the evaluation of eyewitness evidence. These findings can help bridge the transition between empirically demonstrating that limitations in lay knowledge, in fact, exist and identifying the specific eyewitness issues with which laypeople have particular difficulty.

Also diverging from the standard multiple-choice format, Lindsay (1994) reports several studies in which lay knowledge was assessed with the use of a different approach. Rather than assessing accuracy, individuals' perceptions of the relative importance of variables determining eyewitness accuracy were examined. This is an important dimension that multiple-choice instruments cannot adequately reveal; using an instrument specifically designed to yield both absolute and relative importance of different factors can provide greater insight into how laypeople weigh and integrate these variables in relation to their judgments about eyewitness accuracy and attributions of witness credibility.

In multiple surveys respondents were asked how likely a witness would be to make an accurate identification decision under various conditions and to give a rating on a scale with *almost certain to be inaccurate* as one end point and *almost certain to be accurate* as the other. Two items were used to assess the importance of each variable, where one described the absence or minimal level of that variable and the other item described the presence or maximum level of that variable (e.g., *the crime was* versus *the crime was not very stressful for the witness*). Thus, the absolute importance for each variable was determined from the difference between the mean ratings for the two items describing that variable. The general findings were as follows. Across college student samples, the same five variables showed the greatest level of absolute importance. These were perceived to be the most important determinants of eyewitness accuracy and included attention paid to the criminal, opportunity to view the criminal, witness confidence, memory for peripheral detail, and the delay between the crime and identification. First, witnesses were expected to be more accurate if they had paid attention to the criminal during the crime and less accurate if they had not. Second, witnesses were expected to be more accurate if they had a good opportunity to view the criminal and less accurate if they had not. Third, confident witnesses were expected to be more accurate than nonconfident witnesses. Fourth, witnesses with better memory for peripheral details were expected to be more accurate than those with poor memory for these details. Fifth, witnesses were expected to be more accurate after short delays between the crime and identification than after long delays. Furthermore, the relative importance of the variables was similar between samples, where relative importance was based on the rank-order of the size of the absolute differences for each variable.

In contrast, several variables were not perceived as important determinants of eyewitness accuracy by laypeople, including aspects of line-up procedure, such as foil similarity and line-up instructions.

The main conclusion that can be drawn from these results is that clearly there are specific variables that laypeople perceive as important, but some of these are not variables that are important on the basis of research. Laypeople are sensitive to certain variables, such as witness confidence, which has little reliable relation to accuracy, but are insensitive to the impact of line-up procedures in influencing the accuracy of eyewitness evidence. Furthermore, the picture so far indicates that factors related to or indicative of the quality of eyewitness memory are focused on, such as witness confidence and attention paid to the criminal, which correspond to estimator variables. However, there is a marked insensitivity to the influential role that system variables, such as line-up fairness and instruction, play. Unfortunately, estimator variables include those factors that the judicial system cannot control, such as the conditions present at the time of the witnessed event (e.g., lighting, distance from the perpetrator, etc.) and the characteristics of the witness (e.g., age, gender, etc.). In contrast, system variables represent factors that can be controlled, such as preparation and presentation of line-ups, and how interviews are conducted.

Extending this particular observation, Shaw, Garcia, and McClure's (1999) investigation of lay knowledge found that individuals focused overwhelmingly on estimator variables in explaining the factors that affect the accuracy of eyewitness testimony and rarely mentioned system variables. Jury-eligible college students were asked to indicate what variables they believed determined eyewitness accuracy. In contrast to all of the methods used in previous studies, an open-ended and unstructured format was used. Thus, rather than restricting respondents to a predetermined and limited set of variables, six questions were used that gave respondents the opportunity to indicate what factors they believed affect the accuracy of eyewitness testimony. For example, they were asked to think about and explain what might affect accuracy in five categories, which included the eyewitness, the eyewitness's testimony in court, the suspect, the crime situation, the police questioning or identification procedures, and anything else that the respondent could generate. Respondents produced more responses in the eyewitness category than in the other four categories, and the fewest responses in the police and identification procedures category (27% versus 13%). In fact, the one variable mentioned by the greatest percentage of respondents was lighting/time of day associated with the crime situation. Overall, 84% of the responses concerned estimator variables, and only 16% focused on system variables. When respondents were presented with a completely unstructured format, where instructions were given to simply list the 10 things that might possibly affect the accuracy of eyewitness testimony, jury-eligible college students produced an overwhelming number of responses related to estimator variables over system variables (94% versus 6%, respectively). This study is one of the first measuring freely generated responses to issues concerning eyewitness accuracy and further reveals lay people's bias for estimator variables.

Thus, there is clearly a discrepancy between lay understanding of the relevant factors affecting eyewitness accuracy and those that are of lesser diagnostic value. Consistent with the results derived from Lindsay's (1994) ranking format to assess the importance of variables affecting accuracy, laypeople are much more likely to generate and focus on variables associated with the eyewitness, such as individual differences among eyewitnesses and the specific characteristics of the crime scene (i.e., eyewitness attention and lighting conditions). Shaw et al.'s (1999) findings also indicate that respondents rated their own commonsense and everyday life experiences as having a greater impact on their knowledge of eyewitness issues than any other source. In one of the most recent investigations of lay knowledge in this area, Durham and Dane (1999) surveyed college and non-college respondents about their knowledge of published eyewitness memory research. Once again, college students demonstrated better understanding of the effects of memory processes on eyewitness accuracy, the difficulties associated with cross-race identifications, and the relation between confidence and accuracy, based on their level of endorsement of these items. However, whereas the college sample performed better with respect to the relation between confidence and accuracy, both groups tended to *disagree* with the findings of published research, with the non-college sample disagreeing with greater frequency.

The findings derived from different methodologies converge on a common, yet extremely important observation. Results obtained from the structured multiple-choice method clearly indicate that the majority of lay respondents do not provide correct answers to questions concerning a variety of eyewitness factors and particularly those questions about system variables. This finding, in conjunction with results obtained from less structured and completely open-ended formats showing that lay people do not spontaneously use or focus on system variables in their explanations of eyewitness accuracy, provides strong evidence that the poor performance observed is not merely an artifact of the forced-choice questionnaire method. Given that questionnaire results ultimately reflect the quality of the items that compose them, finding corroborating evidence from studies using other methods strengthens the basis for our understanding of what exactly constitutes common knowledge. The fact that laypeople focus on estimator variables to the virtual exclusion of system variables is important when one is considering how to evaluate eyewitness testimony. The recent publication of the DOJ guidelines on how to collect identification evidence provides the court with a clear standard by which to evaluate the procedures used to collect eyewitness evidence. Jurors need to be made aware of the guidelines so they can determine whether the appropriate procedures were used to collect the identification evidence. This would provide jurors with a standard of evaluation that reflects the most recent development in this area.

Studies that have directly examined lay knowledge clearly demonstrate limitations in lay knowledge of eyewitness issues. Although some differences between groups have emerged in some studies, particularly between college and non-college samples of respondents, these have generally been small. Based on the research reviewed, the difference between potential college and community jurors has not been large enough or found consistently enough to indicate that an important gap exists in knowledge. McConkey and Roche's (1989) finding that the performance of advanced psychology students surpassed that of introductory students does suggest, however, the importance of *exposure* to psychological research and theory. Overall, there is a marked lack of correspondence between common knowledge and scientific knowledge. The results of experimental studies converge on the same conclusion.

HOW ACCURATE IS COMMON SENSE?
EXPERIMENTAL STUDIES ON JUROR KNOWLEDGE

In addition to survey studies that specifically focus on measuring the content and breadth of lay juror knowledge of eyewitness issues, a substantial body of experimental research has focused on how a variety of eyewitness factors affect jurors' perceptions of eyewitnesses as well as their evaluations of eyewitness information in jury decision-making. The findings support three general conclusions. First, these studies demonstrate that jurors underestimate the importance of good indicators of accuracy. For example, when mock jurors are presented with information about a variety of factors relevant to eyewitness identification accuracy, such as lineup instructions and fairness, mug-shot search, retention interval, lighting conditions, cross-race identifications, and weapon presence, this information has frequently failed to influence juror verdicts (e.g., Abshire & Bornstein, 2003; Cutler, Penrod, & Dexter, 1990; Cutler, Penrod, & Martens, 1987; Lindsay, Lim, Marando, & Cully, 1986).

Second, these studies further demonstrate that jurors tend to rely heavily on eyewitness factors that are *not* good indicators of accuracy (e.g., Bell & Loftus, 1989; Berman & Cutler, 1996; Brigham & Bothwell, 1983; Cutler, Penrod, & Stuve, 1988; Wells, 1984). Specifically, the relation between witness confidence and accuracy has consistently posed a problem for laypeople, where the accuracy-confidence relation is very often perceived as a strong one (Brigham & Bothwell, 1983). The presence and strength of this belief were also evidenced in many of the survey studies of lay knowledge that were reviewed (e.g., Deffenbacher & Loftus, 1982; Durham & Dane, 1999; Lindsay, 1994). A large number of experimental studies have demonstrated that eyewitness confidence is a better predictor of juror verdicts than eyewitness accuracy, with more confident witnesses being perceived as more believable (e.g., Brewer & Burke, 2002; Cutler et al., 1990b; Fox & Walters, 1986; Lindsay, Wells, & O'Connor, 1989; Lindsay, Wells, & Rumpel, 1981; Penrod & Cutler, 1995).

The third conclusion that can be drawn based on this research is that laypeople tend to overestimate accuracy rates in eyewitness identification situations and have difficulty in distinguishing between accurate and inaccurate witnesses. This implies an underlying belief that eyewitnesses tend to be fairly accurate. Brigham and Bothwell (1983) found that 63% of their jury-eligible respondents believed that more than 50% of eyewitness identifications that are made are correct, whereas only 9% believed that less than 50% are correct. Along similar lines, Lindsay et al. (1989) found that mock jurors evidenced an overall high rate of belief in the testimony of both accurate *and* inaccurate eyewitnesses (68% versus 70%, respectively). Furthermore, in some situations, such as when witnesses are asked nonleading questions, a greater number of mock jurors have been found to believe inaccurate witnesses than to believe accurate ones (86% versus 76%, respectively; Wells, Lindsay, & Ferguson, 1979).

In conclusion, lay knowledge of eyewitness factors is of rather poor quality. First, overall accuracy levels are low—the highest score observed in the survey studies that were reviewed was 61%. Second, what people believe to be important and the information that they focus on are often not diagnostic of and sometimes even irrelevant to eyewitness accuracy. This indicates that intuitive eyewitness theory is limited and does not have a high correspondence with the scientific evidence. Accordingly, it is not surprising to observe that the research findings are not *intuitive* to laypeople. Furthermore, the content of lay beliefs has an impact on jurors' evaluations of eyewitnesses, irrespective of accuracy. Thus, what we can surmise on the basis of years of empirical research is that there is *much* that, in fact, falls *outside* the realm of the average juror's commonsense understanding of eyewitness memory. But what is known about other participants in the legal system? Is the knowledge possessed by those who interact directly with the eyewitness, namely, judges, attorneys, and police investigators, any better than jurors who evaluate their testimony?

IS EYEWITNESS MEMORY COMMON SENSE TO JUDGES, ATTORNEYS, AND POLICE INVESTIGATORS?

There is much less research on what judges know about factors that affect eyewitness memory. To our knowledge, the only survey study published to date that has specifically examined judicial knowledge about a wide range of factors that affect eyewitness accuracy was conducted by Wise and Safer (2004). One hundred sixty judges completed a questionnaire in which they responded to 14 statements about eyewitness factors and provided information about their beliefs concerning how jurors would respond to these items. For example, judges were asked to indicate whether they believed that statements such as, "At trial, an eyewitness's confidence is a good predictor of his or her accuracy in identifying the defendant as the perpetrator of the crime" were (a) generally true, (b) generally false, or (c) I don't know. Only about half of the judges (55%) provided the correct response, averaged across the 14 items, which is not dissimilar to the performance of laypeople across survey studies who average 44% correct on eyewitness knowledge questionnaires. The percentage of judges giving the correct response to individual questions ranged from 19% to 94%, and 80% or more of the judges gave the correct answer for only 3 of the 14 statements. Furthermore, only 32% of the judges correctly disagreed that eyewitness confidence is a good indicator of identification accuracy, and they were frequently incorrect about whether jurors can distinguish between accurate and inaccurate witnesses. Approximately 29% of the judges agreed with the statement that jurors can distinguish between accurate and inaccurate eyewitnesses, 33% neither agreed nor disagreed, and 39% disagreed with this statement. Given that the correct response is disagreement, this implies that 62% of judges, representing almost two-thirds of the sample surveyed, have an inadequate understanding of this issue.

In comparison with Kassin et al.'s (2001) experts, judges diverged significantly from the experts in the accuracy of their responses on the following five items: lineup presentation format (19% versus 81%, respectively), the confidence-accuracy relation (32% versus 87%), the forgetting curve (31% versus 83%), mug-shot-induced bias (74% versus 95%), and weapon focus (69% versus 87%). Judges and the experts did not differ in their rate of correct responses on the effects of attitudes and expectations on memory (94%

versus 95%), the effects of post-event information (84% versus 94%), and confidence malleability (89% versus 95%). Although some correspondence was observed between judges' knowledge of eyewitness issues and that of experts, the limitations are evident.

In predicting the level of juror knowledge of these issues, 64% of the judges endorsed the belief that jurors have limited knowledge of eyewitness factors, whereas fewer judges (41%) endorsed the same belief about attorneys. In predicting how jurors would respond to a subset of these issues, including confidence malleability, weapon focus, mug-shot-induced bias, line-up presentation format, and the forgetting curve, only a minority of judges indicated that jurors would be able to provide an accurate response for these items. Specifically, on the issue of confidence malleability, 89% of judges provided the correct answer, but only 36% of judges believed that the average juror would be able to do so. On the issue of weapon focus, 69% of judges were correct and only 24% of judges believed that jurors would be accurate. For mug-shot-induced bias, 74% of judges were correct and only 38% indicated that jurors would answer accurately. For line-up presentation format and the forgetting curve, judges' accuracy rates and their projected accuracy for jurors were 19% versus 4%, and 31% versus 18%, respectively.

Wise and Safer (2004) also compared judges' projections of juror accuracy with those of Kassin et al.'s (2001) experts. A significant difference was found in the percentage of judges and experts who believed that the average juror could provide the correct answer on two out of the five issues described above, confidence malleability (36% versus 10%, respectively) and mug-shot-induced bias (38% versus 13%, respectively). This indicates that judges show some degree of skepticism about juror understanding of eyewitness issues, but that experts exhibit a greater awareness of the limitations of lay knowledge. Furthermore, judges who showed greater knowledge of eyewitness factors or indicated that jurors cannot distinguish between accurate and inaccurate witnesses were more likely to believe that jurors have limited knowledge concerning these issues. Greater knowledge of eyewitness issues in this sample of judges was also associated with a more cautious appraisal of the value of eyewitness testimony in general.

With respect to other legal professionals' common sense about eyewitness issues, several studies have investigated knowledge of these factors in attorneys, as well as law students. Yarmey and Jones (1983) surveyed a sample of attorneys and a sample of law students and found that neither attorneys nor law students demonstrated a greater overall degree of knowledge than the potential jurors surveyed in their study. Both groups exhibited an accuracy rate of 50% in comparison with jurors who performed at the 41% level. Thus, the level of accuracy was comparably low across all three groups. Similarly, Noon and Hollin (1987) found no difference in accuracy between law students and other potential jurors with the use of the KEBQ. Consistent with these findings, Rahaim and Brodsky (1982) also compared attorneys' knowledge of eyewitness factors with that of potential jurors and found a similar overall accuracy rate between these two groups, 37% and 34%, respectively. A difference was found only for beliefs about eyewitness confidence and accuracy, where the lawyers were correct more often than the jurors. Brigham and Wolfskeil (1983) surveyed attorneys as well as law enforcement officers about knowledge of eyewitness factors and found that prosecuting attorneys and law enforcement personnel endorsed the belief that eyewitness identification is relatively accurate, that it is appropriate to emphasize in court, and overall these groups responded in a similar manner. Defense attorneys, however, were found to believe that eyewitness identifications are more frequently inaccurate and should be regarded with more caution. Specifically, the majority of attorneys and law officers (60% and 63%, respectively) believed that 90% or more of the eyewitness identifications that they had observed were probably correct. Furthermore, 75% of prosecutors and 73% of law officers indicated that witness confidence is positively related to accuracy, whereas fewer defense attorneys responded in this manner (40%). With respect to cross-race identifications, 24% of defense attorneys responded that 90% or more identifications of this type are likely to be accurate; however, much larger percentages of prosecutors and law officers believed that these identifications are likely to be correct (43% and 78%, respectively).

Clearly, we cannot come to the conclusion that eyewitness memory is common sense to judges, attorneys, and law enforcement personnel, as deficits can be observed in samples from these professional populations that are similar to those observed in lay jurors. The implication of this research is that these participants in the legal system are as uninformed as potential jurors, all of whom play a key role in the legal decision-making process. This conclusion raises an important question: If judges, attorneys, and jurors have insufficient knowledge about eyewitness memory, what safeguards exist in the legal system to detect errors in eyewitness testimony, which, if they go unnoticed, may lead to a wrongful conviction?

ARE THERE EFFECTIVE SAFEGUARDS IN THE LEGAL SYSTEM TO PREVENT WRONGFUL CONVICTIONS DUE TO ERRORS IN EYEWITNESS MEMORY?

Given the fallible nature of eyewitness testimony, various constitutional safeguards have been implemented by the legal system in an effort to protect defendants from wrongful conviction based on mistaken identification (Collins, 2003). These safeguards include the right to have an attorney present at a post-indictment line-up, the right to have an identification based on suggestive procedures suppressed (the motion-to-suppress safeguard), the process of voir dire, cross-examination of the witness at trial, expert testimony during trial on issues concerning eyewitness identification, and judicial instructions. Many of these safeguards, however, have been shown to be largely ineffective (Cutler & Penrod, 1995; Devenport, Penrod, & Cutler, 1997; Penrod & Cutler, 1995; Yarmey, 2001). Legal scholars are aware of the shortcomings. With respect to the first two safeguards, the U.S. Supreme Court, in 1967, issued three decisions in cases that involved problems with identification procedures, specifically problematic line-up practices. These cases, known as the "Wade trilogy" (see *United States v. Wade*, 388 U.S. 218, 1967), gave defendants the right to have counsel present at the line-up procedure and the right to challenge unnecessarily suggestive procedures (Koosed, 2002). However, a series of decisions made by the court over the next several years, that either added conditions or included exceptions to the rules, has served to reduce the effectiveness of these safeguards (Collins,

2003). Justice Marshall commented to this effect in his dissent in *Manson v. Braithwaite* [432 U.S. 98; 97 S. Ct. 2243; 53 L. Ed. 2d 140 (1976)], a case in which the Supreme Court declined to adopt a per se exclusionary rule for unnecessarily suggestive line-ups and show-ups, stating, "[T]oday's decision can come as no surprise to those who have been watching the Court dismantle the protections against mistaken eyewitness testimony erected a decade ago in *United States v. Wade*" (Id at 118). Koch (2003) also addresses the ineffectiveness of these safeguards as he explains that the application of the Sixth Amendment to certain identifications has proved to be a hollow victory for defendants. He indicates that the right to counsel will seldom apply to identification procedures because identifications usually occur before the right to counsel goes into effect, and with respect to certain types of identification procedures, such as photograph arrays, the right to counsel will never go into effect (Koch, 2003).

The research community has also demonstrated the ineffectiveness of these safeguards. Stinson, Devenport, Cutler, and Kravitz (1996) designed an experiment to assess the validity of the legal system's hypothesis that attorneys are aware of factors that affect line-up suggestiveness and thus serve as an effective safeguard during line-up procedures. Ninety-seven attorneys were given a written description of an event, shown eight versions of a videotaped eyewitness identification procedure, and then given a questionnaire. The results showed that attorneys rated foil-biased line-ups as more suggestive and less fair than the foil-unbiased line-ups; however, they rated sequential line-ups as significantly *more* suggestive and less fair than simultaneous line-ups, a finding that stands in direct opposition to the research findings. It was also found that biases in line-up instruction and presentation were difficult for attorneys to detect and correct. Furthermore, attorneys reported that they were present at only 5% of their clients' identifications. Stinson, Devenport, Cutler, and Kravitz (1997) assessed judges' sensitivity to line-up suggestiveness and the effects of foil, instruction, and presentation biases, and whether judges are willing to use the motion to suppress a line-up identification in the presence of line-up biases and suggestiveness. The motion to suppress represents an additional safeguard in that a line-up identification can be suppressed on the grounds that the procedure used to obtain the identification was unduly suggestive. A sample of judges was given a description of a hypothetical crime and then completed a questionnaire in which they rated the suggestiveness of the line-up overall, as well as the suggestiveness of the line-up construction, instructions, and presentation. The results reveal that judges show some sensitivity to factors that affect line-up suggestiveness. Specifically, judges rated foil-biased line-ups as more suggestive and less fair than foil-unbiased line-ups, similar to what was found with attorneys, and judges and attorneys both rated the instruction-biased line-ups as more suggestive than instruction-unbiased line-ups. However, judges perceived sequential presentation as *more* suggestive and less fair than simultaneous presentation of a line-up, a finding that was also obtained with attorneys, but one that is inconsistent with the empirical research on line-up presentation and accuracy rates. Although judges were more likely to grant the motion to suppress in the presence of foil-biased line-ups and biased line-up instructions, their rulings on the motion to suppress were not affected by presentation bias. Taken together, these results indicate that the presence of counsel and motion to suppress safeguards may not be as effective as they are believed to be. Based on the review of the research that has examined what both judges and attorneys know about eyewitness factors, it is not surprising that there is a lack of awareness of the important role that system variables play in the accuracy of eyewitness evidence.

Another safeguard implemented is the process of voir dire, the purpose of which is to identify and excuse potentially biased jurors. Attorneys are able to screen potential jurors in order to identify any predispositions that jurors may have relating to their trust of eyewitnesses. In cases where eyewitness identification plays a pivotal role, jurors' ability and willingness to scrutinize and evaluate the credibility of eyewitness testimony are very important in ensuring the fairness of the defendant's trial. Narby and Cutler (1994) examined the effectiveness of this safeguard and found no evidence for a significant relation between attitudes toward eyewitnesses and juror perceptions of defendant culpability. Overall, jurors tended to endorse the positive statements about eyewitnesses (e.g., *Eyewitnesses can usually be believed*) and tended to disagree with negative statements (e.g., *Eyewitnesses generally do not give accurate descriptions*). This finding is, perhaps, not too surprising, in light of research findings showing that laypeople not only possess limited understanding of eyewitness factors, but also fail to display skepticism toward eyewitness evidence in general. Laypeople tend to overbelieve the testimony of eyewitnesses, especially confident ones, irrespective of accuracy (e.g., Lindsay et al., 1989; Penrod & Cutler, 1995) and tend to believe that the majority of eyewitness identifications are, in fact, correct (e.g., Brigham & Bothwell, 1983; Brigham & Wolfskeil, 1983). Furthermore, limits imposed by the court often make it difficult for attorneys to obtain information on prospective jurors' attitudes toward eyewitnesses. On this basis, voir dire would not appear to be an effective safeguard in eyewitness cases.

An additional safeguard is the cross-examination of a witness, which is the most commonly used and is widely believed to effectively protect defendants from erroneous conviction (Walters, 1985). It is also the most commonly used rationale for the exclusion of expert testimony. The purpose of cross-examination is to discover inconsistencies or gaps in the eyewitness's identification. Research findings challenge the effectiveness of cross-examination as a legal safeguard. A study conducted by Wells et al. (1979) demonstrated that jurors are unable to discriminate accurate from inaccurate eyewitnesses based upon cross-examination in a mock trial. Lindsay et al. (1989) further assessed the impact of cross-examination on mock jurors' ability to discriminate between accurate and inaccurate witnesses in a study in which attorneys actually cross-examined the witnesses. Unfortunately, the cross-examination had no effect on improving jurors' ability to differentiate between accurate and inaccurate eyewitnesses. More recently, Devenport, Stinson, Cutler, and Kravitz (2002) investigated the effectiveness of the cross-examination safeguard by testing juror sensitivity to three biases (foil, instruction, and presentation bias), which have consistently been found to affect the suggestiveness of line-up identification procedures. If the goal of cross-examination is to focus on the credibility and accuracy of the eyewitness's identification, then its effectiveness would seem to hinge on jurors' sensitivity to suggestiveness, which can detrimentally affect the accuracy of an identification. Based on juror ratings of foil, instruction, and presentation suggestiveness, jurors showed no sensitivity to presentation bias and some sensitivity to instruction bias, but they were most sensitive to foil bias. Although jurors could discern some forms of bias based on their ratings, the mean ratings themselves reflect a tendency for jurors to use the midpoint of the suggestiveness scale, which is not high in absolute terms. This implies that jurors' perceptions of suggestiveness when bias is present are not especially strong. One reason that cross-examination may be a less than adequate safeguard is that, as evidenced earlier, jurors, attorneys, and judges have insufficient knowledge about eyewitness issues in general. Even more importantly, attorneys lack awareness of specific factors, such as those that affect line-up suggestiveness. If attorneys are not aware of these particular issues, then they cannot adequately cross-examine with respect to them. Consequently, this can impair attorneys' ability to develop truly effective cross-examination strategies in cases where eyewitness testimony plays an important role.

A further safeguard is the admission of expert testimony, which is based on the assumption that such testimony will increase juror sensitivity to the factors that influence eyewitness identification performance and assist jurors in the evaluation of eyewitness evidence. Expert testimony is often admitted in cases as an aide, which can be provided to jurors if the judge determines that the particular subject is outside the jury's realm of knowledge. Psychologists have testified as expert witnesses on eyewitness identification from the beginning of the twentieth century; however, no empirical research on its effectiveness was conducted until 1980 (Hosch, 1980). What influence does this testimony have on jurors' decisions and behaviors?

Studies that have examined the impact of expert testimony on jurors' evaluations of eyewitnesses and their sensitivity to witnessing conditions have produced mixed results. However, there is some evidence that expert testimony can increase juror skepticism, as well as increase juror sensitivity to the factors or conditions that affect eyewitness identification. Sensitivity to eyewitness factors is determined on the basis of whether jurors actually use information about the quality of eyewitness evidence in making judgments about culpability, as well as eyewitness credibility and accuracy. Thus, *sensitization* refers to the process whereby jurors are prompted to reevaluate eyewitness evidence in light of information about eyewitness memory factors, whereas skepticism involves jurors placing less belief in the accuracy of eyewitness identification as a result of expert testimony. Accordingly, the most powerful effect of introducing expert testimony, from a theoretical and applied perspective, would be in promoting *sensitivity* in jurors, because this may alter juror decision-making strategies.

In the earliest three studies assessing the impact of expert testimony (Hosch, Beck, & McIntyre, 1980; Loftus, 1980; Wells, Lindsay, & Tousignant, 1980), the presence of expert testimony was found to increase mock jurors' scrutiny of the evidence, decrease their beliefs in the general accuracy of eyewitness testimony, and reduce jurors' reliance on witness confidence. In a meta-analysis of these studies, Hosch (1980) found that the presence of expert testimony had the largest impact on jurors' deliberation time, followed by changes in their beliefs about and scrutiny of eyewitness identification, and had the smallest effect on their verdicts. Maass, Brigham, and West (1985) found that the presence of expert testimony tended to increase the leniency of mock jurors' judgments about the perpetrator. Along similar lines, Fox and Walters (1986) found that expert testimony served to reduce guilty verdicts, as well as decrease mock jurors' belief in the general accuracy of eyewitness testimony. Furthermore, the impact of general versus specific expert testimony was examined, where general testimony addressed memory processes and the potential for distortion, and specific testimony focused on specific factors affecting eyewitness perception and memory that were highly relevant to the case being tried. Specific testimony was found to reduce jurors' estimates of how likely a person would be to make a correct identification under similar circumstances more than general expert testimony. Similarly, Geiselman et al., (2002) found that only specific expert testimony affected mock jurors' guilty verdicts, where jurors showed a much greater discrimination between good and poor witnessing conditions with specific expert testimony than with either general or no expert testimony, suggesting that this testimony served to sensitize jurors to eyewitness evidence. Devenport et al. (2002) examined the impact of specific expert testimony on juror sensitivity to suggestiveness in line-up identification procedures. Expert testimony increased juror sensitivity to instruction bias but not to foil and presentation bias, and influenced jurors' perceptions of line-up fairness. The results did not indicate that expert testimony increased juror skepticism of eyewitness identification.

Cutler and colleagues, in a series of studies, have examined the effect of introducing adversarial expert testimony on juror evaluations of eyewitness evidence in mock trial situations. They found that this testimony increased juror sensitivity to eyewitness evidence, in that mock jurors were more likely to give guilty verdicts when the conditions of the crime and the eyewitness testimony were conducive to a correct identification, and were less likely to convict if these conditions were conducive to the eyewitness providing an inaccurate identification (Cutler, Dexter, & Penrod, 1989). Furthermore, Cutler, Dexter, and Penrod (1990) attempted to determine whether nonadversarial methods can sensitize jurors to eyewitness issues. Specifically, they assessed the impact of a court-appointed expert, judge's instructions, and no expert advice on mock jurors' evaluations of eyewitness evidence. The results showed that the presence of the expert promoted skepticism toward the eyewitness testimony, but the expert did not increase juror sensitivity to the evidence, indicating that jurors presented with expert testimony were no better at differentiating between good versus poor witnessing conditions than jurors who were not presented with expert testimony. In contrast to the impact of the expert, judicial instructions produced neither effect.

Clearly, the presence of expert testimony affects jurors' decision-making, but other factors likely play an important role in determining its overall effectiveness in sensitizing jurors. These variables would include the perceived credibility of the expert, whether the expert is adversarial or court-appointed, what topics are expounded upon by the expert, as well as other case-specific factors. Along these lines, Maass et al. (1985) report results indicating that providing causal explanations for the unreliability of eyewitness memory is an important factor in the effectiveness of expert testimony. Consequently, more needs to be known about what aspects of expert testimony would be most beneficial to jurors. Specifically, what information is most potent in overcoming jurors' generally inaccurate perceptions, as Hosch (1980) has termed "implicit eyewitness theory," and how should it be structured to maximize its reception by a lay audience? Unfortunately, despite the fact that research shows that expert testimony, particularly specific testimony, can sensitize jurors to the factors affecting eyewitness identification, this type of testimony is rarely admitted, as delineated earlier in this chapter.

Despite the lack of knowledge concerning factors that affect the accuracy of eyewitness testimony in laypeople, as well as legal and law enforcement professionals, the importance of eyewitness accuracy in the judicial system has initiated changes in legal policy. Specifically, judicial instructions represent the last safeguard. Over the last few decades both federal and state courts have encouraged judges to instruct jurors about the factors they should consider in the evaluation of eyewitness evidence. In *Neil v. Biggers* [409 U.S. 188, 93 S. Ct. 375, 34 L. Ed. 2d 401 (1972)], the United States Supreme Court recommended five criteria on which evaluations of eyewitness evidence should be based, including identification certainty, quality of the eyewitness's view of the culprit, the amount of reported attention paid to the culprit, the match between the description of and the actual appearance of the defendant, and the time elapsed between witnessing of the crime and the identification. Unfortunately, research has demonstrated that some of the *Biggers* criteria have serious shortcomings as indicators of eyewitness accuracy (Wells & Bradfield, 1998; Wells & Murray, 1983). However, these criteria are relied on by the court system, and, when satisfied, they are assumed to imply eyewitness accuracy (Bradfield & Wells, 2000). The most widely used standardized set of instructions arose from *United States v. Telfaire* [469 F.2d 552 (D.C. Cir. 1972)] and has been used with the intent to aid jurors' evaluation of identification evidence. Specifically, the *Telfaire* instructions include an instruction that emphasizes to the jury the importance of finding that the circumstances of identification are convincing in determining the guilt of the defendant. To this end, jurors are further instructed to consider factors such as the length of time the witness had to view the offender, the lighting conditions at that time, previous acquaintance with the offender, and circumstances surrounding the line-up identification and to evaluate the credibility and truthfulness of the eyewitness.

What impact do judges' cautionary instructions, such as the *Telfaire* instructions concerning eyewitness testimony, have on sensitizing jurors to eyewitness factors? The research results on this issue are mixed. An early study examining the effects of judicial commentary on mock jurors' decisions produced results indicating that judges' instructions induced skepticism (Katzev & Wishart, 1985). Predeliberation guilty verdicts and deliberation time were reduced the most when judges presented standard instructions, a summary of the witnessing conditions, and commentary on the psychological findings concerning eyewitness identification in comparison with when judges only delivered instructions or delivered the instructions plus a summary. Cutler, Penrod, and Dexter (1990) showed that whereas expert testimony had an impact on jurors' evaluations of eyewitness evidence, judges' presentation of *Telfaire* instructions neither sensitized jurors to eyewitness issues nor increased their skepticism. Greene (1988), however, observed an increase in juror skepticism with these instructions and a greater increase in skepticism of eyewitness testimony when the *Telfaire* instructions were modified to be more understandable to jurors. In contrast, Ramirez, Zemba, and Geiselman (1996) obtained less optimistic results in assessing whether the *Telfaire* instructions, as well as a modified version of these instructions, sensitized jurors to eyewitness issues. The modified version was designed to increase the comprehensibility of the instructions to jurors based on Greene's (1988) modification *and* was further modified to include additional statements concerning factors that affect eyewitness performance based on Kassin et al.'s (1989) survey of experts. The *Telfaire* instructions actually *reduced* mock jurors' sensitivity to the quality of eyewitness evidence and induced either skepticism or overbelief, depending on when these instructions were presented to jurors. The revised version of these instructions did not adversely affect juror sensitivity but did not significantly improve it either.

Although the *Telfaire* instructions have become the most widely used standardized instruction in the country, a general lack of specificity and comprehensibility in these instructions has been a notable problem (Ramirez, Zemba, & Geiselman, 1996). First, these instructions are based on legal precedents rather than empirical research and only make reference to a limited number of factors that affect the accuracy of eyewitness memory (Cutler & Penrod, 1995). Second, research indicates that instructions presented to jurors are often misunderstood, either because they include legal terms or because they are embedded within other, often lengthy, judicial instructions (e.g., Elwork, Sales, & Alfini, 1982; Greene, 1988; Loftus, 1979). Reifman, Gusick, and Ellsworth (1992), in a survey study of 224 citizens called for jury duty, found that actual jurors understood fewer than half of the instructions they received at trial. It has become evident that jurors often have difficulty in comprehending complex legal cases in general and often have difficulty understanding the evidence that has been presented to them (e.g., Goodman, Greene, & Loftus, 1985; Ivkovic & Hans, 2003). Furthermore, research on the impact of judicial instructions has been conducted in jury simulation studies, which by design remove much of the complexity that real court cases possess. If these instructions do not have a dramatic effect on sensitizing jurors in more simplified and controlled contexts, we can only wonder if they are at all effective in more variable and complex situations. Thus, the question that emerges is what benefit can cautionary instructions provide if they, at best, lack specificity and, at worst, are incomprehensible to the average juror and are furthermore given to individuals who are already having trouble understanding the evidence of the case? It appears that cautionary instructions may only serve to compound the problem that jurors have to face in evaluating eyewitness evidence without a sufficient knowledge base.

Given the presence of these various legal safeguards, Wise and Safer (2004) in their survey of judges attempted to determine whether greater knowledge of eyewitness of eyewitness was associated with a willingness to permit legal safeguards. Judges were asked which of five legal safeguards they would permit in order to inform a jury about a variety of factors affecting eyewitness accuracy. On average 80% of judges would permit using cross-examination, 74% would permit closing arguments, 53% would permit voir dire, 44% would permit expert testimony, and 24% would use jury instruction. Unfortunately, the research reviewed indicates that the most popular choices are not necessarily effective safeguards. More importantly, increased knowledge in this sample of judges was associated with not only an increased willingness to allow legal safeguards, including expert testimony, but also a greater reluctance to convict defendants solely on the basis of eyewitness testimony. Even though there are volumes of research by experts on the specific issues that commonly lead to wrongful identification, courts regularly exclude expert testimony on eyewitness issues based on varied and inconsistent reasoning.

CONCLUSION

What is apparent on the basis of our review of state and federal cases is that eyewitness testimony research has penetrated the legal system only to a very limited extent. Our analysis indicates that 32% of the states do not admit testimony of eyewitness experts, either through a per se exclusionary rule, as seen in Tennessee or by language that is highly suggestive of a per se exclusionary rule. Another 43% of the states have ruled that the testimony is admissible but provide multiple reasons for excluding the testimony, suggesting that it is possible, but not probable, that the testimony will be admitted. Taken together, it appears that eyewitness expert testimony has failed to penetrate the majority of the states, yet it appears to be accepted in approximately 25% of the states, but generally only if there is no corroborating evidence.

Reasons given by the courts for excluding eyewitness experts are widely varied. These reasons include the following: eyewitness memory is common sense to jurors and no expert assistance is necessary; cross-examination will reveal any problems with the eyewitness evidence; judicial instructions provide a clear path for jurors to follow in evaluating an eyewitness; expert eyewitness testimony will invade the province of the jury; research on eyewitness memory is "junk science"; and, as stated in *State v. Coley* [32 S.W.3d 831 (Tenn. 2000)], this information has no empirical or scientific basis, it is too general to the case and thus it is not relevant, the prejudicial effect of the testimony outweighs the probative value, and the credibility of the eyewitness should be determined by the jury alone and not be influenced by the testimony of an expert.

Our review of the literature suggests that judges making these decisions appear to lack adequate scientific training to apply the *Daubert* standard, possess inadequate understanding of eyewitness memory, and demonstrate a knowledge base no greater than that seen in jurors. Faith in cross-examination as a solution is also questionable, given that lawyers, who perform this function, also appear to lack the appropriate knowledge of eyewitness memory to construct a genuinely effective cross-examination. Furthermore, the belief that eyewitness testimony is common sense to a jury ignores the large discrepancy between what has been described and identified here as "commonsense understanding" and what the accumulation of scientific research has reliably demonstrated to be true about eyewitness memory. Finally, the skepticism concerning the scientific integrity of eyewitness memory research can be challenged on the basis of the sheer volume of research conducted on factors affecting eyewitness memory over the last century. The picture that emerges from this research, when hundreds of studies are subjected to the meta-analytic approach (see Penrod and Bornstein, this volume), is robust and heartening, from both a theoretical and a forensic perspective. Numerous phenomena are empirically reliable and generalizable enough to not only warrant the demonstrated consensus of expert opinion but also support the admission of expert testimony on these eyewitness issues.

Although this chapter has operationally defined penetration of the legal system as the extent to which eyewitness expert testimony has been admitted in court, there are other options that do portray a promising picture on this front. In particular, the 1999 publication of the Department of Justice *Guide* on the collection of identification evidence is an excellent example of eyewitness research penetrating the legal system (Wells et al., 2000). Our interactions with the Department of Justice indicate that 44,000 copies of this document were distributed to law enforcement across the country, only to be followed by the publication of a training manual to accompany the guidelines that was distributed to approximately 3,000 police training academies. The materials relied heavily upon years of research on eyewitness memory and outline specific procedures for the proper collection of eyewitness evidence.

In 2001 John Farmer, then attorney general of New Jersey, wrote a letter to every law enforcement agency in the state mandating not only the use of the DOJ guidelines, but also many of the suggestions made in a similar set of guidelines developed by a subcommittee appointed by the American Psychology and Law Society and the American Psychological Association, and published by Wells et al. (1998). New Jersey is the only state where the guidelines have been mandated. In our view, the *Guide* serves as a vehicle to further penetrate a legal system that historically has not been receptive to eyewitness research, and the admission of expert testimony focusing on the content of the guidelines represents a solid starting point. First, the guidelines focus primarily on system variables, such as informing the witness that the culprit may or may not be in the line-up, that the verbal description of the witness should be used as the basis to construct the line-up, and that a line-up could be presented sequentially versus simultaneously as a means to reduce false identification. In fact, a recently published study has shown that when mock jurors are provided information that law enforcement personnel made procedural violations of the *Guide*, perceptions of defendant culpability as well as conviction rates were reduced, and eyewitness credibility was challenged (Lampinen, Judges, Odegard, & Hamilton, 2005).

The courts may initially be more receptive to expert eyewitness testimony that focuses on system variables and whether the procedures used to gather the identification evidence followed the appropriate guidelines. Perhaps procedural testimony would be likely to be admitted because system variables are clearly not common sense. Based on the existing research, it is clear that laypeople do not understand the important role that system variables play in eyewitness accuracy. For example, how many jurors would know what a sequential line-up is and why it should be used? In fact, the study by Stinson et al. (1997) found that even judges and lawyers both perceived a sequential presentation to be more suggestive than a simultaneous one. The mere existence of the guidelines is itself a powerful message to the legal system. The procedural issues involved in collecting identification evidence not only have a scientific basis; they also are widely accepted in the field, have nothing to say about the credibility of the witness, are not covered within judicial instructions, clearly are not common sense, and are outside the understanding of judges, lawyers, and jurors. For these reasons, the guidelines could be used by both prosecution and defense to determine whether the line-up procedures were fair and properly conducted. If the courts were to accept expert testimony on the DOJ guidelines, this may encourage more police departments to use them and recognize that eyewitness memory is not common sense and that identification evidence is fragile and must be handled with care before it enters a judicial system that appears to be all too inadequate to evaluate it. Perhaps the solution to the concern over inaccurate eyewitness memory originates in the police station where the identification evidence is collected.

REFERENCES

Abshire, J., & Bornstien, B. H. (2003). Juror sensitivity to the cross-race effect. *Law and Human Behavior, 27*(5), 471–480.

Bell, B. E., & Loftus, E. F. (1989). Trivial persuasion in the courtroom: The power of (a few) minor details. *Journal of Personality and Social Psychology, 56,* 669–679.

Berman, G. L., & Cutler, B. L. (1996). Effects of inconsistencies in eyewitness testimony on mock-juror decision making. *Journal of Applied Psychology, 81*(2), 170–177.

Bloodsworth v. Maryland, 307 Md. 164; 512 A.2d 1056 (Md. App.1986).

Borchard, E. (1932). *Convicting the innocent: Errors in criminal justice.* New Haven: Yale University Press.

Bradfield, A. L., & Wells, G. L. (2000). The perceived validity of eyewitness identification testimony: A test of the five *Biggers* criteria. *Law and Human Behavior, 24*(5), 581–594.

Brandon, R., & Davies, C. (1973). *Wrongful imprisonment.* London: Allen & Unwin.

Brigham, J. C., & Bothwell, R. K. (1983). The ability of prospective jurors to estimate the accuracy of eyewitness identifications. *Law and Human Behavior, 7*(1), 19–30.

Brigham, J. C., & Wolfskiel, M. P. (1983). Opinions of attorneys and law enforcement personnel on the accuracy of eyewitness identifications. *Law and Human Behavior, 7*(4), 337–349.

Brewer, N., & Burke, A. (2002). Effects of testimonial inconsistencies and eyewitness confidence on mock-juror judgments. *Law and Human Behavior, 26*(3), 353–364.

Collins, W. S. (2003). Improving eyewitness evidence collection procedures in Wisconsin. *Wisconsin Law Review,* 529.

Commonwealth v. Abdul-Salaam, 544 Pa. 514; 678 A.2d 342 (Pa. 1996).

Commonwealth v. Christie, 98 S.W.3d 485 (Ky. 2002).

Commonwealth v. Santoli, Jr., 424 Mass. 837; 680 N.E.2d 1116 (Mass. 1997).

Connors, E. T., Lundregan, N., Miller, N., & McEwen, T. (1996). *Convicted by Juries, Exonerated by Science: Case Studies in the Use of DNA Evidence to Establish Innocence After Trail.* Washington, DC: U.S. Department of Justice, National Institute of Justice, NCJ 161258.

Cook v. State, 734 N.E.2d 563 (Ind. 2000).

Criglow v. State, 183 Ark. 407, S.W. 2d.

Cutler, B. L., & Penrod, S. D. (1995). *Mistaken identification: The eyewitness, psychology, and the law.* New York: Cambridge University Press.

Cutler, B. L., Dexter, H. R., & Penrod, S. D. (1989). Expert testimony and jury decision- making: An empirical analysis. *Behavioral Sciences and Law, 7,* 215–225.

Cutler, B. L., Dexter, H. R., & Penrod, S. D. (1990). Nonadversarial methods for sensitizing jurors to eyewitness evidence. *Journal of Applied Social Psychology, 20*(14), 1197–1207.

Cutler, B. L., Penrod, S. D., & Dexter, H. R. (1989). The eyewitness, the expert psychologist and the jury. *Law and Human Behavior, 13*(3), 311–331.

Cutler, B. L., Penrod, S. D., & Dexter, H. R. (1990). Juror sensitivity to eyewitness identification evidence. *Law and Human Behavior, 14*(2), 185–191.

Cutler, B. L., Penrod, S. D., & Martens, T. K. (1987). The reliability of eyewitness identifications: The role of system and estimator variables. *Law and Human Behavior, 11,* 233–258.

Cutler, B. L., Penrod, S. D., & Stuve, T. E. (1988). Jury decision making in eyewitness identification cases. *Law and Human Behavior, 12*(1), 41–56.

Currie v. Commonwealth, 30 Va. App. 58; 515 S.E.2d 335 (Va. 1999).

Daubert v. Merril Dow Pharmaceuticals, Inc., 509 U.S. 579, 125 L.Ed.2d 469, 113 S. Ct. 2786 (1993).

Deffenbacher, K. A., & Loftus, E. F. (1982). Do jurors share a common understanding concerning eyewitness behavior? *Law and Human Behavior, 6*(1), 15–30.

Devenport, J. L., Penrod, S. D., & Cutler, B. L. (1997). Eyewitness identification evidence: Evaluating commonsense evaluations. *Psychology, Public Policy, and Law, 3*(2/3), 338–361.

Devenport, J. L., Stinson, V., Cutler, B. L., & Kravitz, D. A. (2002). How effective are the cross-examination and expert testimony safeguards? Jurors' perceptions of the suggestiveness and fairness of biased lineup procedures. *Journal of Applied Psychology, 87*(6), 1042–1054.

Dunlap, E. E., Ross, D. F., Bradshaw, B., & Thomas, W. N. (2003). *Is eyewitness testimony commonsense to jurors? An empirical test of the reasoning in State of Tennessee v. Coley.* Poster presented at Psychology and Law International, Interdisciplinary Conference, Edinburgh, Scotland, July 7–12, 2003.

Durham, M. D., & Dane, F. C. (1999). Juror knowledge of eyewitness behavior: Evidence for the necessity of expert testimony. *Journal of Social Behavior & Personality, 14*(2), 299–308.

Dyer v. State, 1998 Ark. App. (Ark. Ct. App. 1998).

Elwork, A., Sales., B. D., & Alfini, J. J. (1982). *Making jury instructions understandable.* Charlottesville: Michie Co.

Engberg, v. Meyer, 820 P.2d 70 (Wyo. 1991).

Ex parte Williams, 594 So. 2d 1225 (Ala. 1992).

Findley, K. A. (2002). Learning from our mistakes: A criminal justice commission to study wrongful convictions. *California Western Law Review*, 333.

Fox, S. G., & Walters, H. A. (1986). The impact of general versus specific expert testimony and eyewitness confidence upon mock juror judgment. *Law and Human Behavior, 10*(3), 215–228.

Frank, J., & Frank, B. (1957). *Not guilty.* London: Gollancz.

Garden v. State, 815 A.2d 327 (Del. 2003).

Gatowski, S. I., Dobbin, S. A., Richardson, J. T., Ginsburg, G. P., Merlino, M. L., & Dahir, V. (2001). Asking the gatekeepers: A national survey of judges on judging expert evidence in a post-*Daubert* world. *Law and Human Behavior, 25*(5), 433–458.

Geiselman, R. E., Putman, C., Korte, R., Sharhriary, M., Jachimonwicz, G., & Irzhevsky, V. (2002). Eyewitness expert testimony and juror decisions. *American Journal of Forensic Psychology, 20*(3), 21–30.

Gibbs v. Commonwealth, 723 S.W.2d 871 (Ky.1986).

Goodman, J., Greene, E., & Loftus, E. F. (1985). What confuses jurors in complex cases. *Trial* (November), 65–68.

Green v. United States, 718 A.2d 1042 (D.C. App. 1998).

Greene, E. (1988). Judge's instruction on eyewitness testimony: Evaluation and revision. *Journal of Applied Social Psychology, 18*, 252–276.

Groscup, J., & Penrod, S. D. (2003). Battle of the standards for experts in criminal cases: Police vs. psychologists. *Seton Hall Law Review*, 1141.

Gross, W. D. (1999). The unfortunate faith: A solution to the unwarranted reliance upon eyewitness testimony. *Texas Wesleyan Law Review*, 307.

Hosch, H. M. (1980). A comparison of three studies of the influence of expert testimony on jurors. *Law and Human Behavior, 4*(4), 297–302.

Hosch, H. M., Beck, E. L., & McIntyre, P. (1980). Influence of expert testimony regarding eyewitness accuracy on jury decisions. *Law and Human Behavior, 4*, 287–296.

Huff, R., Rattner, A., & Sagarin, E. (1986). Guilty until proven innocent. *Crime and Delinquincy, 32*, 518–544.

Ivkovic, S. K., & Hans, V. P. (2003). Jurors' evaluations of expert testimony: Judging the messenger and the message. *Law and Social Inquiry, 28*, 441.

Johnson v. State, 272 Ga. 254; 526 S.E.2d 549 (Ga. 2000).

Johnson v. State, 438 So. 2d 774 (Fla. 1983).

Judges, D. P. (2000). Two cheers for the Department of Justice's eyewitness evidence: A guide for law enforcement. *Arkansas Law Review, 53.*

Kassin, S. M., & Barndollar, K. A. (1992). The psychology of eyewitness testimony: A comparison of experts and prospective jurors. *Journal of Applied Social Psychology, 22*(16), 1241–1249.

Kassin, S. M., Ellsworth, P. C., & Smith, V. L. (1989). The "general acceptance" of psychological research on eyewitness testimony: A survey of the experts. *American Psychologist, 44*(8), 1089–1098.

Kassin, S. M., Tubb, V. A., Hosch, H. M., & Memon, A. (2001). On the "general acceptance" of eyewitness testimony research: A new survey of the experts. *American Psychologist, 50*(5), 405–416.

Katzev, R. D., & Wishart, S. S. (1985). The impact of judicial commentary concerning eyewitness identifications on jury decision making. *The Journal of Criminal Law and Criminology, 76,* 733–745.

Koch, R. (2003). Process v. outcome: The proper role of corroborative evidence in due process analysis of eyewitness identification testimony. *Cornell Law Review, 1097.*

Koosed, M. M. (2002). The proposed innocence protection act won't—unless it also curbs mistaken eyewitness identifications. *Ohio State Law Journal, 263.*

Kovera, M. B., & McAuliff, B. D. (2000). The effects of peer-review and evidence quality on judge evaluation of psychological science: Are judges effective gate-keepers? *Journal of Applied Psychology, 85*(4), 574–586.

Lampinen, J. M., Judges, D. P., Odegard, T. N., & Hamilton, S. (2005). Reactions of mock jurors to the Department of Justice guidelines for the collection and preservation of eyewitness evidence. *Basic and Applied Social Psychology, 27,* 155–162.

Lindsay, R. C. L. (1994). Expectations of eyewitness performance: Jurors' verdicts do not follow from their beliefs. In D. F. Ross, J. D. Read, & M. P. Toglia (Eds.), *Adult eyewitness testimony.* Cambridge University Press: New York.

Lindsay, R. C. L., Lim, R., Marando, L., & Cully, D. (1986). Mock-juror evaluations of eyewitness testimony: A test of metamemory hypotheses. *Journal of Applied Social Psychology, 16*(5), 447–459.

Lindsay, R. C. L., Wells, G. L., & O'Connor, F. J. (1989). Mock-juror belief of accurate and inaccurate eyewitnesses: A replication and extension. *Law & Human Behavior, 13*(3), 333–339.

Lindsay, R. C. L., Wells, G. L., & Rumpel, C. M. (1981). Can people detect eyewitness identification accuracy within and across situations? *Journal of Applied Psychology, 66,* 79–89.

Loftus, E. F. (1979). *Eyewitness testimony.* Cambridge: Harvard University Press.

Loftus, E. F. (1980). Impact of expert psychological testimony on the unreliability of eyewitness identifications. *Journal of Applied Psychology, 65,* 9–15.

Maass, A., Brigham, J. C., & West, S. G. (1985). Testifying on eyewitness reliability: Expert advice is not always persuasive. *Journal of Applied Social Psychology, 15*(3), 207–229.

Manson v. Brathwaite, 432 U.S. 98; 97 S. Ct. 2243; 53 L. Ed. 2d 140 (1976).

McConkey, K. M., & Roche, S. M. (1989). Knowledge of eyewitness memory. *Australian Psychologist, 24,* 377–384.

Mims v. State, NO. 12-02-00178-CR (2004 Tex. App.).

Narby, D. J., & Cutler, B. L. (1994). Effectiveness of voir dire as a safeguard in eyewitness cases. *Journal of Applied Psychology, 79*(5), 724–729.

Neil v. Biggers, 409 U.S. 188, 93 S. Ct. 375, 34 L. Ed. 2d 401 (1972).

Noon, E., & Hollin, C. R. (1987). Lay knowledge of eyewitness behavior: A British survey. *Applied Cognitive Psychology, 1,* 143–153.

Pankey v. Commonwealth, 485 S.W.2d 513 (Ky.1972).

Penrod, S., & Cutler, B. (1995). Witness confidence and witness accuracy: Assessing their forensic relation. *Psychology, Public Policy, and Law, 1*(4), 817–845.

People v. Campbell, 847 P.2d 228 (Colo. App. 1992).

People v. Gillis, 1999 Mich. App. LEXIS 2348.

People v. Hill, 84 Mich. App. 90, 269 N.W. 2d 492 (1978).

People v. McDonald, 37 Cal. 3rd 351, 690 P.2d 709 (Cal. 1984).

People v. Smith, 3 Misc. 3d 1007A (NY 2004).

Rahaim, G. L., & Brodsky, S. L. (1982). Empirical evidence versus common sense: Juror and lawyer knowledge of eyewitness accuracy. *Law & Psychology Review, 7*(1), 1–15.

Ramirez, G., Zemba, D., & Geiselman, R. E. (1996). Judges' cautionary instructions on eyewitness memory. *American Journal of Forensic Psychology, 14*(1), 31–66.

Reifman, A., Gusick, S. M., & Ellsworth, P. C. (1992). Real jurors' understanding of the law in real cases. *Law and Human Behavior, 16*(5), 539–554.

Seltzer, R., Lopes, G. M., & Venuti, M. (1990). Juror ability to recognize the limitations of eyewitness identifications. *Forensic Reports, 3*, 121–137.

Shaw, J. S., Garcia, L. A., & McClure, K. A. (1999). A lay perspective on the accuracy of eyewitness testimony. *Journal of Applied Social Psychology, 29*(1), 52–71.

Skamarocius v. State, 731 P.2d 63 (Alas. App. 1987).

State v. Blair, 164 Wis. 2d 64; 473 N.W.2d 566 (Wis. 1991).

State v. Buell, 22 Ohio St. 3d 124; 489 N.E.2d 795 (Ohio 1986).

State v. Coley, 32 S.W.3d 831 (Tenn. 2000).

State v. Fontaine, 382 N.W. 2d 374 (N.D. 1986).

State v. Gaines, 260 Kan. 752; 926 P.2d 641 (Kan. 1996).

State v. Galloway, 275 N.W.2d 736 (Iowa 1979).

State v. George, 264 Neb. 26; 645 N.W.2d 777 (Neb. 2002).

State v. Goldsby, 59 Ore. App. 66; 650 P.2d 952 (Ore. 1982).

State v. Gunter, 231 N.J. Super. 34; 554 A.2d 1356 (N.J. 1989).

State v. Gurley, 565 So. 2d 1055 (La. App. 4 Cir. 1990).

State v. Lee, 154 N.C. App. 410; 572 S.E.2d 170 (N.C. 2002).

State v. Maestas, 63 P.3d 621 (Utah 2002).

State v. Martinez, 774 A.2d 15 (R.I. 2001).

State v. McClendon, 248 Conn. 572; 730 A.2d 1107 (Conn. 1999).

State v. McCord, 505 N.W.2d 388 (S.D. 1993).

State v. McKinney, 74 S.W.3d 291 (Tenn. 2002).

State v. Miles, 585 N.W.2d 368 (Minn. 1998).

State v. Nordlund, 2002 Wash. App (Wash. 2002).

State v. Nordstrum, 200 Ariz. 229; 25 P.3d 717 (Ariz. 2001).

State v. Pacheco, 134 Idaho 367; 2 P.3d 752 (Idaho Ct. App. 2000).

State v. Percy, 156 Vt. 468; 595 A.2d 248 (Vt. 1990).

State v. Rich, 549 A.2d 742, Supreme Judicial Court of Maine 1988.

State v. Schutz, 579 N.W.2d 317 (Iowa 1998).

State v. Taylor, 200 W. Va. 661; 490 S.E.2d 748 (W.Va. 1997).

State v. Tisdel, 338 Ill. App. 3d 465; 788 N.E.2d 1149 (Ill. App. Ct. 2003).

State v. Whaley, 305 S.C. 138; 406 S.E.2d 369 (S.C. 1991).

State v. Whitmill, 780 S.W.2d 45 (Mo. 1989).

Stinson, V., Devenport, J. L, Cutler, B. L., & Kravitz, D. A. (1996). How effective is the presence-of-counsel safeguard? Attorney perceptions of suggestiveness, fairness, and correctability of biased lineup procedures. *Journal of Applied Psychology, 81*(1), 64–75.

Stinson, V., Devenport, J. L, Cutler, B. L., & Kravitz, D. A. (1997). How effective is the motion-to-suppress safeguard? Judges' perceptions of the suggestiveness and fairness of biased lineup procedures. *Journal of Applied Psychology, 82*(2), 211–220.

Technical Working Group for Eyewitness Evidence (1999). *Eyewitness evidence: A guide for law enforcement*. Washington, DC: United States Department of Justice, Office of Justice Programs.

Torres v. State, 1998 OK CR 40; 962 P.2d 3 (Okla. 1998).

United States Code Service. (USCS). Article IV. Relevancy and its limits. Rule 401. Definition of "Relevant Evidence" (Fed. R. Evid. 401).

United States Code Service. (USCS). Article IV. Relevancy and its limits. Rule 403. Exclusion of
    Relevant Evidence on Grounds of Prejudice, Confusion, or Waste of Time (Fed. R. Evid. 403).
United States Code Service. (USCS). Article VII. Opinions and Expert Testimony. Rule 702.
    Testimony by Experts. (Fed. R. Evid. 702).
United States v. Brien, 59 F.3d 274 (1995).
United States v. Brown, 461 F.2d 134 (D.C. Cir. 1972).
United States v. Crotteau, 218 F.3d 826 (7th Cir. 2000).
United States v. Hall, 165 F.3d 1095, 1101 (7th Cir. 1999).
United States v. Kime, 99 F.3d 870 (8th Cir. 1996).
United States v. Labansat, 94 F.3d 527 (1996).
United States v. Langan, 263 F.3d 613 (6th Cir. 2001).
United States v. Lumpkin, 192 F.3d 280 (2d Cir.1999).
United States v. Mathis, 264 F.3d 321 (3rd Cir. 2001).
United States v. Moore, 786 F.2d 1308 (5th Cir. 1986).
United States v. Smith, 122 F.3d 1355 (11th Cir. 1997).
United States v. Smith, 156 F.3d 1046 (10th Cir. 1998).
United States v. Telfaire, 469 F.2d 552 (D.C. Cir. 1972).
United States v. Wade, 388 U.S. 218 (1967).
United States v. Wayne, 254 F. Supp. 2d 602 (2003).
Walters, C. M. (1985). Admission of expert testimony on eyewitness identification. California
    Law Review, 73, 1402–1430.
Weatherred v. State, 15 S.W. 3d 540 (Tex. 2000).
Wells, G. L. (1984). How adequate is human intuition for judging eyewitness testimony? In G. L.
    Wells & E. F. Loftus (Eds.), Eyewitness testimony: Psychological perspectives (pp. 256–272).
    New York: Cambridge University Press.
Wells, G. L., & Bradfield, A. L. (1998). "Good you identified the suspect": Feedback to eyewit-
    nesses distorts their reports of the witnessed experience. Journal of Applied Psychology, 83,
    360–376.
Wells, G. L., Lindsay, R. C. L., & Ferguson, T. J. (1979). Accuracy, confidence, and juror per-
    ceptions in eyewitness identifications. Journal of Applied Psychology, 64(4), 440–448.
Wells, G. L., Lindsay, R. C. L., & Tousignant, J. P. (1980). Effects of expert psychological advice
    on human performance in judging the validity of eyewitness testimony. Law and Human Be-
    havior, 4(4), 275–285.
Wells, G. L., Malpass, R. S., Lindsay, R. C. L., Fisher, R. P., Turtle, J. W., & Fulero, S. M. (2000).
    From the lab to the police station: A successful application of eyewitness research. American
    Psychologist, 55(6), 581–598.
Wells, G. L., & Murray, D. M. (1983). What can psychology say about the Neil v. Biggers crite-
    ria for judging eyewitness accuracy? Journal of Applied Psychology, 68, 347–362.
Wells, G. L., Small, M., Penrod, S., Malpass, R. S., Fulero, S. M., & Brimacombe, C. A. E.
    (1998). Eyewitness identification procedures: Recommendations for lineups and photo-
    spreads. Law and Human Behavior, 22, 603, 647.
White v. Mississippi, 847 So. 2d 886 (Miss. Ct. App. 2002).
White v. State, 112 Nev. 1261; 926 P.2d 291 (Nev. 1996).
Wise, R. A., & Safer, M. A. (2004). What US judges know and believe about eyewitness testi-
    mony. Applied Cognitive Psychology, 18, 427–443.
Yarmey, A. D. (2001). Expert testimony: Does eyewitness memory research have probative value
    for the courts? Canadian Psychology, 42(2), 92–100.
Yarmey, A. D., & Jones, H. P. (1983). Is the psychology of eyewitness identification a matter of
    common sense? In S. Lloyd-Bostock & B. R. Clifford (Eds.), Evaluating witness evidence (pp. 13–
    40). Chichester, England: John Wiley & Sons.

19

Belief of Eyewitness
Identification Evidence

Melissa Boyce
University of Victoria, British Columbia

Jennifer L. Beaudry and R. C. L. Lindsay
Queen's University, Ontario

Imagine you are a juror in a trial. An eyewitness testifies that she saw a man walk into a convenience store, point a gun at the cashier, demand all of the money from the register, and then shoot the cashier. She points to the defendant and identifies him as the stickup man. Are you inclined to believe her? Does it matter how certain she is of her decision? What if she only had a glimpse of the man's face? What if she wasn't wearing her glasses, and as a result had impaired vision? Does it matter if the defendant is of the same race as the witness? Would it matter if the witness had been a young child rather than an adult? Would the police procedures used to question the witness sway your decision in any way? Would the police procedures used to obtain the identification influence your decision?

By now it is clear that eyewitness evidence often is fallible and that many variables influence the likelihood of accuracy. With respect to belief of eyewitness identification evidence, three issues are examined in this chapter: (1) Do jurors believe eyewitnesses? If eyewitness evidence has no impact, then mistaken identification as an issue is less serious than it would otherwise be. However, we show that eyewitness evidence is believed. This leads to the second issue: (2) Can people discriminate between accurate and inaccurate eyewitnesses? If people can make this distinction, then eyewitnesses will be believed only (or primarily) when they are accurate and disregarded when they are not. The innocent would still suffer the social and financial hardships associated with arrest and trial but would rarely be convicted as a result of mistaken identification. However, we show that people are not able to make this distinction, believing accurate and inaccurate eyewitnesses about equally. This brings us to the final issue: (3) Are cues available that can help people to calibrate their belief of the likelihood that an eyewitness is accurate? If so, then eyewitnesses will be believed in those situations in which they are most likely to be correct and not believed when they are least likely to be correct, but only to the extent that jurors can be taught these cues and how to look for them. The importance of this issue arises because of people's inability to discriminate an accurate eyewitness from one who is inaccurate. If people cannot discriminate accuracy, can they effectively increase the probability that their decisions about eyewitness accuracy will be correct by basing their belief on factors that actually affect eyewitness accuracy? The issue is not whether there is evidence that could permit such calibration (see Caputo & Dunning, this volume), but rather whether people in general use the available information to inform their decisions appropriately. Unfortunately, as we will show, the research indicates that this also is not the case, as people tend to base their belief on some factors that do not reflect the likelihood that a correct identification was made and frequently ignore other information that could be useful. We conclude with a discussion of the implications of these findings for the criminal justice system and practitioners within it.

METHODOLOGY USED TO STUDY
EYEWITNESS BELIEF

Before examining the issues of belief, discrimination, and calibration, we provide a brief overview of the methodology used to study eyewitness belief: questionnaires, prediction studies, and simulated testimony. For a more detailed discussion of these techniques, see Lindsay (1994).

1. Questionnaires

The use of questionnaires provides an efficient way to study knowledge of eyewitness issues and the perceived importance of relevant variables. Participants are surveyed about their opinions of factors that can affect eyewitness memory and accuracy (e.g., Deffenbacher & Loftus, 1982; Kassin, & Barndollar, 1992; Yarmey & Jones, 1983). This technique addresses the issue of whether laypeople (often undergraduates, potential jurors, and sometimes eyewitness experts) have an understanding of these factors. A typical item in such surveys may present a scenario such as a woman being mugged by two men, one of her own race and one of another race. Respondents would be asked if later she will be more, equally, or less likely to be able to correctly identify the person of her own or the other race. Although this methodology cannot address the level of belief of eyewitnesses per se, it can shed some light on the issue indirectly. Lack of knowledge about issues that have been associated in past research with the likelihood that an eyewitness will be correct indicates that people may not take these factors into consideration when deciding whether to believe an eyewitness. As well, people may believe that factors not strongly associated with accuracy predict whether an eyewitness will be correct, indicating that these irrelevant factors might be considered by people when they are judging the accuracy of an eyewitness. The worst possible outcome would indicate that people mistakenly believe a factor is predictive of accuracy when it is predictive of inaccuracy. Differences in the views of experts versus other populations indicate lack of knowledge by the public and support arguments for the potential value of expert testimony (e.g., Benton, McDonnell, & Ross, this volume; Kassin & Barnsdollar, 1992).

Questionnaire techniques fail to capture the dynamic aspects of testimony and the interplay of the content of testimony with witness demeanor. Respondents lack information that could put the "case" in context, such as details of the witnessing conditions. Usually, participants are restricted to selecting from a list of possible responses, none of which may perfectly reflect their opinions. Also, there is little or nothing in these studies to indicate how strongly people hold the expressed views, so these views may or may not matter once deliberation begins. On the other hand, questionnaires provide one means of assessing the starting point from which people view eyewitness issues, their naïve expectations of the impact of many variables of interest on eyewitness accuracy.

2. Prediction Studies

Two types of prediction studies could be conducted to examine eyewitness belief. In the first type of prediction research, witnesses view staged crimes and then attempt to identify the perpetrator. Later, other participants view these witnesses to staged crimes testifying about their experiences and the identifications the witnesses made following those experiences. Participants then make judgments about (among other things) whether they believe the eyewitnesses' identifications were accurate or not (e.g., Wells, Lindsay, & Ferguson, 1979). In this type of study, participants often have access to both the witnessing conditions (as reported in the testimony) and the behavior of the eyewitness (demeanor evidence). It is possible to ascertain whether people are able to accurately discriminate between correct and incorrect eyewitnesses based on the participants' judgments, because the witnesses they are viewing actually attempted to identify a previously seen person. Furthermore, prediction research can test whether belief in eyewitnesses is influenced by any witnessing conditions varied in the identification phase of the study.

In the second type of prediction research, participants would read detailed descriptions of past eyewitness identification studies and attempt to predict how accurate the eyewitnesses were (e.g., Brigham & Bothwell, 1983). The accuracy rates estimated by participants are compared with the actual accuracy rates obtained in the original studies to determine the ability of people to realistically estimate eyewitnesses' abilities. However, because only a description of the study is provided, rather than actually viewing witness testimony, these studies look at the anticipated effects of witnessing conditions on identification accuracy, rather than the belief of the eyewitness who made an identification decision after exposure to events under the conditions studied. Clearly it is a (questionable) inference that belief of eyewitnesses exposed to a criminal in specific conditions can be predicted by asking people to estimate the probability that a witness would be accurate under such conditions. This technique has not been used frequently.

3. Simulated Testimony

In simulated testimony studies, participants are presented with a case. This case can be presented in a written format (e.g., Leippe, 1985) or as audio or videotape (e.g., Lindsay,

Lim, Marando, & Cully, 1986). Participants then attempt to reach a verdict based on eyewitness testimony and/or other evidence. The case is created specifically for the study (though the scripts may be based on real cases), and the experimenters manipulate the behavior of the witness as well as other aspects of the evidence. This is in contrast to prediction studies where the witness's behavior is genuine; that is, the testimony truly reflects what the witness recalls from the event witnessed. Using either paradigm, researchers can test for the effects of specific factors (e.g., confidence of the witness); however, whereas in simulated testimony studies the behavior in question is manipulated, in prediction studies the behavior would vary in an uncontrolled manner, and causal inferences would be more difficult to make. The simulated testimony paradigm has frequently been used to examine factors that may contribute to the belief of an eyewitness.

Strengths and Weaknesses. Each of these methodologies has its strengths and its weaknesses. For example, both of the prediction techniques suffer from limitations of the nature of the crimes used to generate eyewitness decisions. Violent, sexual, complex, and lengthy crimes are all unlikely to be studied, for obvious ethical and practical reasons. One advantage of questionnaire and simulated testimony studies is that they do not suffer from such limitations. Another method of studying this phenomenon is the use of field studies (e.g., Devlin, 1976). Results from real cases can be examined to determine whether eyewitness identification evidence has an impact. A single finding from any of these paradigms, although suggestive, will not be conclusive. By comparing the results across studies with the use of multiple methodologies, convergent validity may be achieved regarding the importance of variables influencing belief of eyewitness testimony.

ARE EYEWITNESSES BELIEVED?

In 1974, the Devlin Commission was formed in England to examine eyewitness procedures after several cases of mistaken identification came to light. Devlin (1976) examined all police lineups (or identity parades) conducted in England in 1973. In total, over 2000 parades were analyzed. A suspect was identified in 45% of the parades, and 82% of those identified were subsequently convicted. The identification comprised the only evidence in over 300 cases, and, of these, 75% of the suspects were found guilty. This report (field study) provides compelling real-world evidence that eyewitnesses are believed. Then again, suspect identifications were made in less than half of the cases that the Devlin Report analyzed. It could be argued that the identified suspects were indeed guilty in these cases and that most (perhaps even all) of the eyewitnesses who identified them did so accurately and thus should have been believed.

With the advent of DNA evidence, it is increasingly possible to prove that innocent people are convicted. To date, innocence projects have helped to exonerate at least 142 wrongfully convicted people (Scheck & Neufeld, 2004). Mistaken identification was a contributing factor and probably the primary reason for conviction in over 80% of these cases. Clearly, mistaken eyewitnesses have been believed and have led to the conviction of innocent people. Once again, this evidence is insufficient on its own to lead to the conclusion of a widespread problem. The number of DNA exonerations is trivially small in comparison with the number of convictions based on eyewitness identification evidence. We must rely on the laboratory for evidence of the ease with which witnesses can be enticed into selecting innocent people from lineups (e.g., see Dupuis & Lindsay, this volume; Meissner & Brigham, this volume). The experimental literature demonstrates beyond doubt that eyewitnesses frequently select innocent people from lineups and thus that mistaken identification is likely often to be presented as evidence in court.

Other laboratory research strongly supports the conclusion that eyewitnesses are frequently believed even in the absence of other evidence. Loftus (1974) used a case involving robbery and murder (simulated testimony paradigm) and found that 72% of participants returned guilty verdicts when eyewitness evidence was presented, but only 22% did so in the absence of identification evidence. Wells et al. (1979) found that approximately 80% of people believed the witness they had seen identify a person following a staged crime (prediction paradigm). Generally speaking, laboratory research supports the contention that identification by an eyewitness is a highly credible piece of evidence likely to lead jurors to vote guilty.

Other research has demonstrated that eyewitness evidence is one of the most incriminating types of evidence that can be presented in court. Identification evidence has been shown to be comparable to or more impactive than physical evidence (McAllister & Bregman, 1986; Skolnick & Shaw, 2001), character evidence (Kassin & Neumann, 1997), alibis (McAllister & Bregman, 1989), polygraph evidence (Myers & Arbuthnot, 1997), and even sometimes confession evidence (Kassin & Neumann, 1997).

Interestingly, it seems that eyewitness evidence may actually affect the way in which other types of evidence are viewed. The existence of eyewitness identification evidence increases the perceived strength of the other evidence presented (e.g., McAllister & Bregman, 1986; Kassin & Neumann, 1997). Both legally and scientifically, this may seem to make sense. As multiple sources of information converge on the same conclusion, the evidence supporting the conclusion is stronger. However, what may happen need not be such a positive pattern. Consider the following example.

Assume that the lack of an alibi is of relatively limited probative value in many cases (Turtle, Burke, & Olsen, volume 1). Assume that the probability that a person lacking an alibi is guilty is (arbitrarily) .1. All that is implied here is that most people could not accurately remember and prove their whereabouts at the time of the crime, say 3 weeks ago at 5:45 P.M. When a witness has identified the suspect, the lack of an alibi itself may be perceived as better evidence; thus, the probability that a person lacking an alibi is guilty increases (arbitrarily) to .6. If this altered probability (.6 vs. .1) is used in combination with the identification evidence to estimate the overall probability of guilt or innocence, erroneous conclusions are more likely. Of course the influence could be reciprocal as well. The lack of an alibi may reduce the perceived probability that an identification will be erroneous. The impact of various sources of evidence in combination on the credibility of eyewitness identification evidence is an important issue that has received little attention from researchers to date (but for an example see Cutler, Penrod, & Dexter, 1990).

CAN PEOPLE DISCRIMINATE BETWEEN
ACCURATE AND INACCURATE EYEWITNESSES?

The findings from the Devlin report indicate that eyewitnesses are believed; however, a quarter of suspects whose cases against them rested solely on identification evidence were not convicted. Similarly, laboratory studies indicate that not all eyewitnesses are believed. Is it possible that people are able to discriminate between accurate and inaccurate eyewitnesses, believing only (or primarily) those who are accurate? DNA exoneration cases prove that some inaccurate eyewitnesses are believed. However, exoneration cases are a very small proportion of all eyewitness cases. As a result, the existence of even 142 wrongful convictions is consistent with an argument that identification errors and wrongful convictions based on such errors are extremely rare. Although logically possible, few, if any, researchers believe identification errors to be rare. Many (including the authors) believe DNA cases are the tip of the iceberg, that most identification errors go undetected for a variety of reasons (e.g., once the case is "solved," the investigation is terminated; relatively few cases provide suitable material for DNA testing; etc.). However, this does not alter the fact that DNA exoneration cases are few in number.

Wells developed a prediction paradigm to study this issue (Wells, Lindsay, & Ferguson, 1979). Participants viewed the questioning of witnesses who had just observed a staged theft and identified someone from a lineup. Mock jurors were not able to differentiate between accurate and inaccurate witnesses; both were believed by approximately 80% of participants. Other studies have confirmed that people are not able to make this discrimination (e.g., Lindsay, Wells, & Rumpel, 1981; Wells, Ferguson, & Lindsay, 1981; Wells, Lindsay, & Tousignant, 1980). Even when attempts have been made to increase the ecological validity of the research by having practicing lawyers question eyewitnesses in a real courtroom, mock jurors could not distinguish between accurate and inaccurate eyewitnesses (Lindsay, Wells, & O'Connor, 1989). In fact, only one study using the paradigm of a staged crime followed by a mock trial has ever shown a significant ability to discriminate accurate from inaccurate identification by adult mock jurors listening to the testimony of adult witnesses. In that study, Wells and Leippe (1981) demonstrated that when questioning focused on memory for peripheral details of the event, inaccurate eyewitnesses were believed significantly more often than accurate eyewitnesses.

Interestingly, Leippe, Manion, and Romanczyk (1992) found that people were able to discriminate between correct and incorrect child eyewitnesses (ages 6 and 10). However, the study selected only the most and least accurate children for use in the study, so it is possible that the accuracy of these children may have been obvious. In any case, at least with adults, people consistently demonstrate that they are unable to discriminate between eyewitnesses who are accurate and those who are not.

The staged-event mock-jury paradigm generally presents participants with witnesses, all of whom have seen the same crime and criminal under the same circumstances. Variation in the nature of the crime may significantly influence eyewitness accuracy. If jurors are able to estimate or intuit the impact of such variation, they may be able to calibrate their decisions such that eyewitnesses are most likely to be believed in exactly those situations in which they also are most likely to be accurate. Although this would not elim-inate errors, it would provide some reduction in the rate of wrongful conviction com-pared with random or indiscriminate belief.

IS BELIEF OF EYEWITNESSES WELL CALIBRATED?

People cannot discriminate between individual accurate and inaccurate eyewitnesses. If they could, calibration wouldn't be a concern, but since they can't, people's ability to cal-ibrate their belief to the likelihood that an eyewitness is accurate becomes a useful skill. If people are unable to determine if a particular eyewitness is accurate within a situation, are there factors within situations that can help jurors to determine if the witness is more or less likely to be accurate?

This can be thought of in terms of game theory (McCloskey & Egeth, 1984). In order to maximize correct decisions, people should focus on factors that are related to eyewit-ness accuracy; that way they will optimize their chances of being accurate when deciding whether to believe an eyewitness. If people use the wrong cues, that is, factors that *do not* relate to the accuracy of the eyewitness, then their degree of belief will not be optimally calibrated to the rate of correct identification. How well do people calibrate their belief of eyewitnesses?

Lindsay, Wells, and Rumpel (1981) attempted to address the calibration issue with the use of the staged-crime mock-juror paradigm. Witnessing conditions were manipu-lated to generate poor, moderate, and good witnessing conditions, as indicated by the per-centage of eyewitnesses who were correct when they identified a lineup member (33%, 50%, and 75%). Accurate and inaccurate eyewitnesses from each condition were viewed by mock jurors. Within conditions, the usual result was obtained, indicating no ability to discriminate accurate from inaccurate eyewitnesses based on testimony. However, across conditions, witnesses were more likely to be believed the better the witnessing conditions were (61%, 70%, 78% in the poor, moderate, and good viewing conditions, respectively). This result provides some evidence that jurors may be able to estimate the likely accu-racy of eyewitnesses under varying conditions. Unfortunately, the results were strongly influenced by witness confidence. Confident witnesses were likely to be believed regard-less of witnessing conditions (76%, 76%, 78%, respectively). Thus, people took witnessing conditions into account only when the witness was not confident (46%, 63%, 78%). The pattern in the data from this study is a serious problem for a calibration approach. Wit-nesses who are not confident may be less likely to appear in court because they decline to testify or because the prosecutor believes they will not be convincing. If this reason-ing is correct, the witnesses who would permit some degree of calibration of belief are unlikely to testify, whereas those producing indiscriminate belief are most likely to tes-tify. Furthermore, witness confidence can be altered between the time of identification and testimony (Wells, Ferguson, & Lindsay, 1981) or may be distorted by interactions with police or other witnesses (Wells & Bradfield, 1998). To the extent that this happens, the evidence that could have been used to assist with calibration is distorted, possibly eliminating its usefulness. For a more extensive discussion of the usefulness of witness confidence as an indication of accuracy, see Leippe and Eisenstadt (this volume).

EVIDENCE FOR OVERBELIEF

Research indicates that people overestimate the abilities of eyewitnesses. The Lindsay et al. (1981) study reveals that the percentage of mock jurors who believed eyewitnesses was greater than the percentage of eyewitnesses who made accurate identifications in all conditions. The discrepancy was trivially small when viewing conditions were good (3%) but larger with moderate (20%) and poor (28%) viewing conditions. For confident witnesses drawn from poor viewing conditions, overbelief was very high, as only 33% of witnesses were correct but the witnesses were believed 76% of the time. If this reflects a general pattern, the worse the viewing conditions, the lower the probability that an identification will be accurate, and the greater the discrepancy between eyewitness accuracy and eyewitness belief is likely to be. In other words, as identification accuracy declines, overbelief increases. Since real-world witnessing conditions can be much worse than those found in this laboratory study, very high rates of overbelief would be predicted.

Wells et al. (1979) also exposed students to a staged crime, obtained identifications, and had witnesses testify about their experiences. Although only 54% of witnesses correctly selected the culprit from the lineup, 80% of mock jurors indicated that they believed the witness they saw testify (26% overbelief).

Brigham and Bothwell (1983) conducted a prediction study in which they presented eligible jurors with the procedures from two studies that had previously been conducted to examine eyewitness accuracy, one involving a theft (from Leippe, Wells, & Ostrom, 1978) and the other involving a convenience store interaction (from Brigham, Maass, Snyder, & Spaulding, 1982). Participants were asked to estimate the likelihood of a correct identification.

When presented with information regarding the theft, participants estimated that 71% of witnesses would make a correct identification, when in reality only 12.5% had done so. This supports the earlier speculation that as witnessing conditions deteriorate (12.5% identification accuracy), overbelief escalates (58.5%). Overall, 91% of participants overestimated the percentage of witnesses who would make a correct identification. For the convenience store study, when the target was black, participants thought 51% of witnesses would make an accurate identification when only 32% had (19% overbelief). Over 70% of participants overestimated the percentage of correct identification. It was estimated that 69% of witnesses would make a correct identification when the target was white, although only 31% had (38% overbelief). Over 90% of participants overestimated the percentage of correct identification.

These results indicate that people believe that witnesses are considerably more likely to be accurate than they actually are. Thus, people do not effectively calibrate their belief to the likelihood that an eyewitness is correct; that is, they are not playing the game well. Why might this be? For people to successfully perform this calibration, they must have some understanding of the factors that affect eyewitness memory and accuracy. Past research has shown that people's knowledge of these factors is limited (e.g., Deffenbacher & Loftus, 1982; Benton et al., this volume; Shaw, Garcia, & McClure, 1999). People tend to base their decisions to believe eyewitnesses on at least some factors that are *not* related to eyewitness accuracy.

System versus Estimator Variables

Wells (1978) distinguished two categories of factors that can affect the likelihood that an eyewitness will make a correct identification. System variables are factors that are under the control of the system, and, as such, steps can be taken to ensure that these procedures are used in a way that will optimize eyewitness accuracy. Examples of system variables include such things as identification procedures or questioning strategies. Estimator variables, on the other hand, are factors that are not under the control of police officers but which can affect the likelihood that an eyewitness will make a correct identification. Estimator variables can be further broken down into subcategories pertaining to characteristics of the witness, the culprit, and the situation. Witness characteristics include age, sex, race, and confidence. Culprit characteristics include factors such as race and disguise. Situational variables include such factors as lighting, distance, and exposure time.

   How much consideration do people give to system versus estimator variables? Shaw et al. (1999) asked people to list factors believed to have important effects on eyewitness accuracy. Of the total responses, 42% related to factors describing characteristics of the eyewitness (e.g., vision, age, reputation for honesty), 29% to conditions of the crime scene (e.g., lighting, distance between eyewitness and crime), 26% to characteristics of the eyewitness's testimony (e.g., quality of description, composure in court), 3% to characteristics of the suspect (e.g., race, actions in the courtroom), and only 1% to police procedures (e.g., questioning tactics, handling of evidence). These results indicate that people consider characteristics of the eyewitness to be the strongest determinant of whether the identification is likely to be accurate. More telling, however, is that when the factors are separated into system and estimator variables, 99% of people's responses fell under the category of estimator variables, whereas system variables accounted for only 1% of people's responses. This particular study does not allow us to determine whether people will ignore variance in system variables when deciding whether to believe an eyewitness; however, there is other evidence demonstrating that system variables do not strongly influence juror belief of eyewitness identification evidence (Cutler, Penrod, & Dexter, 1990; Cutler, Penrod, & Stuve, 1988; Lampinen, Judges, Odegard, & Hamilton, 2005).

ESTIMATOR VARIABLES

Characteristics of the Eyewitness

Much of the research on belief of eyewitnesses has focused on estimator variables pertaining to characteristics of the eyewitness, probably because the eyewitness is the most proximal cue, being a primary (and, in legal terms, direct) source of evidence, including identification. Most of the attention is focused on trying to determine witness accuracy by examining the cues provided by the witness. Not surprisingly, it is these variables that have been shown to have the greatest impact on whether an eyewitness will be believed. That is, people calibrate their belief based on characteristics of the eyewitness.

Confidence of the Eyewitness

The research on the effects of eyewitness confidence shows how powerfully a confident witness can sway juror belief. For example, Cutler, Penrod, and Stuve (1988) provided participants with information related to disguise, weapons, violence, mugshot searches, voice samples, length of retention interval, lineup size, similarity of lineup members, and witness confidence. Only witness confidence was related to ratings of the probability that a correct identification was made (60% versus 69%) and a greater proportion of guilty verdicts (39% versus 54%). These findings have been replicated with eligible and experienced jurors (Cutler, Penrod, & Dexter, 1990). Even in courtrooms using actual lawyers, confidence still determined the likelihood that a witness would be believed (Lindsay et al., 1989). In fact, eyewitness confidence is the only variable that consistently predicts belief in every study conducted examining the issue. This is troublesome unless the relationship between confidence and accuracy is strong. Wells et al. (1979) found a small (albeit significant) relationship between confidence and accuracy ($r = .29$), such that confidence accounted for about 10% of the variance in accuracy. In spite of this, witness confidence accounted for 50% of the variance in jurors' accuracy judgments in that study. Such results are typical in eyewitness research, though debate about the strength of the relationship between confidence and accuracy is far from over (see Leippe & Eisenstadt, this volume).

Consistency of Eyewitness Testimony

Consistency of eyewitness statements can have an impact on whether an eyewitness is believed (e.g., Berman, Narby, & Cutler, 1995; Berman & Cutler, 1996). Berman and Cutler found that any type of inconsistency decreased guilty verdicts, whether it was information presented on the stand but originally omitted during pretrial investigations or information presented on the stand that contradicted original statements, or if the testimony on the stand contained contradictions. Lindsay, Lim, Marando, and Cully (1986) manipulated the consistency of a description and the appearance of the perpetrator in court and found it had no effect on belief of the eyewitness. Brewer and Burke (2002) suggest that the effects of witness inconsistency may be confounded with confidence; that is, inconsistency may reduce belief only when it leads to the perception of reduced confidence. This is consistent with the Lindsay et al. data because the witness was portrayed as highly confident in her identification decision regardless of the level of consistency of her other evidence. Fisher and Cutler (1995) examined 612 identification attempts of eight different targets and found that consistency with description was not a powerful indicator of eyewitness accuracy. This finding has important implications because it indicates that consistency (at least with description) is *not* a factor that people should be using to determine whether they believe an eyewitness, and yet many studies suggest they do.

Level of Detail in Eyewitness Testimony

Very few studies have looked at the level of detail provided by the witness during testimony as a determinant of belief about the accuracy of the testimony. Bell and Loftus (1988) found that the level of detail used by the eyewitness did have an effect on guilty verdicts, indicating that eyewitnesses who provide more detail in their testimonies are more likely to be believed. In spite of this, some research has shown that better recall of peripheral details may not mean that the witness was more likely to have made a correct identification. Wells and Leippe (1981) found that people who were better able to remember the peripheral details of a crime scene were actually less likely to make a correct identification. However, participants rated the credibility of the witnesses as though the opposite were true. Again, this is problematic, as the research suggests that detail may not be an indicator of eyewitness accuracy, and yet people seem to use or even misuse it when deciding whether to believe an eyewitness.

Age of the Eyewitness

Overall, the literature examining whether age affects witness belief has converged on two main findings. First, the research generally supports the notion that children's credibility is a multidimensional construct comprising cognitive ability and honesty (e.g., Leippe & Romanczyk, 1989; Ross, Dunning, Toglia, & Ceci, 1990; Ross, Jurden, Lindsay, & Keeney, 2003; Ross, Miller, & Moran, 1987), though there have been some exceptions (e.g., McCauley & Parker, 2001). Although children are believed to be more honest, they are seen to be lacking in cognitive abilities. For this reason, in cases that involve a sexual element, such as child abuse, there is more of a focus on the honesty of the child, and children are typically believed. Alternatively, in cases such as car theft, which focus more on the memory of the child, children are seen as less credible witnesses. The same argument applies to the elderly, as it is believed that memory impairments may compromise their credibility, but, according to stereotypes of the elderly, they are honest.

Second, people have a negative stereotype of children as eyewitnesses, most likely because of their credibility issues related to cognitive skill. Although some studies show that these stereotypes are readily disconfirmed and put aside if people are given the chance to actually view the testimony of the child (e.g., Leippe & Romanczyk, 1989; Ross, Dunning, Toglia, & Ceci, 1990), other studies report the opposite (e.g., Leippe et al., 1992). Research on the elderly has shown that their credibility as witnesses depends on what stereotypes are invoked. Nunez, McCoy, Clark, and Shaw (1999) found that when positive stereotypes of the elderly such as "statesman" were invoked, guilty ratings were significantly higher than when stereotypes such as "senior citizen" or "grandfather" were elicited. It would seem that, based on this evidence, the strongest statement that can be made is that *sometimes* eyewitness evidence is perceived as less credible if the witness is young or elderly, depending on the extent to which certain stereotypes are invoked and the type of case involved. Some have suggested that expectations of poor performance by children and the elderly may create demand characteristics in the research setting that may not generalize to the courtroom (e.g., Kwong-See, Hoffman, & Wood, 2001). This possibility has not been thoroughly evaluated, but the existence of such expectations itself suggests that they may influence real-world trials. Age of the eyewitness can play a role when people are deciding whether to believe an eyewitness.

In light of these findings, does age actually have an effect on eyewitness accuracy? This is one situation where a witness characteristic *has* been shown to have an effect on eyewitness accuracy. Lindsay, Pozzulo, Craig, Lee, and Corber (1997) found that children did not differ in their correct identification rates from adults, but that in target-absent lineups, because of a propensity to guess, they were less likely to correctly reject a lineup (see also Pozzulo, this volume). Likewise, Yarmey (1984), in a review of the literature on the accuracy of elderly eyewitnesses, found that on average the elderly are 7% to 20% less accurate than young adults, although exceptions exist (see also Bartlett & Memon, this volume). Wright and Stroud (2002) determined that it may not be the age of eyewitnesses *per se* that makes them worse at identification, but the age of the eyewitness relative to that of the criminal. People are better at identifying those who are closer to them in age, and the fact that studies typically use young adults as their criminals may account for the findings that children and the elderly are less accurate.

What does this mean in terms of accurate calibration? Perhaps people should only use age as a factor in deciding whether to believe an eyewitness if there is a large age difference between the witness and the suspect. However, research does not suggest that this is what people do, meaning that once again, people are using the wrong cues or applying the correct cues incorrectly when deciding whether to believe an eyewitness.

Credibility of the Eyewitness

The credibility of the eyewitness is an interesting witness variable, as it can exist as its own category, but it can also subsume all other witness characteristics. All of the other witness variables discussed in this chapter (confidence, consistency of testimony, level of detail of testimony, and age of the eyewitness) affect whether an eyewitness is believed because they compromise the perceived credibility of the witness. When an eyewitness's credibility is called into question, his/her impact as an eyewitness is diminished and he/she is less likely to be believed. Whether or not these factors are related to the accuracy of the eyewitness is a separate issue.

Attempts have been made to directly test the effects of a witness's credibility on his/her impact on mock jurors. For example, a number of studies have looked at whether vision impairment will affect a witness's perceived credibility. These studies are more concerned with determining how pervasive findings of eyewitness overbelief are, rather than with the particular variable being used. Vision impairment is something that so obviously will affect whether a person can make an accurate identification that if research can show that people are still willing to believe a witness who has impaired vision, this would provide compelling evidence of people's propensity to believe eyewitnesses.

As mentioned previously, Loftus (1974) used a (simulated testimony) case involving robbery and murder and found that 72% of participants returned guilty verdicts when eyewitness evidence was presented, but only 22% in the absence of identification evidence. In a third condition, 68% of participants found the defendant guilty when the eyewitness who testified was described as legally blind. This study sparked a wave of controversy. Some claimed that eyewitnesses were believed indiscriminately, as it seemed jurors' reliance on eyewitness evidence was so strong that even blind eyewitnesses would be believed! However, since that initial study, very few studies have found any indications that jurors ignore the fact that eyewitness evidence has been discredited (exceptions are Cavoukian, 1981; Hatvany & Strack, 1980; Saunders, Vidmar, & Hewitt, 1983, study 3). The majority of studies report that mock jurors deal with discredited eyewitness evidence either by ignoring it or by slightly overcorrecting (actually returning fewer guilty verdicts than when no eyewitness evidence is presented at all; e.g., Weinberg & Baron, 1982; Saunders et al., 1983, studies 1 & 2; Elliott, Farrington, & Manheimer, 1988; Kennedy & Haygood, 1992). One clear implication of these results is that for years lawyers have been following a sensible practice when they attempt to win cases by discrediting witnesses for the other side.

Characteristics of the Criminal or the Situation

Many of these factors could logically compromise the accuracy of an eyewitness (to varying degrees). Yet very little research has focused on how characteristics of the criminal or the crime scene affect the belief of eyewitnesses. Cutler, Penrod, and colleagues (Cutler et al., 1988, 1990) conducted a series of studies examining the role of multiple factors in eyewitness belief. They found that neither the presence of a disguise nor the criminal's use of a weapon or violence were taken into consideration by mock jurors as potentially compromising eyewitness accuracy. Brigham and Bothwell (1983) found that people recognized that the race of the criminal can play a role in correct identifications but underestimated its effects and continued to overestimate the abilities of eyewitnesses in these situations.

Lindsay et al. (1986) examined the effects of viewing conditions on eyewitness belief by manipulating the time of day (9:00 A.M. on a sunny day versus 1:00 A.M. and 60 feet from a street light) and exposure that the eyewitness had when viewing the criminal (5 seconds, half an hour, or half an hour with eyewitness interaction with the criminal). Lindsay et al. found that fewer people convicted the defendant when the criminal was seen at night (37% versus 57%), though this difference did not reach significance. There were no significant differences in the proportion of guilty votes between the 5-second, half-hour, or half-hour with interaction exposure times (45%, 40%, and 55%, respectively).

Although the evidence is scant, what research has been done indicates that people do not readily consider characteristics of the criminal or the situation when determining whether to believe an eyewitness. Yet a disguise (Cutler, Penrod, & Martens, 1987), a visible weapon (Steblay, 1992), violence (Clifford & Hollin, 1981), and viewing conditions (MacLin, MacLin, & Malpass, 2001) have all been shown to affect eyewitness accuracy.

Thus, people should consider these variables in order to better calibrate their belief of an eyewitness to the likelihood that the witness is actually correct.

SYSTEM VARIABLES

What about system variables? Even less research has examined the effects of system variables than criminal or situational variables on belief of eyewitnesses. Fortunately, a few studies have been conducted that shed light on the impact of system variables when calibrating belief of eyewitnesses.

Fairness of the Lineup

This category includes any type of lineup bias, such as foil bias (members of the lineup are not sufficiently similar to the suspect) and instruction bias (eyewitnesses are told that the suspect either "is" or "may or may not be" in the lineup). Both biases have been shown to greatly increase false identification rates (e.g., Lindsay & Wells, 1980; Malpass & Devine, 1981). Devenport, Stinson, Cutler, and Kravitz (2002) studied jurors' perceptions of these biased lineup procedures. They found that although a foil-biased lineup was rated as significantly more suggestive than an unbiased lineup and that the presence of an instruction bias also led to higher ratings of suggestibility, these biases had little effect on verdicts. Although the presence of a foil bias lowered guilty verdicts, this effect attained only marginal significance (.06). The presence of an instruction bias was not reflected at all in differential guilt ratings. Even though mock jurors were aware that this bias could influence the suggestiveness of a lineup, they failed to consider it important enough to adjust their verdict decisions. Cutler et al. (1988) also found that biased lineups failed to influence belief of eyewitnesses.

Lindsay and Wells (1980) had witnesses to a staged crime attempt identification from foil-biased versus fair lineups and then testify in a mock-court procedure. The lineup fairness manipulation had a dramatic impact on the rate of false identification (70% versus 31%), but mock jurors "were no less likely to believe a witness making an identification from a low- rather than high-similarity lineup" (p. 307).

Lineup Presentation

System variables related to lineup presentation have been included separately from lineup biases. Although the simultaneous lineup is inferior to a properly conducted sequential lineup, most people do not consider it a biased lineup. Devenport et al. (2002) attempted to determine whether lineup presentation, that is, whether eyewitnesses were presented with a sequential or simultaneous lineup, had an effect on mock jurors' belief. The sequential lineup has been shown to be superior to the simultaneous lineup in its ability to decrease false identifications with little loss of correct identifications (Lindsay & Bellinger, 1999; Lindsay et al., 1991; Lindsay & Wells, 1985). In spite of this, people did not find the identification evidence more convincing when a sequential rather than a simultaneous lineup had been used by police.

Modality of the Identification

Research indicates that people are much less likely to accurately identify voices than faces (e.g., Bull & Clifford, 1984; McAllister, Dale, & Keay, 1993, study 1). In fact, we've found in our laboratory that voice identifications have very little probative value (Pryke, Lindsay, Dysart, & Dupuis, 2004). However, McAllister et al. (1993) found that as long as any type of identification was made, witnesses were equally believed and guilty verdicts did not differ by condition. Cutler et al. (1988) also found that people were no less willing to believe voice identifications than face identifications.

Evidence Obtained After Hypnosis

An issue that hasn't received much attention in the literature is whether a witness who makes an identification after undergoing hypnosis to facilitate recall is likely to be believed. Although there are proponents of hypnotically induced witness statements, the evidence generally indicates that hypnosis does not aid witnesses in accurate recall (e.g., Smith, 1983). However, Spanos, Gwynn, and Terrade (1989) found that mock jurors believed eyewitness evidence equally regardless of whether the eyewitness had undergone hypnosis in order to "remember" what her attacker had looked like (40% and 39% guilty verdicts for control and hypnosis groups, respectively).

SUMMARY OF THE LITERATURE

The majority of the research has focused on estimator variables rather than system variables. Studies that relate to the characteristics of the eyewitness are particularly common. The findings so far should raise concern. People do perform a type of calibration process when determining whether to believe eyewitnesses, but they base this process on estimator variables relating to characteristics of the witness, which have, at best, a modest relation and, at worst, no relation to eyewitness accuracy. People pay little if any attention to system variables, even though these variables have consistently been shown to have an effect on the accuracy of identification decisions. Although it is encouraging to think that the factors that seem to have the most impact on the likelihood of a correct identification are factors that are under our control, this knowledge is less valuable if it remains limited to researchers in the area, thus having no effect in the courts. Clearly a goal should be to try to educate people about which variables actually affect eyewitness accuracy and which do not, so that people can better calibrate their belief. This highlights the value of expert testimony in the courtroom (Benton et al., this volume; Van Wallendael, Devenport, Cutler, & Penrod, this volume).

Probative Value of System and Estimator Variables

Some estimator variables definitely have an impact on the likelihood that an eyewitness will be able to make an accurate identification. Consider situational variables. Clearly, a witness to a lengthy crime committed in broad daylight only a few feet from the witness will be more likely to be able to identify the criminal than a witness who caught a brief glimpse of the criminal 30 feet away in the middle of the night from the back of a car window in the pouring rain. Furthermore, characteristics of the criminal can affect how likely he is to be identified. Research has shown that people have difficulty identifying criminals who have changed their appearance, for example, by shaving a beard or cutting their hair (e.g., Cutler et al., 1987). In addition, the own-race bias has received a great deal of attention in the literature for the effects it can have on eyewitness accuracy (Bothwell, Brigham, & Malpass, 1989; Chance & Goldstein, 1996; Meisner & Brigham, this volume).

However, some of these variables may suppress choosing rather than alter the ratio of correct to false identification. Very poor viewing conditions, such as darkness or obstruction of view, may lead witnesses to decline to identify anyone. Since these witnesses will not appear in court, the fact that the viewing conditions reduced accuracy by reducing the proportion of witnesses making correct selections may not be critical. The critical issue is the ratio of accurate to inaccurate "choosers" and "testifiers" and how convincing they are in court. Furthermore, many witness factors are not reliably related to eyewitness accuracy, yet it appears to be these variables that have the largest impact on whether people are willing to believe an eyewitness.

System variables, on the other hand, consistently show a relationship to eyewitness accuracy but are largely ignored by people when they are deciding whether to believe an eyewitness. The experience of one of the authors (RL) when training police, prosecutors, and judges is that the eyewitness is seen as the problem; that is, the eyewitness is seen as the source of error. Police procedures, unless they are obviously biased, are rarely considered a potential problem until people have been exposed to research results documenting the impact on eyewitness accuracy of many standard but poor procedures. Since the public has limited exposure to such information, they do not consider system variables as a concern for evaluating witness testimony. This also is probably due to a general but incorrect expectation that police are aware of and use the best available procedures. Unfortunately, this may mean that jurors are rarely exposed to and thus may not consider system variable issues in court.

DOES BELIEF OF EYEWITNESSES DEPEND ON THE TYPE OF EYEWITNESS EVIDENCE PRESENTED?

Some research has shown that the extent to which eyewitness evidence is utilized compared with other types of evidence may depend on whether mock jurors believe that the defendant is guilty or not. Interestingly, this notion also applies to which types of eyewitness evidence mock jurors focus on (Leippe, 1985; McAllister & Bregman, 1989; Lindsay, 1994). People appear to use a confirmatory strategy to select evidence that will best support their conclusion that the accused person is either guilty or innocent. Evidence supporting this view has been obtained in studies manipulating nonidentification and alibi evidence.

Nonidentification Evidence

A nonidentification occurs whenever an eyewitness selects no one from a lineup or selects a foil rather than the suspect. The research on nonidentification evidence has met with conflicting results. Some studies indicate that nonidentification evidence is highly impactive on mock jurors, whereas other studies have found that this evidence tends to be underutilized. The confirmatory strategy framework can be used to explain these discrepant findings. For example, Leippe (1985) found that nonidentifications had a substantial impact on mock jurors, with guilty verdicts declining from 47% to 14% if nonidentification evidence was included. In a second study, guilty verdicts declined (nonsignificantly) from 29% to 12% if nonidentification evidence was included. Based on the low conviction rates in the control conditions, it seems likely that mock jurors were testing a hypothesis of not guilty based on the other evidence. If mock jurors were using a confirmatory strategy, we would expect them to utilize the nonidentification evidence to support their bias toward a not guilty verdict, which is precisely what they did.

McAllister and Bregman (1986, 1989) also found results supporting the use of a confirmatory strategy. They used a case for which baseline guilty rates were indicative of a not-guilty hypothesis. In line with the confirmatory strategy, they found not only that nonidentifications were overutilized in their study, but also that alibi identifications, which would provide evidence of innocence, also were overutilized, whereas eyewitness identifications and alibi nonidentifications were underutilized.

Conflicting or Corroborated Eyewitness Evidence

At first glance, the results pertaining to how conflicting or corroborated eyewitness evidence affects juror belief are anything but conclusive, since some researchers found that this evidence has an effect and other researchers found that it does not. However, a second look at the findings in terms of hypothesis confirmation reveals another story. Lindsay et al. (1986) manipulated corroborating identification evidence (multiple witnesses identifying the same suspect) versus conflicting evidence (some witnesses stating that the suspect was not the person who committed the crime, whereas others said he was). They concluded that corroborating identification evidence was underutilized, but that conflicting identification evidence resulted in significantly fewer guilty verdicts. It is possible that (based on the other evidence) mock jurors formed a hypothesis of not guilty, causing them to underutilize the corroborating evidence supporting a verdict of guilty and overutilize conflicting evidence confirming a verdict of not guilty.

Leippe (1985) also examined the effects of corroborating evidence and found that the addition of another eyewitness who identified the accused did not significantly increase guilty verdicts (47% and 53%, respectively). It appears from the guilty verdict rate of about 50% that mock jurors in this case were unbiased as to the guilt of the accused, forming no prior hypotheses. McAllister and Bregman's (1986) finding that neither conflicting nor corroborating eyewitness evidence lowered or raised guilty verdicts compared with when just one eyewitness testified supports the notion that when people have no preconceived notions of a suspect's guilt, both corroborating and consistent eyewitness testimony may be underutilized. The idea of a hypothesis confirmatory strategy playing a role in how identification evidence, nonidentification evidence, and the evidence of multiple witnesses is utilized is interesting and deserving of future research. At the moment, the results are too few and inconsistent to draw conclusions. A clear limitation of the existing studies is that they were not designed to explicitly test the possibility that confirmation biases were at work.

IMPLICATIONS AND DIRECTIONS FOR FUTURE RESEARCH

Eyewitness evidence is very compelling to jurors. However, people are not able to tell if a witness is accurate by watching his or her testimony. Jurors appear to base their decisions on whether to believe an eyewitness mostly on characteristics of the witness, such as confidence, which are not strongly related to eyewitness accuracy. Characteristics of the crime scene and the criminal tend to be overlooked, and system variables, which can have a great impact on eyewitness accuracy, are completely ignored when people are deciding whether a witness should be believed. In addition, jurors may focus on evidence that best supports their preconceived hypotheses about a suspect's guilt or innocence. This can lead to the underutilization of nonidentification, conflicting, or corroborating eyewitness evidence, all of which clearly affect the likelihood that a suspect is guilty. The problem is clear. Jurors are unable to determine whether eyewitness evidence is accurate. This may occur because there may be no way to successfully make the discrimination (Caputo & Dunning, this volume). Alternatively, jurors may fail to discriminate eyewitness accuracy because they focus on uninformative variables and disregard at least some variables that do speak to the likelihood that an eyewitness is correct. Or the task of evaluating the available cues in order to accurately assess likely accuracy may be too complex (Smith, Lindsay, & Pryke, 2000).

How can we increase jurors' sensitivity to factors that actually affect eyewitness accuracy? Obviously expert testimony is one option, and there is a great deal of research to be conducted examining that issue. However, based on the resistance expert testimony has received from the courts (Benton et al., this volume), it is important to determine if there are any other options. Once the case is in court, jurors can't tell if an eyewitness is correct. What about at the time of the identification? It would be interesting to test whether people are able to discriminate between accurate and inaccurate witnesses if provided with a tape of the identification procedure (indeed, videotaping identification procedures is recommended by the National Institute of Justice committee on best practices for eyewitness identification procedures; Technical Working Group, 1999). It is possible that jurors base the majority of their opinions, and in turn their verdicts, on their own judgments. That is, when a witness testifies, jurors observe factors related to the witness, such as age, confidence, and consistency. As previously mentioned, these are the variables that are commonly used by experimental participants to determine the credibility of the witness. Perhaps presenting a videotape of the identification would be informative for jurors, since they would be able to see the witness waver or delay for long periods before making the identification versus quickly and confidently selecting the suspect. This information might then be used to discriminate between accurate and inaccurate witnesses.

Are there ways of presenting the case that might cause jurors to focus less on the witness and more on the police procedures in order to better calibrate their belief? Can a judge's instructions about eyewitness identification lead jurors to evaluate eyewitness testimony in more appropriate ways (by taking into account more relevant and less irrelevant variables)? More research is needed on all of the issues discussed in this chapter. We know something about how witness variables affect eyewitness belief, but our knowledge of other variables is lacking. We need to explore more thoroughly the effects of characteristics of the criminal and situation on jurors' perceptions of eyewitness credibility. In addition, more research focused on system variables is needed. In some cases, the conclusions we have come to in this chapter are based on very little data.

Hand in hand with expanding the focus of the research is increasing the breadth of the studies conducted. The majority of these studies look only at the effects of one or two variables on belief. However, in the real world, jurors are faced with a rich palette of information on which to base their belief. Cutler, Penrod, and colleagues are noteworthy exceptions in this regard (e.g., Cutler, Penrod, & Dexter, 1990; Cutler, Penrod, & Stuve, 1988). Their efforts to examine the effects of multiple variables within the same study are commendable. Bradfield and Wells (2000) provide another example with their interesting research on the additive effects of confidence and consistency on belief.

In terms of methodology, the research on belief of eyewitnesses has typically used one of the three paradigms described at the beginning of the chapter. Questionnaires are an easy method for obtaining information; however, problems can arise because of response biases. Questionnaires often use a multiple-choice or forced-choice format that limits the depth and breadth of the information obtained from them. Questionnaires also may make certain issues more salient, leading respondents to answer questions based on demand characteristics when those factors would normally not occur to them if they were on a jury (Shaw et al., 1999). Prediction studies are not without their problems either. A prediction study is only as valid as the description of the original study. If a poor description of what occurred originally is used, people's estimates of the number of people who would make a correct identification are meaningless. Of course, the reliability of the original effect (in the study being described) also limits the validity of prediction studies. It does not matter if people can estimate the frequency of correct lineup decisions from a study if the results of the study do not reflect a general pattern of identification accuracy.

Also, people in prediction studies are making judgments about witnesses on average, rather than a particular witness. Differences in actual versus predicted accuracy rates may reflect people's inability to make overall estimations rather than their inability to determine whether an individual eyewitness is accurate or not (McAllister et al., 1993). Prediction studies where participants watch witnesses testify provide a measure of whether people can discriminate between accurate and inaccurate eyewitnesses based on all of the cues that would be available to jurors. Of course such studies risk lack of validity and generality unless diverse witnesses are used as stimuli (Wells & Windschitl, 1999).

Trial simulation studies are used in an attempt to mimic real life where jurors are making decisions about people's guilt or innocence. Such studies were thoroughly critiqued in the late 1970s (e.g., Bray & Kerr, 1979; Diamond, 1979). Case descriptions may offer little similarity to real life. Descriptions are often very brief. Manipulations may be especially salient because they are in writing, drawing participants' attention to them. Even videotaped trials, which offer an improvement to case descriptions in terms of richness of the stimulus, are limited in length, which may make some information, particularly manipulated variables, more salient than would be the case in a real trial (Ross et al., 1990). The lack of detail may overly simplify the decisions for mock jurors compared with what would be experienced in the real world. Simulated trials often do not include opening statements or judge's instructions. Very few studies have focused on jury deliberation and its effects on eyewitness belief and verdicts. Unrealistic dependent measures may be used, such as asking mock jurors to assign sentences or provide guilt responses on scales rather than as a binary verdict.

It is commendable that a variety of paradigms have been used in the research, as each does have its limitations, and it is reassuring that the results have frequently converged. However, it might be beneficial for researchers to broaden their methods of measuring eyewitness belief in the laboratory in order to decrease the effect of factors such as demand characteristics (e.g., Kwong See, Hoffman, & Wood, 2001). We encourage researchers to "think outside the box" to come up with new ways to test their hypotheses. Finally, leaving the laboratory and collecting field data is essential. It might be interesting for example to ask actual jurors what evidence they based their verdicts on in order to demonstrate the applicability of laboratory studies to the real world.

POLICY IMPLICATIONS

"Postdicting" eyewitness accuracy will never be an exact science. At the moment, we have no reason to believe that people, and thus the courts, are capable of discriminating between cases of correct and mistaken identification based on eyewitness testimony. Although it may be possible to reduce the error rate in estimating accuracy to some degree, our best available information is likely to lead to about a 25% error (wrongful conviction) rate (Smith, Lindsay, & Pryke, 2000). And even this level of performance can only be achieved by regression analysis, not human judgment! Criminal justice systems need to acknowledge the limitations of eyewitnesses and do a better job of deciding when sufficient evidence exists, not only to convict, but also to arrest, charge, and prosecute suspects.

In Canadian legal circles, one factor believed to lead to wrongful conviction is "tunnel vision." Once police and prosecutors become convinced of or committed to the guilt of the suspect, they fail to consider or actively dismiss evidence that may exonerate. Tunnel vision also may lead police and prosecutors to exaggerate the strength of the evidence supporting the hypothesis of guilt. These are examples of confirmation biases and have long been understood by psychologists (Nickerson, 1998). How might such biases be counteracted?

Following the Devlin Commission, the British argued that identification evidence alone should be insufficient to lead to conviction. They argued that corroboration of identification with some form of independent evidence should be required to dispel reasonable doubt. This seems like a good idea up to a point. Certainly wrongful convictions would be reduced by such a policy. However, there are too many cases that lack truly independent, corroborating evidence. Many robbery cases, for example, would fall into this category. Police and prosecutors are not willing to abandon these cases. Thus it is understandable that shortly after proposing this policy the British abandoned it. The fact that the accused fit the description provided by the witness was deemed sufficient to corroborate an identification. Clearly such a trivial level of corroboration will not greatly reduce errors (particularly since research suggests that description accuracy and identification accuracy are not closely related; Wells, 1985.)

Better investigative procedures, particularly better identification procedures, are much more likely to reduce wrongful convictions than efforts to improve postdicting. Tunnel vision and many other considerations strongly support the use of blind testing (Charman & Wells, this volume). If officers are unaware of which lineup member is the suspect, their ability and propensity to influence witnesses would be greatly diminished. The sequential lineup reduces misidentification dramatically with relatively small losses of correct identifications (Lindsay & Wells, 1985; Steblay, Dysart, Fulero, & Lindsay, 2001). This is true even if strong lineup biases are present (Lindsay et al., 1991). As still newer and better procedures are developed, the ability to reduce the rate of false identification may be further enhanced (Dupuis & Lindsay, this volume).

Procedures that reduce false identifications have many advantages over attempts to separate accurate from inaccurate identification decisions in court. Innocent people will be less likely to be arrested, charged, prosecuted, and convicted. Police will continue to investigate cases to find the true perpetrators. Until and unless we can develop highly accurate methods for determining the accuracy of eyewitnesses after identification decisions have been made, the best hope for reducing the unacceptably high rate of false identification and wrongful conviction is to develop improved identification procedures and convince, or better yet, require the police to use them.

ACKNOWLEDGMENT

Preparation of this chapter was supported by grants to R. Lindsay from the Social Sciences and Humanities Research Council of Canada.

REFERENCES

Bell, B. E., & Loftus, E. F. (1988). Degree of detail of eyewitness testimony and mock juror judgments. *Journal of Applied Social Psychology, 18,* 1171–1192.

Berman, G. L., & Cutler, B. L. (1996). Effects of inconsistencies in eyewitness testimony on mock-juror decision making. *Journal of Applied Psychology, 81,* 170–177.

Berman, G. L., Narby, D. J., & Cutler, B. L. (1995). Effects of inconsistent eyewitness statements on mock-juror's evaluations of the eyewitness, perceptions of defendant culpability and verdicts. *Law & Human Behavior, 19*, 79–88.

Bothwell, R. K., Brigham, J. C., & Malpass, R. S. (1989). Cross-racial identification. *Personality & Social Psychology Bulletin, 15*, 19–25.

Bradfield, A. L., & Wells, G. L. (2000). The perceived validity of eyewitness identification testimony: A test of the five Biggers criteria. *Law & Human Behavior, 24*, 581–594.

Bray, R., & Kerr, N. L. (1979). Use of the simulation method in the study of jury behaviour: Some methodological considerations. *Law & Human Behavior, 3*, 107–119.

Brewer, N., & Burke, A. (2002). Effects of testimonial inconsistencies and eyewitness confidence on mock-juror judgments. *Law & Human Behavior, 26*, 353–364.

Brigham, J. C., & Bothwell, R. K. (1983). The ability of prospective jurors to estimate the accuracy of eyewitness identifications. *Law & Human Behavior, 7*, 19–30.

Brigham, J. C., Maass, A., Snyder, L. D., & Spaulding, K. (1982). Accuracy of eyewitness identification in a field setting. *Journal of Personality & Social Psychology, 42*, 673–681.

Bull, R., & Clifford, B. R. (1984). Earwitness voice recognition accuracy. In G. L. Wells & E. F. Loftus (Eds.), *Eyewitness testimony: Psychological perspectives* (pp. 92–124). New York: Cambridge University Press.

Cavoukian, A. (1981). The influence of eyewitness identification evidence. *Dissertation Abstracts International, 42*, 352–353.

Chance, J. E., & Goldstein, A. G. (1996). The other-race effect and eyewitness identification. In S. Sporer & R. Malpass (Eds.), *Psychological issues in eyewitness identification* (pp. 153–176). Mahwah, NJ: Lawrence Erlbaum Associates.

Clifford, B. R., & Hollin, C. R. (1981). Effects of the type of incident and the number of perpetrators on eyewitness memory. *Journal of Applied Psychology, 66*, 364–370.

Cutler, B. L., Penrod, S. D., & Dexter, H. R. (1990). Juror sensitivity to eyewitness identification evidence. *Law & Human Behavior, 14*, 185–191.

Cutler, B. L., Penrod, S. D., & Martens, T. K. (1987). The reliability of eyewitness identification: The role of system and estimator variables. *Law & Human Behavior, 11*, 233–258.

Cutler, B. L., Penrod, S. D., & Stuve, T. E. (1988). Juror decision making in eyewitness identification cases. *Law & Human Behavior, 12*, 41–55.

Deffenbacher, K. A., & Loftus, E. F. (1982). Do jurors share a common understanding concerning eyewitness behavior? *Law & Human Behavior, 6*, 15–30.

Devenport, J. L., Stinson, V., Cutler, B. L., & Kravitz, D. A. (2002). How effective are the cross-examination and expert testimony safeguards? Jurors' perceptions of the suggestiveness and fairness of biased lineup procedures. *Journal of Applied Psychology, 87*, 1042–1054.

Devlin, Hon Lord Patrick. (1976). *Report to the Secretary of State for the Home Department of the Departmental Committee on Evidence of Identification in Criminal Cases.* HMSO.

Diamond, S. S. (1979). Simulation: Does the microscope lens distort? *Law & Human Behavior, 3*, 1–4.

Elliott, R., Farrington, B., & Manheimer, H. (1988). Eyewitnesses credible and discredible. *Journal of Applied Social Psychology, 18*, 1411–1422.

Fisher, R. P., & Cutler, B. L. (1995). The relation between consistency and accuracy of eyewitness testimony. In G. Davies, S. Lloyd-Bostock, et al. (Eds.), *Psychology, law, and criminal justice: International developments in research and practice* (pp. 21–28). Oxford, England: Walter De Gruyter.

Hatvany, N., & Strack, F. (1980). The impact of a discredited key witness. *Journal of Applied Social Psychology, 10*, 490–509.

Kassin, S. M., & Barndollar, K. A. (1992). The psychology of eyewitness testimony: A comparison of experts and prospective jurors. *Journal of Applied Social Psychology, 22*(16), 1241–1249.

Kassin, S. M., & Neumann, K. (1997). On the power of confession evidence: An experimental test of the fundamental difference hypothesis. *Law & Human Behavior, 21*, 469–484.

Kennedy, T. D., & Haygood, R. C. (1992). The discrediting effect in eyewitness testimony. *Journal of Applied Social Psychology, 22,* 70–82.

Kwong See, S. T., Hoffman, H. G., & Wood, T. L. (2001). Perceptions of an old female eyewitness: Is the older eyewitness believable? *Psychology & Aging, 16,* 346–350.

Lampinen, J. M., Judges, D. P., Odegard, T. N., & Hamilton, S. (2005). The reactions of mock jurors to the Department of Justice guidelines for the collection and preservation of eyewitness evidence. *Basic and Applied Social Psychology, 27,* 155–162.

Leippe, M. R. (1985). The influence of eyewitness nonidentifications on mock-jurors' judgments of a court case. *Journal of Applied Social Psychology, 15,* 656–672.

Leippe, M. R., Manion, A. P., & Romanczyk, A. (1992). Eyewitness persuasion: How and how well do fact finders judge the accuracy of adults' and children's memory reports? *Journal of Personality & Social Psychology, 63,* 181–197.

Leippe, M. R., & Romanczyk, A. (1989). Reactions to child (versus adult) eyewitnesses: The influence of jurors' preconceptions and witness behavior. *Law & Human Behavior, 13,* 103–132.

Leippe, M. R., Wells, G. L., & Ostrom, T. M. (1978). Crime seriousness as a determinant of accuracy in eyewitness identification. *Journal of Applied Psychology, 63,* 345–351.

Lindsay, R. C. L. (1994). Expectations of eyewitness performance. In D. Ross, D. Read, & M. Toglia (Eds). *Adult eyewitness testimony: Current trends and developments* (pp. 362–384). New York: Cambridge University Press.

Lindsay, R. C. L., & Bellinger, K. (1999). Alternatives to the sequential lineup: The importance of controlling the pictures. *Journal of Applied Psychology, 84,* 315–321.

Lindsay, R. C. L., Lea, J. A., Nosworthy, G. J., Fulford, J. A., Hector, J., LeVan, V., et al. (1991). Biased lineups: Sequential presentation reduces the problem. *Journal of Applied Psychology, 76,* 796–802.

Lindsay, R. C. L., Lim, R., Marando, L., & Cully, D. (1986). Mock-juror evaluations of eyewitness testimony: A test of metamemory hypotheses. *Journal of Applied Social Psychology, 16,* 447–459.

Lindsay, R. C. L., Pozzulo, J. D., Craig, W., Lee, K., & Corber, S. (1997). Simultaneous lineups, sequential lineups, and showups: Eyewitness identification decisions of adults and children. *Law & Human Behavior, 21,* 391–404.

Lindsay, R. C. L., & Wells, G. L. (1980). What price justice? Exploring the relationship of lineup fairness to identification accuracy. *Law & Human Behavior, 4,* 303–313.

Lindsay, R. C. L., & Wells, G. L. (1985). Improving eyewitness identifications from lineups: Simultaneous versus sequential lineup presentation. *Journal of Applied Psychology, 70,* 556–564.

Lindsay, R. C. L., Wells, G. L., & O'Connor, F. J. (1989). Mock-juror belief of accurate and inaccurate eyewitnesses: A replication and extension. *Law & Human Behavior, 13,* 333–339.

Lindsay, R. C. L., Wells, G. L., & Rumpel, C. M. (1981). Can people detect eyewitness-identification accuracy within and across situations? *Journal of Applied Psychology, 66,* 79–89.

Loftus, E. (1974). Reconstructing memory: The incredible eyewitness. *Psychology Today, 8,* 116–119.

MacLin, O. H., MacLin, M. K., & Malpass, R. S. (2001). Race, arousal, attention, exposure and delay: An examination of factors moderating face recognition. *Psychology, 7,* 134–152.

Malpass, R. S., & Devine, P. G. (1981). Eyewitness identification: Lineup instructions and the absence of the offender. *Journal of Applied Psychology, 66,* 482–489.

McAllister, H. A., & Bregman, N. J. (1986). Juror underutilization of eyewitness nonidentifications: Theoretical and practical implications. *Journal of Applied Psychology, 71,* 168–170.

McAllister, H. A., & Bregman, N. J. (1989). Juror underutilization of eyewitness nonidentifications: A test of the disconfirmed expectancy explanation. *Journal of Applied Social Psychology, 19,* 20–29.

McAllister, H. A., Dale, R. H., & Keay, C. E. (1993). Effects of lineup modality on witness credibility. *Journal of Social Psychology, 133,* 365–376.

McCauley, M. R., & Parker, J. F. (2001). When will a child be believed? The impact of the victim's age and juror's gender on children's credibility and verdict in a sexual-abuse case. *Child Abuse & Neglect, 25,* 523–539.

McCloskey, M., & Egeth, H. E. (1984). Process and outcome considerations in juror evaluation of eyewitness testimony. *American Psychologist, 39*, 1065–1066.

Myers, B., & Arbuthnot, J. (1997). Polygraph testimony and juror judgements: A comparison of the Guilty Knowledge Test and the Control Question Test. *Journal of Applied Social Psychology, 27*, 1421–1437.

Nickerson, R. S. (1998). Confirmation bias: A ubiquitous phenomenon in many guises. *Review of General Psychology, 2*, 175–220.

Nunez, N., McCoy, M. L., Clark, H. L., & Shaw, L. A. (1999). The testimony of elderly victim/witnesses and their impact on juror decisions: The importance of examining multiple stereotypes. *Law & Human Behavior, 23*, 413–423.

Pryke, S., Lindsay, R. C. L., Dysart, J. E., & Dupuis, P. (2004). Multiple independent identification decisions: A method of calibrating eyewitness identifications. *Journal of Applied Psychology, 89*, 73–84.

Ross, D. F., Dunning, D., Toglia, M. P., & Ceci, S. J. (1990). The child in the eyes of the jury: Assessing mock jurors' perceptions of the child witness. *Law & Human Behavior, 14*, 5–23.

Ross, D. F., Jurden, F. H., Linsday, R. C. L., & Keeney, J. M. (2003). Replications and limitations of a two-factor model of child witness credibility. *Journal of Applied Social Psychology, 33*, 418–430.

Ross, D. F., Miller, B., & Moran, P. (1987). The child in the eyes of the jury: Assessing mock jurors' perceptions of the child witness. In S. Ceci, D. Ross, & M. Toglia (Eds). *Children's eyewitness memory* (pp. 121–141). New York: Springer-Verlag.

Saunders, D. M., Vidmar, N., & Hewitt, E. C. (1983). Eyewitness testimony and the discrediting effect. In S. M. A. Lloyd-Bostock & B. R. Clifford (Eds.), *Evaluating witness evidence*. London: John Wiley.

Scheck, B., & Neufeld, P. (2004). *The innocence project.* Retrieved March 12, 2004 from The Innocence Project Homepage: http://www.innocenceproject.org/

Shaw, J. S. I., Garcia, L. A., & McClure, K. A. (1999). A lay perspective on the accuracy of eyewitness testimony. *Journal of Applied Social Psychology, 29*, 52–71.

Skolnick, P., & Shaw, J. I. (2001). A comparison of eyewitness and physical evidence on mock-juror decision making. *Criminal Justice & Behavior, 28*, 614–630.

Smith, M. C. (1983). Hypnotic memory enhancement of witnesses: Does it work? *Psychological Bulletin, 94*, 387–407.

Smith, S. M., Lindsay, R. C. L., & Pryke, S. (2000). Postdictors of eyewitness errors: Can false identifications be diagnosed? *Journal of Applied Psychology, 85*, 542–550.

Spanos, N. P., Gwynn, M. I., & Terrade, K. (1989). Effects on mock jurors of experts favorable and unfavorable toward hypnotically elicited eyewitness testimony. *Journal of Applied Psychology, 74*, 922–926.

Steblay, N. M. (1992). A meta-analytic review of the weapon focus effect. *Law & Human Behavior, 16*, 413–424.

Steblay, N., Dysart, J., Fulero, S., & Lindsay, R. C. L. (2001). Eyewitness accuracy rates in sequential and simultaneous lineup presentations: A meta-analytic comparison. *Law & Human Behavior, 25*, 459–473.

Technical Working Group for Eyewitness Evidence. (1999). Eyewitness evidence: A guide for law enforcement. Washington, DC: U.S. Department of Justice, Office of Justice Programs, National Institute of Justice.

Weinberg, H. I., & Baron, R. S. (1982). The discredible eyewitness. *Personality & Social Psychology Bulletin, 8*, 60–67.

Wells, G. L. (1978). Applied eyewitness-testimony research: System variables and estimator variables. *Journal of Personality & Social Psychology, 36*, 1546–1557.

Wells, G. L. (1985). Verbal descriptions of faces from memory: Are they diagnostic of identification accuracy? *Journal of Applied Psychology, 70*, 619–626.

Wells, G. L., & Bradfield, A. L. (1998). "Good, you identified the suspect:" Feedback to eyewitnesses distorts their reports of the witnessing experience. *Journal of Applied Psychology, 83,* 360–376.

Wells, G. L., Ferguson, T. J., & Lindsay, R. C. L. (1981). The tractability of eyewitness confidence and its implications for triers of fact. *Journal of Applied Psychology, 66,* 688–696.

Wells, G. L., & Leippe, M. R. (1981). How do triers of fact infer the accuracy of eyewitness identifications? Using memory for peripheral detail can be misleading. *Journal of Applied Psychology, 66,* 682–687.

Wells, G. L., Lindsay, R. C., & Ferguson, T. J. (1979). Accuracy, confidence, and juror perceptions in eyewitness identification. *Journal of Applied Psychology, 64,* 440–448.

Wells, G. L., Lindsay, R. C., & Tousignant, J. P. (1980). Effects of expert psychological advice on human performance in judging the validity of eyewitness testimony. *Law & Human Behavior, 4,* 275–285.

Wells, G. L., & Windschitl, P. D. (1999). Stimulus sampling and social psychological experimentation. *Personality and Social Psychology Bulletin, 25,* 1115–1125.

Wright, D. B., & Stroud, J. N. (2002). Age differences in lineup identification accuracy: People are better with their own age. *Law & Human Behavior, 26,* 641–654.

Yarmey, A. D. (1984). Accuracy and credibility of the elderly witness. *Canadian Journal on Aging, 3,* 79–90.

Yarmey, A. D., & Jones, H. P. (1983). Is the psychology of eyewitness identification a matter of common sense? In S. Lloyd-Bostock & B. R. Clifford (Eds.), *Evaluating witness evidence* (pp. 13–40). Chichester, England: John Wiley & Sons.

V

APPLYING PSYCHOLOGICAL RESEARCH TO LEGAL PRACTICE

20

Generalizing Eyewitness Reliability Research

Steven Penrod
John Jay College of Criminal Justice, CUNY

Brian H. Bornstein
University of Nebraska, Lincoln

Hugo Munsterberg's book *On the Witness Stand* (1908) is often credited as the first effort in English to bring basic research in memory and perception to bear on questions such as whether psychologists might be better equipped than judges or juries to assess the validity of eyewitness identifications. Although Munsterberg gives passing reference to the European work of Binet, Stern, Lipmann, Jung, Wertheimer, Gross, Sommer, and Aschaffenburg, he also acknowledges that the volume is really a set of "popular sketches, which select only a few problems in which psychology and law come in contact. They deal essentially with the mind of the witness on the witness stand" (p. 11). Indeed, judge G. F. Arnold (1906) should probably be credited with an earlier, more thoughtful, scientific, legally informed, and expansive treatment of the implications of psychological research for the courts.

Despite the auspicious beginnings of psychological research on legal—particularly eyewitness—issues in the late nineteenth and early twentieth centuries, the enterprise largely foundered and was not revived in a serious way until the late twentieth century (there are some notable exceptions to this trend; see, e.g., Burt, 1931; Robinson, 1935; Weld & Danzig, 1940). There is little question that the volume of eyewitness research grew dramatically in the last quarter of the twentieth century—and may now actually be on the wane (whether this is a sign of fatigue or scientific maturation is a matter we consider later in this chapter). Consider, for example, the distribution of research publication dates for 469 eyewitness experiments conducted in 300 published articles included in a large-scale meta-analysis conducted by the authors and their colleagues:

1965–69	5
1970–74	21

1975–79	47
1980–84	95
1985–89	95
1990–94	89
1995–99	70
2000–02	47
total =	469 experiments

Though the bulk of scientific research on eyewitness issues is predominantly of very recent vintage, enterprising attorneys have long sought to introduce eyewitness expert testimony from psychologists, even before the bulk of this research existed. Fulero (1993) identifies *Criglow v. State* (1931), an Arkansas case, as the first recorded instance in which a psychologist was proffered as an eyewitness expert. By the 1970s a number of psychologists were providing trial testimony about the shortcomings of eyewitness identifications, and appellate courts were paying attention. In 1973 the Ninth Circuit Federal Court of Appeals in *United States v. Amaral* (1973) drew upon the classic *Frye* test (*United States v. Frye*, 1923) to formulate the following admissibility criteria for expert testimony, especially as it pertained to eyewitness evidence:

1. The expert must be qualified to testify about the subject matter.
2. The expert must testify about a proper subject.
3. The testimony must conform to a generally accepted explanatory theory.
4. The probative value of the testimony must outweigh its prejudicial effect.

The *Amaral* court rejected the testimony of the expert (social psychologist Bertram Raven) on yet another criterion—that "it would not be appropriate to take from the jury their own determination as to what weight or effect to give to the evidence of the eyewitness and identifying witnesses and to have that determination put before them on the basis of the expert witness testimony as proffered" (p. 1153). This notion is sometimes referred to as "invading the province of the jury" or the "commonsense" objection (i.e., memory is a matter of common sense, so there is no need for an expert to educate the jury). Although the *Amaral* court was not inclined to admit eyewitness expert testimony, other courts soon took a conflicting view—in 1983 the Arizona Supreme Court ruled in *State v. Chapple* that exclusion of such testimony was a reversible error. A year later the California Supreme Court forcefully argued for the admission of expert psychological testimony on eyewitness memory and ruled that a trial judge abused his discretion in excluding the expert's testimony (*People v. McDonald*, 1984).

In most jurisdictions (the federal courts and most, but not all, states), the admissibility of expert eyewitness testimony is now governed by the criteria set forth in *Daubert v. Merrell Dow Pharmaceuticals* (1993). Unlike previous standards, Daubert deemphasizes general acceptance in the scientific community and requires courts themselves to scrutinize scientific methods in making a determination of scientific validity (Faigman, 1995;

Penrod, Fulero, & Cutler, 1995). With regard to expert eyewitness testimony, this standard explicitly focuses on the ways in which eyewitness memory research is conducted. If the methodology is deemed flawed or otherwise lacking in validity, it is unlikely to be admissible (Faigman, 1995; Penrod et al., 1995; for a thorough review of the legal standards governing the admissibility of eyewitness expert testimony, see Faigman et al., 2002; for examples of recent eyewitness admission decisions, see *N.Y. v. Radcliffe*, 2003 and *People v. Kindle*, 2002—admitting expert testimony in New York and finding ineffective assistance of counsel for failing to call an expert in California).

The courts are not alone in grappling with the issue of psychologists as eyewitness experts—within psychology, questions were being raised about the adequacy of the research as a foundation for such testimony. Despite fairly substantial agreement among eyewitness experts about what research findings on many topics show (Kassin et al., 1989, 2001; Yarmey & Jones, 1983), questions persist about whether the research supports the sort of general conclusions demanded by expert testimony in an adversarial context. The debate was typified by arguments between McCloskey and Egeth (1983) and Loftus (1983; Fishman & Loftus, 1978) over the advisability of psychologists providing expert testimony on eyewitness identification. McCloskey and Egeth asserted that the research findings were, at the time, too scanty or ambiguous to permit an expert psychologist to say much beyond what an average juror knew through common sense; they argued that an expert might be made to look foolish in court (a point they illustrated with a mock cross-examination designed to that end); they questioned whether jurors were over-believing of eyewitnesses; and they questioned whether expert testimony might make juries overly skeptical of eyewitness identification evidence.

In one rejoinder, Wells (1984) argued that McCloskey and Egeth were too concerned with outcomes (i.e., is the ratio of false convictions to convictions of the guilty unacceptably high?) rather than with the process by which jurors evaluate eyewitness evidence. He argued that if there are problems with the process, then there is justification for change, regardless of whether the rate of false convictions is low or high. This debate ebbed and flowed for some time, though the broad indictments of research that appeared in the 1980s have mostly disappeared in the past decade (see, e.g., Bermant, 1986; Egeth, 1993; Elliot, 1993; Loftus, 1993; Yarmey, 1986).

More recent instantiations of the critiques have taken a predominantly methodological focus (e.g., Ebbesen & Flowe, 2002; Yuille, 1993). For example, Yuille (1993) argued that many proponents of eyewitness expert testimony adopt an "unwarranted assumption that the many studies of eyewitness identification provide results that are immediately generalizable to forensic contexts" (p. 572). Yuille cited Yuille and Wells (1991) for the following proposition:

> Caution should be used in generalizing from controlled research studies to real world contexts. The research and forensic contexts must share more than superficial similarities. The variances and covariances among variables that infiltrate actual eyewitness cases are controlled or "randomized out" in experimental research in ways that can make generalization from experiments to actual cases a risky endeavor under certain circumstances. Whenever possible, a comparison of the experimental research and field contexts should be made and their apparent similarities and differences enunciated. (p. 127)

Loftus, Wells, and others have responded to these criticisms at length in other contexts—we do not propose, in this chapter, to recount the point-counterpoint exchanges among critics and respondents. Nonetheless, this criticism, which is grounded on concerns of external validity, raises an extremely important issue, because psycholegal researchers can hardly expect courts or policymakers to adopt their findings if those findings fail to generalize to real-world situations. In the present chapter, we address this concern by focusing narrowly on two of the themes highlighted in the legal cases and psychological debate sampled above.

We start with the question posed by Wells (1993)—Is there a real eyewitness problem and how large might it be? In this section we consider the implications of research on erroneous convictions and DNA exculpations, research on witness errors adduced from police records and, for comparison purposes, the general pattern of errors reported in experimental research.

We next consider the "ambiguity" of findings issue raised by some critics (e.g., McCloskey & Egeth; Elliott) about the size and variability in research findings and Yuille's generalizability argument. In this section we concentrate on meta-analytic studies of eyewitness performance—highlighting variables for which there are moderately large numbers of studies that yield robust patterns of results. We give particular attention to analyses that might reveal whether there are methodological features of studies that would limit their generalizability.

THE ACCURACY OF EYEWITNESS IDENTIFICATIONS—IS THERE A PROBLEM?

Erroneous Convictions Based on Misidentifications

One fundamental consideration that motivates psychologists' interest in the factors that influence eyewitness reliability is a concern that eyewitness identifications are often the source of erroneous convictions. The existence of eyewitness-based false convictions is by now so well established (e.g., Scheck, Neufeld, & Dwyer, 2000; Wells et al., 1998) that it is hardly necessary to belabor the point here. Nonetheless, estimates of the scope of the problem vary widely (Huff, 1987), so it is worthwhile to consider, briefly, the frequency of false identifications.

How often do eyewitness identifications result in erroneous convictions? One way to approach that question is to consider the number of erroneous convictions that might arise from all sources. Huff (1987) conducted a national survey of 54 state attorneys general and in-depth surveys of 229 judges, public defenders, and prosecutors from Ohio and found that 70% of his respondents believed that erroneous convictions comprise less than 1% of all felony convictions. However, another 20% of the estimates fell into the 1–5% range. In addition, Huff undertook a search of major newspapers and 1,100 magazines and journals and located a total of 500 known cases of erroneous conviction. Of course, there are huge numbers of criminal prosecutions in the United States each year, and even if one assumes, as did Huff, that the error rate is only .5%, that yields 7,500 erroneous convictions per year for serious offenses.

What produces these erroneous convictions? A number of scholars, beginning with Borchard (1932), have identified and studied the causes of erroneous convictions in large numbers of criminal cases (see also Brandon & Davies, 1973; Frank & Frank, 1957; Gross, 1987; Gross et al., 2004; Huff, 1987; Huff, Rattner, & Sagarin, 1986; Rattner, 1988). The results of all these studies converge on the conclusion that mistaken eyewitness identifications are among the most—if not *the* most—common sources of erroneous convictions. For example, Huff (1987) concluded from his study of 500 cases of erroneous conviction that the single leading cause of mistaken conviction was erroneous eyewitness identification of the defendants—eyewitness error was involved in nearly 60% of those cases.

More recently, the importance of mistaken identifications as a source of erroneous convictions has been reaffirmed by exonerations based on DNA evidence. In 1998 Wells et al. published a white paper on identification procedures which noted that by 1998 postconviction DNA testing had freed 62 people in the United States—all of whom had been convicted by juries for crimes that they did not commit (see also Scheck, Neufeld, & Dwyer, 2000). Although some cases involved coincidental circumstantial evidence or perjury, 52 of the 62 cases were mistaken eyewitness identification cases, with a total of 77 mistaken eyewitnesses (for more recent figures, see the Innocence Project website—http://innocenceproject.com—which reported 181 DNA exculpations as of July 2006; and Gross et al., 2004).

The cases reviewed by these observers are unique in that there was some basis for concluding that the identifications were mistaken. Of course, it is impossible to know how representative those cases are of all cases where there have been erroneous convictions. DNA exculpations arise solely from cases in which DNA is available; as a result, the likelihood of misidentifications is almost certainly many times greater than these estimates suggest (Gross et al., 2004).

Witness Errors at the Police Station

Some additional insight into the identification accuracy rates of actual eyewitness identifications emerges from studies of actual witnesses. The largest number of these studies comes from the United Kingdom. For example, Slater (1994) examined identification attempts by 843 British witnesses who viewed 302 suspects. Slater found that suspects were identified by 36% of witnesses, and foils were mistakenly identified by 190 witnesses (22.5%). Wright and McDaid (1996) examined identification attempts of 1,561 British witnesses who viewed 616 suspects in live lineups and obtained comparable results: 611 witnesses (39.1%) picked the suspect, 310 witnesses picked a known-innocent foil (19.9%), and 640 (41%) made no identification. Similar results emerge from a recent study by Valentine, Pickering, and Darling (2003), who examined the performance of 584 witnesses in 295 cases and found that 41% picked the suspect, 21% picked a known-innocent foil, and 39% made no identification (total = 101% due to rounding). The results of these studies are remarkably consistent: In all three studies, slightly more than one in three positive identifications were of innocent foils. It is likely that witnesses in these studies were confronted with nine-person arrays, the British standard.

The only comparable American study is that of Behrman and Davey (2001), who examined police records in the Sacramento, California area in 271 cases involving 349 crimes (the vast majority armed robberies). They examined 289 photographic lineups and 58 live lineups. Unfortunately, because police records were incomplete, Behrman and Davey could not determine how many of the identifications from photo lineups, in which 48% of the witnesses identified the suspect as the perpetrator, were of known-innocent foils. In live lineups (which did report mistaken identifications of foils), Behrman and Davey found that 50% of the witnesses identified the suspect (an unknown percentage of those identifications were errors), the false identification of foils rate was 24%, and 26% of the witnesses were not able to make a choice—again, roughly one-third of positive identifications were errors.

In fact, the error rate in all of these studies is likely to be greater than one in three—partly because the high foil choosing rate suggests that many witnesses are doing little more than guessing and some suspect "choices" are simply guesses—some correct or lucky guesses and some erroneous guesses. Penrod (2003) used the Behrman and Davey data—in combination with data from a number of other studies—to estimate the proportion of Sacramento witnesses who identified a suspect but were merely guessing (more than one in four) and to estimate the likelihood that witnesses had mistakenly identified an innocent suspect—nearly one in seven positively identified suspects. Penrod's analysis suggests that fewer than half of the Sacramento witnesses who made a choice actually identified a guilty suspect from memory, and another 18% of witnesses failed to identify a guilty suspect. And of course, some of the positively identified suspects were undoubtedly innocent.

Witness Errors in Experimental Field Studies

Another source of data pertaining to accuracy rates of actual eyewitness identifications is field studies of eyewitness identification. Some researchers (e.g., Brigham, Maass, Snyder, & Spaulding, 1982; Hosch & Platz, 1984; Krafka & Penrod, 1985; Pigott, Brigham, & Bothwell, 1990) have attempted to reap the benefits of both laboratory experiments and realistic crime conditions by conducting well-controlled experiments in realistic field settings. The primary purpose of this research is, like that of laboratory experiments, to estimate the effects of an isolated factor on identification accuracy. Because such studies are conducted in realistic settings, their identification accuracy rates might be a better indication of those in actual crimes (at least nonviolent crimes), as compared with less realistic experiments (though note that if anything, laboratory studies, in which witnessing conditions tend to be relatively good, will tend to overestimate the abilities of actual witnesses).

In the four cited studies, data were gathered from a total of 291 mock eyewitnesses, who performed 536 separate identification tests. The correct identification/foil identification rates for target-present lineups in these experiments were 34%/45% (Brigham et al., 1982), 41%/14% (Krafka & Penrod, 1985), 44%/37% (Platz & Hosch, 1988), and 48%/

33% (Pigott et al., 1990), yielding unweighted averages of 42%/32%. False identifications (in target-absent lineups) were assessed in two of the studies: the rates were 34% (Krafka & Penrod, 1985) and 37.5% (Pigott et al., 1990).

What we learn from these experiments is that identifications for persons seen briefly, in nonstressful conditions, and attempted after brief delays, are frequently inaccurate. In one of these studies (Pigott et al., 1990), the mock eyewitnesses were bank tellers, 70% of whom reported that they had received training for eyewitness situations.

In short, research on actual eyewitness performance at the police station and on mock witnesses in realistic field settings supports the conclusions of examinations of erroneous convictions, which is that eyewitnesses are making large numbers of errors. Correct identification rates from target-present arrays appear to be accurate less than half the time, and about one-quarter of witnesses mistakenly identify a foil. In target-absent arrays, the mistaken identification rate appears to be about 35–40%. In real police lineups, the known (minimum) error rate is about one-third. Because the suspect in these lineups might or might not actually be guilty, the true error rate is undoubtedly higher. The research on exculpations indicates, moreover, that a significant number of eyewitness errors are not detected and eliminated as a result of normal police, prosecutorial, and court processes.

GENERALIZABILITY: META-ANALYZING
EYEWITNESS RESEARCH

Our emphasis in this section is on meta-analytic studies of eyewitness research. An advantage of the meta-analytic approach is that it allows an exploration not only of methodological main effects, but also of interactions between methodological variables and other factors. In assessing the generalizability of various research methods, knowledge of how different methodological approaches—such as live versus videotape target presentation—interact with other variables of interest can be more informative than knowledge of their main effects (Bornstein, 1999; Bray & Kerr, 1982). An understanding of how various research methodologies affect witness performance has implications for both theory development and forensic practice (Koehnken, Malpass, & Wogalter, 1996; Wells et al., 1998), especially given that, as noted above, many of the critiques of expert eyewitness testimony have a methodological basis. The present section summarizes the major findings of extant meta-analyses of the eyewitness literature, with a particular emphasis on methodological variables as possible moderators.

Among the major advantages of meta-analysis are the following:

1. Meta-analyses systematically use prior research findings to generate a fairly precise estimate of the effect sizes detected in a body of research and thereby provide a succinct summary of the status of scientific research in a particular domain. Simply looking at the numbers of significant and nonsignificant findings, in contrast, can yield an extremely distorted picture of the relationships involved. For which variables are there insufficient numbers of studies or studies with such low statistical power that further

investigations are needed in order to pin down effect sizes and causal relationships? Variables that play a key role in theoretical formulations probably deserve the most research attention.

2. Meta-analyses permit identification of variables where there is substantial variability in findings (e.g., conflicting findings or findings in which effect sizes are highly variable) that makes interpretation of findings difficult.

3. Meta-analysis permits tests of interactions or moderating effects across studies that have not been examined within studies. There are, for example, sound reasons to believe that field and laboratory studies may yield different estimates of the effect size of at least some independent variables. Hypotheses about such interactions can be tested, and a number of such hypotheses are specified below. Thus, with meta-analysis it is possible to assess the extent to which variability across studies can be accounted for by moderating variables such as research methods, operational definitions of independent variables, differences in participants, and so on. Where it is impossible to account for such variability, further research is clearly required.

4. The results of meta-analysis can provide guidance about avenues of further research that are likely to be more or less fruitful. Theories designed to provide explanatory, causal accounts of particular phenomena are not all equal. Some theoretical accounts are more elegant than others, some encompass more findings than others, and some, importantly, account for more of the variability in critical dependent variables (i.e., some theories embody relationships that capture larger effect sizes). Although explained variance is only one of the criteria by which theories should be evaluated, it can be an important criterion—especially insofar as knowledge about the explanatory power of theories can serve as an important guide to where research and policy resources ought to be applied. Meta-analysis is extremely useful in assessing the relative sizes of effects examined in a body of research and in distinguishing the explanatory power of alternative theories.

Shapiro and Penrod (1986)

Shapiro and Penrod (1986) published the first general quantitative assessment of the factors influencing facial identification. Their meta-analysis drew on over 190 individual studies from 128 articles on face recognition and eyewitness memory, spanning 960 experimental conditions and including more than 16,950 participants. Virtually all of that research had been reported in peer-reviewed scientific journals through 1985.

A preponderance (80%) of the studies analyzed by Shapiro and Penrod (1986) were laboratory-based studies of facial recognition, as opposed to more realistic eyewitness simulations. Though they do not report precise numbers, they note that overall performance levels were higher in the laboratory studies, which is a potential concern for generalizability of the findings. In related work, Lindsay and Harvie (1988) conducted a meta-analysis that compared a somewhat haphazard sample of face recognition and staged-crime studies. The overall hit rate (.64) in face recognition studies ($N \approx 113$ results) was somewhat higher than the proportion of correct identifications (.58) in staged-crime studies ($N \approx 47$ results), though this difference was not statistically significant. The false alarm rate in the face recognition studies (.18, $N = 64$) was significantly lower than two types of mistaken identifications in staged-crime studies—those made from target-present arrays (.29, $N = 47$) and target-absent arrays (.41, $N = 12$).

Thus, at the superficial level of comparing laboratory-based face recognition and more realistic eyewitness studies, the concerns about external validity appear to have some merit. Upon closer inspection, however, the difference between the two types of studies was almost entirely mediated by methodological variables, such as retention interval, that tend to covary with study type. Shapiro and Penrod (1986) demonstrated this by employing two analytic techniques. The first was an "effect size" analysis, which combined the effect sizes of factors across studies that manipulated a particular factor. This analysis comprises what is typically done in traditional meta-analysis. The second approach was a "study characteristics" analysis. Here, experiments were grouped on various factors (e.g., viewing conditions, the manner in which identification accuracy was tested, and methodological factors that might influence identification accuracy). The influence of these grouping variables on identification accuracy rates was then examined. The analyses of study characteristics have more than 950 data points (based on judgments from more than 16,500 participants) for correct identifications, whereas effect size analyses have fewer than 30 data points (even though they are often based on between 1,000 and 2,000 participants). For variables that appear in both sets of analyses, each analysis can be considered a validity check for the other.

In the following section we consider, first, the Shapiro and Penrod effect-size results that bear on experimental methodology, such as aspects of the eyewitnessing environment; second, we consider characteristics that differ across studies and tend to distinguish between relatively artificial face recognition studies and more realistic eyewitness studies. We do not attempt otherwise to review the underlying research.

Effect Size Analyses

Expectation of Future Identification Test.   Expecting an identification test had no significant effect on either correct ($d = .10$; 56% vs. 58% for expected/not expected) or false ($d = .27$; 27% for both) identifications.

Orienting/Processing Instructions and Strategies.   Two types of orienting strategies were examined. Encoding instructions and degree of elaboration were analyzed separately. Both variables produced large effects on correct identifications: for encoding instructions, $d = .97$ (74% vs. 66%); for elaboration, $d = 1.0$ (78% vs. 72%). The effects on false identifications were smaller: for encoding instructions, $d = .38$ (21% vs. 27%); for elaboration, $d = -.06$ (10% vs. 11%). Although these variables had a statistically significant effect (d) on correct identifications, the improvements in performance were small.

Exposure Duration.   Exposure time significantly influenced correct identifications (69% vs. 57%) but not false alarms (34% vs. 38%) in the studies where exposure time was manipulated.

Retention Interval.   Longer delays led to fewer correct identifications (d = .43; 51% vs. 61%) and more false identifications (d = .33; 32% vs. 24%). Across all experimental cells in all the studies examined in the meta-analysis (including those that did not directly manipulate retention interval), retention interval proved an important determinant of correct identifications (r = −.11, p < .05), though there was no significant relationship with false identifications.

Study-Characteristics Analysis

As noted above, in addition to effect size analyses, Shapiro and Penrod also undertook a larger-scale analysis looking for patterns of relationships between variables and performance across studies. The analysis essentially used variability—across studies—in study characteristics (including many of the variables that had been manipulated within studies) to examine the explanatory value of individual variables while controlling for the influence of other variables. Unsurprisingly, Shapiro and Penrod's data displayed multicollinearity—that is, some study characteristics proved somewhat redundant because they varied together across the studies. This occurred primarily because laboratory researchers make use of one set of procedures, whereas field researchers characteristically make use of somewhat different procedures. For example, laboratory studies frequently use large numbers of faces for subjects to remember, frequently expose participants to faces for shorter periods of time, and frequently test memory after shorter delay periods. To clarify the analyses and results, correlated variables were combined into groups for analysis, and variables that were independent of one another were analyzed independently.

Shapiro and Penrod noted that when the effects of all other variables are removed from the analyses, most variables and blocks of variables still explained significant portions of variance. With regard to correct identification rates, a block of *Attention* variables accounted for a significant unique portion of variance (attention, knowledge, and mode of presentation made significant individual contributions). The duration of exposure per face was positively related to hit-rate performance, whereas its quadratic component was not. Pose accounted for a significant amount of variance. A group of variables related to *Load at Study* also accounted for significant variance (with number of targets making the significant contribution). Retention interval accounted for significant variance (though the quadratic component of retention interval did not). *Load at Recognition* did not account for any unique variance. *Type of Study* (facial recognition versus eyewitness) also accounted for significant variance. In sum, these 11 sets of variables accounted for 47% of the variance in hit rates (with an adjusted R^2 of .45).

We would particularly note the significant effect of *Type of Study*, as the performance of this variable is quite informative with respect to the generalizability of the effects—across studies—of the other variables noted above. When considered separately, *Type of Study* accounted for 35% of the variance in performance across the approximately 700 experimental conditions examined in the correct identification analysis—that is to say, there were quite substantial differences in performance between facial recognition studies (where performance was much better) and eyewitness studies (where performance was much worse). However, in Shapiro and Penrod's multivariate analysis, the difference in performance between the two types of studies is largely accounted for by the systematic differences in the methods used in those studies (that is, by the other variables in the analysis)—the multivariate R^2 drops to 3% when the other variables are considered.

Although a somewhat different pattern of results emerged from the study of which methodological variables affected identification errors, as opposed to hit rates, the take-home point was the same: the effect of study type was mediated by other study characteristics. Specifically, *Attention* block variables (attention, knowledge of the identification task, and mode of presentation—frontal views led to fewer false alarms) were significant. Load at study also accounted for significant variance (with number of targets and faces positively associated with false-alarm rates). Retention interval did not reach significance. In contrast with its weaker effects on hits, *Load at Recognition* uniquely accounted for 5% of the variance in false alarms. Mode of presentation at recognition accounted for a large portion of this effect—the B weights indicate a 15% higher false-alarm rate when subjects are confronted with live targets as opposed to still photographs. There was a negative correlation between false-alarm rate and number of foils. In all, the variables accounted for 43% of the variance in false-alarm performance.

Again, *Study Type* was significant—though its zero-order R^2 of .3 dropped to a negligible .02 in the multivariate analysis—a result paralleling that detected in the hit-rate analysis. The main conclusion from Shapiro and Penrod's examination of methodological differences is that once the different methods used in facial recognition and eyewitness studies are accounted for, the categorical distinction is largely meaningless. Results from artificial laboratory studies and more realistic eyewitness studies are influenced by the same factors—and systematically so. Thus, one can generalize, with a reasonable degree of confidence, from tightly controlled experimental research to more realistic eyewitnessing situations.

FOCUSED META-ANALYSES

More focused meta-analyses of specific topics in the eyewitness literature have reached similar conclusions; that is, methodological variables have less of an impact on results than do more substantive variables. We briefly review here the major methodological findings of these focused meta-analyses.

Witness Confidence and Witness Accuracy

A number of studies indicate there is a strong cross-cultural belief there is a strong relation between eyewitness confidence (especially the confidence level expressed post-identification) and identification accuracy (Brigham & Wolfskiel, 1983; Brigham & Bothwell, 1983; Deffenbacher & Loftus, 1982; McConkey & Roche, 1989; Noon & Hollin, 1987; Rahaim & Brodsky, 1982; Sporer, 1983; Yarmey & Jones, 1983). Other studies indicate that the confidence that an eyewitness expresses in his or her identification is the most powerful single determinant of whether or not observers believe that the eyewitness made an accurate identification (Cutler, Penrod, & Dexter, 1990; Leippe

& Romanczyk, 1987, 1989; Leippe, Manion, & Romanczyk, 1991; Lindsay, Wells, & O'Connor, 1989; Lindsay, Wells, & Rumpel, 1981; Turtle & Wells, 1988; Wells, Ferguson, & Lindsay, 1981; Wells, Lindsay, & Ferguson, 1979; Wells & Murray, 1984).

Overall, it is clear that jurors do rely on witness confidence as an indicator of witness accuracy. These observations highlight the importance of knowing whether confidence is predictive of eyewitness identification accuracy (see chapters by Leippe & Eisenstadt and Boyce, Beaudry & Lindsay in this volume for a more detailed consideration of this issue). A substantial body of research has examined the association between the witness's confidence and the accuracy of the identification. The most common statistical metric for the eyewitness identification confidence/accuracy literature has been the point-biserial correlation (with accuracy as a dichotomous variable and confidence as a continuous variable). Over the years, several relevant meta-analyses of such data have been conducted.

Although some research has addressed the relationship between pre-identification confidence and accuracy (e.g., Cutler & Penrod, 1989a, which found a negligible correlation), witnesses' reported confidence after making (or failing to make) a lineup identification is of greater forensic relevance than their pre-identification confidence. Deffenbacher (1980) reviewed a set of studies conducted since the turn of the century and concluded that there was little support for a strong reliance on witness confidence as a guide to witness accuracy. Penrod (reported in Penrod, Loftus, & Winkler, 1982) offered confirmation of this conclusion by meta-analyzing 16 eyewitness studies with an average correlation (weighted for degrees of freedom) of $r = .23$. In a larger review of 31 studies Wells and Murray (1984) reported an average $r = .07$.

Several studies have indicated that an important moderator of the confidence-accuracy correlation is whether or not the witness chooses someone from the lineup. For example, Sporer, Penrod, Read, and Cutler (1995) analyzed 30 studies from their laboratories ($N = 4,036$ participants) that used staged crime scenarios. The overall confidence-accuracy correlation in these studies ($r = .29$) corresponds to that reported in previous reviews. The correlation was significantly higher for choosers ($r = .41, N = 2,467$) than for nonchoosers ($r = .12, N = 1,569$). These findings indicate that, when limited to witnesses who make positive identifications, confidence appears to be a modest predictor of accuracy, whereas, among witnesses who reject lineups, confidence appears to be very weakly related to accuracy (see also Brigham, 1988; Fleet, Brigham, & Bothwell, 1987; Sporer, 1992, 1993). Sporer et al. found that whether the event was presented live or on videotape moderated the strength of the C/A relationship as well, with the C/A relationship stronger for live than for videotaped presentations.

An earlier study by Bothwell, Deffenbacher, and Brigham (1987) provides an answer for why presentation medium moderates the C/A relationship. They meta-analyzed 35 studies involving staged incidents, which yielded a statistically significant average post-identification confidence and accuracy correlation of $r = .25$. This finding, which was somewhat more optimistic than most previous research, suggests that witnesses who are highly confident in their identifications are somewhat more likely to be correct as compared with witnesses who display little confidence.

More importantly, Bothwell et al. also found that the strength of the relationship between confidence and accuracy was moderated by study characteristics, such as the duration of target face exposure. The correlation of exposure duration and the accuracy-confidence correlation was .51: longer exposures allowed for greater predictability of accuracy from confidence. They proposed an "optimality hypothesis," according to which the C/A correlation is relatively good under optimal eyewitnessing conditions, but poor or nonexistent under suboptimal eyewitnessing conditions. It seems reasonable to assume that live event presentations provide more diverse cues, and hence more optimal conditions, than videotaped event presentations.

As Bothwell et al. note, many, if not most, genuine crimes are likely to have relatively poor witnessing conditions, because of brief exposure, high stress level, etc. Thus, it is not at all clear that the identification conditions that give rise to moderately high confidence-accuracy correlations are likely to prevail in the real world. A major reason for such a concern is evidence that, under less than pristine conditions, witness confidence is highly malleable and may be "pushed around" in ways that weaken or destroy even the modest confidence-accuracy relation reported by Sporer et al. for choosers. We discuss this in greater detail in the later section called "confidence malleability."

Cross-Race Performance

One interaction examined by Shapiro and Penrod (1986) was that between witness race and target race. Based on an analysis of 17 studies with a total of 1,571 participants, they found that the "cross-race effect" was quite robust (mean $d = .53$ for hits [$r = .26$], $d = .44$ for false alarms [$r = .21$]). Bothwell, Brigham, and Malpass (1989) meta-analyzed 14 samples of data on differential recognition for own- versus other-race faces. They found that the magnitude of the own-race bias was similar for both Black and White witnesses ($r = .33$). They also reported considerable consistency across studies, with both Black and White witnesses exhibiting own-race bias in 79% of the samples reviewed.

This conclusion was confirmed by Anthony, Copper, and Mullen (1992), who examined 15 studies with 1,725 participants (mean $r = .28$). Anthony et al. also identified an interesting interaction with the duration of exposure to the target, such that the magnitude of the own-race bias increased with briefer exposure times, though this effect was limited to White participants.

Meissner and Brigham (2001) have most recently meta-analyzed the relevant research. The analyzed data were from 39 research articles, with 91 independent samples involving nearly 5,000 witness participants. Because one of the criteria for inclusion was that the studies must have included a within-subjects test of own- versus other-race identification, the vast majority of studies (91%) used a laboratory-based face-recognition paradigm, as opposed to a lineup identification task. They examined hit and false-alarm rates, as well as measures of discrimination accuracy and response criterion. Overall, they reported that the chance of a mistaken identification was 1.56 times greater with other-race faces than with same-race faces and that witnesses were 1.4 times more likely to correctly identify a previously viewed own-race face as compared with performance on other-race faces (overall, participants were more than 2.2 times as likely to accurately identify own-race faces as new versus old, when compared with performance on other-race faces).

Meissner and Brigham explored the question of possible moderators, including a number of methodological characteristics, such as whether the studies utilized identical or different faces at study and test, exposure time, and retention interval. They found that altering the facial photographs significantly increased the ORB, as did reducing the amount of viewing time and increasing the retention interval. These study characteristics that heighten the ORB are precisely those that tend to characterize real-world eyewitnessing situations: different views of the perpetrator at the time of the event and the subsequent identification, brief view of the perpetrator during the crime, and a long retention interval. Thus, despite the considerable variability in research methodologies, more realistic simulations increase, rather than decrease, the research implications.

Eyewitness Test Media

Cutler et al. (1994) examined the impact of the modality of the lineup identification tests in a meta-analysis that compared the effect of live lineups, videotape lineups, and photo lineups on witness identification accuracy. The effect of live versus videotaped lineups was small and nonsignificant for both hits and false alarms, although slightly more hits and false alarms were obtained with videotaped lineups. Live and videotaped lineups did produce slightly more hits ($d = .08$, $p < .07$) and significantly fewer false alarms ($d = .19$, $p < .0001$) than did more impoverished presentation media such as photo arrays, slides, and line drawings. This difference can likely be attributed to the additional cues, such as gait and posture, provided by moving media (Cutler & Penrod, 1988; Cutler, Penrod, & Martens, 1987; O'Rourke et al., 1989).

Cutler et al. (1994) note that the effectiveness of a test medium is likely to depend on the quality of exposure to the perpetrator at the time of the crime. For example, if the witness views only the face of the perpetrator, the additional cues provided by live and videotaped lineups are unlikely to improve recognition accuracy. Nonetheless, these findings are significant, because, as noted by Cutler et al. (see also Shapiro & Penrod, 1986), videotaped (and especially live) lineups are much less common in the research literature than slides or photo arrays. Although the frequency of photo lineups appears to exceed that of live or videotaped lineups in the real world as well (e.g., Behrman & Davey, 2001), the preponderance of highly impoverished media in research could limit the external validity of research findings, *but only if* substantive variables exert differential effects with different kinds of media. The research conducted by Cutler and colleagues (summarized in Cutler et al., 1994) suggests that a variety of system variables, such as lineup type, tend to exert comparable effects regardless of identification test medium. Thus, it does not appear to pose a serious threat to external validity.

Weapon Focus

Weapon focus refers to the deleterious effect on eyewitness performance of a visible weapon held by the target (Loftus, Loftus, & Messo, 1987). Steblay (1992) conducted a meta-analysis of the weapon focus phenomenon. As Steblay points out, the experimental manipulation of weapon presence is important because of the variability of weapon use in actual crimes, as well as its relationship to the emotional response of witnesses (Kramer et al., 1990). Of 19 studies representing 2,082 participants, the mean effect size for lineup identification was a modest, but statistically significant, .13. The size of the effect varied, depending on methodological factors relating to the realism of the event. The effect was generally stronger in more realistic, crime-like situations, such as events involving live presentations, and where a crime scene (viewed via video or slides) was likely to be perceived as relatively threatening or arousing; in less realistic situations (e.g., where a weapon was present but no crime occurred), the effect was greatly reduced.

Other methodological variables with forensic relevance moderated the effect as well. For example, the effect was larger for relatively long (i.e., 2+ days) retention intervals ($h = .22$) than for same-day tests ($h = .12$), though it was statistically significant in both cases. The bad news (if there is bad news) from Steblay's (1992) meta-analysis of the weapon focus effect is that methodological differences, such as event realism and retention interval, do matter; but the good news is that, as with the ORB (Meissner & Brigham, 2001), relatively artificial simulations *underestimate* the magnitude of the effect. In simulations with high verisimilitude (live presentations, high arousal levels, long retention intervals), the effect of weapon presence is at its greatest.

Instructions to Witnesses

Eyewitness lineup performance can also be adversely affected by how witnesses are instructed prior to and during lineups. For example, witnesses who are given biased instructions leading them to believe that the suspect is in the lineup are more likely to make false identifications (Wells, 1993). Biased instructions can either suggest to the eyewitness that the perpetrator is in the lineup or discourage witnesses from saying the perpetrator is not in the lineup. Steblay (1997) conducted a meta-analysis of 18 studies ($N = 2,588$) of such lineup instruction effects—looking at three types of biased instructions: 1. *Leading Instructions*, which imply that the suspect is in the lineup, as opposed to an unbiased instruction stating that the suspect "may or may not be present." 2. *Pressure Instructions*, which do not include the option of "not present" or "no choice." 3. *Task-oriented Instructions*, which stress the importance of successfully making an identification and/or the serious consequences of a failure to identify the perpetrator.

Overall, Steblay (1997) obtained a reliable effect of bias instructions on choosing rates ($h = -.46$ in target-present lineups and $-.48$ in target-absent lineups); that is, biased instructions simply make witnesses more likely to make a positive identification. Moreover, the overall effect size for accuracy was $h = .26$—the overall proportion of correct identifications for unbiased lineups was 56% versus 44% for the biased condition. Biased instructions had a much more negative effect on accuracy in target-absent than in target-present lineups ($h = .58$ vs. $.02$; see Table 20.1 for means).

With respect to methodological moderating variables, the effect size in studies using live and video presentations produced somewhat larger effects ($h = .39$ and $.33$) than those using photo displays ($h = .19$). Tests conducted at relatively long retention intervals (2–3 days) yielded a larger effect size ($h = .46$) than tests conducted at both shorter and longer time periods (h ranging from $.15$ to $.23$). Student and non-student witnesses did not differ markedly, though the effect was slightly stronger for non-student witnesses ($h = .26$ and $.34$, respectively). Steblay also examined a subset of studies in which participants witnessed what they believed, at the time, to be actual events. In four tests involving such staged events, participants were told that the event was not real before the lineup task; in six tests, participants were debriefed after the lineup task. The instruction effect was considerably larger when they knew at the time of the lineup that the event was fake ($h = .50$ vs. $.04$). In all of these instances, the biased instruction effect was concentrated in target-absent lineups—with h typically ranging from $.5$ to $.9$. For pre- and post-task debriefings the effect sizes in target-absent lineups were $h = .61$ and $.21$ respectively.

These findings are partially consistent with those of the meta-analyses described above. On the one hand, the effect of biased lineup instructions was greater for tests that were more realistic in some respects (e.g., live or video presentation, non-student witnesses). On the other hand, the effect was lower for tests that were more realistic in other respects (e.g., witnesses who believe the lineup is for genuine crime-investigation purposes), or heightened realism exerted an ambiguous effect (e.g., retention interval, where the effect is greatest at intermediate delays).

Witness Age

Although most child witness studies emphasize their recall abilities and, in particular, their suggestibility (e.g., Ceci & Bruck, 1993; Doris, 1991), a number of experiments have addressed their facial recognition skills. Shapiro and Penrod (1986) found (in nine studies) that children were significantly worse than adults in terms of both hits and false alarms. A larger (total $N = 2,086$, compared with 603) and more recent meta-analysis by Pozzulo and Lindsay (1998), summarizing 13 studies with 51 hypothesis tests, has qualified these findings somewhat. Although children of all ages were less likely than adults to reject (correctly) a target-absent lineup, only children younger than age 5 performed worse than adults at target-present lineups. This finding is consistent with other re-

TABLE 20.1
Lineup Instructions

	Unbiased (% correct)	Biased (% correct)	Effect Size (h)
Target-absent	60	35	.58
Target-present	54	53	.02
Overall	56	44	.26

search showing that young witnesses are not uniformly inferior to adults (e.g., Ceci et al., 1987; Goodman & Bottoms, 1993).

Showups

To date, most eyewitness research has focused on photo and live lineups, with much less attention given to showups (single-suspect presentations to witnesses). Arguably, the research is skewed in the wrong direction, as studies of police practices indicate that the showup is perhaps used much more often than more time-consuming and complicated photo and live lineups. For example, Gonzalez, Ellsworth, and Pembroke (1993) enlisted the help of a detective to record all identifications (lineups and showups) in which he was involved until he reached 50 lineups. The final total included 172 showups and 52 lineups—77% were showups. Flowe, Ebbesen, Burke, and Chivabunditt (2001) found that showups were used for 55% of identifications in 488 cases they studied in a U.S. metropolitan area. McQuiston and Malpass (2001) reported a showup rate of 30% in El Paso County, Texas. Behrman and Davey (2001) studied 271 cases involving 349 crimes in the Sacramento County area—the identification procedures they analyzed included 258 field showups, 289 photographic lineups, 58 live lineups, and 18 single photo showups.

Traditional legal and psychological concerns about showups have focused on the fact that showups do not contain known-innocent foils who might draw erroneous choices of witnesses who are merely guessing and that showups can more clearly underscore police suspicions about an individual than would a lineup (and might, therefore, be "inherently suggestive"). More recently it has been noted that showups might actually inhibit choosing by witnesses because showups do not permit comparative or relative judgments in which witnesses might be inclined to pick the "best match" to their memory. Noting these conflicting theories, Steblay et al. (2003) recently meta-analyzed the existing research on showups versus lineups. They located 8 papers with 12 comparisons of lineups and showups including 3013 participants.

With respect to choosing rates across conditions, 71% of participants viewing a target-present lineup made a choice from the array (either a correct or a foil identification) and 46% of showup participants made a choice—necessarily a correct identification. In target-absent displays, lineups also produced a higher choosing rate: 43% versus 15% for showups.

Overall, showups produced a mean of 69% correct decisions versus 51% in lineups. However, that analysis does not differentiate the types of errors being made. Correct identification rates in target-present showups (47%) and lineups (45%) were quite comparable. False identification rates are slightly higher in showups (16%) than in lineups (11%) when lineup foil choices are excluded from analysis. And, in a subset of the studies that permitted an analysis of the situation where an innocent suspect resembled the perpetrator, dangerous false identifications were more numerous for showups (23%) than for lineups (17%).

Using the numbers above, for showups 47% of witnesses choose the suspect in the target-present condition and 23% in the target-absent resemblance condition, generating a diagnosticity ratio of 2.0 (Wells & Lindsay, 1980). For lineups, 45% of witnesses choose the suspect from the present lineup and 17% from the absent lineup, generating a diagnosticity ratio of 2.6. Thus, it appears that despite the significantly lower choosing rates in showups, the presence of foils in lineups actually does afford innocent suspects an extra margin of protection.

Stress

The literature on witness stress or arousal has been somewhat contradictory, with some studies showing beneficial effects of arousal and others showing detrimental effects (Christianson, 1992). Deffenbacher, Bornstein, Penrod, and McGorty (2004) conducted a meta-analysis on 27 tests of the effects of heightened stress on eyewitness identification. The proportion of correct identifications was higher for low-stress (54%) than for high-stress (42%) conditions. This effect was considerably larger for TP lineups ($h = -.52$) than for TA lineups ($h = .01$). They addressed other moderators relevant to the research's experimental verisimilitude. As shown in Table 20.2, the effect of stress was negligible (albeit still significant, $h = -.10$) in face recognition studies but robust in the more ecologically valid eyewitness paradigm ($h = -.36$). Not surprisingly—given that the research paradigm distinction overlaps with whether or not the stimulus involves a staged crime—mean effect sizes were larger for staged-crime studies ($h = -.58$) than for studies manipulating stress by other means ($h = -.28$). Table 20.2 shows the mean proportion correct for high- and low-stress conditions as a function of these variables. As with the meta-analyses described above, the analysis shows that the effect of a substantive variable—here the witness's stress level—is greater in more realistic conditions.

Sequential Lineups

Given the relatively poor performance of eyewitnesses overall, much research has focused on how to improve their capabilities (e.g., Fisher & Geiselman, 1992; Koehnken & Malpass, 1996; Wells, 1993). One of the more effective techniques—especially for reducing the rate of false identifications—is to present lineup members sequentially, one at a time, rather than all at once (Lindsay & Wells, 1985). A number of studies have now compared sequential and simultaneous lineup presentation.

In a meta-analysis summarizing 12 studies totaling 1,829 participants, Cutler and Penrod (1995, Chapter 8) reported that sequential lineups reduced false identifications in

TABLE 20.2
Stress Effects (values are mean percentage correct)

	High Stress (%)	Low Stress (%)	Effect Size (h)
Face recognition research paradigm	56	58	−.10
Eyewitness research paradigm	39	53	−.36
Staged crime	33	50	−.58
Non-staged crime	56	69	−.28

target-absent lineups from an average of 53% (in simultaneous lineups) to only 16%. In 2001, Steblay, Dysart, Fulero, and Lindsay published a larger-scale meta-analysis of this topic, examining 23 papers, containing 30 comparisons of sequential and simultaneous procedures, based on 4,145 research participants. These experiments were conducted in the United States, Canada, Britain, South Africa, Germany, and Australia and employed a wide array of research participants, formats (photo, video, both), types of crime (robbery, theft, other, no crime), and event stimuli (video, live, slides, transparencies).

Steblay et al. reported that overall, there was a slight advantage in correct decisions for sequential lineups (56% vs. 48%). However, the pattern was markedly different, depending on whether the perpetrator was in the array. For target-present lineups, there was a somewhat higher correct identification rate for simultaneous arrays (50%) than for sequential arrays (35%). Conversely, witnesses were also nearly half as likely to make a false identification from a target-absent sequential array (28%) than from a simultaneous array (51%). This advantage of sequential lineups held up even in studies in which research teams further tested the perpetrator-absent scenario by placing a particular suspect in the lineup who closely matched the description of the true target. The difference largely boils down to the fact that witnesses are considerably less likely to choose when presented with a sequential lineup than when presented with a simultaneous lineup. A larger meta-analysis (113 experiments from 82 papers) of the topic by Ebbesen and Flowe (2002) found a comparable advantage for sequential presentation in TA lineups (29.3% vs. 48.6% false identifications), while failing to show a significant decrement in the hit rate for TP lineups (48.8% simultaneous vs. 44.6% sequential).

With respect to methodological variables, Steblay et al. found, generally, that the advantage of simultaneous presentation in TP lineups was *less* for more realistic simulations, whereas the advantage of presentation in TA sequential lineups was *greater* for more realistic simulations. For example, the effect sizes (r) for hits in TP lineups were $-.30$ for slide stimuli versus $-.11$ for both live and video stimuli; whereas for correct rejections in TA lineups, the effect sizes were .18 for slide stimuli versus .24 and .28 for video and live stimuli, respectively. Thus, "[g]eneralizing to real world identification situations, the tradeoff between correct and false identifications would appear to be not a serious problem" (p. 470). They concluded:

> [u]nder the most realistic simulations of crimes and police procedures (live staged events, cautionary instructions, single perpetrators, adult witnesses asked to describe the perpetrator), the differences between the correct identification rates for simultaneous and sequential lineups are likely to be small or nonexistent. On the other hand, correct rejection rates are significantly higher for sequential than simultaneous lineups and this difference is maintained or increased by greater approximation to real world conditions. (p. 471)

Using the numbers from the Steblay et al. paper, one can calculate a hit-to-false alarm diagnosticity ratio for identifications of suspects in sequential versus simultaneous lineups. The simultaneous ratio is 50:27 or 1.85. The sequential ratio is 35:9 or 3.9. Thus, the odds that a suspect identified in a sequential lineup is guilty are about twice that of one identified from a simultaneous lineup.

Penrod (2003) decomposed the Steblay et al. data even further and argued that the numbers conceal a substantial amount of witness guessing. Recall that Steblay et al. reported that false identifications of designated innocent suspects was higher in simultaneous compared with sequential lineups (27% vs. 9%) and that witnesses were about twice as likely to make a false identification (innocent suspect plus foils) from simultaneous target-absent arrays (51%) as compared with sequential target-absent arrays with (28% foil guesses). Given the 27%/9% innocent suspect identifications (bad guesses) noted earlier, this implies that in simultaneous target-absent lineups, 51% erroneous identifications—27% innocent suspect identifications "bad guesses" = 24% foil identifications. Similarly, in sequential target-absent lineups, 28% erroneous identifications—9% suspect identifications "bad guesses" = 19% foil identifications (see Tables 20.3 and 20.4, where Steblay et al. results are indicated in bold and Penrod estimates are in brackets).

Extracting the designated innocent suspects from the totals suggests that roughly the same proportion of witnesses identified foils in target-present and target-absent arrays (24% in simultaneous arrays and 19% in sequential) and guessed innocent suspects in target-present and target-absent arrays (27% in simultaneous arrays and 9% in sequential). This implies that nearly three-fourths of witnesses who identified the suspect in sequential target-present arrays (26% of 35%) did so without guessing—we might expect that these witnesses, if presented a target-absent array, would shift to "not there" (whereas the 9% who guessed the suspect might erroneously shift to the designated/similar suspect in a target-absent lineup)—all as shown in Table 20.4. In the simultaneous arrays where 50% of target-present witnesses identified the suspect, a similar analysis suggests that more than half (27% of the 50%) would have shifted to the similar-looking designated suspect and 23% would have said (correctly) "not there" had they been presented a target-absent array—Table 20.3.

The Penrod analysis suggests that the sequential method substantially reduces the tendency to guess and may particularly reduce the tendency to guess the innocent suspect. The sequential method also reduces lucky guesses of suspects in target-present

TABLE 20.3
Simultaneous Presentations

	Target Present (%)	Target Absent (%)
No choice	**26**	**49**
Correct	—	[23]
Guess	**26**	[26]
Identifications	**50**	**51**
Correct	[23]	—
Suspect guess	[27]	**27**
Foil guess	**24**	**24**
Total	**100**	**100**

(Column percentages indicated) [Bracketed percentages are explained in the text]

TABLE 20.4
Sequential Presentations

	Target Present (%)	Target Absent (%)
No choice	46	72
Correct	—	[26]
Guess	46	[46]
Identifications	35	28
Correct	[26]	—
Suspect guess	[9]	9
Foil guess	19	19
Total	100	100

(Column percentages indicated) [Bracketed percentages are explained in the text]

lineups—from 27% in simultaneous to 9% in sequential, as shown in the two tables—though some may be inclined to consider this a loss in "hits," it actually appears to be a suppression of lucky guesses. The reduction in the bias against the innocent (and guilty) suspects is consistent with evidence from studies by Lindsay et al. (1991) showing that sequential procedures can reduce a variety of forms of lineup bias. The Penrod analysis also underscores that the ostensible loss in positive identifications might actually be entirely attributable to guessers—"lucky guessers" in target-present lineups are being converted into people declining to make a choice in sequential arrays. It perhaps goes without saying that if we believed that identifications based on lucky guesses were acceptable evidence of guilt, we might be content to allow the police to run lineups with obscenely high levels of suspect bias—of course we do not because there has been an intuitive sense that such a practice would snare too many innocent suspects.

Knowledge of Research Participation

The research of Haber and Haber (2001) supports the conclusion that witnesses who believe that they have witnessed actual crimes will perform similarly to witnesses who know they are participating in an experiment. They performed a meta-analysis of experiments (some of which are included in the Ebbesen and Flow and Steblay et al. meta-analyses) in which witness-participants observed a crime and then attempted to identify the perpetrator. In 23 studies participants watched a video, slide presentation, or movie of a crime and subsequently performed a lineup task (Demo-crime/Demo-lineup). In 14 studies, a crime was enacted in the presence of the participants, but later—before attempting identifications—the witnesses were told the crime had been staged (Real-crime/Demo-lineup). In seven studies, the participants believed they observed a real crime and believed the lineup presentation was real (Real-crime/Real-lineup).

As shown in Table 20.5, the percentages are very close across the three groups of studies, and the small differences are not significant ($p > 0.05$).

TABLE 20.5
Witness Performance as a Function of Knowledge About Real
Versus Demonstration Studies

| | Perpetrator Present | | | Perpetrator Absent | | Overall |
	Hit (%)	FA (%)	Miss (%)	CR (%)	FA (%)	Correct (%)
Demo-crime/Demo-lineup	43	34	24	49	51	46
Real-crime/Demo-lineup	52	24	24	48	52	50
Real-crime/Real-lineup	47	24	28	53	47	50

Lessons from Focused Studies

In sum, the focused meta-analyses that have appeared since Shapiro and Penrod's (1986) broader review strongly support its use as an analytic tool for three reasons. First, it is capable of summarizing research findings that address the same question with slightly different methodologies, allowing for confident conclusions about the main question of interest. In the field of eyewitness memory research, meta-analyses have demonstrated quite convincingly that myriad factors (e.g., exposure time, retention interval, lineup type and instructions, etc.) exert an effect on eyewitness performance. Some of these conclusions are, by now, sufficiently well grounded to have led to major policy innovations (Technical Working Group on Eyewitness Evidence, 1999; Technical Working Group for Eyewitness Evidence, 2003; Wells et al., 1998).

Second, and more importantly, meta-analysis allows for comparisons between research methodologies that vary across studies, something that traditional reviews cannot accomplish. In debating the external validity of a field of research—especially a field with the sort of policy implications inherent in eyewitness memory research—it is helpful to know whether methodological variables affect performance, but even more helpful, if not crucial, to know whether methodological variables interact with substantive variables (Bornstein, 1999). The focused meta-analyses described above directly address this issue. For example, they have justified Shapiro and Penrod's call for more research employing both target-present and target-absent lineups, as they have conclusively demonstrated that main effects such as witness age (Pozzulo & Lindsay, 1998), lineup presentation (Cutler & Penrod, 1995; Steblay et al., 2001), stress (Deffenbacher et al., 2004), and lineup instructions (Steblay, 1997) are not at all consistent across these different methodologies. An understanding of how eyewitness performance differs for TA and TP lineups is crucial, because in the real world, no one knows for certain whether the suspect in the lineup is genuinely guilty (assuming the suspect protests his innocence, as nearly all do).

Third, the meta-analyses that have been conducted on eyewitness memory consistently show that when the effects of substantive variables vary across different research methodologies, they are larger for more realistic procedures. Factors such as lineup presentation (simultaneous vs. sequential), weapon focus, stress, the cross-race effect, etc. exert larger effects on eyewitness performance when the situation closely matches real witnessing circumstances (e.g., live or video stimulus, staged crime or other eyewitness event) than when the situation is relatively contrived and controlled (e.g., slide presentation, nonthreatening event, or sequence of faces). This pattern of findings provides a powerful answer to the criticism (e.g., Elliott, 1993; Yuille, 1993; Yuille & Wells, 1991) that eyewitness research lacks external validity: If anything, much eyewitness research *underestimates* the magnitude of effects. Eyewitness researchers and the courts can therefore be reasonably certain that the findings do generalize to genuine eyewitness situations. Although we would not be so foolhardy as to claim that all of the empirical questions have been answered, we do assert that many phenomena—such as those reviewed here—are robust enough and generalizable enough to warrant the broad consensus found among eyewitness experts and to support expert testimony on these topics.

CONCLUSIONS

Despite the relatively broad consensus among researchers about which variables do (and do not) affect eyewitness identification performance, the direction of those effects, and whether or not the findings are sufficiently reliable to testify on in court (e.g., Kassin et al., 2001), both the courts and some eyewitness researchers have raised questions about the methods used in eyewitness research. Evidence illustrating the scope and frequency of eyewitness misidentifications comes from several sources—studies of false convictions (e.g., DNA exonerations), studies of station-house identifications, and laboratory experiments. At the beginning of the twenty-first century, the field of eyewitness memory research is sufficiently large and well established that it has begun to identify several causes of these misidentifications. Concerns that this research lacks generalizability are unfounded; rather, the more ecologically valid the research becomes, the larger—and potentially more problematic from a forensic perspective—the effects tend to be. Future research should continue to explore the role of methodological characteristics, such as target-absent versus target-present lineups, but a purported lack of external validity should not be used as an excuse to exclude expert testimony in eyewitness cases.

REFERENCES

Anthony, T., Copper, C., & Mullen, B. (1992). Cross-racial facial identification: A social cognitive integration. *Personality and Social Psychology Bulletin, 18,* 296–301.

Arnold, G. F. (1906). *Psychology applied to legal evidence and other constructions of law.* Calcutta: Thacker, Spink and Co.

Bermant, G. (1986). Two conjectures about the issue of expert testimony. *Law and Human Behavior, 10,* 97–100.

Behrman, B. W., & Davey, S. L. (2001). Eyewitness identification in actual criminal cases: An archival analysis. *Law & Human Behavior, 25,* 475–491.

Borchard, E. M. (1932). *Convicting the innocent: Errors of criminal justice.* New Haven: Yale University Press.

Bornstein, B. H. (1999). The ecological validity of jury simulations: Is the jury still out? *Law and Human Behavior, 23,* 75–91.

Bothwell, R. K., Brigham, J. C., & Malpass, R. S. (1989). Cross-racial identification. *Personality and Social Psychology Bulletin, 15,* 19–25.

Bothwell, R. K., Deffenbacher, K. A., & Brigham, J. C. (1987). Correlation of eyewitness accuracy and confidence: Optimality hypothesis revisited. *Journal of Applied Psychology, 72,* 691–695.

Brandon, R., & Davies, C. (1973). *Wrongful imprisonment.* London: Allen & Unwin.

Bray, R. M., & Kerr, N. L. (1982). Use of the simulation method in the study of jury behavior: Some methodological considerations. *Law and Human Behavior, 3,* 107–119.

Brigham, J. C. (1988). Is witness confidence helpful in judging eyewitness accuracy? In M. M. Gruneberg, P. E. Morris, & R. N. Sykes (Eds.), *Practical aspects of memory* (Vol. 1, pp. 77–82). Chichester, England: Wiley.

Brigham, J. C., & Bothwell, R. K. (1983). The ability of prospective jurors to estimate the accuracy of eyewitness identifications. *Law and Human Behavior, 7,* 19–30.

Brigham, J. C., Maas, A., Snyder, L. D., & Spaulding, K. (1982). Accuracy of eyewitness identifications in a field setting. *Journal of Personality and Social Psychology, 42,* 673–681.

Brigham, J. C., & Wolfskeil, M. P. (1983). Opinions of attorneys and law enforcement personnel on the accuracy of eyewitness identification. *Law and Human Behavior, 7,* 337–349.

Burt, H. E. (1931). *Legal psychology.* New York: Prentice-Hall.

Ceci, S. J., & Bruck, M. (1993). Suggestibility of the child witness: A historical review and synthesis. *Psychological Bulletin, 113,* 403–439.

Christianson, S.-Å. (1992). Emotional stress and eyewitness memory: A critical review. *Psychological Bulletin, 112,* 284–309.

Criglow v. State, 36 S.W.2d 400 (1931).

Cutler, B. L., Berman, G. L., Penrod, S. D., & Fisher, R. P. (1994). Conceptual, practical and empirical issues associated with eyewitness identification test media. In Ross, D., Read, J. D., & Toglia, M. (Eds.), *Adult eyewitness testimony: Current trends and developments.* New York: Cambridge University Press.

Cutler, B. L., & Penrod, S. D. (1988). Improving the reliability of eyewitness identification: Lineup construction and presentation. *Journal of Applied Psychology, 73,* 281–290.

Cutler, B. L., & Penrod, S. D. (1989). Forensically relevant moderators of the relation between eyewitness identification accuracy and confidence. *Journal of Applied Psychology, 74,* 650–652.

Cutler, B. L., & Penrod, S. D. (1995). *Mistaken identification: The eyewitness, psychology and law.* New York: Cambridge University Press.

Cutler, B. L., Penrod, S. D., & Dexter, H. R. (1990). Juror sensitivity to eyewitness identification evidence. *Law and Human Behavior, 14,* 185–191.

Cutler, B. L., Penrod, S. D., & Martens, T. K. (1987). Improving the reliability of eyewitness identifications: Putting context into context. *Journal of Applied Psychology, 72,* 629–637.

Daubert v. Merrell Dow Pharmaceuticals, Inc., 125 L. Ed. 2d 469, 113 S. Ct. 2786, (1993).

Deffenbacher, K. (1980). Eyewitness accuracy and confidence: Can we infer anything about their relationship? *Law and Human Behavior, 4,* 243–260.

Deffenbacher, K. A., Bornstein, B. H., Penrod, S. D., & McGorty, K. (2004). A meta-analytic review of the effects of high stress on eyewitness memory. *Law and Human Behavior, 28,* 687–706.

Deffenbacher, K. A., & Loftus, E. F. (1982). Do jurors share a common understanding concerning eyewitness behavior? *Law and Human Behavior, 6,* 15–30.

Doris, J. (1991). *The suggestibility of children's recollections.* Washington, DC: American Psychological Association.

Ebbesen, E., & Flowe, H. (2002). *Simultaneous v. sequential lineups: What do we really know?* Unpublished manuscript. Retrieved 7/13/06 from http://www.pucsd.edu/~ebbe/SimSeq.htm

Egeth, H. E. (1993). What do we not know about eyewitness identification? *American Psychologist, 48,* 577–580.

Elliott, R. (1993). Expert testimony about eyewitness identification: A critique. *Law and Human Behavior, 17,* 423–437.

Faigman, D. L. (1995). The evidentiary status of social science under Daubert: Is it "scientific," "technical," or "other" knowledge? *Psychology, Public Policy, and Law, 1*, 960–979.

Faigman, D. L., Kaye, D. H., Saks, M. J., & Sanders, J. (2002). *Modern scientific evidence: The law and science of expert testimony* (2nd ed.). St. Paul: West Group.

Fisher, R. P., & Geiselman, R. E. (1992). *Memory-enhancing techniques for investigative interviewing: The cognitive interview.* Springfield: Charles C. Thomas.

Fishman, D. B., & Loftus, E. F. (1978). Expert psychological testimony on eyewitness identification. *Law & Psychology Review, 4*, 87–103.

Fleet, M. L., Brigham, J. C., & Bothwell, R. K. (1987). The confidence-accuracy relationship: The effects of confidence assessment and choosing. *Journal of Applied Social Psychology, 17*, 171–187.

Flowe, H., Ebbesen, E., Burke, C., & Chivabunditt, P. (2001, July). *At the scene of the crime: An examination of the external validity of published studies on line-up identification accuracy.* Paper presented at the American Psychological Society Conference, Toronto, Canada.

Frank, J., & Frank, B. (1957). *Not guilty.* London: Gollancz.

Fulero, S. M. (1993). *Eyewitness expert testimony: An overview and annotated bibliography, 1931–1988.* Unpublished manuscript, Sinclair College.

Gonzalez, R., Ellsworth, P. C., & Pembroke, M. (1993). Response biases in lineups and showups. *Journal of Personality & Social Psychology, 64*(4), 525–537.

Goodman, G. S., & Bottoms, B. L. (1993). *Child victims, child witnesses: Understanding and improving testimony.* New York: Guilford.

Gross, S. R. (1987). Loss of innocence: Eyewitness identification and proof of guilt, *Journal of Legal Studies, 16*, 395–453.

Gross, S. R., Jacoby, K., Matheson, D. J., Montgomery, N., & Patel, S. (2004). *Exonerations in the United States, 1989 through 2003.* Unpublished manuscript downloaded from http://www.law.umich.edu/newsandinfo//exonerations-in-us.pdf

Haber, R. N., & Haber, L. (2001). *A meta-analysis of research on eyewitness lineup identification accuracy.* Paper presented at the Annual convention of the Psychonomics Society, Orlando, Florida, November 16.

Hosch, H. M., & Platz, S. J. (1984). Self-monitoring and eyewitness accuracy. *Personality and Social Psychology Bulletin, 10*, 289–292.

Huff, C. R. (1987). Wrongful conviction: Societal tolerance of injustice. *Research in Social Problems and Public Policy, 4*, 99–115

Huff, R., Rattner, A., & Sagarin, E. (1986). Guilty until proven innocent. *Crime and Delinquency, 32*, 518–544.

Kassin, S. M., Ellsworth, P. C., & Smith, V. L. (1989). The "general acceptance" of psychological research on eyewitness testimony: A survey of the experts. *American Psychologist, 44*, 1089–1098.

Kassin, S. M., Tubb, V. A., Hosch, H. M., & Memon, A. (2001). On the "general acceptance" of eyewitness testimony research. *American Psychologist, 56*, 405–416.

Koehnken, G., Malpass, R. S., & Wogalter, M. S. (1996). Forensic applications of line-up research. In S. L. Sporer, R. S. Malpass, & G. Koehnken (Eds.), *Psychological issues in eyewitness identification* (pp. 205–231). Mahwah, NJ: Lawrence Erlbaum Associates.

Krafka, C., & Penrod, S. (1985). Reinstatement of context in a field experiment on eyewitness identification. *Journal of Personality and Social Psychology, 49*, 58–69.

Kramer, T. H., Buckhout, R., & Eugenio, P. (1990). Weapon focus, arousal, and eyewitness memory: Attention must be paid. *Law & Human Behavior, 14*, 167–184.

Leippe, M. R., & Romanczyk, A. (1987). Children on the witness stand: A communication/persuasion analysis of jurors' reactions to child witnesses. In S. J. Ceci, M. P. Toglia, & D. F. Ross (Eds.), *Children's eyewitness memory* (pp. 155–177). New York: Springer-Verlag.

Leippe, M. R., & Romanczyk, A. (1989). Reactions to child (versus adult) eyewitnesses: The influence of juror's preconceptions and witness behavior. *Law and Human Behavior, 13*, 103–132.

Leippe, M. R., Manion, A. P., & Romanczyk, A. (1991). Eyewitness memory for a touching experience: Accuracy differences between adult and child witness. *Journal of Applied Psychology,* 76, 367–379.

Lindsay, R. C. L., & Harvie, V. L. (1988). Hits, false alarms, correct and mistaken identifications: The effect of methods of data collection on facial memory. In *Practical aspects of memory: Current research and issues: Vol. 1. Memory in everyday life* (pp. 47–52). Oxford, England: John Wiley & Sons.

Lindsay, R. C. L., & Wells, G. L. (1985). Improving eyewitness identifications from lineups: Simultaneous versus sequential lineup presentation. *Journal of Applied Psychology,* 70, 556–564.

Lindsay, R. C. L., Lea, J. A., Nosworthy, G. J., Fulford, J. A., Hector, J., LeVan, V., et al. (1991). Biased lineups: Sequential presentation reduces the problem. *Journal of Applied Psychology,* 76, 796–802.

Lindsay, R. C. L., Wells, G. L., & O'Connor, F. J. (1989). Mock juror belief of accurate and inaccurate eyewitnesses: A replication and extension. *Law and Human Behavior,* 13, 333–339.

Lindsay, R. C. L., Wells, G. L., & Rumpel, C. M. (1981). Can people detect eyewitness identification accuracy within and across situations? *Journal of Applied Psychology,* 66, 79–89.

Loftus, E. F. (1983). Silence is not golden. *American Psychologist,* 38, 564–572.

Loftus, E. F. (1993). Psychologists in the eyewitness world. *American Psychologist,* 48(5), 550–552.

Loftus, E. F., Loftus, G. R., & Messo, J. (1987). Some facts about "weapon focus." *Law & Human Behavior,* 11(1), 55–62.

McCloskey, M., & Egeth, H. (1983). Eyewitness identification: What can a psychologist tell a jury? *American Psychologist,* 38, 550–563.

McConkey, K. M., & Roche, S. M. (1989). Knowledge of eyewitness memory. *Australian Psychologist,* 24, 377–384.

McQuiston, D. E., & Malpass, R. S. (2001, June). *Eyewitness identifications in criminal cases: An archival study.* Paper presented at the 2001 Biennial Meetings of the Society for Applied Research in Memory and Cognition, Kingston, Ontario, Canada.

Meissner, C. A., & Brigham, J. C. (2001). Thirty years of investigating the own-race bias in memory for faces: A meta-analytic review. *Psychology, Public Policy, & Law,* 7, 3–35.

Munsterberg, H. (1909). *On the witness stand: Essays on psychology and crime.* Garden City, NY: Clark, Boardman.

Noon, E., & Hollin, C. R. (1987). Lay knowledge of eyewitness behaviour: A British survey. *Applied Cognitive Psychology,* 1, 143–153.

O'Rourke, T. E., Penrod, S. D., Cutler, B. L., & Stuve, T. E. (1989). The external validity of eyewitness identification research: Generalizing across subject populations. *Law & Human Behavior,* 13, 385–395.

Penrod, S. D. (2003). Eyewitness identification evidence: How well are witnesses and police performing? *Criminal Justice Magazine,* Spring, 36–47.

Penrod, S., Loftus, E. F., & Winkler, J. (1982). The reliability of eyewitness testimony: A psychological perspective. In N. Kerr & R. Bray (Eds.), *The psychology of the courtroom.* New York: Academic Press.

Penrod, S. D., Fulero, S. M., & Cutler, B. L. (1995). Expert psychological testimony on eyewitness reliability before and after Daubert: The state of the law and the science. *Behavioral Sciences and the Law,* 13, 229–259.

People v. Kindle, 2002 Cal. App. Unpub. LEXIS 6453 (Cal. 2002).

People v. McDonald, 37 Cal.3d 351, 690 P.2d 709, 716, 208 Cal.Rptr. 236, 245 (1984).

Pigott, M. A., Brigham, J. C., & Bothwell, R. K. (1990). A field study of the relationship between quality of eyewitnesses' descriptions and identification accuracy. *Journal of Police Science and Administration,* 17, 84–88.

Platz, S. J., & Hosch, H. M. (1988). Cross racial/ethnic eyewitness identification: A field study. *Journal of Applied Social Psychology,* 18, 972–984.

Pozzulo, J. D., & Lindsay, R. C. L. (1998). Identification accuracy of children versus adults: A meta-analysis. *Law and Human Behavior, 22*, 549–570.

Rahaim, G. L., & Brodsky, S. L. (1982). Empirical evidence versus common sense: Juror and lawyer knowledge of eyewitness accuracy. *Law and Psychology Review, 7*, 1–15.

Rattner, A. (1988). Convicted but innocent: Wrongful conviction and the criminal justice system. *Law and Human Behavior, 12*, 283–293.

Robinson, E. S. (1935). *Law and the lawyers.* New York: Macmillan.

Scheck, B., Neufeld, P., & Dwyer, J. (2000). *Actual innocence.* Garden City, NY: Doubleday.

Shapiro, P. N., & Penrod, S. D. (1986). Meta-analysis of facial identification studies. *Psychological Bulletin, 100*, 139–156.

Slater, A. (1994). *Identification parades: A scientific evaluation.* Police Research Award Scheme, Police Research Group, Home Office [reported in Tim Valentine & Pamela Heaton. (1999). An evaluation of the fairness of police line-ups and video Identifications, *Applied Cognitive Psychology, 13*, S59–S72].

Sporer, M. (1983). Allgemeinwissen zur psychologie der zeugenausage [Common understanding concerning eyewitness testimony]. In H. J. Kerner, H. Kury, & K. Sessar (Eds.), *Deutsche forschungen zur kriminalitaetsentstehung und kriminalitaetskontrolle* (pp. 1191–1234). Cologne, Germany: Heymanns.

Sporer, S. L. (1992). Post-dicting eyewitness accuracy: Confidence, decision times and person descriptions of choosers and non-choosers. *European Journal of Social Psychology, 22*, 157–180.

Sporer, S. L. (1993). Eyewitness identification accuracy, confidence, and decision times in simultaneous and sequential lineups. *Journal of Applied Psychology, 78*, 22–33.

Sporer, S. L., Penrod, S., Read, D., & Cutler, B. (1995). Choosing, confidence, and accuracy: A meta-analysis of the confidence-accuracy relation in eyewitness identification studies. *Psychological Bulletin, 118*, 315–327.

State v. Chapple, 135 Ariz. 281, 660 P.2d 1208 (1983).

Steblay, N. M. (1992). A meta-analytic review of the weapon focus effect. *Law and Human Behavior, 16*, 413–424.

Steblay, N. M. (1997). Social influence in eyewitness recall: A meta-analytic review of lineup instruction effects. *Law and Human Behavior, 21*, 283–297.

Steblay, N., Dysart, J., Fulero, S., & Lindsay, R. C. L. (2003). Eyewitness accuracy rates in police showup and lineup presentations: A meta-analytic comparison. *Law & Human Behavior, 27*, 523–540.

Steblay, N., Dysart, J., Fulero, S., & Lindsay R. C. L. (2001). Eyewitness accuracy rates in sequential and simultaneous lineup presentations: A meta-analytic comparison. *Law and Human Behavior, 25*, 459–473.

Technical Working Group for Eyewitness Evidence. (1999). Eyewitness evidence: A guide for law enforcement (Booklet). Washington, DC: United States Department of Justice, Office of Justice Programs. http://www.ojp.usdoj.gov/nij/pubs-sum/178240.htm

Technical Working Group for Eyewitness Evidence. (2003). *Eyewitness evidence: A trainer's manual for law enforcement* (Booklet). Washington, DC: United States Department of Justice, Office of Justice Programs. http://www.ojp.usdoj.gov/nij/eyewitness/188678.html

Turtle, J. W., & Wells, G. L. (1988). Children versus adults as eyewitnesses: Whose testimony holds up under cross examination? In M. W. Gruneberg et al. (Eds.), *Practical aspects of memory* (pp. 27–33). New York: Wiley.

U.S. v. Downing 753 F2d 1224. (3d Cir.) (1985)

United States v. Amaral, 488 F.2d 1148 (9th Cir.) (1973).

United States v. Frye, 293 F. 1013 (D.C. Cir.) (1923).

Valentine, T., Pickering, A., & Darling, S. (2003). Characteristics of eyewitness identification that predict the outcome of real lineups *Applied Cognitive Psychology, 17*, 969–994.

Weld, H. P., & Danzig, E. R. (1940). A study of the way in which a verdict is reached by a jury. *American Journal of Psychology, 53*, 518–536.

Wells, G. L. (1993). What do we know about eyewitness identification? *American Psychologist, 48*, 553–571.

Wells, G. L. (1984). How adequate is human intuition for judging eyewitness testimony. In G. L. Wells & E. F. Loftus (Eds.), *Eyewitness testimony: Psychological perspectives* (pp. 256–272). New York: Cambridge University Press.

Wells, G. L., & Lindsay, R. C. L. (1980). On estimating the diagnosticity of eyewitness nonidentifications. *Psychological Bulletin, 88*, 776–784.

Wells, G. L., & Murray, D. M. (1984). Eyewitness confidence. In G. L. Wells & E. F. Loftus (Eds.), *Eyewitness testimony: Psychological perspectives*. Cambridge: Cambridge University Press.

Wells, G. L., Lindsay, R. C. L., & Ferguson, T. J. (1979). Accuracy, confidence, and juror perceptions in eyewitness identification. *Journal of Applied Psychology, 64*, 440–448.

Wells, G. L., Small, M., Penrod, S., Malpass, R. S., Fulero, S. M., & Brimacombe, C. A. E. (1998). Eyewitness identification procedures: Recommendations for lineups and photospreads. *Law and Human Behavior, 22*, 603–647.

Wells, G. L., Ferguson, T. J., & Lindsay, R. C. L. (1981). The tractability of eyewitness confidence and its implications for triers of fact. *Journal of Applied Psychology, 66*, 688–696.

Wright, D. B., & McDaid, A. T. (1996). Comparing system and estimator variables using data from real line-ups. *Applied Cognitive Psychology, 10*, 75–84.

Yarmey, A. D. (1986). Ethical responsibilities governing the statements experimental psychologists make in expert testimony. *Law and Human Behavior, 10*, 101–115.

Yarmey, A. D., & Jones, H. P. T. (1983). Is the psychology of eyewitness identification a matter of common sense? In S. Lloyd-Bostock & B. R. Clifford (Eds.), *Evaluating witness evidence* (pp. 13–40). Chichester, England: Wiley.

Yuille, J. C. (1993). We must study forensic eyewitnesses to know about them. *American Psychologist, 48*, 572–573.

Yuille, J. C., & Wells, G. L. (1991). Concerns about the application of research findings: The issue of ecological validity. In *The suggestibility of children's recollections.* (pp. 118–128). Washington, DC: American Psychological Association.

21

Mistaken Identification = Erroneous Conviction? Assessing and Improving Legal Safeguards

Lori R. Van Wallendael and Brian L. Cutler
University of North Carolina, Charlotte

Jennifer Devenport
Western Washington University

Steven Penrod
John Jay College of Criminal Justice, CUNY

Alejandro Dominguez was a 16-year-old from Mexico, a legal resident alien in the United States, when he was arrested for the rape of a Caucasian woman in the town of Waukegan, Illinois. Dominguez protested his innocence, and although he had no criminal record, he was tried as an adult. On the advice of his attorney, he waived his right to a jury trial and was tried before Circuit Court Judge Harry D. Hartel in 1990. Hartel found Dominguez guilty and sentenced him to 9 years in prison. With credit for time served in jail before trial, plus day-for-day good time in prison, Dominguez was released from prison in December, 1994. But six years later, the specter of the crime came back to haunt him again, when the U.S. Immigration and Naturalization Service threatened to deport Dominguez for failing to register as an ex-sex offender. By this time, Dominguez was married and the father of a child. He retained defense attorneys Jed Stone and John P. Curnyn to seek DNA testing of the biological evidence in the rape case, and in 2001, Circuit Court Judge Raymond McKoski granted their motion for DNA testing (at Dominguez' expense). In March, 2002, results of the test positively excluded Dominguez as the rapist, and he was officially exonerated on April 26, 2002 (Warden, 2003).

How did an innocent teenager find himself in the midst of such a 12-year nightmare? The major evidence against Alejandro Dominguez was the report of an eyewitness—

an identification that was shaky, at best. The victim's initial description of her rapist was inconsistent with Dominguez' appearance in a number of ways. The victim told police that her attacker wore a diamond earring in a pierced ear and had a tattoo. Dominguez had no ear piercings and no tattoos. Moreover, the victim told police that the rapist spoke to her in English. Several witnesses testified in court that Dominguez spoke only Spanish at the time. Finally, the Waukegan Police used a suggestive identification procedure during the lineup. The victim stated during cross-examination that the lead detective in the case told her to "watch the one sitting on the chair. Tell me if that is the one" (Warden, 2003).

In the case of Alejandro Dominguez, a mistaken eyewitness identification led to the conviction of an innocent man. But is the Dominguez case an isolated exception to the rule? Studies suggest that it is not. Researchers investigating cases of erroneous convictions, in which the convicted person was later proven to have been innocent (often by DNA testing in recent years), have consistently pointed to mistaken eyewitness identification as a significant factor in the majority of such convictions (Borchard, 1932; Huff, 1987; Scheck, Neufeld, & Dwyer, 2001).

Yet the law has never been blind to the danger of mistaken identification. Numerous safeguards are built into the legal system in order to protect the innocent from wrongful accusations, including those resulting from eyewitness identifications. Unfortunately, research suggests that traditional safeguards are ineffective in protecting people like Alejandro Dominguez from erroneous conviction. These safeguards are ineffective in part because they assume a high level of knowledge on the part of attorneys, judges, and juries, or assume that the principles of eyewitness memory are common sense. Attorney presence at lineups, for example, can be effective only insofar as the attorney knows what to look for in terms of lineup composition, number of foils, instructions to the witness, and other, more subtle biasing factors in the administering officer's vocal tone or body language. Motions to suppress an eyewitness's testimony, assuming the attorney recognizes a serious problem, are unlikely to meet with success unless a judge (1) is well educated about eyewitness testimony and (2) recognizes that the jury may not be knowledgeable about the factors that impeach the eyewitness's credibility. Empirical research addressing attorney and judge sensitization to eyewitness factors suggests that the above conditions often are not met within the court system. Similarly, cross-examination of eyewitnesses during a trial depends upon the attorney's sensitivity to the factors influencing eyewitness accuracy, as well as the judge's or jury's awareness of the importance of those factors. For example, in the Alejandro Dominguez case, although a significant biasing instruction was revealed during cross-examination, the judge apparently did not give this bias much weight in his verdict.

Rather than inferring a certain amount of knowledge on the part of attorneys, judges, and particularly jurors, we argue that more effective safeguards will focus on the education of those parties, before or during a trial. As currently implemented, judges' cautionary instructions tend to emphasize only a limited number of eyewitness factors while ignoring others and may inappropriately encourage jurors to use eyewitness confidence as an indicator of accuracy. Research has provided little evidence that the standard instructions given by judges can reduce erroneous convictions; however, we hold out hope that improvements in judges' instructions could better sensitize jurors to factors affecting eye-witness reliability. The use of expert testimony about eyewitness research is also a promising avenue for educating jurors to make them better able to evaluate the testimony of an eyewitness to a crime.

This chapter first examines existing research on the effectiveness of a number of traditional safeguards against mistaken identification: presence of counsel at the identification, motions to suppress eyewitness testimony, voir dire, and cross-examination of eyewitnesses. We then examine research on the effectiveness of expert testimony, a less traditional safeguard that appears to be growing in acceptance (Kassin et al., 2001). Finally, we present suggestions for improvements to traditional safeguards.

PRESENCE OF COUNSEL SAFEGUARD

The presence of counsel safeguard serves to protect criminal defendants from mistaken eyewitness identifications by allowing defense attorneys to be present during their clients' eyewitness identification procedures. Specifically, this safeguard enables attorneys to observe the identification procedure and to record any suggestive procedures that may be used. This safeguard, however, is effective only if attorneys are knowledgeable about the factors that influence lineup suggestiveness and are present at their clients' lineups to view any biased lineup procedures.

Are Attorneys Knowledgeable about Lineup Suggestiveness?

In order to examine attorney sensitivity to factors that influence lineup suggestiveness, Stinson, Devenport, Cutler, and Kravitz (1996) showed 97 public defenders one version of a videotaped lineup where foil (biased vs. unbiased), instruction (biased vs. unbiased), and presentation (simultaneous vs. sequential) biases were manipulated between sub-jects. The foil-biased, instruction-biased, and simultaneous presentations are known to produce more false identifications than the foil-unbiased, instruction-unbiased, and se-quential presentation conditions, respectively (Steblay, 1997; Steblay et al., 2001; Wells, Rydell, & Seelau, 1993). After viewing the lineup, the attorneys evaluated the lineup's suggestiveness and indicated whether they would submit a motion to suppress the iden-tification. The results revealed that attorneys who were shown foil-biased lineups, as compared with attorneys shown foil-unbiased lineups, rated the lineups as more sugges-tive and less fair and were more likely to indicate that they would submit a motion to suppress the identification. Attorneys who were shown instruction-biased lineups, as compared with those shown instruction-unbiased lineups, also rated the lineups as more suggestive; however, they did not find the lineup to be less fair, nor were they more likely to indicate that they would submit a motion. Last, attorneys' responses were not influ-enced by presentation bias. Thus it would appear that attorneys are sensitive to some of the factors influencing identification accuracy, but not to others.

Likelihood of Attorney Presence at Lineups

Although research suggests that attorneys are somewhat sensitive to factors influencing eyewitness identifications, the presence of counsel safeguard is effective only if attorneys are present at their clients' lineups to document these factors for the purpose of filing a subsequent motion to suppress the identification. Researchers, however, have reported that attorney presence at lineups may be the exception rather than the rule. Specifically, attorneys and police officers surveyed in Brigham and Wolfskeil's (1983) study reported that attorneys are typically present at lineups occurring after their clients' first court appearance but rarely present at lineups occurring before the initial court appearance. Furthermore, Stinson et al. (1996) found that when the defense attorneys were asked how often they attended their clients' identifications, they reported being present at only 5% of the identification tests. Thus, the effectiveness of the presence of counsel safeguard appears to be limited not only by attorney knowledge of the factors influencing eyewitness identification performance, but also by the absence of attorneys at their clients' lineups. An important contributor to this pattern may be the failure of many suspects to demand legal representation until after the initial identification is made. Certainly police are not required to and rarely do suggest that suspects be represented during identification procedures.

MOTION-TO-SUPPRESS SAFEGUARD

In cases in which the defense attorney believes that the identification procedures were impermissibly suggestive, she or he may file a motion to suppress the identification evidence on the grounds that the procedures were unduly suggestive. The trial judge then considers the evidence put forth in the motion (and the testimony in the hearing on the motion if one is granted) and decides whether to grant or deny the motion. Granting the motion means that the eyewitness identification evidence will not be presented to the jury. Denying the motion means that the prosecution is free to proffer the identification evidence at trial.

For the motion-to-suppress safeguard to be effective, three things must happen. First, the procedures must be sufficiently suggestive to surpass some threshold. Second, as discussed earlier, the attorney must be sufficiently sensitive to suggestive procedures so that she or he can recognize them and describe them in a compelling way to the judge. Third, the judge must be capable of accurately distinguishing between suggestive and nonsuggestive procedures, and his or her decisions should reflect this accuracy.

How capable are judges at discriminating between suggestive and nonsuggestive identification procedures? To date, we know of only one study that empirically addressed this question. Stinson, Devenport, Cutler, and Kravitz (1997) examined the decisions of judges who were asked to rule on a simulated motion to suppress identification evidence. The authors solicited the participation of 197 circuit judges in Florida, 99 of whom participated. Each judge received a survey containing (1) a description of the event and perpetrator, (2) a high-quality color photocopy of a photoarray, (3) a description of the identification procedure, (4) a motion to suppress, and (5) a questionnaire. The following photoarray factors were manipulated in a $2 \times 2 \times 2$ design: Foils (Unbiased vs. Biased), Instructions (Unbiased vs. Biased), and Presentation (Simultaneous vs. Sequential). These factors were manipulated via the descriptions of the lineup procedures and through the use of the photocopied photo array. The questionnaire contained the major dependent variables, which included judges' ratings of the suggestiveness of the identification procedure and decision on the motion (grant or deny).

The results showed that judges were sensitive to both Foil Bias and Instruction Bias. For example, of the judges who received Foil-Unbiased photo arrays, 17% granted the motion. In contrast, of the judges who received Foil-Biased photo arrays, 43% granted the motion, a statistically significant difference. Likewise, of the judges who received Instruction-Unbiased photo arrays, 16% granted the motion. By contrast, of the judges who received Instruction-Biased photo arrays, 46% granted the motion—again, a significant difference. Suggestiveness ratings mirrored the results of the motion decision. Although these results are encouraging, a less encouraging pattern emerged for Presentation Bias. Judges' decisions to grant or deny the motion were not significantly influenced by Presentation Bias, and there was a nonsignificant tendency to grant the motion more frequently following a sequential photo array (40%) than a simultaneous photo array (23%). Comparably, sequential photo arrays were rated as significantly more suggestive than simultaneous photo arrays, a pattern that directly conflicts with the psychological research on presentation bias.

Thus, Stinson et al.'s findings suggest that judges are sensitive to some identification test biases (i.e., Foil and Instruction Biases) but not others (Presentation Bias). One significant limitation to this study is that motions to suppress are often argued in a hearing following testimony from the officer who conducted the identification test and sometimes from the eyewitness. In this study judges made their decisions solely on the basis of written descriptions and arguments.

VOIR DIRE AS A SAFEGUARD

The voir dire process, that is, the procedure by which a jury is selected, also serves as a potential safeguard against erroneous conviction in eyewitness cases. In theory, voir dire can be used to identify venire persons who are unable or unwilling to scrutinize eyewitness testimony. The attorney can exercise causal or peremptory challenges to excuse venire persons who are unable or unwilling from serving on the jury. In practice, however, identifying venire persons who are unable or unwilling to scrutinize eyewitness testimony is easier said than done. Voir dire is effective as a safeguard only insofar as the following two assumptions are met: (1) the legally imposed restrictions on voir dire permit the attorney to query jurors about their potential biases and (2) the information revealed during such inquiries is in fact indicative of juror bias. In this section we review the evidence on the validity of these two assumptions.

Research on the effectiveness of voir dire generally reveals that juror bias is most reliably predicted by case-relevant attitudes (Kovera, Dickinson, & Cutler, 2003). In eyewitness cases, therefore, we would expect that attitudes toward eyewitnesses would be the best predictor of juror bias. By attitudes toward eyewitnesses we mean jurors' predispositions to believe or disbelieve eyewitness testimony. A juror who is predisposed to put high levels of trust in eyewitness memory is unlikely to scrutinize it by, for example, considering carefully the conditions under which the event was witnessed and the identification made.

The opportunity to question venire persons about their attitudes during voir dire—a practice referred to as *extensive voir dire* (Kovera et al., 2003)—varies considerably. Extensive voir dire is not only limited to the United States jury system, it is limited within the United States as well. In the federal court system, the voir dire process is brief and superficial. The questions are typically posed by the judge, with little or no input from the attorneys. Questioning jurors about their attitudes is unusual. Voir dire practices in the state courts vary more widely. Some states (e.g., California, Massachusetts) follow the federal courts in conducting minimal voir dire. In other state court systems (e.g., Connecticut, Florida, North Carolina), attorneys conduct the voir dire, and they are given discretion to question jurors about their attitudes (though the degree of latitude varies from courtroom to courtroom). Thus, in most courtrooms, attorneys do not have the opportunity to question venire persons about their biases for or against eyewitnesses.

Given that at least in some courts attorneys have the opportunity to question jurors about their attitudes toward eyewitnesses, it behooves us to ask whether these attitudes do, in fact, reveal bias toward or against believing eyewitness testimony. Toward this end, Narby and Cutler (1994) devised an instrument for reliably assessing venire persons' attitudes toward eyewitnesses as a way of screening for juror ability and willingness to scrutinize eyewitness testimony.

Narby and Cutler's Attitudes Toward Eyewitnesses Scale (ATES) consists of nine statements to which respondents rate their agreement on a Likert agreement scale. Examples of items include "Eyewitnesses frequently misidentify innocent people just because they seem familiar," and "Eyewitness testimony is more like fact than opinion." Their first study of this instrument examined its reliability. In data from 511 undergraduates and 140 jury-eligible community members from Miami-Dade County, Florida, the instrument showed strong evidence of unidimensionality (Tucker-Lewis Index of .96) and internal consistency (Coefficient Alpha of .80). Their second study attempted to replicate the instrument's psychometric properties and examine the instrument's predictive validity. Participants were 62 students and 46 community residents from south Florida. In addition to completing the ATES, each participant viewed a videotaped enactment of a robbery trial in which eyewitness identification played a pivotal role and then rendered a verdict and evaluated the evidence. Once again, the ATES showed acceptable levels of unidimensionality (Tucker-Lewis Index of .90) and internal consistency (Coefficient Alpha of .70). Unexpectedly, the ATES score did not correlate significantly with verdict or ratings of the defendant's culpability ($r = .14$ and .08, respectively). Narby and Cutler's third study tested the same hypotheses and used the same procedures and materials as their second study, but in the third study the eyewitness's confidence in her identification (100% vs. 80% confident) was manipulated. Once again, the ATES scores were found to be unidimensional (Tucker-Lewis Index of .81) and internally consistent (Coefficient Alpha of .84). As in their second study, ATES scores did not correlate significantly with verdict or ratings of defendant culpability ($r = -.15$ and $-.01$, respectively).

In summary, Narby and Cutler's (1994) studies show that, although attitudes toward eyewitnesses can be reliably assessed, these attitudes show little utility for predicting juror bias toward or against eyewitnesses during voir dire. Tempting as it may be to simply endorse this conclusion a decade later, recent research contradicts the conclusion. Devenport and Cutler (2004) conducted a trial simulation experiment to examine the impact on juror decisions of defense-only expert testimony and opposing expert testimony about the psychology of eyewitness memory. Participants were 257 jury-eligible community members and 240 students from Nebraska. Each participant completed the ATES (included as a randomization check), viewed one of 12 versions of a videotaped trial (Foil-Biased vs. Foil-Unbiased Lineup X Instruction-Biased vs. Instruction-Unbiased Lineup X No Expert vs. Defense Expert vs. Opposing Experts), rendered a verdict, and evaluated the evidence. The ATES scale scores were internally consistent (Coefficient Alpha of .89) and correlated in the expected directions with verdict ($r = -.41$; $p < .01$), rating of the defendant's culpability ($r = -.36$, $p < .01$), and perceived accuracy of the identification ($r = -.37$, $p < .01$). We have no clear indication why ATES scores correlated with juror decisions in Devenport and Cutler (2004) but not in Narby and Cutler (1994). We can only conclude that the results are mixed.

The Attitudes Toward Eyewitnesses Scale is the most direct measure of juror bias toward or against eyewitnesses. As for whether it actually predicts juror bias, the jury is still out on this question. Nevertheless, given the mixed results for the most direct measure, there is little reason to believe that less direct measures, such as personality, demographic characteristics, or other attitudes, will fare better at predicting juror bias. If given the opportunity to assess juror attitudes toward eyewitnesses, it seems at least plausible that attorneys can identify potentially biased venire persons during voir dire. More generally, given the lack of opportunity attorneys have for questioning venire persons about their attitudes toward eyewitnesses and the questionable predictive validity of such attitudes, we can only conclude that the utility of voir dire as a safeguard against erroneous conviction based on mistaken identification is marginal at best.

CROSS-EXAMINATION SAFEGUARD

The cross-examination of eyewitnesses is one of the most regularly implemented safeguards protecting defendants from erroneous convictions resulting from a mistaken eyewitness identification. Similar to the presence of counsel safeguard, there are several assumptions regarding attorney knowledge and behavior underlying the effectiveness of the safeguard. Specifically, in order for the cross-examination safeguard to be effective, attorneys must (1) have access to information regarding the eyewitness event and identification for the purpose of identifying any factors that may have enhanced the suggestiveness of the identification, (2) be sensitive to factors influencing identification performance, and (3) be able to effectively highlight the suggestiveness of these factors for the jury during the trial. Furthermore, the cross-examination safeguard assumes that jurors, when presented with information regarding the reliability of the eyewitness' identification, will be sensitive to this information and will use this information effectively in their decision-making.

Attorney Access to Information about Identification

Essential to the preparation of an effective cross-examination of an eyewitness is the opportunity for the attorney to (1) obtain information regarding the events surrounding the crime and (2) observe and record the suggestive aspects of the eyewitness identification procedure. Unfortunately, in order to obtain information regarding the witnessing conditions surrounding the event, attorneys must rely on the memories and records of the individuals present (i.e., the witness and police). Thus, attorney access to information regarding factors that may have influenced the eyewitness's memory and subsequent identification may be limited by the accuracy and completeness of the information obtained from both the witness and the police. Furthermore, for this information to be helpful in the preparation of an effective cross-examination, the attorney must be knowledgeable about how witness conditions affect eyewitness accuracy.

More importantly, attorneys are often limited by the type and timing of the identification procedure. Specifically, the Supreme Court has ruled that the presence of counsel safeguard does not extend to the use of photo arrays (*United States vs. Ash*, 1973) or to identifications obtained prior to the defendant's indictment (*Kirby vs. Illinois*, 1972). Thus, attorneys are essentially excluded from identification tests that occur early in the investigation of the defendant. And as indicated earlier, attorneys are rarely present at their client's live, post-indictment lineups.

Attorney Knowledge of Factors Affecting Accuracy

Effective cross-examination of an eyewitness also requires that the attorney question the eyewitness in such a way as to highlight to the jury the factors present during the witnessing of the event that are known to influence eyewitness performance. This, however, can only be done if the attorney knows which factors have deleterious effects on identification accuracy.

To assess attorney knowledge of factors known to influence eyewitness identification performance, Rahaim and Brodsky (1982) had 43 attorneys read a brief scenario and then selected one of four alternative answers. Overall, the majority of attorneys appeared to be sensitive to the negative effects of race and violence/stress on eyewitness identification performance but insensitive to the lack of relationship between eyewitness confidence and identification accuracy. In a larger-scale study, Brigham and Wolfskeil (1983) assessed attorney knowledge in a survey of 235 prosecutors and defense attorneys. The results of an open-ended question revealed that, when asked what factors are most likely to influence identification accuracy, attorneys correctly identified factors such as the physical characteristics of the suspect, lighting at the scene of the crime, and length of viewing time. Although identified less frequently, attorneys incorrectly mentioned eye-witness characteristics such as witness temperament, intelligence, and whether the witness has a good memory. Furthermore, factors such as weapon focus, disguises, retention internal, and suggestive identification procedures were not mentioned, suggesting that attorneys may not be aware of a number of factors known to influence eyewitness identification accuracy.

Studies of Effectiveness of Cross-examinations

Assuming that attorneys are sensitive to and highlight for the jury factors known to influence eyewitness identification performance, the cross-examination of the eyewitness will not be effective unless jurors (1) are sensitive to the factors influencing eyewitness identification accuracy and (2) use this information when evaluating eyewitness testimony.

Research assessing juror sensitivity to factors affecting eyewitness reliability and their ability to discriminate between accurate and inaccurate eyewitnesses is extensive and has utilized various methodologies (i.e., surveys, post-diction studies, and trial simulation experiments). Across all of the various types of studies, however, the results appear to be remarkably similar. Specifically, prospective jurors appear to be somewhat aware of the detrimental effect of race and prior photo array identifications on identification accuracy (Deffenbacher & Loftus, 1982; McConkey & Roche, 1989; Noon & Hollin, 1987) but insensitive to other factors, such as the influence of crime seriousness (Kassin, 1979) and instruction bias (Wells, 1984, as cited in Kassin, 1979). Furthermore, when presented with factors that are known to influence identification accuracy, jurors appear to be insensitive to the importance of this information and to pay little attention to it when evaluating the evidence and rendering verdicts (Cutler, Penrod, & Dexter, 1990; Cutler, Penrod, & Stuve, 1988). In addition, this body of research suggests that jurors may (1) place too much emphasis on eyewitness testimony (as cited in Weinberg & Baron, 1982; Loftus, 1974), (2) have difficulty distinguishing between accurate and inaccurate eyewitnesses (Lindsay, Wells, & O'Connor, 1989; Wells, Lindsay, & Ferguson, 1979), and 3) base their decisions in part on witness confidence, a poor predictor of identification accuracy (Lindsay, Wells, & Rumpel, 1981; Wells, Lindsay, & Ferguson, 1979).

EXPERT TESTIMONY SAFEGUARD

The legal admissibility of expert testimony regarding eyewitness accuracy is discussed at length elsewhere in this volume; in this chapter, we focus solely on studies that examine the effectiveness of such testimony, if admitted. In theory, expert testimony could have at least three different types of effects on jurors' decisions: (1) the expert could simply confuse the jurors; (2) the expert's testimony could cause the jurors to become more skeptical of eyewitness testimony in general; or (3) the expert's testimony could actually sensitize

jurors to the factors that make a particular identification more or less likely to be accurate. There is, thankfully, no empirical evidence to date that suggests the first effect, but
evidence is mixed regarding the expert's ability to elicit the second and third effects.

Early studies of eyewitness expert testimony were designed primarily to look for skepticism effects. For example, Loftus (1980) constructed a brief, written description of an
actual assault case that included an identification of the defendant by an eyewitness.
College student participants read either a no-expert version of the case, in which the
summary of defense evidence consisted only of the defendant's denial of guilt, or an expert version, in which the defense summary included a psychologist's testimony about
factors influencing eyewitness accuracy. Participants in the expert condition showed increased skepticism regarding eyewitnesses, finding the defendant guilty only 39% of the
time as opposed to 58% for the no-expert condition. In a second study, when college student participants were asked to deliberate after reading the same materials, 7 of 10 juries
reached a guilty verdict in the no-expert condition, as compared with only 3 of 10 in the
expert condition. Although these studies are limited in their use of college student participants and written trial summaries, the second study remains one of the few attempts
to examine actual deliberation after an expert has testified.

Another study that included deliberation was done by Maass, Brigham, and West
(1985). They presented student participants with a one-page written description of a
court case and manipulated the presence or absence of an eyewitness for the prosecution
who had confidently identified the defendant on two occasions. When the eyewitness
was present, some participants were presented with expert testimony by a criminologist
regarding high error rates in eyewitness identification. Again, expert testimony decreased
belief in the defendant's guilt in individual mock jurors' judgments both before and after
a 30-minute deliberation period. Without any eyewitness, the average post-deliberation
rating of likelihood of guilt (on a 7-point scale, where 7 indicates certainty of guilt) was
2.54. Adding the eyewitness (with no expert testimony) increased the average guilt rating
to 5.18; adding the expert reduced the average guilt rating to 3.57. Thus, the expert diminished but did not entirely negate the effect of the eyewitness identification.

In a more realistic simulation, Hosch, Beck, and McIntyre (1980) enacted a trial
about a fictitious burglary in front of a group of non-student, jury-eligible participants.
The trial was also videotaped and later shown to college student participants. An eyewitness provided key evidence for the prosecution. Half of the participants in the live
simulation were removed from the room while a psychologist gave expert testimony about
the effects of such factors as exposure duration and witness stress on memory. At the
conclusion of the trial, participants were divided into groups of six jurors to deliberate
and reach a verdict. Unfortunately, the evidence against the defendant was so weak that
all of the participant juries acquitted the defendant, with or without the expert testimony. Juries who heard the expert, however, did spend more time discussing both the
eyewitness and non-eyewitness evidence and rated eyewitness testimony as less reliable
and less important on subsequent questionnaires.

Finally, Leippe and colleagues (2004) recently examined the timing of eyewitness
expert testimony, the strength of the case against the defendant, and jurors' need for cognition as potential moderators of skepticism effects. College students read a transcript of

a robbery/murder trial that included the identification of the defendant by a single eye-witness. The strength of the prosecution's case was manipulated, as was the presence of an expert testifying for the defense about the factors that affect eyewitness reliability. When included, the expert testimony was introduced either before or after the eyewit-ness was actually presented. In addition, the judge either did or did not remind the jury of the expert's testimony in his instructions at the end of the trial. An individual differ-ence variable, need for cognition (NC), also was measured for each participant. With or without expert testimony, there was a greater likelihood of a guilty verdict with a strong prosecution case than with a weak one. Strength of prosecution case, however, did not moderate the effect of the expert's testimony. Skepticism was seen, but only in the con-ditions in which the expert testified after the eyewitness's testimony (as is the norm in American trials) and the judge reminded the jury of the expert's testimony. Under those conditions, guilty verdicts were 41% with the expert's testimony and 58% without it when the prosecution's case was strong, and 21% with the expert's testimony as com-pared with 42% without it when the prosecution's case was weak. Participants with a moderate need for cognition score were the most sensitive to the manipulation of case strength, but need for cognition did not interact with any effects of expert testimony.

None of the previously discussed studies systematically varied the witnessing condi-tions, lineup instructions and procedures, or other variables believed to influence eye-witness accuracy. Thus, none were capable of determining whether mock jurors became more sensitive to factors predictive of accuracy. Several more recent studies, however, addressed the issue of sensitization, with mixed results. Blonstein and Geiselman (1990) asked college student participants to read a one-page summary of an armed robbery case, a one-page description of the testimony of an eyewitness, and a one-page summary of testimony by a court-appointed expert. Two variables were manipulated: the eyewit-ness's view of the perpetrator (good or poor) and the expert's conclusions about the eye-witness (credible or not very credible). Participants judged the eyewitness's credibility both before and after reading the expert's conclusions. The expert's conclusions had a substantial impact on participants' judgments of the eyewitness's credibility, with partic-ipants showing increased skepticism if the expert found the witness not very credible, and increased belief in the witness if the expert found the witness credible. The effect of the good versus poor viewing conditions was considerably smaller but still statistically significant. The conclusions of the expert did not interact with the viewing conditions, suggesting no sensitization effects. However, the written materials used in this study were fairly minimal, the participants were all students, and the realism of the methodology was limited. Furthermore, having the expert's actual opinion about the credibility of the eyewitness in question may have discouraged participants from actively evaluating the witnessing conditions for themselves.

Fox and Walters (1986) used a combination of written trial summary and video-taped testimony to examine the effects of expert testimony in the context of a conve-nience store robbery. Mock jurors read a brief summary of the crime and the defendant's testimony and then watched videotaped enactments of the testimony of the key eye-witness, presented as having either high or low confidence in the identification. Half of the participants also viewed the testimony of an expert witness who emphasized the lack of validity of confidence as a cue to accuracy. Fox and Walters found a strong effect of eyewitness confidence and a strong skepticism effect, but no interactions that would indicate that the expert's testimony mitigated the mock jurors' reliance on confidence as a cue.

Lindsay (1994) also found evidence of skepticism but not sensitization in a study in which college students watched a videotaped trial enactment in which the evidence included the actual photo spread from which the defendant had been identified. For half of the participants, the photo spread was constructed fairly, with all of the foils resembling the eyewitness's description of the perpetrator. The other half of the participants saw a biased photo spread in which the defendant was the only person who fit the eyewitness's description. Expert testimony that discussed limitations of eyewitness testimony (including the construction of lineups) had the effect of reducing the rate of guilty verdicts for both fair and unfair lineups, but not of increasing sensitivity to lineup bias. In fact, the manipulation of lineup construction showed that mock jurors believed the biased lineup to be fairer than the unbiased lineup, and guilty verdicts were most frequent in the biased lineup condition, regardless of expert testimony.

Outside of the context of a full trial, Wells and colleagues have found mixed evidence of sensitization increases following the presentation of expert testimony (Wells, 1986). In their paradigm, witnesses watched a live, staged theft under poor, moderate, or good witnessing conditions, made an identification, and then were videotaped being cross-examined about their identification. Then mock jurors viewed the videotaped cross-examinations and were asked to state whether they believed that the witness had made an accurate or inaccurate identification. In one study (Wells, Lindsay, & Tousignant, 1980), half of the participants watched a videotaped expert discussing the prevalence of misidentifications and the low correlation between accuracy and confidence. In this study, participants who did not hear the expert believed accurate witnesses 59% of the time and inaccurate witnesses 64% of the time. Those who heard the expert believed accurate witnesses 41% of the time and inaccurate witnesses 40% of the time. Thus, there was a pronounced skepticism effect, but no heightened ability to detect accuracy after hearing the expert. A second study using the same paradigm (described in Wells, 1986), however, found heightened sensitization using more elaborative testimony by the expert, who gave specific suggestions such as noting that good memory for trivial details can actually suggest poorer memory for the culprit's face. Participants in this second study who did not hear the expert testimony were unable to tell accurate from inaccurate witnesses (belief rates of 53% and 55%, respectively). Those who heard the expert, however, believed accurate witnesses 60% of the time and inaccurate witnesses only 45% of the time—solid evidence for increased sensitization.

Mixed evidence for sensitization has been provided by Cutler and colleagues. Cutler, Penrod, and Dexter (1989) created four versions of a videotaped armed robbery trial, manipulating witnessing conditions (good vs. poor, with poor featuring a disguised robber, presence of a weapon, long retention interval, and suggestive lineup instructions) and eyewitness confidence (stated as 80% or 100%). Over 500 college students and almost 100 experienced jurors saw one of the versions of this trial, provided judgments of guilt, and answered a questionnaire about eyewitness psychology. About half of the participants also saw an eyewitness expert, called by the defense, who gave elaborate testimony about memory processes and the factors that influence eyewitness accuracy. In the absence of expert testimony, mock jurors showed no sensitivity to witnessing conditions and gave equal guilty verdicts and ratings of belief in the eyewitness in both the good and poor conditions. However, when the expert was presented, guilty verdicts and belief in the eyewitness were significantly higher for the good conditions. With respect to witnessing conditions, at least, expert testimony appeared to increase sensitization without producing higher overall skepticism. On the other hand, mock jurors' use of confidence as a cue to accuracy was not systematically affected by the expert's testimony.

The source of expert advice also appears to be an important mediator of skepticism and sensitization affects. Cutler, Dexter, and Penrod (1990) replicated the above design but varied whether the expert was court-appointed or was replaced by a judge's presentation of instructions concerning eyewitness evidence. For both sources, there was no evidence of increased sensitization to eyewitness factors, but there was evidence of heightened skepticism regarding eyewitnesses.

Mixed evidence regarding sensitization effects was again found by Devenport and colleagues (2002). They asked 800 students and jury-eligible citizens to watch one of 16 versions of a videotaped trial. The versions varied in the presence of expert testimony, the selection of foils in the lineup, the instructions given to the eyewitness, and the manner of lineup presentation (simultaneous vs. sequential). Results revealed no overall skepticism effects and no increased juror sensitivity to the manner of lineup presentation or to the influence of foil bias (of which the jurors were already somewhat aware without the expert). There was some evidence of sensitization to instruction bias in jurors' evaluations of lineup fairness, ratings of the defendant's guilt, and verdicts, but only in the foil-unbiased conditions.

More recently, Devenport and Cutler (2004) examined the impact of defense-only expert testimony and opposing expert testimony about the psychology of eyewitness memory, as described earlier in the context of voir dire. Participants viewed one of 12 versions of a videotaped trial (Foil-Biased vs. Foil-Unbiased Lineup X Instruction-Biased vs. Instruction-Unbiased Lineup X No Expert vs. Defense Expert vs. Opposing Experts), rendered a verdict, and evaluated the evidence. There was no significant main effect of expert testimony on participants' verdict judgments: 37% found the defendant not guilty in the no-expert condition, 41% found the defendant not guilty in the defense-expert condition, and 47% found the defendant not guilty in the opposing-expert condition. Participants in the opposing-expert condition did perceive the defense expert's testimony to be less credible, less influential, and less useful than participants in the defense-only expert condition. They also felt that the opposing experts had a more negative impact on the credibility of psychology than those who heard only the defense expert. There was no evidence of sensitization effects in any condition.

In conclusion, existing research on the impact of expert testimony has provided more questions than answers. Increased skepticism seems to be a common effect, and some studies suggest that expert testimony can sensitize jurors to certain factors that affect eyewitness accuracy. Juror belief in certain factors such as confidence, however, seems to be remarkably tenacious. Further research is needed to determine the conditions under which skepticism and sensitization are seen.

POLICY IMPLICATIONS

Lack of relevant knowledge of the factors that influence eyewitness testimony, on the part of attorneys, judges, and jurors, places significant limitations on the effectiveness of traditional safeguards against mistaken identification. Athough a certain amount of education of the jury may be conducted during the trial itself, through judge's cautionary instructions or expert testimony, such education will take place only when the attorney and judge are sensitive to its potential importance. For researchers in this area to have a real impact on erroneous convictions, we must increase our efforts to "give psychology away" to legal professionals at all levels. Researchers in our field must take every opportunity to share their knowledge through workshops, seminars, and writings directed toward attorneys and judges.

Furthermore, even a knowledgeable attorney must have adequate access to information in order to effectively file a motion to suppress, cross-examine a witness, or present an expert witness. Given that attorneys are typically not present at their clients' identifications, it is imperative that lineups are adequately documented. Photo lineups need to be preserved so that attorneys and experts can examine the adequacy of the foils and the composition of the lineup. Sadly, we have consulted in cases where the foils were simply put back into a foil box after the identification was made, and the lineup could not be reconstructed. Similarly, for live lineups, an accurate record of the entire procedure should be kept, preferably on videotape. At minimum, a photographic representation of the lineup must be kept, and the exact instructions given to the eyewitness need to be recorded, as well as any feedback given to the witness during or subsequent to the identification.

Adjustments and improvements to existing safeguards can go only so far, however, toward preventing erroneous convictions. The research reviewed here suggests that there is no sure way to protect from conviction an innocent person who has been mistakenly identified. The best cure for mistaken identification is prevention, and this is best undertaken through the adoption of guidelines for better identification procedures. The identification procedures recommended by the National Institute of Justice, as well as states such as New Jersey, Illinois, and North Carolina, attack the problem by attempting to prevent mistaken identification through the use of standardized instructions for lineups, double-blind lineups, sequential presentations, and other procedural modifications, the effectiveness of which is documented elsewhere in this volume. Once a bad identification has been made, it may be difficult to undo the damage.

REFERENCES

Blonstein, R., & Geiselman, R. E. (1990). Effects of witnessing conditions and expert witness testimony on credibility of an eyewitness. *American Journal of Forensic Psychology, 8*, 11–19.

Borchard, E. M. (1932). *Convicting the innocent.* Garden City, NY: Garden City Publishing.

Brigham, J. C., & Wolfskeil, M. P. (1983). Opinions of attorneys and law enforcement personnel on the accuracy of eyewitness identification. *Law and Human Behavior, 7*, 337–349.

Cutler, B. L., Dexter, H. R., & Penrod, S. D. (1990). Nonadversarial methods for sensitizing jurors to eyewitness evidence. *Journal of Applied Social Psychology, 20*, 1197–1207.

Cutler, B. L., Penrod, S. D., & Dexter, H. R. (1989). The eyewitness, the expert psychologist, and the jury. *Law and Human Behavior, 13*, 311–332.

Cutler, B. L., Penrod, S. D., & Dexter, H. R. (1990). Juror sensitivity to eyewitness identification evidence. *Law and Human Behavior, 14*, 185–191.

Cutler, B. L., Penrod, S. D., & Stuve, T. E. (1988). Jury decision making in eyewitness identification cases. *Law and Human Behavior, 12*, 41–56.

Deffenbacher, K. A., & Loftus, E. F. (1982). Do jurors share a common understanding concerning eyewitness behavior? *Law and Human Behavior, 6*, 15–30.

Devenport, J. L., & Cutler, B. L. (2004). Impact of defense-only and opposing eyewitness experts on juror judgments. *Law and Human Behavior, 28*, 569–576..

Devenport, J. L., Stinson, V., Cutler, B. L., & Kravitz, D. (2002). How effective are the cross-examination and expert testimony safeguards? Jurors' perceptions of the suggestiveness and fairness of biased lineup procedures. *Journal of Applied Psychology, 87*, 1042–1054.

Fox, S. G., & Walters, H. A. (1986). The impact of general versus specific expert testimony and eyewitness confidence upon mock juror judgment. *Law and Human Behavior, 10*, 215–228.

Hosch, H. M., Beck, E. L., & McIntyre, P. (1980). Influence of expert testimony regarding eyewitness accuracy on jury decisions. *Law and Human Behavior, 4*, 287–296.

Huff, C. R. (1987). Wrongful conviction: Societal tolerance of injustice. *Research in Social Problems and Public Policy, 4*, 99–115.

Kassin, S. (1979). Personal communication cited by Wells, G. L. (1984). How adequate is human intuition for judging eyewitness testimony? In G. L. Wells & E. F. Loftus (Eds.), *Eyewitness testimony: Psychological perspectives* (pp. 256–272). New York: Cambridge University Press.

Kassin, S. M., Tubb, V. A., Hosch, H. M., & Memon, A. (2001). On the "general acceptance" of eyewitness testimony research: A new survey of the experts. *American Psychologist, 50*(5), 405–416.

Kovera, M. B., Dickinson, J. J., & Cutler, B. L. (2003). Voir dire and jury selection: Practical issues, research findings, and directions for future research. In A. M. Goldstein (Ed.), *Handbook of Psychology: Volume 11. Forensic Psychology* (pp. 161–175). New York: John Wiley & Sons.

Leippe, M. R., Eisenstadt, D., Rauch, S. M., & Seib, H. (2004). Timing of eyewitness expert testimony, jurors' need for cognition, and case strength as determinants of trial verdicts. *Journal of Applied Psychology, 89*, 524–541.

Lindsay, R.C.L. (1994). Expectations of eyewitness performance. In D. Ross, D. Read, & M. Toglia (Eds.), *Adult eyewitness testimony: Current trends and developments* (pp. 362–384). New York: Cambridge University Press.

Lindsay, R. C. L., Wells, G. L., & O'Connor, F. J. (1989). Mock juror belief of accurate and inaccurate eyewitnesses: A replication and extension. *Law and Human Behavior, 13*, 333–339.

Lindsay, R. C. L., Wells, G. L., & Rumpel, C. M. (1981). Can people detect eyewitness identification accuracy within and across situations? *Journal of Applied Psychology, 66*, 79–89.

Loftus, E. F. (1974). Reconstructive memory: The incredible eyewitness. *Psychology Today, 8*, 116–119.

Loftus, E. F. (1980). Impact of expert psychological testimony on the unreliability of eyewitness identification. *Journal of Applied Psychology, 65*, 9–15.

Maass, A., Brigham, J. C., & West, S. G. (1985). Testifying on eyewitness reliability: Expert advice is not always persuasive. *Journal of Applied Social Psychology, 15*, 207–299.

McConkey, K. M., & Roche, S. M. (1989). Knowledge of eyewitness memory. *Australian Psychologist, 24*, 377–384.

Narby, D. J., & Cutler, B. L. (1994). Effectiveness of voir dire as a safeguard in eyewitness cases. *Journal of Applied Psychology, 79*, 724–729.

Noon, E., & Hollin, C. R. (1987). Lay knowledge of eyewitness behaviour: A British survey. *Applied Cognitive Psychology, 1*, 143–153.

Rahaim, G. L., & Brodsky, S. L. (1982). Empirical evidence versus common sense: Juror and lawyer knowledge of eyewitness accuracy. *Law and Psychology Review, 7*, 1–15.

Scheck, B., Neufeld, P., & Dwyer, J. (2001). *Actual innocence*. New York: Signet.

Steblay, N. (1997). Social influence in eyewitness recall: A meta-analytic review of lineup instruction effects. *Law and Human Behavior, 21*, 283–297.

Steblay, N., Dysart, J., Fulero, S., & Lindsay, R. C. L. (2001). Eyewitness accuracy in sequential and simultaneous lineup presentations: A meta-analytic comparison. *Law and Human Behavior, 25*, 459–473.

Stinson, V., Devenport, J. L., Cutler, B. L., & Kravitz, D. A. (1996). How effective is the presence-of-counsel safeguard? Attorney perceptions of suggestiveness, fairness, and correctability of biased lineup procedures. *Journal of Applied Psychology, 81*, 64–75.

Stinson, V., Devenport, J. L., Cutler, B. L., & Kravitz, D. A. (1997). How effective is the motion-to-suppress safeguard? Judges' perceptions of the suggestiveness and fairness of biased lineup procedures. *Journal of Applied Psychology, 82*, 211–220.

Warden, R. (2003). *The Illinois exonerated: Alejandro Dominguez*. Northwestern University School of Law, Center on Wrongful Convictions. Retrieved December 30, 2003 from http://www.law.northwestern.edu/depts/clinic/wrongful/exonerations/Dominguez-IL.htm

Weinberg, H. I., & Baron, R. S. (1982). The discredible eyewitness. *Personality and Social Psychology Bulletin, 8*, 60–67.

Wells, G. L. (1984). The psychology of lineup identifications. *Journal of Applied Social Psychology, 14*, 89–103.

Wells, G. L. (1986). Expert psychological testimony: Empirical and conceptual analysis of effects [Special issue: The ethics of expert testimony]. *Law and Human Behavior, 10*, 83–95.

Wells, G. L., Lindsay, R. C. L., & Ferguson, T. J. (1979). Accuracy, confidence, and juror perceptions in eyewitness identification. *Journal of Applied Psychology, 64*, 440–448.

Wells, G. L., Lindsay, R. C. L., & Tousignant, J. P. (1980). Effects of expert psychological advice on human performance in judging the validity of eyewitness testimony. *Law and Human Behavior, 4*, 275–285.

Wells, G. L., Rydell, S. M., & Seelau, E. P. (1993). The selection of distractors for eyewitness lineups. *Journal of Applied Psychology, 78*, 835–844.

22

Giving Psychology Away to Lawyers

James M. Doyle

Center for Modern Forensic Practice,
John Jay College of Criminal Justice, CUNY

Psychological researchers' generosity with scientific knowledge has never been in doubt; their eager efforts to share eyewitness research findings with the legal system date at least from Hugo Munsterberg's *On The Witness Stand* in 1908. This *Handbook* includes just the latest in a very long line of calls on researchers to "give psychology away" to the legal system (Miller, 1969; Van Wallendael, Davenport, Cutler, & Penrod, this volume), and through the years psychologists have responded energetically to those calls (Loftus, 1983).

Still, the researchers are usually depressed by the reception their gifts receive from their legal beneficiaries. What good, after all, is applied psychology that no one will agree to apply? Will the contributions to this handbook meet the same ingratitude as their forerunners? A glance at past misunderstandings may suggest a new approach to how psychological research can be introduced to the judicial system.

The trouble started as soon as Munsterberg's pioneering effort drew a response from Dean John Henry Wigmore, the towering eminence of American evidence law, in a lengthy article in the *Illinois Law Review* (Wigmore, 1909).

Engaging so revered a legal figure as Wigmore at that infant stage in the dialogue might seem to promise a productive relationship, but Wigmore's article has gone down in the annals of psychological commentary as a scathing broadside, creating a situation in which psychology was "so vilified by legal scholars that it almost irreparably damaged early attempts to apply the behavioral sciences to the law" (Bershoff, 1993, p. 172). Wigmore's response to Munsterberg was certainly a clumsy thank-you note, but it should not be dismissed as a superstitious rant by an ignorant legal tribesman. Wigmore did chide Munsterberg, but Wigmore also sternly attacked American lawyers for failing to grasp the significance of what Munsterberg offered, asserting that "In no country had the legal profession taken so little interest in finding out or using what the other sciences were doing." Wigmore even proposed a solution: urging "earnestly, as the lawyers in

Europe are urging, friendly and energetic alliance of psychology and law in the noble cause of justice" (Wigmore, 1909, p. 406).

What went wrong? Certainly, the articles collected in this handbook prove that there *should* be a friendly and energetic alliance between psychology and law, and yet examples of lawyers' and judges' indifference to psychological methods and findings abound (Van Wallendael, Davenport, Cutler, & Penrod, this volume). Even so, the chapters collected here also provide an occasion to view the psychology/law relationship through a new lens. How much of the problem lies not in the lawyers' response to Munsterberg and his heirs, but in the researchers' response to Wigmore and his? Nearly a century after Munsterberg and Wigmore collided, it might be time to question whether the scientific community's default response to the lawyers' ingratitude—that is, "They just don't get it"—is adequate to the situation. Wigmore, after all, said some things worth hearing.

Consider, for example, Wigmore's anticipation of one of the happier products of the relationship between the two disciplines: the consideration and adoption by the National Institute of Justice and a variety of state and local jurisdictions of eyewitness investigation protocols derived from the burgeoning "system variable" research. (Wells et al., 2000). For many commentators, the publication by the NIJ of *Eyewitness Evidence: A Guide for Law Enforcement* represents the belated triumph of scientific enlightenment over obdurate legal ignorance—certainly not a panacea, but a ray of hope, warranting two cheers, even if it does not earn three (Judges, 2000).

More than 60 years earlier Wigmore had outlined an eyewitness identification protocol that required an immediate measurement of eyewitness confidence, a double-blind testing procedure, and the sequential display of suspect and fillers. It also mandated the use of at least 25 foils in every witness test, and it included the dynamic display of fillers and suspects speaking and in motion: features supported by the research, but not included in the National Institute of Justice's *Guide* (Wigmore, 1937). In short, Wigmore's revolutionary program tracks modern system variable research *better* than does almost any contemporary *Guide*. There is no evidence that any psychological researcher has ever heard of Wigmore's version of a system variable approach to identifications, but attending to Wigmore as we approach the 100th anniversary of his lesson to Munsterberg helps to explain why "giving eyewitness psychology away" succeeded in the NIJ *Guide* context and not in others. Among other things, reading this handbook with Wigmore in mind reminds us of the truism known to every veteran spouse who has ever confronted a 40th birthday or a 10th anniversary: gift-giving is a rewarding but also a difficult and complex enterprise.

STATISTICAL GIFTS TO DIAGNOSTIC ADVERSARIES

Gift giving requires attention not only to what we like to give, but to who our beneficiaries are and what they might want to receive.

On that point, Wigmore offered psychologists a warning it is not clear they have quite absorbed. Wigmore pointed out that Munsterberg's gift, although fascinating and well intended, was largely useless. In part this was because of the infant state of the research. In 1908 there was too little research and too few researchers, and most of the research was in German; practically speaking, there was no way to use it in an American courtroom. Wigmore was right about these things, and right as a matter of science, not as a matter of insular legal reasoning.

But Wigmore's technical critiques should not mask Wigmore's deeper theme—a theme that remains pertinent even after the extensive and scrupulous research exemplified in this handbook has filled many of the gaps that Munsterberg ignored. Wigmore described permanent structural barriers to collaboration that even the mature science reflected in this handbook must acknowledge.

Munsterberg gave the lawyers a catalogue of remarkably prescient insights into misconceptions about eyewitness performance, and to an uncanny degree his insights have been vindicated by modern research. But Wigmore pointed out that the legal system's concern is not with the reliability of *witnesses*; it is with the reliability of *verdicts*. Witnesses make mistakes, but if the legal system catches the mistakes, then Munsterberg's jeremiad was largely beside the point. Psychological studies generate statistical, probabilistic results: they tell you what happens 7 times out of 10. But a *verdict* requires something more: a verdict requires a clinical, diagnostic decision about whether *this* case is one of the 7 or one of the 3. On this point, Munsterberg had very little to offer.

The collaboration of law and psychology that produced the reforms included in the NIJ *Guide* was triggered by a perfect storm of circumstances that included an uniquely receptive attorney general in Janet Reno and a drumbeat of DNA exonerations in eyewitness cases, but the most important reason for progress was that the *Guide*, unlike the protagonists in the expert testimony debate, did not face the problem of translating statistical information into a diagnostic process. New procedures founded on system variable research (Malpass, Tredoux, & McQuiston-Surrett, this volume; Dupuis & Lindsay, this volume) do not require clinical or diagnostic decisions to justify their *preventive* application. They can be employed from a public health perspective, and from that perspective a protocol that gets the right guy 7 times out of 10 is simply better than one which is right 5 times out of 10. The achievement of the Technical Working Group that drafted the *Guide* was to focus the research exactly on the reliability of *witnesses* as that reliability was affected by investigative processes—to focus it, that is, exactly where Wigmore had claimed Munsterberg's learning should properly be confined.

A subsidiary lesson from Wigmore's response to Munsterberg also helps to explain the relative success of the law/psychology relationship in the NIJ *Guide*—that is, it is easier to give psychology away around a conference table than in a courtroom. Gift giving is not only a question of what is given; where and how the gift is delivered make a difference, too.

This lesson is one that Wigmore not only taught, but exemplified. Wigmore's response to Munsterberg is regarded as "scathing" because Wigmore chose, in a moment of ponderous academic whimsy, to cast his article as a trial of Munsterberg for libeling the legal system. In Wigmore's article, a fictionalized Munsterberg testified in his own defense and was subjected to withering adversary attack. In that attack Wigmore enjoyed to the fullest the lawyer's ultimate fantasy of writing both the cross-examination questions *and* the answers. Still, Wigmore wrote within the conventions of adversary advocacy, and he exemplified the shortcomings of adversarial slash-and-burn as a method for discussing cutting-edge research. The effect of Wigmore's travesty trial was to destroy Munsterberg, not to correct or modulate him, and along the way, Wigmore effectively obscured the broad range of agreement that Wigmore and Munsterberg actually shared.

The NIJ *Guide* effort at giving psychology away succeeded because Janet Reno did not permit an adversarial confrontation between the disciplines to arise. Instead, she pursued a policy of bringing everyone to the table and forcing them to engage each other outside the courtroom process (Wells et al., 2000; Doyle, 2005).

Reno's determination to bring *everyone* to the table provided one more lesson for psychologists to consider: interactions with the legal system should pursue that system broadly and include the investigative community. Once the interaction has been focused on an error-prevention (rather than post-hoc error-catching) effort, the police investigators become consumers of system variable research and allies of system variable researchers. The lawyers (prosecutors and defenders both) encounter the science of memory after the litigation is well advanced and there are only two choices available: win the case or lose it. The investigators encounter eyewitnesses at a point where a new suspect can still be found, and other investigative avenues can still be explored. The investigators not only see many mistaken eyewitnesses in cases that never make it to the lawyers because the witnesses have identified a filler; the investigators are also conscious of the fact that when they get the wrong suspect, the real perpetrator gets away. They are motivated by ideals of professionalism and workmanship that do not depend entirely on the advocates' reflexive question, Who wins? In the end, it was the investigators, acting on their realization that memory evidence can and should be treated with "CSI" professionalism, who tipped the balance toward creating the NIJ's *Guide* rather than burying it (Doyle, 2005; Patenaude, 2003).

The most direct application of many of the contributions to this handbook is to the daily lives of serious police investigators. Show-up identifications (Dysart & Lindsay), mug books, (McAllister), facial composites (Davies & Valentine), the varieties of line-up construction (Malpass, Tredoux, & MicQuiston-Surrett) and alternative approaches to line-ups (Dupuis & Lindsay) are all equipment from the everyday police toolbox. The investigative community may be temperamentally conservative, but that does not mean that it will persist in the promiscuous use of, for example, facial composites because "That's what the media wants," once they are aware of research that questions whether the current composite routines actually interfere with the eyewitness's ability to identify a perpetrator. The fact is, the investigators are hungry for information about how their tools function (Patenaude, 2003).

There can be other allies mobilized in a preventive, professionalizing effort at the application of science, unless psychological researchers insist on going it alone. The world of expert scientific testimony in the courts in the United States was revolutionized by the Supreme Court's opinion in *Daubert v. Merrell-Dow Pharmaceuticals*. The fundamental idea of science on which *Daubert* pivots is borrowed explicitly from an opinion of the United States Court of Appeals for the Third Circuit in *Downing v. United States*: a case that considered and endorsed as a model of "good science" expert psychological testimony on the question of eyewitness performance. A broad range of forensic scientists—fingerprint experts, tool marks and ballistics examiners, for example—are now struggling with the criteria that have shaped the research contained in this handbook. Moreover, a parade of highly publicized trials, including the O. J. Simpson case, and the stunning popularity of the television series *CSI: Crime Scene Investigation* and its spin-offs have put the science of evidence collection and preservation in the forefront of investigative and public consciousness. Psychologists who study memory are no longer the only scientists who must fight to promote the use and oppose the abuse of science in the criminal investigative process; forensic scientists (not to mention near-scientists, folk scientists, and pseudo-scientists) are now heavily involved in infiltrating their knowledge into the business of collecting and preserving evidence. Legal system ignorance of scientific procedures and findings may be profound, but it is also under persistent assault from many directions. Cross-fertilization between, for example, the American Psychology-Law Society and the American Academy of Forensic Sciences seems long overdue.

Forming alliances with these other scientists is particularly important at this moment because anyone trying to promote the science of eyewitness memory in the criminal justice system faces a practical turning point: the looming computerization of the eyewitness investigation business. The days of detectives carrying greasy "six-packs" of mug-shots in their pockets will linger for a while, but the days of *some* sort of identification procedure carried out on a Palm Pilot are on the near horizon. Whether these procedures will be good ones or bad ones is up for grabs. There is an opportunity to intercept the technological wave with good science, but there is a corresponding danger that once departments and institutions have invested in new hardware, new software, and new training—even if these are defective in terms of the science of memory—it will be extremely difficult to dislodge the newly embedded practices.

Interposing the justice system's lawyers as a membrane through which the research must pass on the way to the police investigators obviously creates the potential for dangerous refractions of the message, but the lawyers will not be easy to dislodge. No discussion of eyewitness reform in the legal system will ever manage to completely quarantine the diagnostic and the preventive goals; there will always be lawyers, and the lawyers will always be looking over their shoulders into the courtroom. In the struggle over the issuance of the NIJ *Guide*, for example, vehement prosecutorial resistance was provoked by the quite accurate prediction that whenever the police did not follow a recommended error prevention procedure, that preventive shortfall—despite its statistical and probabilistic origins—would infect the diagnostic trial process, enhancing indiscriminate juror skepticism and threatening the conviction rate (Judges, 2000). Still, every opportunity should be taken to identify and create forums where the needs—and doubts—of the investigative community can be addressed directly on the basis of research.

The battle over expert testimony was in its historical context the most natural vehicle for interaction between eyewitness researchers and the legal system, but it is not the best. Prevention and diagnosis are two different things, and to make prevention's claims as strongly as possible, a way has to be found to make those claims directly to those elements of the legal system most interested in preventing errors before they happen. The adversarial worries of the courtroom advocates will always be a drag on movement toward error-prevention reform, but they will be less of a drag if they are confronted face to face.

Finally, it is important to recognize that the NIJ *Guide* and the state-level reforms that built upon it are, at this moment, merely episodes, not fundamental changes. It would be a tremendous mistake to declare victory—even to declare real progress—until the error-prevention initiatives themselves become the subject of an ongoing reciprocal relationship with the system. Instituting, for example, sequential lineup procedures is not enough—not until a venue is created where the operation of sequential lineups in the field can be reported, evaluated, and critiqued, in a critical dialogue that can inform new adjustments founded on scientific research.

TELLING STORIES TO THE LEGAL SYSTEM

Even if an ongoing, improved error-prevention collaboration is achieved, the future of the application of eyewitness psychology to the law will be inextricably tied to the legal system's retrospective, diagnostic needs (Benton, McDonnell, Ross, Thomas, & Bradshaw, this volume).

The advances of science in identifying post-dictive indicators of eyewitness accuracy (or inaccuracy) are very striking (Caputo & Dunning, this volume), and the ignorance and lethargy of the legal system in utilizing science's findings are, to say the least, impressive. Still, even here, attention to the challenges of gift giving repays the effort. The research contained in this handbook shows a striking deepening and elaboration of the research, but it is not so qualitatively different from what has gone before that it will force a fresh reaction from the legal system. Is it possible to avoid having these advances shrugged off as more of the same? The best advice might be: Give them a story.

Pioneering efforts to present psychological knowledge on eyewitness performance to the legal system relied on expert testimony as their vehicle and foundered on the fact that the best that experts from Munsterberg, through, say, Robert Buckhout in the 1970s could offer was an adjustment in the degree of general skepticism regarding eyewitness testimony (1975). This drew criticism even from some experimentalists whose research agenda included investigations of eyewitness memory (e.g., McCloskey & Egeth, 1987), as well as virulent hostility from some members of the legal system who recognized that the only way to prevent all wrongful convictions was to guarantee wrongful acquittals by freeing the violent guilty along with the innocent. Subsequently, a reorientation exemplified in the early work of Elizabeth Loftus and others led to controlled laboratory research into the observable impact of specific factors concerning an event, a witness, or an investigation on eyewitness performance. From the mid-1970s on—and certainly by the time of this handbook—psychology can claim to have generated an enormous amount of good science regarding factors such as weapons focus, own-race bias, and stress that are present in most eyewitness encounters leading to trials.

This factor-based expertise is certainly an advance over simply testifying that "nearly 2,000 eyewitnesses can be wrong" (Buckhout, 1975) on the basis of Munsterbergian classroom demonstrations of eyewitness unreliability, but this does not mean that the factor-based research translates automatically, or even easily, into the legal system's diagnostic procedures.

Wells' 1978 article, "Applied eyewitness testimony research: System variables and estimator variables," which was published in the *Journal of Personality and Social Psychology*, is best remembered for its introduction of the "system variable" formulation that provoked a substantial shift in interest toward preventive procedural reforms. But in that article Wells made another point regarding the unwieldiness of factors-based research product. By Wells's calculation, in a routine criminal eyewitness case in which you could identify 20 researched factors, even if you arbitrarily limited each factor to only high or low influence, there would be 1,048,576 potential outcomes when you attempted to combine the factors. (Wells, 1978). Conscientious efforts have been made to study the interaction of two or three factors, but no one has (or could) study the interaction of the hundreds of factors present in an individual crime or accident.

The crucial point is that a trial is *required* to combine the factors; no single factor can be dispositive. Own-race bias matters, but it matters a lot less when the eyewitness has a 3-hour encounter with the robber than it does when the encounter is fleeting. Even though an expert witness may know quite a lot about what factors were influential, *listing* those factors makes a very limited contribution to the trial's post-diction of error. It simply isn't the case that whenever the danger factors (say, violence + weapon + race) outnumber the reliability factors (say, lighting + duration), the identification can be post-dicted as erroneous (Caputo & Dunning, this volume).

Furthermore, in the minds of the diagnostic functionaries of the courtroom world, the fact that the contribution of these lists of factors is small (and potentially misleading) is aggravated by the fact that they must recur in many, many eyewitness cases—75,000 each year according to one estimate (Cutler & Penrod, 1995). "With little to distinguish this case from the general rule against admitting expert testimony on eyewitness identifications," one judge complained, "we are left with no guidelines to decide the deluge of similar issues which are sure to result" (*State v. Chapple*, dissenting opinion, p. 300). Even judges who have read and recognized the significance of the scientific material on the difficulty of diagnostic evaluation of eyewitness memory are predisposed against expert testimony: "Altogether, it is much better for judges to incorporate scientific knowledge about the trial process *into* that process, rather than to make the subject a debatable issue in every case" (*United States v. Hall*, p. 1120).

But if expert testimony that recites and explains a list of factors makes a problematic way to "give psychology away" to lawyers, what is the alternative?

If we recognize that the law goes about its business by identifying, developing, and evaluating narratives and then assigning them categories, we open a new path (Amsterdam & Bruner, 2000). This is an oversimplification, of course; a fascinating body of legal and social science literature addresses the complexity of the trial performance (Burns, 1999), but the relationship between the narrative and the category—even if that relationship is an endlessly elaborated and nuanced one—captures the adversary trial's method of combining the myriad factors present in any event. Pennington and Hastie (1991), for example, have investigated jury behavior and confirmed that jurors typically understand trials by a process of weighing competing stories.

Too often psychology's attempts to intervene in the legal system have been (or anyway have *seemed* to lawyers to be) efforts to skip the individual eyewitness's narrative and immediately assign a category—that is, *reliable* or *unreliable* identification. What if the purpose of the gift of psychology could be reconceived as enriching and elaborating the narratives that lawyers and judges develop in the courtroom for evaluation by jurors as they pursue their task of placing the unique narrative into its category (or evaluation by judges hearing motions to suppress evidence)? What if the narrative, not the list of factors, became the vehicle for gift giving?

Take, for example, a routine simultaneous line-up. An eyewitness, a doctor, is the victim of a beating when his office is burglarized for drugs. The next morning, he receives a telephone call at work from the detective, who asks him to come to the police station. He knows the detective is looking for a suspect; he knows that other potential doctor victims are in jeopardy; he has told the detective how busy he is with his patients, and he knows the detective would not drag him to the station for no reason. At the station, as the detective shows him the line-up, there is an air of expectation. He is directed to evaluate the line-up, and no one tells him that the perpetrator may not be present. He does not choose immediately, but carefully studies the line-up for several minutes. He asks that the individuals be turned sideways. He has always done well on standardized tests and he has taken hundreds of them. He makes his choice, and, eager to know how he has done, he looks to the detective. The detective simply nods and checks a box. The next day, the doctor receives a subpoena to testify before a grand jury.

This schematic version of the forced choice/relative judgment story does not do justice to the enormous flexibility and richness of the trial's numerous performative languages (Burns, 1999), but it will serve to illustrate the contribution that psychology can make to the courtroom's evaluation once the defense lawyers understand the story implicit in the research. The witness's expectations, the social pressures on the witness, the possibility of a witness's high need for cognition, the witness's careful comparison of the choices he is offered, the witness's experience and comfort with multiple choice tasks, the witness's high motivation to successfully make a choice (even when *none of the above* is not an option), and the witness's life-long interest in how he scored on his tests can all be mobilized by a defense lawyer who understands the relative judgment research. Similarly, the absence of countermeasures—pre-line-up instructions, blind and sequential administration, immediate confidence measurement—can also be underlined once the lawyers understand the story.

The criminal defendant's right to tell his story through, for example, cross-examination is well understood and well protected through a variety of mechanisms, all of them more effective if psychology manages to communicate the story to the legal system. Defense lawyers who might otherwise have imagined psychological experts to be "silver bullet" solutions to their problems will begin to understand the need to investigate, for example, time-to-decision measures (Caputo & Dunning, this volume). Judges who have grasped the story will understand that they should utilize the option of instructing jurors that, just as a line-up is more reliable than a show-up, a sequential line-up is more reliable than a simultaneous one, or that the lack of an uncontaminated, immediate confidence measurement (NIJ) requires that the witness's statement of confidence be treated with caution (Lieppe & Eisentstadt, this volume).

Of course it will sometimes be true that the best way to tell the story will be through expert testimony, but the expert testimony will be more effective if it is fueled by the facts developed with the story in mind and is utilized in service of the narrative.

It is also worth remembering that this storytelling vision of psychology's contribution also permits the easy mobilization of scientifically based *counter*-stories. The forced-choice story can be met, when the facts allow it, by the response that the eyewitness was properly instructed that the perpetrator may or not be present in the line. The fact that contaminated confidence may be misleading can be met (again, where the facts allow) by the counternarrative of a correctly conducted double-blind line-up procedure including an immediate statement of uncontaminated confidence.

A new concentration on service to the narrative properties of adversary fact-finding may help to extricate psychology from the predicament in which it has found itself (Munsterberg, 1908). Too often the legal system has rejected psychological science on the grounds that it does not deliver something it has never promised to give in the first place: a categorical statement of identification accuracy or inaccuracy in the manner of a DNA comparison.

If Wigmore's "friendly and energetic alliance" is finally to be achieved—and the contributions to this handbook provide a very clear incentive—some new orientation is worth a try. The lawyers probably can't—and certainly won't—do it on their own.

REFERENCES

Amsterdam, A., & Bruner, J. (2000). *Minding the law.* Cambridge: Harvard University Press.
Bershoff, D. N. (1993). Preparing for two cultures: Education in law and psychology, in R. Roesch & S. D. Hart (Eds.), *Psychology and law: The state of the discipline.* New York: Plenum.
Buckhout, R., (1975). Nearly 2000 witnesses can be wrong. *Social Action and the Law, 2,* 7.
Burns, R. (1999). The lawfulness of the American trial. *American Criminal Law Review, 38,* 205.
Cutler, B., & Penrod, S. (1995). *Mistaken identification: The eyewitness, psychology and the law.* Cambridge: Cambridge University Press.
Daubert v. Merrell-Dow Pharmaceuticals, 509 U.S. 79 (1993).
Downing v. United States, 753 F.2d 1224 (3d Cir. 1985).
Doyle, J. M. (2005). *True witness: Cops, courts, science, and the battle against misidentification.* New York: Palgrave.
Judges, D. (2000). Two cheers for the Department of Justice's *Eyewitness evidence: A guide for law enforcement. Arkansas Law Review, 53,* 21.
Loftus, E. F. (1983). Science is not golden. *American Psychologist, 65,* 564–572.
McCloskey, M., & Egeth, H. (1986). The experimental psychologist in court: The ethics of expert testimony. *Law and Human Behavior, 10,* 1–13.
Miller, G. (1969). Psychology as a means of promoting human welfare. *American Psychologist, 24,* 1063.
Munsterberg, H. (1908). *On the witness stand.* New York: McClure.
National Institute of Justice, Technical Working Group on Eyewitness Evidence (1999). *Eyewitness evidence: A guide for law enforcement.*
Patenaude, K. (2003, October). Improving eyewitness identification. *Law Enforcement Technology, 178.*
Pennington, R., & Hastie, L. (1991). Cognitive theory of juror decision making: The story model. *Cardozo Law Review, 519.*
United States v. Hall, 165 F.3d 1095 (7th Cir. 1999).
Wells, G. (1978). Applied eyewitness testimony research: System variables and estimator variables. *Journal of Personality and Social Psychology, 30,* 330.

Wells, G., Fulero, S., Malpass, R., Turtle, J., & Lindsay, R. C. L. (2000). From the lab to the police station: a successful application of eyewitness research. *American Psychologist, 55,* 581–598.

Wigmore, J. H. (1909). Professor Muensterberg and the psychology of testimony: Being a report of the case of Cokestone v. Muensterberg. *Illinois Law Review, 3,* 399.

Wigmore, J. H. (1937). *The science of judicial proof* (3d ed.). Boston: Little, Brown & Co.

Author Index

Numbers in *italics* indicate pages with complete bibliographic information.

A

Abberton, E., 116, *129*
Abdi, H., 72, 82, 95, *100*
Abshire, J., 484, *496*
Ackil, J. K., 314, *338*
Adachi, K., 51, *57*
Adams, F., 22, *29*
Adams-Price, C., 312, 327, *334*
Aiken, S. J., 112, *129*
Akamatsu, S., 93, *99*
Akehurst, L., 405, *418*
Alexander, J. F., 36, *57*
Alfini, J. J., 493, *497*
Allan, K., 17, *29*, 314, *335*
Allison, H. C., 62, 79, 310, *335*
Alper, A., 429, *446*
Amador, M., 19, *29*
Amsterdam, A., 579, *581*
Anderson, C. A., 408, *418*
Anderson, N. D., 310, 311, 315, 316, 320, *334*
Anthony, T., 258, 261, *276*, 541, *551*
Aperman, A., 53, *58*
Arbuthnot, J., 505, *524*
Argenti, A. M., 260, *280*
Armstrong, H. A., 115, *129*
Arnold, G. F., 529, *551*
Arocha, J. F., 264, *280*
Aronovitch, C., 119, *129*
Autry, M. W., 346, *359*
Avetissian, I. V., *29*

B

Babinsky, R., 346, *357*
Bäckman, L., 311, 322, 323, 324, 326, *334*
Baddeley, A. D., 275, *281*, 392, *425*
Baenninger, M., 264, *276*, 290, 292, *303*
Bahrick, H. P., 18, *27*, 434, *446*
Bahrick, P. L., 434, *446*
Bailis, K. L., 114, *131*
Baker, E. J., 55, *57*
Baker-Ward, L., 300, *303*
Bala, N., 190, *199*
Baldwin, H., *81*
Baldwin, J., 102, 120, *129*
Balota, D. A., 310, 320, *334*
Banaji, M. R., 352, *357*
Banka, L., 36, *58*
Baranski, J. V., 209, 211, *215*
Barkan, H., 351, *357*
Barkowitz, P., 261, 266, 267, *276*, 277, 373, *374*
Barnard, M., 351, *358*
Barndollar, K. A., 479, *498*, 502, *522*
Barneby, A., 122, *129*
Baron, R. S., 513, *524*, 565, *572*
Baron-Cohen, S., 285, *303*
Barron, A., 117, *130*
Bartholomeus, B., 108, 116, *129*
Bartlett. J. C., 14, *32*, 44, *58*, 146, *151*, 265, *280*, 289, *303*, 309, 313, 316, 317, 318, 321, 322, 323, 324, 326, 327, 328, 329, 330, 332, 333, *334*, 335, 336, 337, 368, 370, *375*

Subject Index

A

Absolute judgment, 76, 139, 141, 151, 184, 192, 196, 239, 240, 243, 244, 250, 299, 404, 445
Accuracy of descriptions, 7, 20, 175, 278, 349
Accuracy of eyewitness identification, 33, 57, 153, 250, 277, 361, 362, 375, 419, 421, 428, 446, 449, 463, 490, 496, 522, 532, 544, 552, 570
Accuracy of memory for violent or nonviolent crimes, 373, 379, 396
Accuracy-confidence relationship, 422, 423, 431, 448
Acoustic identification, 102, 118, 129, 130, 131, 132, 133, 134, 135, 355
Admissibility of expert testimony, 457, 468, 565
Admissibility of eyewitness experts, 455, 456, 458
Age-invariant edict, 329, 332
Alcohol, 4, 11, 31, 34, 107, 118, 147, 148, 149, 151, 152, 153, 352, 359, 360, 374, 480
Alternative lineup procedures, 438, 440
Artist's impressions, 59, 60, 61, 64
Attorneys' knowledge of eyewitness memory, 486
Attribution of character, 81, 83
Aural-perceptual, 101, 102, 106, 107, 113

B

Belief of eyewitness identification evidence, vii, 501, 509
Benton Face Recognition Test (BFRT), 326, 327
Biased instructions, 43, 174, 181, 182, 187, 203, 272, 399, 441, 543, 556, 561

C

Calibration of confidence, 208, 20, 217, 253
Calibration , 208, 210, 216, 217, 253, 278, 381, 385, 386, 387, 388, 393, 394, 396, 397, 402, 404, 405, 406, 413, 415, 416, 419, 420, 422, 424, 502, 507, 508, 512, 515
CCTV, 78, 79, 87, 88, 98, 341, 359
Characteristics of the eyewitness, 509, 510, 515
Choosers versus non-choosers, 423, 438, 446, 448, 516, 540, 541, 555
Choosing behavior, 139, 202, 203, 204, 205, 206, 208, 212, 214, 215, 364, 366, 394
Clothing Bias, 138, 143, 145, 149, 151, 182, 187, 197, 374

Cognition of correspondence, 389
Cognitive influences on eyewitness identification, 204, 205, 206, 215, 217
Cognitive interview, 16, 19, 29, 30, 61, 70, 75, 81, 124, 133, 286, 311, 312, 313, 335, 553
Commitment effects, 41, 43, 57, 151, 335
Computer-based retrieval systems, 51, 57
Computer-based systems, 56, 61, 80, 94, 176
Confidence malleability in eyewitness identification, 213, 214, 480, 486, 541
Confidence measurement, 211, 580
Confidence scaling, 212, 213
Confidence-accuracy relationship, vi, 110, 111, 208, 212, 213, 215, 216, 217, 265, 377, 378, 383, 418, 419, 420, 422, 423, 432, 472, 553
Configural encoding, 31, 448
Consistency, 9, 10, 46, 107, 114, 135, 458, 510, 511, 512, 518, 519, 523, 541, 562
Construction methods, 60, 159, 177
Correspondence between lay and expert knowledge, 480, 481
Creating profiles, 439
Cross-contamination, 17
Cross-race identification, 142, 143, 147, 151, 198, 236, 261, 279, 438, 439, 440, 476, 479, 483, 484, 487

D

Daubert , 456, 457, 458, 470, 472, 473, 494, 497, 530, 552, 553, 576, 581
Development factors (in composite construction), 56, 71, 83
Discrimination, x, 25, 68, 109, 110, 130, 134, 211, 258, 261, 262, 268, 278, 279, 321, 322, 357, 491, 502, 506, 518, 541
Distributed exposures, 121, 125
DNA-based exonerations, 155, 221, 233, 377, 455, 458, 496, 504, 505, 506, 532, 533, 551, 558, 575
Duration estimation, 121
Dynamic information, 36, 37, 38, 79, 93

E

Earwitness confidence, 106
Earwitness descriptions, 105, 124, 136